Lecture Notes in Computer Science 11003

Commenced Publication in 1973
Founding and Former Series Editors:
Gerhard Goos, Juris Hartmanis, and Jan van Leeuwen

More information about this series at http://www.springer.com/series/7409

Ting-Ting Wu · Yueh-Min Huang
Rustam Shadiev · Lin Lin
Andreja Istenič Starčič (Eds.)

Innovative Technologies and Learning

First International Conference, ICITL 2018
Portoroz, Slovenia, August 27–30, 2018
Proceedings

Springer

Editors
Ting-Ting Wu
National Yunlin University of Science and Technology
Yunlin
Taiwan

Yueh-Min Huang
Kun Shan University
Tainan City
Taiwan

and

National Cheng Kung University
Tainan City
Taiwan

Rustam Shadiev
Nanjing Normal University
Nanjing
China

Lin Lin
University of North Texas
Denton, TX
USA

Andreja Istenič Starčič
University of Ljubljana
Ljubljana
Slovenia

ISSN 0302-9743 ISSN 1611-3349 (electronic)
Lecture Notes in Computer Science
ISBN 978-3-319-99736-0 ISBN 978-3-319-99737-7 (eBook)
https://doi.org/10.1007/978-3-319-99737-7

Library of Congress Control Number: 2018952238

LNCS Sublibrary: SL3 – Information Systems and Applications, incl. Internet/Web, and HCI

This Springer imprint is published by the registered company Springer Nature Switzerland AG
The registered company address is: Gewerbestrasse 11, 6330 Cham, Switzerland

Preface

The International Conference of Innovative Technologies and Learning provides a platform for those working on educational technology to get together and exchange experiences. Benefiting from the use of a variety of emerging innovative technologies, the e-learning environment has become highly diversified along the way. Diversified innovative technologies have fueled the creation of advanced learning environments by adopting appropriate pedagogies. Moreover, these technologies not only facilitate learning but also actively help students reach maximized learning performances. However, owing to the rapid evolution of these new technologies, how to make use of them by complying with effective pedagogies to create adaptive or smart learning environments has always been a challenge. Therefore, this conference intends to provide a platform for those researchers in education, computer science, and educational technology to get together and share their experiences in effectively applying cutting-edge technologies to learning as well as initiating future projects. It is hoped that the findings of each work presented at the conference will enlighten researchers or education practitioners to create more effective learning environments. ICITL is always open to the public for sharing their works.

This year's conference, ICITL 2018, was held in Portoroz, a Slovenian Adriatic seaside resort located in the Municipality of Piran of southwestern Slovenia, one of Slovenia's major tourist areas. This year we received 160 submissions from 17 countries worldwide. After a rigorous double-blind review process, 66 papers were selected as full papers and four papers were selected as short papers, yielding an acceptance rate of 44%. These contributions cover the latest findings in the areas, including: (1) application and design of innovative learning software, (2) augmented and virtual reality in education, (3) collaborative learning, (4) design and framework of learning systems, (5) educational data analytics techniques and adaptive learning applications, (6) instructional strategies, (7) learning analytics and education data mining, (8) mind, brain, and education, (9) pedagogies to innovative technologies, (10) personalized and adaptive learning, (11) social media and online learning, (12) technology-enhanced language learning, and (13) innovative thinking education, and future trend developments. Moreover, ICITL 2018 featured two keynote presentations by renowned scholars: Prof. Chin-Chung Tsai, Prof. Cathleen Norris, and Prof. Elliot Soloway. They offered insight into the interplay between students' concepts of learning and curricula in an open world.

We would like to thank the Organizing Committee for their effort and time spent to ensure the success of the conference. We would also like to express our gratitude to the Program Committee members for their timely and helpful reviews. And last but not least, we would like to thank all the authors for their contribution in maintaining a high-quality conference – we count on your continued support in playing a significant role in the innovative technologies and learning community in the future.

August 2018

Yueh-Min Huang
Ting-Ting Wu
Lin Lin
Rustam Shadiev
Andreja Istenic Starcic

Organization

Conference Co-chairs

Yueh-Min Huang	National Cheng-Kung University, Taiwan
Andreja Istenic Starcic	University of Ljubljana, Slovenia

Program Co-chairs

Ting-Ting Wu	National Yulin University of Science and Technology, Taiwan
Lin Lin	University of North Texas, USA
Rustam Shadiev	Nanjing Normal University, China

Program Committee

Ann-Therese Arstorp	The Norwegian Directorate for Education and Training, Norway
Charoenchai Wongwatkit	Mae Fah Luang University, Thailand
Charuni Samat	Khon Kaen University, Thailand
Chi-Cheng Chang	National Taiwan Normal University, Taiwan
Chengjiu Yin	Kobe University, Japan
Daniel Spikol	Malmo University, Sweden
Demetrios G Sampson	Curtin University, Australia
Di Zou	The Education University of Hong Kong, SAR China
Edward J. Coyle	Georgia Institute of Technology, USA
Eric Bruillard	Université Paris Descartes, France
Frode Eika Sandnes	Oslo and Akershus University College of Applied Sciences, Norway
Gabriella Dodero	Free University of Bozen-Bolzano, Italy
George Ghinea	Brunel University, UK
Gunnar Sivertsen	Nordic Institute for Studies in Innovation, Research and Education, Norway
Haoran Xie	The Education University of Hong Kong, SAR China
Ian Solomonides	Victoria University, Australia
Maria Dardanou	The Arctic University of Norway, Norway
Mariann Solberg	The Arctic University of Norway, Norway
Kinshuk	University of North Texas, USA
Lisbet Rønningsbakk	The Arctic University of Norway, Norway
Michael Spector	University of North Texas, USA
Neil Yen	University of Aizu, Japan
Roza Valeeva	Kazan Federal University, Russia
Rong-Huai Huang	Beijing Normal University, China

Sumalee Chaijaroen	Khon Kaen University, Thailand
Tim Engels	University of Antwerp, Belgium
Thrasyvoulos Tsiatsos	Aristotle University of Thessaloniki, Greece
Tristan E. Johnson	Northeastern University, USA
Wai Hong Chan	The Education University of Hong Kong, SAR China
Wu-Yuin Hwang	National Central University, Taiwan
Yao-Ting Sung	National Taiwan Normal University, Taiwan

Main Organizer

Co-organizers

Contents

Augmented and Virtual Reality in Education

ARPiano Efficient Music Learning Using Augmented Reality

Fernando Trujano(✉), Mina Khan, and Pattie Maes

Massachusetts Institute of Technology, Media Laboratory, 77 Massachusetts Avenue, Cambridge 02139, USA
Trujano.Fernando@gmail.com

Abstract. ARPiano uses a MIDI keyboard and a multifunction knob to create a novel mixed reality experience that supports visual music learning, music visualizations and music understanding. At its core, ARPiano provides a framework for extending a physical piano using augmented reality. ARPiano is able to precisely locate a physical keyboard in order to overlay various objects around the keyboard and on individual keys. These augmented objects are then used for music learning, visualization and understanding. Furthermore, ARPiano demonstrates a novel way to utilize the keys in a piano as an interface to interact with various augmented objects.

Keywords: Augmented reality · Piano · Learning · Education · Music

1 Introduction

This paper describes ARPiano, a mixed reality application that augments a physical keyboard. ARPiano uses a MIDI (Musical Instrument Digital Interface) keyboard and a multifunction knob to create a novel mixed reality experience that supports visual music learning, music visualizations and music understanding. ARPiano is able to precisely locate a physical keyboard in order to overlay various objects around the keyboard and on individual keys. These augmented objects are then used for music learning, visualization and understanding. Furthermore, ARPiano demonstrates a novel way to utilize the keys in a piano as an interface to interact with various augmented objects.

1.1 Goals

ARPiano is designed to allow for better visual music learning, music visualization and music understanding.

Music Learning. The main goal of ARPiano is to facilitate visual music learning using augmented reality. Traditional music learning focuses on reading symbols in the form of sheet music. However, these symbols are abstract and there is no intuitive correlation between the symbol and the note that it represents. For example, notes of different lengths are differentiated by whether the symbols are filled in or not (quarter note and half notes)

T.-T. Wu et al. (Eds.): ICITL 2018, LNCS 11003, pp. 3–17, 2018.
https://doi.org/10.1007/978-3-319-99737-7_1

or whether they have an extra tick attached to them (eighth notes and sixteenth notes). This notation is not immediately intuitive and requires that the user learn the symbols in order to make sense of them. Current theories of learning show that using multiple modalities in learning is an effective strategy to form mental constructs and schemas [1–4]. The visual aspect of traditional music learning depends on these abstract symbols and could be stronger.

ARPiano aims to facilitate visual music learning by providing a deeper connection between the song the user is learning and what they are seeing. This is accomplished by intuitive and spatially accurate visuals, real time feedback, and performance statistics. ARPiano visually renders a song in the form of a sequence of cuboids where the length of the rectangle represents the length of the note and the position relative to the keyboard represents the note value.

Music Visualization and Understanding. ARPiano also allows for music visualization and music understanding. Music visualization is accomplished by emitting a sprite from the physical key location whenever the key is pressed. This provides the user with a visual counterpart to what they are hearing and allows them to better see patterns in the music. Additionally, while the user is playing, ARPiano is able to augment the interface to point out specific musical artifacts, such as chords, which aids in music understanding.

2 Previous Work

Music learning software is not a new field and there are many applications available that try to facilitate music learning by creating visuals or providing performance statistics. However, none of the applications provide spatially accurate visuals.

2.1 Smart Music

Smart Music [5] is a music learning software that provides helpful feedback on a player's performance. A user is displayed the sheet music as well as a bar indicating the current measure that they are on. While playing a song, Smart Music uses a microphone to determine whether the user is playing the correct notes. While Smart Music provides helpful statistics to the user, such as which sections had the most mistakes, it still relies on sheet music and does not offer a more intuitive musical representation of a song.

2.2 Synthesia

Synthesia [6] is a piano learning software that, like ARPiano, renders songs in the form of a piano roll. Each note in the song is represented by a rectangle that slowly approaches its corresponding key on a virtual keyboard on the display. This representation is more intuitive than sheet music and allows the user to see patterns in the song. Synthesia is also able to track a player's performance and provide statistics to help them guide their practice. While Synthesia provides an intuitive visual representation of the song, it does so on a traditional 2D display and requires that the user look back and forth between the virtual keyboard on the display and the physical keyboard they are playing on.

2.3 Andante/Perpetual Canon

Andante [7] and Perpetual Canon [8] are part of a collection of research projects developed by Xiao Xiao from the MIT Media Lab. They augment a piano with a projector and are able to provide visualizations of pre-recorded or live music. These projects did not however, focus on music learning or analyzing what is being played.

3 Design

ARPiano is implemented as a Unity application that runs on a Hololens and wirelessly receives messages from a server running on a PC. The application augments the physical keyboard with sprites and annotations and receives input from the keyboard in order to support various interactions. ARPiano adopts a modular design in the form of Keyboard Components (see Sect. 4).

3.1 Integrated Sensors

ARPiano uses a MIDI Keyboard and a multifunction knob for input. Both of these devices communicate over USB. Since the Hololens does not have any USB ports, additional steps had to be taken to integrate these devices into a Mixed Reality experience. The application also uses the built in Hololens camera to get the initial position of the keyboard in three dimensional space.

The keyboard sends MIDI commands to the computer over USB and is the main interface for ARPiano. When a key is pressed the keyboard emits the corresponding sound and sends a MIDI message to the connected computer. MIDI is well established and documented so many libraries exist to parse these messages. I used the open source Midi Jack Unity plugin [9] to parse each incoming MIDI message into its corresponding channel, note and velocity. The computer then sends each event (either noteOn or noteOff) to the Hololens using the HoloToolkit sharing service. These messages are then used by the Hololens to support various interactions.

The multifunction knob serves as an additional controller to change several parameters of the keyboard. An augmented interface can be rendered on top of the controller to show which parameter is being changed (see Sect. 4.3). I used the Griffin Power mate to map knob rotations and presses to different keypress events. These events are then picked up by the computer using Unity's Input library and sent to the Hololens via the Sharing Service. The Hololens then decides what to do depending on the current state of the keyboard.

Lastly, ARPiano uses the built in Hololens camera to detect the three dimensional position of the first and last keyboard keys as described in the following subsection.

3.2 Physical and Augmented Keyboard

At its core, ARPiano consists of a main Keyboard class that handles incoming messages from the server and is responsible for the initial calibration. The keyboard class is responsible for parsing these messages and making them available to Keyboard Components (see Sect. 4). Each message consists of the pressed note (as a midi integer) and the velocity of the pressed note (as a float).

Calibration of the physical keyboard allows the Hololens to know precisely where each key on the keyboard is in three dimensional space. This process is done by placing two key-sized Vuforia markers on the first and last key of the keyboard. When the application is first opened, the user is instructed to look at the first and last key of the keyboard until the keys turn green, indicating successful detection of the markers (Fig. 1). In order to accommodate keyboards with different number of keys, the user then presses the first and last key. This finalizes the calibration procedure and allows the Keyboard class to accurately determine the correct position of the keyboard and each individual key therein.

Fig. 1. Calibration ensures that the Hololens knows the exact location of the physical keyboard. The markers show the perceived location of the first and last keys. (Color figure online)

The Keyboard Class exposes several methods such as GetNotePosition which returns the position of a key in the physical space given the corresponding midi number. This allows components like NoteSpawner to place sprites in the position of a corresponding key (see Sect. 4.4). The Keyboard class also allows KeyboardComponents to subscribe to three different events: calibrationComplete, noteOn, and noteOff.

3.3 Component Menu

The Component Menu utilizes the keyboard keys as an interface to enable or disable individual Keyboard Components. To open the menu, the user must press and hold the first key in the keyboard. While the key is being held, a loading ring appears on top to indicate how much longer until the menu opens. ARPiano avoids accidental opening of the menu by requiring the user to hold the lowest key for a couple of seconds, which does not happen often in regular music.

Once the menu is opened, all keyboard components are paused and icons representing keyboard components are rendered on the keyboard. Each icon consists of a colored rectangle that spans four white keys on the keyboard along with a three dimensional representation of the keyboard component, as seen in Fig. 2. The rectangle appears green or white depending on whether the corresponding component is enabled or disabled. To change the state of a component, the user simply needs to press any of the keys under the icon. Once the state of a component changes, the menu closes. Alternatively, the user can press the first key again to close the menu.

Fig. 2. 3D icons representing Keyboard Components are overlayed on top of the keyboard. From left to right, the icons represent: Keyboard Labels, Note Spawner, Chord Suggestion, Chord Detector and Song Tutorial. In this figure, the Note Spawner component is enabled. (Color figure online)

4 Keyboard Components

ARPiano is designed to allow for easy addition of new features in the form of Keyboard Components. A Keyboard Component subscribes to messages from the main Keyboard class and can be enabled or disabled independently of other Keyboard Components. Keyboard Components use helper methods from the Keyboard class to correctly position objects relative to the keyboard or the desired key.

At this time, ARPiano consists of six different Keyboard Components that enable music learning, understanding and visualization. The main goal of ARPiano is to facilitate visual music learning through augmentations on the physical keyboard. This is accomplished by the Chord Suggestion, Keyboard Labels and Song Tutorial Components. Music visualization complements the music listening experience by providing a visual counterpart to the song being played. It can also provide a history to each note and allow for easier recognition of patterns in a song. In ARPiano the Note Spawner and Flashy Visualizer Components visualize the notes as they are being played. Music understanding reinforces the music learning aspect by creating deeper connections between what is being played and what is being learned. ARPiano allows users to better understand music by pointing out interesting note intervals through different colors and annotations. The Note Spawner and Chord Detector components aid in music understanding.

4.1 Chord Suggestion

The Chord Suggestion component gives hints to a user as they are learning different chords. When a key is pressed, other keys next to it are highlighted to indicate that those keys, together with the pressed key, form part of a chord (Fig. 3). More specifically, the pressed key is treated as the root key in the cord and the third and fifth notes of the triad are highlighted. Different color highlights indicate different chord qualities, though at this time only major and minor chords are supported.

Fig. 3. The Chord Suggestion component highlights keys that can form chords. In this figure, both major (green highlight) and minor (pink highlight) chords are suggested with shared keys being highlighted blue. (Color figure online)

The Chord Suggestion component works by doing MIDI math on the pressed midi notes. Since the intervals between the notes in the triads are fixed regardless of the root note, this is a straightforward calculation.

4.2 Keyboard Labels

The Keyboard Labels component adds note labels to each key of the keyboard to assist the user in recognizing the position of notes in the keyboard (Fig. 4). The Component loops from the first key of the keyboard (as determined during the calibration procedure) to the last key and adds the corresponding note label. In MIDI, each note is represented as an integer with Middle-C being 60 and subsequent indices corresponding to the next semitones (so 61 corresponds to C#, for example). Knowing this, it is possible to label all of the keys in the keyboard.

Fig. 4. The Keyboard Labels component augments each key by labeling its corresponding note.

4.3 Song Tutorial

The Song Tutorial Component is the most complex Keyboard Component in ARPiano. It enables music learning by allowing the user to play any MIDI song in a visual and intuitive way. The component works by rendering a virtual piano roll of the song that precisely matches the physical piano. That way, as the piano roll moves down, the user can press the indicated keys in a similar way to popular music games like Guitar Hero. The speed and current position of the song can be adjusted using the multifunction knob and interactive performance statistics are displayed at the end in order to increase practice efficiency.

PianoRoll. The piano roll consists of a series of TutorialNotes depicted as cuboids whose position in the left/right axis represent the key to be played while the position in the vertical axis represents the time when the key should be played. Furthermore, the length of the cuboid represents the amount of time the note should be held for, and black keys are differentiated from white keys by the their position and color (Fig. 5). The piano roll starts on top of the keyboard and slowly moves down, causing some Tutorial Notes to lay directly on top of the keys of the keyboard. Each time a Tutorial Note does this, the user is instructed to press the key on the keyboard. By following these simple instructions, a melody can be played.

Fig. 5. SpectatorView image of AR PianoRoll representation of Beethoven's Für Elise

The piano roll is rendered by taking any MIDI song and translating it to a Tone.js compatible JSON file. Tone.js is a java script library to parse and create MIDI files, and includes an automatic script to convert a midi file to a json file [10]. It was chosen specifically to avoid working with MIDI files to speed up development as I was already familiar with parsing JSON files in Unity. From the MIDI file, the JSON file is able to obtain a list of notes, each consisting of a time, duration, and midi integer. These can be easily mapped into their corresponding Tutorial Note cuboids using the main Keyboard class.

As the piano roll moves down, the user must press the correct keys in order to play the melody. In addition to the auditory feedback the user gets from the piano, Tutorial Notes change color to indicate whether they were correctly played or not. Note verification, as described above, is accomplished by maintaining a list of notes are currently touching the keyboard and thus, should be played. If a note in this list is played, it is marked as correct and turns green, otherwise if the note leaves the keyboard without being played, it is marked as incorrect and turns red. This visual feedback provides another way for the user to gauge their performance in real time as they are playing the song.

Song Adjustments. The Song Tutorial Component allows the user to adjust the current position of the piano roll and the speed at which it moves down by turning a multifunction knob. The song can also be paused and resumed by pressing the knob. More specifically, I connected a Griffin Power mate to the server computer and mapped various types of rotations and presses to different keyboard presses that get forwarded to the Hololens through the sharing service. The knob supports two kinds of rotations: a regular rotation, and a pressed rotation. These are both sent to the Hololens.

The knob is augmented with two sets of half rings around it that represent two song parameters. The outer ring depicts the current position of the song and the inner ring represents the speed at which it is being played. When the knob is turned, the corresponding ring value changes and its exact value is shown on top of the ring (Fig. 6). The knob UI is an interesting demonstration of how augmented reality can create a multi-function interface using a single device. The knob is kept on the keyboard close by so that it can be reached easily. During music practice, a user is able to use the visual feedback and quickly "scroll" back to a difficult section in order to practice it at a slower tempo, for example.

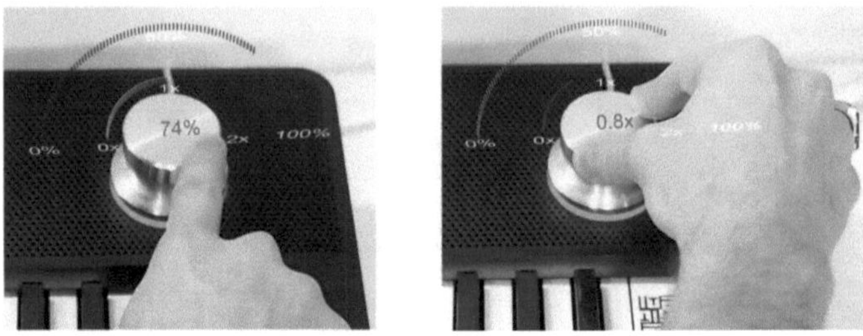

Fig. 6. The knob can be used to see and control the position of the song being played (left) or the speed at which it is being played (right)

Song Tutorial Results. After a song is played, the Song Tutorial component displays helpful statistics about the performance in the form of Song Tutorial Results. These results use the keyboard as an interactive canvas to visually show different statistics. An arrow is rendered on the last key to signify that pressing it will render the next available result. Currently, ARPiano supports two types of results: mistakes over time, and mistakes per key.

The first graph maps each key in the keyboard to a section of the song and color codes the keys depending on the number of mistakes that occurred during that section. This allows the user to quickly see which sections of the song need more practicing, as seen in Fig. 7. Additionally, pressing a key will automatically scroll to that section of the song so the user can practice it immediately.

The second graph color codes each key to the ratio of times that that key was pressed correctly. This allows the user to quickly identify which hand needs more practice. Pressing a key will reveal the exact number of times that that key was supposed to be played, and the number of times it was actually played.

Song Tutorial Results demonstrate a novel way to utilize the keyboard as an interactive canvas while providing useful statistics to help maximize practice efficiency.

Fig. 7. At the end of a Song Tutorial, the keyboard is transformed into a visual representation of the user's performance. In this graph, it is clear that the user made more mistakes in a specific section near the beginning of the song.

4.4 Note Spawner and Flashy Visualizer

The Note Spawner and Flashy Visualizer both emit sprites when a key is pressed from the location of the pressed key. These components subscribe to the noteOn and noteOff events and use the Keyboard's helper methods to position the sprites at the correct location.

The Flashy Visualizer, as the name implies, aims to complement a live music performance by providing colorful visuals corresponding to the notes being played. This Component renders various sprites when a key is pressed, or when a combination of keys is pressed (such as a chord) in order to provide a visual counterpart to the notes being played.

The Note Spawner emits a cuboid from the pressed key that slowly travels up. The length of the emitted sprite represents the length that the note was held for while the speed at which the sprite moves up represents the velocity of the corresponding key press. The NoteSpawner creates a temporal dimension to the music being played while allowing the user to see patterns within the song (Fig. 8).

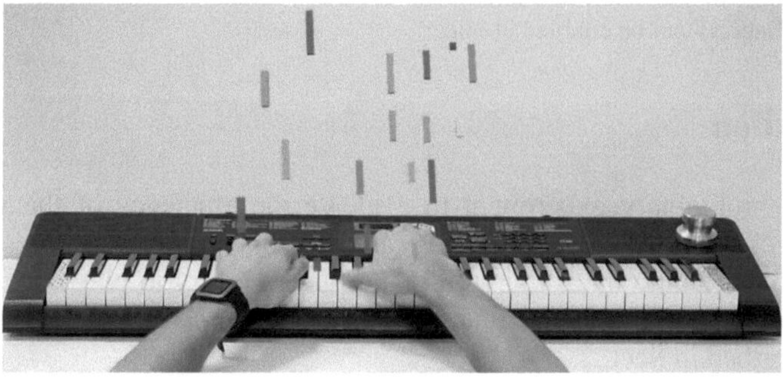

Fig. 8. The Note Spawner component emits cuboids as the user plays the keyboard in order to visualize rhythmic and tonal patterns in the song.

The Note Spawner Component can be configured to spawn notes whose color corresponds to that of a color wheel overlayed on top of the circle of fifths. This harmonic coloring provides an interesting visualization of the note intervals so a close relationship in sound is described visually by a close relationship in color [11]. Using these colors, tonal patterns can be seen in many songs, such as Chopin's Prelude, Opus 28, No. 3 in G major, which remains entirely in a single tonal area [4]. The note positions and lengths in combination with the harmonic coding provide a way to observe the tonal and rhythmical patterns of a song in a way that sheet music can simply not capture.

4.5 Chord Detector

The Chord detector component makes the user more aware of chords by creating an annotation of the chord name every time a chord is played (Fig. 9). By reminding the user of the chord name whenever a chord is played a deeper connection can be formed between the notes and the corresponding chord. I hypothesize that this aids in music understanding by making the user more aware of common chord intervals. Similarly to the Chord Suggestor, the Chord Detector works by analyzing the intervals of all notes being pressed. On each key press, the Chord Detector analyzes every subset of three notes and tries to match them to a major or minor chord. Once the chord is detected, an annotation with the chord name is rendered on top of the root note. The positioning of the annotation allows the user to see which inversion of the chord was played.

Fig. 9. The Chord Detector component analyzes the keys as they are pressed in order to label chords when they are played. This figure also shows how multiple components (ChordDetector and KeyboardLabels) can be enabled at once.

5 Evaluation

I designed a preliminary experiment to evaluate the efficiency of the visual music learning aspect of ARPiano. More specifically, I wanted to analyze the strengths and weaknesses of ARPiano by asking non-piano players to try to play various melodies without practicing them ahead of time. As a baseline comparison, I used the Synthesia software described in Sect. 2.2.

Each participant was asked to play 4 songs in total, 2 using ARPiano, and 2 using Synthesia. I chose the following songs: Twinkle twinkle (easy difficulty, both parts), Beethoven's Ode to joy (easy difficulty, both parts), Beethoven's Für Elise (medium difficulty, melody only), and Bach's Minuet in G (medium difficulty, melody only). The songs were chosen because of their popularity and varying degrees of difficulty.

For each participant, the starting method (ARPiano or Synthesia) and song pairing (one from each difficulty level) was randomly selected such that each song got played an equal amount of times on each method.

Users were briefly instructed on how to use each method and played a short chromatic exercise using the method in order to make sure they understood how to use the method correctly. After the method tutorial, each user played two songs using the selected method, filling out a quick survey in between songs.

After the first method was completed, the same exercise was conducted with the other method and the other two songs.

5.1 Study Results

I conducted this study with 14 participants (11 Female, 2 Male, 1 Agender) aged between 18–22. 57% participants had played instruments before (35.7% had played one instrument, 21.4% had played two), and exactly 50% of participants could read sheet music. None of the participants reported having played the piano before.

All participants agreed (7.1%) or strongly agreed (92.9%) that they "found ARPiano fun to use". In comparison, 35.5% of participants agreed (28.6%) or strongly agreed (7.1%) that they "found Synthesia fun to use". 35.5% of participants agreed that they would use Synthesia again to learn piano while 85.7% of participants agreed (21.4%) or strongly agreed (64.3%) that they would use ARPiano again. 85.7% of participants agreed (35.7%) or strongly agreed (50%) that "ARPiano was intuitive to use" while only 42.8% of participants agreed (21.4%) or strongly agreed (21.4%) that "Synthesia was intuitive to use".

After each performance, participants were ask to rate their performance based on their initial expectations. 78.57% of ARPiano players reported performing about the same (42.85%) or better than (25%) or much better than (10.72%) what they originally expected. In comparison, only 21.4% of Synthesia players reported performing about the same (14.3%) or better than (7.1%) what they originally expected, with 46.4% of them performing "much worse than" what they expected.

On average, users performed better using ARPiano and commented on the convenience of having the note sprites land on the corresponding physical key instead of on a virtual keyboard on the monitor. One participant was even able to play both songs (Ode to Joy and Bach Minuet) with fewer than 2 errors in each. Interestingly, for song sections with consecutive notes (key-wise), participants were often able to play the melodies correctly with both methods. However, ARPiano performed much better in sections where the notes were not consecutive. With Synthesia, users often missed any jumps in the notes because they were unable to determine how far to move their hand to hit the correct note and there was not enough time to look back and forth between the keyboard and the monitor. With ARPiano, users were able to see exactly where their hand should move to without having to look away from the keyboard.

It should be noted that the limited field of view of the Hololens made it difficult to play notes that were more than an octave an a half away from each other. For example, there is a section of Für Elise where a single high note must be played. All ARPiano players missed the jump since they could not see the note coming into the keyboard.

Synthesia players saw the jump, but usually hit the wrong note. These types of mistakes should decrease as AR technology improves.

6 Challenges

While ARPiano was designed to overcome many Hololens specific challenges, there were still different challenges to overcome in order to make ARPiano a reality. These include UI specific challenges when working with AR, imperfect Vuforia tracking and a lack of a music theory background.

For ARPiano all UI Elements must be relative to the keyboard. This means that to move something to the right it is not sufficient to move it in it's x direction as the definition of "right" depends on the initial position and rotation of the keyboard. I solved this by exposing the position, rotation, and directional vectors (forward, up, right) of the physical keyboard to other classes, and making all UI elements relative to that. However, this was not always sufficient as the Vuforia markers provided imperfect tracking.

For the most part, the Vuforia marker positioning was accurate to a centimeter which was good enough for the purposes of positioning objects relative to the keyboard. The rotation of the markers however, was not as accurate and caused issues with some UI elements, such as the piano roll in the Song Tutorial component. To support tilting of the piano roll, I initially rendered the piano roll vertically and rotated it around the right vector of the keyboard. I then moved the entire piano roll in a vector such that the first note would hit it's correct position. In theory, this should make all notes hit the correct position. However, due to small imperfections on the axis of rotation (i.e., the rotation of the keyboard as determined by the Vuforia markers) a small drift was introduced and the Tutorial Notes quickly became out of place, making it impossible to continue playing the song. I solved this challenge by expanding the Tutorial Note Class and making each note move towards its end location individually of all other notes. This effectively cancels out the imperfections on the rotation and guaranteed that all notes would always hit the correct spot on the keyboard.

This project required a surprising amount of knowledge of music theory. I had to familiarize myself with the underlying music theory to be able to implement components such as the Chord Detector. Some helper functions, particularly those in the keyboard class pertaining to the structure of notes in the keyboard, are written naively and inefficiently. While these do not have an adverse effect on performance, I'm sure I could find a more elegant way to write them if I had a stronger music theory background.

7 Future Work

ARPiano explores the different applications and benefits that an augmented instrument can provide. These applications range from music learning to music visualization and understanding. As it stands, with its various Keyboard Components, ARPiano is able to show the potential of an augmented keyboard to the above applications. However, the possibilities of an augmented instrument are far greater than those implemented in the current version of ARPiano.

Keyboards are not the only type of instruments that can benefit from augmentation. I hypothesize that many other instruments, such as string or brass instruments can benefit in their own way from various augmentations. These instruments would be trickier to implement because unlike a keyboard, they can move around while they are being played, which would require constant, real-time tracking from the headset. On the music visualization end, augmented instruments have direct applications to live performances where each instrument can be visualized independently in order for the audience to get a better feel and understanding on what each instrument is contributing to the overall song. For easier adoption, a smartphone version using current AR technologies like ARCore and ARKit can be created.

More research is needed to better understand the benefits of an augmented instrument in regards to music visual learning. For example, it would be interesting to see the a similar study as the one described in Sect. 5 over a longer time period to see whether the augmented keyboard allowed users to master a song more efficiently than other methods.

With an augmented instrument, music learning can take a more traditional approach or a completely different, gamified approach. With a traditional approach, the system could present the user with each song section and allow them to practice it independently. When the user has shown mastery of the current section, the next section can be rendered and practiced. Using devices such as the Muse [12] the system could be able to detect when the user is ready to move onto the next section by measuring the level of concentration of the user as they play. High brain activity would signify that the user is still struggling with the piece while low activity would signify that the section is likely committed to muscle memory since the user is more comfortable playing it. This allows the system to take full control of the learning space in an attempt to maximize the efficiency of the learning process.

An augmented keyboard also allows the possibility to take a completely different approach to music learning. For example, the learning experience could be masked in the form of various games where the correct combination of keys need to be pressed in order to pass each level. This experience would be especially appealing to kids, who may find it difficult to get started with a piano due to the lack of visual stimulation. Without even being aware of it, kids could be learning about chords structures while playing a fun and entertaining game.

8 Conclusion

ARPiano uses the Microsoft Hololens to augment a physical MIDI keyboard in order to facilitate visual music learning, understanding and visualization. This novel application is accomplished by combining existing peripherals such as a MIDI keyboard and multi-function knob with Augmented Reality technology.

ARPiano provides a way to track the position of each key on the keyboard in order to render various sprites and annotations on the physical keyboard depending on what the user is playing. With the Component Menu and Song Tutorial Results, ARPiano also demonstrates a way to use an existing physical peripheral as an intuitive interface to various supported interactions. Lastly, ARPiano provides a helpful way to visualize music where both tonal and rhythmic patterns can be observed.

Before augmented reality, adding visual learning functionality to instruments required expensive hardware and visuals were limited to that hardware. With augmented reality, there is no limit to the type and position of objects that can be rendered on the keyboard. Furthermore, adding new functionality does not require any additional hardware as all new functionality can be virtually rendered into the user's field of view. I believe this opens the possibility to rethink the way we approach music learning.

Acknowledgments. Redacted to maintain submission anonimity.

References

1. Campbell, P.S., Scott-Kassner, C., Kassner, K.: Music in childhood: from preschool through the elementary grades. Schirmer Cengage Learning, Boston (2014)
2. Gault, B.: Music learning through all the channels: combining aural, visual, and kinesthetic strategies to develop musical understanding. Gen. Music Today **19**(1), 7–9 (2005). https://doi.org/10.1177/10483713050190010103
3. Morris, C.: Making sense of education: sensory ethnography and visual impairment. Ethnography Educ. **12**(1), 1–16 (2016). https://doi.org/10.1080/17457823.2015.1130639
4. Harmonic Coloring: A method for indicating pitch class (n.d.). http://www.musanim.com/mam/circle.html. Accessed 11 Dec 2017
5. Music Learning Software for Educators & Students (n.d.). https://www.smartmusic.com/. Accessed 11 Dec 2017
6. Synthesia, Piano for Everyone (n.d.). https://www.synthesiagame.com/. Accessed 11 Dec 2017
7. Xiao, X.: Andante: a walking tempo (n.d.). http://portfolio.xiaosquared.com/Andante. Accessed 11 Dec 2017
8. Xiao, X.: Perpetual Canon (n.d.). http://portfolio.xiaosquared.com/Perpetual-Canon. Accessed 11 Dec 2017
9. Takahashi, K.: MidiJack, 5 November 2016. https://github.com/keijiro/MidiJack. Accessed 11 Dec 2017
10. Tone.js (n.d.). https://tonejs.github.io/. Accessed 11 Dec 2017
11. Color Music Theory (n.d.). https://www.facebook.com/Virtuosoism/. Accessed 11 Dec 2017
12. How does Muse work? (n.d.). http://www.choosemuse.com/how-does-muse-work/. Accessed 11 Dec 2017
13. Smith, T.F., Waterman, M.S.: Identification of common molecular subsequences. J. Mol. Biol. **147**, 195–197 (1981)
14. May, P., Ehrlich, H.C., Steinke, T.: ZIB structure prediction pipeline: composing a complex biological workflow through web services. In: Nagel, W.E., Walter, W.V., Lehner, W. (eds.) Euro-Par 2006. LNCS, vol. 4128, pp. 1148–1158. Springer, Heidelberg (2006)
15. Foster, I., Kesselman, C.: The Grid: Blueprint for a New Computing Infrastructure. Morgan Kaufmann, San Francisco (1999)
16. Czajkowski, K., Fitzgerald, S., Foster, I., Kesselman, C.: Grid information services for distributed resource sharing. In: 10th IEEE International Symposium on High Performance Distributed Computing, pp. 181–184. IEEE Press, New York (2001)

17. Foster, I., Kesselman, C., Nick, J., Tuecke, S.: The physiology of the grid: an open grid services architecture for distributed systems integration. Technical report, Global Grid Forum (2002)
18. National Center for Biotechnology Information. http://www.ncbi.nlm.nih.gov

Improving the Skills Training by Mixed Reality Simulation Learning

A Pilot Case Study of Nasogastric Tube Care

ChinLun Lai[1(✉)] and Yu-mei Chang[2]

[1] Communication Engineering Department, Oriental Institute of Technology, Taipei, Taiwan
fo001@mail.oit.edu.tw

[2] Nursing Department, Oriental Institute of Technology, Taipei, Taiwan
fk001@mail.oit.edu.tw

Abstract. In this paper, an innovative simulated learning model to improve the efficiency of nursing skills training by the help of mixed reality technique is proposed and the nasogastric tube care is selected as our first training course example. An interactive self-training methodology containing step by step operation directions, as well as the on line test after the course is designed using mixed reality scenario and wearable device platforms. This method fulfills the strategy of learning by practice while reducing the related cost and effort significantly. From the implemented system, it is observed by some test samples feedback that the teaching auxiliary system can not only improves the student's interest in skill training but enhances the learning performance than the traditional teaching methods, and can be applied in other skill training fields successfully.

Keywords: Mixed reality technology · Nasogastric tube care
Nursing skills training · Simulation learning · Teaching auxiliary system

1 Introduction

Observing that the nursing profession is facing a problem of shortage of nursing manpower due to the rapid development of high-tech medical care environment, it is not possible to nurture the talents needed in the industry by traditional nursing education [1]. Traditional teaching methods such as lecturing, discussion, role-playing, and laboratory demonstration exercises can neither meet the current needs of education and practice again, nor meet the highest principle of patient safety in medical institutions [2]. However, via the nursing situation simulation teaching method, it can replicate a real situation of clinical practice in a safe environment and provide students necessary skills training in much efficient and effective.

Due to the property of nursing education which emphasizes the integration of knowledge, skills and attitudes, it is necessary to improve the quality of nursing education [3] for obtaining better quality of care under the increasing complex medical environment hence ensure patient safety. To achieve this goal, nursing students need to learn how to link classroom teaching with clinical practice by using contextual simulation teaching

T.-T. Wu et al. (Eds.): ICITL 2018, LNCS 11003, pp. 18–27, 2018.
https://doi.org/10.1007/978-3-319-99737-7_2

strategies which is widely used as a worldwide nursing teaching curriculum. Different from the traditional teaching strategy, students today can learn in full digital contents environment. Thus the nursing educators must think about how to use situational simulation to achieve the expected learning goals. The simulation-based learning is a learner-centered based strategy which provides constructive and stimulates discussion of clinical practice. Students in can achieve maximum learning performance through try-by-errors and self-reflection [4] under a non-threatening environment. It is proved that the simulation-based learning can promote students' clinical decision-making power, self-efficacy and self-confidence, and can overcome learning that cannot be achieved due to the limitations of real clinical situations [5, 6], thus had been heavily used in clinical nursing education, situational simulation activity design and effective laboratory planning and innovation.

Mixed Reality (MR or Hybrid Reality) technology is an extension of Virtual Reality (VR) or Augmented Reality (AR) [7]. In simple terms, AR is the superimposition of computer information into the real world, allowing us to obtain the correct information at the right place and time, while VR only replace the real word scene by a computer-based virtual environment, and the objects and information are placed in it and projected to the user. The user can also use the controller (keyboard, mouse, or others) to control the virtual environment and interaction with the environment. In contrast, MR further integrates the real environment with the need of the environment to create a new mixed environment so that the real and virtual human things can interact and communicate with each other, and it links the real world objects with computer-generated objects. The earliest implementation of MR systems can be traced back to the results developed by Armstrong Laboratories of the US military in the early 1990s [8].

In recent years, AR/VR/MR technologies have been widely used in different technical fields. In addition to art and music, many applications have also been branched out in manufacturing, commerce, and educations. The more significant ones include IPCM, RAVE, Aviation, Healthcare, Remote working, and Military Training [9]. The actual cases are such as: pre-rehearsal surgery, virtual operation of the machine, handheld information prompting service device, interactive games of virtual objects, instant home application devices, and so on. In medical research, the AR/VR/MR is developed extremely rapidly in the hospitals and medical schools. The main reason is that such technologies can effectively save much time, reduce costs, and facilitate collaboration in personnel skills training. There are many medical schools/hospitals using AR/VR/MR for teaching or surgical training. In teaching, students can wear AR/VR glasses to view 3D stereoscopic human structures and organs, and even "take out" an organ for more detailed observation. In surgical training, students or trainees wear AR/VR glasses and perform surgical exercises on the virtual corpse through a 3D Holographic Anatomy program. This allows students to save tens of hours in traditional cadaveric laboratories. The more practical aspect is that the body is not easy to obtain, so surgical simulation can reduce the burden on hospitals or schools.

There are various AR/VR medical applications in the world. For example, the "Visible Human" project carried out by the National Medical Library, it offers a good potential for the understanding and learning of the 3D structure of human anatomy. In terms of surgical simulations, there are bronchial endoscopic surgery simulation system and gallbladder removal surgery simulation system which provided by Immersion and KISMET respectively to train the surgical skill which required hundreds of real operations surgeons in the past. In domestic cases, the Chang Gung Memorial Hospital and University Medical Augmentation Reality Research Center uses medical AR technology to transform the patient's computed tomography scans and magnetic resonance imaging images into a 3D stereoscopic image with a sense of depth. Thus the doctor can observe the bone structure and muscle tissue in different spaces and even remove each bone and find lesions, just like playing video games by wearing the AR tools. In addition, by using of 3D skull repair software, it is possible to make a more beautiful bone implants and repair the broken skull accurately. They had successfully repaired nearly 50 patients form this tool, not only shortened the operation time, but also to ensure good-looking, and even can be used in plastic surgery. Similarly, for AR applications in nursing education, Immersion also provides an intravenous simulation training system which can provide different grades needles and feedback force when the needle in the simulation screen is inserted into the patient's arm to increases the operator's immersive feeling. In addition, the system will also generate an evaluation report for the operator as a reference for improving his skills when the training course is finished. From this perspective, the AR technology had been proved to be very effective in reducing learning barriers, enhancing learning motivation, enhancing learning effectiveness, and reducing staff training time and costs in the field of medical education [10–14].

As stated previously, it is observed that the teaching and learning methods designed by AR/MR technique had been rapidly developed and test in medical education field to evaluate the relative learning performance. It is expected that there will be a large number of physical lesson plans and research results in the near future, thus can be used as a powerful aid for teachers, researchers, and students in teaching activities and technology research such as in [15]. On the other hand, current nursing skills testing methods still rely on more traditional models and it is short of MR techniques. The nursing skill training process still requires a lot of manpower, equipment, as well as the time-space resources, thus increase the restrictions for students' needs in self-study, practice, and pre-testing. That is, it is the most urgent thing in nursing education to develop a strategy to help students achieve automated skills exercises/tests, and self-monitoring without being limited by time, space, and equipment.

In view of this, this study develops a MR training prototype system for automated nursing skills training/exercise to achieve the goal of S-Learning by combining the related content knowledge including nursing skills testing process, designing of hybrid reality imaging system, motion sensing technology, 3D object modeling and dynamic performance, interactive situation design, and video content recognition technology. With the help of this system, students can train themselves without being limited by the time, space, and special equipment to achieve the goal of nursing skills training. In addition, different to the current digital teaching aid system, the proposed system incorporates motion sensing and computer vision technology as a human-machine interface to facilitate the operation. From this it is able to achieve fully automated self-test objectives without an instructor monitoring, and obtain a similar effect as the students are in the real test site field. In this way, the training and testing of nursing skills can not only greatly reduce the investment in real equipment, manpower, and space, but also increase the effectiveness of the training process by means of repeated exercises and system automation and quick feedback. Thus increase the design and implementation of innovative application testing and teaching systems required in the nursing teaching field.

2 The Research Methodology

The realization of MR reality should consider the sensing method in the human-machine interaction for environment and objects. At the same time the imaging mode and equipment are also the key role for successful field application since the HM interaction is the foundation form the traditional digital E-Learning to immersive S-Learning strategy. The commonly used imaging systems include CAVE (Cave Automatic Virtual Environment), HMD (Head Mounted Display), HUD (Head Up Display), Desktop or Tabled PC, and Mobile Phone. Although the holograms can enable users to achieve a best immersive sense of environmental integration, it is not practical since the high cost and complexity for implementing the whole system. Therefore, the development and use of alternative products with similar performance and low cost is the goal of equipment manufacturers in recent years. For example, the Hololens, developed by Microsoft, is simulated by HUD as an omni-directional display [16], or 3D projective holographic display applications [17] can be the good practices. In addition, such as Magic Leap's Retina Projective Reality (Synthetic Reality, which is currently not available for sale) [18], or Oculus Rift VR, and the upcoming Oculus Gloves [19] are also claimed to has exciting effect. From the foregoing, the key issue for MR is the acquisition and identification (including location, time, and style) of users themselves and the present content, while the content, methods, timing, and interaction techniques of the information are also crucial. Therefore, the development of effective methodology to achieve the information retrieval and then combined with appropriate processing procedures to complete the integration of real-world application case requirements is the main goal of this paper.

In order to develop the prototype of MR teaching system, the design considerations of the system platform and the simulation scenarios are the most important. For system platform design, the main considerations include complexity and cost of the system construction (or duplication difficulty), experience comfort and security, integration of real and virtual contents, degree of immersive fusion, difficulty of operation interface, maintenance and adaptation of the system, and the ability for future extensive applications [20, 21]. In general, the helmet-mounted system has the advantages of simple hardware configuration and good immersive fusion degree, while the omnidirectional projection or surround field-covered CAVE design has the most natural and realistic telepresence. However, it brings the drawback of high system complexity and cost. In this paper, the helmet-mounted system design such as the Magic Leap, Holoens and Oculus of the helmet type (HUD/HMD), is adopted to achieve the good immersive perception and low construction cost. The whole system design concept is described as follows:

2.1 Design of the Display Platform

In the initial stage of the prototype system construction, a lightweight head-mounted device which is similar to the Google Cardboard, and an Android OS based mobile phone are used to be combined as the MR system platform. It is observed that the low hardware cost, low construction complexity can be obtained while achieving high complex MR functions integration ability by programming the mobile phone simply to manipulate the built-in various sensing modules. In other words, MR functions such as the external control command input (gesture control or touch I/O), video contents projection, sound effect output, real word image capture and the integration with virtual objects, can be accomplished easily by just writing suitable mobile phone programs. Therefore, it is suitable for the initial development stage of the prototype system as a basis of hardware structure and functions testing. Figure 1 show the proposed MR teaching platform architecture of this paper.

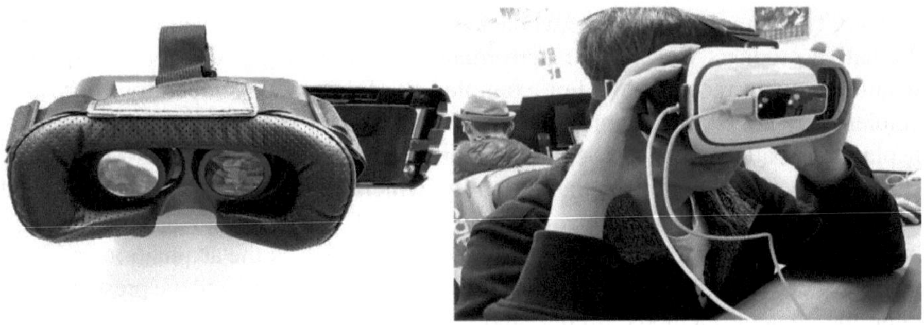

Fig. 1. (Left) The proposed MR teaching platform architecture (with phone inserted), and (Right) Easy to use by wearing the MR training system

2.2 UI Interface and Gesture Control Recognition

In order to attend the goal of interaction with MR system intuitively, the gesture control method is adopted. To reduce the time consuming and noise interference, an optical device module (Leap Motion) is incorporated in the system UI interface for gesture commands recognition rather than traditional video analysis methods. Thus, the system can achieve more accurate and rapid detection of detailed hand movements under a variety of environmental conditions. The Leap Motion sensor functions can be easily developed through the Unity package software which is a 3D game development tool. The goal of the sensor is to transform the actions of the entity gesture operations into the object control in the virtual space, and combine object control on the projection display platform to achieve intuitive situational simulation requirements. The Leap Motion sensor periodically detects the movement information of the hand and each detection package contains a list of information including finger numbers, direction and shape of hands, thus the desired control command can be defined by analyzing the time-varying gesture behavior and control the MR system accordingly. In other words, through the hand-featured information provided by Leap Motion, tracking the static information such as the position, angle, direction, and fingertip position of the hand in space, and the aforementioned time-varying signals, etc., the various gesture commands are defined. Once the gesture behavior recognition is completed, it is converted into the corresponding 3D object control command and then changes the output contents of the projection video.

2.3 The System Software Development Platform

The Unity package software is used as the system software development platform for environment integration. Unity is a cross-platform game engine with very powerful functions for 3D objects and scene processing and can be easily developed and implemented in PC, Mac OS, stand-alone games, or mobile devices such as iOS or Android OS. In addition, it owns comprehensive support for various types of AR/MR software and hardware and the relative public resources are widely used. Due to these factors, it is selected as the integrated development platform for the real-world system. After importing the 3D scene or object model workouts into the Unity and integrate the detected Leap Motion commands, the programmed scenario will be performed and the corresponding videos output is displayed according to the perceived user's gestures to achieve the effect of simulating operations when testing or training process.

2.4 The MR Contents Development Tool

In MR content development consideration, there are many development tools available on the market such as ARToolKit, Wikitude, Unifeye, Apple's AR Kit, and Google's AR Core. However, due to the expensive cost of the commercial products licensed version and the limited support for different platforms, the Vuforia software package, which is an augmented reality suite provided by Qualcomm Inc., is selected as the AR/MR content development tool at the initial stage in our work. In addition to offering the iOS and Android mobile device platform SDKs, it also provides the Unity engine plug-in modules thus it can be easily integrated into our Unity platform for creating the MR application on PCs or mobile devices. Moreover, since the Vuforia is free to download and use but only needs additional payment if advanced features and services are used for commercial purpose, it is in line with our first-phase project requirements.

2.5 Nursing Experts Conduction

On the other hand, in order to confirm the clinical nursing skill test module established in the initial stage, clinical expert consultation was conducted by six clinical practice experts. At the same time they are also served as a collaborative teaching faculty for the industry sector and help to listed important and basic clinical nursing skilled to be trained. These skills comprise nasogastric tube care, urinary catheterization, intravenous administration, suction, and change position. Considering the complexity of the operation steps, required time, manpower, and resources, the nasogastric tube care should be firstly built and tested at the initial stage. Therefore, the operation steps for nasogastric tube care are defined and made according to the nursing textbooks and clinical nursing standards of major hospitals, and then programmed into the MR system prototype as the training/learning contents.

3 Simulation Results and Discussions

To test and evaluate the proposed methodology, a prototype of the MR training system with realistic scenario is planned and implemented on the PC and mobile devices. Although there is variety of nursing skill exercise to be constructed, the nasogastric tube care is selected and built first as the MR contents for self-training and exercise purpose thus to improve the nursing skills of students. The real scenario and objects needed in this nursing skill and the corresponding virtual 3D models can be shown in Fig. 2, while the implemented prototype and the snapshots during the training process are shown in Figs. 3 and 4. This system was applied to ten students of 2-years Nursing program in adult-nursing course as a precursor study. It is observed that via the designed interactive exercise scenarios, students are able to practice their hands-on skill under an immersive environment by watching the HDM and performing skill procedure through hand gestures. During the practice/testing process, the video outcome of each practice from the MR support is varied according to student's gesture under the imported nursing skill standards. In other words, students can gain the learning feedback immediately by the system thus can improve their learning outcomes after each training practice. On the other hand, students can also watch the demonstrations tips and receive instructions for completing the learning course when they met some problems during the training process. A simple result is obtained, from the subjective feedback of students, that the learning motivation and efficiency are increased by the help of the proposed MR teaching support system. Moreover, expensive resources such as nursing teaching aid, educational hardware, and realistic material can be reduced significantly by the virtual 3D models and scenario. That is, the proposed teaching support system provides an eco-friendly and self-learning practical environment anytime and anywhere with gaining immediate learning feedback and practical experiences for the students. However, since only a preliminary analysis was conducted on the reflections of students in this study, an objective evidence of the enhancement of learning effectiveness by using this system

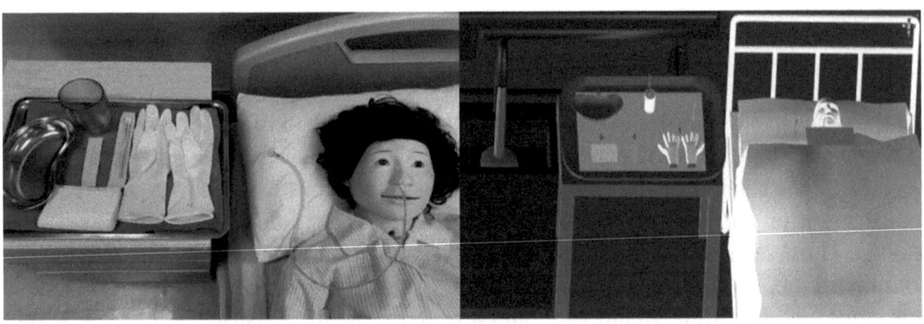

Fig. 2. (Left) The real scenario and the necessary objects used in the nasogastric tube care, and (Right) The MR contents of the 3D scenario and models.

was not obtained. The reliability and validity of this system must be further tested, and rigorous interventional measures must be developed to test the effectiveness of this system and its influence on learning effectiveness.

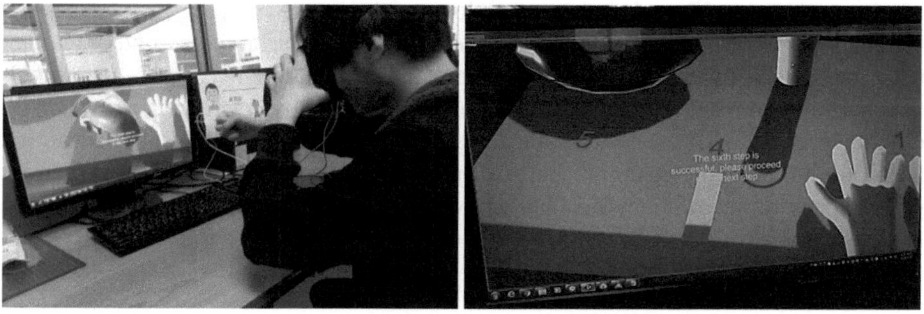

Fig. 3. (Left) Self-train the nasogastric tube care skill by intuitive gesture control, and (Right) User can obtain immediate feedback during the training/testing process

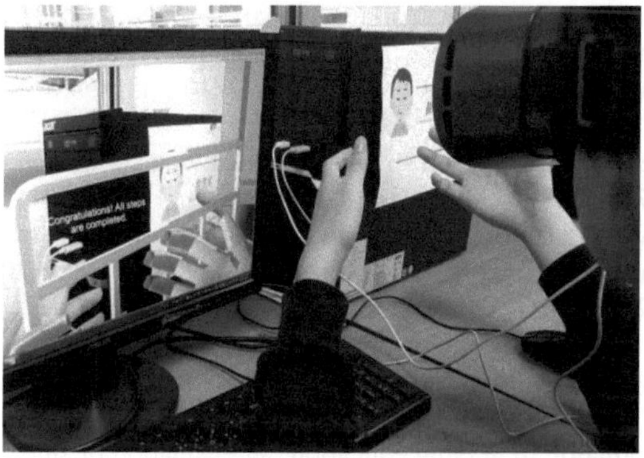

Fig. 4. Completing the training/testing without limitation of tutor manpower, space, and time

4 Conclusions

This paper proposes a powerful teaching/learning assistant system based on mixed reality technology. By combining the techniques including hybrid reality imaging system design, gesture commands recognition, 3D object and scenario modeling, interactive contents design, and AV content output design, an automatic self-learning/testing system prototype is constructed and test to achieve the goal of S-Learning. Through the proposed MR system, various training script in real world can be implemented as corresponding MR contents and be practiced under very low cost while the extra limitations of time, space, manpower, can be removed. It is observed from the test samples feedback that the learning motivation are quite satisfactory in the determined nursing skill test items and can be easily applied to other skill training fields. The large experiment results will be applied to the field courses to collect feedback data from students to verify the effectiveness of proposed learning method.

On the other hands, the students can gain feedback from the MR support system immediately once they finished the test or training process thus to improve their learning efficiency by watching the demonstrations and receive correct instructions for completing the whole operations, while the teachers or educators can find where and what the students often doing wrong and then modify the teaching contents accordingly to help students do better in the future. To sum up, the proposed MR support system not only replaces the traditional medical teaching tool by reduce the exhaust of educational hardware and realistic material, but also provides an eco-friendly and self-learning practical environment in anytime and anywhere with immediate practical experiences feedback to help the students improve their learning motivation, effectiveness, and efficiency.

References

1. Jeffries, P.R. (ed.): Simulation in Nursing Education: From Conceptualization to Evaluation. National league for Nursing, New York (2007)
2. Waxman, K.: The development of evidence-based clinical simulation scenarios: guidelines for nurse educators. J. Nurs. Educ. **49**(1), 29–35 (2010). https://doi.org/10.3928/01484834-20090916-07
3. Landeen, L., Nielson, A.: Focus on simulation-integrating simulation into teaching practice. J. Nurs. Educ. **47**(11), 487–488 (2008)
4. Handwerker, S.M.: Transforming nursing education: a review of current curricular practices in relation to Benner's latest work. Int. J. Nurs. Educ. Scholarsh. **9**(1) (2012). http://dx.doi.org/10.1515/1548-923X.2510, (Article 21)
5. Ahn, H., Kim, H.: Implementation and outcome evaluation of high-fidelity simulation scenarios to integrate cognitive and psychomotor skills for Korean nursing students. Nurse Educ. Today **35**(5), 706–711 (2015)
6. Khalaila, R.: Simulation in nursing education: an evaluation of students' outcomes at their first clinical practice combined with simulations. Nurse Educ. Today **34**, 252–258 (2014). https://doi.org/10.1016/j.nedt.2013.08.015
7. Milgram, P., Kishino, A.F.: Taxonomy of mixed reality visual displays. In: IEICE Transactions on Information and Systems, pp. 1321–1329 (1994). Accessed 17 Oct 2013
8. Hettinger, L.J., Riccio, G.E., Visually induced motion sickness in virtual reality system: implications for training and mission rehearsal, In Interagency Conference on Visual Issues in Training and Simulation, Armstrong Laboratory, Aircrew Training Research Division, Williams Air Force Base, AZ (1991)
9. Shumaker, R., Lackey, S.: Virtual, augmented and mixed reality. designing and developing virtual and augmented environments. In: 6th International Conference Proceedings, Part I, Heraklion, Crete, Greece, 22–27 June (2014)
10. Hussein, M., Nätterdal, C.: The Benefits of Virtual Reality in Education-A Comparison Study, Bachelor Dissertation. Chalmers University of Technology, University of Gothenburg, Sweden (2015)
11. Freina, L., Ott, M.: A literature review on immersive virtual reality in education: state of the art and perspectives. In: Proceedings of eLearning and Software for Education (eLSE), Bucharest, 23–24 April (2015)

12. Zhu, E., Masiello, I., Hadadgar, A., Zary, N.: Augmented reality in healthcare education: an integrative review, PeerJ PrePrints, pp. 1–22 (2014)
13. Reinald, A.D.L., et al.: Augmented reality in nursing education: addressing the limitations of developing a learning material for nurses in the Philippines and Thailand. IJODeL, **2**(1), (2016)
14. Carlson, K.J., Gagnon, D.J.: Augmented reality integrated simulation education in health care. Clin. Simul. Nurs. **12**(4), 123–127 (2016)
15. Lai, C., Chu, Y.: Increasing the learning performance via augmented reality technology. In: Wu, T.-T., Gennari, R., Huang, Y.-M., Xie, H., Cao, Y. (eds.) SETE 2016. LNCS, vol. 10108, pp. 58–64. Springer, Cham (2017). https://doi.org/10.1007/978-3-319-52836-6_8
16. Karthika, S., Praveena, P., GokilaMani, M.: HOLOLENS. Int. J. Comput. Sci. Mobile Comput. **6**(2), 41–50 (2017)
17. Lai, C.: An intuitive and interactive holographic instructional support system. Int. J. Electr. Electron. Data Commun. **5**(9), 32–35 (2017)
18. van der Vlugt, N.: An ontological enquiry into the MagicLeap and Augmented Reality, Master thesis of Philosophy of Science Technology and Society in University of Twente, February 2017
19. Conn, M.A., Sharma, S., Immersive telerobotics using the oculus rift and the 5DT ultra data glove. In: 2016 International Conference on Collaboration Technologies and Systems, pp. 387–391, October 2016
20. Kiyokawa, K.: 3D collaboration using mixed reality technology. In: Proceedings of the First International Symposium on Universal Communication, pp. 100–109 (2007)
21. Krichenbauer, M., Yamamoto, G., Taketomi, T., Sandor, C., Kato, H.: Towards augmented reality user interfaces in 3D media production. In: proceedings of IEEE/ACM International Symposium on Mixed and Augmented Reality (ISMAR), Munich, Germany, pp. 23–28, September 2014

Using Scaffolding Strategy and Real-Time Assessment Programming Tool to Develop a VR-Based Application

Yu-Lin Jeng[1(✉)], Qing Tan[2], and Ya-Chang Wang[1]

[1] Department of Information Management, Southern Taiwan University of Science and Technology, Tainan, Taiwan R.O.C.
jackjeng@mail.stust.edu.tw, 4A490142@stust.edu.tw

[2] School of Computing and Information Systems, Athabasca University, Athabasca, Canada
qingt@athabascau.ca

Abstract. A computer programming course is a great way to foster students' ability in critical thinking and logical thinking. Computer programming skill enables students to build applications using their creativity, and scaffolding strategy helps lecturers to guide students by providing appropriate support. In this study, we proposed a learning activity that combines scaffolding strategy with a real-time assessment programming tool to develop a VR-based game application. During the process of building the VR-based game, the developing logs are collected and analyzed and the error type is sent to the lecturer so that the lecturer is able to provide instant support to the students. After the project, we validated the project results and evaluated the effectiveness of the proposed learning activity by a survey. The survey results indicate that the proposed learning activity is helpful and useful. The experiment results are discussed at the end of the paper.

Keywords: Programming learning · Scaffolding strategy
Real-time assessment

1 Introduction

Papert [1] mentioned that by learning programming language, one can develop logic thinking, cultivate critical thinking, and gain learning competence. Likewise, according to Shafto's observation [2], learning programming design students can enhance their mathematical and scientific capability since software program design allowed learners to solve problems by correcting, defining, implementing, and verifying methods. Jonassen stated that in the process of program design, students must recognize and use various rules of programs [3]. Thus, they have to considerably apply high-level competence such as logic thinking, critical ability, and creativity. Brusilovsky [4] argued that learning program design allows students to develop accurate logic thinking and abstract deduction competence. Thus, students should approach programming design course as early as possible. Barker [5] indicated that children's learning of program design could reinforce their logic thinking, organization, critical and problem-solving capacities. Based on previous literature, learning programming design leads to cultivation of

T.-T. Wu et al. (Eds.): ICITL 2018, LNCS 11003, pp. 28–35, 2018.
https://doi.org/10.1007/978-3-319-99737-7_3

students' high-level thinking competence. In order to enhance students' programming skill, the authors have developed a real-time assessment programming tool which can collect the programming logs from students and identify the error types of those logs. After the analysis of students' error logs, lecturers are able to understand the students' programming ability and coding problems in real-time manner. In this paper, the authors presents using the real-time assessment programming tool [6] and scaffolding strategy to help students to develop a VR-based application. Accordingly, the authors design a learning activity for students to achieve their project goal efficiently. In the end of the learning activity, we validate their project outcome and evaluate the effectiveness of the proposed learning activity conducted by a survey.

The rest of the paper is organized as follows: Sect. 2 describes the related works, Sect. 3 illustrates the proposed learning activity. Then, the project outcome and the survey results are presented in Sect. 4. Finally, the conclusions for this study are provided in Sect. 5.

2 Related Works

Scaffolding means the instructional assistance to enhance students' learning ability by sufficient support when students learn new concept or skill. The main concept is derived from Zone of Proximal Development (ZPD) which is the learning theory developed by Vygotsky [7]. The theory classifies learners' tasks accomplished into three degrees, as shown in Fig. 1. The first is the task which learners can accomplish independently. The second is the task which learners accomplish with assistance. The third is the task which learners cannot accomplish. The second one refers to ZPD called by Vygotsky. Learners are in the state between "being able" and "being unable" to independently accomplish the task. Hence, these learners need the guidance or assistance from lecturers or more

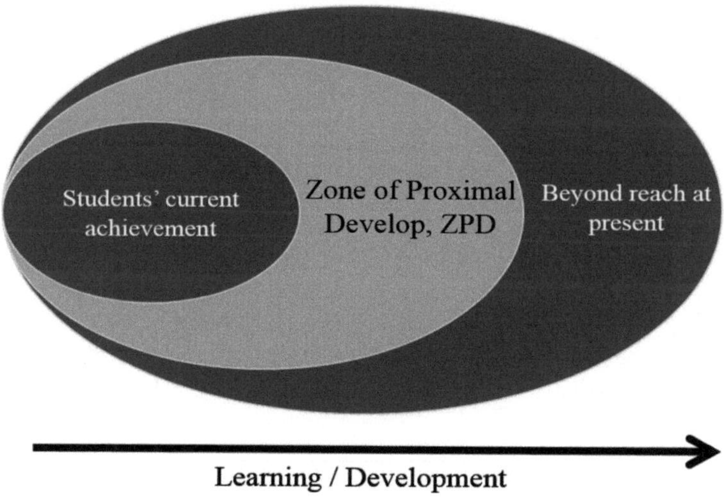

Fig. 1. ZPD illustration

competent peers. In other words, with the intervention of scaffolding assistance, learners can successfully accomplish the task and obtain related skills. Vygotsky argued that ZPD learners cannot independently overcome the obstacle of the task. Thus, they require others' assistance. With others' guidance and assistance, learners are able to finish the task, strengthen personal learning skill and further expand the range of task that they can handle independently.

Scaffolding supports not only learners' learning process, but also lecturers' instruction. Thus, lecturers can establish scaffolding at any time according to students' learning situations to provide guidance and assistance as needed. Hence, learners can successfully achieve their learning objectives. According to related research, scaffolding application in learning activities upgrades learners' learning outcome and enhances learners' learning potential. Although scaffolding positively enhances learning outcome, it should be cautious when practicing scaffolding. Teachers' scaffolding assistance must match students' personal competence level or prior knowledge. When learning content provided by teachers is too difficult, students could be confused and frustrated. When it is too simple, students could not be interested in. Thus, scaffolding assistance is mostly presented by guidance or hints instead of allowing learners to repetitively practice by directly using complete solution. Therefore, learners can establish new knowledge structure based on prior knowledge to enhance the competence to independently accomplish the task, which fulfills the goal of scaffolding guiding instruction.

As to the characteristics to apply scaffolding, Van de Pol [8] proposed three principles. The first is contingency, the second is scaffolding fading and the third is transfer of responsibility, as shown in Fig. 2. Contingency of the first phase means teachers should provide scaffolding according to students' current learning situation, diagnose students' learning outcome at any time and immediately modify scaffolding assistance. At the same time, teachers should be aware that intervention of scaffolding assistance results in improvement of students' learning outcome in order to provide the most appropriate scaffolding assistance. Scaffolding fading of the second phase means

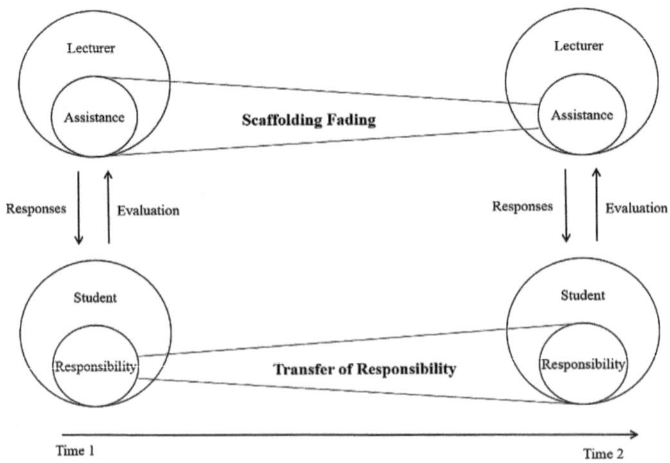

Fig. 2. Scaffolding principles [8]

teachers should constantly progress with students' competence and successively reduce intervention of scaffolding assistance to allow students to gradually and independently accomplish the task. Finally, transfer of responsibility means when intervention of scaffolding assistance is diminishing and students' competence is enhancing, learning responsibility should be gradually transferred to students. Thus, students are able to finish the task independently.

In addition, Van de Pol [8] generalized the research findings of Wood [9] and Tharp and Gallimore [10], and further proposed six instructional methods of Scaffolding, as described below:

(1) Feeding back: Lecturers provide feedback to students regarding students' learning performance.
(2) Hints: Lecturers provide suggestions or clues to students to allow students to ponder on possible solution instead of directly providing students with solution in detail.
(3) Instructing: Lecturers explain to students regarding what and why they should do.
(4) Explaining: Lecturers provide students with more information in detail or in-depth description.
(5) Modeling: Lecturers demonstrate some specific skills to students who can thus imitate and learn from them.
(6) Questioning: Lecturers pose some questions to students and hence students can ponder on and result in cognitive structure.

Based on the above, it shows that Scaffolding enhances students' development of high level of intellectual competence. Through temporary scaffolding guiding instruction assistance, students can initialize learning and successively learning responsibility can be transferred. Therefore, students are able to accomplish the task independently. In addition, in Scaffolding based instruction, learning can be integrated in learning activity. Based on their prior knowledge, learners gain new knowledge, which results in active learning. In learning process, learners only receive suggestions or assistance. As to the rest, it relies on their active learning behaviors.

3 Research Design

3.1 Learning Activity Design

The goal of this research is to use the real-time assessment programming tool to help lecturer to understand the learning status of students so that lecturer can provide real-time assistance for students. The architecture of the proposed idea is illustrated in Fig. 3. Students uses Visual Studio as development tool to develop VR-based application. In the developing process, the real-time assessment programming tool will collect the developing logs and the analytic server will analyze the logs and provide graphical analysis results for lecturers. Lecturers as the experts in this learning activity will then provide their learning assistance according to students' need.

In order to help students to develop a VR-based project, we proposed a learning activity combine with scaffolding strategy and the real-time assessment programming

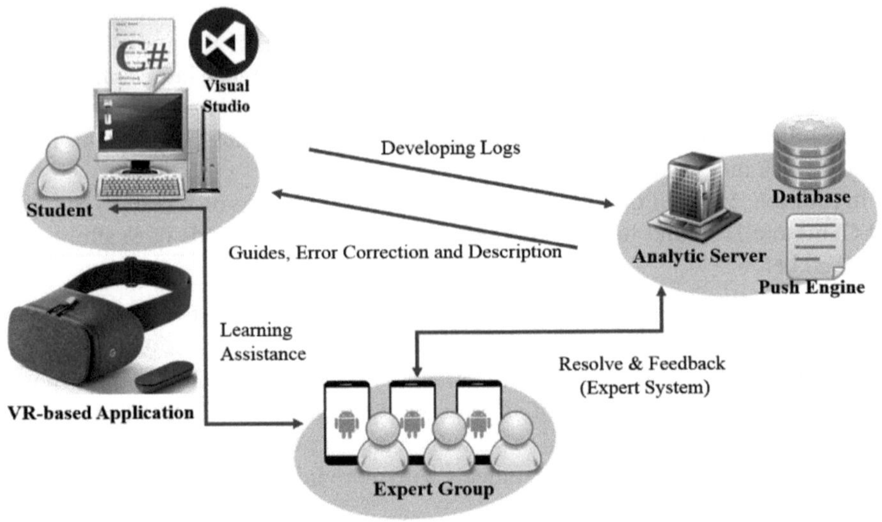

Fig. 3. The proposed architecture of the research

tool. The learning sequences include the following six instructional activities. And the process of instructional activities is shown in Fig. 4:

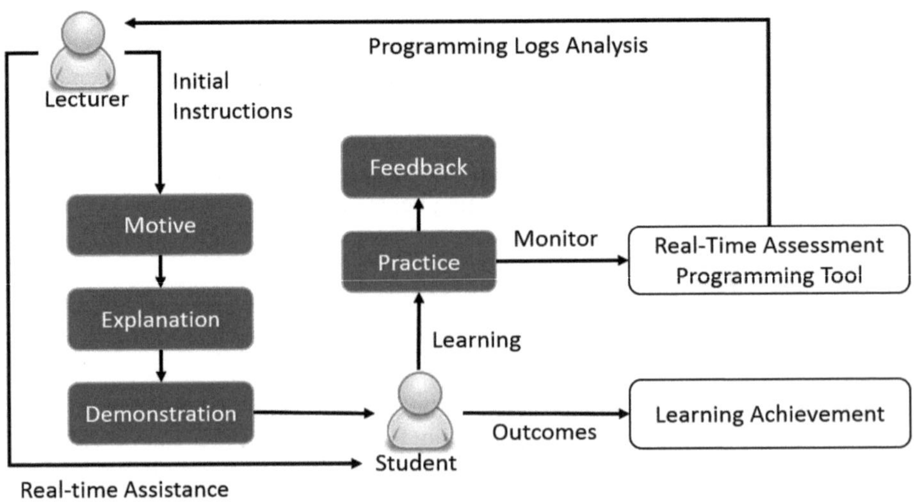

Fig. 4. Learning activity process

(1) Development of motive: lecturers elaborate the application of program examples in real environment
(2) Explanation of concept: lecturers explain learning concept
(3) Demonstration of example: lecturers propose appropriate examples regarding the topics and demonstrate the operation

(4) Operation and practice: according to lecturers' demonstration of example, students operate and practice the system independently.
(5) Scaffolding assistance: lecturers provide assistance according to students' problems
(6) Learning/feedback: students present learning and feedback of project development

With the help of the real-time assessment programming tool, lecturers are able to receive students' developing logs analysis results and its error types so that lecturers can provide the real-time assistance.

3.2 Implementation Interfaces

After the learning activity and the implementation of the project, students have completed a VR-based application which runs on Google DayDream device. The demonstration picture is shown in Fig. 5. The left-hand side interface shows the running VR game and the right-hand side shows the student who plays with the VR game. In this VR game, student use the DayDream controller as the dart and shoot the dart in VR environment. In this project, students need to use two developing tool to complete this project. Students use Unity 3D to create 3D models and environment, use Visual Studio to control the game logic and motion definition. Therefore, the assistance from the lecturer is important due to the complex developing settings. In the proposed learning activity, lecturer is able to receive the real-time developing reports from real-time assessment programming tool so that the lecturer can provide more support in time.

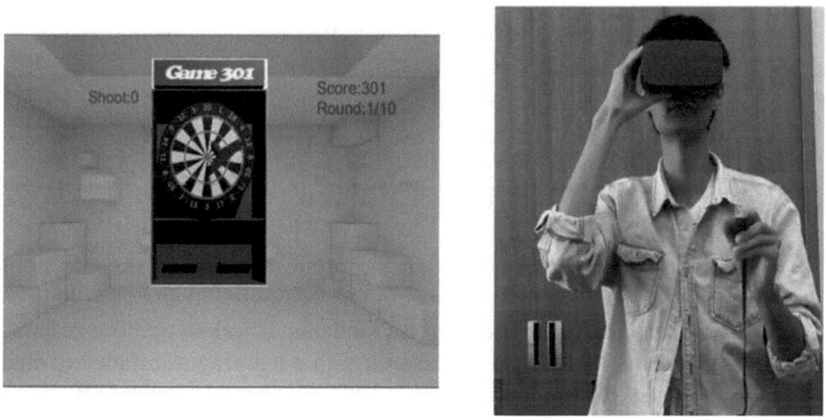

Fig. 5. The implementation interfaces of the project

4 Experimental Results and Discussions

In the proposed learning activity, we develop the motive of students and then guide them with practice program examples. After the learning stage, students need to implement a project by solving all kinds of problems. During this stage, students usually need specific help from lecturer. However, students sometimes do not know what is the problem they are facing at the particular time. Therefore, the real-time assessment programing tool will provide the programming logs analysis results to lecturer who can accordingly provide learning support in time. In this experiment, we want to inspect the responses from students to understand the effectiveness of the proposed learning activity.

In this experiment, we asked 12 students who joined the development of the VR-based application project to provide their feedback by answering a questionnaire. The response portion of each question in the questionnaire was designed using a 5-point Likert scale. Typically, an item in a Likert scale is given as a statement and the invited experts need to respond the statement using a scale from 1 to 5, in which 5 stands for "strongly agree" and 1 stands for "strongly disagree". The 5 level responses also stand for the score of each question thus we can calculate the mean value of each item. The questionnaire item and statement includes:

(1) The proposed learning activity accelerates the developing process.
(2) The proposed learning process is easy to follow up.
(3) The lecturer usually provides useful suggestions for me.
(4) Most problems during project development can be solved by this learning activity.
(5) The proposed learning activity helps me to avoid making the same developing error.

The responses data from students were collected from online survey system and it can be further analyzed and discussed. The statistical results were presented in Table 1. The 5th column describes the percentage of each item score that are greater or equal to 4.

Table 1. Questionnaire results

Item	Mean	Stand deviation	Variance	Score >= 4
1	4.17	0.799	0.639	75.0%
2	4.08	0.640	0.410	83.0%
3	4.25	0.722	0.521	83.0%
4	3.75	0.433	0.188	75.0%
5	4.25	0.595	0.354	91.7%

The responses to Item (1) indicate that the proposed learning activity helps the developing process of the VR game project. The responses to Item (2) indicate the proposed learning process is not too hard for students to follow up. The responses to Item (3) indicate the lecturer can provide appropriate learning assistance to students. These responses reflect the proposed learning activity is useful and effective in project development. However, the score of the responses to Item (4) is less than 4. It shows that the students still have problems in this activity. According to the interview with those students, it indicates that completing the practice project needs not only programming skills but also system design and analysis knowledge. The proposed learning activity focuses too much on the programming skill and lacks other important theoretical knowledge. Therefore, extra learning resources are needed in the proposed learning activity to enhance students' domain knowledge. Finally, the responses to Item (5) indicate that students are able to aware of their programming error type and they have learned to avoid making the same error when programming.

5 Conclusions

VR-based game is a very popular type of digital game. Students are getting more and more interested in developing their own VR game at school. However, it is hard for them to develop a complete VR game without extra assistance. This research proposed a learning activity for lecturers and students to follow and to accomplish the VR project step by step. In the proposed learning activity, a lecturer can get the program developing status of students through the real-time assessment programming tool so that the lecturer is able to know what kind of support that the students need. With implementing the scaffolding assistance, students can finally complete their VR-based project. After they finish their project, we evaluated their project results and collected their feedback by a survey. The survey results indicate that the proposed learning activity is useful for students to learn programming. However, it also indicates that extra learning resources are also needed for students to fulfill the requirement of the project, such as, the theory of system design and analysis.

Acknowledgement. The authors would like to thank the Ministry of Science and Technology of the Republic of China, Taiwan, for financially supporting this research under Contract No. MOST 105-2511-S-218-003-MY2.

References

1. Papert, S.: Mindstorms: Children, Computer, and Powerful Ideas. Basic Books, New York (1980)
2. Shafto, S.A.S.: Programming for learning in mathematics and science. ACM SIGCSE Bull. **18**(1), 296–302 (1986)
3. Jonassen, D.H.: Computers in the Classroom: Mindtools for Critical Thinking. Prentice-Hall, Englewood Cliffs (1996)
4. Brusilovsky, P., Calabrese, E., Hvorecky, J., Kouchnirenko, A., Miller, P.: Mini-languages: a way to learn programming principles. Educ. Inf. Technol. **2**(1), 65–83 (1997)
5. Barker, G., Lao, A.C., Reynolds, B.L., Wu, F.: Learning efficiencies using multi-agent based game simulations. In: Proceedings of the 16th International Conference on Computers in Education, Taipei, Taiwan, pp. 737–741 (2008)
6. Jeng, Y.L., Tan, Q., Shu, Y., Huang, S.B.: A real-time assessment of programming through debugging log analytic. In: International Symposium on Emerging Technologies for Education, pp. 438–445 (2017)
7. Vygotsky, L.S.: Mind in Society: The Development of Higher Psychological Processes. Harvard Universisy Press, Cambrige (1978)
8. Van de Pol, J., Volman, M., Beishuizen, J.: Scaffolding in teacher-student interaction: a decade of research. Educ. Psychol. Rev. **22**(3), 271–297 (2010)
9. Wood, D., Bruner, J.S., Ross, G.: The role of tutoring in problem solving. J. Child Psychol. Psychiatr. **17**(2), 89–100 (1976)
10. Tharp, R.G., Gallimore, R.: Rousing Minds to Life: Teaching, Learning, and Schooling in Social Context. Cambridge University Press, Cambridge (1988)

Virtual Reality and Knowledge Rediscovery in Sub-Sahara Africa: A Review of Literature

Newton Buliva(✉)

University of North Texas, Denton, TX, USA
newtonbuliva@my.unt.edu

Abstract. Even as the effectiveness of Virtual Reality (VR) in education begins to be understood in the US and western Europe, the potential for this technology to lead to knowledge rediscovery and lifelong learning in Sub-Saharan Africa remains unexploited. This region has unique educational-delivery problems that position VR as a premier instrument that may respond to learners' needs. Factors hindering education in Sub-Sahara Africa include the high expenses for students attending brick-and-mortar schools; the long distances learners must travel to access these schools; the lack of learning materials like books and writing instruments; and few educational technology professionals. This present research reviewed published research articles on how VR, as an educational tool, can be used to address these problems and lead to knowledge rediscovery and lifelong learning in Africa. The review suggested that, at this time, VR can only be used as a supplementary teaching aid to assist learner understanding.

Keywords: Virtual Reality · Sub-Sahara Africa · Educational technology Knowledge rediscovery · Lifelong learning

1 Introduction

As technology becomes ubiquitous in education, and as its use spreads rapidly, Virtual Reality (VR) is becoming an essential tool for education, especially in industrialized countries. A successful VR is a user interface that involves real-time simulation and interaction through multiple sensorial channels which include vision, audio, touch, smell and even taste [1]. Thus, a successful VR platform allows users to interact with it, to be fully immersed in it and it also fires up users' imaginations. A system that can have users so absorbed in it, can also be used for educational and training purposes. This versatility allows both instructors and learners to construct and reconstruct knowledge [2], further blurring the boundary between instructor and learner, and instead building a community of learners. Students learn best when they enjoy a rich, multi-modal experience that facilitates teaching and learning, and takes into consideration the real-life world [3, 4]. It is no longer sufficient for learners to just read books, look at a computer screen, or listen to an instructor. These forms of learning and teaching are only partially engaging. Instead, as Furness, Winn and Yu note, students need to experience the concepts and principles contained in the content as much and as directly as possible for effective learning to occur. Virtual Reality offers this experiential learning, which often requires mental and physical engagement, appropriate

T.-T. Wu et al. (Eds.): ICITL 2018, LNCS 11003, pp. 36–47, 2018.
https://doi.org/10.1007/978-3-319-99737-7_4

amounts of challenge and an appropriate pedagogical framework for learning to be effective. Research has also suggested that intrinsic motivation is increased if the learner has ownership of experience and control over and personal involvement in the experience [3]. VR offers learners the ability to construct their own ideas directly from experience, thus increasing intrinsic motivation.

This explosion in the use of virtual reality as an educational tool is becoming well-established in the developed world, especially in western Europe and north America. Considering the traditional limits to mass education in sub-Saharan Africa, VR as an educational tool is under critical consideration as a tool for alternative access to learning. However, the introduction of VR requires a reliable supply of electric power, the necessary bandwidth and professional expertise to prepare the content and to instruct learners. Nevertheless, these costs are relative compared to the costs of building brick-and-mortar learning institutions, the costs of maintaining educational buildings, and personnel costs, which have all limited the expansion of learning opportunities for Sub-Sahara Africa's learners.

2 Purpose and Research Question

The purpose of this paper is to review research on the use of VR in sub-Sahara Africa and to evaluate its importance in knowledge rediscovery. This present review reflects on the need to deploy VR as a learning tool in these countries. The research questions considered by this current review include: To what extent is VR a viable tool of education in sub-Sahara Africa? To what extent is VR limited as an educational tool in these countries? To what extent can VR be used as a tool that leads to knowledge rediscovery and lifelong learning in sub-Saharan Africa?

3 Method

A search was conducted on the major research databases including: ProQuest, ERIC, EBSCOhost, PsycInfo, JSTOR, Project MUSE, Google Scholar, and databases that focus on African research (for example, African Journals Online, and Africa Research). The search was conducted from March 25th, 2018 to April 23rd, 2018 and targeted the year 1970 to the present. The search used these terms: Africa Virtual Reality, Virtual Reality in African education, and immersive technology in Africa.

4 Findings

Using these terms, the review identified 26 articles that directly addressed VR in African education or training. This report focused on these 26 research articles which were then grouped into the two themes: VR for educational purposes and VR in commercial use. Four of the research pieces addressed VR in training for industries like mining, tourism, and healthcare. Four other items addressed VR regarding student learning and education, but the rest of the articles (18) treated VR in Africa in general terms, as part of other learning technologies.

The review summarized the articles, identifying the main points addressed. The main points were:

- There is poor digital infrastructure in sub-Sahara Africa that may not sustain the use of VR in mass education
- There is insufficient and unreliable supply of electricity which is fundamental for successful use of educational technology
- The prices of VR hardware are often out of reach for local educators and institutions
- Inadequate bandwidth to support VR technologies
- Few trained personnel that are inadequate to address the VR interaction for learners

These findings are noted in Table 1 below:

Most of the articles on VR in African education identified poor digital infrastructure on the continent that at this time is unable to sustain the use of VR in mass education. Most of the articles also identified the insufficient supply of electricity to African learning institutions as a hindrance to the establishment of VR in these institutions. Other drawbacks included: inadequate telecommunications, lack of VR hardware, low bandwidth and limited trained personnel.

Researchers [20] have found that connectivity, capacity and content still elude African educational planners in their attempt to implement robust digital learning infrastructures.

The extent of the use of VR in education in Africa remains unclear. There is a pan-African university, African Virtual University (AVU), that offers distance education to learners in 30 African countries. It was launched in 1997 in Washington, DC, with assistance from the World Bank and is headquartered in Nairobi, Kenya. Although its title includes the word 'virtual', it does not offer VR experiences to learners. Instead, it mostly provides distance, asynchronous learning using open sources to learners in 54 learning centers in sub-Saharan Africa countries.

In a review of the AVU, researchers [5] evaluate the role of the university in the education of youth in Africa. These researchers contend that the university does not support local development but has been foisted on the locals because the western countries that are backing it have deep financial wherewithal. It is important that foreign-local partnerships in the transfer of educational technology be sensitive to local needs.

It is also important that authentic local content is utilized if VR should lead to knowledge rediscovery. These investigators [5] note that in the case of the AVU most of the learning content is directly imported from the US and Europe via satellite, with minimal local input. These authors state that foreign and culturally-inappropriate content offered by the university do not resonate with the needs of local learners. They claim that the university is a debt trap that peddles obsolete products by discouraging local innovation and establishing dependency. These authors conclude that this virtual university is unsuitable for sub-Sahara Africa.

VR offers one way to reach learners who cannot rediscover knowledge through traditional learning forms. Conventional forms of learning limit access to educational and learning opportunities to those with financial ability. VR could present to these

Table 1. Articles reviewed, and the main points addressed.

Ref#	Author(s)	Main Points Addressed
[5]	Amutabi, Oketch	a. The authors review the performance of the African Virtual University (AVU) b. They note that the AVU delivers content that is not appropriate to the learners c. They state that the AVU approaches all the learners from the region as if they are in a homogenous setting, yet they are from various countries d. They conclude that the AVU is not appropriate for learners in the region
[6]	Gulati	a. Author presents an overview of technology-facilitated learning for deprived populations b. Discusses challenges by learners in developing countries in trying to access education c. Questions whether developing nations should invest resources in e-learning
[7]	Guttentag	a. Author considers application of VR in tourism because of its immersive experience b. VR allows visits to inaccessible or insecure places c. Practical application of VR in developing countries
[8]	Hawkins	a. A review of failures and successes of educational technology in developing countries b. Call for educational policies to be formulated that are recognize the importance of educational technologies c. the need for local communities to have a buy-in in educational technologies
[9]	Keengwe, Bhargava	a. Reviews the relevance of social and cultural context of mobile technologies on educational opportunities in developing countries b. They note that some technologies may not be appropriate for developing countries
[10]	Morris, Louw, Crous	a. Offers a practical use of VR in conjunction with pharmacological analgesia to reduce paid and anxiety in adult burn patients b. Based in South Africa, the study suggested that VR systems can be a useful adjunct therapy for burn pain management
[11]	Sife, Lwoga, Sanga	a. A review of Information and Communications Technologies (ICT) in developing countries b. Discusses pedagogical, costs and technical implications of educational technologies in developing countries
[12]	Squelch	a. A study on real-world application of VR technology in South African mining

(*continued*)

Table 1. (*continued*)

Ref#	Author(s)	Main Points Addressed
		b. Training of miners to reduce accidents and fatalities in South African mines c. Effective alternative mode of training for safety and hazard awareness
[13]	Tichon, Burgess-Limerick	a. A review of VR in mining in South Africa b. Training using VR gives miners improved motor and cognitive skills, thus reducing accidents b. VR for safety training
[14]	Zymberg, Vaz-Guimarães Filho, Lyra	a. Although study is not based on Africa, it is based on a developing country – Brazil, and has relevance to Africa b. VR use in medical training – skull surgical training techniques c. Recommend the use of VR to improve skills
[15]	Eschenbrenner, Nah, Siau	a. Though not based on Africa, this study helped explain benefits of VR and how it responds to pedagogical needs b. Underscores the unexplored potential of VR in education
[16]	Czerniewicz	a. Study based at the University of Cape Town, South Africa on challenges of educational technologies b. Discusses the need to overcome the digital divide, respond to a new communication order and transforming higher education in post-apartheid South Africa
[17]	Dawley, Dede	a. Article helps in reviewing examples of virtual worlds and immersive simulations b. Explores the designs, adaptation and support of situated learning experiences using VR c. Reviews educational purposes of VR, theoretical foundations and learning affordances and limitations
[18]	Etzo, Collender	a. Although not on VR, this article helps us understand the infrastructure of African technology b. In addition to VR, m-learning may prove important because of the widespread use of mobile phones in Africa
[19]	Global System for Mobile Communication (GSMA)	a. This report helps to review the reach of mobile phones in sub-Sahara Africa b. M-learning may also prove important in the region
[20]	Gunga, Ricketts	a. Article explores collaboration between public and private partners in bringing e-learning to African universities

(*continued*)

Table 1. (*continued*)

Ref#	Author(s)	Main Points Addressed
		b. Emphasizes the need for collaboration among stakeholders for success of e-learning in the region
[21]	Lee	a. Explores human capital development arising from expansion of educational technology in developing countries b. Discusses measures to build appropriate human capacity for new technologies in developing countries
[22]	Klopfer, Yoon	a. Although not about Africa, the articles helps understand how to develop VR content for tech savvy learners
[23]	Mtebe, Raisamo	a. Discusses the adoption of LMS in higher education in Sub-Sahara Africa b. Article was useful in understanding the infrastructure of African educational technology
[24]	Nafukho, Muyia	a. Article concludes that the design of the African Virtual University was flawed because it did not involve the local communities b. The AVU did not lower costs of learning for the students despite the region becoming a booming market for e-learning markets
[25]	Pineteh	a. Examines virtual interactions at a South African university b. It notes that traditional forms of teaching are still important despite virtual interactions c. Calls for both forms of teaching
[26]	Hicks	a. Discusses the set-up of the AVU following reduced funding for public education in sub-Sahara Africa b. Concludes that the AVU is a top-down system and that most learners do not have the infrastructure to access the content
[27]	Perkins	a. A series of concise reports on ICT and the African continent
[28]	Lockwood	a. Describes VR projects in Africa b. Argues for PCs to be used to access VR because of their affordability c. Highlights the need to preserve and promote African culture through VR
[29]	Makransky, Lilleholt	a. Although not based on Africa, this paper discusses VR as it is projected to play an important role in education by increasing student engagement and motivation

(*continued*)

Table 1. (*continued*)

Ref#	Author(s)	Main Points Addressed
		b. It explores the differences of using either immersive or desktop VR to administer a virtual science learning simulation
[30]	Monahan, McArdle, Bertolotto	a. Although this is not based on Africa, it suggests that VR affords lifelong learning as it is innovative and can motivate learners
[31]	Van Wyk, De Villiers	a. Another article that explores VR in the service of the mining industry in South Africa b. It discusses how VR training tools can provide simulated exposure to real-world working conditions without the associated risks
[32]	Dewailly	a. This article discusses the role of VR in tourism, which is a major income earner for countries in sub-Sahara Africa

countries a solution to overcome the rigid educational infrastructures that restrict knowledge rediscovery and lifelong learning. VR offers flexibility in terms of time and place where learning occurs; it does not limit knowledge rediscovery to a traditional classroom. An author [6] notes that lack of resources in developing countries, results in learners having a limited number of textbooks, desks, libraries, laboratories and writing spaces. Some of these inequalities may partly be addressed using VR technology. Most disadvantaged learners in sub-Sahara Africa are marginalized, live in rural areas, are often isolated, poor, neglected, and they attend schools staffed with unqualified teachers with little access to information [32]. It is these sorts of learners that VR educational may assist in rediscovering knowledge.

Some researchers have advocated for the use of mobile technologies in knowledge acquisition in sub-Sahara Africa because of the broad penetration of mobile phones in the region (for example, [9]). According to an organization that represents the interests of mobile network providers worldwide [19], there were 420 million unique mobile subscribers in sub-Sahara Africa in 2016, representing a mobile penetration rate of 43%. This represents a growth of 6.1% and is 50% higher than the global average. By the end of 2016, the total number of SIM connections in this region had reached 731 million and are projected to rise to nearly 1 billion connections by 2020. Despite this phenomenal growth in mobile phone connections, fully integrated use of VR can offer a more significant advantage to learners than mobile connections.

However, some VR learning technologies are being used in this region. An author [7] notes that tourism is important for the economies of most African countries. He indicates that because it provides an immersive experience, VR can be used to have visitors tour inaccessible touristic destinations. Inaccessibility of touristic destinations could be due to concerns over security and safety, the fragility of the site, the distance and costs of travelling, among others, he notes. By employing VR in the service of the tourism sector, these countries can attract more visitors, and may spur greater tourist traffic to their countries' attractions.

VR technologies can also lead to knowledge rediscovery in the medical area in sub-Sahara Africa. One of the most common uses of VR technology is in the medical area. An example of VR use in the medical field was a study conducted by researchers [10] who considered the feasibility of low-cost VR system in reducing pain in adult patients in South Africa. They examined the possibility of using VR in conjunction with pharmacological analgesia, to reduce pain and anxiety in adult burn patients undergoing treatment. The researchers measured pain and anxiety for patients using VR and analgesia and those using analgesia only. The study did not find any significant difference between the two sets of patients, despite the growing trend to employ VR as an additional tool in alleviating pain in South Africa.

These researchers' study [10] provides an instructive case study on the use of VR for knowledge rediscovery. The researchers suggest that low-cost VR systems show promise as a clinically useful adjunct therapy to the current burn pain management regimens in South Africa.

Mining companies in South Africa are also investing in VR as an alternative form of training. Mine safety is crucial for these companies and VR gives learners opportunities to practice without being in the actual mines. Another researcher [12] presents an interesting case study on the use of VR and its real-world application in the service of South African mining companies. The researcher reports that there are high incidences of accidents and fatalities in South African mines, which are mostly attributed to ineffective or inappropriate training methods and materials. The researcher recommends the use of VR as an alternative training solution to improve the effectiveness of safety and hazard awareness training which is a rediscovery of knowledge.

Other researchers [13], also consider the use of VR in mines. Because of its financial clout, which is a result of significant mineral riches, South Africa is a leading utilizer of Virtual Reality in Africa, especially in the training of miners. The researchers note that mining is a high-risk industry which results in loss of life and limb for miners. Compromised human safety also results in a slow-down of production which impacts the mining companies financially. In this regard, VR simulation offers the opportunity to develop perceptual expertise, improved motor, and cognitive skills among miners. The use of VR in such dynamic ways thus leads to lifelong learning and growth.

5 Discussion

VR holds the promise of playing a significant role in knowledge rediscovery and lifelong learning in sub-Sahara Africa. Because of its affordances that allow learners to visualize concepts and form accurate mental images of hard-to-understand concepts, its potential on the continent remains untapped. It is pointed out [28] that VR offers new ways to visually communicate ideas, skills and knowledge such that it overcomes literacy barriers so often experienced in education and training.

For sub-Sahara Africa, VR can lead to knowledge rediscovery by facilitating the transfer of context-specific knowledge, thus overcoming traditional verbal and written barriers to communication, according to Lockwood. He notes that knowledge can be successfully transferred through this medium because it is rich in context and concept, in addition to providing learners with a rewarding visual experience when well-designed.

Knowledge rediscovery can be aided when learners renew interest in learning concepts when they are presented in a new and engaging manner. Perhaps a concept was taught, but the learner did not understand it because of the way it was explained. Enter VR, which can enable the learner to look at the content in a new light. Through VR, learners can visualize, for example, production processes, scientific and engineering processes and rediscover past historical and cultural worlds. For centuries, Africa's traditional forms of communication, and the preservation and promotion of local history, have relied on oral transmission from one generation to the next. As Lockwood notes, VR affords people in sub-Sahara Africa a medium to visually facilitate the transfer of context-specific knowledge that is inhibited by traditional verbal and written barriers to communication.

VR technologies in Africa can be applied to the farming community, where learners can rediscover knowledge by virtually experiencing how successful farmers care for their crops and livestock. Additionally, most rural sub-Saharan Africa farmers rely heavily on micro-finance schemes to develop their businesses and farming. A VR platform can guide potential borrowers through the borrowing process and even successful use and repayment of micro-finance loans.

Furthermore, Africa is a continent inundated with refugees escaping hunger, famine, war and political oppression. It is possible that a VR program can allow government officials, donors, and others, to experience what these refugees experience such that they can understand their problems and address them; a rediscovery of knowledge, as it were. Learners can also experience, through VR, examples of good governance and learn from these. Additionally, a VR experience of better health services can be determined by medical personnel so that they can rediscover knowledge on how to care for patients.

The review suggests that VR is not yet standardized in education and training in sub-Sahara Africa. Most VR use is on an experimental basis, with much of it being used in mining industries in South Africa and some usage in the medical field. This review failed to find any research on VR use in public education systems in sub-Sahara Africa. However, VR as an educational tool still holds great promise for learners in this part of the world. According to research [21] many developing countries, including those in sub-Sahara Africa, have not caught up with developed countries technologically because of poverty. This also means that they cannot absorb any technology diffused from the developed countries. Additionally, these countries lack the human capacity to utilize and promote advanced technologies such as VR.

Another challenge facing learners in sub-Sahara Africa is that national educational policies do not address learning through instructional technologies. Additionally, the instructors who are required to teach distance courses are not adequately trained to teach in digital environments, and often lack teaching experience. If VR is to be successfully integrated into learning institutions in sub-Sahara Africa, then national policies should be adjusted to accommodate learners who use this technology. Some research [8] recommends consideration for the support of teachers' professional development so that they can operate new educational technology. This research calls for a review of national educational technology policies to bring them in line with interaction with current technologies. It states that for digital technologies to be successful in the region, there is need to have buy-in from the local community. It also emphasizes the need to have private-public sector partnerships and the importance of empowering girls in the utilization of educational technology.

One way to address the costs of VR equipment is to deploy it on personal computers (PCs). PCs are readily available in African countries, and they can handle the intensive 3D graphics used in VR [28]. Furthermore, the costs of VR equipment have been declining over the last few years. Learners can take advantage of lower cost Google Cardboard Kit(T) which are now available for under US$ 10.00.

Sub-Saharan Africa countries can also enter into partnerships with much established VR providers in developed countries to learn from them and facilitate the transfer of technology. There is need to assist local educators and trainers with the capacity to comprehensively use these systems. Although many researchers have criticized the model of the African Virtual Universities, it is a starting point through which locals can be empowered to influence the content of the learning material so that it incorporates local cultures and traditions. Unless learners identify with the content, local knowledge will remain undiscovered, and foreign content will be viewed as a short-term way to merely earn certificates.

6 Conclusion

In a continent where 35% of the adult population (about 153 million people) are illiterate, two-thirds of whom are women [34], VR tools present the possibility for these learners to rediscover knowledge and experience life-long learning since it de-emphasizes the use of written text and promotes learner interaction in authentic settings.

References

1. Burdea Grigore, C., Coiffet, P.: Virtual Reality Technology. Wiley-Interscience, London (1994)
2. Pineteh, E.A.: Using virtual interactions to enhance the teaching of communication skills to information technology students. Br. J. Educ. Technol. 85–96 (2012). https://doi.org/10.1111/j.1467-8535.2011.01193.x
3. Furness III, T.A., Winn, W., Yu, R.: The Impact of Three Dimensional Immersive Virtual Environments on Modern Pedagogy: Global Change, VR and Learning. A report of workshops held in Seattle, Washington, and Loughborough, England (1997)
4. Istenic Starčič, A., Cotic, M., Solomonides, I., Volk, M.: Engaging preservice primary and preprimary school teachers in digital storytelling for the teaching and learning of mathematics. Br. J. Educ. Technol. 29–50 (2016) https://doi.org/10.1111/bjet.12253
5. Amutabi, M.N., Oketch, M.O.: Experimenting in distance education: the African Virtual University (AVU) and the paradox of the World Bank in Kenya. Int. J. Educ. Dev. **23**(1), 57–73 (2003). https://doi.org/10.1016/S0738-0593(01)00052-9
6. Gulati, S.: Technology-enhanced learning in developing nations: a review. Int. Rev. Res. Open Distrib. Learn. **9**(1) (2008). http://dx.doi.org/10.19173/irrodl.v9i1.477

7. Guttentag, D.A.: Virtual reality: applications and implications for tourism. Tourism Manage. **31**, 637–651 (2008). https://doi.org/10.1016/j.tourman.2009.07.003
8. Hawkins, R.J.: Ten lessons for ICT and education in the developing world. In: CID (Center for International Development), The Global Information Technology Report 2001–2002: Readiness for the networked world (chap. 4). Oxford University Press, Oxford (2002)
9. Keengwe, J., Bhargava, M.: Mobile learning and integration of mobile technologies in education. Educ. Inf. Technol. **19**, 737–746 (2014). https://doi.org/10.1007/s10639-013-9250-3
10. Morris, L.D., Louw, Q.A., Crous, L.C.: Feasibility and potential effect of a low-cost virtual reality system on reducing pain and anxiety in adult burn injury patients during physiotherapy in a developing country. Burns **36**, 659–664 (2010). https://doi.org/10.1016/j.burns.2009.09.005
11. Sife, A., Lwoga, E., Sanga, C.: New technologies for teaching and learning: Challenges for higher learning institutions in developing countries. Int. J. Educ. Dev. Using ICT **3** (2007)
12. Squelch, A.P.: Virtual reality for mine safety training in South Africa. J. S. Afr. Inst. Min. Metall. **101**, 209–216 (2001)
13. Tichon, J., Burgess-Limerick, R.: A review of virtual reality as a medium for safety related training in mining. J. Health Saf. Res. Pract. **3**(1), 33–40 (2011)
14. Zymberg, S., Vaz-Guimarães Filho, F., Lyra, M.: Neuroendoscopic training: presentation of a new real simulator. min-minimally invasive. Neurosurgery **53**(01), 44–46 (2010). https://doi.org/10.1055/s-0029-1246169
15. Eschenbrenner, B., Nah, F.F., Siau, K.: 3-D virtual worlds in education: applications, benefits, issues and opportunities. J. Database Manage. **19**(4), (2008). https://doi.org/10.4018/jdm.2008100106
16. Czerniewicz, L.: Cape of storms or cape of good hope? Educational technology in a changing environment. Br. J. Educ. Technol. **35**(2), 145–158 (2004). https://doi.org/10.1111/j.0007-1013.2004.00377.x
17. Dawley, L., Dede, C.: Situated learning in virtual worlds and immersive simulations. In: Spector, J., Merrill, M., Elen, J., Bishop, M. (eds.) Handbook of Research on Educational Communications and Technology, pp. 723–734. Springer, New York (2014). https://doi.org/10.1007/978-1-4614-3185-5_58
18. Etzo, S., Collender, G.: The mobile phone 'revolution' in africa: rhetoric or reality? Afr. Aff. **109**(437), 659–668 (2010). https://doi.org/10.1093/afraf/adq045
19. Global System for Mobile Communication (GSMA). The Mobile Economy of Sub-Saharan Africa (2017). https://www.gsmaintelligence.com/research/?file=7bf3592e6d750144e58d9dcfac6adfab&download
20. Gunga, S.O., Ricketts, I.W.: Facing the challenges of e-learning initiatives in African universities. Br. J. Educ. Technol. **38**(5), 896–906 (2007). https://doi.org/10.1111/j.1467-8535.2006.00677.x
21. Lee, J.: Education for technology readiness: prospects for developing countries. J. Hum. Dev. **2**(1) (2001). https://doi.org/10.1080/14649880120050219
22. Klopfer, E., Yoon, S.: Developing games and simulations for today and tomorrow's tech savvy youth. TechTrends **49**(3), 33–41 (2005). https://doi.org/10.1007/BF02763645
23. Mtebe, J.S., Raisamo, R.: A model for assessing learning management system success in higher education in Sub-Saharan countries. Electron. J. Inf. Syst. Developing Countries **61**, 1–7 (2014). https://doi.org/10.1002/j.1681-4835.2014.tb00436.x
24. Nafukho, F., Muyia, M.H.: The world bank's Africa virtual university project: a revisit. Eur. J. Training Dev. **37**, 646–661 (2013). https://doi.org/10.1108/EJTD-02-2013-0020

25. Pineteh, E.A.: Using virtual interactions to enhance the teaching of communication skills to information technology students. Br. J. Educ. Technol. **43**, 85–96 (2012). https://doi.org/10.1111/j.1467-8535.2011.01193.x
26. Hicks, E.K.: Can the African virtual university transform higher education in Sub-Saharan Africa? Comp. Technol. Transf. Soc. **5**(2), 156–177 (2007). https://doi.org/10.1353/ctt.2007.0027
27. Perkins, R.A.: Spotlight Africa: selected articles and reports (2003–2007). TechTrends, **51**(6) (2007). https://doi.org/10.1007/s11528-007-0086-9
28. Lockwood, D.: Virtual reality in Africa – for Africa. Digit. Creativity **13**(1), 3–6 (2002). https://doi.org/10.1076/digc.13.1.3.3214
29. Makransky, G., Lilleholt, L.: A structural equation modeling investigation of the emotional value of immersive virtual reality in education. Assoc. Educ. Commun. Technol. 1–24 (2018). https://doi.org/10.1007/s11423-018-9581-2
30. Monahan, T., McArdle, G., Bertolotto, M.: Virtual reality for collaborative E-Learning. Comput. Educ. **50**(4), 1339–1353 (2008). https://doi.org/10.1016/j.compedu.2006.12.008
31. Van Wyk, E., De Villiers, R.: Virtual reality training applications for the mining industry. In: Proceedings of the 6th International Conference on Computer Graphics, Virtual Reality, Visualisation and Interaction in Africa, pp. 53–63 (2009). https://doi.org/10.1145/1503454.1503465
32. Dewailly, J.M.: Sustainable tourist space: from reality to virtual reality? Tourism Geographies **1**(1), 41–55 (1999). https://doi.org/10.1080/14616689908721293
33. Lewins, K.M., Stuart, J.S. (eds.): Educational Innovation in Developing Countries: Case Studies of Change Makers. Macmillian, London (1991)
34. UNESCO Office in Dakar. (n.d.). Literacy and non-formal education. http://www.unesco.org/new/en/dakar/education/literacy/. Accessed 19 April 2018

Collaborative Learning

Understanding the Effects of Online Collaborative Knowledge-Building Activities on Pre-service Teachers' Views of "Learning": A Case Study Using Triple Cross-Validation Analysis

Chih Hui Seet(✉) and Huang-Yao Hong

Department of Education, National Cheng Chi University, Taipei 11605, Taiwan
105152014@mail2.nccu.tw, hyhong@nccu.edu.tw

Abstract. This research study aimed to understand the concept of "learning" held by current Taiwanese pre-service teachers from the information and communication technology (ICT) generation in order to establish a new digital learning theory for the future. Over the course of an entire semester, 38 participants took an elective course that adopted a project-based teaching strategy named "Educational Media" administered in an online, collaborative, knowledge-building environment. Using grounded theory and a design-research method, an open-ended survey questionnaire was administered to compare the pre-test and post-test definitions of learning generated from each pre-service teacher. A triple cross-verification of qualitative and quantitative forms was then analyzed by up to three assistants from the course. Results showed that participants altered their thinking about learning, which was reflected in their assignments and narratives documented on the questionnaires after experiencing knowledge-building activities. Correlation analysis showed that the perceived learning dimension moved from a traditional mode to a more constructive mode compared to the beginning of the course. In summary, this triple cross-validation method may improve the effect of objective explanation and analysis results.

Keywords: Conception of learning · Collaborative knowledge building
Triple cross-validation

1 Introduction

To support the knowledge economy age, recent pedagogies are already transforming to develop new, 21st-century competencies for today's learners [1]. Through the convenience of the Internet and advanced learning facilities, many technological tools are used in schools to improve learning efficacy so learners can learn whatever and whenever they want. Undoubtedly, information and communication technology (ICT) in education may enhance students' learning of basic knowledge [2]. For example, MOOCs, Coursera, and Moodle provide great learning opportunities, but these types of learning that emphasize and claim effectiveness with knowledge absorption are no longer adequate. Knowledge is not the only way to access the

T.-T. Wu et al. (Eds.): ICITL 2018, LNCS 11003, pp. 51–60, 2018.
https://doi.org/10.1007/978-3-319-99737-7_5

unknown world any longer [3]. Because of this, knowledge-building activities were conducted to test how much participants could deepen their conceptualization of learning.

The aforementioned digital learning sources were not only an alternative channel to access learning but also agents of change regarding the way people learned imperceptibly [4]. On the other hand, with the rapid development of the digital learning sector, there has been a consensus to establish a new and suitable theory to fulfill the demands of modern teaching and learning [5]. Current students still adopt traditional ways of learning policies despite living in this digital native's world [6]. Despite vast growth and investigation of global digital learning, the digital learning theoretical framework was rarely researched [7]. Research on the definition of learning showed that it is necessary to have a concept of learning in light of empirical studies [8]. [9] researched metaphors and thoughts associated with educational frameworks. He mentioned tension among the implicit substrates of figurative association. Hence, this research study attempts to provide some assistance to ease this tension as well.

However, to survive in this complex and rapidly changing world, learning as a factor of "global competition" [10] will be more important than teaching in the future. Its significance affects not only the traditional classroom but also new trends in digital learning. How teachers define and understand learning will have a direct influence on their daily teaching as well as determining their instructional design. As a result, both teachers and students must learn how and what to learn. This study aims to clearly explain the significance and understanding of the word "learning." Additionally, like most qualitative research studies, it would not seem objective or accurate to utilize only one kind of method to analyze subjective data. Therefore, this research study attempts to measure the cross-validation results for three different types of analysis to see whether validation could be improved from these multiple perspectives.

2 Literature Reviews

Learning is a lifelong process for everyone; contemporary generations even learn ubiquitously through the convenience of the Internet and advanced technical support. [11] conducted a study that discussed how to refine learning and share knowledge among IT facilities in a collaborative way. The research of [12] redefined learning as an ontogenetic adaptation, which has fortified other definitions and has pointed to important advantages for cognitive learning research. Even so, there is still not enough research to satisfactorily explain the concept of learning.

In Asia, learning always be passive and for examination purpose only, the concept-based didactics classroom existing everywhere [13]. Parents and school teachers prefer knowledge acquisition; the National College Entrance Examination in China is the most competitive selective examination in the world [14, 15]. Despite changes ushered in by the new era and environment and even the global revolution of teaching and learning, it is deeply ingrained in the minds of Chinese people that "learning as rote memorization of knowledge" still cannot be changed. Influenced by the impact of globalization, some educators in Asia have shunned rote learning [16], this shows a little improvement of different learning concept and strategies are in progress.

[17] claimed that despite computer-supported, collaborative learning, group interaction within student-centered learning could enrich knowledge construction. In future 21st-century learning, students must be able to multi-task, have the ability to integrate cross-domain problems, and possess an open attitude toward learning. [18] investigated collaborative learning on students' openness to diversity and showed that through collaborative learning, students interacted with others and claimed to gather different experiences. Another study also mentioned the importance of the environment on collaborative knowledge-building activities, asserting that students could be more progressive and productive if they are in a creative climate [19]. In these situations, knowledge is the product of community-collaborative learning where students are not merely exposed to teacher-centered instruction.

In a knowledge-building environment, being student-centered is essential to allow students to generate ideas and engage in critical thinking. Recent studies found a trending approach toward these types of learning strategies [20]. Many researchers have proven that it is functional to promote significant learning. In addition, many schools in Europe have already adopted thinking designs as a learning strategy [21] to generate opportunities for learning in an idea-centered and knowledge-building classroom. There are many studies on learning and its metaphor; [22] investigated the metaphorical interpretation of learning by Chinese students and concluded that in Chinese society, moral and interpersonal dimensions are most important and represented in the Chinese education system, which expresses more traditional negative connotations and a lack of originality, creative inspiration, active participation, and active interaction in learning. Another study by [23] divided learning into four metaphorical dimensions: learning as behavior changing, learning as acquisition, learning as participation, and learning as knowledge creation. [24] surveyed the concepts and metaphors of teaching and discussed conceptual aspects of acquisition and participation, suggesting further research to explore each epistemology and the concepts of the relationship between teaching and learning within these metaphors. [25] conducted research on metaphorical learning and argued that the process of learning does not plausibly take place only within an individual, but that every kind of professional practice should include both individual and group learning.

Recent methodologies in the qualitative research included documentation, interviewing, observation, content analysis, secondary qualitative studies, and open-ended questionnaire analysis, to name a few. The collected data were then analyzed according to the unit of analysis that was previously set. [26] explored a hybrid method for group interviews and focus groups to generate new theoretical developments. Additionally, [27] assessed online textual feedback by using an amend coding scheme. From much of the literature reviewed, a phenomenon has been noted that qualitative analysis prefers using one method to complete an entire data interpretation [28].

3 Research Methodology

The main purpose of this research study is to investigate teachers' cognition and conception of "learning" under new trends of learning styles in this ICT generation. Our research also serves as an opportunity to test the effects of online, collaborative, knowledge-building activities. The study sample was composed of 38 college students who took a university course about educational media. They were then randomly divided into 10 groups, each group comprising three to five students. This research study was conducted over a semester (18 weeks), using a design research method to collect data. Before this course began, online, open-ended, structured questionnaires were surveyed on the learning community "Knowledge Forum 6," which is also a part of the entire semester's learning environment. The online questionnaires asked participants, "Please define learning in your own words," encouraging participants to share their unique perspectives (the replies were written in Chinese in a postscript form within an online community). Based on the knowledge-building environment and activities, we expected to find that the participants' concepts toward "learning" would be upgraded from a traditional learning module to a higher constructive learning model.

Three types of hybrid analytical methodology (SPSS22, MAXQDA 2018, and NVivo-12) were used to analyze the collected data. The methodologies, which were conducted by up to three assistants from the course, were:

Method 1: Keywords listed according to the frequency of appearance and a driven coding method.
Method 2: Disassembled sentences reviewed with both a given code and driven code.
Method 3: Subjective markings on the entire narratives documented on questionnaires according to the self-created rubrics.

Table 1 shows the analysis for Method 1.

Method 2 disassembles sentences with the use of both a given code and a driven code shown in Tables 1 and 2. This subjective marking also reviewed the sentences according to [23] learning metaphors, and a revision of the metaphors were done to fit the data (Table 2). For Method 3, the entire narrative recorded on the questionnaires was once again subjectively marked by also using this table as one part of the analysis reference. The marking scores ranged from 0 to 5, with the coding form shown in Table 2.

Method 3 subjectively marked the entire narrative from questionnaires, except for the cross-validation reviews shown in the tables for Method 1 and Method 2. A self-created rubric was also applied (Table 3). The scores also ranged from 0 to 5.

These three methods were first analyzed several times before a peer debriefing and a marking procedure. In summary, these three types of analyses could be a remedy for "insufficient meaning retrieval" thus avoiding the occurrence of "quoting out of context." Although this kind of triple cross-validation was not intended to improve the reliability or validity of the qualitative and quantitative forms, consolidating the results could appear more convincing by achieving the interrater agreement, which compares the three types of script coding.

Table 1. Keywords listed by frequency of appearance and driven coding

New encoding name	Definition
Self-satisfaction and instinctual needs	The description is more biased toward traditional physical and psychological aspects and the basic needs of biology
Traditional learning module	In the past decade, we experienced teachers as the center of the classroom, knowledge as authority, and more emphasis on results
Ubiquitous and lifelong learning	Over past, contemporary, and future decades, the forms of this type of learning are not same due to revolutions of learning
Cross-traditional learning in knowledge economy era	Every new era has its mainstream technology; for example, when computers or the Internet first appeared, the Internet age emerged
Life-emotional learning mode	Seeking emotional states when learning, which is both rote teaching and learning toward some specific target
Cooperative learning	In order to construct a project or encourage interaction between the student and teacher on both sides could be seen in the classroom
High-level mental learning activities	Emphasis on student-centered activities and highly valued skills that may benefit future environments
Experiential learning	Applying real experience when one needs to respond to a future task
The reality of learning in the 21st century	Design thinking, which states there is no end to the process of learning, or the journey of learning as an ongoing pursuit of truth

4 Analysis of Results

4.1 Words Count

First, questionnaires were run through t-tests, and the total words used in the questionnaires were counted (Table 4). From the results, there was an increase in words being used to describe "learning" between the beginning of the course and the end of course. These results showed that students were trying to use more descriptive words and more samples to define the word "learning" from multiple perspectives (Fig. 1).

4.2 Method 1: Keywords Searched by Frequency and Driven Coding

Even though we measured the frequency of keywords that did not define the meaning of sentences, a regrouping of words according to the relevant concept was performed, and these groupings were given a new title to complete the encoding of driven data. We found that all of the concepts had a positively increasing phenomena; this can be identified as an indication of the basic understanding for the next part discussed below. We considered that the positively increasing phenomenon occurred because we only counted word without classifying whether it was a positive or negative description.

Table 2. The standard of marking.

Score given and meaning	Definition
No relevance = 0: *Learning (other theory)	Not related to this theory
Low level = 1: Learning as absorption and sharing of skill or knowledge	Exchange on only the basic concepts of knowledge, short narrative length that only contained basic information
Low level = 2: Learning as acceptance and internalization of skill or knowledge	Understanding and acceptance of the basic concepts of knowledge, attempt to internalize the received information into a personal schema
Intermediate level = 3: Learning as participation or socialization	Learning as knowledge exchange and viewed as practical in the community; each participant contributes to some advancement of knowledge through a short discussion
High level = 4: Learning as reflection, revision, and idea generation	An activity of mindfulness as an ongoing process of participation, trying to fix the problem by imagining, thinking, revisioning, and generating new ideas
High level = 5: Learning as knowledge creation	An advanced level of skill that attempts to achieve problem-solving and create something by coming out with new ideas or customizing designs or practical activities; a high level of participation, indicating much interest and attention to this topic

Table 3. Rubrics for entire passage or paragraph marking

Score	Description
0	Learning as a basic and fundamental physical and psychological need that fulfills one's desires in order to survive
1	Traditional teacher-centered learning module (didactic learning orientation) treats learning as purely knowledge absorption or internalization to instill a sense of some general truth
2	Learning that is connected to traditional, modern, or future boundaries (such as lifelong learning or technology support learning; these concepts cross regardless of the past or future, but are not the same form of implementation)
3	Learning as participation, interaction, or socialization within a team or community
4	Learning as a student-centered module (such as inquiry, creating, or reflection), which gives priority to the expression of students' thinking and ideas
5	Future, authentic experiences learning module (learning through real situations such as some problem solving, design thinking, or learning in virtual reality; experiencing what was learned and what has contributed to society), learning as knowledge creation, to solve problems in real life using relevant experiences

Table 4. Word count on pretest and posttest questionnaires (Two-Tailed)

Types	*M*	*SD*	*t*
Word count before course	109.750	95.405	9.557^{**}
Word count after course	200.28	132.531	

$^{**}p < .001$

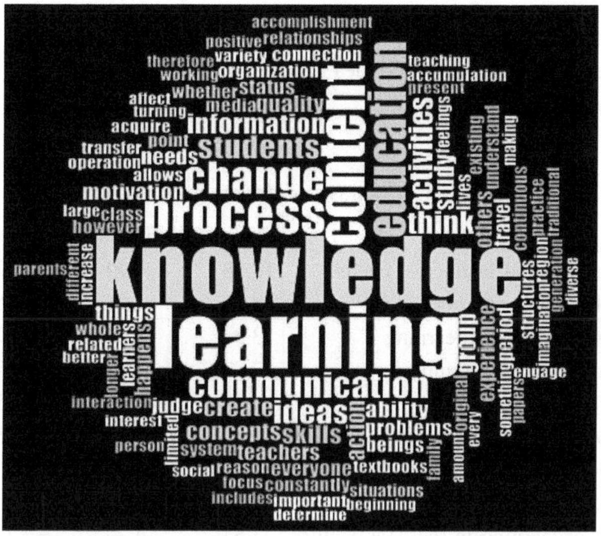

Fig. 1. Word cloud after the course (NVivo 12).

Therefore, the proportion of elements like "collaborative learning" (+3%) and "high-level mental learning activities" (+5%) exhibited the most increased percentage after the semester of course.

4.3 Method 2: Sentence Analysis (by Given Code and Driven Code)

See Tables 5 and 6.

4.4 Method 3: Paragraph and Whole Passage Marking (with Self-created Rubrics)

Although these were subjective markings, a reliability scale was run in SPSS to test the intra-class coefficient of each assessor. The Cronbach's alpha for 38 students was .874 in the beginning of the course and .925 at the end of the course. Method 3 showed an improvement at the end of the course (Tables 7 and 8).

Table 5. Contrasts of given code results

Description	Initial (%)	Final (%)	Average (%)
Learning (Other theory)	26.36	15.94	−10.42
Learning as absorption and sharing of skill or knowledge	19.57	6.3	−13.27
Learning as acceptance and internalization of skill or knowledge	11.6	2.02	−9.58
Learning as participation or socialization	10.32	18.02	+7.7
Learning as reflection, revisioning, and idea generation	13.27	19.29	+6.02
Learning as knowledge creation	2.31	7.98	+5.67

Table 6. Contrasts of driven code results

Renaming keywords	Initial (%)	Final (%)	Percentage (%)
Self-satisfaction and instinctual needs	12.28	4.49	−7.79
Traditional learning module	8.31	4.96	−3.35
Ubiquitous and lifelong learning	3.3	4.69	+1.39
Cross technology era learning	2.87	5.13	+2.26
Life-emotional learning mode	1.01	4.16	+3.15
Cooperative learning	5.37	12.62	+7.25
High-level mental learning activities	10.17	13.77	+3.6
Experiential learning	5.23	8.03	+2.8
The reality of learning in the 21st century	7.51	4.72	−2.79

Table 7. Paired samples statistics for five assistances (Self-created rubrics)

Assessor	M (Difference between pre and post)	SD	t
1	−2.289	1.784	-7.909^{**}
2	−1.895	1.984	-5.888^{**}
3	−1.500	1.689	-5.476^{**}
4	−1.921	1.583	-7.479^{**}
5	−1.737	1.537	-6.967^{**}

* p <. 05 **p <. 001

Table 8. Results from participants' T-Tests for Method 3

	M (Difference between pre and post)	SD	t
Results after the course	−1.8684	1.44766	-7.956^{**}

* p <. 05 **p <. 001

5 Discussion and Conclusions

In this research study, most of the participants were sophomores; they received traditional, didactic teaching methods more than previous generations. We concluded that participants' subjective conceptualizations toward learning had a latent divergence of change from a single focus to multiple and generalized foci, and from broad meanings and beliefs based on more traditional beliefs on learning to a complex and modernized set of beliefs on learning. Although a traditional learning module is an important necessity since the world is continuously developing, learning should also keep up with the times. Teachers should include more teaching materials instead of just using one didactic teaching method. Classes can be livelier and customized to a specific teaching target.

Additionally, by using online, collaborative, knowledge-building activities, students are allowed to learn by sharing their ideas with different people. This suggests that using these types of teaching strategies may improve the quality of courses and indicates that student-centered teaching can be easily achieved by sharing authority with students to focus on a specific topic they are interested in. At the end of the semester, this project-based course had resulted in ten groups of different online learning platforms containing many creativity ideas at the stories and design dimensions, the core conception of learning also reflected directly from their project. Finally, with using the analysis methods discussed in this study, different points of view can be interpreted. Objectivity could be improved in this study, along with the reliability of collected data, which were obtained from open-ended, structured narratives.

References

1. Cynthia, L.S.: The futures of learning 3: what kind of pedagogies for the 21st century? UNESCO (2015)
2. Simin, G., Athirah, W., Rosdy, W.: Teaching and learning with technology: effectiveness of ICT integration in schools. Int. J. Res. Educ. Sci. (IJRES) **1**(2), 175–191 (2015)
3. Huang, G.J., Chen, H.D. (eds.): Future Classroom, Mobile and Ubiquitous Technologies-Enhanced Learning. Higher Education Books Series, Taiwan (2014)
4. Ravenscroft, A.: From conditioning to learning communities: implications of fifty years of research in e-learning interaction design. ALTJ **11**(3), 418 (2016). https://doi.org/10.1080/0968776030110302
5. Hong, H.Y., Chang, H.Y.: From Method to Theory: Test and Establishment of Digital Learning Theory. Advanced Research Methodology for e-learning. Higher Education Books Series, Taiwan (2017)
6. Charles, K.: Theoretical perspectives of how digital natives learn. Int. J. High. Educ. **3**(1), 94–109 (2014). Retrieved from ERIC database (EJ1067467)
7. Manuela, A., Fernando, B., Oliver, T.: An e-learning theoretical framework. Educ. Technol. Soc. **19**(1), 292–307 (2016)
8. Ane, Q., Merete, W., Gerd, C., Mikala, H.: On the Definition of Learning. University Press of Southern Denmark, Odense (2016)
9. Davis, B.: On the many metaphors of learning … and their associated educational frames. J. Curric. Stud. **50**, 182–203 (2017)

10. Jarvis, P.: Globalisation, Lifelong Learning and the Learning Society. Sociological Perspectives. Routledge Taylor and Francis Group, New York & London (2007)
11. Wei, F.H., Chen, G.D.: Collaborative mentor support in a learning context using a ubiquitous discussion forum to facilitate knowledge sharing for lifelong learning. Br. J. Edu. Technol. **37**(6), 917–935 (2006)
12. Houwer, J.D., Barnes-Holmes, D., Moors, A.: What is learning? On the nature and merits of a functional definition of learning. Psychon. Bull. Rev. **20**(4) (2013). https://doi.org/10.3758/s13423-013-0386-3
13. Li, J.H.: China's schools teach kids to take tests, obey the state, and not much more. Daily Beast (2013). https://www.thedailybeast.com/chinas-schools-teaches-kids-to-take-tests-obey-the-state-and-not-much-more
14. Benjamin, S.: Stressful times for Chinese students. Times Mag., Hong Kong Tuesday, 12 June 2007. http://content.time.com/time/world/article/0,8599,1631854,00.html
15. Jaime, F.: Making the grade in China: Grueling college exams. CNN, 11 June 2010. http://edition.cnn.com/2010/WORLD/asiapcf/06/11/china.gaokao.national.college.exam/index.html
16. Natasha, B.: Don't copy Asia on rote learning, schools told. The Australian, 28 May 2015. https://www.theaustralian.com.au/national-affairs/education/dont-copy-asia-on-rote-learning-schools-told/news-story/ffc663483187d93e490d75e747f305c0
17. Zhu, C.: The effect of cultural and school factors on the implementation of CSCL. Br. J. Edu. Technol. **44**, 3 (2012)
18. Loes, C.N., Culver, K.C., Trolian, T.L.: How collaborative learning enhances students' openness to diversity. J. High. Educ. (2017). https://doi.org/10.1080/00221546.2018.1442638
19. Hong, H.Y., Chang, Y.H., Chai, C.S.: Fostering a collaborative and creative climate in a college class through idea-centered knowledge-building. Instr. Sci. **42**(3), 389–407 (2013)
20. Marlies, B., Eva, K., Katrien, S., Filip, D.: Using student-centred learning environments to stimulate deep approaches to learning: factors encouraging or discouraging their effectiveness. Educ. Res. Rev. **5**(3), 243–260 (2010)
21. Design thinking: breaking the frame from education. National Taiwan University, Design for Change Taiwan, Parenting Magazine Taiwan
22. Xiong, C.: Metaphors of learning Chinese students live by. J. Lang. Teach. Res. **6**(4), 877–882 (2015). https://doi.org/10.17507/jltr.0604.23
23. Hong, H.Y., Sullivan, F.R.: Towards an idea-centered, principle-based design approach to support learning as knowledge creation. Educ. Tech. Res. Dev. **57**(5), 613 (2009)
24. Wegner, E., Nückles, M.: Knowledge acquisition or participation in communities of practice? Academics' metaphors of teaching and learning at the university. Stud. High. Educ. **40**(4), 624–643 (2015)
25. Hager, P.: Learning and metaphors. Med. Teach. **30**(7), 679–686 (2009). https://doi.org/10.1080/01421590802148899
26. Yardley, S., Brosnan, C., Richardson, J.: Sharing methodology: a worked example of theoretical integration with qualitative data to clarify practical understanding of learning and generate new theoretical development. Med. Teach. **35**(3), 1011–1019 (2013)
27. Shroff, R., Deneen, C.: Assessing online textual feedback to support student intrinsic motivation using a collaborative text-based dialogue system: a qualitative study. Int. J. e-learning **10**(1), 87–104 (2010)
28. Roberts, D.L., Breen, L.J., Symes, M.: Teaching computer-assisted qualitative data analysis to a large cohort of undergraduate students. Int. J. Res. Method Educ. **36**(3), 279–294 (2013)

Attitude Toward Online Peer-Assessment Activity: Experiential Learning Theory Viewpoint

Wan-Hsuan Yen(✉) and Chi-Cheng Chang

Department of Technology Application and Human Resource Development, National Taiwan Normal University, No. 162, Section 1, HePing E. Road, Taipei 106, Taiwan
gordonwyen@gmail.com

Abstract. Kolb's Experiential Learning Theory (ELT) can help educators design learning activities with holistic view in mind. By understanding student's learning preference, educators may choose the methods that interest students most. From our study of 175 Taiwanese postgraduate students, 49.7% of them are assimilating (AS) type who learn best through reflection and conceptualization. Online peer-assessment activity is found to be preferred in attitude by AS type students over diverging (DI) type. As a result, the utilization of seminars with online peer-assessment can provide real world simulation and may interest the majority of postgraduate students. The implication of using ELT in learning activity design is also discussed.

Keywords: Experiential Learning Theory (ELT) · Peer-assessment
Online peer-assessment · Learning style

1 Introduction

Nowadays, experiential learning theory has become more important in higher education because it helps learners "learn how to learn" [1]. Information explosion forced postgraduates and future researchers to obtain and organize knowledge more effectively. In response to increasing competition and pressure in the academic field, scholars have to learn and adapt to changes more quickly. As a sequence, teachers in higher education system need to continue developing more effective and engaging pedagogical methods, where experiential theory can be used as guidance.

One of the goals of higher education is to develop independent scholars, who can observe the status quo, propose the research question, read through relating publications, communicate about one's research, and critically review others' research. Although teachers can teach the basic principles about above issues, it is difficult for students to really learn and master these without experiencing. While most postgraduate students might learn from discussing with their own advisors or other senior students, a well-designed course should also be benefit for them.

Seminars with online peer-assessment provide a learning experience where students are able to develop the academic ability: students are required to study a topic

T.-T. Wu et al. (Eds.): ICITL 2018, LNCS 11003, pp. 61–70, 2018.
https://doi.org/10.1007/978-3-319-99737-7_6

independently, to present one's own knowledge in public, and to evaluate and give feedback to others' performance. These activities simulate real world academic tasks that students will face in the future. In addition, if students want to succeed in the academic field, they need to master the above tasks. This design, seminars with online peer-assessment, allows students to experience and learn like no others.

Kolb's experiential learning theory, one of the well-known educational theories, may be the best to describe the process people learn from experience such as seminars with online peer-assessment. This theory shows how experience is translated through reflection into concepts. These concepts are then used as guides for active experimentation and the choice of new experiences [2]. Kolb and Kolb [1] believe this process is portrayed as an idealized learning cycle or spiral where the learner "touches all the bases"—experiencing, reflecting, thinking, and acting—in a recursive process that is responsive to the learning situation and what is being learned.

However, not all learning activities can guide students through the whole learning cycle. Take seminars with online peer-assessment as an example, it may emphasize some aspects of the learning cycle over the others. For instance, students need to prepare for the seminar by searching and reading academic journals and books. They also need to organize the information pieces into concrete presentation materials and present to the class. These activities make students actively engage and "experience" on their own. On the other hand, when assessing peer's presentations, students compare their classmates' works with their existing knowledge. This activity triggers students to "reflect" and to possibly form new "concepts". Similarly, upon receiving peer's assessment result, students might be aware of some needs for improvement. Which cause them to "reflect" then modify existing "concepts". Later, students may "experiment" newly learned concept in future assignments, but it is beyond the scope of current design.

Furthermore, Kolb and Kolb [3] considered the match between learning style and the demands of learning tasks can increase learning interests and effectiveness. Although seminars with online peer-assessment seems to be an ideal learning method for postgraduate students, whether students with different learning style have similar motivation remains a question. To discover the relationship, we focus on the online peer-assessment activity in this research. Not only does this relationship not researched thoroughly before, but the discovery of it can also guide teacher design activities for various students.

2 Literature Review

2.1 Experiential Learning Theory and Kolb Learning Style

Drawing from scholars like John Dewey, Kurt Lewin, and Jean Piaget, Kolb [4] developed experiential learning theory as a holistic model of the learning process. This theory is built on six propositions that are shared by these scholars:

1. Learning is best conceived as a process, not in terms of outcomes.
2. All learning is relearning.

3. Learning requires the resolution of conflicts between dialectically opposed modes of adaptation to the world.
4. Learning is a holistic process of adaptation to the world.
5. Learning results from synergetic transactions between the person and the environment.
6. Learning is the process of creating knowledge.

ELT defines learning as "the process whereby knowledge is created through the transformation of experience. Knowledge results from the combination of grasping and transforming experience" [4]. The ELT model portrays two dialectically related modes of grasping experience—Concrete Experience and Abstract Conceptualization —and two dialectically related modes of transforming experience—Reflective Observation and Active Experimentation. It is a process of constructing knowledge that involves a creative tension among the four learning modes. Learning is ideal when the learner "touches all the bases"—experiencing, reflecting, thinking, and acting—in a recursive process. Immediate or concrete experiences are the basis for observations and reflections. These reflections are assimilated and distilled into abstract concepts from which new implications for action can be drawn. These implications can be actively tested and serve as guides in creating new experiences (see Fig. 1).

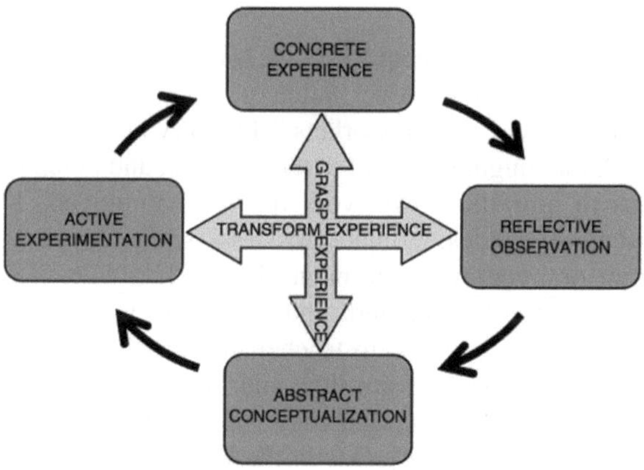

Fig. 1. The experiential learning cycle [1]

In short, Kolb's model includes a learning cycle that involves four processes that must be present for learning to occur. These are "feeling" in Concrete Experience, "watching" for Reflective Observation, "thinking" for Abstract Conceptualization, and "doing" for Active Experimentation. According to Kolb, individuals perceive information by feeling and thinking, and process it by watching and doing. The learning style of an individual is the combination of these four ways of learning and not determined by a single ability [5].

Individuals with diverging style (DI) have Concrete Experience and Reflective Observation as dominant learning abilities. DI type people are best at viewing concrete situations from many different points of view. In formal learning situations, people with the DI style prefer to work in groups, and listening with an open mind. Individuals with an assimilating style (AS) have Abstract Conceptualization and Reflective Observation as dominant learning abilities. AS type people are best at understanding a wide range of information and putting into a concise and logical form. In formal learning situations, people with this style prefer readings, lectures, exploring analytical models, and having time to think things through. Converging style (CO) individuals have Abstract Conceptualization and Active Experimentation as dominant learning abilities. CO type people are best at finding practical uses for ideas and theories. In formal learning situations, people with this style prefer to experiment with new ideas, simulations, laboratory assignments, and practical applications. Those with an accommodating style (AC) have Concrete Experience and Active Experimentation as dominant learning abilities. AC type people perform best when learning primarily from "hands-on" experience. In formal learning situations, people with the AC learning style prefer to work with others to get assignments done, set goals, do field work, and test out different approaches to completing a project [3, 4].

Numerous studies have evaluated and proved validity and reliability of the KLSI [3, 6, 7]. Researches also show that determining the learning styles of students may help teachers develop appropriate teaching methods [8–10].

2.2 Peer-Assessment

Topping [11] defines peer-assessment (PA) as "an arrangement for learners and/or workers to consider and specify the level, value or quality of a product or performance of other equal-status learners and/or workers." In a PA activity, a student generates grading and feedback that might be useful to the assessee, and potentially gives the peer assessor insights as to how their own work might be improved. These assessments could be quantitative (i.e., grades; ratings across assessment criteria) and/or qualitative (feedback; written or oral comments) in nature [11, 12].

With the development of computers and networks, web-based peer-assessment system is widely used, since it can help teacher manage the process and let students complete their PA assignment free from time and location constrains [13].

Both theoretical and empirical researches supported that PA provides learning benefit to assessors and assessees [14]. One of the key benefits is social learning effect, that student learns from each other [15]. In addition, it requires assessors to use their knowledge and skills to review, clarify, and correct others' work. These tasks are cognitively demanding, as they trigger students actively reviewing new but relative information. When evaluating other's performance, assessors might discover the difference between assesse and themselves. This process helps assessors reflect and discover new insights. Additionally, PA encourages students to be critical and independent learners because they become more familiar with the assessment rubric. Such a learning process develops students' knowledge base and critical thinking [16, 17]. Alternatively, assessees may find the content and context in peer-assessment data more likely to students' own language, and the chance for acceptance and possibility to implement the feedback comment also increase [18, 19]. Peer assessors could provide candid, rich and multi-perspective feedback as opposed to instructors' feedback. In sum, peer-assessment provides multiple growth opportunities for assessors and assessees.

As mentioned above, we can summarize: Geographically, there are different dominating learning styles among professions. The matching of the teaching method and the learning style may enhance student's learning interests. We propose our research questions below:

1. What is the dominating learning style of these doctoral students?
2. For online peer-assessment, are there preference (attitude) differences between different learning styles?
3. Does online peer-assessment activity fit the preference of the dominating learning style of these doctoral students?

3 Method

3.1 Participants and Procedures

Two hundred postgraduate students (109 males and 91 females) among thirteen courses, such as Organizational Learning and Adult Learning, using seminar with online peer-assessment were surveyed. 175 students completed the survey. Nearly 70% of them had experience in assessing peers online and over 90% of them had working experiences, which is 15.98 years in average.

In each course, seminars with online peer-assessment were embedded as a learning activity. Students prepared their presentations by searching and studying assigned topics independently. They then presented their topics orally in front of peers. After the presentation, presenter's classmate logged in to the online peer-assessment system to grade the presenter's performance and provide feedback within a period of time. Finally, at the end of each course, students were asked to complete the survey about their attitude toward the online peer-assessment activity, as well as their Kolb's Learning Style.

We then analyzed the between-group variance versus within-group variance to test if there are different attitudes toward online peer-assessment activity between different learning styles. If the between-group difference is significant, then we would use Post Hoc to specify the source of variance.

3.2 Attitude Toward Online Peer-Assessment Inventory

To assess students' attitude toward online peer-assessment activity, we developed "Attitude toward online peer-assessment inventory". It has 11 items such as: "I think online peer-assessment is very meaningful." and "I completed online peer-assessment activity with care." Students rated their attitude on Likert 5 point scale. The Cronbach's α is 0.915, which shows the questionnaire is high in reliability.

3.3 Kolb Learning Style Inventory

The Kolb Learning Style Inventory (KLSI) is designed to measure the degree to which individuals display the different learning styles derived from experiential learning theory. KLSI format requires students to rank their preferences for the abstract, concrete, active and reflective orientations.

KLSI have a short questionnaire (12 items) that asks respondents to rank four sentence endings that correspond to the four learning modes – Concrete Experience, Reflective Observation, Abstract Conceptualization, and Active Experimentation.

The format of the KLSI is a forced choice format that ranks an individual's relative choice preferences among the four modes of the learning cycle. It assesses six variables, four primary scores that measure an individual's relative emphasis on the four learning orientations – Concrete Experience, Reflective Observation, Abstract Conceptualization, and Active Experimentation and two combination scores measure an individual's preference for abstractness over concreteness (AC-CE) and action over reflection (AE-RO). The four primary scales of the LSI are ipsative because of the forced choice format of the instrument.

The four basic learning style types—AC, DI, AS, and CO—are then created by dividing the AC-CE and AE-RO scores at the 50th percentile of the total norm group and plotting them on the Learning Style Type Grid. The cut point for the AC-CE scale is +7 and the cut point for the AE-RO scale is +6. The Accommodating type would be defined by an AC-CE raw score <= 7 and an AE-RO score >= 7, the Diverging type by AC-CE <= 7 and AE-RO <= 6, the Converging type by AC-CE >= 8 and AE-RO >= 7 and the Assimilating type by AC-CE >= 8 and AE-RO <= 6.

3.4 Data Analysis

We used SPSS 23 for the descriptive statistics and ANOVA with Welch test to examine whether the attitude and perception between learning style groups are significantly different. This is because our data do not obey the assumption of homogeneity of variance. As for the items which are significantly different between groups, we then use Games-Howell (GH) test as Post Hoc test for specific group comparison.

4 Results

4.1 Descriptive Analysis

The numbers of people in each Kolb's learning style and its percentage is listed in Table 1. As shown in Table 1, the majority of postgraduate students are AS type. The second highest type is DI type. Both CO and AC are similar in numbers. This shows these postgraduate students mostly use reflection and conceptualization as learning mode.

Table 1. Numbers of people and percentage of Kolb's learning style

Kolb's learning style	Diverging (DI)	Assimilation (AS)	Converging (CO)	Accommodation (AC)
No. of people	43	87	23	22
Percentage	24.6%	49.7%	13.1%	12.6%

Table 2. Average and Standard Error of attitude toward online peer-assessment

Item	Average	S.D.
1. I think online peer-assessment is very meaningful	4.22	.671
2. I am very interested in online peer-assessment activity	3.99	.864
3. I like online peer-assessment activity	3.89	.798
4. I consider online peer-assessment a very important activity	4.09	.742
5. I completed online peer-assessment activity with care	4.57	.582
6. I take my online peer-assessment score seriously	3.75	.872
7. I take my online peer-assessment feedback seriously	4.17	.769
8. I am very interested in the online peer-assessment feedback from my classmates	4.28	.692
9. I think the result of online peer-assessment is very reliable	3.64	.838
10. I think my scores from classmates are very reliable	3.70	.739
11. I think my scores to classmates are very reliable	3.94	.803

Table 2 shows the average and standard deviation of student's attitude toward online peer-assessment activity. Since all item averages are above 3.0, the students' attitude toward online peer-assessment activity is positive.

4.2 Attitude Toward Online Peer-Assessment Between Different Learning Styles

The Welch's ANOVA and Post Hoc G-H test result is shown in Table 3. Six out of eleven items show significant different responses between different learning styles. Four Post Hoc tests revealed significant difference between specific groups: AS type people think online peer-assessment activity is very meaningful and interesting than DI type people do. Although AS type and DI type people both learn from reflection, AS type people prefer extracting their reflection to abstract concepts. In peer-assessment activity, assessors are required to use their knowledge and skills to review, clarify, and correct others' work. Such learning process provides a strong chance of developing students' knowledge base and critical thinking awareness, which is highly conceptualized. As a sequence, AS type people are also more confident in the scores they provided to their peers.

Table 3. Welch's ANOVA and Post-Hoc GH test result of attitude toward online peer-assessment between different learning styles

Item	*F*	dF1	dF2	*p*	Post Hoc (G-H test)
1. I think online peer-assessment is very meaningful	2.888	3	60.260	.043*	AS > DI
2. I am very interested in online peer-assessment activity	4.784	3	58.647	.005**	AS > DI, AC
3. I like online peer-assessment activity	2.604	3	58.012	.060	_
4. I consider online peer-assessment a very important activity	2.790	3	58.980	.048*	_
5. I completed online peer-assessment activity with care	1.041	3	54.335	.382	_
6. I take my online peer-assessment score seriously	5.981	3	56.024	.001**	AC > DI
7. I take my online peer-assessment feedback seriously	1.193	3	58.277	.320	_
8. I am very interested in the online peer-assessment feedback from my classmates	3.041	3	55.199	.036*	_
9. I think the result of online peer-assessment is very reliable	.857	3	59.187	.468	_
10. I think my scores from classmates are very reliable	1.366	3	58.355	.262	_
11. I think my scores to classmates are very reliable	5.799	3	58.465	.002**	AS > DI, CO

$^*p < .05$, $^{**}p < .01$, $^{***}p < .001$

5 Discussion and Conclusion

Our research found AS type people are the majority in the postgraduate courses. This type of people generally have more positive attitude toward online peer-assessment activity. Since AS type was the dominant type in these postgraduate courses, online peer-assessment was well accepted, appreciated, and fit for the students' interests. On the contrary, DI type people, that use less conceptualization, have less positive attitude. This finding echoes the statement of Kolb and Kolb [3], where the matching of learning style and pedagogical approach may trigger the best interests.

According to "ARCS (Attention, Relevance, Confidence and Satisfaction) Model of Motivational Design", the proper matching between students' learning preference and teaching method is an important factor for students' motivation [20]. Although Kolb's learning style is different from the learning styles that generally known by the public, such as visual and auditory, it helps educators understand how students prefer to learn at the conscious level.

Learning theory plays an important role in the field of education. Moreover, it explains why some students learn better than others and can even help educators design more effective activities. Experiential learning theory emphasizes the learning cycle starting from concrete experience. It provides a holistic view about how people grasp and transform experience. If a learning activity focuses only on pieces of the learning cycle, it may cause imbalance effects on students: a problem solving method may be ideal for conceptualization and experimentation learning mode, but not the other two. It is important to diagnose matching between learning styles and teaching methods, so educator can design the optimized combination of activities for target students. Additionally, learning activities should be developed in ways that draw on abilities from each stage of the experiential learning cycle and take the students through the whole process in sequence. Teachers may also consider blending students of different learning styles in group learning, so they may also learn from each other.

6 Limitations and Future Direction

There are several limitations of this research. First of all, the sample of postgraduate students might be biased since only the registered students for these courses were surveyed. This may decrease the external validity. Second, there is no analysis between courses to see if there is interaction among course topic and students' attitudes, perception, and learning styles, which might miss the opportunity for the holistic understanding about the interaction between learning styles and learning space. Third, only online peer-assessment activity was surveyed while the whole learning process includes students' preparing and presenting. Last but not least, due to the page limit, only the preference aspect was presented while other aspects such as learning effect and performance need to be omitted.

In the future, two possible directions can be considered: First, in addition to analyzing the relationship between learning styles and activities, the learning space should also be considered to help teachers choose the proper pedagogical approach. Second, learning styles may influence more than student's learning interests. Other aspects such as performance and its cause might also be affected by the interaction of teaching methods and learning styles. With a better understanding of this relationship, educator might have a better criteria when selecting suitable teaching methods and teaching roles.

References

1. Kolb, A.Y., Kolb, D.A.: The learning way: meta-cognitive aspects of experiential learning. Simul. Gaming **40**(3), 297–327 (2009)
2. Almeida, P.A.: Kolb's experiential learning theory revisited. Adv. Psychol. Res. **102**, 63–76 (2015)
3. Kolb, A.Y., Kolb, D.A.: The Kolb learning style inventory 4.0: a comprehensive guide to the theory, psychometrics, research on validity and educational applications. Hay Resources Direct, Boston, MA (2013)
4. Kolb, D.A.: Experiential Learning: Experience as the Source of Learning and Development. Prentice-Hall, New Jersey (1984)

5. Ogut, E., Senol, Y., Yildirim, F.B.: Do learning styles affect study duration and academic success? Eur. J. Anat. **21**(3), 235–240 (2017)
6. Mainemelis, C., Boyatzis, R.E., Kolb, D.A.: Learning styles and adaptive flexibility - testing experiential learning theory. Manage. Learn. **33**(1), 5–33 (2002)
7. Platsidou, M., Metallidou, P.: Validity and reliability issues of two learning style inventories in a Greek sample: Kolb learning style inventory and Felder Soloman's index of learning styles. Int. J. Teach. Learn. High. Educ. **20**(3), 324–335 (2008)
8. Cassidy, S.: Learning styles an overview of theories, models and measures. Educ. Psychol. **24**(4), 419–444 (2004)
9. Kolb, A.Y., Kolb, D.A., Passarelli, A., Sharma, G.: On becoming an experiential educator: the educator role profile. Simul. Gaming **45**(2), 204–234 (2014)
10. Novak, S., Shah, S., Wilson, J.P., Lawson, K.A., Salzman, R.D.: Pharmacy students' learning styles before and after a problem-based learning experience. Am. J. Pharm. Educ. **70**(4), 74 (2006)
11. Topping, K.: Self and peer assessment in school and university: reliability, validity and utility. In: Segers, M., Dochy, F., Cascallar, E. (eds.) Optimising New Modes of Assessment: In Search of Qualities and Standards, pp. 55–87. Springer, Dordrecht (2003)
12. Hsia, L.H., Huang, I., Hwang, G.J.: Effects of different online peer-feedback approaches on students' performance skills, motivation and self-efficacy in a dance course. Comput. Educ. **96**, 55–71 (2016)
13. Cheng, K.H., Tsai, C.C.: Students' interpersonal perspectives on, conceptions of and approaches to learning in online peer assessment. Australas. J. Educ. Technol. **28**(4), 599–618 (2012)
14. Huisman, B., Saab, N., van Driel, J., van den Broek, P.: Peer feedback on academic writing: undergraduate students' peer feedback role, peer feedback perceptions and essay performance. Assess. Eval. High. Educ. **43**, 1–14 (2018)
15. van Gennip, N.A.E., Segers, M.S.R., Tillema, H.H.: Peer assessment as a collaborative learning activity: the role of interpersonal variables and conceptions. Learn. Instr. **20**(4), 280–290 (2010)
16. Hovardas, T., Tsivitanidou, O.E., Zacharia, Z.C.: Peer versus expert feedback: an investigation of the quality of peer feedback among secondary school students. Comput. Educ. **71**(Suppl. C), 133–152 (2014)
17. Wang, X.M., Hwang, G.J., Liang, Z.Y., Wang, H.Y.: Enhancing students' computer programming performances, critical thinking awareness and attitudes towards programming: an online peer assessment attempt. Educ. Technol. Soc. **20**(4), 58–68 (2017)
18. Murillo-Zamorano, L.R., Montanero, M.: Oral presentations in higher education: a comparison of the impact of peer and teacher feedback. Assess. Eval. High. Educ. **43**, 1–13 (2017)
19. Yu, F.Y., Wu, C.P.: Predictive effects of online peer feedback types on performance quality. Educ. Technol. Soc. **16**(1), 332–341 (2013)
20. Li, K., Keller, J.M.: Use of the ARCS model in education: a literature review. Comput. Educ. **122**, 54–62 (2018)

Sharing the World and Sharing the Word. Using Technology for Pre-service Teachers' International Collaboration

Lisbet Rønningsbakk(✉)

UiT the Arctic University of Norway, Postbox 6050, Langnes, 9037 Tromsø, Norway
Lisbet.ronningsbakk@uit.no

Abstract. Teachers today need multicultural competence and understanding to address both global as well as the local possibilities and challenges in their teaching. One way to develop such understanding during teacher education can be meeting with pre-service teachers from different parts of the world. This was our main objective in a collaborative project between an American University and two Norwegian Universities. The pre-service teachers designed lesson plans about cultural diversity, human rights and technology in education, which were implemented in the pre-service teachers' practice in US and Norway. The paper presents the project and findings of an action research case study. The discussion focuses on the role of technology to scaffold international collaboration in teacher education.

Keywords: Cultural diversity · Human rights · Technology
Online collaboration · Hermeneutic phenomenology · Culture education
Developing professional practice · Freire

1 Sharing the World and Sharing the Word

The title mirrors a text of Paolo Freire; "Reading the world, reading the word", from the book "Teachers as cultural workers" [1]. Freire was occupied by the idea that describing the world with words has an emancipating function to people. His context was the poor labor population of Brazil and his means was literacy. However, his thoughts seem to be valuable for teachers in a broader and more general view because it pinpoints the need of describing the world, or what we see and experience, with words, to develop understanding. In the project, our focus was on sharing experiences with teaching about culture and human rights, perspectives that will need to be shared with consideration of the different contexts they appear in, like culture and language. Technology can provide new perspectives to the dimension of sharing because it adds other forms of artifact to communication, like symbols (e.g. emojis), pictures, videos, multimedia texts, that makes mutual understanding possible across language barriers. Technology allows us to connect across the globe and provide distributed teaching and learning experience by sharing stories digitally [13]. In this project, one of the objectives is to find out if and

T.-T. Wu et al. (Eds.): ICITL 2018, LNCS 11003, pp. 71–80, 2018.
https://doi.org/10.1007/978-3-319-99737-7_7

how technology can be used to give access to discovering the similarities and differences between the contexts through discussing and sharing experiences.

2 Methods

2.1 The Project in Few Words

This project was made possible by a US grant, and took part in two pre-service teacher groups from US and Norway. Both groups were at 4th year of their study and had about 12 students.

Through the academic year of 2015–16 the pre-service teachers from US and Norway worked together in five project groups. The main assignment was to develop and implement a lesson plan that was addressing one of the thematic fields: cultural diversity, human rights and technology in education, in their school practices in US and Norway. As a preparation we had a couple of web meetings where students from US and Norway could get to know each other and learn about the US and Norwegian school systems.

The five groups designed different learning activities for their students; exploring the concept of culture through presenting cultural assets, analyzing the way postcards from United States and Norway express cultural concepts, reflect on the situations for refugees and immigrants, using drama to learn about children's rights around the world, and discuss how technology interfere with real-life interactions between people.

The lesson plans were modified and adapted to the different contexts where the pre-service teachers had their practice. The collaboration during the preparations, took place in different social media, like email, facebook-groups, and online video meetings through various platforms. The final stage of the collaboration was the conference in United States in April 2016, where the participants presented their projects and discussed the results of the project.

2.2 Research Design and Methods

The study has elements of both action research [2] and case study method [3]. The project description identifies two studies within the project [4]. One study is the collaborative project that the pre-service teachers conduct together in cross continental groups, developing lesson plans to be implemented in practice schools [4]. This can be regarded as an action research study because it is a participant driven project where the researchers and the practitioners work together to develop new and better practices [2]. Action research is a method that is well suited for practice oriented research in Education [5].

The other study is the one that the research team conduct on the pre-service teachers' collaborative projects [4], in which my focus is on how international collaboration can help to develop a better awareness of multicultural contexts, and how technology can facilitate such collaborations. This can be regarded as a case study [3], investigating a phenomenon in its real context, and are well suited where the researcher has access to a variety of data as well as being able to interview participants about their experiences [6]. During the project, we have gathered different types of data. All online activities have been recorded and transcribed. We also have collected all written material, like written assignments and instructions for the pre-service teachers' activities, lesson plans, and email-conversations during the project period and after. The students have given their written response to questions pre and post the project. We also recorded the final conference presentations. All institutions, places and study programs have been made anonymous.

Data analysis in a case study research is to elaborate the collected data to identify themes and descriptions that are important for understanding the case [7], and work them into gradually more theoretical concepts [7]. In this case it has been done by reviewing the data repetitively to identify statements and narratives that clarify the main objectives in the study: how international collaboration can help the pre-service teachers and the university teacher to a better awareness of multicultural contexts, and how technology can facilitate international collaboration.

3 Results

3.1 Important Experience for All Parties

It was no doubt that the project was a great experience for all collaborators. The pre-service teachers' presentations at the project conference in US showed that they had had valuable experiences from the project collaborations. The researchers from US and Norway concluded that the project had had impact on the pre-service teachers' professional development. The close collaborations between pre-service teachers from both countries resulted in a mutual understanding of both cultural similarities and differences. The experiences also led to developing the course Culture in Education in the Norwegian program, adding new titles to the reading list. We are also working to implement international collaboration in the course curriculum, and will conduct a new pilot based on experiences from this project, in 2019.

3.2 *Culture* Has Different Connotations in US and Norway

The project collaboration showed both implicit and explicit differences in the way we understand the concept of *culture* in US and Norway. One project developed a lesson plan where students should present their culture to students in the other country. It showed that US and Norwegian students had different understanding of the concept. One of the US pre-service teachers concluded: "In US students automatically linked culture to where is my family from and in Norway what am I doing in my life." The US students automatically turned to their ethnic heritage which for them defined their culture, while the Norwegians told about their home town, how it was to live there, about their interests and the activities they engaged in. The pre-service teachers saw that this gave an opportunity to discuss different concepts of culture with the students because they got new knowledge about how culture can be understood and could elaborate their own understanding using the others' concept of *culture*.

3.3 Huge Differences in Cultural Variance in US and Norway

In comparison, US and Norway have huge differences when it comes to cultural diversity. The US pre-service teachers told about classes with lots of different ethnicities represented. One of the US student classes had more than 90% Latino students and that the rest of them represented a variance of other ethnic origins. The US pre-service teachers also told that bilingual students are on different levels of English language performance. Discussing and analyzing cultural concepts and matters demand a certain level of language skills and many adaptions and adjustments were needed to make it work.

In Norway, the population is quite homogenous and the only places we have large groups of populations with other ethnic origins, is in a few large cities. 2015 was as a year of refugee crisis in Europe with more than 1 million refugees entering Europe [8]. More than 30.000 [8] refugees made it to Norway. Many people are very skeptical towards refugees and the government practice a restriction politics to make it difficult to get accepted for a permanent stay in Norway. This is a worry because school is a place where every child and youth should feel welcomed. The schools and teachers therefore have to act towards discrimination. The Norwegian pre-service teachers had had focus on this in their course and some also wanted to bring these perspectives into their projects.

One of the groups talked about the difference between Norwegian and US teachers. In US the teachers feel obliged to address questions about cultural diversity directly to avoid oppression. One of the US students said: "And I think that we found that one reason why we approach diversity (different) is because of our historical context. The US has a more recent history of oppression than your (country) and for that reason as social justice educators we have an obligation to address diversity in a direct way and address oppression…".

3.4 Different School Cultures

The project also identified differences in school cultures in US and Norway. The US participants pointed at the strong tendency to stick to the curriculum, not having the time to explore other ways of learning and moving the teaching a bit "out of the box". They reflected that the Norwegian teachers had more possibilities to use creative and artistic expressions in the work. It seemed that the US pre-service teachers were more occupied with adapting the lesson plan to the curriculum while the Norwegians had more flexibility. One of the US pre-service teachers told that exchanging postcards with the Norwegians were not quite in line with the curriculum so she changed the activity to instead discuss the concepts of cultures that was represented on US postcards during the 1960s and 70 s to see how the strong liberation movements at that time (race, women) were represented on the postcards. Other presentations showed that the students also hesitated doing new activities. One US pre-service teacher said: "When presented this lesson, students got weirded out and asked why are we doing this? This is not important. I don't understand why we have to talk about this. (…) we got a lot of resistance saying I don't want to do this and I don't understand the meaning of this for school». This showed that some of the US students had difficulties adapting to new ways of working in class, an observation that might express different school cultures. Blikstein refers to Cohello when explaining how a concept of traditional schooling tend to underestimate the importance of experience different approaches to learning than the students are used to: “The underlying theory of mind is apparently that “playing around” and learning are literally incommensurate. The epistemological belief of the teachers is that there must be concrete goals, plans to get there, and orderly sequences of knowledge construction” [9]. I believe that students inherit this belief from their teachers and parents and that they can oppose doing things in school that they find not valuable for tests or exams.

3.5 The Role of Technology

The role of technology was important in many ways. Technology made the collaboration possible. In the different projects technology also was used as part of the lesson plans. We found that the technology worked well for our purpose in the project, when it comes to the technical part of the issue. Common lectures were implemented using a video meeting tool that can provide both video of participants, shared files and chat. The video meeting tool was used for meetings between researchers and between pre-service students. The project groups also used social media to chat and share documents, and email for correspondence. It seemed that the pre-service teachers were familiar with using technology for collaborative purposes. They could use the platforms and devices they usually used.

However, we also knew that access to the technology itself was not enough to establish a good relationship within the project groups. We needed to facilitate the work to make good relations possible. We had planned to use the first common online meeting to discuss some prepared questions to two texts by Freire [1] and Blikstein [9] in project groups. But the Norwegian pre-service teachers refused to do this. Even if we had published the questions in good time before the web meeting, they told me that they felt insecure using English as a professional language, discussing with peers who were native speakers. I had underestimated the role of language when it came to the Norwegian students. We had to adjust the assignments to just presenting themselves to their peers. We learnt that we had to adjust our lesson plans to what the Norwegian students were ok with when it came to language.

We also saw that the Norwegian and the US students had different possibilities using technology. One of the projects involved Norwegian students making a video for presenting their home town to the US students. The conference participants at US were impressed that Norwegian students at the age of 12–13 years old could produce videos of such good quality. The US pre-service teachers reported their students to be much more diverse in their approach to using technology while the Norwegian students gave the impression of having good access to technology at home. One of the participants from US said: “some of the things that we noticed, was an obvious difference in access to technology. (…) The movies they made were really impressing, (…) and it definitely gave us the sense that the kids have access to technology at home where they created these parts that are really giving them an advantage when they want to make products». He continued: “It is always near to me when we go in to the computer lab that a lot the basic functions and technology are new to the kids and they are spending a lot of time learning how to set things up". This showed the different possibilities in US and Norway for using technology in classroom activities.

4 Discussion

4.1 The Difficulty of Seeing and Understanding Across Contexts

For me as a university teacher, it is of the most importance to facilitate a learning experience for the pre-service teachers that help them develop a sensitivity towards the cultural differences they will meet in their work. All teaching practice is embedded in cultural contexts that can obscure our understanding and make critical reflection difficult because we don't see all that is necessary to see. Our perception involves both cognition and intuition. What we notice by our senses is transformed to meaning by our conscious minds but in a context that we intuitively take for given. In other words, we tend to understand social phenomenon by automatically put it into a context that we are familiar with. That means that we can overlook contextual conditions that might be important to really see and understand.

This I know. Still this was an important learning during the project. Implementing the project involved a lot of detailed planning for the two teachers directly involved with the pre-service teachers. During this interaction I saw that even when in a professional relation where cross-cultural discovering is the main issue, I was not able to discover all cultural differences at once. When we discussed practical solutions I automatically translated it to the actual situation in Norway. As two skilled professionals we had a lot of experience about teaching that made it possible for us to adapt the common activities to our respective contexts. But in a situation when we were busy and had limited possibilities to discuss I saw that I could tend to underestimate the need of contextual knowledge about the situation our common plan should work in. I more than once discovered that even if we had agreed about something I wasn't really sure if we had the same comprehension of what we actually had decided. This was of minor importance and caused no problems. But they made me realize how difficult it is to really see situations where cultural differences are involved.

The Norwegian philosopher Jakob Meløe has developed a theory of seeing based on a phenomenology hermeneutic philosophical tradition. Meløe's concern is that we can view a professional situation with three different sights depending on how we judge our own knowledge and ability to understand a social phenomenon in relation to its context [10]. Meløe defines three different sights: the professional sights, the non-professional sight and the dead sight, according to our sensitivity for the contextual matter in the situation [10]. The professional sight describes the way professionals with contextual knowledge understand the practice situation. They are insiders within the professional field they are interacting with. The non-professional sight describes professionals who know that they are not familiar with the context and therefore know that there could be contextual information they do not see. The dead sight is taken by those who believe they understand a situation even without the contextual knowledge of the situation [10]. I understand that Meløe's theory is pinpointing the difficulty that both pre-service and in-service teachers' experience: that one has to recognize not only what we see but also what we do not see or understand in a certain situation. One important aim in this project was to get the pre-service students to develop a sensitivity to the contextual matters of their teaching practice that make them aware of what they do not understand, to avoid them using Meløe's "dead sight" [10] in professional situations. I believe that for teachers who work in cultural diversities this is of the most importance because a traditional school paradigm easily can underestimate students' cultural context and take away the focus of understanding on behalf of transferring knowledge in school. Gadotti, inspired by Freire, says: "We read the world from the space, from the place where we are located. (…) We are located in many places. This diversity is the wealth of humanity. Without it, there would be no change; the world would be static." [11]. The development of sensitivity towards culture, to be able to use the non-professional sight instead of the dead one, is crucial to those who are the professional teachers of tomorrow because cultural diversity is a resource for human change and development.

4.2 The Importance of Pre-service Teachers' International Collaboration

Freire states the importance of respecting our students' cultural identities [12] and warns that it is difficult to understand the difference between our own culture and others: "We have a strong tendency to affirm that what is different from us is inferior. We start from the belief that our way of being is not only good but better than that of others who are different from us. This is intolerance. It is the irresistible preference to reject differences" [12]. Knowing this, it is most important to give the pre-service teachers experiences through their studies that can help them taking the necessary steps to avoid this tendency and to be able to meet all students with respect. International collaborations like this seem to be a good way to gain necessary knowledge of diversity.

To the pre-service teachers, designing lesson plans to conduct in both countries, was a significant experience to understand the concept of culture in a critical way. One of the US participants quotes Freire: "To study is to uncover; it is to gain a more exact comprehension of an object; it is to realize its relationship to other objects" [1]. And he reflects on the quote: "… and I think specifically the last part of the quote: to relate it to other objects, is picturing our projects because through understanding the Norwegian culture more did we come to a deeper understanding of our own culture". The pre-service teachers realized that getting to know their international peers' culture, made them able to take a step back and get new perspectives of their own culture. Freire meant that teaching involves learning as well because all teachers learn from their students. In this case the pre-service teachers learned about the concept of culture through their students in both countries in addition to the learning they did during their collaboration. The students also learnt from each other, as well as the university teachers who learnt from each other and from the pre-service teachers from both countries. Through the projects all parties would develop texts in various formats, about their worlds, to share with peers that might not have an inside understanding of its context. They would experience how their steps backwards made it possible to view their culture in a more critical way, in Freire's terms. Or, they were able to understand the importance of seeing in a critical light, knowing that they did not have the insiders' implicit understanding of the context, or with Meløe's non-professional sight [10]. As a teacher, the respect for the student is a fundament that all teaching must be placed upon. And to develop the sensitivity for the cultural context is way to develop respect for all students.

4.3 The Role of Technology

Technology can bridge gaps between places in the world and bring students and teachers together in communication and collaboration. But it is important to understand that using technology also has limitation. Even if we found that the technology was quite easy to use, there were problems. We had to prepare the common meetings to be sure that the technology worked. We ordered a specific network that was more stable than the one we used every day and cable connections to the network to be sure that it would work. We also used better microphones than we usually had the need for to be sure that the audio quality was the best possible. It worked quite well for the on-campus students. When the pre-service teachers met in their groups, we saw that not everyone's devices were sufficiently set up for working with the social media platforms we had chosen. Not all our pre-service teachers had the digital literacy needed to be sure their own technology worked well. Most problems seemed to be solved by sharing devices and by helping each other within the project groups.

We seem to take for given that today's pre-service teachers have the digital competencies that is needed for using different digital resources for online collaboration. We experienced that this was not the real situation when the project started. Some of our pre-service teachers did not have the right equipment to take part in the collaboration. They seemed to use the applications easy as long as they worked, but it was obvious that some did not have the sufficient skills to solve problems with their own device to make the audio and video work properly. This was, however, connected to the technical part of the use. Using social network sites for collaboration was no problem because the participants were familiar with collaborating through social network sites. Starcic et al. [13] also confirm that students can benefit from using social network sites in their formal learning, and emphasize the importance of stimulating student-teachers to use social network sites for global networking purposes [13].

When the pre-service teachers made their lesson plans, the Norwegians seemed to be able to use quite advanced technology in their learning activities with the students. One example was the videos that Norwegian students made to present themselves to the US students. The video had very good qualities, showing that the Norwegian students had both skills and resources to make products of high quality.

Another issue is developing relations in technology supported collaborations. For the researchers' group we planned to establish good relations through face-to-face meetings. First the researchers met in Oslo to get to know each other and elaborate the project plan. This was followed up with regular video meetings during the next couple of months before we first met together with the pre-service students. We also had mail contact through the project period and my colleague was in US with the Norwegian participants at the conference in April 2016. (I did not have the possibility to go but followed the conference online using a video conference tool). That is how we could establish good relations between the US and the Norwegian researchers in the project.

But we underestimated the Norwegian pre-service teachers' language barrier towards their US peers. Norwegians are in average quite well English spoken, but working together in a professional matter seemed to challenge their language skills. Several of the Norwegians showed negative attitudes towards speaking English in this situation and they kept on having this fear all through the project, even after experiencing that the presentations went very well at the US conference. When we first tried to make the groups discuss articles they had worked with in the lessons, the Norwegians denied totally to do that. We tried instead to ease the start of the collaboration with meetings within the groups where the participants could tell a little bit about themselves. That worked quite well even if some of the Norwegians did not say so much. During the collaboration the language barrier for the Norwegians got a bit lower, but it must be emphasized that also language is an important matter when it comes to collaboration in profession oriented projects.

4.4 The University Teacher's Learning

For my own learning as a university teacher, the observation of the pre-service teachers' project presentations was important to understand what they did conclude about their own learning in light of the collaborative activities we had during the project. I am convinced that the project really made a difference for the Norwegian pre-service teachers. When listening to the project presentations from US, it was obvious that the groups had caught interesting points about their own learning about cultural challenges that teachers meet in their profession. The way the used Freire [1] to account for their arguments, showed this clearly. I also saw the emerging sensitivity towards cultural contexts that occupied Meløe's mind when developing the theory of the sights [10]. Sharing the world through sharing the word is an exercise that can bridge gaps between the local and the global contexts and make them possible to investigate through new perspectives. One of the Norwegian students in the project presentation said that the project was broadening the perspectives for the students and got them away from an abstract academic approach. "Suddenly it is not about reproducing knowledge but applying subject matters to a context". With this conclusion she showed that new perspectives also opened up for her as a pre-service teacher. This is promising when it comes to her professional development as a teacher who will see all her students with a curiosity towards their cultural context, to give them all the respect they need and deserve.

Technologies give access to possible collaborations with pre-service teachers from other parts of the world, that would be impossible without technology. They can learn about cultural contexts together with their students and university teachers through sharing the world and sharing the word in Freire's spirit.

References

1. Freire, P.: Teachers as cultural workers. Letters to those who dare teach. In: First Letter: Reading the World/Reading the Word, pp. 17–26. Westwood Press, USA/UK (1998)
2. Tiller, T.: Aksjonslæring. Forskende partnerskap i skolen. Høyskoleforlaget, Kristiansand (1999)
3. Hammesley, M., Gomm, R.: Introduction. In: Gomm, R., Hammersley, M., Foster, P. (eds.) Case Study Method, pp. 1–16. Sage, London (2000)
4. Mahiri, J., Stien, K., Bostad, I, Babaci-Wilhite, Z.: Pre-Service Teacher Collaboration: Integrating Technology, Diverse Student Cultures, and Human Rights in Instruction. Project Narrative for Peder Sæther Center Award (2015)
5. Leming, T.: Action research: well suited to change and development of an education student's attitude? In: Furu, E.M., Lund, T., Tiller, T. (eds.) Action Research. A Nordic Perspective, pp. 95–109. Høyskoleforlaget, Kristiansand (2007)
6. Yin, R.K.: Applications of Case Study Research, 2nd edn. Sage, Thousand Oaks (2003)
7. Christoffersen, L., Johannesen, A.: Forskningsmetode for lærerutdanningene. Abstrakt forlag, Oslo (2012)
8. Tjernshaugen, K.: Her er grafene som forklarer asylåret (2015). https://www.aftenposten.no/norge/politikk/i/wAjA/Her-er-grafene-som-forklarer-asylaret-2015. Aftenposten nett 05 Jan 16
9. Blikstein, P.: Travels in troy with Freire: technology as an agent for emancipation. In: Noguera, P., Torres, C.A. (eds.) Social Justice Education for Teachers: Paulo Freire and the possible dream, pp. 205–244. Sense, Rotterdam (2008)
10. Saus, M.: Det kyndige blikk, det ukyndige blikk og det døde blikk. Barnevernets utviklingssenter i Nord-Norge, Tromsø (2006)
11. Gadotti, M.: Paulo Freire and the culture of justice and peace. In: Noguera, P., Torres, C.A. (eds.) Social Justice Education for Teachers: Paulo Freire and the Possible Dream, pp. 147–159. Sense, Rotterdam (2008)
12. Freire, P.: Teachers as cultural workers. Letters to those who dare teach. In: Eight Letter: Cultural Identidy and Education, pp. 69–74. Westwood Press, USA/UK (1998)
13. Starcic, A.I., Huang, P.-S., Valeeva, R.A., Latypova, L.A., Huang, Y.-M.: Digital storytelling and mobile learning: potentials for internationalization of higher education curriculum. In: Huang, T.-C., Lau, R., Huang, Y.-M., Spaniol, M., Yuen, C.-H. (eds.) SETE 2017. LNCS, vol. 10676, pp. 400–406. Springer, Cham (2017). https://doi.org/10.1007/978-3-319-71084-6_45

Construction of Artificial Intelligence Mechanical Laboratory with Engineering Education Based on CDIO Teaching Strategies

Yu-Ting Tsai[1(✉)], Chi-Chang Wang[1], Hsin-Shu Peng[1], Jin H. Huang[1], and Ching-Piao Tsai[2]

[1] Feng Chia University, Taichung 407, Taiwan
yuttsai@fcu.edu.tw
[2] National Chung Hsing University, Taichung 402, Taiwan

Abstract. Artificial Intelligence (AI) education breaks a new ground with the recent approaches to let students understand how people being activated by their thinking rule. In the beginning of systematic instruction of AI, the organization should be lateral and subjacent supported with students and teachers. To construct the Artificial Intelligence mechanical laboratory (AIML) may require a vibrant community of inventive problem solvers due to the underrepresented populations of engineering students in the field of AI, and the applications of different science field for the AIML are also needed. In this paper, we introduce the way to correlate the research and teaching process for the construction of the AIML based on the CDIO teaching philosophy. During the AIML building progress, the construction indicators and design strategies may help the students to improve their learning initiative. Through the joining and support of experimental equipment, students' academic knowledge can be accelerated and more certain for the direction of applications. The close combination of the experimental teaching and practical ability with CDIO project-based learning are consistently found in good practices of active learning for the engineering education.

Keywords: CDIO · Artificial Intelligence · Project-based learning

1 Introduction

Over the last decade, the undergraduate academic program is engaged the new education way to encourage the students for their adaptive learning improvement. Many education centers are now moving to a new synthesis of the real practice and engineering science. The live interactions with the real projects can help students envision their career possibilities from studying science, technology, engineering and mathematics. From the past, the university education has focused on academic knowledge and changed it by using computer-assisted methods to enable students to gain enlightenment, feel interest from practical problems, and then think about basic science. These would help them to clarify their future development. However, the courses offered by university education are usually full of pluralistic knowledge. Students should determine the direction of the learning subject under the guidance of the professors in order to clearly move toward

T.-T. Wu et al. (Eds.): ICITL 2018, LNCS 11003, pp. 81–87, 2018.
https://doi.org/10.1007/978-3-319-99737-7_8

the correct learning path. Our ambition with our academic program is to provide students around the world with the technology that they need to do groundbreaking research into mechanics, mathematics, computer science and become part of a vibrant, global community of cross-domain experts.

Referred to CDIO (conceive-design-implement-operate) [1] presented an exploration and practice of CDIO educational idea in teaching reform of computer foundation is a kind of learning based on the whole process of an engineering project as well as a revolution against the lecture-oriented teaching model. Zhang [2] studied the nature, research content, research methods and expected goals of the course of analog electronic technology to improve the level of college students. The model [3] based on CDIO guide deals with a model providing a structured method for engineering curriculum design for electrical engineering. Moreover, a CDIO practice scheme in telecommunication engineering program described in [4]. Jeppson et al. [5] reported on the design and implementation of a Master's program in Integrated Electronic System Design at Chalmers University of Technology from the perspectives of CDIO and constructive alignment. Jiancheng et al. [6] proposed the "Experiment-Guidance-Theory" teaching mode in optics course by integrating the theory of optics courses with corresponding experiments.

In this paper, we introduce the teaching orientation based on CDIO which can guide students in different fields to work together for the feasibility of the implementation system, such as a smart mechanical sensing layer for information retrieval and intelligent decision applications. Students are also allowed to work through the implementation of real project, then in order to find valuable topics in the machinery manufacturing, and try to come up with solutions to develop their ability through the conceive and design. We guide students to apply to the automatically machine production line as an example, and to establish a mechanical and electrical integration technology in the AIML construction.

2 CDIO Approaches

With the introduction of the new departmental resources and the establishment of the teacher's laboratory, students play a very important role. To construct the Artificial Intelligence mechanical laboratory (AIML), teachers and students need to inject new technology and teaching together. Now AI technology has been widely spread around the world, so the establishment of students from the laboratory can be guided by the theme of the task, then understand what the lack is, and to learn from the related courses for engineering reasoning and problem solving. Incorporated the mode of CDIO, the teacher may provide a set of personal experiences which will allow early fundamentals to be more deeply understood, and motivate students for innovating their engineering idea in the conceive stage. As shown in Fig. 1, the self-assessment, reflection on learning achievement through internet things, creative thinking from group discussion, and the guided of team leader who lead to communicate directly with their instructor. Also, the teaching mode should be changed from the general textbook mode to project-based assign mode. The goal is to provide the information from teachers' expert experiences to teach the student how to construct their flow charts for thinking.

Fig. 1. The illustration for allowing early fundamentals to be more deeply understood to motivate students for innovating their engineering idea in the Conceive stage.

2.1 Goal of Artificial Intelligence Mechanical Laboratory

The purpose of this project is to plan and develop the personnel of our group team and the employees of co-op industrial Co., Ltd. together to develop a smart machine production line which is contained the integrate image vision, conveyor tracking, route generation and automation peripherals, x-y-z pressure platform, and mechanical wisdom handling. Though the basic technologies from teacher and corporation of company, we actively train students for learning the production technology required for automated production line. The production line planned in this case can be used as a practical teaching material for allowing students and practitioners to obtain related theories, techniques for learning automation, and train automation talents with the manufacturing industry. According to the reason and demand for cooperation proposed by co-op Industrial Co., the CDIO project propose a practical technology development and the talent cultivation program.

In the beginning of Conceive stage of CDIO, we give a course which is to cultivate professional knowledge and talents in the manufacturing industry to reduce academic gaps for students. To achieve this goal, each student has the ability to master the manufacturing process, computer graphics design, simulation and analysis, coordination to test the equipment. Each of these competencies is distributed in different courses, in other words, students are required to personally complete the various stages of the independent goal of each part. They may get the opportunity for system integration and verification. Therefore, we establish the several necessary technical projects in the program of the department of precision and mechanical systems. Now, we have completed the performance indicators for the four courses during 2017 to 2018.

2.2 The Design Stage of Leading Technical Construction

Due to the innovation of the Internet of Things and automation technology, computer automation production technology has been increasingly concerned and applied by various industries. For the needs of automation manufacturing, the students propose the idea to use the intelligent robotic automation machine system. It uses the current professional robot arm hardware/software as the mainstay, and the computer plane production line to establish automated intelligent programs. The integration of teaching and practice corresponds to intelligent automatic machinery technology, and it is oriented towards the self-device development. The smart automation industrial technique now so-called artificial intelligence control is contained with the image computing processing capabilities, so that the computer has the ability to connect with the machine control as shown in Fig. 2.

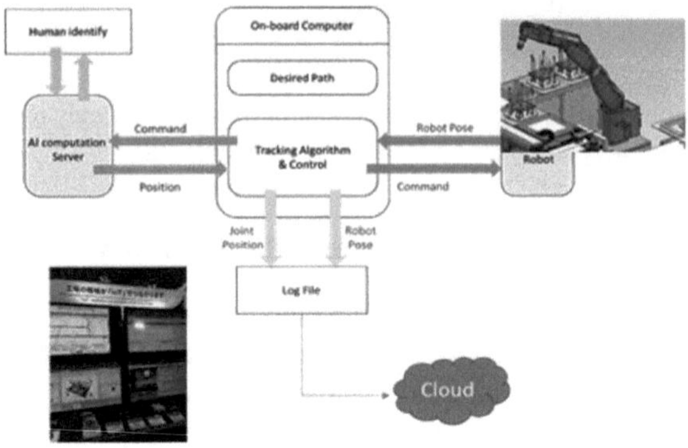

Fig. 2. The illustration for constructing the idea through computer aided graphic creation and design programming flowchart in the design stage.

2.3 The Implementation Stage Cooperated with Machinery Co.

In the initial design of the CDIO project, an automated manufacturing production line system was proposed in the Design stage. The research direction is trying to make the machinery process of making the products and let the student to do the practice with today's automated equipment company. The implementation steps include fabric positioning, bonding, unilateral sewing, flipping and stitching. Therefore, a draft automation process from the student group team is proposed in implementation stage for the machinery production process. It is intended to each design step corresponding to the design of the automation equipment, and takes the necessary technology for the automation as a CDIO guideline, and leads the student group team to create the corresponding equipment with Machinery Company. The design and technology demonstration is shown in Fig. 3, which includes the demonstration design of the turning mechanism, the viscose mechanism, the computer vision and the automatic XY platform.

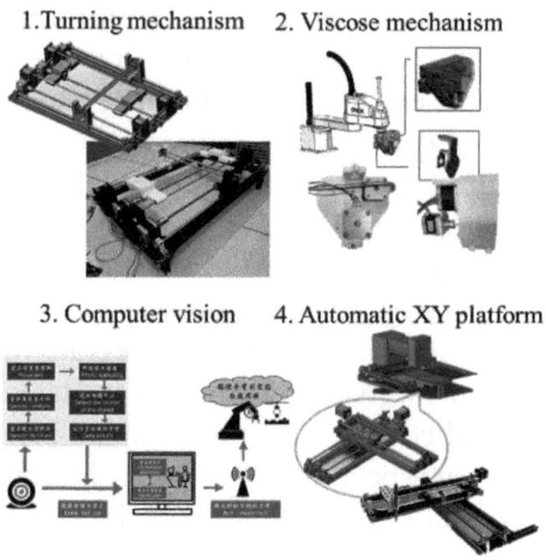

Fig. 3. The illustration for manufacturing the demonstration design in the implementation stage.

On the other hand, students are allowed to simulate and confirm the establishment and editing of the smart agent program from AI technology. To improve the scope of motion before the imported of the robot arm, and the schedule of the production line which including the station time (Tact time), faulty operation, post-operation status and fault monitoring etc. This allows students to learn how to use AI technology to do the system's run-to-run control (Fig. 4).

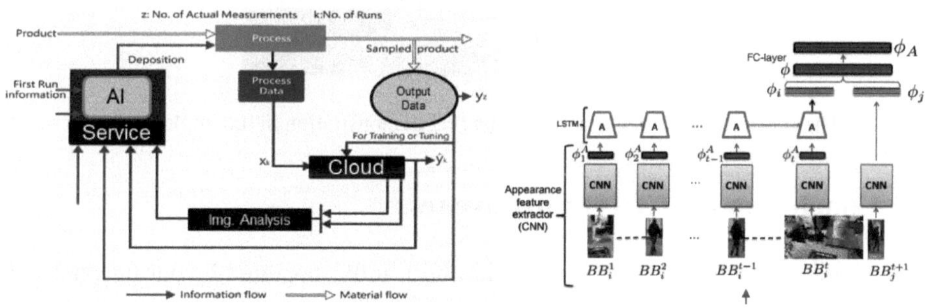

Fig. 4. Including the AI technology to let students learning how is the smart system to do the run-to-run control.

2.4 The Operation Stage for Production Exhibition

Students in this stage create and replace existing technologies for their products. The result may break through the previous steps of the hand-making of the specific products through the first three stages with the cooperation of the company to shape its production line. The actual results of the project based on the above steps are shown in Fig. 5, which is the actual product output of the CDIO project. The change designs for all organizations with new start-ups are collated with the manufacturer's revised CAD file for automation machinery process in design stage. According to the results, each single point operation can be performed. The automated path motions are performed around the robot arm for each single point process. The robot arm can be expanded and simulated to assess whether any combination of the existing production line and other points has any interference. In this case, it is expected that the future production line can have multiple replacements, such as multiple combinations of parallel, cycle, and before and after processes for the manufacturing purpose.

In view of this, the students produce a set of single-station production line integration and tracking systems that can be arranged in multiple combinations. The development target is the automated production line system, and integrate various stations to develop a needle automated production line. Key technologies and talent development programs focus on the development and education of program and production line engineering support software. The technical aspects emphasis on key technologies such as machine vision image identification, End-effect of robot arm and cutting path planning, as well as the use of robotic arm and shoe manufacturing fixtures. Finally, this CDIO project guides the students to develop the production process line for constructing a real automation management platform (Fig. 5).

Fig. 5. The illustration for manufacturing the real demonstration in the implementation stage.

3 Conclusion for CDIO Effectiveness

The laboratory produced by the project has been fully supported by our university. In order to continue the CDIO project, the school will successively employ the teacher support of the relevant expertise, and will also combine the existing teaching space and curriculum of the school and the development of the teachers of the intercollegiate teachers. With the CDIO project-based construction rule for the manufacturing of the smart manufacturing industrial application, it can effectively improve students' learning ability to increase their competitiveness.

Acknowledgement. The authors would like to thank the Ministry of Science and Technology of Taiwan for financial support under Contract Nos. MOST 105-2511-S-035 -012 -MY3, MOST 106-2218-E-035-011-, MOST 106-2221-E-035-051-, and MOST106-2221-E-005-046-MY3. Authors are also thankful for partial financial support from Co-op Industrial Co. Taichung, Taiwan.

References

1. Shen, Y., Xue, H., Zhang, M., Fan, Y.: Exploration and practice of CDIO educational idea in teaching reform of computer foundation. In: 2009 International Conference on Computational Intelligence and Software Engineering, Wuhan, pp. 1–3 (2009)
2. Zhang, T., Shi, Y.: Research and practice on the teaching of analog electronic technology under the innovative talents training mode. Adv. Comput. Sci. Res. (ACSR) **76**, 947–950 (2017)
3. Erik, B., Claus K.: A model for the development of a CDIO based curriculum in electrical engineering. In: Proceedings of the 7th International CDIO Conference, Technical University of Denmark, Copenhagen, 20–23 June (2011)
4. Wang, T., Cheng, W.: CDIO practice in telecommunication engineering program. In: Proceedings of the 8th International CDIO Conference, Queensland University of Technology, Brisbane, Australia, 1–4 July (2012)
5. Jeppson, K., Peterson, L., Svensson, L., Edefors, P.L.: Implementing Constructive Alignment in a CDIO-oriented Master's Program in Integrated Electronic System Design. ResearchGate (2018). https://www.researchgate.net/publication/267375424_Implementing_Constructive_Alignment_in_a_CDIO-oriented_Master%27s_Program_in_Integrated_Electronic_System_Design)
6. Jiancheng, L., Zhenhua, L., Yunjing, J., Jing, Q., Yang, S.: Research on Experiment-Guidance-Theory teaching mode in optics course. In: Liu, X., Zhang, X. (eds.) ETOP 2017 Proceedings, paper 104526 M, Optical Society of America (2017)

Design and Framework of Learning Systems

Using Educational Websites and Platforms in Russia: Cognitive Needs of Children and Problems of Teachers

Gulshat Shakirova(✉) and Elvira Sabirova

Institute of Psychology and Education, Kazan Federal University,
18 Kremlevskaya Street, 420008 Kazan, Russia
gkharis@gmail.com

Abstract. The educational environment at the present stage is characterized by implementation and integration of intensively developing digital technologies. Popularization of educational websites and platforms for children on various electronic devices is under way. The purpose of the study is to reveal the peculiarities of using educational websites in Russia in the process of teaching children of 6–8 years. The study was conducted during 2017 in conjunction with preschool and elementary educational institutions in Kazan. Questionnaires for teachers and parents were created to determine specifics of using educational websites and platforms. They consist of demographic, technological, innovative, motivational units, parental attitude to technologies, and depend on the sample of subjects. To identify the problem areas in the organization of teaching with digital resources the focus group method was applied. This article can be interesting for teachers, parents, administrations of educational institutions.

Keywords: Education · Digital technologies · Teaching children
Cognitive needs of children · Using interactive technologies in teaching
Educational websites · Interactive educational platforms

1 Introduction

Cognitive needs are one of the main aspects in child's personality growth. Researchers found out that cognitive needs are independent needs of individual, having their own tasks in the structure of behavior. Though, its structure, dynamics and connection with other needs remain as a subject of serious discussions. Definition of cognitive needs essence stays controversial.

Development of child's eagerness to cognition connects with increasing needs for communication [1, 2]. D.E. Berlain ascertained relations in development of research and cognitive actions with searching information and adaptation process of a person [3]. M.A. Kholodnaya outlined properties of cognitive activity, such as non-saturability, unselfishness, no need for external stimulation [4].

We understand cognitive needs as independent needs intended on gaining new information. At the initial level, realization of cognitive needs is based on wish to get new impression. At this level child reacts on novelty of stimulus. At the higher level

T.-T. Wu et al. (Eds.): ICITL 2018, LNCS 11003, pp. 91–100, 2018.
https://doi.org/10.1007/978-3-319-99737-7_9

child shows needs in inquisitiveness. This is expressed in child's interest to phenomenon and inclination to study it.

Inquisitiveness has non-systematic, spontaneous, emotional character and as a result frequently does not have socially significant product. At the higher level cognitive needs are characterized by intentional activity and lead to significant results in a form of new knowledge [5].

Purpose of our research is to reveal specifics of using educational websites in Russia when teaching 6–8 years old children.

Objectives of research:

(1) Create questionnaires to identify needs in using educational websites and platforms according to demographic, technological, innovative and motivational units.
(2) Define possibilities of using educational websites taking into account problem zones in teaching 6–8 years old children.
(3) Describe cognitive needs of 6–8 years old children in process of using educational websites and platforms.

2 Literature Review

Digital educational websites and platforms are actively introduced in preschool and elementary education [6–9]. Scientists agree that the capacity of digital technologies as one of the powerful instruments in education of children is beyond question [10, 11]. Researches of International academic community confirm that digital educational platforms serve as main instrument for improving process of education and development [12]. It helps preschool and school age children to get new knowledge, to learn advanced concepts which are considered to be incompatible with this age group [13–15]. Teachers are facing a requirement for innovative integration of platforms and other educational technologies in teaching and learning to respond to students' diverse needs [16]. For successful integration, teacher needs to integrate pedagogical, technological and content knowledge [8]. Educational platforms have a potential to connect formal and informal and can be used in formal and non-formal education of preschool and elementary school children [17].

Analysis of psychological and pedagogical literature shows that researches of educational websites and platforms in Russia are intended on teaching children mathematics [18], native and foreign languages [19], development of children with disabilities [20], development of educators' informational competence [21]. These researches showed:

(1) lack of theoretical basis and diagnostic tools for wide use of digital websites and platforms needed for effective education and evaluation of programs' quality;
(2) ambiguity in quality and level of digital education system [3, 22].

3 Materials and Methods

3.1 Experimental Base and Research Methods

Survey was conducted in Kazan (the Republic of Tatarstan, Russian Federation). The sample of the study consist of 202 people: 73 preschool teachers, 70 teachers of elementary school, 30 parents of 6–7 years old children, 30 parents of 7–8 years old children.

Psychological and educational methods: questionnaires «Educational websites and platforms' use» for teachers and parents [23, 24]; «Diagnostic of cognitive needs of children» [12, 25]; observation and focus groups. For data processing it was used mathematical and statistical methods.

3.2 Description of Questionnaires «Educational Websites and Platforms' Use» for Teachers and Parents

Questionnaire for teachers includes demographical indicators of preschool and elementary school teachers such as "work experience, age of children, residential area". Technological unit includes questions about equipment of preschools and elementary schools with digital technologies (computer, tablet, video projector, smart boards etc.). Next unit consists of questions and statements about possibilities of using innovation teaching forms during educational process («I use digital technologies at the lesson», «I do not have an idea about possibilities of using digital ways of teaching», «Using educational platforms and websites at the lessons improve effective learning" etc.). Motivational unit is intended to identify incentives that encourage educators to use websites and platforms («Soon I plan to master new educational websites and platforms», «The work with digital resources lets…» etc.).

Questionnaire for parents consists of demographic, technological, motivational units and parental attitude to technologies. Demographic unit has such indicators as "age, gender, frequency of using digital devices; time spent in the Internet". Technological unit consist of statements that indicates access for children to digital technologies and the Internet («My child has access to digital devices», «My child has free internet access» etc.). Motivational unit includes questions intended on mediated revealing of the interest to gadgets («What is the reason of child's interest to gadgets…» etc.), identifying meaningful aspect in using digital devices («What games most of all attract your child?», «What games and platforms does your child use frequently?», «Does your child shows interest to educational websites» etc.). Parental attitude to technologies helps to specify whether they agree or disagree to use technologies and websites in educational process and at home («It is impossible to educate children without digital devices and platforms», «I do not like when my child spends time in virtual world»).

Cognitive needs of children are evaluated with the help of questionnaire by V.S. Yurkevich for junior pupils, modified and adapted questionnaire by E.A. Baranova for preschool children. Both variants of questionnaires have 7 questions and addressed to parents. The answers to these questions allow detecting cognitive needs and development level of children.

3.3 Description of Focus Group Research

Method of focus groups is applied to define problem zones in using websites and platforms during educational process of preschool and elementary school teachers. This psychological method allows getting wide individualized material, to identify unaware factors of relation to definite subjects and phenomena, to reveal cause and effect links of functioning social and psychological phenomena.

Preparation stage of focus groups consisted in formulating hypothesis and problem issue for discussing. The main question was «What factors make the educational process difficult when using websites and platforms?».

Main stage of focus groups started with opened question to show various opinions of participants («What barriers bother you in using websites and platforms in teaching?»).

During discussion, moderator imperceptibly controlled the group using 5 s pauses and "inquiries" such as: «Would you explain more clearly?», «Could you show an example?».

At the final stage moderator summarized opinions of teachers. Records of discussions are interpreted and printed. The analysis of the main difficulties in organizing educational process of 6–8 years old children using educational websites and platforms was done.

4 Results

4.1 Questionnaire Results of Teachers

According to demographic indicators it was found that preschool teachers are younger (30 years on average) than teachers of elementary schools, respectively elementary school teachers have more educational experience. Digital technologies are presented in preschools (87%) and elementary schools (91%) on high level. At pre-school educational institutions equipment mostly represented by computers and in elementary schools additionally, there are video projectors and interactive boards. Innovation forms of teaching are used by both groups of respondents: preschool teachers - 62%, elementary school teachers - 91%. Although work with educational websites and platforms in preschool educational institutions practically is not done (8%), at the same time elementary school teachers use various digital platforms (66%). Motivation of elementary school teachers about mastering new educational websites is higher (44%) in comparison with preschool teachers (17%). Both kinds of teachers agree that work with digital resources helps clearly explain educational material, increases interest of learners, helps to carry out tasks in non-standard way and also independently repeat studied material (Table 1).

Correlation analysis of preschool teachers shows negative relation between innovation and motivation units ($r = -0.45$; $p < 0.01$). Disintegration between these blocks indicates about problems that decrease interest and interfere in realizing innovation forms of education with websites and platforms. At the same time positive interrelation between technological and innovation units ($r = 0.58$; $p < 0.01$) shows active inclusion of innovation education forms that are not connected with educational websites.

Table 1. «Educational websites and platforms use» questionnaires' main indicators of teachers.

Units	Indicators	Preschool teachers	Elementary school teachers
Demographic unit	Average age of teachers (years)	30	42
	Work experience (years)	10	26
Technological unit	Equipping with digital technologies	87%	91%
	Basic types of digital devices	Computer	Computer, projector, interactive board
	User experience (years)	13	15
Innovation unit	Innovative forms of training	62%	91%
	Individual work with children using educational websites and platforms	8%	66%
Motivational unit	In the nearest future intend to develop new educational websites	17%	44%
	Working with digital resources allows …	To present the material colorfully; to show many examples; to increase the interest of children in learning	To accomplish tasks in a non-standard way; to get acquainted with the phenomenon under study independently; possibilities in repeating material

Demographic indicators have inverse relation with innovation ($r = -0.42$; $p < 0.01$) and motivational units ($r = -0.51$; $p < 0.01$) and reflects that digital technologies mostly are used by young specialists of preschools but with age teachers have lower motivation in mastering new educational technologies.

Correlation analysis of elementary school teachers shows direct correlation between all units. Demographic indicators correlates with innovation unit ($r = 0.51$; $p < 0.01$). Technological unit correlates with innovation ($r = 0.5$; $p < 0.01$) and motivational units ($\mathrm{r} = 0.61$; $p < 0.01$). These results show that there is no age limitation in using websites and platforms, and there are technical possibilities and eagerness to work on perfection of innovative teaching forms.

4.2 Questionnaire Results of Parents

The results of demographic unit shows that the number of boys and girls of preschool (42%, 58%) and elementary school age (49%, 51%) is almost the same. Preschool children spend about 3 h per day in the Internet, while elementary school age children spend about 2 h per day. Technologically 86% of preschool and 92% of elementary school children have access to digital technologies and nearly all of them have free access to the Internet. Motivational unit indicates interest and frequent use of the following educational websites and platforms of preschool age children: «iQsha» (http://iqsha.ru/), «Educating games» (http://golopuz.org/), «Igraemsa» (http://igraemsa.ru/), «Chudo-Udo» (http://chudo-udo.com/), «Poskladam.ru» (http://poskladam.ru/). Elementary school children use «Uchi.ru» (http://uchi.ru), «Open school» (http://openschool.ru/ru/home), «InternetUrok.ru» (http://interneturok.ru), «Yaklass» (http://yaklass.ru/). Most children of both age groups (78%, 76%) use digital resources to the same extent. The use of educational platforms and entertainment applications remains on the same level. Parental attitude to use digital technologies in education is rather negative than positive in both groups (Table 2).

Table 2. «Educational websites and platforms use» questionnaires' main indicators of children.

Units	Indicators	Preschool teachers	Elementary school teachers
Demographic unit	Boys	42%	49%
	Girls	58%	51%
	Time, spend in the Internet	185 min	130 min
Technological unit	Availability of digital technologies to children	86%	92%
	Access to the Internet	80%	90%
Motivational unit	Educational websites and platforms used by children	«iQsha» https://iqsha.ru/ «Educating games» http://golopuz.org/ «Igraemsa» http://www.igraemsa.ru/ «Chudo-Udo» http://chudo-udo.com/ «Poskladam.ru» http://poskladam.ru	«UCHi.ru» https://uchi.ru/ «Open school» http://openschool.ru/ru/home «InternetUrok.ru» https://interneturok.ru «Yaklass» http://www.yaklass.ru/
	Digital resources usage: Educational websites and platforms Games and cartoons	78% 41% 59%	76% 45% 55%
Parental attitude to digital technologies	Positive attitude to use digital technologies in education	35%	45%
	Negative attitude to use digital technologies in education	65%	55%

Correlation analysis of preschool children indicates direct correlation between technological and motivational unit (r = 0.51; $p < 0.01$). It means that the availability of digital devices helps to raise interest in using resources. Inverse correlation between negative attitude of parents in using digital technologies and motivational unit (r = −0.68; $p < 0.01$) reduces children's willingness to study.

4.3 Analysis of Cognitive Needs Average of Pre-school and Elementary School Children

Cognitive needs of preschool and elementary school children that actively use digital resources are highly expressed, differences are insignificant. Boys' cognitive needs indications are alike with the indicators of girls (Table 3). It shows that cognitive needs of children are typical for both genders. Preschool children cognitive needs are expressed in eagerness to novelty and characterized by wishes of a child to new stimulus coming externally. Such children need constant shifting of digital resources and non-systematic use of applications. Elementary school children's cognitive needs are determined by inquisitiveness and personal selection of incoming information. It means that children at this age select websites and platforms in accordance with their inner criteria and interests.

Correlation analysis shows positive relations between cognitive needs and the use of websites and platforms of preschool (r = 0.58; $p < 0.01$) and elementary school children (r = 0.61; $p < 0.01$) who use digital technologies frequently. This indicates that needs in novelty and inquisitiveness realizes with the help of educational platforms.

Table 3. Cognitive needs average of preschool and elementary school children

	Preschool children	Elementary school children
Boys	21.8	23.6
Girls	19.1	22.4

4.4 Results of Focus Groups Work

Focus groups revealed the following problem zones in teaching 6–8 years old children.

1. There are a small percentage of educators who do not consciously accept the implementation of educational websites and platforms in the process of teaching children. Educational institutions should achieve a compromise on the integration of educational websites and platforms in order to meet the needs of learners. It is also necessary to observe continuity in the training of preschool children and junior schoolchildren using educational interactive websites and platforms.
2. Informational competency of the older teachers is not sufficient. Aged teachers do not have formed abilities and skills in using interactive educational websites and platforms which are needed for delivering educational materials to children. It is necessary to organize training courses in order to develop their informational

competency so that they could give children correct abilities and skills on using interactive educational websites and platforms.

3. Insufficient financing is reflected on the quality of providers' service. As a rule, using interactive educational websites and platforms demands uninterruptable service. If educational institution has modest budget, there should be considered option of using platforms on the basis of free software, and also employing compatibility standards for connecting to other web resources.
4. Providing informational security. There should be minimized transmission of private data (author's programs creation for teaching children with the help of interactive educational websites and platforms), and if such transmission is necessary, it is necessary to implement it in accordance with the national legislation and the rules of the educational institution.

5 Discussions

A.M. Matyushkin considers cognitive needs as system property of a person. It is characterized by age specifics and represents combination of motivational-conceptual and instrumental-stylistic features with regard to which there are readiness built and constant strive of human being acquired new information [26].

The cognitive needs, the needs to acquire new knowledge, especially during the period of the development of the psyche are the source and the basis of the cognitive activity of a child. These all set the tone and speed up the development of cognitive and personal structures, and the creative activity of a child.

Modern researches of teachers intended on studying various aspects of teaching children, show that productivity of children's intellectual development depends on position of a child and one's activity. Intensive development of digital technologies, popularization of educational applications and websites leads to active usage of various devices by children. All this in its turn contributes introduction the interactive educational websites and platforms into process of teaching.

Many Russian psychologists believe that a small child, at least up to three years old, does not need to provide digital devices - for the development of his cognitive abilities, the entire sensorial range is needed: not only visual, but also tactile and auricular. It is more useful for a child to play toys than to touch smartphone. Since the moment when child gets acquainted with virtual games, these games take all children's attention and child does not spend time for other activities. At the age of 6–8 years, it is better to give preference to Internet applications, where in the game form tasks for the development of memory, attention, and visual perception are suggested.

6 Conclusion

To solve these problems successfully, education system of preschool and elementary school institutions has to provide conditions for making appropriate informational and educational environment.

(1) Questionnaires «Educational websites and platforms use» for teachers includes demographic (age of teachers; work experience), technological units (digital devices that are presented in preschools and elementary schools), innovation (traditional forms of teaching, innovation forms of teaching, individual work with children with help of education websites and platforms), motivational (aim to master new educational websites, time spent in the Internet, frequently used educational websites and platforms),

Questionnaires «Educational websites and platforms use» for parents includes demographic indicators of children (child's age, gender), technological unit (availability of digital devices and access to the Internet), motivational unit (frequently used education websites and platforms by children) and parental attitude to technologies (positive or negative).

(2) Possibilities of using educational websites due to the problem zones of teachers are defined. They are:

- teachers that deliberately do not accept implementation of educational websites and platforms in teaching process;
- reduction of digital skills of aged teachers;
- insufficient financing and as a result low quality of provider service;
- protection authors' rights of teachers who make teaching programs for children.

(3) Realization of today's children cognitive needs is fulfilled with direct interest to digital devices provided with applications and games, and also by their wish to achieve results in educational game. Educational websites and platforms, on the one hand, help to visualize ready-made knowledge, and, on the other hand, they are a way of gaining new knowledge, they increase the need for cognition.

Acknowledgments. The work is performed according to the Russian Government Program of Competitive Growth of Kazan Federal University.

References

1. Lisina, M.I.: Problems of communication in the ontogeny, Moscow (1986)
2. Park, Y.: A pedagogical framework for mobile learning: categorizing educational applications of mobile technologies into four types. Int. Rev. Res. Open Distance Learn. **12**, 78–102 (2011)
3. Berline, D.E.: Curiosity and information search. Questions Psychol. 54–60 (1966)
4. Kholodnaya, M.A.: Psychology of the intellect: the paradoxes of research, Moscow (1997)
5. Menshikova, E.A.: On the issue of the psychological and pedagogical nature of cognitive needs. Sib. Pedagogical J. **1**, 311–322 (2009)
6. Berson, I.R., Berson, M.J. (eds.): High Tech Tots: Childhood in a Digital World, pp. 5–22
7. Goodwin, K.: Use of tablet technology in the classroom. Curriculum and Learning Innovation Centre, NSW Department of Education and Communities, Strathfield, NSW (2012)

8. Istenic Starcic, A., Cotic, M., Solomonides, M., Volk, M.: Engaging preservice primary and preprimary school teachers in digital storytelling for the teaching and learning of mathematics. Br. J. Edu. Technol. **47**(1), 29–50 (2016)
9. Yelland, N.J.: Shift to the Future: Rethinking Learning with New Technologies in Education. Routledge, New York (2007)
10. Chiong, C., Shuler, C.: Learning: is there an app for that? Investigations of young children's usage and learning with mobile devices and apps. Int. J. Mob. Learn. Organ. **9**(3), 271–283 (2010). The Joan Ganz Cooney Distance Learners, New York
11. Sukstrienwong, A.: Animo math: the role-playing game in mathematical learning for children. TEM J. **7**(1), 147–154 (2018)
12. Yin Yin, K., Fitzgerald, R.: Pocket learning: a new mobile learning approach for distance learners. Int. J. Mob. Learn. Organ. **9**(3), 271–283 (2015)
13. Fallon, G.: What's going on behind the screens? J. Comput. Assist. Learn. **30**, 318–336 (2014)
14. Kucirkova, N.: Children's interactions with iPad books: research chapters still to be written. Front. Psychol. **4**, 995 (2013)
15. Pitchford, N.J.: Development of early mathematical skills with a tablet intervention: a randomized control trial in Malawi. Front. Psychol. **6**, 485 (2015)
16. Istenic Starcic, A.: Educational technology for the inclusive classroom. TOJET Turk. Online J. Educ. Technol. **9**(3), 26–37 (2010)
17. Dua, S., Meacham, K.: Navigating the Digital Wild West of educational apps with millions of apps to choose from, how do parents and educators find apps that pass the test? (2016)
18. Kardash, A.I., Levitskaya, S.M., Dudykevich, A.T.: Development of online testing in mathematics. Vestnik Vinnitckogo politechnicheskogo instituta **2**(119), 157–161 (2015)
19. Lenintseva, V.A., Burukina, T.N.: Websites in teaching the Chinese language. In: Modern Technologies and Tactics in Teaching Professionally-Oriented Foreign Language, pp. 106–108 (2013)
20. Kozhalieva, Ch.B., Shulekina, Yu.A., Kireeva, I.P.: Educational opportunities as a platform for educational inclusion. Problemy sovremennogo pedagogicheskogo obrazovanija **52**(3), 335–345 (2016)
21. Stepanova, L.V.: Formation of ICT - the competences of the future teacher-psychologist. E-learning in the University and School, pp. 261–263 (2014)
22. Traxler, J.: Defining, discussing and evaluating mobile learning: the moving finger writes and having writing. Int. Rev. Res. Open Distrib. Learn. **8**(2), 1–12 (2007)
23. Sabirova, E.G., Zakirova, V.G., Masalimova, A.R.: Development of junior pupils research skills in interrelation with universal learning activities. Int. J. Environ. Sci. Educ. **11**(4), 505–514 (2016)
24. Shakirova, G.F.: Psychological features of children in the digital age. Int. J. Sci. Stud. **5**(6), 176–179 (2017)
25. Baranova, E.A.: Diagnosis of cognitive interest in younger schoolchildren and preschoolers, Saint Petersburg (2005)
26. Matyushkin, A.M.: To the problem of situational cognitive needs of generation. Psychological research of intellectual activity. Moscow (2009)
27. Judge, S., Floyd, K., Jeffs, T.: Using mobile media devices and apps to promote young children's learning. In: Heider, K.L., Renck Jalongo, M. (eds.) Young Children and Families in the Information Age. EYC, vol. 10, pp. 117–131. Springer, Dordrecht (2015). https://doi.org/10.1007/978-94-017-9184-7_7
28. Yurkevich, B.C.: Technique "Cognitive Need". In: Ilin EP. Motivation, pp. 370–371 (2002)

Reducing Language Speaking Anxiety Among Adult EFL Learners with Interactive Holographic Learning Support System

YingLing Chen(✉)

Central of General Education, Oriental Institute of Technology, Taipei, Taiwan
cil0226@mail.oit.edu.tw

Abstract. In this paper, an interactive holographic learning support system is implemented in the course for reducing language speaking anxiety among adult EFL learners. The interactive holographic platform can be intuitively controlled by hand gesture thus the learner's control intention can be easily converted into the learning system. 12 adult EFL students were selected for interviews in the study. The use of semi-structure interview technique was implemented to be the main method of gathering research data. The data were obtained through adapted and modified open-ended questions. Participants were asked to reflect after each English conversation practice with interactive holographic learning support system. The study identified several language learning issues and indicated language anxiety become difficulties and had debilitating effect in communication through English language. Moreover, the proposed 3D holographic platform did create the environment and provide opportunities for EFL learners applied their target language and reduced their foreign language speaking anxiety.

Keywords: 3D holographic projection technology
English as a foreign language · Foreign Language Anxiety
Interactive learning support system

1 Introduction

Foreign Language Anxiety (FLA) has been noticed by many language educators. According to a variety of researchers [1–5], FLA can be a predictor of success in learning the foreign language. Second language learners feel hesitant, frustrated and confused; their emotions influence their performance on their target language learning and their motivation in learning English [6]. Consequently, it is critical for language teachers to be aware of the learners' diverse aspects in order to assist their learning and improve their performance. Technology support can be a practical tool for educators enhance their instruction. Holography, or holographic projection, is an imaging technique that records all the information of the reflected or transmitted light waves when an object is imaged; the illusion of 3D object is formed from different angles and perspectives [7]. Unlike conventional 3D display techniques, holographic images can be viewed without 3D glasses. As a result, the cost is declined; the value of the educational implication is raised. Technology-assisted learning provides convenient

T.-T. Wu et al. (Eds.): ICITL 2018, LNCS 11003, pp. 101–110, 2018.
https://doi.org/10.1007/978-3-319-99737-7_10

access to interactive conversational contents especially by providing students a learning bridge with a 3D holographic display technology. According to interactionist approaches to SLA [8], interaction is the most important way in which learners obtain data for language learning. This study developed a 3D holographic character with interaction, and "photosensitive layer to achieve a transmittance rate of 99.99% mirror-like appearance" [7] to investigate whether speaking activities such as role-plays and conversation drills help decrease students' speaking anxiety. Effective instruction enables learners to internalize knowledge and skills.

2 Literature

2.1 Foreign Language Anxiety

FLA is defined as "a distinct complex of self-perceptions, beliefs, feelings, and behaviors related to classroom language learning arising from the uniqueness of the foreign language learning process" [1]. Therefore, language learning anxiety is related to performance. Language learning anxiety appears across both genders when learners face pressure, learners meet unfamiliar material, assessments for learners, and students are confused by different grammar rules [6].

According to [1] "FLA is the subjective feeling of tension, apprehension nervousness, and worry associated with an arousal of the autonomic nervous system." Meanwhile, [1] divide FLA in three related behavioral performances: (1) communication apprehension, (2) test anxiety, and (3) fear of negative evaluation. Consequently, a person who has anxiety worries and displays unconfident behavior. Furthermore, according to previous research, not only the obvious behavioral performances were discovered but also physical conditions were recorded. [9] further explained that "anxiety can be measured in three different ways: by behavioral tests, where the actions of a subject is observed; by the subject's self-report of internal feeling and reactions; or by physiological tests, where measures of heart rate, blood pressure, or palmar sweating are taken". [10] claimed that "emotionality" refers to physiological reactions, such as blushing or racing heart, and behavioral reactions.

2.2 How to Reduce Language Anxiety

It has been observed by the researcher, students are reluctant to use the foreign language they have been learning. Also, the EFL teachers complain about their students' couch potato like during EFL setting. [6] further investigated that English is not their official language which means students cannot use and practice their target language frequently. Hence, teaching strategy becomes a major determinant of student reticence or participation. [11] proposed that the more speaking activities in which students engaged, the better they rate their ability in speaking the target language. The result indicates students who have more opportunities in applying what they have learned in class have higher confidence about their oral proficiency. Besides, teachers' willingness to work with their students to improve low academic performance has a positive effect on reducing students' anxiety [12].

2.3 Technology Assists Language Learning

Technology is very much part of language learning throughout the world at all different levels [13]. Language instructors try to find ways for learners to do meaningful spoken language practice in a class; linking the class to the real world, using tools for learners to ask questions and understand their response can be challenging sometimes. Another benefit of using technology for language learning instruction is that the computer technology offers immediate practice and it also provides added practice when necessary. According to [14], students have been able to improve their sight word vocabulary, fluency, and comprehension by the technology support. Technology support increases interaction with texts, concentration to individual needs, and independence to learning through an ability to produce the target language. Students need to learn vocabulary in context and with visual clues to help them comprehend. Technology provides EFL learners wealthy, contextual environment. [13] explained technologies are ideally placed to help teachers working with learners, and learners working independently, to do the necessary language. The importance of technology use is its potential to create new opportunities for curriculum and instruction by bringing real-world instruction into the classroom for students to explore.

2.4 Interactive Holographic Learning Support System

Digital environments are a big part of learners' education and lifestyles in the 21 century. Incorporating existing technologies and techniques such as 3D simulation, virtual reality (VR), and augmented reality (AR) as teaching support is an inevitable trend of future education [15]. Holography allows the user or learner to view fully parallax, auto-stereoscopic 3D images. The scheme for presentation and manipulation of 3D visualizations is important; student controlled visualizations with multi-view capability yield improvements in learning over automatically rotating visualizations. Interactive 3D Holography decreases the gap between classroom theory and reality; it also provides a personalized virtual instructor with human learning experience by focusing on the achievement of the practical knowledge and skills. The 3D graphical representations satisfy a basic human need; they provide a visual perception much closer to real life than 2D images [7]. [16] reported 7 ways of holographic technology make learning more fun. The technologies that can have the best impact on education are evolving quickly from year to year, and the pace seems to be quickening. Interactive Holographic Learning Support System is not a technology in itself, but rather a technology-enabled teaching technique and students' learning outcome.

3 Methodology

3.1 Learning System Design

In this paper, two techniques are incorporated to design the interactive learning system: the holographic 3D projection and hand gesture recognition. First, we developed a multi-perspective projection system to project the virtual instructor realistically. The system projected 2D objects into a 3D space to produce the holographic display of the object. The holographic projection platform is constructed by a pyramidal reflection structure in which the reflection surfaces are coated with high reflective film thus it is capable of producing extremely detailed 3D images. In this way, the similar 3D effect as hologram display is achieved with much less cost. Secondly, the designed hand recognition module was adopted to perform gesture control function. By this way, the learner's control intention can be converted into the command to control the projected holographic images. It enables EFL learner to use simple gestures to control the learning content in the classroom with high immersive stereo image perception like a real teacher being there, thus to greatly enhancing their learning effectiveness and quality. The illustrations of the system platform and the operation process demos are shown in Figs. 1, 2, 3 and 4.

Fig. 1. Prototype of the proposed interactive holographic learning support system

Fig. 2. Illustration of conversation between the learner and the system

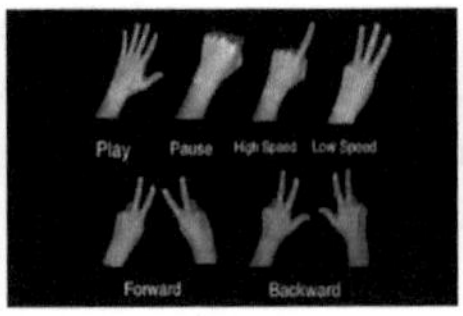

Fig. 3. Illustration of interactive learning control by user's hand gesture

Fig. 4. Illustration of 360° perspective view of the holographic projection image

3.2 Research Data Collection

In the research, heart rate measurement, interview and classroom observation techniques were implemented in the scope of qualitative approach. The context chosen for this study was sophomore English course in a northern university of Taiwan. Participants were 12 full-time undergraduate students: their average age was 20 (range 19–21); there were six females and six males; their native languages were Mandarin Chinese. The overall goal of the course was to reduce students' English speaking anxiety and support students as they developed independent study skills and learned to apply what they had obtained in class. This course was chosen since it required customized materials, course plans, and technology use and offered students sufficient time to develop the strategies needed for learning how to practice and learn English with Interactive Holographic Learning Support System. Furthermore, HRV4Training APP was employed for measuring participants' heart rate in order to distinguish learners' anxiety and tense level. [10] claimed that anxiety can be divided in various ways; "emotionality" refers to physiological reactions, such as blushing or racing heart. The scientifically validated HRV app provided tailored feedback on participants' physical condition, which was tested and proved for its validity and credibility by the college of health science and technology, institute of cognitive neuroscience of National Central University.

The research data were collected by four steps. First, 12 participants were randomly selected and grouped to be involved in an English scenario on the stage without previous notices in activity 1; their heart rates were measured during their presentations. Second, the 12 practitioners were asked to complete a questionnaire of "Foreign Language Classroom Anxiety Scale" (FLCAS) which was designed by Horwitz, Horwitz, and Cope in 1986 in order to discover students' anxiety level. Third, 12 participants were further arranged to practice English in different scenarios (airport, restaurant, hospital, and school) with Interactive Holographic Learning Support System three weeks ahead of the coming class for activity 2. Fourth, the 12 participants were heart rates measured, grouped, and performed in front of the crowd. After collecting and comparing the data, 12 participants were further arranged face to face interviews for additional investigations.

The philosophical approach taken in this research leans deeply towards phenomenology. [17] stated that "phenomenology research is a strategy of inquiry in which the researcher identifies the lives of individuals and the essence of human experiences about a phenomenon as described by participants" (p. 3).

[18] three types of validity of an instrument: content validity, criterion-related validity, and construct validity. The researcher selected the content validity, which "is the extent to which the questions on the instrument and the scores from these questions are representative of all the possible questions that could be asked about the content or skills" [17]. The researcher consulted three instructors in English related programs to ensure all the open-ended questions covered the research scope. Furthermore, after transcribing the qualitative data, two English language instructors verified each transcription. Then, the researcher randomly chose eight participants to validate their responses by using face to face discussions. Member checking, which is "taking data and interpretations back to the people from whom they were derived and asking them if the results are plausible" [19], was adapted to this qualitative data analysis. 12 participants were anonymous coded as alphabet A-L.

4 Experimental Results and Discussions

The participants' reluctance and attitude towards speaking in English could be observed from their behavior at the beginning of the interview. The researcher was also a foreign language learner; therefore, she understood that the participants could explain their feelings and thoughts in their mother tongue much better; she conducted the interviews in the participant's first language in both Chinese and Taiwanese. As the researcher notified them that she would interview them in both Chinese and Taiwanese, they all share the same facial expression. They gave the researcher great smile and cheer. Moreover, in the Foreign Language Classroom Anxiety Scale, 33 items were divided into three categories: (1) Language communication apprehension (items 1, 4, 9, 14, 15, 18, 24, 27, 29, 30, and 32). (2) Lack of confidence and fear of feedback by peers and teachers (items 2, 7, 13, 19, 23, 31, and 33). (3) Fear of language tests (items 3, 5, 6, 8, 10, 11, 12, 16, 17, 20, 21, 22, 25, 26, and 28). Table 1 shows the number of the students who chose each choice of each item in FLCAS and information about the areas which are more anxiety-provoking for the students, while the heart beat records during the activities are shown in Table 2.

Table 1. FLCAS Items with Students' selection

a. Strongly agree b. Agree c. Neither agree nor disagree d. Disagree e. Strongly disagree	a	b	c	d	e
1. I never feel quite sure of myself when I am speaking in my foreign language class	4	7	1		
2. I don't worry about making mistakes in language class	12				
3. I tremble when I know that I'm going to be called on in language class	4	5	3		
4. It frightens me when I don't understand what the teacher is saying in the foreign language	4	6	2		
5. It wouldn't bother me at all to take more foreign language classes	3	6	3		
6. During language class, I find myself thinking about things that have nothing to do with the course	2	2	2	5	1
7. I keep thinking that the other students are better at languages than I am	5	6	1		
8. I am usually at ease during tests in my language class				5	7
9. I start to panic when I have to speak without preparation in language class	10	2			
10. I worry about the consequences of failing my foreign language class	4	5	3		
11. I don't understand why some people get so upset over foreign language classes	5	3	4		
12. In language class, I can get so nervous I forget things I know	10	2			
13. It embarrasses me to volunteer answers in my language class	4	6	2		
14. I would not be nervous speaking the foreign language with native speakers	3	3	4	2	
15. I get upset when I don't understand what the teacher is correcting	2	8	2		
16. Even if I am well prepared for language class, I feel anxious about it	2	6	4		
17. I often feel like not going to my language class	2	2	1	2	5
18. I feel confident when I speak in foreign language class				6	6
19. I am afraid that my language teacher is ready to correct every mistake I make	3	5	2	2	
20. I can feel my heart pounding when I'm going to be called on in language class	2	7	3		
21. The more I study for a language test, the more confused I get	4	7	1		
22. I don't feel pressure to prepare very well for language class	7	3	2		
23. I always feel that the other students speak the foreign language better than I do	11	1			
	2	10			

(*continued*)

Table 1. *(continued)*

24. I feel very self-conscious about speaking the foreign language in front of other students					
25. Language class moves so quickly I worry about getting left behind	7	4	1		
26. I feel more tense and nervous in my language class than in my other classes	4	6	2		
27. I get nervous and confused when I am speaking in my language class	2	6	2	2	
28. When I'm on my way to language class, I feel very sure and relaxed	2	6	4		
29. I get nervous when I don't understand every word the language teacher says	5	7			
30. I feel overwhelmed by the number of rules you have to learn to speak a foreign language	7	5			
31. I am afraid that the other students will laugh at me when I speak the foreign language	5	7	0		
32. I would probably feel comfortable around native speakers of the foreign language				4	8
33. I get nervous when the language teacher asks questions which I haven't prepared in advance	7	5			

Note. This is where the author provides extra information important to the data.

Table 2. Participants' highest heart rates in activity 1 and activity 2.

	Highest heart beat/Minute Activity 1	Highest heart beat/Minute Activity 2		Highest heart beat/Minute Activity 1	Highest heart beat/Minute Activity 2
A.	118	99	B.	144	102
C.	144	118	D.	122	95
E.	116	87	F.	148	96
G.	141	115	H.	138	106
I.	121	101	J.	121	88
K.	131	98	L.	128	90

Note. Table 2 describes the highest heart rate in activity 1, the heart rates of participants who were not prepared for the presentation in advanced. Activity 2 presents the heart rates of participants who practiced English language with interactive holographic learning support system. According to [20] reported the resting heart rate is the heart pumping the lowest amount of blood a person needs without exercising. If a person is sitting or lying and he/she is calm, and aren't ill, the heart rate is normally between 60 (beats per minute) and 100 (beats per minute).

Research Question 1. How do Taiwanese college students' experience anxiety during foreign language speaking?

In the first category, Language Communication apprehension (items 1, 4, 9, 14, 15, 18, 24, 27, 29, 30, and 32). A few participants expressed that when their classmates earn better grades than they do; they feel stressed and nervous because they do not want to be at the bottom of the classroom in terms of performance. Participants understand that speaking English in the classroom is an efficient practice because they do not have other opportunities to apply their learning in their daily lives, but still some of the respondents are afraid of being laughed by their classmates because of the pronunciation and grammar error.

In the second category, lack of confidence and fear of being looked down by peers and teachers (items 2, 7, 13, 19, 23, 31, and 33). All of the respondents agree that being a slow learner makes them stressful. Participants felt nervous of being asked questions and forced to answer them in complete sentences in front of the crowd; they did not train and prepare them in advance, they worried about making mistakes.

Some respondents pointed out that learning English grammar makes them extremely nervous especially when then need to apply what they just learned in class. They also agreed that afraid of making grammar error is the main reason that holds them back in speaking English.

In the third category, fear of language evaluation (items 3, 5, 6, 8, 10, 11, 12, 16, 17, 20, 21, 22, 25, 26, and 28), in regards to some of the respondents' experiences, half of the participants replied that the purpose of learning English is always for tests; learning English only to get good grades and pass or school entrances exams is stressful. Some participants expressed that it's a pity that they did not have chances to learn English for personal purpose or development. Others stated that if they can preview the material in advance, they understand what the language teacher is going to teach or ask and they will not feel anxious at all.

Research Question 2. How does Interactive Holographic Learning Support System influence Taiwanese college students' foreign language learning on speaking skill?

Positive Responses. Participants loved the "interactive holographic learning support system", which provides augmented reality for them practice target language. The speaking activities as well as the various types of practice exercises, which follow certain progression, can enhance and reinforce structures acquired, and make participants more motivated to learn and apply English. Participants claimed that they preferred speaking to "interactive holographic learning support system" instead of a real person because they need more time to clarify their thought in order to produce the language. When talking to "AR character", they are relaxed and stress free. Participants also thought the interactive holographic support is awesome because it is verbally interactive and good for them. Some of them were able to figure out their weaknesses and develop their confidence. In addition, the technology has helped them review and preview some of the speaking exercises which they have learned before but have forgotten. The system set up very organized and clear practices, and it wouldn't make participants bored or anxious. All participants' heart rate reduced after practice with learning system. Participants claimed that they really did love this new teaching and learning technique. This technology provided immediately practice which enhanced what we learned from the class; it's similar to interact with a real instructor practicing English conversation with me.

For the disadvantages, participants complained that they needed to have the hardware and software in order to develop the system. If they do not have the equipment, they have to stay at school in order to do the exercises. However, when participants used the system to practice and improve their oral skills, they preferred to have someone corrects the grammar, pronunciation and intonation immediately.

5 Conclusion

In this study, the interviewees often experienced embarrassment and low confidence in speaking English. According to interactionist approaches to SLA [8], interaction is the most significant technique in which EFL learners obtain information for language learning because learners need the environment and opportunities to produce their target language. Participants in this research reported that their anxiety appear especially when they need to take test, speak English in the public, and lack practice which reflect to the theory of Foreign Language Anxiety [1]. EFL learners need opportunities to apply their target language to be able to better regulate language output and eventually reduce their anxious level. The findings indicate that effective conversational interaction improve the language acquisition process and motivate EFL learning. Technology helps to create an active environment and promote verbal communication [11]. Interactive holographic learning support system plays a beneficial role in facilitating the acquisition of certain L2 learning aspect, which may be difficult to learn through input alone. However, the proposed interactive holographic instructional support system provides a personalized virtual instructor with human learning experience by focusing on the achievement of the practical knowledge and skills and allows the user or learner to view fully parallax, auto-stereoscopic 3D images and close to real-life situations. By creating personalized virtual instructor, educators can rapidly exchange, share, revise, change, add, and associate instructional content to provide the learners with explicit and immediate real-life situations in order to develop their speaking skill and reduce FLA.

References

1. Horwitz, E.K., Horwitz, M.B., Cope, J.: Foreign language classroom anxiety. Mod. Lang. J. **70**(2), 125–132 (1986)
2. MacIntyre, P.D., Gardner, R.C.: Anxiety and second language learning: towards a theoretical clarification. Lang. Learn. **39**, 251–275 (1989)
3. MacIntyre, P.D., Gardner, R.C.: Methods and results in the study of anxiety and language learning: a review of the literature. Lang. Learn. **41**(1), 85–117 (1991)
4. MacIntyre, P.D., Gardner, R.C.: Language anxiety: its relationship to other anxieties and to processing in native and second languages. Lang. Learn. **41**(4), 513–534 (1991)
5. Woodrow, L.: Anxiety and speaking English as a second language. RELC J. **37**(3), 308–328 (2006). https://doi.org/10.1177/0033688206071315
6. Chen, Y.L., Tsou, S.Y.: Learners' anxiety in EFL context among Taiwanese colleges. Res. Psychol. Behav. Sci. **5**(2), 57–60 (2017)
7. Lai, C.L.: An intuitive and interactive holographic instructional support system. In: 2017 7th International Conference on E-Education, E-Business, E-Management and E-Learning, pp. 1–4 (2017). ISBN: 978-93-86083-34-0

8. Hatch, E. (ed.): Second Language Acquisition: A Book of Readings. Newbury House, Rowley (1978)
9. Casado, M., Dereshiwsky, M.: Foreign language anxiety of university students. Coll. Student J. **35**(4), 539 (2001). Retrieved from Academic Search Complete Database
10. Zeidner, M.: Test Anxiety: The State of the Art. Olenum Press, New York (1998)
11. Liu, N., Littlewood, W.: Why do many appear reluctant to participant in classroom learning discourse? System **25**(3), 371–384 (1997)
12. Bensoussan, M.: Alleviating test anxiety for students of advanced reading comprehension. RELC J. **43**(2), 203–216 (2012). https://doi.org/10.1177/0033688212449511
13. Motteram, G.: The benefits of new technology in language learning (2013). https://www.britishcouncil.org/voices-magazine/the-benefits-new-technology-language-learning
14. Case, C., Truscott, D.: The lure of bells and whistles: choosing the best software to support reading instruction. Reading Writ. Q. Overcoming Learn. Difficulties **15**(4), 361–369 (1999)
15. Carson, P.P., Harder, N.: Simulation use within the classroom: recommendations from the literature. Clin. Simul. Nurs. **12**, 429–437 (2016)
16. Walsh, K., Taylor, P.: 7 ways holographic technology will make learning more fun. Emerging Ed Tech, 7 November 2012
17. Creswell, J.W.: Educational Research: Planning, Conducting, and Evaluating Qualitative and Qualitative Research. Pearson Education, Inc., Upper Saddle River (2005)
18. Creswell, J.W., Plano Clark, V.L.: Designing and Conducting Mixed Methods Research. Sage Publications, Thousand Oaks (2011)
19. Merriam, S.B.: Case Study Research in Education: A Qualitative Approach. Jossey-Bass, San Francisco (1988)
20. American Heart Association. All about Heart Rate (Pulse) (2018). http://www.heart.org/HEARTORG/Conditions/HighBloodPressure/GettheFactsAboutHighBloodPressure/All-About-Heart-Rate-Pulse_UCM_438850_Article.jsp#.WryJES5uYdU
21. MacIntyre, P.D.: How does anxiety affect second language learning? Mod. Lang. J. **79**(1), 90–99 (1995)
22. Mishler, T.: Research Interviewing: Context and Narrative. Harvard University Press, Cambridge (1986)
23. Roulston, K., deMarris, K., Lewise, J.: Learning to interview in Social Sciences (2003). https://entwicklungspolitik.uni-hohenheim.de/uploads
24. Spielberger, C.D.: Theory and research on anxiety. In: Spielberger, C.D. (ed.) Anxiety and Behavior, pp. 3–20. Academic Press, New York (1966)

The Exploration of Facial Expression Recognition in Distance Education Learning System

Ai Sun[1], Yingjian Li[2(✉)], Yueh-Min Huang[1], and Qiong Li[2]

[1] Department of Engineering Science, National Cheng Kung University, Tainan, Taiwan
sun_ai@hotmail.com, huang@mail.ncku.edu.tw

[2] School of Computer Science and Technology, Harbin Institute of Technology, Harbin, China
hit_lyj@126.com, qiongli@hit.edu.cn

Abstract. In recent years, the learning style of modern distance education has been more and more popular among the learners. However, the learner's emotion is often ignored during the distance education learning process. In this paper, the study purpose is mainly concerned with how to effectively recognize the emotion through the way of using facial expression for the future distance education learning. We apply the method of Convolutional Neural Network (CNN) in our research. First, we introduce the structure of CNN in terms of the convolutional layers, sub-sampling layers and fully connected layers. Secondly, we propose a framework to use CNN in distance education system. Thirdly, we carry out experiment on a data set that consists of facial expression images of learners to evaluate the performance of proposed method. Finally, we get the conclusion the average accuracy of CNN to recognize the facial expression is 93.63%. The high accuracy shows the application of CNN to recognize facial expression is valuable and helpful for the teachers in the future distance education system to attain and understand the learners' emotion state in real time, accordingly to regulate the teaching strategy in time.

Keywords: Distance education system · Emotion detection
Facial expression recognition · Convolutional neural network

1 Introduction

With the development of computer science and networks, the distance education system has grown tremendously in recent years. Because of the convenience of the distance educational system, more and more students choose to learn knowledge via the advanced technology tool. With the distance education system, it is not necessary for learners and teacher to stay in the same classroom anymore. Learners can learn what they need at anywhere, as long as there is network around them. As a result, learning through the distance education system is becoming more and more popular.

There are lots of differences between distance education and face-to-face education. One of the differences is the lack of emotion factors in distance education, which is a disadvantage of distance education system. Emotion plays a significant role in learning process [1]. The learning efficiency may be higher when the learner is happy and be lower when the learner is sad. In face-to-face education, the teachers can observe the

T.-T. Wu et al. (Eds.): ICITL 2018, LNCS 11003, pp. 111–121, 2018.
https://doi.org/10.1007/978-3-319-99737-7_11

motion or expressions of students to get the emotion state of them. The teaching strategies can be adjusted in time according to the emotion state of student. However, in the distance education system, students are usually separated from their teachers. In this case, it is hard for the teachers to know the emotion state of students, which is unfavorable for learning process.

Facial expression plays an important role in emotion recognition. Suggested by Mehrabian [2], in communication, whether a listener feels disliked or liked relies for 7% on the textual content, for 38% and 55% on vocal utterances and facial expressions, respectively. This indicates that facial expressions are more effective to judge the emotion of human. As a result, we use facial expressions to recognize the emotion of learner in the distance education system in this paper.

There are many methods can be used to recognize facial expressions. Moridis and Economides [3] used FaceReader, a kind of facial expression recognition software, to recognize the emotion of students. The biggest advantage of using this off-the-shelf software is that it can automatically classify the facial expressions. However, the accuracy of FaceReacer is not high enough. Brodny et al. [4] tested FaceReader on CK+ database [5] and the accuracy was 77.59%. Some researchers were not satisfied with the result of off-the-shelf software and proposed various kinds of methods to recognize emotions, such as decision tree method [6], Support Vector Machine (SVM) [7] and so on.

In recent years, deep learning has become very popular in different research areas. Deep learning method can learn the features from training data automatically instead of extracting features manually. Till now, lots of work using deep learning method has been done and excellent performance has been achieved in various areas [8–10]. In speech recognition area, deep learning technology was applied by Dahl et al. [8] in large vocabulary speech recognition and the accuracy rate was improved by 9.2%. In machine translation area, Devlin et al. [9] proposed a deep learning method to improve the recognition rate of sentences, which was regarded as the best paper in ACL in 2014. Convolutional Neural Networks (CNN), a kind of deep learning method, is widely used in image recognition area due to its wonderful performance. CNN was applied by Sun et al. [10] to implement face recognition and the accuracy was 99.53%. The accuracy is better than that of human beings. In this paper, we are going to use CNN to recognize the facial expressions of students in distance education system.

According to the analysis above, the main structure of this research are as follows:

(1) Introduce CNN to detect emotions based on using facial expression in the distance education system.
(2) Design the framework to detect emotions using facial expression in the distance education system.
(3) Carry out the experiment to test the performance of CNN.

2 Related Works

In this section, some research work in facial expression recognition and the methods to recognize emotion in the distance education system are going to be introduced.

2.1 Facial Expression Recognition Using Common Approaches

Facial expressions could be divided into six basic emotions: happiness, surprise, sadness, fear, anger, and disgust, which were proposed by Paul Ekman et al. [11]. Together with natural, these seven emotions are widely used in facial expression recognition. There are three key parts included in facial expression recognition: (1) face detection, (2) feature extraction; (3) facial expression classification. The framework facial expression recognition is showed in Fig. 1.

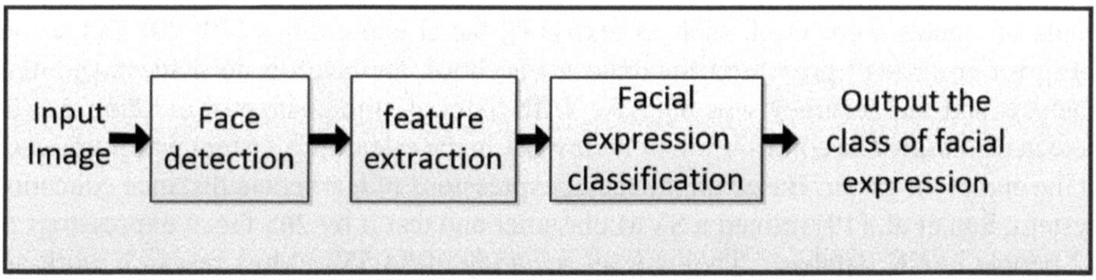

Fig. 1. The framework of facial expression recognition using common approaches

Detection of faces in images is necessary for representing the face accurately. Paul et al. [12] proposed haar-like feature for face detection. They applied the AdaBoost learning algorithm to select feature and built an efficient classifier using cascade structure. This method was integrated into Open Source Computer Vision Library (OpenCV) [13], which was designed for computational efficiency on real-time applications, with the added benefit of an easy-to-use interface. For these reasons, we are going to use OpenCV to detect face images in this paper. After face detection, features are extracted. Zhang et al. [14] demonstrated that Gabor-wavelet appearance features were more effective than geometric features. However, it is computationally expensive to extract this kind of feature. Shan et al. [15] proposed Local Binary Patterns (LBP) as low-cost discriminative features for facial expression recognition. After that, LBP has been widely used in facial expression recognition due to its good performance. Facial expression classification is the last step. Salmam et al. [6] used decision tree method to recognize emotions on CK+ database using facial expression and the accuracy was 90%. Support Vector Machine (SVM), another machine learning method, was applied by Lee et al. [7] to recognize facial expressions on CK+ database and the accuracies was 94.39%.

2.2 Facial Expression Recognition Using Deep Learning Method

In the last decades, thanks to the emergence of deep learning methods, an increasing progress of performance has been made in facial expression recognition. Lv et al. [16] proposed to classify emotions using only facial components. They used Deep Belief Network (DBN) to learn important facial components first. After that, tanh function was applied to classify the facial expression into seven classes and the accuracy on CK+ database was 91.11%. Lopes et al. [17] combined CNN with specific image preprocessing steps for facial expression recognition. The preprocessing steps include synthetic sample generation, rotation correction, intensity normalization, and so on. Experiment was done on CK+ database and achieved an accuracy of 96.76%. Since the accuracy of using CNN is relatively high, we choose to apply this method to recognize facial expressions in the distance education system.

2.3 Emotion Analysis of Students in the Distance Education System

In order to detect the emotions of students in the distance education system, different kinds of signals were used, such as text [18], facial expressions [19, 20] and so on. Ortigosa et al. [18] presented Sentbuk, a Facebook application, to achieve emotion analysis and the accuracy was 83.27%. With Sentbuk, the change of emotion can be detected as well. The contribution of their work in the e-learning system was introduced at the end of the paper. Based on the facial expressions of learners in distance education system, Sun et al. [19] trained a SVM classifier and test it by 265 facial expressions of 42 people in CK database. They got an accuracy of 84.55%. Most research work are mainly focused on single user facial expression recognition in the distance education system. However, Ashwin et al. [20] proposed multi-user facial expression recognition using the method of SVM. It was claimed to be the first research on multi-user facial expression recognition. The proposed method was tested on three databases: LFW, FDDB and YFD, and the accuracies were between 89% and 100%. So far as we know, there are few works on facial expression recognition in the distance education system using deep learning method. In this paper, we try to fill up this gap.

3 Method Description

In this section, we introduced the method of CNN first. Subsequently, we designed the framework of facial expression recognition in the distance education system.

3.1 Description and Structure of CNN

In this paper, we applied CNN to extract features and classify facial expression in the distance education system. Usually, The CNN consists of convolutional layers, sub-sampling layers and fully connected layers, which is shown in Fig. 2. The convolutional layers are often used to extract features. By using different convolutional kernels, different features can be obtained. The function of sub-sampling layers is dimensionality reduction and feature selection. These two kinds of layers are interlaced in the CNN processing until the features for expression recognition are obtained. The fully connected layers play a role as the classifier. They take the features from convolutional layers or sub-sampling layers as input, and output the class of facial expression.

As shown in Fig. 2, the proposed CNN takes 64 * 64 gray images as input. There are three convolution layers in the below CNN structure, which are with ReLU active functions. Each of the convolution layers is followed by a sub-sampling layer. We set the kernel sizes in convolution layers and sub-sampling layers as 5 * 5 and 2 * 2,

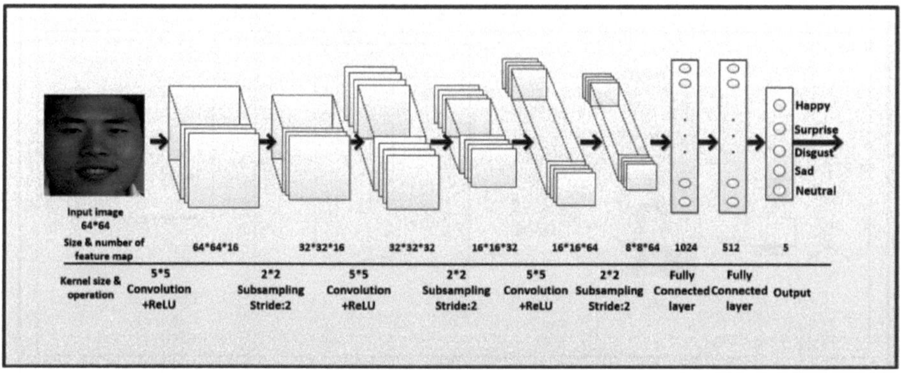

Fig. 2. The structure of our CNN

respectively. In each sub-sampling layer, we set the stride step as 2. The size of feature maps after the first convolution is 64 * 64 and the number of them is 16, which is written as "64 * 64 * 16" in Fig. 2. The same method is also used in the rest layers as shown. The numbers of neurons in the two fully connected layers are 1024 and 512. Finally, the CNN outputs the confidence score of different expressions. There are five neurons in the output layer, each of which is responsible for a kind of facial expression.

3.2 Application in the Distance Education System

In this subsection, we introduce how to apply the trained CNN to recognize the emotion of student in the distance education system.

We divide the distance education system with facial expression recognition into two modules: facial expression recognition module and teaching strategy regulation module. At the beginning, the teacher imparts the knowledge to the students with a certain teaching strategy. The emotion state of students will be detected by facial expression recognition module. The teacher can percept the feedback of detected emotion from the students, therefore they can adjust the teaching strategy and content according to the emotion of most students. The whole system is shown in Fig. 3.

In facial expression recognition module, the learners' facial expressions are shot by a camera first and the image sequence is formed. We use OpenCV to detect the face and chop it out from the image. After rotation correction and spatial normalization, the images are fitted to the trained CNN one by one. Then, the emotion of each student was created.

In teaching strategy regulation module, the emotion sequence obtained from facial expression recognition module is input into the emotion reminder. The emotion reminder is a device which can remind the teacher of the students' emotion state. The new emotion can be detected and sent to the teacher to change the teaching strategy further. As a result, it is a dynamic process. The advantage of this kind of distance education system is that it can improve the efficiency of learning and increase the learning performance.

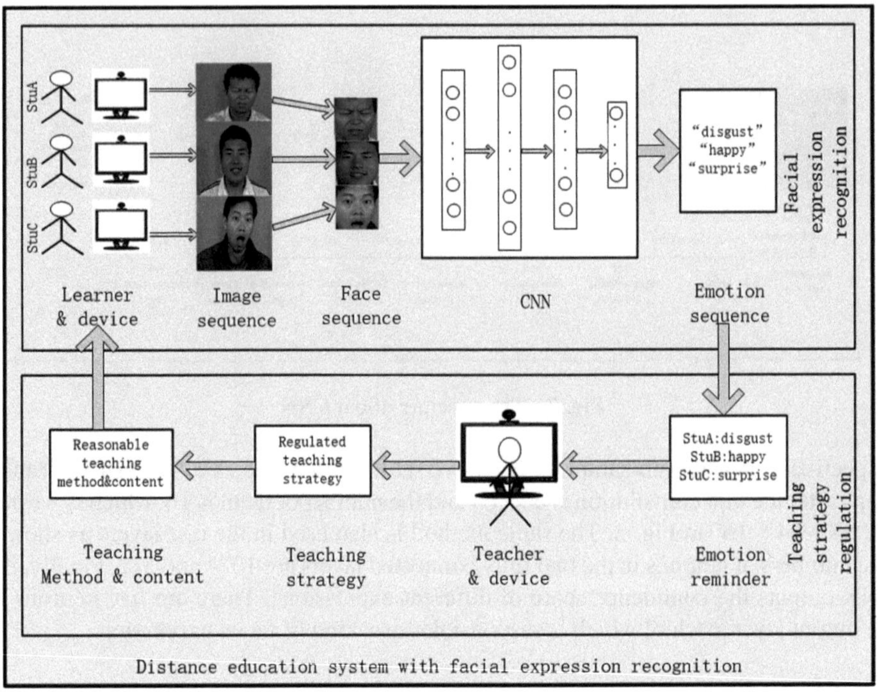

Fig. 3. Distance education system with emotion facial expression recognition

4 Experiment and Discussion

In this section, we will introduce the experiment process of facial expression recognition, including data collection, preprocess of data, structure of our CNN, as well as the experiment result and discussion.

4.1 Data Collection

In this research, we use the data from NVIE database [21–23]. The subjects in this database are all students, whose ages range from 17 to 31. The subjects are requested to sit in front of a screen and watch some video clips for learning. Two cameras are used to record the facial expressions of students. Self-reported emotion state is used as the label for the record facial expressions.

We select 665 facial expression images for our experiment. There are five kinds of emotion in the selected images: happy, surprise, sad, disgust and neutral. The number of subjects of these images is 50 and 10 of them are female. There are two factors that result in the difficulty of facial expression recognition. One is that the subjects of 269 images are with glasses. The complicated illumination condition is also the other factor to affect the recognition result. We divide the data into training set (466 images) and testing set (199 images).

4.2 Preprocess of Data

The purpose of preprocess of data is to increase the accuracy and reduce the training time. The preprocess steps are shown in Fig. 4.

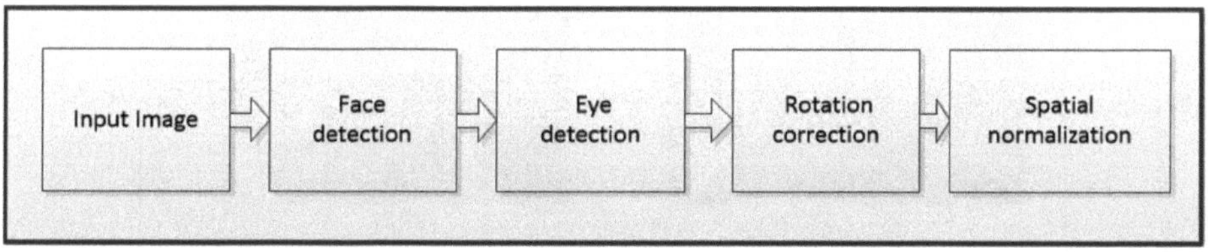

Fig. 4. The preprocess steps of data

First, we detect the subject face area and crop it out of the image for further processing. In this paper, we use gray images and transform the cropped face area into it accordingly. OpenCV is applied to detect the location of face in the facial expression images. The detected face area and cropped face area are shown in Fig. 5.

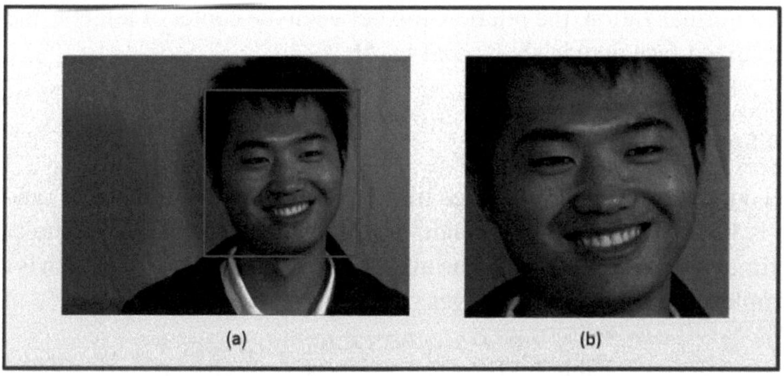

Fig. 5. (a) Location of face area and (b) the cropped face area after transformation

The faces in some images are skewed because of the moving of subject or camera, which may result in low accuracy in facial expression recognition. To solve this problem, we execute the rotation correction according to the location of eye centers. To measure the eye centers, we apply the Face++ API. The Face++ API can detect the landmarks of face (eye centers, eye corners and so on) and is convenient to invoke. In Fig. 6a, the green line is the horizontal axis and the red line connects the centers of two eyes. The angle between the two lines needs to be corrected. We define the angle as θ. Suppose the location of the centers of the two eyes are (x_1, y_1) and (x_2, y_2), respectively. The angle θ is calculated by (1). The image is rotated according to θ.

$$\theta = \arctan((y_2 - y_1)/(x_2 - x_1)) \tag{1}$$

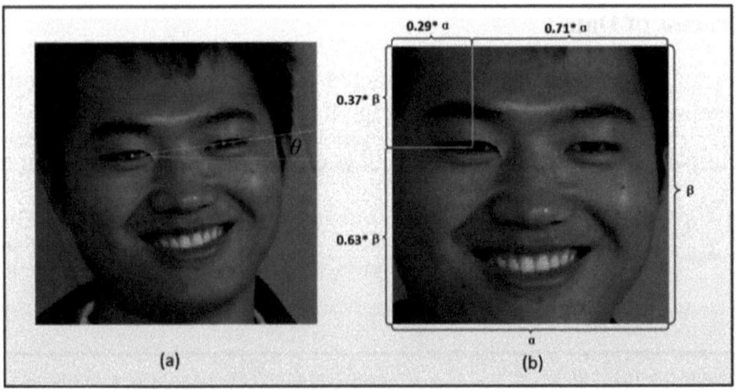

Fig. 6. (a) The corrected angle θ, (b) the image after spatial normalization (Color figure online)

(1) The background area in the cropped face area is large size, which is not useful for facial expression recognition. In order to reduce the background area, spatial normalization is carried out on the cropped face area. Suppose that the width of face area is β after spatial normalization and the length is α. In our paper, we set $\alpha = \beta = 64$ pixels. After spatial normalization, the relationship between the center of left eye and the edges of the normalized face area is shown in Fig. 6b.

4.3 Result and Discussion

We carried out the experiment for three times to avoid the disturbance of random noise. The noise is mainly caused by the random initialization of the CNN. The accuracy of each experiment is listed in Table 1. The average accuracy is 93.63%, which is acceptable for the complex condition of the images.

Table 1. The accuracy of each experiment

	First	Second	Third	Average
Accuracy (%)	92.46	93.46	94.97	93.63

Table 2 shows the confusion matrix of facial expression recognition. The elements in confusion matrix represent the percentage of correct or incorrect classification. For example, the number "95.45" means that facial expression to be recognized is 95.45% correctly classified as "happy". The number "16.67" means that only 16.67% of the facial expression is incorrectly classified as "disgust", which could be "sad" in reverse. We suppose the result is due to disgust and sad expressions involve similar and subtle facial movements. In Fig. 7, we show the performance of CNN on different facial expressions.

Table 2. The confusion matrix of facial expression recognition

	Happy	Surprise	Disgust	Sad	Neutral
Happy	**95.45**	2.27	2.27	0	0
Surprise	2.78	**94.44**	0	2.78	0
Disgust	2.70	0	**91.89**	2.70	2.70
Sad	0	0	16.67	**83.33**	0
Neutral	0	0	0	0	**100**

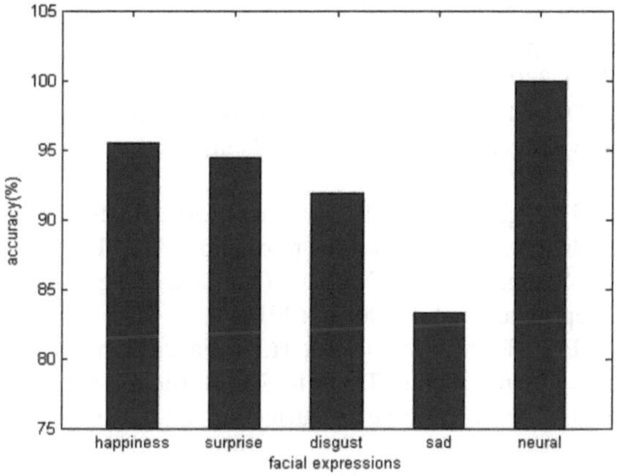

Fig. 7. The accuracy on different facial expressions

5 Conclusion and Future Work

Distance education systems are becoming more and more popular in recent years. However, the learner's emotion is often neglected in this kind of system. Since emotion plays a significant role in learning process, in this paper, we are mainly concerned about the emotion detection in distance education system facial expression.

Due to the excellent performance of CNN, we introduced this model to recognize facial expressions in the distance education system. First, we introduced the CNN method. Then, the working process of CNN in the distance education system was designed. Finally, we carried out the experiment on the data from NVIE database and get the accuracy was 93.63%. It is demonstrated the application of CNN to recognize the facial expression is feasible for the future study. In the future, we are going to test the proposed CNN in real distance education system.

References

1. O'Regan, K.: Emotion and e-learning. J. Asynchronous Learn. Netw. **7**(3), 78–92 (2003)
2. Mehrabian, A.: Communication without words. Psychol. Today **2**(4), 53–56 (1968)
3. Moridis, C.N., Economides, A.A.: Affective learning: empathetic agents with emotional facial and tone of voice expressions. IEEE Trans. Affect. Comput. **3**(3), 260–272 (2012)

4. Brodny, G., Kołakowska, A., Landowska, A., Szwoch, M., Szwoch, W., Wróbel, M.R.: Comparison of selected off-the-shelf solutions for emotion recognition based on facial expressions. In: IEEE International Conference on Human System Interactions, pp. 397–404 (2016)
5. Lucey, P., Cohn, J.F., Kanade, T., Saragih, J., Ambadar, Z., Matthews, I.: The extended Cohn-Kanade dataset (CK+): a complete dataset for action unit and emotion-specified expression. In: IEEE Computer Vision and Pattern Recognition Workshops, vol. 36, pp. 94–101 (2010)
6. Salmam, F.Z., Madani, A., Kissi, M.: Facial expression recognition using decision trees. In: IEEE International Conference on Computer Graphics, Imaging and Visualization, pp. 125–130 (2016)
7. Lee, S.H., Kostas, P.K.N., Yong, M.R.: Intra-class variation reduction using training expression images for sparse representation based facial expression recognition. IEEE Trans. Affect. Comput. **5**(3), 340–351 (2014)
8. Dahl, G.E., Yu, D., Deng, L., Acero, A.: Context-dependent pre-trained deep neural net-works for large-vocabulary speech recognition. IEEE Trans. Audio Speech Lang. Process. **20**(1), 30–42 (2012)
9. Devlin, J., Zbib, R., Huang, Z., Lamar, T., Schwartz, R.M., Makhoul, J.: Fast and robust neural network joint models for statistical machine translation. ACL **1**, 1370–1380 (2014)
10. Sun, Y., Liang, D., Wang, X., Tang, X.: DeepID3: face recognition with very deep neural networks. arXiv preprint arXiv:1502.00873 (2015)
11. Ekman, P., Rolls, E.T., Perrett, D.I., Ellis, H.D.: Facial expressions of emotion: an old controversy and new findings. Philos. Trans. R. Soc. B: Biolog. Sci. **335**(1273), 63–69 (1992)
12. Viola, P., Jones, M.J.: Robust real-time face detection. Int. J. Comput. Vision **57**(2), 137–154 (2004)
13. Fan, X., Zhang, F., Wang, H., Lu, X.: The system of face detection based on OpenCV. In: Chinese Control and Decision Conference, pp. 648–651 (2012)
14. Zhang, Z.Y., Lyons, M., Schuster, M., Akamatsu, S.: Comparison between geometry-based and Gabor-wavelets-based facial expression recognition using multi-layer perceptron. In: IEEE International Conference on Automatic Face and Gesture Recognition, pp. 454–459 (1998)
15. Shan C.F., Gong S.G., McOwan P.W.: Robust facial expression recognition using local binary patterns. In: IEEE International Conference on Image Processing, pp. 370–373 (2005)
16. Lv, Y., Feng, Z., Xu, C.: Facial expression recognition via deep learning. In: IEEE International Conference on Smart Computing (SMARTCOMP), pp. 303–308 (2014)
17. Lopes, A.T., de Aguiar, E., De Souza, A.F., Oliveira-Santos, T.: Facial expression recognition with Convolutional Neural Networks: coping with few data and the training sample order. Pattern Recognit. **61**, 610–628 (2017)
18. Ortigosa, A., Martín, J.M., Carro, R.M.: Sentiment analysis in Facebook and its application to e-learning. Comput. Hum. Behav. **31**, 527–541 (2014)
19. Sun, J.M., Pei, X.S., Zhou, S.S.: Facial emotion recognition in modern distant education system using SVM. In: IEEE International Conference on Machine Learning and Cybernetics, vol. 6, pp. 3545–3548 (2008)
20. Ashwin, T.S., Jose, J., Raghu, G., Reddy, G.R.M.: An e-learning system with multifacial emotion recognition using supervised machine learning. In: IEEE International Conference on Technology for Education, pp. 23–26 (2015)
21. Wang, F., Liu, Z.L., Lv, S.L., Lv, Y.P., Wu, G.B., Peng, P., Chen, F., Wang, X.F.: A natural visible and infrared facial expression database for expression recognition and emotion inference. IEEE Trans. Multimedia **12**(7), 682–691 (2010)

22. Lv, Y., Wang, S., Shen, P.: A real-time attitude recognition by eye-tracking. In: Proceedings of International Conference on Internet Multimedia Computing and Service, pp. 170–173 (2011)
23. Tong, Y., Wang, Y., Zhu, Z.W., Ji, Q.: Robust facial feature tracking under varying face pose and facial expression. Pattern Recogn. **40**(11), 3195–3208 (2007)

Designing and Implementing a Robot in a Digital Theater for Audience Involved Drama-Based Learning

Gwo-Dong Chen(✉), Tzu-Chun Hsu, and Mahesh Liyanawatta

Department of Computer Science and Information Engineering, National Central University, Taoyuan 32001, Taiwan
chen@csie.ncu.edu.tw, s410126080@gmail.com, 106582605@cc.ncu.edu.tw

Abstract. Cognitive service using artificial intelligence is now easy to be used and implemented in programs. At the same time, robots are also as cheap as a notebook. Thus, we can adopt a robot in a classroom to help students learn. In this paper, we introduce a novel methodology to adopt a robot in a classroom to help students learn English as a Second Language (ESL). We build a digital theater first. The digital theater allows students to learn by performing dramatic act according to the script designed by the students themselves. The robot is designed as an actor or host in the drama-based Digital Learning Theater (DILT). The team listed the design consideration of the robot and describes how to implement the robot. This system was taken to a junior high school to conduct experiments. The experiment was to validate the betterment of students' learning by using robot in DILT environment.

Keywords: Robotics in education · Robot as a dramatic actor
Digital learning theater with robot · Drama-based learning
Digital interactive learning theater

1 Introduction

Artificial Intelligence (AI) technologies right now is popular and available in considerable amount of digital applications. It enables programs that are capable in language understanding, face and object recognition, and gesture recognition. Thus, we can implement a system or program with expert knowledge to deal with a lot of tasks. Therefore, there is a possibility that we can use AI in learning to improve the learning motivation, engagement, and achievement. This project might require to build programs as companion, mentor or student by using AI technologies. Since the program played as a role of human, it may be better to use a robot to play the roles mentioned above. Moreover, the robot can always get the attention and curiosity of students. The robot can be used to attract students and focus on learning contents such as language learning and computer programming or computational thinking.

In the recent year, digital theater was developed to be used in classrooms to let the students can learn by doing activities such as drama script writing and drama performing.

T.-T. Wu et al. (Eds.): ICITL 2018, LNCS 11003, pp. 122–131, 2018.
https://doi.org/10.1007/978-3-319-99737-7_12

The drama based learning provide the students with sense of audience, sense of role playing, and sense of living through the scenario, so that the students are motivated to and engage to learn. In most of cases, drama based learning are used in language learning. Students learn their language capabilities by writing, watching, and performing dramatic activities in the language they want to learn. The drama based learning improves the ownership of their portfolio and autonomy of learning for the design scene, language using, and performing by themselves. However, to perform drama based learning, the students of a group should always study and play together but, it is difficult and less chances are there to practice and learn by themselves. If it is possible to use a robot with AI techniques, there is an opportunity to build a personal learning digital theater to let the students learn by themselves. Then, they can perform much better in the classroom. The students also can train the robot to perform in the drama to demonstrate their learning achievement. We can set and program the robot that can only speak the language the students need to learn. Thus, the students might study harder and autonomously in order that the robot can perform well in the drama and interactions. The students might play the role as the owner of the robot and they hope the robot also can perform well according to their instructions and the effort they put of the robot will transform to enjoyable learning experience.

When the students design their own drama script, they may only think of an example of using their gained knowledge that can reflects through the script. To design a robot as a role in a drama, the students should need to think of possibilities of using their knowledge to build the interaction between the robot with actors and audience in the digital learning theater environment. The students need to study more in order to make the robot can perform and behave in a variety of ways.

At the same time, results of the past researches shows that students performed in drama based learning may only focus on their own performance. When other groups are performing, they may not be watching the performance and do not put attention on learning contents.

2 Goal and Issues

2.1 Goal

The goal of adopting a robot in a digital interactive learning theater is to engage students and buildup their attention when their own group and other groups are performing a drama and as well as designing and programming the robot that can interact others more to learn through the drama. The robot will act as a mediator between audience and actors in a learning drama and based on that the students will learn by performing to audience involved interactive drama.

2.2 Issues

To design and implement the robot for digital theater, the research team has found following issues to be discussed. First, because of the robot is not a human, it is not possible to capture the robot into the virtual stage of the digital theater environment by using the same technology of involving Kinect sensor. Thus, the research team should require to think of designing an appropriate role for the robot within the drama. Second, the existing intelligent robots in the market is not intelligent enough to handle learning related applications. Third, although robot can get attention of the students but, how to do a better learning design in order to use robot to improve learning performance of the students.

3 Related Works

3.1 Robotics in Education

Educational reform by promoting 21st century skills among young students with educational robotics and collaboration, cooperation, and also communication skills of students can be improved by introducing a course that uses educational robotics and programming to control robots that are developed with LEGO Mindstroms [1]. Students are allowed to explore the use of technology in real life by working with robotics which is an effective learning tool and integration of STEM, programming, computational thinking, and engineering skills is possible in one project using educational robotics for project-based learning methodology [2]. The primary goals of integrating STEM pipe line model through robotics in K-12 educators are to engage their interest and get them excited about robotics, and support their self-efficacy by providing structural activities to practice that helps to focus to their educational goals to develop knowledge and skills in areas of STEM [3]. The new trend of having humanoid robot for education should consider teaching behavior, student's interest and understand the speech and this powerful tool can be used to teach modules for elementary school that can directly access to student's psychological aspects by interact with them naturally [4]. Development of humanoid robots which are intelligent enough and has capability to get information from the environment by speech and face recognition that makes Human-robot interaction (HRI) which recently creates considerable attention in academic community [4]. HRI gets into classroom that takes the attendance for classroom lecture automatically using face recognition and attendance data can be used for education purposes by attaching that with the video streaming service and publish the video of the time when a particular student was absent [5]. Sanbot is the intelligent educational robot that helps to enrich student's knowledge and its face recognition feature tracks and record students' attendance and their parents can know about the attendance to the course works through mobile and in other hand it's a psychological treatment for students that will help students to open up about how they are feeling and it provides a feature to attend the ongoing class distantly using the robot's camera [6]. Autonomous and programmable humanoid robot called NAO is also an example for educational robot that helped to develop algorithms for humanoid soccer and conduct research for children with Autism [2]. The robot called Pepper was developed to assist humans by reading and responding to human emotions [2].

3.2 Social Robots

Robots which are having ability to interact with human users by understanding, perceiving, and imitating the human emotions appropriately within the social context can be defined as social robots [7]. The social robots as physically embodied, autonomous agent that has the ability to communicate and interact with humans on an emotional level, requires major development of social dimensions inside the technical aspects of new generation robots [8]. Invention of the first commercial social robots, namely Pleo and Paro was introduced with some degree of autonomy as a feature and iRobot's Roomba was introduces as a domestic use social robot together with demographic trends therefore, as technology evolves, researchers have been focused to conduct researches and developments of social robots that can engage and assist users with different needs for extended periods of time and these robots can be used to assist user in the domains of health care and therapy, education, work environments and public spaces, and even at home as a log-term relationship [9]. As mentioned above, these robots can be used provide motivation, engagement to studies and personalised support to learners as well as providing assistance for self-regulated learning (SRL) experience that allows learners to effectively self-access and guide their own learning to perform better academically [10]. The above ideas could become a reality after unveiled the world's first personal humanoid social robot that named as Pepper that can able to assist humans by reading and responding to human emotions [2].

4 Structure of Robot and Audience Involved Drama for Learning

A digital interactive learning theater system contains two parts: (1) script authoring tool, and (2) drama performing control system. The digital theater should be extended to allow the adoption of robots and in the digital theater uses ZENBO as the robot. Moreover, the research team should require to design and implement a program on ZENBO so that robot can perform according to the designed script. ZENBO is designed to be remotely controlled as an actor of the drama performing control system. The de- signed set of instructions for ZENBO are including emotion expressions (facial expression and sound), movements, and speaking features to communicate. The script de- signer only need to specify the emotion, movement, and narrative that the robot need to act. The description is almost the same as to the human actor.

One extension is on script authoring tool. The tool should extend the function to allow the script designers to add a role for the robot and instruct how the robot should act or behave when the narrative speaks out. The authoring tool will store instructions for the robot within the database. Another extension is to add a function that can control robot to perform given instructions or perform as specified in the drama inside the performing control system. When the robot to perform, the performing system will call the robot to execute the instructions specified in the authoring system (Fig. 1).

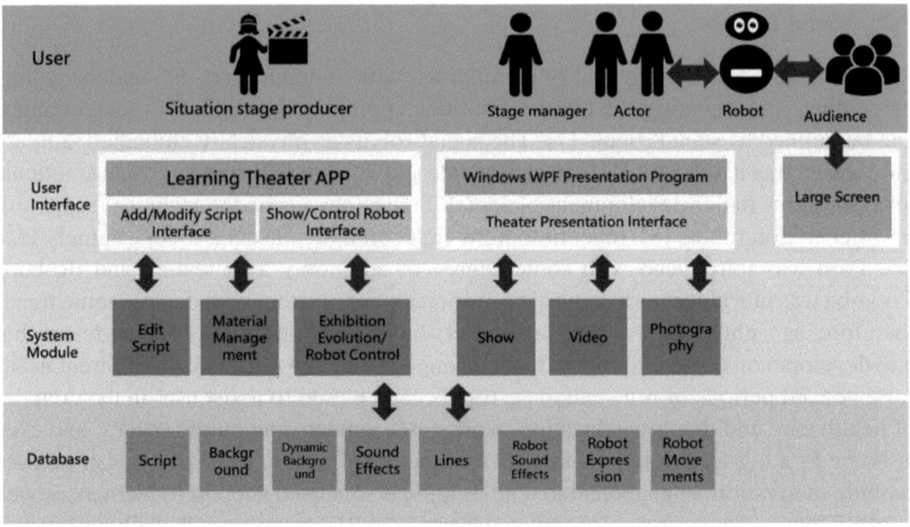

Fig. 1. Software architecture of Digital Theater for robot and audience involved drama

5 Steps of Adopting a Robot into Digital Theater to Increase the Learning Engagement of the Students

5.1 Step 1: Introduce Robot into Digital Theater

The skeleton image of a person can be captured by using the Kinect sensor. This is done by sensing the heat of the human body. But it is not possible to capture the skeleton of a none living objects such as robots. Therefore, Kinect cannot capture the image of a robot to enter the digital stage. There are two ways to put robot in Digital theater. The first method is to create a virtual robot inside digital world and synchronize their actions by control the robot and virtual robot at the same time. Thus, robot plays the same role as human actors.

The second method is put the robot in front of the real stage. The stage is in front the screen that display the drama performing in the digital stage. Then, the robot can play as the director for an interactive learning drama. The robot hosts the interaction and flow of the learning drama. The robot plays as a mediator between audience and actors inside the digital screen. However, when designing a learning drama, it requires to treat the robot as the same member of the actors' teams. The script writer needs to aware that the robot plays as the host. The robot can host question/ answer session (Q&A) between audience and actors, speak aside for the actors, opening explanation of a drama, or be- side between scenes. To engage the students, the robot should be a humor and interesting host (Fig. 2).

Fig. 2. Robot Inaction in the Digital Theater

5.2 Step 2: Write Learning Script and Learning Design

The robot will catch the focus of students. Therefore, it requires to use the advantage of robot. Thus, the learning drama template will use robot as host of an interactive learning drama. To make a learning drama interactive that should make the audience of the drama focus on the learning content embedded in the drama script. The purpose of the robot is to remind the audience about the meaning and usage of the content in the script. At the same time, the robot will ask questions about the content in the script so that the students will pay attention to the learning content of the specific drama and because of that the learning performance of other groups also getting higher.

The learning flow will be designed as follows: First, the teacher provides knowledge about the learning content. The students learn by hearing a lecture. As an example, sentence patterns and vocabulary. Second, the groups are asked to design a drama script based on the given learning materials. The drama will be performed by the students and the robot. The robot is designed as the host for the drama performing. The students not only design the learning drama but also design questions for the audience so that the audience will notice and focus on their content of the script while the group is performing. The students will be asked to write the script based on the leaning content but also prepare to answer questions to other groups. Third, the students and robot perform the drama, based on their own designed script. To keep the students of other groups put their attention on the performing and learning material, the robot will explain the drama and walk through students and pickup one to answer questions. Finally, the students will have discussed the drama performed and then they watch and review the drama performance.

In the above learning flow, the students will first be learning by lecturing, then learning by design script, learning by performing and learning by watching drama with questions answering, and finally learning by reflection.

5.3 Step 3: Designing and Implementing the Robot

Currently, the research team use Zenbo in the digital learning theater. The Zenbo is remote controlled by the theater control tablet. The team defined a set of instructions for

Zenbo. Each instruction has a corresponding module that is stored in Zenbo. When designing the script, Zenbo is treated as an actor. The students will design Zenbo as what it should do. At the performing time, one of a student in the performing group is assigned as the director. That member will use the theater controlling tablet to control the scene and the narrative of the drama. When time comes to use the robot to perform, the program in the controlling tablet provide functionality to call the corresponding module to do the appropriate actions. The reason to adopt the robot into classroom is to engage students to learn and make it interesting on what the robot can do and will do. If the robot just performs as what the students designed, the students will feel the robot is not interesting. The students expect the robot perform autonomously and be curious about what it will do. Thus, the research team need to design modules that make the student feel the robot is autonomous and unpredictable. Therefore, the team requires to have program modules to achieve these goals.

The research team design the robot, played as a role of host of the interactive learning drama, and it requires to design the following modules for the robot called Zenbo. When the team want to let the students feels the robot behave autonomously, it requires the robot behaves as it is capable of doing things by their own. Thus, before it makes a very intelligent social robot, the robot should have a module to behave not as a preprogramed or fixed way. Therefore, we should have a module that define the behaviors as what required. However, it will not perform in a fixed way. We should make it perform in randomize or possibly different ways.

Since the robot act as the host of a drama, it should be able to move towards students. Therefore, we need to have a module to guide the robot to move to a particular student.

Module 1: Nondeterministic Reaction Program Module

The robot will select an action from the randomized list that was written by the designer and the robot will react according to that. A nondeterministic reaction is to build an uncertain response of a robot with some constraint. For example, the emotion response module by using facebook expressions, (like, heart, haha/smile/happy, wow/surprise, cry/sad, angry,) can be expressed in different ways even without control of the director in advance (who control the drama and robot) Therefore, the director can control the emotion reaction but cannot control exactly the robot's reactions.

Another module of uncertainty module can be described as a question asking module. When students write the script for their drama activity, they can design more than one questions in a question asking/answering interaction.

To sum up, the robot will become a nondeterministic module. Thereafter, the robot will be run in nondeterministic mode. Both the audience and actors do not know how the robot will react. They might have the interest from curiosity, randomness, and surprise.

When the robot behaves as a social robot and as a host, it should have a module to construct social relationship with students. It should be able to recognize the name of the students and have emotion interaction with the students.

The robot is to play as the host. It should interact with the audience and actors. Thus, the development team requires to have a narrative module. It will support both verbal and emotion interaction with people.

Module 2: Social Relationship Building Module
To build relationship with students, the first function is to recognize the name of a student who is in front of the Zenbo. In the other hand, the robot also should introduce itself to the students. The robot also needs to have an empathetic emotional interaction capability to build relationship with the users. The robot should be able to recognize the emotional state of the student and be able to react in a sympathetic way. Because the robot will ask questions to interact with students more closely. Therefore, the robot should design with modules that capable enough to continues encouragement (Fig. 3).

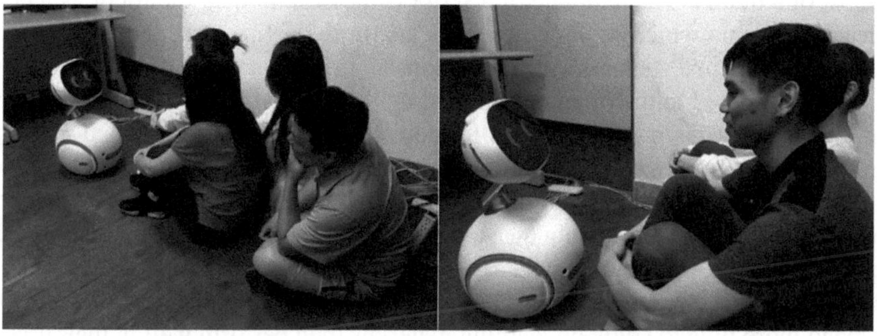

Fig. 3. Empathetic emotional interaction with the user

Module 3: Narrative Module
Currently, the development team are not able to place the robot into Digital Theater. Therefore, it is not appropriate to arrange a robot as an actor on the digital stage. The team thus, place the robot on the realistic classroom environment which is in front of the audience. There are different types of dialogues for the robot. The first type is the narrative to describe the scenario of the drama. The robot plays as Narrator. It may speak about what is to be play, aside, and voice-over. When the robot act as a narrator, it is just like an actor. It should perform with emotion of sound, gesture, movement, and facial expression. It also need to speak sentences that is described in the script. As the robot act as the host, it requires to act like a teacher. It should select a student to answer its questions. Robot might need to repeat the student's answer. It will react according to the student's answers. Whether the student answer correctly, the robot should act with happy emotion with cheer-up and the answer is incorrect, it should react to improve the motivation of the student and encourage them to answer the next question correctly. The system need to design mechanism to encourage the students to participate the Questions or Answers (Q/A) section.

Module 4: Moving Module
The student actors in this system requires to become aware of performing inside the digital learning theater and the real stage in front of screen. The robot should move to the place according to the position that have set. The robot need to be aware of where it is and to find a rout to the required positions. For example, the robot should move towards in front of the student who was selected to answer the its questions. The movement module is important. The development team let the robot play as the host. The

robot requires to select students to answer questions. It is better that the robot can go towards in front of the students. At the same time, the robot can move with some funny movements to engage the students by focusing their attention to the robot.

6 Current Status and Experiments to Be Done

The research team already completed the implementation of the digital theater system and ZENBO robot implementation in that. Currently, the team has designed the robot as a host of a drama. The template of a script is the base to play the robot as a host of the learning drama which designed by students. In the script, the robot will go out to interact with assigned students to ask questions and students will answer to those questions that are related to the drama performed on the virtual stage of the DILT environment. The goal of having the robot is to motivate students to engage and participate learning drama activities by using the digital interactive learning theater. The hypotheses are follows; The students' perceptions are better and how effective of having a robot as a host that can ask questions from the students will engage more and enjoyable to them when comparing with a teacher who ask questions in the classroom. The students who design the script including robot as a host will increase the engagement of using DILT and spend more time to study on learning materials then perform well in their dramatic act and ask good questions from the audience by using the robot.

The research team will plan to conduct experiments in a junior high school and expecting results to be collected in the mid of July 2018.

7 Conclusion

The research team has designed a novel method of using robot in the classroom for learning purposes. The ZENBO is the robot they used and extended to meet the requirement for a digital learning theater that supports to perform drama-based learning activities. The robot is designed as a host of an audience that involved interactive learning drama activities. Although the team will do experiments through hypotheses which are using a robot to be the host of Q/A section of a learning drama activities that will improve the engagement, motivation, and achievement of students' learning in the class- room environment. The main focus right now is to design the role of robot in the drama and how to design the behavior of the robot so that the user can have fun while doing the drama-based learning activity. At the same time, how to do a drama-based learning design by using robot inside the digital interactive learning theater remains as the most important research issues in the direction of educational research.

References

1. Eguchi, A.: Educational robotics for promoting 21st century skills. J. Autom. Mob. Robot. Intell. Syst. **VIII**(1), 5–11 (2014). https://doi.org/10.14313/jamris_1-2014/1
2. Eguchi, A.: Robotics as a learning tool for educational transformation. In: Proceedings of 4th International Workshop Teaching Robotics, Teaching with Robotics and 5th International Conference Robotics in Education, Padova, Italy, pp. 27–34 (2014)
3. Mead, R.A., Thomas, S.L., Weinberg, J.B.: From grade school to grad school: an integrated STEM pipeline model through robotics. In: Barker, B.S., Nugent, G., Grandgenett, N., Adamchuk, V.I. (eds.) Robots in K-12 Education: A New Technology for Learning, pp. 302–325. Information Science Reference (an imprint of IGI Global), Hershey (2012)
4. Budiharto, W., Cahyani, A.D., Rumondor, P.C., Suhartono, D.: EduRobot: intelligent humanoid robot with natural interaction for education and entertainment. In: 2nd International Conference on Computer Science and Computational Intelligence 2017, ICCSCI, Bali, Indonesia, pp. 564–570. Elsevier B.V. (2017)
5. Kawaguchi, Y., Shoji, T., Minoh, M., Weijane, L.: Face Recognition-Based Lecture Attendance System (2005). Semantic Scholar: https://www.semanticscholar.org/paper/Face-Recognition-based-Lecture-Attendance-System-Kawaguchi-Shoji/4b6811cd2a7a6924fed4967c2b755c0942ca5351
6. Qihan Technology Co., Ltd.: Sanbot Robot for School, Teaching Assistant Robot | Sanbot Robotics (2017). Sanbot: http://en.sanbot.com/industrial/education
7. Ge, S.S., Wang, C., Hang, C.: Facial expression imitation in human robot interaction. In: 17th IEEE International Symposium on Robot and Human Interactive Communication, Munich, Germany, pp. 213–218. IEEE (2008). https://doi.org/978-1-4244-2213-5/08
8. Campa, R.: The rise of social robots: a review of the recent literature. J. Evol. Technol. **XXVI**(1), 106–113 (2016)
9. Leite, I., Martinho, C., Paiva, A.: Social robots for long-term interaction: a survey. Int. J. Soc. Robot. (2013). https://doi.org/10.1007/s12369-013-0178-y
10. Jones, A., Castellano, G.: Adaptive robotic tutors that support self-regulated learning: a longer-term investigation with primary school children. Int. J. Soc. Robot. (2018). https://doi.org/10.1007/s12369-017-0458-z

Instructional Strategies

Using Constructivist Instructional Design for Flipped Classroom to Enhancing Cognitive Learning Performance

Issara Kanjug[1(✉)], Niwat Srisawasdi[2], Sumalee Chaijaroen[1], and Parnpitcha Kanjug[3]

[1] Department of Educational Technology, Faculty of Education Khon, Kaen University, Khonkean, Thailand
issaraka@kku.ac.th

[2] Division of Science, Mathematics, Technology Education Khon Kaen University, Khonkean, Thailand

[3] Department of Educational Technology, Faculty of Education Prince of Songkla University, Patani, Thailand

Abstract. A flipped classroom pivots from a traditional learning style which learners contribute to outside-of-class exercises or self-learning to, instead, building knowledge or apprehending contents before coming to class. This study brings in the constructivist theory as a foundation of the instructional design as an online self-study management outside of class as well as hands-on activities in actual classrooms. The researchers developed constructivist learning management system (CLMS) and collected the data from the students to investigate how they built knowledge during the knowledge transfer, in particular. The study on students' cognitive ability found that on the correlation between students' learning retention and transfer of learning, there was a moderate positive correlation ($r = 0.569$). According the findings, students employed three processes to transfer their learning: (1) accessing the prior knowledge or schema from the existing cognitive structure; (2) constructing a link between new contexts and prior knowledge; and (3) utilizing that connection to resolve problems in the new contexts at hand.

Keywords: Flipped learning · Learning management system
Knowledge transfer · Constructivist learning environment
Technology enhance learning

1 Introduction

A flipped classroom pivots from a traditional learning style which learners contribute to outside-of-class exercises or self-learning to, instead, building knowledge or apprehending contents before coming to class. Thus, they will experience a hands-on practice and exchange their pre-class knowledge with their instructors in class so as to achieve an integrated body of knowledge [1, 2]. To bring knowledge outside of class and share with others in class, thus, is a contributing factor to effective learning. Yet, the students need to be equipped with a knowledge transfer skill, which involves the ability to apply

T.-T. Wu et al. (Eds.): ICITL 2018, LNCS 11003, pp. 135–145, 2018.
https://doi.org/10.1007/978-3-319-99737-7_13

or transfer a solution found in a similar context to a new situation [3]. Apart from retaining the contents, the students need to be able to transfer them. Hence, there are two essential factors which support the process of 'knowledge transfer': (1) retention and (2) ability to transfer. These factors are, however, born out of meaningful learning by the students [4].

A learning style grounded in Constructivist theory focuses on the students drawing knowledge from experiences and practicing through thorough thinking processes. With linking what they have learned from past experiences with real situations, they will be able to build a new body of knowledge that is called meaning-making' through problem-based learning. This approach will give the students an opportunity to analyze problems, create varying alternatives, decide to choose a means to problem that fits such specific contexts. To succeed a task, the students must seek new knowledge through problem-solving processes, collaborate in learning and solving problems with classmates, exchange ideas and intellectual processes. At the same time, teachers take a coaching or guiding role as to supervise and motivate the students to acquire or build new knowledge on their own [5–7]. The flipped classroom is, all in all, a learning style which amplifies integrative learning environments suitable for interdisciplinary teaching.

Instructional design of the flipped classroom normally requires the students to commit to the pre-class self-study while time spent in actual classrooms mainly contributes to hands-on learning or a laboratory part. The problem the instructors need to bear in mind is 'how to design class activities that effectively supplement self-study at home', so that the students come to classrooms with concepts. They can, then, apply and connect those prepared concepts with experiences and knowledge they attain in actual classes. Online learning technology or learning through networks eliminates several limitations such as time-and-place limit, large numbers of users' access and up to date upgrade of the technology. Apart from that, the students can also control a learning pace, so it fits each user's needs. Hence, this study brings in the constructivist theory as a foundation of the instructional design as an online self-study management outside of class as well as hands-on activities in actual classrooms. The researchers developed constructivist learning management system (CLMS) and collected the data from the students to investigate how they built knowledge during the knowledge transfer, in particular.

2 Literature Review

2.1 Constructivist Learning Environment (CLEs)

CLEs focus on learning environment management from experiences, which enhances knowledge creation, active learning and real situation-based learning. The students need to build a connection between schema and new knowledge or situations at hands, so that they achieve meaning-making' on their own. Jonassen [8] suggested a model of learning environment based on Constructivism, which aims to improve a problem-solving skill particularly, for complicated problems. The model encourages the students to prepare relevant case studies, so that they learn to transfer their learning from those case studies to real problems. The students also need a source of information to find out about relevant information, apprehend the problems at hands, suggest potential results and use a cognitive tool to help them interpret meanings and solve the problems. In addition to that, the students should be encouraged to use the cognitive tool to solve problems and co-create a learning community. To ensure that learning is meaningful and applicable to real life, these compositions need to be counted in the process: (1) question, case study, problem or project; (2) related case: this is very effective for the students, who have few experiences. Hence, this will provide them with relevant experiences to the problems. (3) Information resources; (4) cognitive tools; (5) communication and collaboration tools and (6) Social/ context support: This is required for efficient application and is important to the instructors as much as the knowledge facilitators. The students will be well-prepared through knowledge-enhancing projects guided by the instructors whether in forms of a workshop or a meeting. Also, the instructors can seek help from the researchers by consent. Also, the instructors can raise questions, which to be answered within the group of instructors or technicians. All in all, social or context support from the instructors is imperative to the students' learning processes.

2.2 Flipped Learning Environment

Flipped learning is a pedagogical approach in which direct instruction moves from the group learning space to the individual learning space, and the resulting group space is transformed into a dynamic interactive learning environment where the educator guides students as they apply concepts and engage creatively in the subject matter [9]. The idea of shifting instruction to students before the class and using class time for assignments allows students to learn the basic concepts on their own and explore the concepts in depth during the class. Such engagement allows students to construct their own knowledge. Basically, the flipped classroom is the result of the effective integration between learning outside the classroom and inside the classroom [10, 11]. Learning outside the classroom enables students to construct declarative knowledge, e.g. theoretical principles, facts and any relevant principles, which is normally taught in the classroom. It, however, has been changed in this study in a way that students can do the self-study of this kind of content at home through video-lectures, together with written materials and online tasks and quizzes [12, 13]. This method is regarded as passive learning in which students are merely required to study the content. The present study intended to propose the student-centered teaching approach which enabled students to study the content through the online learning technology named SOCIALClassnet. For in-class learning, students will engage in active knowledge creation in which they need to apply knowledge acquired through self-studies at home to solving problems and creating projects or new tasks with their classmates [14]. In particular, students will be involved in in-class learning activities which facilitate transferring such acquired knowledge and integrating it in learning activities through the practical use of knowledge described as procedural knowledge. In implementing this approach, teachers will no longer focus on lectures but rather will provide students with questions or problems to challenge their thinking and to promote knowledge. Apart from that, teachers and students may need equipment or technological devices to facilitate learning activities such as problem-based learning, use of information resources and case studies. In this study, LMS (Learning Management

System) was employed to facilitate all learning processes inside and outside the classroom. This particular technology will be further discussed below.

2.3 Cognitive Performance and Evaluation

Cognitive performance in this study can be referred to as learning outcomes which reflect students' learning abilities. In particular, there are two goals of education, namely remembering and understanding. The former goal remembering is a cognitive ability to remember what has been taught and to make use of such knowledge. Therefore, a test of memory in general will ask students about what they have already learned; this test is most concerned with how much students can remember. The latter understanding refers to the cognitive ability to create representations for understanding what has been learned; it reflects students' abilities to use the acquired knowledge to deal with problems at hand. This cognitive ability can be assessed with a transfer test. This test normally asks students to solve problems in contexts differing from classroom contexts, so students will have to apply their knowledge to new situations. Thus, this transfer test is mainly concerned with the quality of learning or more specifically to what extent students can apply their knowledge. Hence, improving the quality of learning requires the promotion of students' remembering and understanding [4, 15]. In addition, Gentner, Holyoak and Kokinov [3] gave a description about mechanisms of knowledge transfer in that when dealing with new problems or situations, students will tap into their prior knowledge and schema within the existing cognitive structure. In doing so, they will take into account shared features between old and new cognitive structures, create a linkage of the features and build new knowledge related to the new contexts. This process reflects students' ability to transfer knowledge effectively, which will in turn reflect cognitive performance in flipped learning.

2.4 Constructivist Learning Management System for Flipped Classroom

The designed learning management will focus on students' learned content outside classrooms to facilitate their understanding of the content before doing in-class activities to expand their knowledge; then, they will do the self-study to review and reflect what they learn. In designing the teaching approach for a computer programming class, it was found that the teacher would prepare the activities which would encourage students to solve theoretical problems outside the classroom. Meanwhile in the classroom, the teacher provided the students with the problems to solve, which required them to rely on pre-class knowledge acquired outside the classroom; in this activity, the students would work together with their classmates while the teacher acted as a coach. This form of teaching was considerably effective. Although the computer class was scheduled only one period a week, this approach allowed more opportunities for learning, revision and discussion. All learning activities of the constructivist-based learning management system for a flipped classroom would be based on constructivism which focuses on creating knowledge through hands-on experience and practice by integrating schema with real contexts to make meaning out of it. In implementing that, problem-based learning was used to enable students to analyze the given problems and make a decision fitting the contexts. Through this way, students would in turn acquire new knowledge by seeking answers to complete the given tasks on their own by means of resources, collaboration and sharing cognition. In the meantime, the teacher acted as a coach to advise and encourage them to think in order to make meaning by themselves. This framework aimed to develop students' ability to transfer prior knowledge and experience acquired through self-studies and to integrate it in the classroom. Then, it was transformed into LMS named SOCIALClassnet. The following figure explains the development of SOCIALClassnet.

We purposed the framework design as Fig. 1. It consisted with 5 stages of learning outside the classroom activity and during class learning activity. From these learning processes, we form the elements of CLMS which are essential to use in each process; (1) knowledge acquisition, (2) knowledge transfer, (3) knowledge construction, (4) knowledge reflection and, (5) knowledge sharing. The description of each key element is shown in Table 1.

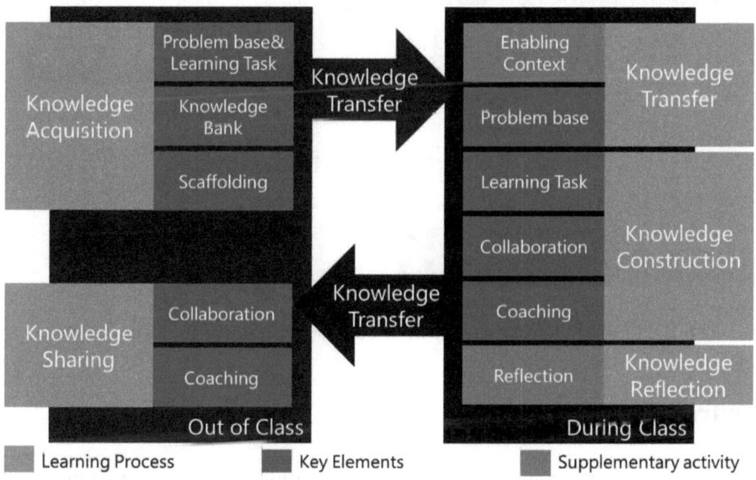

Fig. 1. Framework of constructivist learning for flipped classroom

Table 1. The key elements and descriptions of purpose SCOCIALClassnet.

Key elements	Description
Problem base & Learning Task	Authentic problems with meaningful tasks
Knowledge Bank & related case	Knowledge repository for student to accomplish their goals
Scaffolding	Scaffolding composes of 4 types: conceptual scaffolding, metacognitive scaffolding, strategic scaffolding and procedural scaffolding
Collaboration & cognitive tools	Place for collaborative learning and sharing. Tools for manipulate problem and task
Coaching & social support	Teacher provide supports to help the student perform a task

Figure 1 illustrates framework design. There are 5 stages of learning process which are separated into 2 stages outside classroom activity and 3 stages during class activity. Students begin to perform knowledge acquisition by studying problem base and learning task. Knowledge bank and Scaffolding are provided to support students. After finishing individual preparations, they share their knowledge by using collaboration tool. Teacher provides feedback and facilitates students by observing learning activity. At the same time, other students learn from multiple perspectives from their classmates. During the class, students transfer their knowledge to perform activity. Outside classroom task and during class activity was shared common knowledge. This leads students to transfer their prior knowledge into new situation or problem solving. Enabling context and reflection are supplement activities when students are lack of attention or confuse with the lesson they learned.

Some of user interfaces are shown in Fig. 2

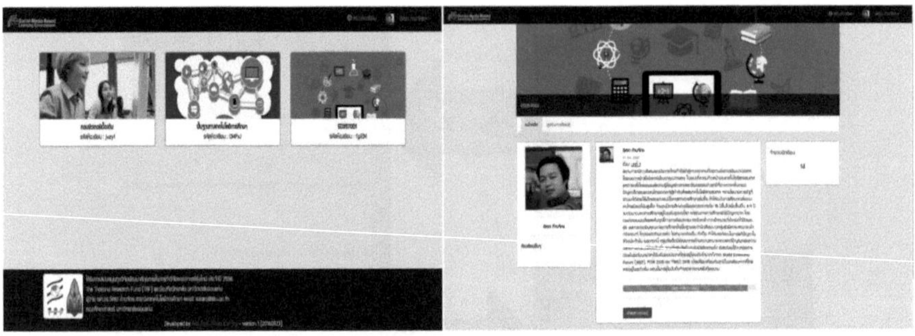

Fig. 2. Online classroom screen of each subject in SCOCIALClassnet.

3 Research Results

This section discusses the results of the students' cognitive ability based on the retention test and transfer test. In this study, the data were collected from twenty-two participants and analyzed with Pearson product moment correlation. The results are shown below.

According to the above figure, there was a moderate positive correlation between learning retention and transfer of learning ($r = 0.569$), which indicated that the students' high scores of learning retention would result in the high scores of transfer of learning as well. In relation to the correlation between learning achievement and transfer of learning shown in Fig. 3, no correlation was found ($r = 0.108$). Based on Mayer's concept on learning outcomes [4], the students' learning styles can be distinguished into three styles: no learning gained, rote learning and constructivist-based learning.

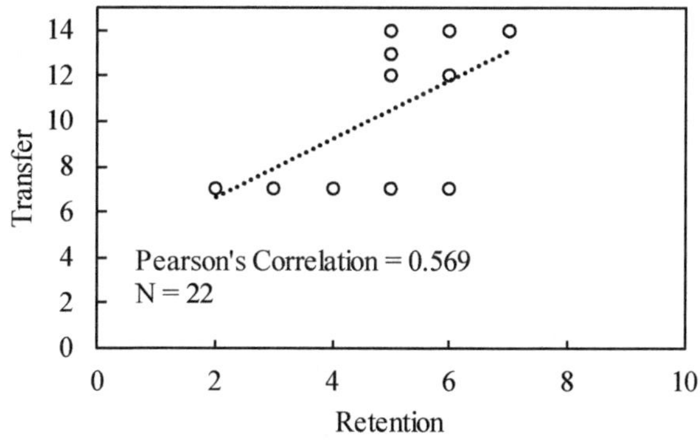

Fig. 3. displays the correlation between learning retention and transfer of learning.

In studying students' transfer of learning, this study was derived from Genter, Holyoak and Kokinov's concept of transfer of learning [3] which consists of the following processes: (1) tapping into the prior knowledge or schema from the existing cognitive structure; (2) creating a connection between new contexts and prior knowledge; and (3) using that connection to solve problems in such contexts. To collect the data, three of the students were interviewed, and then the collected data were analyzed with a protocol analysis. The study found that the students used the following processes to transfer their learning

Student No.1

During the interviews, all three students were asked how they dealt with or solved the problem when facing the new mission or context. It was found that the first student tapped into prior knowledge and created a connection to deal with the new situation as can be seen from the following dialogue.

Researcher: How did you figure it out?

Student no.1: Well, I looked at its source. So, I tried to figure out that if I used this code, what would the result be? Then, I thought about the new lab assignment and tried to see if there was anything that could be used further.

Researcher: So, does that mean you focused on any similarity between the old and new lab assignment and then applied such a similarity to the new one?

Student no.1: Yes, I looked at their shared aspects.

Researcher: So, once you spotted such a similarity, what did you do next? As in the new lab assignment, the teacher wanted the word Distance Calculation, so what would you do to achieve that?

Student no.1: I'd write the command System.out.print.

Researcher: How did you know that you had to use that command?

Student no.1: I knew that because I've already done it before. So to speak, I applied the prior lab assignment to the new one

According to the above dialogue, the student attempted to access his prior knowledge as he said in the interview, "I looked at its source". He also created the linkage between the prior and new problem by trying to change the command and used that command to achieve the task as he said, "if I used this code, what would the result be?", "..see if there was anything that could be used further." and "I applied the prior lab assignment to the new one".

Apart from that, the student was asked about their transfer of learning when encountering the new problem differing from what they had experienced before. It was discovered that the student would consult a book first, and unless it helped solve the problem, he would consult his teacher as indicated in the following dialogue.

Researcher: Suppose the new problem, as in the distance calculation program, completely differed from the old one and you have never done it, what would you do?

Student no.1: I would consult a book first to see if there was any similarity. Otherwise, I would figure out their differences and the solution to the problem. Other than that, I would consult my teacher

Student No.2

It was discovered that the student tapped into her prior knowledge but was unable to link such knowledge with the new situation, so she could not solve the problem in such a situation. The following dialogue illustrates how she dealt with the new situation.

Researcher: So, did you use your prior knowledge from the old lab assignment when doing the new one?

Student no.2: Yes, I did.

Researcher: How did you do it?

Student no.2: Well, the teacher gave us the examples related to the assignment and described the steps as well as how we could use certain aspects from the examples. I would also apply the old lab to the new one. For instance, the new lab required students to use BMI Calculator. I would apply knowledge gained from the old lab to the new one, like adjusting the numbers or values

In relation to the dialogue above, this student accessed her prior knowledge and created a connection between the prior knowledge and new situation. Finally, she solved the problem with such a connection as she said in the interview, "…apply knowledge gained from the old lab to the new one…".

Apart from that, the student tried changing some parts of the command she had learned before to produce the outcome as needed, which is described in the following dialogue.

Researcher: So, did you compare the new lab with the old one to see if there was any similarity?

Student no.2: Yes, I did. I may have changed some parts, too.

Researcher: So, what were the similarities that you found?

Student no.2: Since it was about BMI calculation, I just changed numbers just to understand that both assignments were the same. I just had to change some parts or numbers, but other parts stayed just the same.
Researcher: Suppose there were some differences, what would you do to complete this lab assignment?
Student no.2: In that case, I would take a look at the old lab

Given the statement "…changed some parts…", it means that the student just tried changing the command she had learned before. It indicates that the student attempted to create a link between the old and new assignment by specifically considering their similarities.

Apart from that, the student was asked during the interview about her problem-solving method when facing the new situation that she had never experienced before. The student stated that when she did not have sufficient knowledge, she would do more research by consulting a book. The dialogue below shows her response to that question.

Researcher : What if both assignments were totally different, what would you do?

Student no.2: I would have to do more research.
Researcher: Where exactly?
Student no.2: from a book

In addition, the student was found to do trials and errors when she realized that she could not find any more information from the book, as can be seen in the following dialogue.

Researcher: Supposing you did not find anything useful in the book. What would you do next?
Student no.2: I would rely on myself.
Researcher: And when you had written the program and it was a dead end, what would you do in this case?
Student no.2: I would try to spot the errors and try running the program again and again

Considering the interview with the second student, it can be concluded that the transfer of learning did occur, which was in conformity to Gentner et al.'s concept. More specifically, the student used her prior knowledge to link such knowledge with the new problem and solved that problem. Also, when she found herself having inadequate knowledge, she would ask her teacher about how to solve it. More ever, students tapped into their prior knowledge and linked the knowledge with the new situation by means of observation and trials and errors to solve the assigned new problem.

4 Discussion

The study on students' cognitive ability found that on the correlation between students' learning retention and transfer of learning, there was a moderate positive correlation ($r = 0.569$). That is, when the students had high scores of learning retention, they would have high scores of transfers of learning. On the other hand, the low scores of learning retention would result in low scores of transfers of learning. The study also discovered that 59.09 percent of the students were equipped with constructivist-based learning while 18.18 of them were with rote-learning; 22.73 of them did not gain learning. This was consistent with Mayer [4, 15] stating that there were three learning styles. The goal of this study was to enable students to possess constructivist-based learning, which was dependent on two factors, namely learning retention and transfer of learning. Thus, in enhancing students' information memorization and applicability, the design of learning environments is an important element. According to this study, learning environments were designed based on ID Theory which used problems and learning missions to promote transfer of learning. Hence, learning through computer programming would allow students to think systematically, which would lead to understanding. Learning through media attributes, e.g. color emphasis and use of images, could also help build understanding while learning through networks allowed students to control their learning pace, which would affect their retention or remembering. Apart from that, methods for using learning environments played an important role. In this study, a flipped classroom was applied following constructivism pedagogy, which helped promote students' pre-class understanding. All the aforementioned factors had effects on students' learning retention and transfer of learning. According the findings, students employed three processes to transfer their learning: (1) accessing the prior knowledge or schema from the existing cognitive structure; (2) constructing a link between new contexts and prior knowledge; and (3) utilizing that connection to resolve problems in the new contexts at hand this corresponded to Gentner, Holyoak & Kokinov's conceptual framework [3]. It exposed students to the hands-on practice through computer programming and simultaneously allowed the teacher to motivate the students during learning. Moreover, the creation of LMS was based on ID Theory. In particular, the design of the instruction was based on media attributes, which enabled students to understand the overall content easily. In the meantime, the flipped classroom helped build their pre-class understanding, leading students to transfer their learning.

Acknowledgement. This research supported form Thailand Research Found (TRF); Faculty of Education; and Research and Technology Transfer Affairs, Khon Kean University

References

1. Bergmann, J., Sams, A.: Flip Your Classroom: Reach Every Student in Every Class Every Day. International Society for Technology in Education, Washington (2012)
2. Yarbro, J., Arfstrom, K.M., McKnight, K., McKnight, P.: Extension of a review of flipped learning. In: Flipped Learning Network (2014). http://goo.gl/jZ2yBf. Accessed 13 June 2016
3. Gentner, D., Holyoak, K.J., Kokinov, B.N.: The Analogical Mind: Perspectives from Cognitive Science. Cambridge MIT Press, Cambridge (2001)
4. Mayer, R.E.: Learning strategies for making sense out of expository text: the SOI model for guiding three cognitive processes in knowledge construction. Educ. Psychol. Rev. **8**, 357–371 (1996)

5. Bransford, J.D., Brown, A.L., Cocking, R.R. (eds.): How People Learn: Brain, Mind, Experience and School. National Academy Press, Washington (2000)
6. Mayer, R.E.: The promise of multimedia learning: using the same instructional design methods across different media. Learning and Instruction **13**, 125–139 (2003)
7. Sousa, D., Tomlinson, C.: Differentiation and the Brain: How Neuroscience Supports the Learner-Friendly Classroom. Solution Tree, Bloomington (2011)
8. Jonassen, D.H.: Designing constructivist learning environments. In: Reigeluth, C.M. (ed.) Instructional-Design Theories and Models: A New Paradigm of Instructional Theory, vol. 2, pp. 215–239. Lawrence Erlbaum Associates, Mahwah (1999)
9. Flipped Learning Network (FLN). The Four Pillars of F-L-I-P™ (2014). https://flippedlearning.org/. Accessed 13 June 2016
10. Sams, A., Bergmann, J.: Flip your students' learning. Educ. Leadersh. **70**(6), 16–20 (2013)
11. Bergmann, J., Sams, A.: Flipped learning. In: ISTE, Washington & Eurospan, London (2014)
12. Tourón, Santiago.: Flipped learning model and the development of talent at school. Revista de Educación **368**, 198–231 (2015)
13. González-Gómez, D., Jeong, J.S., Rodríguez, D.A., Cañada-Cañada, F.: Performance and perception in the flipped learning model: an initial approach to evaluate the effectiveness of a new teaching methodology in a general science classroom. J. Sci. Educ. Technol. **25**(3), 450–459 (2016)
14. Moraros, J., Islam, A., Yu, S., Banow, R., Schindelka, B.: Flipping for success: evaluating the effectiveness of a novel teaching approach in a graduate level setting. BMC Med. Educ. **15**(1), 27 (2015)
15. Mayer, R.E.: Multimedia Learning. Cambridge University Press, New York (2001)

Synthesis of Theoretical Framework of Constructivist Creative Thinking Massive Open Online Courses (MOOCs) for Higher Education

Benjaporn Sathanarugsawait[1] and Charuni Samat[2(✉)]

[1] School of Information Technology, Sripatum University, Khon Kaen, Thailand
[2] Department of Education Technology, Faculty of Education, Khon Kaen University, Khon Kaen, Thailand
thaibannok@hotmail.com

Abstract. This research study aimed to synthesize of theoretical framework of constructivist creative thinking massive open online courses (MOOCs) for Higher Education. Several methods used were document analysis, survey and case study. The following were: (1) examined the principles and theories (2) to synthesize theoretical framework, (3) to synthesize designing framework. The result revealed that: (1) to synthesize theoretical framework comprise of 5 components as following that. Contextual base, Psychological base, Technologies base, Creative Thinking base and Pedagogies base Model learning environments. (2) To synthesize theoretical framework of Constructivist Creative Thinking Massive Open Online Courses (MOOCS) for Higher Education.

Keywords: Constructivist · Massive open online course · Creative thinking Higher education

1 Introduction

Thailand needs to adapt to the changing world and strengthen its immunity in the country. Countries can adapt to change. And to strengthen the knowledge. Science, technology, innovation and creativity. It is the driving force behind Thailand's economic and social development. In accordance with the National Education Act B.E. 2002. Section 7 requires Thais to be creative [1]. Continuing Education and Continuing Education Sustainable Development Strategy for Lifelong Learning. The changes in Thai society have impacted both political, social, economic and technological. Economic trends are adapting to digital economies. Enhancement of creative thinking on learner based on the web-based learning environment was achieved using the principles and theories for synthesizing the theoretical framework and the environmental design which promote creative thinking. The theories and web-based characteristics were brought into the design of instruction that utilized the learning environment media and methods with important components of the Constructivist Theory. Massive open online course (MOOCs) can be used for promoting learner's creative thinking in order to have meaning learning. MOOCs are online education platforms accessed Online

T.-T. Wu et al. (Eds.): ICITL 2018, LNCS 11003, pp. 146–150, 2018.
https://doi.org/10.1007/978-3-319-99737-7_14

courses taught in universities draw a lot of interest, and provide a complete distance learning environment through assignments, presentations, videos and other course materials [2]. This accordingly happens from interaction with the learning environment.

Thus, this research was aimed at synthesize of theoretical framework of constructivist creative thinking massive open online courses (MOOCs), from synthesizing of the theoretical framework and learning environment. In order to obtain the basis for theoretical framework of constructing the appropriate and efficient learning environment models for the learners.

2 Methodology

This study was aimed to synthesize theoretical framework of constructivist creative thinking massive open online courses (MOOCs) for Higher Education. Research methodology is Document analysis method of research design. To study the theories about constructivist creative thinking massive open online courses (MOOCs) for Higher Education.

3 Theoretical Framework

We purposed the framework design. The theoretical framework was synthesized based on studying and analyzing the principles, theories, and related literature regarding design, cognitive theories, constructivist theories, the constructivist learning environment model, web base learning, media symbol system, and creative thinking. The theoretical framework showed five important theoretical foundations, which were as followed: (1) Psychological base, (2) Pedagogies base, (3) Media and technologies base (4) Creative Thinking base and (5) Context of student in Higher education base.

4 Method and Result

4.1 Data Collection

In this study, researchers have created tools to study and collect data. Tools used for document research. Here are the details. (1) Documentation, Inspection and Analysis To build a theoretical framework. Theoretical frameworks are used for recording, analyzing, and analyzing documents on theoretical principles. And research related to the online teaching system open. Including how to create a record. This is the basis of an open online learning system. (2) A survey for learners and instructors on the context of learning management. The style is open-ended. There are learning issues that promote creative thinking skills for students in higher education. Identify reasons for the issues.

Data analysis are the details. (1) Theoretical Framework Use analytical methods by analytical and summative narratives. Interpretation of data on theoretical principles involved. Document Research and from analyzing documents from data. (2) Contextual condition of the learner's teaching. Use the data analysis method. Analytical and summative analysis based on survey data for learners. Context of teaching (3) Contextual context of teaching and learning. Use the data analysis method. Analytical and summative narrative based on data from the survey for the instructor Context of teaching as "Fig. 1".

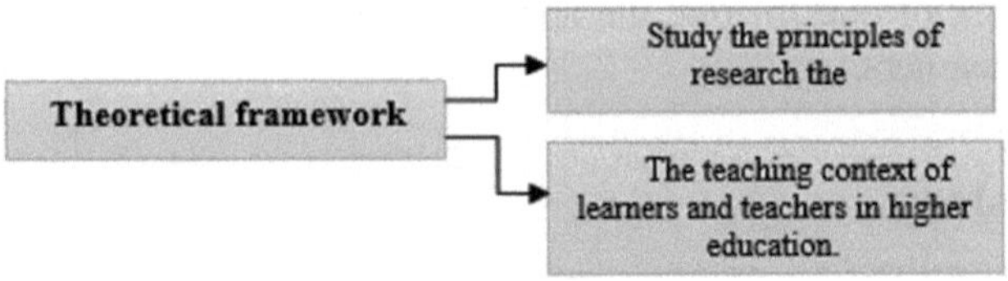

Fig. 1. Show how to collect data, how to conduct research.

4.2 Research Result

The research was synthesized from the literature review (literature review). Research papers from theoretical studies on constructivist creative thinking massive open online courses (MOOCs) for Higher Education. The theoretical framework showed five important theoretical foundations, which were as followed: (1) Psychological base, (2) Pedagogies base, (3) Media and technologies base (4) Creative Thinking base and (5) Context of student in Higher education base as Fig. 2.

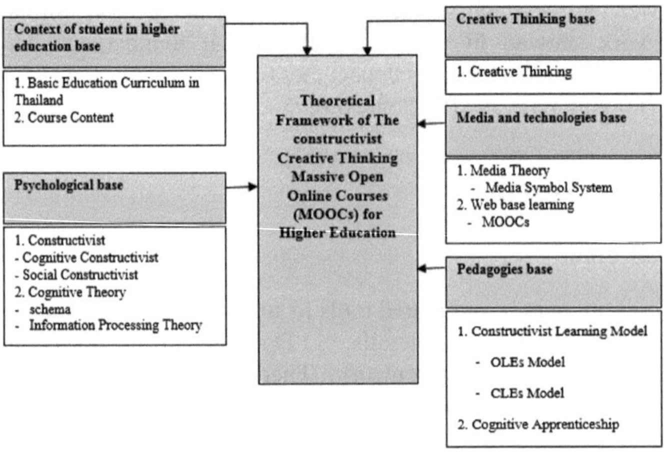

Fig. 2. Theoretical framework of the constructivist creative thinking massive open online courses (MOOCs) for Higher Education.

Figure 2 shows the theoretical foundations of an open online teaching system. The creativity that promotes creativity for all five tertiary learners has been synthesized. Review of literature and related research. The researcher will present the results of each of the fundamentals related to creativity for students in higher education in each component.

Psychological Base: Constructivist creative thinking massive open online courses (MOOCs) for Higher Education based on two principles, Piaget's cognitive constructivist theories and Vygotsky's social constructivist theories have been applied [3].

Pedagogies Base: Principles of learning environment design. The Hannafin OLEs [4] focus on the development of multiple thinking, [4] which allows the learner to create. Many alternatives with various elements and principles. Is to enter the context (Enabling Context). In addition, Jonassen [4] Suggested principles for designing a learning environment based on a constructivist approach. Constructivist learning environments focus on the development of knowledge-based learning and complex problems (Ill-structure) [5].

Media and Technologies Base: The media and technology fundamentals are The principle of the symbol of the media (Media symbol System) that describes the effects of web base learning environment. Each type of media has a symbolic system. Symbolic systems are the basis of design. Features of each type of media design [6].

Creative Thinking Base: The foundation of creative thinking is in line with Creative thinking. Creativity. It is the ability of the person to solve the problem. It is the thought that creates new things, the ability of the person. It applies to many jobs, including:

Initiative Originality, Fluency, Flexibility, Elaboration [7].

Context of Student in Higher Education Base: Curriculum design consistent with the criteria. Course Syllabus Standard framework for national higher education and the creation of a supportive environment for the production of graduates [1] is consistent with the standard framework. National Higher Education (TQF) is a framework that shows the system of higher education in the country.

5 Conclusion

Synthesize of theoretical framework of constructivist creative thinking massive open online courses (MOOCs) for Higher Education. Research methodology is Document analysis method of research design. The theoretical framework was synthesized based on studying and analyzing the principles, theories, and related literature regarding design, cognitive theories, constructivist theories, the constructivist learning environment model, web-based learning, media symbol system, and creative thinking. Researchers have created tools to study and collect data. Tools used for document research. Documentation and A survey for learners and instructors on the context of learning management. Data analysis are the Theoretical Framework Use analytical methods by analytical, summative narratives, Contextual condition of the learner's teaching and Contextual context of teaching and learning. Research papers from theoretical studies on constructivist creative thinking massive open online courses (MOOCs) for Higher Education. The theoretical framework showed five important theoretical foundations, which were as Psychological base, Pedagogies base, Media and technologies base, Creative Thinking base and Context of student in Higher education base. This research will be developed as a MOOCs and will be applied to Higher Education.

Acknowledgements. This work was supported by the Academic and Research Affairs, Innovation and Cognitive Technology Research Group, Faculty of Education, and the Research and Technology Transfers Affairs Division, Faculty of Education, Khon Kaen University.

References

1. Office of the National Education Commission. National Education Plan (2002–2016): the conclusion. Sweet graphics, Bangkok (2011)
2. Kesim, M., Altınpulluk, H.: A theoretical analysis of MOOCs types from a perspective of learning theories. Soc. Behav. Sci. **186**, 15–19 (2015)
3. Sumalee, C., et al.: A study of thinking potential of students studying instructional innovation enhancing thinking potentiality. A Research Report (2007)
4. Hannanfin, M., Land, S., Oliver, K.: Open learning environments: foundations, methods, and models. In: Reigeluth, C.M. (ed.) Instructional Design Theories and Models: A New Paradigm of Instructional Theory. Volume II. Lawrence Erlbaum Associates, Newjersy (1999)
5. Jonassen, D.: Designing constructivist learning environments. In: Charles, M.R. (ed.) Intuitional Design Theories and Models: A New Paradigm of Instructional Theory Volume II, New Jersey (1999)
6. Samat, C., Chaijaroen, S.: Design and development of learning environment to enhance creative thinking and innovation skills for teacher training in the 21st century. In: Proceedings of the 23rd International Conference on Computers in Education, ICCE 2015, pp. 667–672 (2015)
7. Guilford, J.P.: The Nature of Human Intelligence. McGraw Hill, New York (1967)

Learning Analytics and Education Data Mining

Multimodal Learning Recommendation - Using Adaptive Neuron-Fuzzy Inference System for Microlearning

Kun-Te Wang[1], Ming-An Lin[1], Tien-Chi Huang[2](✉), and Neil Yuwen Yen[3]

[1] Faculty of Computer and Software Engineering, Huaiyin Institute of Technology, Huai'an, China
wangtaito@gmail.com, andylin1979@yahoo.com.tw
[2] National Taichung University of Science and Technology, Taichung, Taiwan
tchuang@nutc.edu.tw
[3] Information Security Laboratory, The University of Ainu, Sapporo, Japan
neilyyen@u-aizu.ac.jp

Abstract. This paper presents a multimodal learning strategy based on learners' preferences to improve adaptive learning processes. At present, the use of fragmented content is considered a more effective learning method for online learners. Access to an idea or news in various ways makes it easier for students to understand and retain information. However, this challenges learners' pace of learning, because too much digital information can interfere with their goals. To predict learners' preferences for what they are learning, this study first uses the neuro-fuzzy reasoning method to diagnose learners' activities related to their styles in a microlearning learning environment. Then, based on the results, a recommendation model is developed to help learners participate in adaptive learning activities and digital contents. This study makes the tracking of online learning activities consistent with the multimodal learning mode. Our results show that the identification model divided the sample of 154 learners into 9 learning categories. Learning activities corresponding to learning preferences enables learners to obtain answers quickly through the recommendation mode. The study also demonstrates that the effectiveness of the learning mechanism can facilitate the teaching process, generate rich learning guidance, and help teachers design a better, well-structured course. Therefore, learners can easily achieve their learning goals when the recommended content is received.

Keywords: Multimodal learning · Learner preferences
Neuro-Fuzzy Inference · Micro-learning

1 Introduction

1.1 Different Learning Styles

People have different preferred styles for interacting with others on the job and for solving problems that arise in the course of learning. For instance, learners can verify facts and learn what they want to on Google and can participate in a MOOC for the

T.-T. Wu et al. (Eds.): ICITL 2018, LNCS 11003, pp. 153–164, 2018.
https://doi.org/10.1007/978-3-319-99737-7_15

program language Python. Moreover, learners can visit the international space station on Google Earth. Besides being able to watch and listen to the introduction of a video, learners can discuss the experience with other participants. All ways in which to obtain information on what we need is ubiquitous on the Internet.

Learning-Subject research contends that the use of short content may increase information retention by 20% [1]. This learning format has spawned the micro-learn movement [2]. Furthermore, studies confirm that the use of technical learning has changed the traditional way of teaching and learning [3, 4]. For example, high wireless network performance is correlated with the positive experience of students. Regarding meeting the technological support needed, students' are likely to figure out solutions to technology problems by themselves, search online sources, or ask friends [5]. Therefore, learners have the greatest control in terms of obtaining Internet guidance. Acquiring rich digital content through a multiple-method learning strategy, the demand is that adaptive learning be tailored to individual learners as much as possible. In general, learners' characteristics can be linked to their so-called learning style [6]. We need tools to research and develop models suitable for the online learning environment. Numerous studies related to the learning domain have been conducted in the past decades.

John Carroll proposed a model to account for school learning. His premise was that school learning was a function of time. Specifically, Carroll proposed that the degree of learning $f = (\text{time spent} / \text{time needed})$ [7]. In other words, if the degree of learning for each student was that the time spent on actual learning was equal to the time the learning actually needed, learners could achieve their learning objectives. In addition, Bloom proposed mastery learning in accordance with Carroll's learning model. He recommended that the course or units be organised into relatively small learning units, and that each unit have its own objectives and assessments [4]. Hwang and Wang considered that students' ability and motivation negatively affect their reading behaviours. This means that learning efficiency is a variable dependent on reading time and students' motivation [8].

Different students have different preferred ways to learn [9]. Michael stated that a learner's recognition style should be considered in an individualised learning environment [10]. Individuals learned with ease when meaningful contents were linked to their learning style. David Kolb published his experiential learning cycle to clarify the way in which learners learn [11]. As we all learn in different ways; the model gave rise to related terms such as Kolb's experiential learning theory (ELT) and learning styles inventory (KLSI 4.0) [12]. The inventory explores how learners interpret and reflect on facts to determine their preferred ways to learn. The newer KLSI 4.0 is a 20-item assessment tool that identifies 9 styles delineated as 4 learning dimensions: (1) Reflective Observation (RO): combines preferences for experiencing and reflecting, (2) Abstract Conceptualisation (AC): combines preferences for reflecting and thinking, (3) Active Experimentation (AE): combines preferences for thinking and doing, and (4) Concrete Experience (CE): combines preferences for doing and experiencing, as shown in Fig. 1. The nine learning styles can support to account for differences in individuals' learning. For example, an 'acting' learner may need to enhance learning through discussion and peer interaction, while 'imagining' learners may learn best through abstract concepts and imagination.

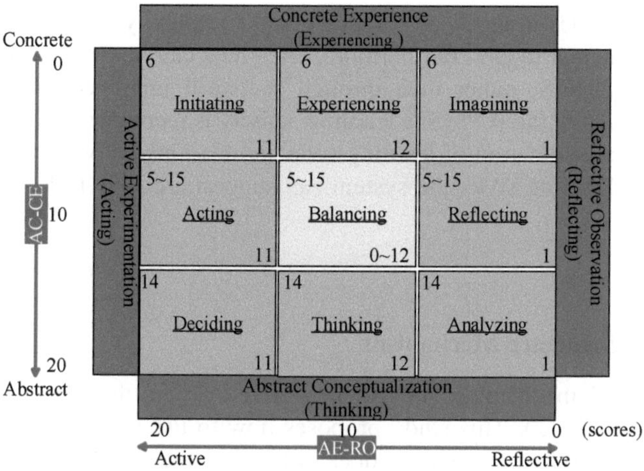

Fig. 1. Features of learning styles according to Kolb's LSI 4.0 model. (*Kolb's Experiential Learning Model: Concrete Experience (CE) and Abstract Conceptualisation (AC), Reflective Observation (RO), and Active Experimentation (AE).) (**The KLSI consists of 20 questions about the ways in which one learns best. In addition, the nine types are as follows: (1) Initiating - ACCE (labelled score in top left corner) < 6, AERO (labelled score in bottom right corner) > 11; (2) Experiencing - ACCE < 6, AERO > 0 & < 12; (3) Imagining - ACCE < 6, AERO < 1; (4) Reflecting - ACCE > 5 & < 15, AERO < 1; (5) Analysing - ACCE > 14, AERO < 1; (6) Thinking - ACCE > 14, AERO > 0 & < 12; (7) Deciding - ACCE > 14, AERO > 11; (8) Acting - ACCE > 5 & < 15, AERO > 11; (9) Balancing - ACCE > 5 & < 15, AERO > 0 & < 12. [12])

Numerous studies have confirmed the benefit of adaptive learning systems that individually adjust to the specific characteristics of students such as their learning style, exercise varying levels of difficulty, and provide recommendations for navigation. These adaptive hypermedia systems positively affect students' performance, meet learning goals, and facilitate learning processes [13]. Spring considers how to use the concept of learning styles in planning information literature or other teaching sessions [14]. Jia Jiunn Lo and Pai-Chuan Shu also suggest that learners' learning behaviours have influenced the development of an adaptive hypermedia-learning system depending on learning style [15]. Considering the above, we speculated that learning styles and learning activities are closely correlated (e.g. learning time and updating the time of a course) and use our approach to find evidence thereof.

1.2 Adaptive Neuro-Fuzzy Inference System (ANFIS)

To study multimodal learning, we refer to Kolb's learning styles, which pointed out the functions of learning schedule, score, forum interaction, and reviews learning frequency. Depending on these operational variables, this study first utilised the Adaptive Neuro-Fuzzy Inference System (ANFIS) to develop a network-based model to identify the learning activity preferences of e-learners. ANFIS techniques have effectively been applied to student diagnostic models [16]. In addition, the ANFIS identity network can process these variables in terms of computational complexity and optimum control in parallel with the actual model. Furthermore, e-learners can be designated into learning groups through ANFIS, rather than through statistical inference using Kolb's LSI. Based on the results of the ANFIS, a learning activity is recommended to learners. This study presents a classification of learning style and learning activity, so that according to the estimated learning style, the system can suggest a course task to the learner.

2 Method

2.1 Learning Sequence Mechanism

A learning control mechanism aims to support e-learners through a micro-learning environment (see Fig. 2). This study proposes how to use the threshold to conduct a learning sequence. When the learner does not across the threshold in the process of learning, the learning control mechanism will be triggered to provide the assisted learning activities. After obtaining a token (learner's score), the learner can cross the threshold to the next level. If the token (learner's score) is not sufficient to open the threshold, the ANFIS method is used to recommend more activities and contents to the learner corresponding to his/her learning preference, in other words, to use more tokens to open the threshold to the next knowledge point. The learning control mechanism is shown in Fig. 2.

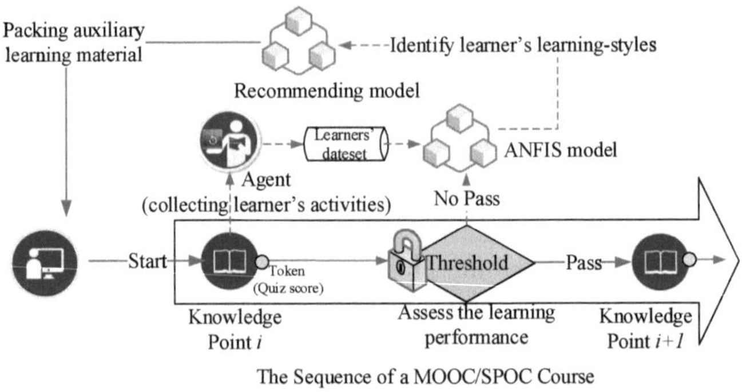

Fig. 2. The learning control mechanism consists of the Neuro-Fuzzy model and recommending model in the micro-learning environment

First, learners have many learning activities in a MOOC course. For example, they can click on knowledge points, search and read articles, test their understanding, or visit discussion forums. These learning activities (learners' views, time, frequency) are monitored from a knowledge point to the next point through a software agent. All learners' learning behaviours are recorded as a dataset, and fuzzy inference rules and neuron networks applied to ascertain the e-learner's learning type and learning style. Their learning styles further reflect relevant learning activities to generate recommendations for the learning control models. These recommendations are involved in a set of closed terms and as the domain classification related to learning style. Therefore, the studying model can satisfy the learner and provide assistance to complete a course sequence based on his/her individual learning style.

2.2 Fuzzy Inference Rules for Learning Activities Representation

To infer the relationship between learners' activities and learning styles, generating records is a critical part of the process. The model needs to capture records of learning activities into dataset *B*, where for example, each response is the time of the learning course unit, number of posts in the forum, speed of the test response, and the review frequency of topics, which can be addressed and indexed, as shown in the records in Fig. 3.

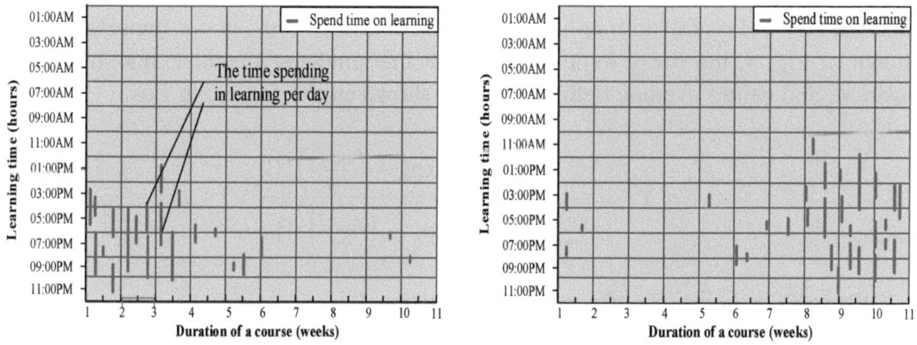

(a) The learning activities of an active learner

(b) The learning activities of a passive learner

Fig. 3. Learning activities of learners who participated in one course according to learning time and frequency. In addition, (a) (b) illustrate two different learning activities.

Depending on the learning activities, records are assigned to the linguistic value *v*, represented as the learning schedules (learning time and frequency) = {always, passable, less}, participation in the forum = {more, normal, less}, quiz reaction = {fast, normal, slow}, and review topic = {often, even, seldom}. Each *Bi* has term *v* consisting of *m* linguistic values $B_i = \{V_1, V_2, \ldots V_m,\}$. The values of the evaluated activities were then summarised into *k* groups. Furthermore, the dataset $T(B_i) = \{B_1, B_2, \ldots B_k,\}$, where $B_i(i = 1, 2, \ldots, k)$, represents a sentence describing the *i*th type of response of the learners' activities. For example, considering the set $T(B_i) = \{learning\ time\ on\ course\ unit\} = \{short,\ normal,\ long\}$, where the linguistic variable *m* = *3*. In our study, fuzzy set $B_i(i = 1, 2, 3, 4)$ and term $V_m(m = 1, 2, 3)$ formulates an input to the identifying process. Furthermore, involving the fuzzy variables and using the *IF-THEN* rule infer the consequents of the nine styles of KLSI.

If B_1 *is* v_{11} *AND* B_1 *is* v_{12} *AND*. . .B_1 *is* v_{1m} *AND*

. . .

If B_k *is* v_{k1} *AND* B_k *is* v_{k2} *AND*. . . B_k *is* v_{km} *AND*
THEN Y_1 *is CE AND* Y_2 *is AC AND* Y_3 *is RO AND* Y_4 *is AE*

2.3 Tuning Learning Styles Using the ANFIS Model

Implementing fuzzy inference rules enabled the construction of a neural network for identifying the relationships between learning activities and learning styles. Furthermore, based on the reasoning output, the desired data $D_i(i = 1, \ldots, 4)$ in the training set represents the results of KLSI (CE, AC, RO, and AE). $T(D_i) = \{D_1, D_2, \ldots D_k\}$ could be used to provide supervised data in the identify network. If the outputs of network Y_i miss the desired variables D_i, the network is backward calculated to minimise the error function $E = \frac{1}{2}(Y - D)^2$ to fine-tune the results of KLSI. Thus, in our implementation, shown in Fig. 5, the fuzzy logic system with the singleton fuzzifier, max-min composition, and centre average defuzzifier is as shown in the following Eqs. (1)–(2).

$$Y = \frac{\sum_{l=1}^{k} \overline{y_l}\{\prod_{i=1}^{n} \exp[-\left(\frac{x_i - \bar{x}_{li}}{\sigma_{li}}\right)^2]\}}{\sum_{l=1}^{k}\{\prod_{i=1}^{n} \exp[-\left(\frac{x_i - \bar{x}_{li}}{\sigma_{li}}\right)^2]\}} \tag{1}$$

Where $\overline{y_l}$ *is the center of membership function* B_i
σ_{li} *is inflection point and* $\bar{x}_{li}$ *is the highest point of membership function* B_i

$$z_e = \exp\left[-\left(\frac{x_i - \bar{x}_{li}}{\sigma_{li}}\right)^2\right], \tag{2}$$

$$= \sum_{l=1}^{k} \overline{y_l} z_e, \tag{3}$$

$$b = \sum_{l=1}^{k} z_e \tag{4}$$

Using the Gaussian membership function is $u_{Ali}(x_i) = \exp\left[-\left(\frac{x_i - \bar{x}_{li}}{\sigma_{li}}\right)^2\right]$

Where $\overline{x_1}$ *is the center of* x_i

Therefore, the ANFIS network needs to adjust error function E by three variables, $\overline{y_l}, \sigma_{li},$ *and* $\bar{x}_{li}$, to minimise it. In addition, the training network in Fig. 4 also uses the steepest descent algorithm given by Eqs. (5)–(7).

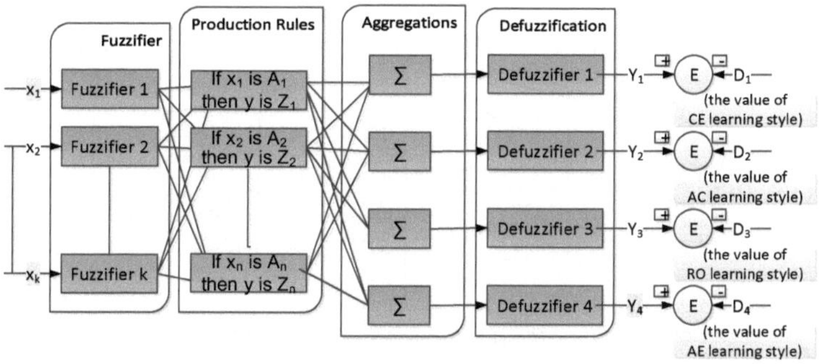

Fig. 4. Schematic of the inference model to identify learning styles (CE, AC, RO, and AE)

$$\overline{y_l}(k+1) = \overline{y_l}(k) - \alpha \frac{(Y-D)}{b} Z_l|_k \tag{5}$$

$$\overline{x_{li}}(k+1) = \overline{x_{li}}(k) - \alpha(Y-D) \cdot \frac{\overline{y_l} - Y}{b} \cdot Z_l \frac{2(x_i - \overline{x_{li}})}{\sigma_{li}^2}|_k \tag{6}$$

$$\sigma_{li}(K+1) = \sigma_{li}(k) - \alpha(Y-D) \cdot \frac{\overline{y_l} - Y}{b} \cdot Z_l \frac{2(x_i - \overline{x_{li}})^2}{\sigma_{li}^3}|_k \tag{7}$$

Updating these variables as in (5), (6), and (7) enables adjusting the neuro-fuzzy network to evaluate the input of the network (learner's activities). The membership function in Eq. (2) also describes a reversible learning curve. This enables the identification of learning activities to determine learning styles, rather than through the KLSI questionnaire.

2.4 Constructing the Types of Recommended Learning Activities

First, when learners do not cross the threshold of a certain knowledge point, a few recommended activities are triggered. The system's recommendation model will provide learning materials based on the relationship between learning style and structured learning activities.

Figure 5 shows the domain relationship between learning styles and learning activities. Therefore, categorising the domain can indicate the relevant learning activities with the learning system at the knowledge points learners need. The categorisation consists of two knowledge domains, namely learning styles, as mentioned in Sect. 1, and the learning-activity domain, which is represented as an aggregation consisting of reading articles, forum dialogues, quizzes, multimedia materials, using search tools, simulations and examples, and annotations. There is an association domain between learning style and learning activities to guide machine-assessable semantic contents.

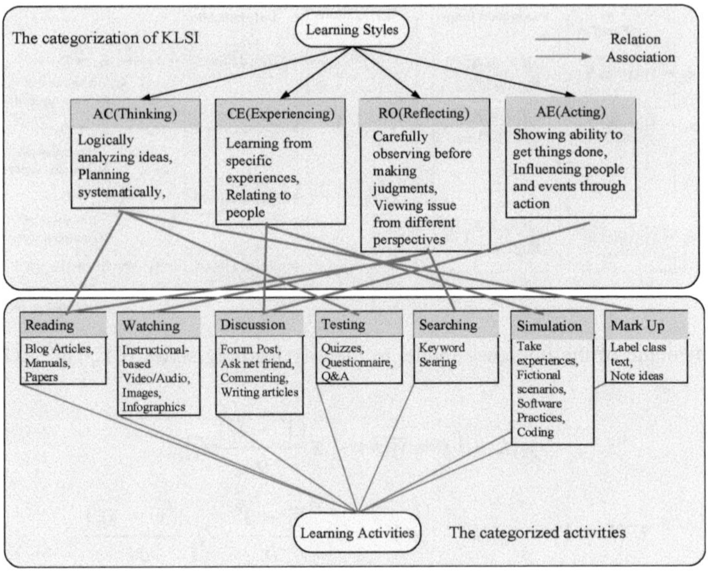

Fig. 5. Categorization of learning styles and learning activities

3 Experimental Results and Discussions

3.1 Aggregate Learning Activities in the MOOC Environment

First, three courses were created and put onto a MOOC platform. All three courses consist of sequences of 15 knowledge points. Therefore, we required a software agent to collect learners' learning activities including the time spent on reading and watching. The system also gathered test scores, the frequency of reading articles, posts to the forum, keyword searches, and annotations, as shown in Fig. 6

In the above learning scenario, agents retrieved the activities of 154 learners. For these activities, the data were extracted, transferred, and loaded. For example, the learning process is divided into three levels (active by >=0.7, progress by >=0.4, passive by <0.4) according to students' learning progress. There are seven dimensions including learning progress, watching multimedia, and testing. These data will be prepared as the parameters for the next stage of the neuro-fuzzy model.

3.2 The Tuning Process of Neuro-Fuzzy Model

The experiment was completed according to the following steps. The study first investigated the learning styles of 154 learner samples based on the 80 items of the KLSI program. The individual learning styles of the samples can be calculated in advance and are considered a training set so that we can monitor the output of the network-fuzzy model (see Fig. 4) to adjust the error function E (see Sect. 2.3). It was assumed that each input layer has seven variables $x_1, x_2, \ldots, x_7$. Each variable has three language variables and the hidden layer provides 81 possible combinations of rules.

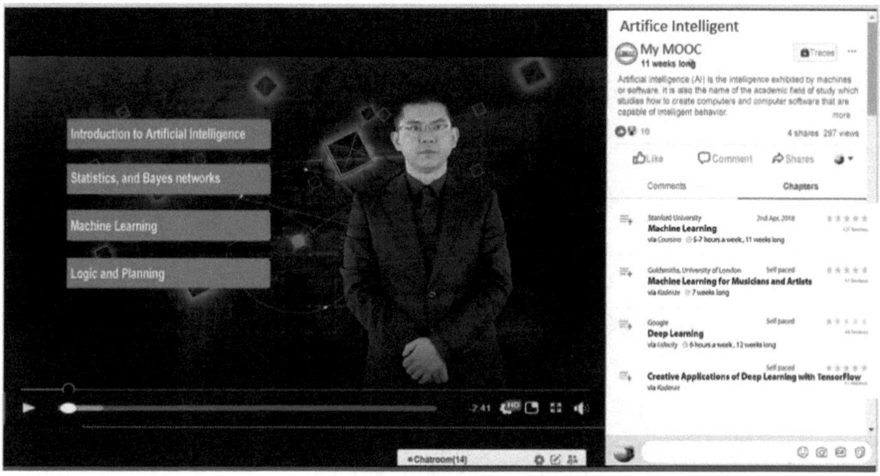

Fig. 6. Navigating a course on the MOOC platform and collecting learners' learning activities through a learning agent.

The output of the reasoning process is projected to the four outputs of the language values $y_i = \{CE, AC, RO, AE\}$ (see Fig. 1), and then the KLSI included nine style types, which were calculated based on the output of the fuzzy-network model. The membership function is bound to $0 \leq x_1, x_2, \ldots, x_7 \leq 1$. The training data was substituted into a neuro-fuzzy network and run 150 times to adjust the network parameters associated with the membership function and fuzzy model. The experimental results of network convergence for training times increased, but the root mean square error gradually decreased by about 100 training times. The actual data error is between 0.1 and -0.1 (Fig. 7).

The goal at this stage was to tailor the parameters of the initial model via a training procedure to match the optimising outputs. Important is that the initial model structure was not optimised, but optimal parameters are needed so that the antecedent Gaussian membership functions have a uniform standard deviation. The functional consequent parameters are only optimal with respect to membership functions using the ANFIS.

3.3 Evaluating the Effectiveness of the Learning Mechanism

To evaluate the learning mechanism in a MOOC course, the study first used the samples of the pretest and posttest to predict the learning performance of 154 undergraduate students, and then conducted the final test after the learning activity recommendations. Figure 8 displays the progress bar showing the learning rates of three subject-learning activities as 24.9%, 18.8%, and 19.7% respectively. The recommendations of the learning-activities model show the assisting functionality of the learning mechanism that can enhance learners' self-learning ability.

Furthermore, four experimental questions were designed, and each answer put into a separate learning activity. According to learners' preferences, they carried out the learning activities related to these four problems. It was assumed that the learner's

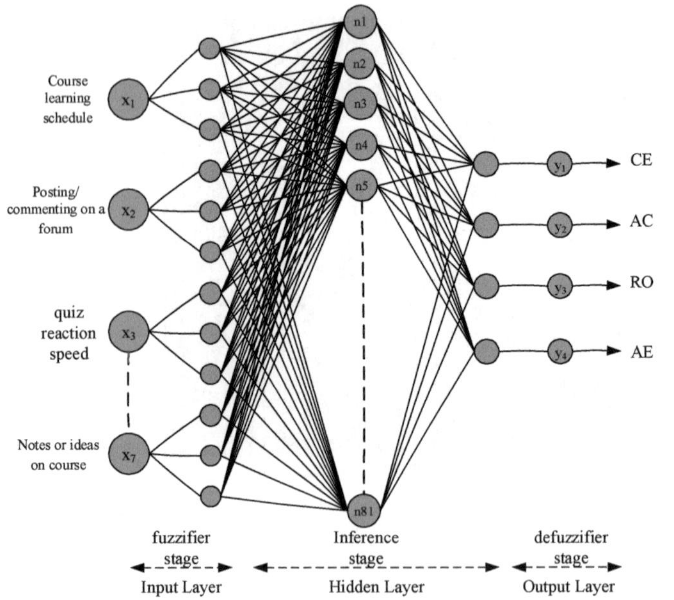

Fig. 7. Network implemented to identify learning styles by monitoring the four types of learning activities

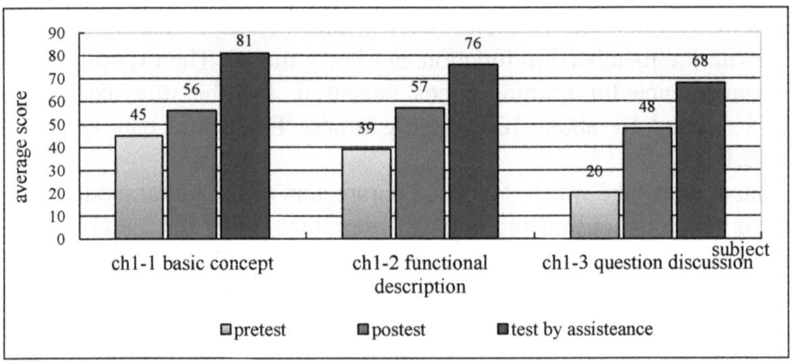

Fig. 8. Three learning progress rates, including the learning average score after offering the recommended content.

learning preference has a strong advantage over experimental problems and that they can quickly find a solution. For example, we put the Q1 answer into the activities needing experimentation. A learner with an 'initiating' style, characterised by the ability to initiate action to deal with an experience and situation, should be able to find Q1 answers quickly (Table 1).

In the experiment, 30 of 154 learners with significant characteristics (15 on AC–CE dimension by >14 (raw scores) and 15 on AE-RO dimension by >11) were selected. Response time (Q1–Q4) refers to the time taken for learners to search for the answers to

Table 1. Response time for finding solutions based on a learner's learning style

Learning dimension	Question and its characteristic			
	Q1	Q2	Q3	Q4
	Need to experiment	Need to read and think	Need to watch	Need to discuss on forum
AC	29	11*	25	16
CE	13	20	18	25
AE	8*	19	24	14*
RO	17	30	17*	18

*The value represented the average time spent (min) on finding a solution.
**The superscript (*) shows the advantage of the learning-style type.

a question. This result is essentially in line with the assumption above. A learner will quickly find answers through the recommendation mode when the learning activities correspond to his/her learning preferences.

4 Conclusion

This study posited that a semi-automated evaluation of learning can provide the system to recommend what short contents learners need. For example, in one MOOC, students participated in a problem-based activity in which groups of three students used the concepts with concrete examples, which taught them to solve problems. This problem-based activity engages both 'experiencing' learners, who need concrete data to absorb new information, and 'thinking' learners, who like to think about abstract concepts.

The study provides an evaluation method, which substantiates the value of the research. This matrix reorganises teaching techniques, individual learning styles, and course structures to encourage learning by reconsidering teaching and learning. In addition, the learning mechanism can be integrated into a MOOC/SPOC learning system, which aims to provide recommendations for learners with different styles. It helps to (1) provide clustering features: the learning mechanism has the ability to cluster learner groups with learning preferences and make various recommendations for learning activities and subject matter to better satisfy the needs of each group. (2) Improves performance with online efficiency: in the learning system, it is not necessary to evaluate learning styles or conduct a survey before the pretest. Utilising the ANFIS approach is suitable for learning in a dynamic micro-learning environment. Further work is needed on recording the data on learning activities and on more accurately measuring these learning activities to determine how to develop truly individualised computer-assisted learning.

References

1. Giurgiu, L.: Microlearning an evolving eLearning trend. Sci. Bull. **22**(1) (2017)
2. Göschlberger, B.: A platform for social microlearning. In: Verbert, K., Sharples, M., Klobučar, T. (eds.) EC-TEL 2016. LNCS, vol. 9891, pp. 513–516. Springer, Cham (2016). https://doi.org/10.1007/978-3-319-45153-4_52
3. Zhao, Y., Yan, M.A.: Research on the construction of robotics micro-learning mode in primary and secondary schools based on the WeChat platform. Digital Education (2017)
4. González-Martínez, J.A., et al.: Cloud computing and education: a state-of-the-art survey. Comput. Educ. **80**, 132–151 (2015)
5. Christopher Brooks, D., Pomerantz, J.: ECAR study of undergraduate students and information technology, EDUCAUSE Center for Analysis and Research (ECAR) [R], 18 October 2017. https://library.educause.edu/resources/2017/10/ecar-study-of-undergraduate-students-and-information-technology-2017
6. Sankey, M., Gardiner, M.: Engaging students through multimodal learning environments: the journey continues. In: ASCILITE-Australian Society for Computers in Learning in Tertiary Education Conference (2010)
7. Berliner, D.C.: Telling the stories of educational psychology. Educ. Psychol. **27**(2), 143–161 (1992)
8. Yuin, H.W., Wang, C.Y.: A study of learning time patterns in asynchronous learning environments. J. Comput. Assist. Learn. **20**(4), 292–304 (2004)
9. Truong, H.M.: Integrating learning styles and adaptive e-learning system. Comput. Hum. Behav. **55**(PB), 1185–1193 (2015)
10. Workman, M.: Performance and perceived effectiveness in computer-based and computer-aided education: do cognitive styles make a difference? Comput. Hum. Behav. **20**(4), 517–534 (2014)
11. Kolb, A.Y., Kolb, D.A.: Experiential Learning Theory. Springer, New York (2012)
12. Kolb, D.A.: Learning style inventory version 4.0 Hay resources direct (2011). www.learningfromexperience.com
13. Hurtado, C., Licea, G., Garcia-Valdez, M.: Integrating learning styles in an adaptive hypermedia system with adaptive resources (2018)
14. Spring, H.: Learning and teaching in action. Health Inf. Libr. J. **29**(2), 172–176 (2012)
15. Lo, J.J., Shu, P.C.: Identification of learning styles online by observing learners' browsing behaviour through a neural network. Br. J. Educ. Technol. **36**(1), 43–55 (2005)
16. Stathacopoulou, R., et al.: Neuro-fuzzy knowledge processing in intelligent learning environments for improved student diagnosis. Inf. Sci. Inform. Comput. Sci. Int. J. **170**(2–4), 273–307 (2005)

Exploring Learners' Cognitive Behavior Using E-dictionaries: An Eye-Tracking Approach

Xuesong Zhai[1,4], Nanxi Meng[2], Jing Yuan[3(✉)], Yalong Yang[4], and Lin Lin[5]

[1] Faculty of Education, School of Educational Technology, Beijing Normal University, 19, Xinjiekou St., Beijing, China
zhxs@bnu.edu.cn

[2] Department of World Languages, Literatures and Cultures, College of Liberal Arts and Social Sciences, University of North Texas, 1155 Union Circle, Denton, USA
Nanxi.Meng@unt.edu

[3] School of Foreign Studies, Anhui Sanlian University, 47, Hean St., Hefei, China
Janeyuan1980@hotmail.com

[4] Anhui Provincial Key Laboratory of Intelligent Building and Building Energy Saving, Anhui Jianzhu University, 856, Jinzhai St., Hefei, China
yangyl@ahjzu.edu.cn

[5] Department of Learning Technology, College of Information, University of North Texas, 1155 Union Circle, Denton, USA
Lin.Lin@unt.edu

Abstract. E-dictionaries applications (apps) have been widely used as tools for language learning. There has been little experimental research examining what learners focus or learn when they use the e-dictionaries, although some studies have looked at the user satisfaction and feature requirements of e-dictionaries. This current study used eye-tracking technology to examine what information the participants paid attention to, and how the participants processed information when using e-dictionaries. Fifteen college students participated in the study. The participants were asked to fill a survey and then to view eight vocabulary interfaces from three e-dictionaries. The participants' eye fixations and viewing paths suggested that the interface layouts of the e-dictionaries affected their attention and displaying patterns. The eye-tracking data by the participants, however, did not match with the reported data filled out by the participants. Detailed results and implications for design and learning are discussed.

Keywords: E-dictionary · Eye-tracking · Cognitive load · Fixation Scanning path

1 Introduction

Online or e-dictionaries have become one of the most popular tools for language learners and the general public. The e-dictionaries are widely used online resource among university students [1]. It is easy to check up meanings of words or find connections of knowledge and information. Many e-dictionaries companies try to conduct surveys to investigate users' perceptions and satisfactions of their products while overlooking

T.-T. Wu et al. (Eds.): ICITL 2018, LNCS 11003, pp. 165–171, 2018.
https://doi.org/10.1007/978-3-319-99737-7_16

users' cognitive processing of the materials. The purpose of this study is to fill in the gap and explore an objective measurement of e-dictionary users' cognitive processes and learning behaviors.

Eye-track technique, which is usually used to detect users' eye fixations and scanning paths, was selected as an experimental method in this study. The eye-tracking technique may allow researchers to visualize the users' attention and cognitive processes, which has been documented for analyzing readers' text-processing in the context of various format and text genre [2]. Additionally, studies from the perspective of cognitive load have documented that the complexity of searching tasks and the layout of a website affect consumers' shopping behaviors [3].

The current research, based on cognitive load theory, aims to examine the validity and reliability of using eye-track technology to analyze users' cognitive behaviors using e-dictionaries. The study has potential to provide insights for design and learning of online materials.

2 Theoretical Foundation

Cognitive Load Theory (CLT), based on the limited theory and schema theory [4] refers to the cognitive resources in the process of accomplishing the tasks,which put forward two primary hypotheses: First, Working Memory (WM) is limited when processing new information. Second, Long-term Memory can store information and schemas without limitation. Three elements are included in CLT: intrinsic cognitive load, extraneous cognitive load and germane cognitive load [5].

Intrinsic load refers to the load that is imposed by the nature of what is to be learned, including the amount of information and activities. The larger the intrinsic load is, the more the learner's cognitive resources will be taken. Intrinsic load may be reduced by effective instruction, esp. when learners lack prior knowledge [6]. Extraneous cognitive load (ECL) refers to the cognitive load that is imposed by instructional designs. Such design requires learners to engage in activities that are not directed at schema acquisition. Extraneous load is generated by improper interface design and is directly related to the presentation of information. The larger the extraneous load is, the more the learner's cognitive resources will be taken. So the design of information and interface should be improved to reduce extraneous load. Germane cognitive load, also called effective cognitive load, refers to the consuming load in the process of establishing schema and schematic automation. The construction of schema is an inevitable stage, during which knowledge will be stored in long-term memory. Schematic automation can help store established schema in long-term memory quickly and automatically without taking up the cognitive resources of Working Memory. Germane cognitive load comes from learners' effective cognition and explanation when performing cognitive tasks.

All the three kinds of load constitute the total cognitive load in the process of task accomplishments. Because of the limitation of the cognitive capacity in WM, learners will suffer from learning difficulties and negative learning experiences if total cognitive load exceeds learner's WM capacity. As a result, when designing interfaces, designers should try to reduce intrinsic and extraneous cognitive loads and avoid cognitive overload.

The purpose of this study was to examine students' attention and use of e-dictionaries though eye-tracking technologies. The following are the questions:

(1) What areas of the e-dictionaries do students pay most attention?
(2) What are the students' viewing patterns or paths?
(3) Which of the e-dictionaries do students like most and why?

3 Methods

3.1 Participants

A total 15 college students (5 males and 10 females) from a Chinese university participated in the study. The average age was 24, ranging from 21 to 28 years old. All participants were asked to complete two parts of the study, the eye-tracking experiment and the post-survey. The e-dictionaries used in the study included Bing, Eduic, and Youdao.

3.2 Instruments

Survey questionnaires and a set of eye-tracking device were used in the study. The survey consisted of two open-ended questions asking the participants of the preferential functions and reasons for using e-dictionaries based on their prior experiences. The Eye Tribe was utilized to conduct the eye-tracking part of the study. The equipped eye tracker enabled users to use gaze as the major input modality, combined with other input devices including mouse, keyboard, touch and gestures. The calculated gaze point was referred as the active application. Eye gaze data collected by the eye-tracker is referred as the passive application, which will be described more thoroughly later in this paper.

3.3 Procedure

The experiment was conducted in a laboratory with sound insulation. Upon the arrival at the lab, all the participants were asked to sign a release form, granting permission to record their actions and comments while completing the tasks. The participants were asked to fill out an open-ended questionnaire about their preferential e-dictionary, followed by the experiment in which participants were (1) informed of the purpose of the study, introduced to the equipment and procedures; (2) asked to view the result pages of a group of English words from different e-dictionaries; (3) instructed that the software, not the time they spent on viewing the page or their performance would be evaluated in the study; and (4) asked to complete all the scanning tasks in maximum of 15 min. Due to the limited number of device (one eye-tracking device), the participants completed the experiment each at a time. The participants each were asked to place their chin on the chin rest, adjust their body to a comfortable sitting position, and keep the head static. The distance between the monitor and the chin rest was approximately 60 cm (approx. 23.6 in.). After each of the participants completed the eye-tracking task, they were asked to rank the format and content of the e-dictionaries. The participants were then asked to complete a post-survey on gender, age, major, and their e-dictionary software experiences. Each participant took 10–15 min to complete the entire study, including the eye-tracking experiment and the post-survey.

The presentation sequence of the e-dictionaries was balanced between the 15 participants to prevent sequence bias towards any particular e-dictionaries, with five participants receiving the result page screens of one e-dictionary respectively. The eye-tracking data from browsing the screenshots were recorded automatically by the eye-tracker and analyzed the software named Eyeproof matched to the eye-tracker. Once situated, the participants were told to begin the Eye Tribe calibration to ensure that the data collected were precise and accurate. At the end of the calibration, the eye-tracker displayed whether the calibration was sufficient, or would need to be repeated. Three participants were asked to repeat the calibration processes. After the completion of calibration, the results pages were shown to the participants, and the actual viewing processes began.

4 Results

4.1 Survey Results

According to the content analysis, the survey results showed that the participants preferred e-dictionaries that would (1) run fast; (2) be easy to use; (3) have a simple interface design, (4) have accurate translation; and (5) be multifunctional. They also preferred dictionaries that would have fewer advertisements but show more examples.

4.2 Heat Maps and Scanning Paths

The cumulative fixation data were translated into a heat map which can be interpreted as the degree of visual attention. It provided a more intuitive understanding of fixation results. Colors on the heat maps represent the degree of fixations. Red indicates the highest level of fixation, followed by green and yellow. The area with no color received no fixation. The solid red diamonds in the heat maps indicated the users' mouse clicks and were irrelevant to fixation analysis. The denser the information on the image, the more fixations it received and the larger the fixation areas became.

The heat maps of result pages are shown in Fig. 1 below. It can be observed that the participants appeared to pay more attention to the Example Sentences area, followed by Meaning, Pictures, Phrase, Spelling, Synonym and Pronunciation. With more than five example sentences listed on the result page, the first two received more attention than the rest. The figures indicate that the Example Sentences and Meaning of a word were the critical components for all the dictionary users.

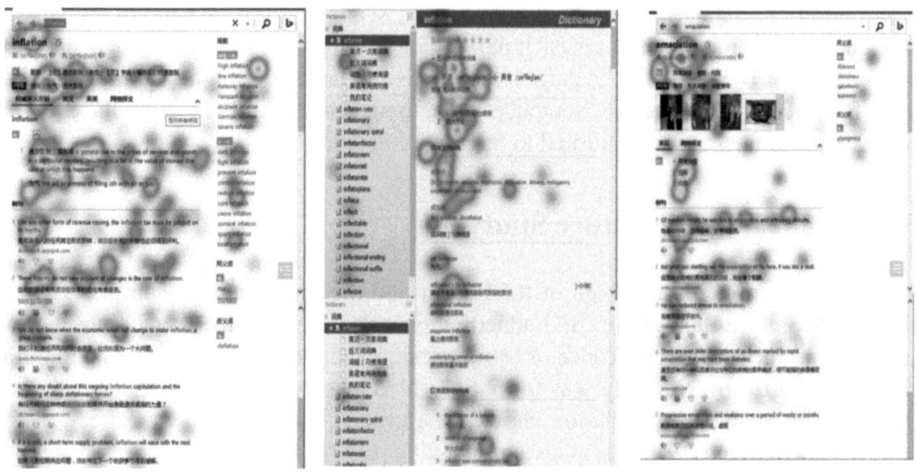

Fig. 1. Heat map samples

The number of fixations on a particular Area Of Interest (AOI) indicated the importance, or in other words, the noticeability of that AOI to a user while accomplishing the task. The alternative explanation of this metric is the number of words or 'chunk' needing processing. Hence, high fixation counts for certain AOI could be attributed to the length of the sentence that grabbed the users' attention.

For the three dictionaries, the Example Sentences areas received the most fixation. Observed in Bing and Eudic dictionary, the area received the second most fixations is the Meaning area. For Youdao dictionary alone, Phrase received more fixations than Meaning. As for the rest of AOI, Pronunciation received the least fixations for Bing dictionary while Spelling drew the least fixations for Eudic and Youdao dictionary respectfully. Interestingly, Meaning and Example sentences attracted far more fixations than the left AOIs for Bing dictionary.

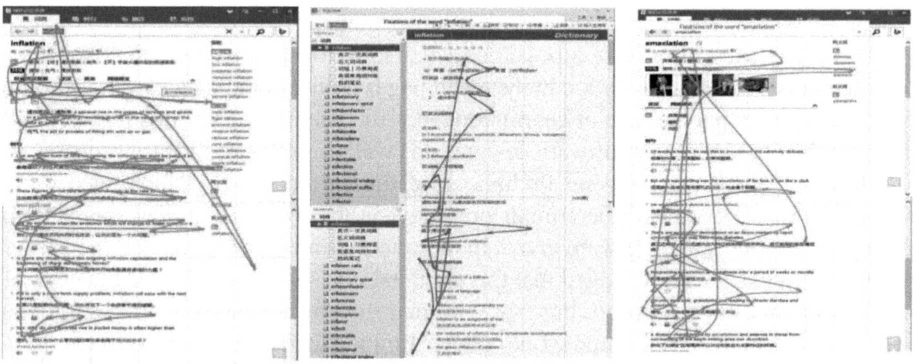

Fig. 2. Scanning path samples

In addition, as shown in Fig. 2 above, each scanning path represents the spatial sequence of eye-movements for each participant during the eye tracking session. The scanning paths indicate that the participants tended to pay attention first to the Meaning area, followed by the Example Sentences area, then areas of AOI. Towards the end, the participants almost always returned to the Meaning area.

5 Conclusion and Future Study

This study examined the design of the format and the presentation of information in three frequently e-dictionaries and added empirical evidence of eye-tracking metrics testifying to the great significance of format design and the amount of information of a dictionary software. Not only was format revealed as being important holistically but also the personalized information showed the crucial factor which can affect users' learning performance [7]. Heat maps and scanning path further jointly indicated the three most engaging areas: Example sentences, Meaning and Pictures. Particularly, Meaning and Example sentences in Bing dictionary attracted nearly five times fixations than the sum of the left AOI's. One explanation of Bing dictionary received such high fixation could be that the Meaning and Example sentences make up about 80% of the total area in the images, therefore containing more words for users to process. Another possible explanation could be attributed to the format of Bing dictionary, which presented the information and functions significantly differently from the other two. Pictures and Meaning, in this study, were equally important. The picture captured the users' attention at a much faster rate than text, therefore, receiving high fixation. The findings are consist with the load theory of attention proposed by Lavie [8], a perceptual selection mechanism exists in the human cognitive behavior, and an individual can ignore irrelevant stimuli when he or she is under circumstances of high perceptual load [9].

Interestingly, according to the survey, participants preferred dictionaries with following features: easy to use, simply designed, with diversified functions and with more example sentences. When comparing the result of post survey to heat map and scanning path, participants, in fact, paid little attention to those excessed example sentences, which directly contradict with what participants stated.

This study tried to provide a possible explanation for the inconsistent conclusions on whether too much information in the result pages reduces or enhance user's learning efficiency from a perspective of cognitive load [10]. The findings of this research will be of interest to dictionary software designers as well as online dictionary users.

However, there exist several limitations of the current study, which need future research. First, the size of the stimuli presented in the experiment was small. Eight exemplars in each software were given, in order to minimize the burden on the participants. It should be acknowledged that this small number of stimuli limited the generalizability of this study. Second, this study limited the physical activity to eye tracking and only to participants recruited at one college, limiting the generalizability of the study. Finally, future research could investigate by including more questions in the post-survey as a means to check the participants' understanding of the stimuli, to see if eye-tracking play a role in the participants' understanding of the texts.

Acknowledgments. Thanks are due to for funding by Anhui provincial research projects (foundation NO.: 2015zdjy115, SK2015A632, SK2017ZD42 & SK2017A0015), the Chinese Science Funding for Post-doctors (foundation NO.: 2018m630092), and the National Key Research and Development Program of China (foundation NO.: 2017YFC0704100)

References

1. Lebenicnik, M., Pitt, I., Istenic Starcic, A.: Use of online learning resources in the development of learning environments at the intersection of formal and informal learning: the student as autonomous designer. Ceps J. **5**, 95–113 (2015)
2. Clark, M., Ruthven, I., O'Brien Holt, P., Song, D., Watt, S.: You have e-mail, what happens next? Tracking the eyes for genre. Inf. Process. Manage. **50**, 175–198 (2014)
3. Wang, Q., Yang, S., Liu, M., Cao, Z., Ma, Q.: An eye-tracking study of website complexity from cognitive load perspective. Decis. Support Syst. **62**, 1–10 (2014)
4. Sweller, J.: Cognitive load during problem solving: effects on learning. Cogn. Sci. **12**, 257–285 (1988)
5. Yuan, L., Kekang, H.E.: The Construction of the central radio and TV University teaching quality guaranteeing system. Radio and TV System Quality Guaranteeing Research. Problem group. Modern Dist. Educ. **5,** 7–9 (2006). (in Chinese)
6. Paas, F., Van Gog, T., Sweller, J.: Cognitive load theory: new conceptualizations, specifications, and integrated research perspectives. Educ. Psychol. Rev. **22**, 115–121 (2010)
7. Zhai, X., Gu, J., Liu, H., Liang, J.C., Tsai, C.C.: An experiential learning perspective on students' satisfaction model in a flipped classroom context. Educ. Technol. Soc. **20**, 198–210 (2017)
8. Lavie, N., Hirst, A., de Fockert, J.W., Widing, E.: Load theory of selective attention and cognitive control. J. Exp. Psychol. Gen. **133**, 339–354 (2004)
9. Klemz, B.R., Thomas, S.G.: Dueling or the battle royale? The impact of task complexity on the evaluation of entry threat. Psychol. Mark. **20**, 999–1016 (2003)
10. Zhai, X., Yan, D., Jing, Y.: Investigating learners' technology engagement - a perspective from ubiquitous game-based learning in smart campus. IEEE Access **6**, 10279–10287 (2018)

Understanding Inquiry-Based Searching Behaviors Using Scan Path Analysis: A Pilot Study

Wan-Ting Sun[1], Feng-Ru Sheu[2(✉)], and Meng-Jung Tsai[3(✉)]

[1] National Taiwan University of Science and Technology, Da'an District, Taipei 10607, Taiwan
sun05121@gmail.com

[2] Kent State University, 1125 Risman Drive, Kent, OH 44242, USA
fsheu@kent.edu

[3] National Taiwan Normal University, No. 162, Section 1, Heping East Road, Da'an District, Taipei City 106, Taiwan
mjtsai99@gmail.com

Abstract. The purpose of the study is to explore user's online information searching behavior via incorporating eye tracking tool with conventional user research methods and an emphasis on how eye tracking data can reveal a deeper understanding of user behaviors, specifically of interest is scan path analysis. The National Central Library (NCL) website was selected to test out two common searching tasks for libraries or library alike. And an eye-tracking device was used to detect the visual pathway. Scan path video was further used to analyze the user's visual behavior patterns. Eight participants, four male and four female with ages from 24 to 26, were recruited for the study. A Tobii 4C eye-tracker was used to collect eye movement data and a self-developed eye-tracking data analyzer was utilized for data analysis, including fixation data and scan-path visualization. The results showed that participants who completed the task correctly had more regular and strategic searching patterns. On the opposite, participants did not find the correct answer showed no particular patterns regarding the visual path when conducting the task. The paper reported the examination of information search for the two most common inquiry on a live library website by eight Taiwanese participants in regards to search efficiency (i.e. task completion, task time, and browse pages). The paper also illustrated the additional value eye tracking tools can provide in support of user research.

Keywords: Online searching behavior · Browse path · Scan path
Eye tracking

1 Introduction

Searching information online is a daily task in the age of information exploration. People extensively access and exchange information via the Internet. Searching information quickly and correctly is the fundamental and critical skill at the information age. Therefore, understanding how users perform online information searching is an interest of educators, researchers, and information designers. Conventional user research methods have some limitations. For example, the verification of whether or not the users/participants actually "look at" or "read" the information on the present screen (or Web pages)

T.-T. Wu et al. (Eds.): ICITL 2018, LNCS 11003, pp. 172–177, 2018.
https://doi.org/10.1007/978-3-319-99737-7_17

traditionally can be obtained through follow-up interview/clarification or self-report/think-aloud. With eye tracking data (i.e. scan paths, fixation counts and fixation duration), the researchers were able to know so without interrupting participants or the limitation of memories. In short, applying eye tracking allowed researchers to explore a reader's searching behavior directly by accessing visual path track. For instance, the study of Ranyner [1] found the difference in detailed question response of speedreading people and general readers that speedreading people could not answer the question required detailed information without saccade-related information. The result further indicated two possible reasons for the occurrence of word skimming included word-length information and textual variable. Short words were more likely to be skipped comparing to long words. Also, a contextual constraint may affect reader's decision to proceed to next fixation, skipping to the word or go back to the earlier part of text [1].

Eye movement is also considered relevant to understanding different aspects of the cognitive process and attention patterns. For instance, Just and Carpenter [2] proposed an idea called 'eye-mind hypothesis,' which means the location that eyes gaze correspond to human thoughts. Inhoff and Liu [3] examined the perceptual processes and visual activity of Chinese text reading. Results showed the difference in perceptual processes and the area of effective vision (perceptual spans) between an English text reader and a Chinese text reader. Similarly, Tsai and Liu [4] examined the association between online searching strategies visual attention path via eye movement. Results suggested a significant difference in visual attention distribution on task problem between female and male. The results provided the possible explanation that users missed the correct answer even when their fixation location was around the relative information.

The above studies demonstrated the benefits of using eye tracking tool in various aspects as well as suggest eye-tracking tools may help researchers better understand user behaviors and provide additional data on visual pattern and attention. Therefore, the purpose of the study is to explore user's online information searching behavior via incorporating eye tracking tool with conventional user research methods with an emphasis on how eye tracking data can reveal a deeper understanding of user behaviors, specifically of interest is scan path analysis.

2 Methods

2.1 Participants

As the target audience of the national central library website is for the general adult population, we limited our participants to adult 20 years old or older with no severe visual impairments. A total of eight participants, four female and four male with ages ranging from 24 to 26 years old, were recruited through a recruitment post on Facebook and PTT, a social media tool used by college students in Taiwan. They were all students from a public university in Taipei, Taiwan.

2.2 Apparatus

This study utilized a Tobii 4C eye-tracker (sampling rate 60 Hz) to collect participants' eye-tracking data and the Eye-tracking Data Analyzer (EDA), a self-developed Unity programing to calculate eye-tracking data, including fixation data using the dispersion-based algorithm [5]. The EDA has been used and validated in a previous study [6]. Also, EDA can general scan-path visualization which allows video analysis visualizations for video analyses [7].

2.3 Procedure and Tasks

Each participant signed up an individual session in a lab setting, a computer station with internet access. The facilitator first gave an overview of the study and then allowed the participants to read the consent form with study information as well as to ask questions. During the session, each participant was asked to conduct a live website search on the national central library website for the answers to two information-based inquires. Library hours and eligibility to use services are among the most commonly asked questions for public libraries or museums. Therefore, the tasks were derived from these two areas and presented in a format of questions on purpose. They were: (1) what the library hours are on Tuesday in general, and (2) whether or not a 15-year-old high school student can apply for a library card. Once the participants indicate that they finished and returned the task sheet to the facilitator, the task performance portion was considered 'complete.' The session was recorded, including the computer screen, audio conversation, and eye movement (collected by Tobii 4C).

3 Results and Discussion

3.1 Task Completion Rate, Browse Page Count, and Time Spent

Task Completion Rate. Overall, the participants have no problem finding information in responding to the given tasks. All eight participants completed both tasks within three minutes. The completion rate is 100%. The definition of technical completion is to ***arrive*** at the "target web page," where necessary information for completing tasks is located. There were two target pages for each task. The soft definition for completion was when the participant indicated they were finished (writing down answers and return the task sheet to the facilitator).

Browse Page Count. Goldberg, Stimson, Lewensteln, Scott, and Wichansky [8] indicated the browse page count is associated with search efficiency. Results showed that all users completed two tasks within seven pages, including the home page (the starting page). Three out of eight persons browsed just three pages to complete both tasks. In other words, there is only one mouse click per task, which is considered rather efficient.

Time Spend. Time spent is another performance indicator for online information searching [9]. For task 1, the mean of searching time for task 1 was 36.92 s. The mean time spending on the result page (target page) was 28.95 s. Moreover, the total time spending was 65.87 s. For task 2, the average searching time was 13.998 s, the mean of the result page time was 14.07 s, and total time spending was 28.07 s. In other words, all participant completed the first task within about one minute and the second task within 30 s.

3.2 Accuracy of the Performance

Although all participants located/arrived at the target page and completed the tasks, there was a difference regarding quality in their responses/answers. For library hours inquiry, the answer is straightforward. All participants fulfill the inquiry correctly. As for the eligibility, there was a slight difference regarding accuracy. In general, only 16 years old or older can apply for a library card. However, full-time students under 16 can also apply for a card. Both pieces of information were listed on the target pages. Three out of eight participates did not answer the answer correct although they were on the target pages and the necessary information was nearby. In other words, we know that participants have 'arrived' at the target page and possibly 'look at' the necessary information to answer the questions. However, we do not know if the participants actually "read" the information. This is one of the areas where eye tracking data can provide additional information for better understanding without interrupting task process.

3.3 Scan Path Video Analyze

The Scan path video analysis provided further information about user's visual path. The results suggested that some participants spent more time on relevant information (see Fig. 1). The visual path regularly moved in the information box (the red box) to compare the information between right and left columns. Some spend more time on irrelevant information. As shown in Fig. 2, although the participant was on the right page, the 'reading' was all over the place. Some participants highlighted the content in the table to remind themselves of the content previously read. On the other hand, the saccades of users who answer inaccurately showed no obvious strategies, move fast (scan path and

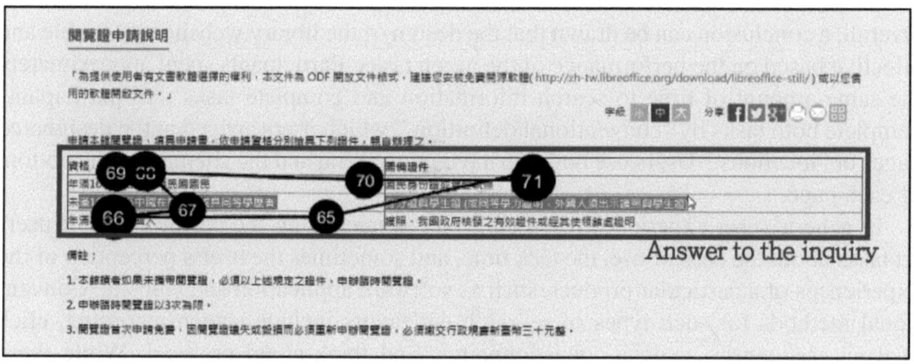

Fig. 1. Example scan path of the user who gets the answer correct (Color figure online)

gaze/fixation data), and did not focus on the relevant information (based on fixation data). In short, the participants who had correct answer conducted the task strategically.

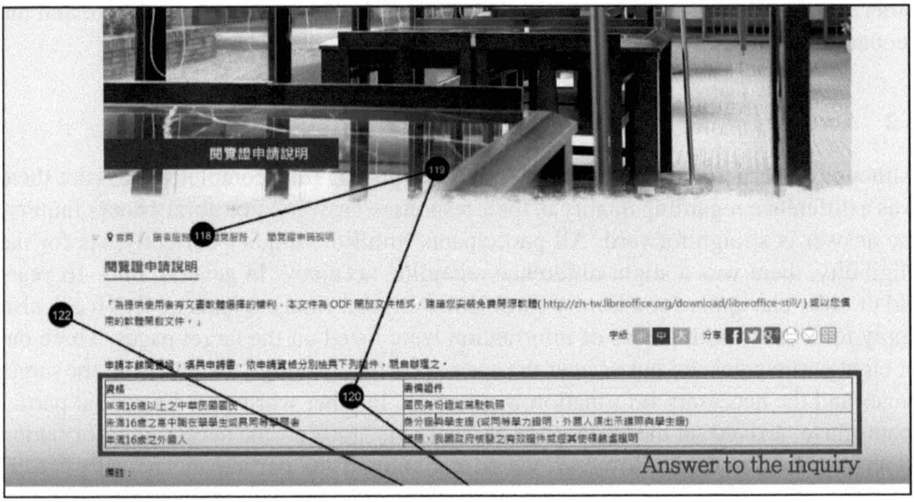

Fig. 2. Example scan path of the user who gets the answer wrong (Color figure online)

It is interesting to find that the user did not find the answer in the results page; even their visual path showed they have browsed/looked at the information. Some users just fixed near the relevant data, but still did not answer it right. Such results might align with a study of Inhoff and Liu [2]. Inhoff and Liu found the perceptual spans was small while reading Chinese sentences, a possible explanation why some users gazed near the information and still could not make the correct answer. First, it was that they saccaded around and did not cogitate. Another explanation was that they did not "see" the information.

4 Conclusion

Overall, a conclusion can be drawn that the design of the library website was usable and effective based on the performance of the given tasks. Participants spent approximately the same amount of time to search information and complete tasks. All participants complete both tasks by "conventional definition," which users arrived at the designated pages or "locations." Users use both top navigation menu and the sitemap on the bottom of each page.

In general, user experience research involves measuring the performance of users on tasks about the ease of use, the task time, and sometimes the user's perception of the experiences of a particular product, such as software application and website. Conventional methods for such types of research endeavors include screen recording, click analysis, sequences analysis, questionnaires, and think-aloud protocol. While these provide valuable sources of data, eye tracking data provide additional information that conventional methods cannot obtain, which helps to confirm or triangulate a specific phenomenon, and, therefore, better understand user behaviors.

Results in the present study confirmed the benefits of using eye tracking tool in user research, specifically in exploring online information search using Scan Path Video analysis. Results showed all the eight participants completed task 1 (the library hours on Tuesday in general), while part of the users passed task 2 (whether or not a 15-year-old high school student can apply for a library card). The scan path analysis further showed qualitative differences in visual path between users who answered correctly and those answered incorrectly that otherwise could not be obtained through conventional methods. Future studies may further expand the use of eye tracking tool to explore the user's searching behavior patterns with different learning contexts and user tasks or goals.

References

1. Rayner, K.: Eye movements in reading and information processing: 20 years of research. Psychol. Bull. **124**(3), 372–422 (1998). https://doi.org/10.1037/0033-2909.124.3.372
2. Just, M.A., Carpenter, P.A.: A theory of reading: from eye fixations to comprehension. Psychol. Rev. **87**(4), 329–345 (1980). https://doi.org/10.1037/0033-295X.87.4.329
3. Inhoff, A.W., Liu, W.: The perceptual span and oculomotor activity during the reading of Chinese sentences. J. Exp. Psychol. Hum. Percept. Perform. **24**(1), 20–34 (1998). https://doi.org/10.1037//0096-1523.24.1.20
4. Tsai, M.J., Liu, W.Y.: Undergraduates's online search strategies and visual attention distribution. Master's thesis (2012). http://hdl.handle.net/11296/c983vv
5. Salvucci, D.D., Goldberg, J.H.: Identifying fixations and saccades in eye-tracking protocols. In: Proceedings of the Eye Tracking Research and Applications Symposium, pp. 71–78. ACM, New York (2000)
6. Hsu, C.Y., Chiou, G.L., Tsai, M.J.: A pilot study on developing and validating a fixation-based scaffolding learning system. Poster presented at 2016 International Conference of East-Asian Association for Science Education, Tokyo, Japan (2016)
7. Tsai, M.J., Hsu, P.F., Pai, H.T.: Eye-tracking Data Analyzer (EDA) developed for educational researchers: a sample module of LSA. In: 4th International Symposium on Educational Technology, Proceedings of ISET 2018, Osaka, Japan (2018)
8. Goldberg, J.H., Stimson, M.J., Lewensteln, M., Scott, N., Wichansky, A.M.: Eye tracking in web search tasks: design implications. In: Proceedings of the Symposium on Eye Tracking Research and Applications, New Orleans, Louisiana, USA, pp. 51–58. ACM (2002). https://doi.org/10.1145/507072.507082
9. Hsu, C.Y., Tsai, M.J., Hou, H.T., Tsai, C.C.: Epistemic beliefs, online search strategies, and behavioral patterns while exploring socioscientific issues. J. Sci. Educ. Technol. **23**(3), 471–480 (2014). https://doi.org/10.1007/s10956-013-9477-1

Big Data Analysis in Drug Offense Crime to Advice Education Training Course in Police Academy

Kuo-Ching Wu[1], Yeong-Ching Lin[2], and Chun-Yi Lu[2](✉)

[1] Central Police University, Taiwan, Republic of China
wkc@mail.cpu.edu.tw
[2] National Penghu University of Science and Technology, Taiwan, Republic of China
{yclin,jamesleu}@gms.npu.edu.tw

Abstract. With the rapid development of emerging drug industry, Drug traffickers have more knowledge in marketing packaging and thus crime rate increased. Police are facing more and more investigations in drug-related offenses. This work uses Big-Data analytics technology and SEM Model which drawing on a large-scale sample of 87,926 court judgment documents for drug-related crime in Taiwan and Fujian. The result show reduced processing time significantly by Spark and No-SQL database technology. Simultaneously, Motel is a hotbed of drug-related offenses, Internet chat rooms are virtual places for cyber drug transactions, and Drug abusers always carry both gun and bullets. Based on the above results, the findings in this work may use for education training courses in the police academy.

Keywords: Big data · Data mining · Drug offense crime

1 Introduction

"Drug Trafficking and Abuse" is an essential issue for national security [1–3]. Most opiate and Methamphetamine made in golden triangle area: Myanmar, Thailand, and Laos [4]. A statistics from NNCC (National Narcotics Control Commission, NNCC-Official Organization in China) display that there are 60% drug supply come from the north of Laos and Myanmar in 2013 [5]. Su takes drug offense Crime as Non-Traditional Security Challenge because drug trafficking belongs to international trade [6]. Therefore, both drug abuse and offense crime are a global issue.

The purpose of drug offense crime strategies, including of Eradication- root out illegal planting, Destruction-destroy factory and Consumer Market Interdiction, is to reduce the number of unlawful use of drugs [7]. Eradication means to root out illicit farming and Destruction is means to discover and destroy the factory. And then, Blockade marketing channel will cause Consumer Market interdiction.

This work expected to get some useful information which will assist to investigate drug abuse cases from past drug offense criminal records with Big-Data analytics technology. It draws on a large-scale sample of 87,926 court judgment documents for

T.-T. Wu et al. (Eds.): ICITL 2018, LNCS 11003, pp. 178–185, 2018.
https://doi.org/10.1007/978-3-319-99737-7_18

drug-related crime in Taiwan and Fujian. In NIST (National Institute of Standards and Technology, NIST) Big-Data Interoperability Framework (NBDIF), it was defined as "they consist of extensive datasets-primarily in the characteristics of volume, variety, velocity, and/or variability-that require a scalable architecture for efficient storage, manipulation, and analysis." In NIST Special Publication (#1500-1), There are more detailed definitions for Volume, Velocity, Variability, and Variety [8]. More simply put, Big -Data associated with processing in time. While complicated documents or files operated by SPARK or other computing architectures, it must be output report in tolerance time so that can use for decision support in some events, such as the spread of infectious diseases, terrorist attack, etc.

This paper divided into four main sections. Section 1 provides some background information about both drug offense crime and the definition of Big-Data. Section 2 outlines the design of Big-Data analytics, describing some of the Big-Data frameworks. Section 3 discusses the result. Finally, Sect. 4 outlines some suggestions to Advice Education Training Course in Police Academy.

2 Design and Development Big-Data Analytics

There are several phases in Big-Data procedures. First of all, the work gets court judgment documents which associated with drug-related crime from both Taiwan Court Information Search System and Government Information Open Platform. After that, there are 87,926 files were selected manually by the judgment date between Jan 2012 and Dec 2017. All files size is approximate to 1G bytes (1,079,599,104 bytes). All phases described as follows:

1. ***Collection Phase:*** To Get Data from both Taiwan Court Information Search System (http://jirs.judicial.gov.tw/index.htm) and Government Information Open Platform (https://data.gov.tw/) and process data initially as above described. Finally, Valid Sample is 64,418.
2. ***File Conversion Phase:*** Convert PDF files to Text Files by software -"UniPDF."
3. ***Extract-Transform-Load Phase:*** The process of data Extract, Transform and Load from source to destination. In this Phase, we use some software, such as SPARK, SCALA and MongoDB, and coding some procedures to deal with Chinese for literal consistency. Besides, MD5 Hash Function used for removing redundancy data.
4. ***Processing Phase:*** Import Data (including of Database and Data Collection) into MongoDB. In this stages, our procedures face to the out of memory problem. Some solutions, such as BufferedWriter, PrintWrite, and SparkContext.Parallelize. saveASTextFile, are all failed. Finally, To reset JVM parameters and increase the memory size for JVM runtime is one of the solutions.
5. ***Transfer Output Data to Excel Phase:*** Transfer files- the result of Processing Phase into Excel Format.
6. ***Text Mining Phase:*** Transfer Excel file into SAS as a data set by SAS Enterprise Guide 7.1. The Text Miner function of SAS Enterprise Miner is responsible for Text Parsing and output 20,000 Chinese Words which is related to "Drug offense

Words." At the same time, Operator must pay attention to the maximum size (32,676 bytes) of string type filed in SAS for preventing system halt. Then, To import these output into a new Excel file for next Phase.

7. ***Words Screening Phase:*** First, the phase combined the previous stage Excel file with MongoDB to set up the critical value of term frequency. Second, using Excel VBA to reduce "Drug offense Words." from 20,000 to 5,000. Third, Operators will determine which keyword can be satisfied for this work. Finally, To merge "Drug offense Words." and these keywords. After filter redundancy words, 1,116 Chinese words obtained.
8. ***Words Variable Computing:*** Computing 1,116 Chinese words with defined eight variables in 64,418 samples.
9. **Filter and Select Variable:** To get rid of sparse value from 1,116 × 8 matrix.
10. ***Data Mining Phase:*** First, this stage takes observation sample from the files which generated while variables select process. Second, Using Regression Analysis to examine the correlation between multiple explanatory variables and dependent variables, including three-degree drugs classify in Taiwan and involves various crimes. Finally, Because of the amount of data is too significant result in out of memory, this work will use Linear Structure Relationship Model for next phase.
11. ***Reduce Sample Phase:*** Given the formula for 64,418 samples and reduce Sample from 64,418 to 11,486.

$$\text{Reserved}_{\text{Value}} = \text{PROBNORM}\left(\frac{\text{PRIN1}}{\text{SQRT(EigenValues)}}\right) * 100$$

$$\text{where Reserved}_{\text{Value}} \geq 50$$

12. ***Factor Analysis:*** filter the Eigenvalues > 1.0 and factor loadings > 0.35 by Varimax. Method. Moreover, for simplifying research, only top 30 elements will be selected.
13. ***Getting Behavioral Pattern:*** To try to build Linear Structure Relationship Model from the top 30 elements by IBM SPSS AMOS.

3 Experimental Result

This section divided into two parts. One is the result of Data Mining, describing some findings in the process, the other one is the Linear Structure Relationship Model, showing the analysis results of the drug offense crime pattern.

3.1 The Result of Data Mining

An argot is a secret language used by offenders to prevent outsiders from understanding their conversations. Drug offenders use argot words-e.g., slang, trap, rock, roll, star, smacked, etc. - are present in some English-speaking countries. Similarly, some

Table 1. The behavior pattern of first grade drug offense crime in Taiwan.

N=64,418, Variables=1,116 Definition of First Grade Drugs: Heroin, Opium, Morphine, and Cocaine						
No.	Argot word 1	Argot word 2	Argot word3	Argot word4	Argot word5	Argot word6
1	海洛因	收受	取走	毒品次數	追查	證人身份
2	無期徒刑	收款	拘提	桃園機場	大包	廣東
3	甲基安非它命	改造	一手交錢	快遞	九月	藏匿
4	施用	進價	男子	鹽酸鹽	六月	冰
5	轉讓	新臺幣	分量	代價	毒品成份	友人
6	所得價金	二級毒品	教唆犯	未遂	檢舉	含混
7	一手交貨	原料	幫助	重量	中盤毒梟	微信
8	持有	高度行為	無罪	借貸	承租	耗損
9	想像競合	槍管	調查局	查禁	原料藥	上線
10	交易時間	制式子彈	監聽	買賣價差	工具	償還
11	併罰	分擔	紙	收貨	交保	海巡署
12	機票	遊藝	書證	證據方法	牙保	租屋處
13	銷毀	女生	朋友	通路	公共電話	付款
14	所得	因果	七月	關係人	牽連	進貨
15	酮	接聽	交通	分工	害怕	
16	行動電話	汽車旅館	搭機	收件人	化學	
17	純質	車站	分裝	鑑定	投宿	
18	低度行為	彈殼	陷害	中山	夜市	
19	拘役	大盤	毛重	供需	三月	
20	磅秤	聯繫	文書	貨運	掩飾	
21	現金	小盤	起運	出鏡	記憶	
22	警察局	製毒	態樣	合成	交易對象	
23	粉末	十月	同一性	麥當勞	夾藏	
24	累犯	查獲	沒收	差價	接觸	
25	連帶	擊發	兜售	八月	水果	
26	價量	郵局	自由意志	檢查	進口物品	
27	交易毒品	晶片	佐證	出口	心理狀況	
F value=532.31, (Prob.>F)< .0001 , R^2=0.7975,adjust R^2=0.796						

Table 2. Classify the behavior pattern of first grade drug offense crime into 16 categories

Category	Chinese Argot Words
Ingredients of Drugs	海洛因、甲基安非他命、酮、鹽酸鹽、原料、原料藥、女生、冰、水果、純質、含混、合成、粉末、二級毒品、化學
Drug & Crime	施用、持有、製毒
Delivery by Transportation	起運、廣東、中山、分裝、貨運、快遞、大包、桃園機場、夾藏、掩飾、紙、進口物品、出口、進貨、查獲、收件人、檢查、藏匿、郵局、租屋處
Delivery by People	機票、桃園機場、搭機、取走、代價、出境、檢查、夾藏、分工、分擔、接觸、男子、朋友、友人、交通
Law Enforcement Agency	警察局、調查局、海巡署
Delivery Place	交易時間、交易對象、汽車旅館、車站、麥當勞、夜市、遊藝
Payment Method	接觸、交易毒品、一手交貨、一手交錢、現金、收受、收款、進價、新臺幣、收貨、牙保、付款、分量、重量、磅秤、耗損
Contact	行動電話、聯繫、公共電話、微信
The Scale of Delivery	大盤、小盤、通路、兜售、中盤毒梟、分裝
The Profits of Delivery	現金、所得價金、新臺幣、所得、價量、買賣價差、差價、供需
Psychological Condition	陷害、害怕、記憶
Money Demand	借貸、償還
Gun & Bullet	改造、槍管、制式子彈、工具、擊發、彈殼、藏匿
Month	十月、七月、八月、九月、六月、三月
Investigation Pattern	查獲、晶片、拘提、監聽、接聽、因果、書證、文書、態樣、自由意志、佐證、證據方法、關係人、鑑定、檢查、追查、檢舉、證人身份
Sentencing	無期徒刑、想像競合、併罰、銷毀、拘役、低度行為、累犯、連帶、高度行為、教唆犯、幫助、無罪、陷害、沒收、牽連、未遂、交保、同一性

Chinese argot words appear in our analysis results. In analyzing the data, some tables as below will show Chinese argot words instead of translating to English for adequately present the true meaning and correlations. From the perspective of academic research, we may take these Chinese argot words as symbols.

In data mining phase, this study refers to the viewpoint of Newman and obtain some interpretability analysis results from the content eigenvalues in court judgment documents [9]. There are 64,418 samples and 1,116 variables in the analysis. To simplified results, the study only shows the behavior pattern of First Grade Drug Crimes (See Table 1). The argot words in Table 1 sorted by significant from left to right, top to bottom. Moreover, Table 2. shows the Chinese argot words classification into 16 categories.

3.2 The Linear Structure Relationship Model

This study also uses Linear Structure Relation (LISREL) to verify the cause-effect relation by SEM (Structural Equation Model, SEM). There are 30 eigenvalues, 192 variables and 11,486 records in this work. Figure 1 adapted MLE (Maximum Likelihood Estimates, MLE) to show the SEM model. Also, the fit index of SEM show as Table 3.

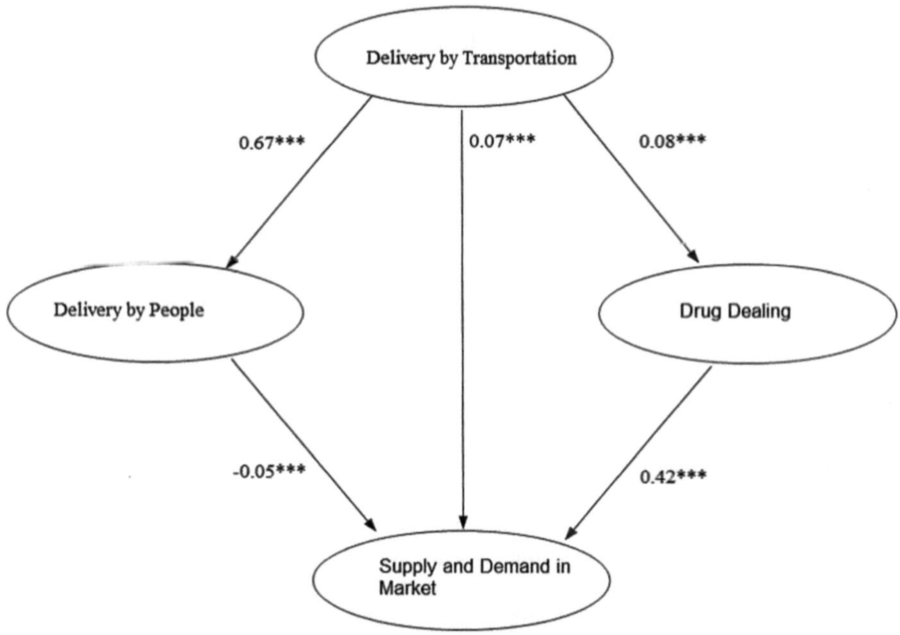

Fig. 1. The LISREL model

Table 3. Fit index for SEM model

Fit index	Value	Acceptable standard
RMSEA	**0.086**	**Excellent: RMSEA < 0.05** **Good: 0.05 ≤ RMSEA < 0.08**
CFI	0.753	0 < CFI < 1
GFI	0.808	0 < GFI < 1
AGFI	**0.781**	**AGFI < GFI & AGFI > 0.9**
PNFI	0.699	0 < PNFI < 1
PCFI	0.701	0 < PGFI < 1

In Table 3 and Fig. 1, Both RMSEA and AGFI outlook not so good. It may require more precise filter parameters in CFA phase. We will try to use second-order factor analysis in the futures. Moreover, this work will also try to prune covariate by M.I. Value (Modification Indices, M.I.) for SEM optimization.

Table 4. Ten significant finding in the study

No.	Directions
1	Severe Crimes recruit Mild Crime
2	The motel is a hotbed of drug crimes; Internet chat rooms is a virtual place, and coffee shop is a physical location for drug dealing
3	Drug abusers always carry a gun and bullets
4	Drug smuggling Via air transport
5	The monitoring of telephone and telephone records is a necessary tool for judicial investigation
6	Drug offender communicates with others by using argot words
7	Drug offenders declare "I forgot the phone call." to conceal criminal intent
8	March and August are peak seasons for drug activities
9	Both cell phone and apps, such as WeChat, Line and What's app, are tools for drug crimes
10	Bit-Coin becomes a payment mechanism

4 Conclusion and Suggestions

To conclude, the present study is preliminary research on drug crime by Big-Data technology, but its relevance to Chinese argot words, using by criminals, can also be seen. There are ten significant finding that may be used as crime investigation teaching material in police academy (See Table 4.). However, whether this will also apply to a criminals investigation in other parts of the world cannot be determined based on this study. Further research is therefore warranted in different countries.

Acknowledgment. This work supported by Ministry of Science and Technology, Taiwan, R.O.C. under Grant No. MOST 106-2511-S-346-002-MY2

References

1. Swanstrom, N.: The narcotics trade: a threat to security national and transnational implications. Glob. Crime **8**(1), 1–25 (2007)
2. Walther, M.F.: Insanity: four decades of U.S. counterdrug strategy. Strategic Studies Institute, U.S. Army War College, Carlisle, PA (2012)
3. Weimer, D.: Seeing Drugs: Modernization, Counterinsurgency, and US Narcotics Control in the Third World, 1969-1976. Kent State University Press, Kent (2011)
4. Chin, K.L.: The Golden Triangle: Inside Southeast Asia's Drug Trade, 1st edn. Cornell University Press, Ithaca (2009)
5. National Narcotics Control Commission.: Annual Report on Drug Control in China. NNCC, Beijing (2013)
6. Su, X.: Nontraditional security and China's transnational narcotics control in Northern Laos and Myanmar. Polit. Geogr. **48**, 72–82 (2015)
7. Mejia, D., Restrepo, P.: The Economics of the War on Illegal Drug Production and Trafficking. Documento CEDE No. 2013-54 (2013). SSRN: https://ssrn.com/abstract=2353939 or https://doi.org/10.2139/ssrn.2353939
8. NIST NBDIF HomePage. https://bigdatawg.nist.gov/V1_output_docs.php NBDIF
9. Newman, E.: Critical human security studies. Rev. Int. Stud. **36**(1), 77–94 (2010)

Mind, Brain and Education

Design and Development of Learning Innovation Enhancing Learning Potential Using Brain-Based Learning

Sumalee Chaijaroen[1] and Charuni Samat[2(✉)]

[1] Department of Education Technology, Faculty of Education, Khon Kaen University, Khon Kaen, Thailand
sumalee@kku.ac.th

[2] Department of Computer Education, Faculty of Education, Khon Kaen University, Khon Kaen, Thailand

Abstract. The purpose of this research was to design and develop learning innovation enhancing learning potential of the learners using brain-based learning. The target group consisted of 9 administrator, teachers teaching science learning substance in grade 4–6, total of 36 teachers, and 4–6 grade students from 9 schools, total of 928 students in primary school. The research and development was employed in this study. The procedure were as following: (1) to examine the principles and theories regarding brain-based learning, constructivist and cognitive theories (2) to explore the school context concerning brain-based learning (3) to synthesize designing framework of learning innovation enhancing learning potential of the learners using brain-based learning (4) to design and develop learning innovation according to above mentioned designing framework. The result revealed that: (1) The learning innovation enhancing learning potential of the learners using brain-based learning comprise of 9 components as following: (1) Problem base (2) Knowledge bank (3) Scaffolding (4) Meaningful experience (5) Multiple intelligence development center (6) Relaxation room (7) Edutainment room (8) Brain-gym room (9) Collaboration (2) The efficiency of the learning innovation illustration as following: (1) The Experts review (2)The learners' opinions from 9 schools (3) The learners' multiple intelligences and learning achievement.

Keywords: Design and develop learning innovation · Brain-based learning Constructivism · Learning environment

1 Introduction

Instructional design has played important role in order to improve the learning potential of learners, allowing them to perform better on the learning process, especially brain-based learning. The studies revealed that the learning management which compatible with the operation of brain, which we called brain-based learning is leading to effective learning. Not only, effective learning on the dimension of achievement scores but also increases more connection between brain cell which we called synapse [1]. This, intern it may influence on learning both achievement scores and brain compatible. With this

T.-T. Wu et al. (Eds.): ICITL 2018, LNCS 11003, pp. 189–195, 2018.
https://doi.org/10.1007/978-3-319-99737-7_19

attention to brain-based learning, some studies [2] have demonstrated the effectiveness and efficiency of brain-based learning such as processes of brain-based learning have relationship with multiple intelligences development, including, 8 important principles of brain-based learning.

Based on above mentioned reasons the researchers recognize how importance of brain-based learning. Thus, the purpose of this study was to design and develop learning innovation enhancing learning potential of the learners using brain-based learning. In order to address this purpose, this study proposed a theoretical and designing framework from the review of related literature including empirical exploration of contextual study of the school context concerning brain-based learning. This study will be influence to effective learning that can be enhancing brain operation of learners. This leading to efficiency of learning potential development simultaneously increasing brain cell and synapse of brain cell. This in turn, will be influence learning potentials.

2 Methodology and Result

This study was aimed to synthesize theoretical framework and design of Constructivist augment reality web-based learning environment to enhance creative thinking. Research methodology is developmental research consisted of 3 processes; (1) Designing process and (2) Developing process research methods are document analysis, and (3) Evaluate process the efficiency of the design framework. The procedures were as following: (1) To examine and analyze the principles and theories, (2) To synthesize theoretical framework, (3) To synthesize designing framework, and (4) To evaluate the efficiency of the learning environments.

2.1 Data Collection

The target group consisted of 9 school directors and 36 teachers, teaching science learning substance in grade 4–6 from 10 schools, and 4–6 grade students, during the first semester of 2006 school year from 10 schools, total of 828 students in primary school level under the Office of Khon Kaen Educational Service Area 5 Chumpae District, Khon Kaen Province, Northeastern Thailand.

2.2 Instruments

The research instruments consisted of:

1. Learning innovation enhancing learning potential of the learners using brain-based learning.

The learning innovation enhancing learning potential of the learners using brain-based learning was design and developed as the following details: the researchers reviewed and analyzed principles and theories and research related to the learning potential of the learners using brain-based learning including contextual study. Based on the above mentioned study concerning (1) 12 Brain-based learning principles, based on brain research [2] (2) Constructivist theories (3) Multiple intelligences [3, 4] and the result of school contextual study. Designing framework was synthesized 9 essential components was shown as following: (1) Problem base, (2) Knowledge bank, (3) Scaffolding, (4) Meaningful experience, (5) Multiple intelligence development center, (6) Relaxation room, (7) Edutainment room, (8) Brain-gym room, and (9) Collaboration.

The efficiency of Learning innovation was assessed on 5 dimensions as followings: (1) Product examination, (2) Contextual utilization, (3) Learners' opinions toward learning innovation, (4) Cognitive ability, and (5) Learning achievement.

2. The instruments for collecting data consisted of (1) The learners' opinionnaire toward learning innovation (2) The interview form of learning innovation enhancing learning potential of the learners using brain-based learning (3) The learners' multiple intelligent test (4) Learning achievement test.

2.3 Data Collection and Analysis

The data were collected both quantitative and qualitative methods as following:

1. Synthesis of designing framework and components of the learning innovation enhancing learning potential of the learners using brain-based learning.
2. Design and develop Learning innovation. The researchers designed and developed the learning innovation based on above mentioned designing framework and Components. This learning innovation was tried out and the data were collected and analyzed by the researchers as following details:
   2.1 expert review such as content expert, multimedia expert, instructional designer, especially in brain-based learning and measurement and evaluation expert, for checking the gathering data instruments. The data were analyzed by summarization, interpretation and analytic description.
   2.2 The learners' opinions toward the learning innovation enhancing learning potential of the learners using brain-based learning. The data were analyzed by summarization, interpretation and analytic description.
   2.3 The learners' multiple intelligence. The data were analyzed by descriptive statistics: Mean, S.D. and Percentage.
   2.4 The learners' learning achievement. The data were collected and analyzed by using descriptive statistics: Mean, S.D. and Percentage.

2.4 Research Result

1. The learning innovation enhancing learning potential of the learners using brain-based learning was constructed based on Designing framework. These data were collected by analyzing principles, theories, related research and school contextual study as above mentioned. Designing framework and Components of Learning innovation were synthesized. The details are illustrated in Fig. 1.

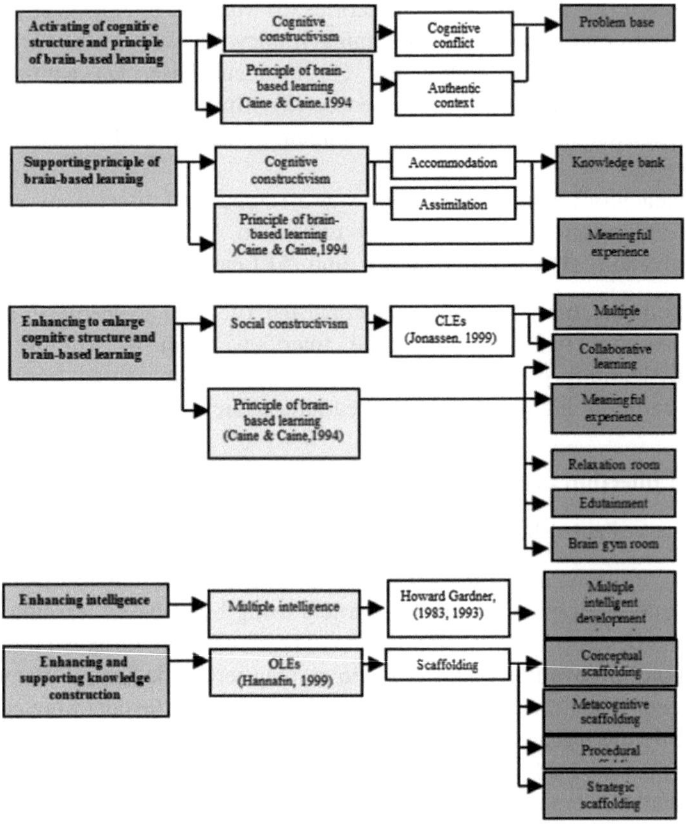

Fig. 1. Designing framework of learning innovation enhancing brain-based learning potential

It comprises of 9 components as following: (1) Problem base, (2) Knowledge bank, (3) Scaffolding, (4) Meaningful experience, (5) Multiple intelligence development center, (6) Relaxation room, (7) Edutainment room, (8) Brain-gym room, and (9) Collaboration. They were designed and developed by researcher team. The components of learning innovation were shown as below Figs. 2, 3, 4, 5, 6, 7, 8 and 9.

Fig. 2. Problem base

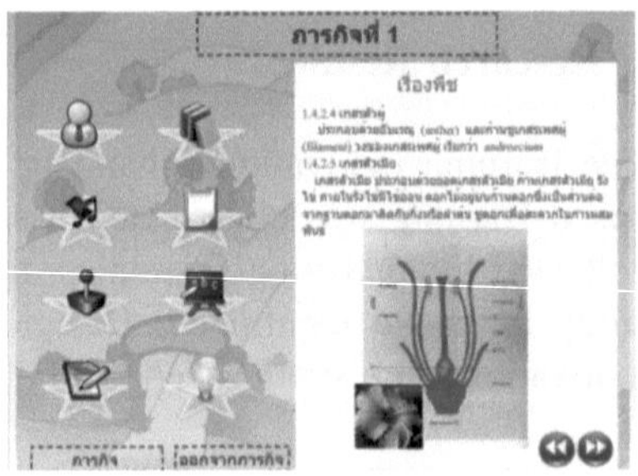

Fig. 3. Knowledge bank

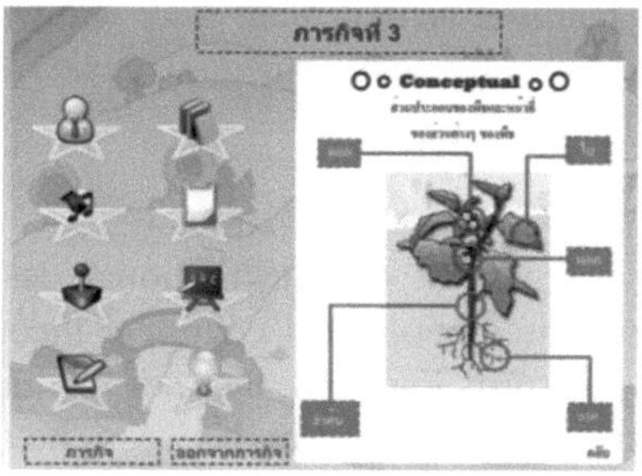

Fig. 4. Conceptual scaffolding

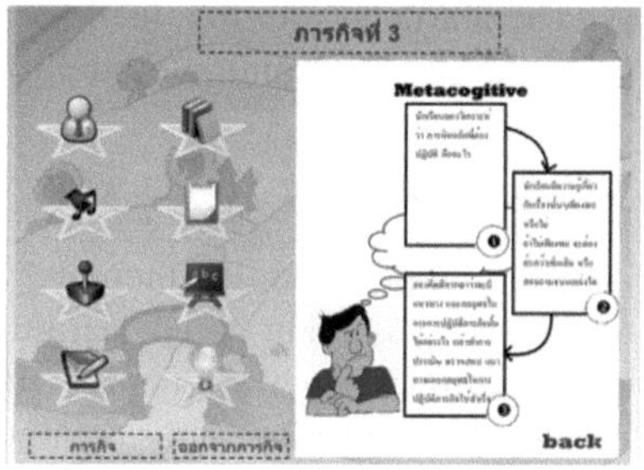

Fig. 5. Metacognitive scaffolding

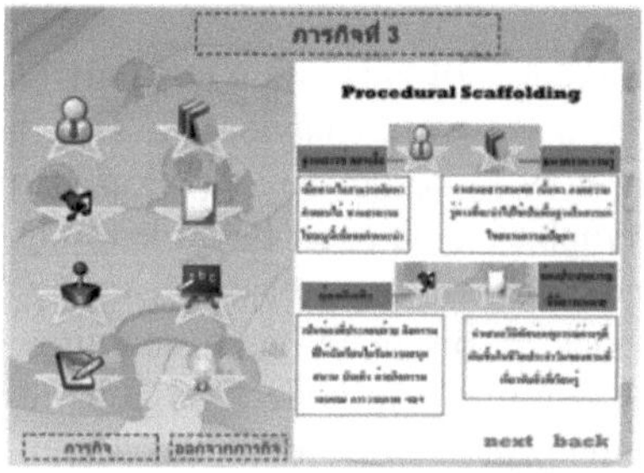

Fig. 6. Procedural scaffolding

Fig. 7. Strategic scaffolding

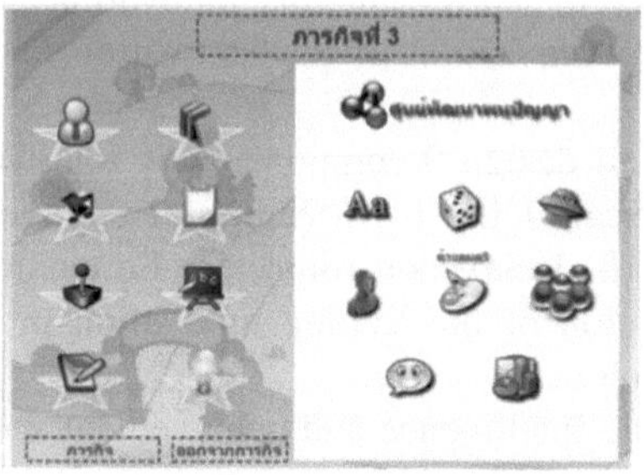

Fig. 8. Multiple intelligence

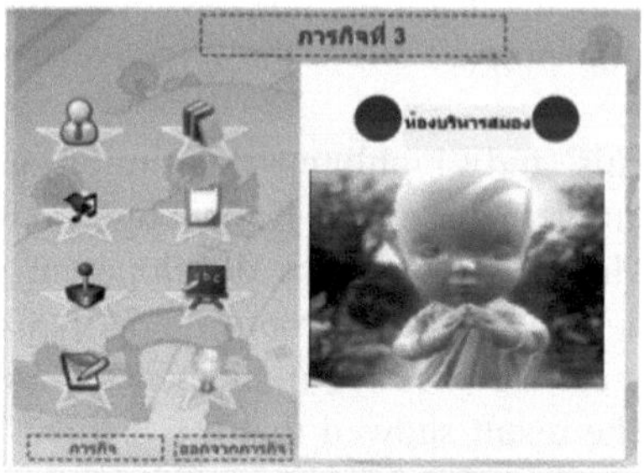

Fig. 9. Brain-gym room

2. The efficiency of the learning innovation was revealed in several dimensions as following:
   (1) The Experts review showed that the designing of learning innovation was appropriate and congruent with the theories and principles as above mentioned designing framework. That can be enhancing brain based learning.
   (2) The learners' opinions showed that the learning innovation was appropriate and help them in the learning process. And they prefer to learn with this innovation learning process. And they prefer to learn with this innovation.

(3) The learners' multiple intelligences and learning achievement were shown the higher level of multiple intelligences and learning achievement scores.

2.5 Conclusions

The results support the ID theories, which employed in this instructional design. Theories used was brain-based learning, multiple intelligence and cognitive theories. Designing framework was synthesized based on principle and theories including contextual study results. This framework show the relationship between how to implement principles and theories into practice. Based on this reason it resulted in the implementation of this innovation effective. It can be utilized in the real world practically. The results of the study further showed all dimensions of the innovation effectiveness such as expert reviewer, contextual utilization appropriate, enhancing both multiple intelligence and achievement.

Previous research pointed mainly to the effectiveness of innovation just only on the dimension of achievement score scores based on a view of Behaviorism. This study provides a possible research issue by proposing how to design and develop learning innovation underlying with Cognitivism which emphasize on brain-based learning and multiple intelligence. Cognitivism which emphasize on brain-based learning and multiple intelligence. Cognitivism which emphasize on brain-based learning and multiple intelligence. In addition to offering how to utilization it effectively, the results of this study may also contribute to the conceptualization of instructional design and implementation of learning innovation enhancing learning potential of the learners using brain-based learning. What happens in the learning process, it was illustrated by the learners' opinions showed that the learning innovation was appropriate and help them in the learning process. And they prefer to learn with this innovation. This learning process show the effectiveness of implementation of the innovation in this study.

This study highlights this notion and how to design 9 components as following: (1) Problem base, (2) Knowledge bank, (3) Scaffolding (4) Meaningful experience (5) Multiple intelligence development center, (6) Relaxation room, (7) Edutainment room, (8) Brain-gym room, and (9) Collaboration of the leaning innovation in this study can be effective implement in similar context.

The result showed that the learners' multiple intelligence and achievement scores were higher. This can be confirmed the actual classroom. Although some implications can be expected to impact in practice, care must be taken when generalizing the findings into other context. This study examines one school in a Thailand context. Future research needs to examine the research issues proposed from this study in more diverse settings.

Acknowledgment. This work was supported by the Academic and Research Affairs, Innovation and Cognitive Technology Research Center, Faculty of Education, the Research and Technology Transfers Affairs Division, Khon Kaen University, and National Research Council of Thailand.

References

1. Sternberg, R.J.: Wisdom, Intelligence, and Creativity Synthesized. Cambridge University Press, New York (2003)
2. Caine, R., Caine, G.: Making Connections: Teaching and the Human Brain. Addison-Wesley, Menlo Park (1994)
3. Gardner, H.: Frames of Mind: The Theory of Multiple Intelligences. Basic Books, New York (1983)
4. Gardner, H.: Multiple Intelligences: The Theory in Practice. Basic Books, New York (1993)
5. Jonassen, D.H.: Designing constructivist learning environments. In: Reigeluth, C.M. (ed.) Instructional Design Theories and Models: A New Paradigm of Instructional Theory, pp. 217–239. Lawrence Erlbaum Associates, Mahwah (1999)
6. Hannafin, R.D.: Open learning environments: foundations and models. In: Reigeluth, C. (ed.) Instructional-Design Theories and Models (Volume II), pp. 372–389. Lawrence Erlbaum, New Jersey (1999)

Designing of the Learning Innovation Enhance Learning Potential of the Learners Using Brain-Based Learning

Charuni Samat[1(✉)], Patcharee Saengjan[2], Sumalee Chaijaroen[2], Issara Kanjug[2], and Pornsawan Vongtathum[1]

[1] Department of Computer Education, Faculty of Education, Khon Kaen University, Khon Kaen, Thailand
thaibannok@hotmail.com

[2] Department of Educational Technology, Faculty of Education, Khon Kaen University, Khon Kaen, Thailand

Abstract. Brain-based learning is generally defined as the understanding of the relationship between the educational environment and the complexities of the human brain. Brain-based learning requires basic knowledge of the specific areas of the brain that are impacted and then manipulating the classroom to provide a positive learning environment to increase academic growth. Also, the purposes of this research was to synthesize theoretical framework and designing framework of The Learning Innovation Enhance Learning Potential of the Learner's Using Brain-based Learning. The document analysis research and survey research was employed in this study. The procedure were as following: (1) to examine the principles and theories of brain-based learning, constructivist and cognitive theories (2) to explore the contextual study for brain-based learning (3) to synthesize designing framework of learning innovation (4) to design and develop learning innovation according to above mentioned designing framework. The data analysis was preceded by analytical description and interpretative summary. The result revealed that: The learning innovation enhance learning potential of the learners using brain-based learning comprise of 9 components as following: (1) Problem base (2) Knowledge bank (3) Scaffolding (4) Meaningful experience (5) Multiple intelligence development center (6) Relaxation room (7) Edutainment room (8) Brain-gym room and (9) Collaboration.

Keywords: Cognitive learning potential · Brain-based learning
Multiple intelligence · Constructivist

1 Introduction

In the present, the world of information and technology has advanced and changed quickly. There are many different data and information. Become a society of learning is linked to knowledge and knowledge worldwide, must be designed to provide an effective learning to guide the development of better learning. As a result, teachers, educational staffs, and educational organization had to adapt themselves to be Learning

T.-T. Wu et al. (Eds.): ICITL 2018, LNCS 11003, pp. 196–204, 2018.
https://doi.org/10.1007/978-3-319-99737-7_20

Organization. The advancement of neurological science are greater [1]. Scientists are beginning to understand the biological mechanisms and processes of the nervous system, which controls emotions, behavior, thought and intelligence as well as knowledge of various factors that affect the development and function of the nervous system [2]. Describe the process by which human beings. Intellectual development and learning all of these processes occur in the brain [3], which is the most important organ of the human nervous system. This allows researchers to study and discover about the brain mechanisms used in human learning [1].

Research intelligence students of Thailand in year 2011 found that the average intelligence level students Thailand in the country was 98.59 (the average IQ in the normal range 90–109), which is the level of intelligence that is normal but slightly low. Especially when compared to children in many countries in Southeast Asia such as Hong Kong, Singapore, China, Japan, Learning directly related to the brain, requires a learning process of the brain (Mental process) [4], from receiving and processing incoming (Sensory information) thinking, cognitive, planning and memory The brain is a complex organ and adaptability over time it can be a complex process, or processing multiple tasks simultaneously [3]. The brain can perceive and remember information better if it is meaningful [4], to develop the multiple intelligences of students, a more potent should be taught in accordance with the principles of multiple intelligences and learning principles to enhance learning potential using Brain-based Learning.

According to the above reasons, the researcher was interested in synthesize the Theoretical Framework as foundation of analysis the Designing Framework The Learning Innovation Enhance Learning Potential of The Learner's using Brain-based learning comprise of 9 components as following: (1) Problem base, (2) Knowledge bank, (3) Scaffolding, (4) Meaningful experience, (5) Multiple intelligence development center, (6) Relaxation room, (7) Edutainment room, (8) Brain-gym room, and (9) Collaboration, for improving the students to obtain knowledge with strength, develop excellence competency, and promoting for students' multiple intelligence.

2 Research Objective

To synthesize the Theoretical Framework and Designing Framework of The Learning Innovation Enhance Learning Potential of the learner's using brain-based learning.

3 Research Design

The document analysis research and survey research was employed in this study. The procedure were as following: (1) to examine the principles and theories of brain-based learning, constructivist and cognitive theories (2) to explore the contextual study for brain-based learning (3) to synthesize designing framework of learning innovation (4) to design and develop learning innovation according to above mentioned designing framework. (See Fig. 1).

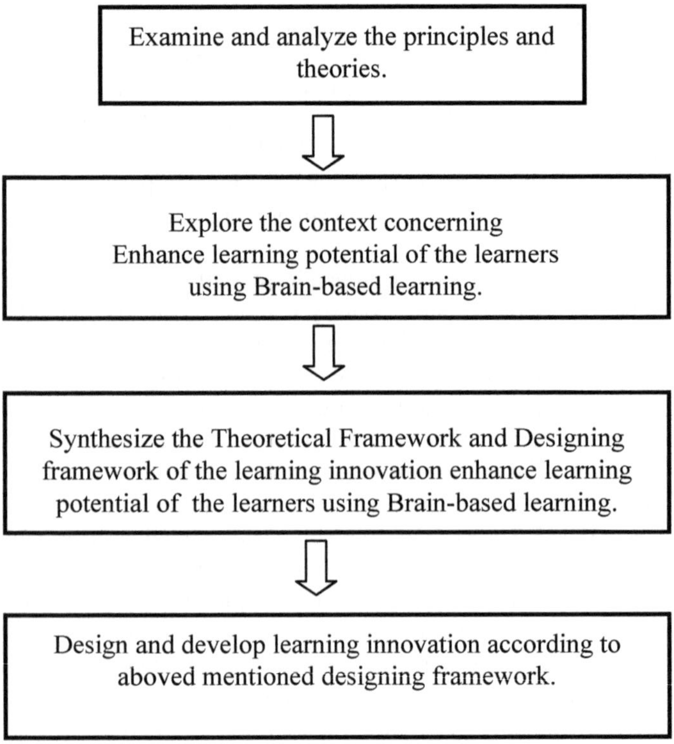

Fig. 1. The step of synthesize the theoretical framework and synthesize the designing framework of the learning innovation enhance learning potential of the learners using Brain-based learning.

4 Data Collection

(1) The Literature review, study of rationale, theory, and related literature with related Theory of Learning, consisted of Theory of Knowledge Construction based on Constructivist Theory [5], and enhance learning potential of the learners using Brain-based learning. For using as basis of research, and recording in the Recording Form of document Investigation.
(2) The synthesis of Theoretical Framework from theories and related literatures, consisted of theory of knowledge construction based on Constructivist Theory, and enhance learning potential of the learners using Brain-based learning.
(3) The synthesis of Designing framework was based on Theoretical Framework.
(4) The design framework was presented to the thesis advisor, and experts for considering, improving, and correcting.

5 Data Analysis

The obtaining data analysis of this study included the Qualitative Data Analysis.

The researcher would present data analysis as follows:

The designing framework of this study was the framework in designing based on ID Theory.

(1) Theoretical Framework obtained from rationale, theory, and related literature by documentary analysis. Data were analyzed by descriptive analysis and Interpretation conclusions.
(2) Designing framework obtained from rationale, theory, and related literature by Documentary analysis. Data were analyzed by descriptive analysis and Interpretation conclusions.

6 Research Findings

According to Literature review for synthesizing Theoretical Framework, the rationales, theories, and related literature of designing the learning innovation enhance learning potential of the learners using Brain-based learning, as basis for of research as Fig. 2: Theoretical Framework, the rationales, theories, and related literature of designing the learning innovation enhance learning potential of the learners using Brain-based learning, including major components as: Foundation of Psychology of Learning, Media Theory, Science of Teaching, and Technology as following details.

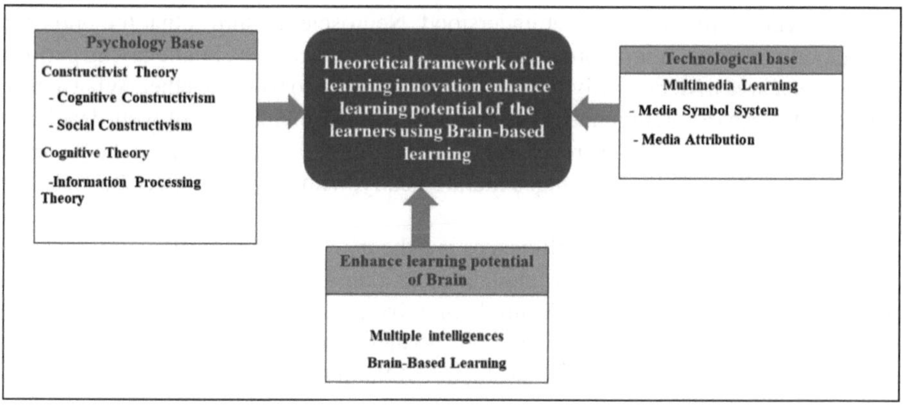

Fig. 2. Theoretical framework of the learning innovation enhance learning potential of the learners using Brain-based learning

6.1 Psychology Base

The knowledge management had major basis from Psychology of Learning especially the changing society, the information technology played role in educational management. So, different forms of theories and rationales in Educational Technology were administered in integrated way for quality of teaching. Foundation of psychology was an important part in designing the learning environment appropriate with human's learning potential to be efficient focusing on Cognitive processes so that the students would construct knowledge and learn throughout their life.

1. Constructivist Theory consisted of important basic approaches viewing that learning occurring inside students who construct knowledge from relationship between what be seen, and former knowledge. The approach occurred from report of psychologist and educator as Jean Piaget, and Lev Vygotsky, classified into 2 approaches as: (1) Cognitive Constructivism with foundation from Jean Piaget. According to this approach, the students constructing knowledge through action. If they were stimulated by problem causing their Cognitive Conflict, (2) Social Constructivism with foundation from Lev Vygotsky, the viewpoint that "the social interaction played an important role in cognitive development [6]." The students had limitation in the developmental zone called Zone of Proximal Development.

2. Cognitive Theory, is an approach to psychology that attempts to explain human behavior by understanding the thought processes. The assumption is that in humans, thoughts are the primary determinants of emotions and behavior. Information processing is a commonly used description of the mental process, comparing the human mind to a computer.

6.2 Enhance Learning Potential of Brain

1. Brain-based learning, the differences of opinion and theory in psychology indicate that the learning process is not yet understood. Neuroscience shows that the brain can be modeled not with a central processor where "intelligence" lies, but in having perhaps 70 functional areas. Mental activity requires several areas to work together. What appear as different types of intelligence result from different combinations of well-developed functional areas, Learning is a process by which neurons join by developing the synapses between them, Knowledge is arranged hierarchically, with new knowledge being linked to existing neural networks

2. The theory of Multiple Intelligences is a theory of intelligence that differentiates it into specific (primarily sensory) "modalities", rather than seeing intelligence as dominated by a single general ability. Multiple intelligences of 8 components as following: (1) Musical–rhythmic and harmonic (2) Visual–spatial (3) Verbal–linguistic (4) Logical–mathematical (5) Bodily–kinesthetic (6) Naturalistic (7) Interpersonal (8) Intrapersonal.

6.3 Technological Base

Our world today is changing rapidly in terms of whether it is in terms of education, economy and society, particularly in terms of information technology. In an era of education reform. Also accelerate the development of education to improve the quality of education. In order for people to help develop the country. Information and communication technology (ICT) is a powerful tool to enhance quality of education. The competency of computer shown in combining many kinds of media including: the letter, picture, sound, animation, videotape, and interaction. All of these things could help multi-media computer to be interesting, and could convey meaning very well.

The Media Symbol Systems theory developed by Salomon is intended to explain the effects of media on learning. States: To summarize, the symbol systems of media affect the acquisition of knowledge in a number of ways [7]. First, they highlight different aspects of content. Second, they vary with respect to ease of recoding. Third, specific coding elements can save the learner from difficult mental elaborations by overtly supplanting or short-circuiting specific elaboration. Fourth, symbol systems differ with respect to how much processing they demand or allow. Fifth, symbol systems differ with respect to the kinds of mental processes they call on for recoding and elaboration. Thus, symbol systems partly determine who will acquire how much knowledge from what kinds of messages (See Fig. 2).

According to the synthesize the designing framework base on Theoretical framework and put into practice, the components in designing of The Learning Innovation Enhance Learning Potential of the Learners using Brain-based learning comprise of 9 components as following: (1) Problem-base, (2) Resources, (3) Scaffolding, (4) Meaningful experience, (5) Multiple intelligence development center, (6) Relaxation room, (7) Edutainment room, (8) Brain-gym, and (9) Collaboration.

Figure 3(a) Problem base; designed for stimulating the cognitive structure, applied from the approach of Cognitive Constructivism using OLEs Model as situation from Authentic Context [5]. In the design, the picture, statement, sound, and animation should be used to stimulate the students to have Recognition, and Attention by using Externally imposed for helping student to refer to or associate with their own experience; (b) Resources is knowledge source was an origin in collecting the information, content, and information the students would use in solving the problem they faced with. They had discovery learning through various information technologies for organizing data to be easy to analyze and storing the students' information [8].

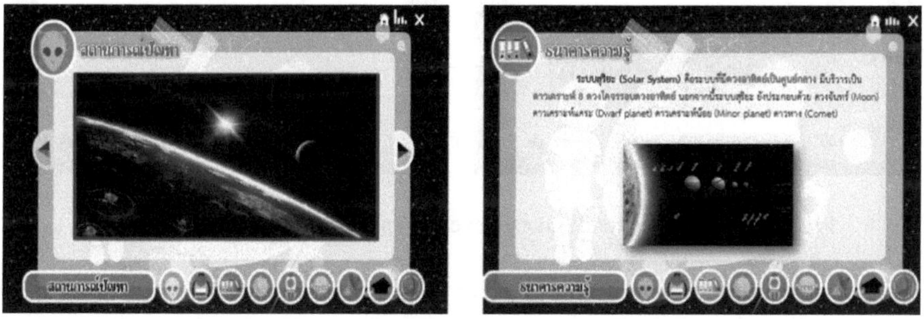

Fig. 3. (a) Problem base; (b) Resources

Figure 4(c) Scaffolding; designed by OLEs Model, since the students had limitation in duration of development called Zone of Proximal Development would base on helping or scaffolding classified into 4 scaffoldings: (1) Conceptual Scaffolding, (2) Metacognitive Scaffolding, (3) Procedural Scaffolding, and (4) Strategic Scaffolding; (d) Meaningful experience; this element is based on the principle the brain is meaning-driven – meaning is more important to the brain than information.

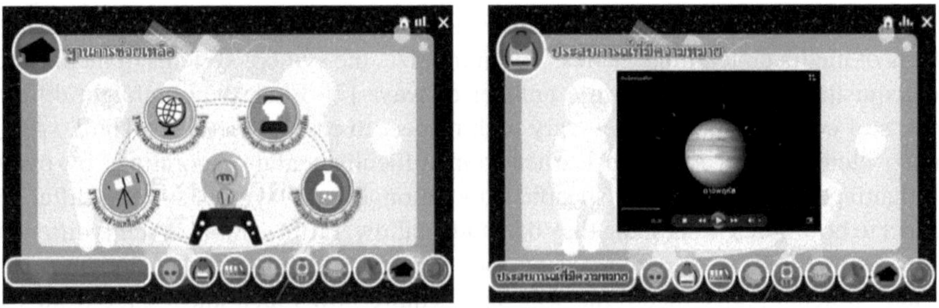

Fig. 4. (c) Scaffolding; (d) Meaningful experience

Figure 5(e) Multiple intelligence development center; the study research involves developing brain. Multiple Intelligences Theory, which can help support [9] has proposed a theory of cognitive development consisting of eight sided as follow: (1) Musical–rhythmic and harmonic (2) Visual–spatial (3) Verbal–linguistic (4) Logical–mathematical (5) Bodily–kinesthetic (6) Naturalistic (7) Interpersonal (8) Intrapersonal; (f) Relaxation room; this element of the principle that "the state of stress and danger that will stop. A barrier to learning including the destruction of brain cells," so the design of learning to reduce fear. Apprehension Tension in children and create a more interesting challenge for children. Encourage children to alert [10]. The relaxation room is designed with an educational game for students to relax and have fun with the knowledge together.

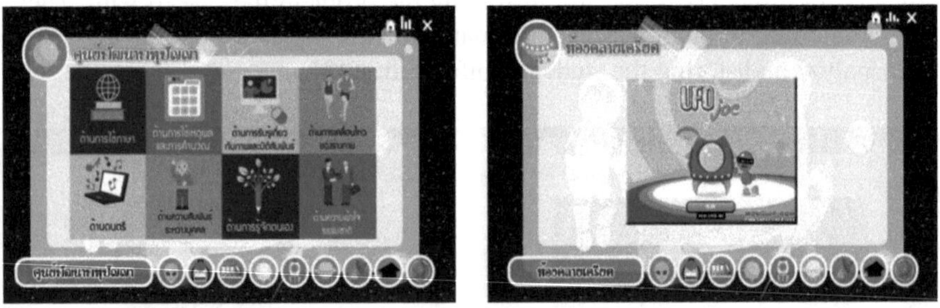

Fig. 5. (e) Multiple intelligence development centre; (f) Relaxation room

Figure 6(g) Edutainment room; this element of that principle. Emotions are critical to learning - they drive our attention, health, learning, meaning and memory; (h) Brain-gym [11]; the principle that all learning is mind-body – movement, foods, intentional cycles, drugs and chemicals all have powerful modulating effects on learning.

Figure 7(i) Collaboration; to provide opportunity in obtaining guidelines in cooperating in creating society for knowledge sharing, and the students collaborated in solving the problems. They would exchange similar objective to solve problem.

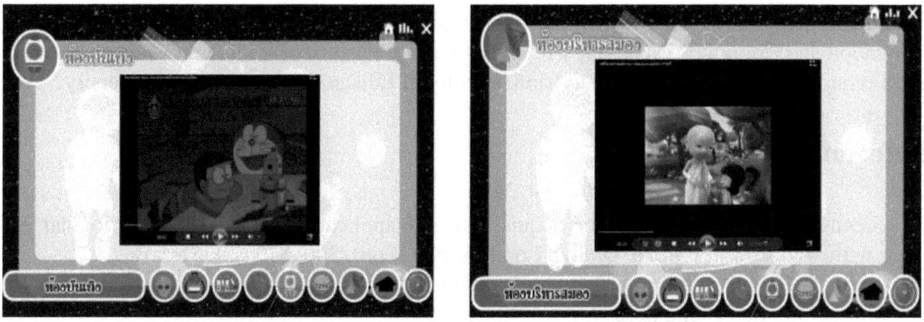

Fig. 6. (g) Edutainment room; (h) Brain-gym

Fig. 7. (i) Collaboration

7 Conclusion

The purposes of this research was to synthesize theoretical framework and designing framework of The Learning Innovation Enhance Learning Potential of the Learner‘s Using Brain-based Learning. The data analysis was preceded by analytical description and interpretative summary. The result revealed that: The learning innovation enhance learning potential of the learners using brain-based learning comprise of 9 components as following: (1) Problem base, (2) Knowledge bank, (3) Scaffolding, (4) Meaningful experience, (5) Multiple intelligence development center, (6) Relaxation room, (7) Edutainment room, (8) Brain-gym room, and (9) Collaboration. The next study for this research, we will planning to study of the efficiency of the learning innovation illustration as following: the experts review, the learners' opinions, the learners' multiple intelligences and the learning achievement. The further study should be studied about other factors such as gender, age, emotions affected multiple intelligences in order to develop a Learning Innovation Enhance Brain-based Learning, media attribute affected multiple intelligences for using such attributes to design and develop the learning innovation as a multimedia learning environment more efficiently and brain wave or specific brain area affected learners' multiple intelligences for more useful in development and enhancement of learners.

Acknowledgements. This work was supported by the Academic and Research Affairs, Innovation and Cognitive Technology Research Group, Faculty of Education, and the Research and Technology Transfers Affairs Division, Faculty of Education, Khon Kaen University.

References

1. Greenwood, R.G.W.: Educator acquisition and application of recent Neurological and cognitive research. Proc. Roy. Soc. Lond. A **295**(1966), 300–319 (2006)
2. Amanda, P., Jeri, S.: Increasing student achievement through brain-based strategies. The Brain Store, San Diego (2007)
3. Caine, R., Caine, G.: Making Connections: Teaching and the Human Brain. Addison-Wesley, Menlo Park (1994)
4. Call, N., Featherstone, S.: Thinking Child – Brain – Based Learning for the Foundation Stage. Network Educational Press Ltd., Stafford (2003)
5. Chaijaroen, S.: Educational Technology and Instructional System Development. Khon Kaen University, Khon Kaen (2006)
6. Tubar: The effect of brain- based learning to success and retention in social studies elementary education online. lkö_retim Online **6**(1), 62–75 (2007)
7. Salomon, G., Clark, R.: Re-examing the methodology of research on media and technology in education. Rev. Educ. Res. **47**, 99–120 (1977)
8. Wattanachai, S.: Learners' cognitive learning potential using learning innovation enhancing brain-based learning potential. Khon Kaen University (2008)
9. Davis, L.: Using the theory of multiple intelligences to increase fourth-grade students' academic achievement in science, Doctoral dissertations, Nova Southeastern University, Fischer Graduate School of Education and Human Services (2004)
10. Daman, B.: The effect of brain-based instruction to improve on students' academic achievement in social studies instruction. In: Paper Presented in 9th International Conference on Engineering Education, 23–28 July 2006
11. Jensen, E.: Brain-Based Learning: The New Science of Teaching & Training. The Brain Store, San Diego (2000)

Exploring the Correlation Between Attention and Cognitive Load of Students When Attending Different Classes

Shu-Chen Cheng[1(✉)], Yu-Ping Cheng[2], Chien-Hao Huang[1], and Yueh-Min Huang[2]

[1] Department of Computer Science and Information Engineering, Southern Taiwan University of Science and Technology, Tainan, Taiwan
{kittyc,ma5g0207}@stust.edu.tw

[2] Department of Engineering Science, National Cheng Kung University, Tainan, Taiwan
yuping.cheng0413@gmail.com, huang@mail.ncku.edu.tw

Abstract. Brainwaves are the signals produced by the activities of nerve cells in the human brain. When recorded and shown on scientific instruments, they have the appearance of a wave, thus earning it its name. This study was conducted by wearing a non-invasive head-mounted brainwave detecting instrument to measure the attention level of students when attending different classes. Those results are then combined with the cognitive load scale to explore the correlation between the attention and the cognitive load of each student when attending different classes. According to the study results, a student attending English class will show a higher level of attention than one attending algorithm class. Furthermore, the learner showed lower cognitive load when reviewing previously learned content than when learning for the first time. However, the learner showed higher attention value when learning for the first time than when reviewing previously learned content.

Keywords: Attention · Cognitive load · Brainwave

1 Introduction

As technology continues to advance, students can conveniently and efficiently learn or review material using technological applications. Many researchers have previously mentioned the importance of attention as the starting point for learning [1]. When learners can consistently concentrate on studies and link them to what they have already learned, they can gradually memorize what they learned for the long term. Therefore, this study adopts an instrument to detect brainwaves to record the attention and cognitive load of the learner when applying different educational materials. In this study, we aim to explore the attention and cognitive load of the learners using a brainwave instrument and the cognitive load scale and then analyze whether the association between these two factors would be significant in different classroom environments.

T.-T. Wu et al. (Eds.): ICITL 2018, LNCS 11003, pp. 205–214, 2018.
https://doi.org/10.1007/978-3-319-99737-7_21

2 Literature Review

2.1 Brain Wave

The classification of the brain's electrical waves is based on the different frequencies of the brain's previously discovered electrical wave signals, which have been named using the Greek letters α (Alpha), β (Beta), θ (Theta), δ (Delta), and γ (Gamma) waves. Figure 1 shows the waves classified by frequency, with the α wave, β wave, and γ wave classified as fast waves due to their quickly changing frequency and the θ wave and δ wave classified as slow waves due to their slowly changing frequency. The slow waves are usually generated during sleep, so they are also referred to as sleep waves. These five waves with their different frequencies represent the following [2–4]:

1. Alpha activity: These waves keep people awake and clear in a relaxed situation. The parietal lobe and occipital lobe of the brain transmit waves with a frequency of about 8–15 Hz and an oscillation of about 50 μV, which keeps people standing by for any new initiation with limited energy consumption. The brain stores relatively higher energy to quickly re-activate when new stimulation occurs to ensure smooth operation, and the individual is alert and keen to respond to any new situation. When the brain enters such a state, it is referred to as α block, that is to say, the α wave plays a role as the bridge between consciousness and unconsciousness.
2. Beta activity: These waves keep people clear and alert to any sudden change, that is to say, the β wave is only produced when people are conscious. When the parietal lobe and frontal lobe of the brain transmit a cycled wave with a frequency of 13–30 Hz and oscillation of 5–20 μV, the physical and psychological status of human beings is under the super mode of frequency to elevate the attention level with considerable energy consumption. Stress increases if the energy supply is inadequate.
3. Gamma activity: Since the frequency of γ waves is excessively fast, it is barely observed on a traditional brainwave detection instrument. However, thanks to the updated technological development, these waves can now be detected on digital brainwave detection instruments. This wave represents when people are under meditation, with a cycle wave with a frequency of about 30 ~ 60 Hz and an oscillation of 5–10 μV transmitted by the temporal lobe of the brain. This condition selectively influences people to focus, recognize, and be aware.
4. Theta activity: This wave shows when people are in a relaxed status with an interrupted consciousness. When people are under a subconscious condition, their parietal lobe and temporal lobe transmit a cycled wave with a frequency of about 4–8 Hz and an oscillation of around 30 μV. Their physical and psychological status is to renew and enhance the deep memory of the brain and re-collate memories.
5. Delta activity: This wave shows when people are in a relaxed condition with an interrupted consciousness. That is to say, for people at rest, the brain transmits a cycled wave with a frequency of about 0–4 Hz and an oscillation of around 100–200 μV. Their physical and psychological status is under deep sleep, so the δ wave directly influences the quality of sleep.

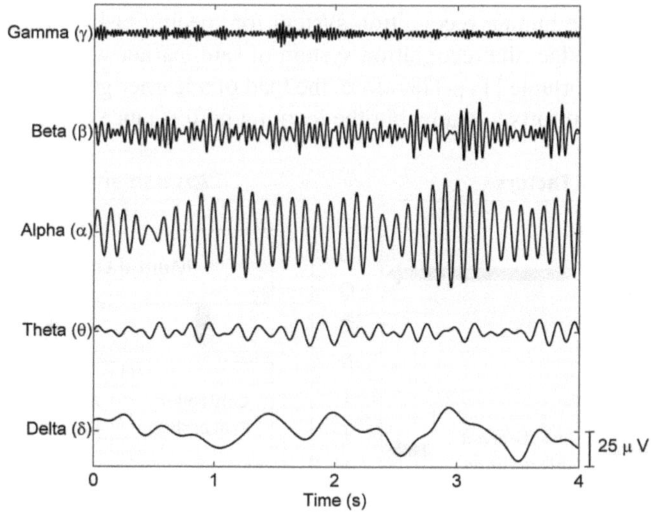

Fig. 1. Example EEG signals acquired during a rest state with closed eyes [2]

2.2 Attention

Attention is a very critical factor influencing learning performance [5]. Attention has been explained as the inert psychological activities produced by the brain [6]. Research and applications related to attention are broad, such as the investigation of attention-related brainwave signals to explore the learning performance and attitude of university students in English listening courses [7]. Through an electronic learning environment, learners provide some dynamic and static clues to explore whether their attention is influenced in different situations [8]. For example, if cell phones are used excessively in a classroom environment, the attention of the students toward the courses will be influenced [9]. The study herein was conducted to explore whether the attention of students differs with varying educational materials of courses or classroom environments.

2.3 Cognitive Load

The cognitive load is proposed to be composed of two dimensions [10], which are the assessment factors and the causal factors. As shown in Fig. 2, the causal factors are constructed by the following three factors: the more stable learner factor, the unstable task/environment factor, and the mutual interactions between those two factors. Meanwhile, the assessment factors are the results of the cognitive load, which can be discussed with regard to three aspects: the mental load, which is influenced by the task/environment factor to cause fluctuations of the cognitive load; mental effort, which is internally influenced and controlled by the learner to cause fluctuations of the cognitive load; and learning performance, which is influenced by the consequences of cause and effect to cause fluctuations of the cognitive load. Furthermore, the cognitive load refers to the load produced in the human recognition system for specific tasks. When a learner is studying for knowledge, the recognition system of said learner will study harder if he or she feels uncomfortable [11]. Therefore, the load of a learner grows relatively larger when making more efforts to study, but the learning performance decreases [10].

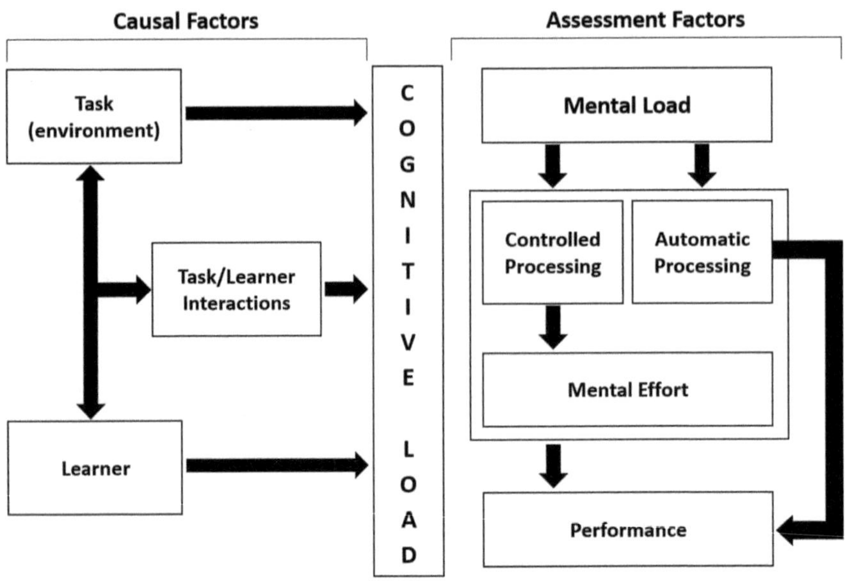

Fig. 2. Schematic representation of the cognitive load construct [10]

3 Method

By analyzing brainwave data and cognitive load scale in this study, we were able to explore the association between the attention and cognitive load of students attending an algorithm course and an English course, performing the experiments in the two different classes. The algorithm course and the English course are taught by the same teacher once a week. The students wore the instrument for brainwave detection and filled out the cognitive load scale after each class or chapter. Furthermore, in the review session of the algorithm course, each student was monitored for testing the same contents to compare the differences of the attention. Then, the students filled out the cognitive load scale for the cognitive load variation analysis between the two learning instances.

3.1 Subjects

The subjects for this experiment were students in their junior year in the Information Engineering Department of the Colleague of Engineering of some university.

3.2 Experimental Process

Prior to the experiment, we explained the overall procedure and objective of the experiment to all the learners. After confirming that all the learners properly understood, the experiment could be implemented smoothly. A demonstration about how to wear the brainwave detection instrument and prevent signal detection failure or interruption of the brainwave detection instrument due to some other factors was performed. Then, the learners started their studies in the classes while wearing the instrument and were monitored by the brainwave monitoring program to ensure that the brainwave data were transported normally.

Data were recorded when the classes moved to the next chapter or the educational materials were changed by the teachers. The brainwave signals were observed for changes at such points. The student was then asked to fill out the cognitive load scale after the courses. All the attention data collected in the study were analyzed in seconds to explore the attention value change for every second of the learner compared with the cognitive load scale questionnaire filled out by the learner.

3.3 Research Tool

We adopted laptops in this study to easily implement the experiment in the classrooms. To ensure that the testing process could receive stable brainwave signals and record them smoothly, the minimum requirements of the laptops were as follows: equipped with at least 8G of memory, Windows 10, and more than 128 G of capacity, which allowed us to save and analyze the data and relationship of attention value and cognitive load.

The subjects of the study wore a non-invasive head-mounted brainwave detecting instrument (BrainLink) produced by Macrotellect Ltd. to detect the attention value and relaxation value of the learners when attending different classes with different educational materials.

The delicate instrument is designed to detect brainwaves through the TGAM electroencephalogram module. Collecting students' brainwave signals through the dry electrode placed as the front head sensor and transmitting them to the system by bluetooth module can transform them into digital signal parameters. They were then recorded by the brainwave monitoring system for further analysis of the association between waves. The apparatus is illustrated in Fig. 3.

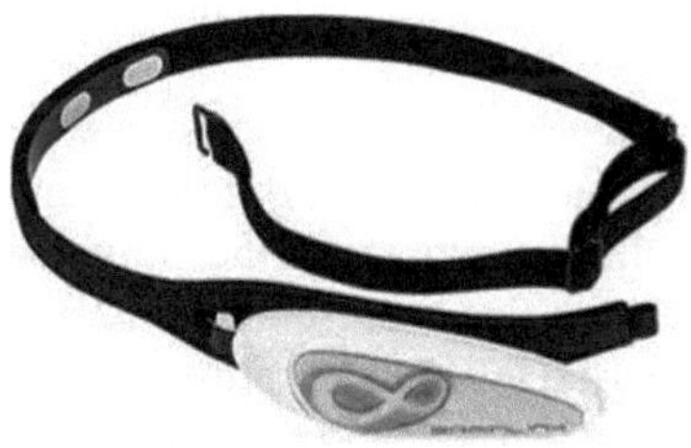

Fig. 3. Head-mounted brainwave detecting instrument (BrainLink) [12]

4 Experimental Results

This study applied a brainwave detecting instrument to measure the data of students during algorithm and English classes. Figure 4 shows the difference of attention value in the algorithm and English course, with the horizontal axis referring to the time sustained and the vertical axis representing the attention value. As shown in Fig. 4, the solid blue line represents the individual average value in the algorithm class, while the dotted blue line represents the group average value in the algorithm class; the solid orange line represents the individual average value in the English class; and the dotted orange line represents the group average value in the English class. Between the individual average value and the group average value, the attention while attending the algorithm course was lower than that while attending the English class. Furthermore, in the aspect of cognitive load, Fig. 5 shows the difference of cognitive load while attending the algorithm class and attending the English course, with the solid orange line representing the cognitive load in the English class and the solid blue line representing the cognitive load in the algorithm class. According to the results shown here, the cognitive load while attending the algorithm class was higher than that while attending the English course.

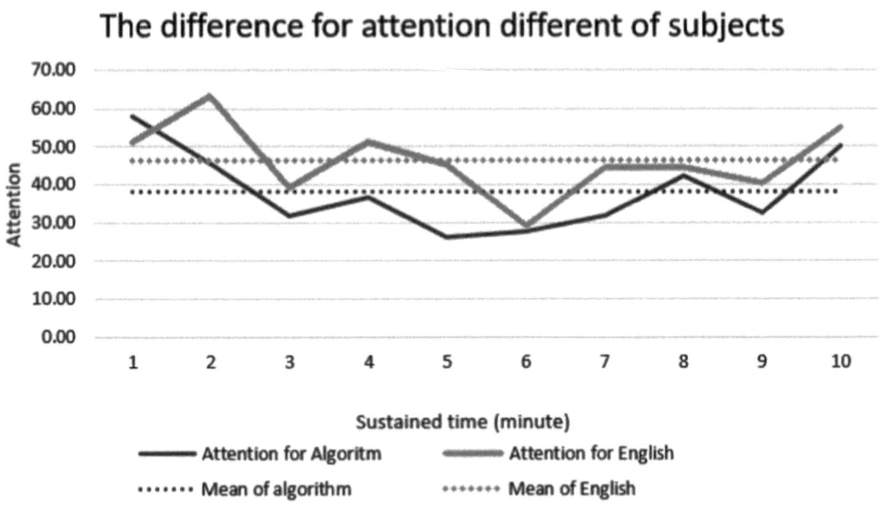

Fig. 4. The attention values of students attending different classes (Color figure online)

This study explored the attention values of students when learning new content and reviewing the same one previously learned while attending the algorithm course. As indicated in Fig. 6, the solid blue line represents the individual average value for learning new content, and the dotted blue line represents the group average value for learning new content; meanwhile, the solid green line represents the individual average value for reviewing the same content just learned, and the dotted green line represents the group average value for reviewing the same content just learned. The learners were found to show different attention levels for learning new contents and for reviewing the same

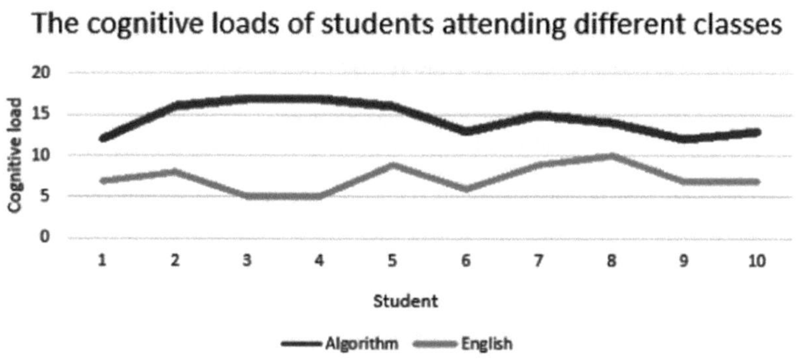

Fig. 5. The cognitive loads of students attending different classes (Color figure online)

contents just learned during the algorithm course. However, neither of them differed much from each other, though a lower attention value was observed for reviewing the contents just learned.

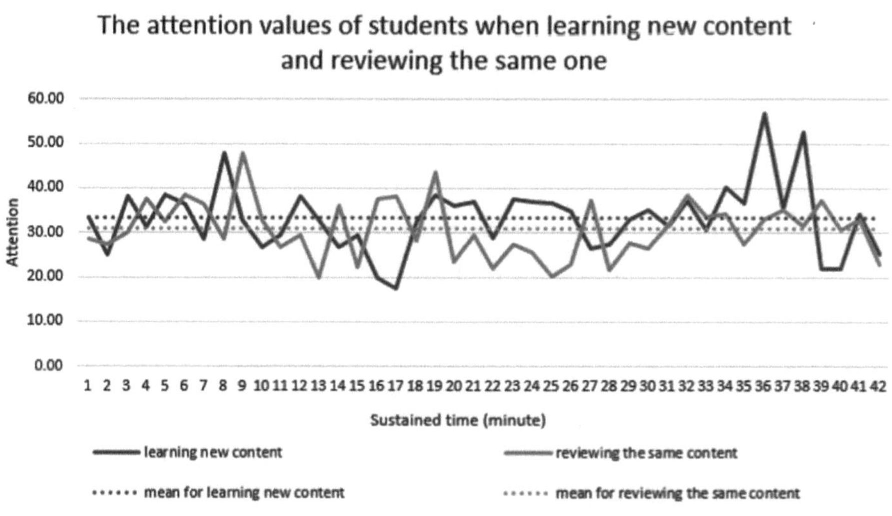

Fig. 6. The attention values of students when learning new content and reviewing the same one (Color figure online)

This study has classified the cognitive load into the three different levels of low, medium, and high. The classification criteria was calculated using the sum of the scores of the four questions on the questionnaire filled out by the learner after the classes. The cognitive load and classification determined the level of the load. Figure 7 illustrates the average attention value of 22 learners with different cognitive loads during the algorithm and English classes; the solid orange line represents that the load was low, the solid green line represents medium, and the solid blue line represents high. The dotted lines represent the group average value respectively. With these three classification levels, the range of each classification was: low (4–8), medium (9–15), and high (16–20). The questions of the cognitive load questionnaire were as follows:

Cognitive load questionnaire
I feel like I have made a lot of effort to be able to learn in this way.
1 2 3 4 5
I feel like I need to make a lot of effort to learn the content of this study course.
1 2 3 4 5
In this kind of situation, I cannot concentrate on my studies by way of the educational materials applied.
1 2 3 4 5
In this kind of situation, I feel very stressed by the educational materials applied.
1 2 3 4 5

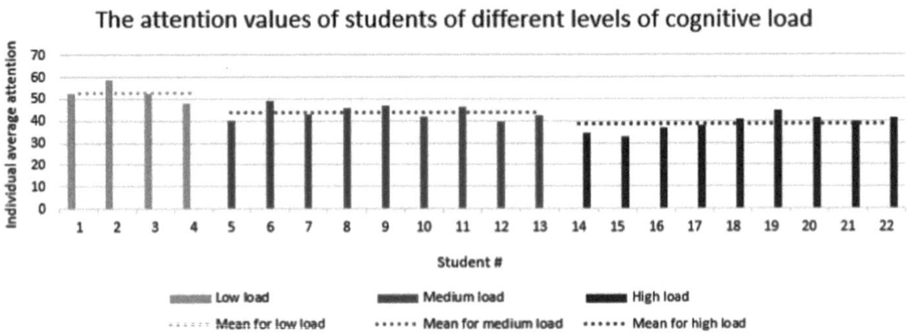

Fig. 7. The attention values of students of different levels of cognitive load (Color figure online)

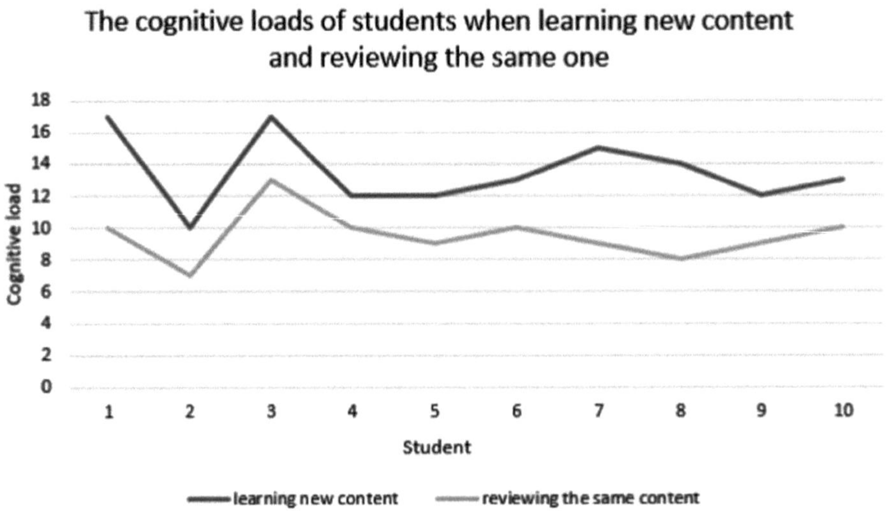

Fig. 8. The cognitive loads of students when learning new content and reviewing the same one (Color figure online)

In this study, we compared the cognitive load of 10 learners for learning new content with the one for reviewing the same content just learned while attending the algorithm class. As indicated in Fig. 8, the solid blue line represents the cognitive load for learning new content, and the solid green line represented the cognitive load for reviewing the same content just learned. As shown by the results, the cognitive load for learning new content was significantly higher than the one for reviewing the same content just learned.

5 Conclusion

This study adopted an instrument to measure brainwaves to explore correlation between the attention value and the cognitive load of the learner while attending different classes. As the study results show, the English course induces higher attention and lower cognitive load than the algorithm course does. On the other hand, while attending the algorithm class, the learner showed higher attention for learning new content than for reviewing the same content just learned, while the learner showed lower cognitive load for reviewing the content learned before than learning the content at the first time.

Acknowledgements. This study is supported in part by Ministry of Science and Technology, Taiwan under Contract No. MOST-106-2511-S-218-001-MY3 and MOST-106-2511-S-006-001-MY3

References

1. Kuo, Y.C., Chu, H.C., Tsai, M.C.: Effects of an integrated physiological signal-based attention-promoting and English listening system on students' learning performance and behavioral patterns. Comput. Hum. Behav. **75**, 218–227 (2017)
2. Campisi, P., La Rocca, D., Scarano, G.: EEG for automatic person recognition. Computer **45**(7), 87–89 (2012)
3. Gregory, T.K., Pettus, D.C.: An electroencephalographic processing algorithm specifically intended for analysis of cerebral electrical activity. J. Clin. Monit. **2**(3), 190–197 (1986)
4. Sanei, S., Chambers, J.A.: EEG Signal Processing. Wiley (2013)
5. Avery, M.: Preschool physical education: a practical approach. J. Phys. Educ. Recreation Dance **65**(6), 37–39 (1994)
6. Hanslmayr, S., Gross, J., Klimesch, W., Shapiro, K.L.: The role of alpha oscillations in temporal attention. Brain Res. Rev. **67**(1–2), 331–343 (2011)
7. Kuo, Y.-C., Chu, H.-C., Tsai, M.-C.: Effects of an integrated physiological signal-based attention-promoting and English listening system on students' learning performance and behavioral patterns. Comput. Hum. Behav. **75**, 218–227 (2017)
8. Ilgaz, H., Altun, A., Aşkar, P.: The effect of sustained attention level and contextual cueing on implicit memory performance for e-learning environments. Comput. Hum. Behav. **39**, 1–7 (2014)
9. Mendoza, J.S., Pody, B.C., Lee, S., Kim, M., McDonough, I.M.: The effect of cellphones on attention and learning: the influences of time, distraction, and nomophobia. Comput. Hum. Behav. **86**, 52–60 (2018)
10. Paas, F.G., Van Merriënboer, J.J.: Variability of worked examples and transfer of geometrical problem-solving skills: a cognitive-load approach. J. Educ. Psychol. **86**(1), 122 (1994)

11. Feinberg, S., Murphy, M.: Applying cognitive load theory to the design of web-based instruction. In: Paper Presented at the Proceedings of IEEE Professional Communication Society International Professional Communication Conference and Proceedings of the 18th Annual ACM International Conference on Computer Documentation: Technology & Teamwork (2000)
12. SH Ltd. http://www.brain-sh.tw/product_content.php?p_id=134

Human Connectedness to Nature: Comparison of Natural vs. Virtual Experiences

Mary D. Smith[1,3(✉)], Sean Getchell[2,3], and Megan Weatherly[1]

[1] Center for Teaching and Learning, Stephen F. Austin State University, 1936 North Street, Nacogdoches, TX 75962, USA
{smithmd1,msweatherly}@sfasu.edu

[2] Harris Health System, Houston, USA
seangetchell@my.unt.edu

[3] College of Information, University of North Texas, 1155 Union Circle, Denton, TX 76203, USA

Abstract. There is a growing number of studies completed in which virtual environments have been and are being evaluated for their effectiveness with regard to a more positive learning experience and improved learning outcomes. Though the impact of virtual learning environments has been researched most thoroughly in the fields of medicine and military and police operations, an increasing number of studies focus on the virtual learning environment as a whole. This study will attempt to determine student experience a more significant potential positive impact on stress and well-being in nature or a simulated natural environment experienced via virtual reality. This study is a connectedness to nature study where students report how connected to life they feel after being immersed in the setting for a period.

Keywords: Virtual reality · Nature · Educational technology
Multimedia learning · Affordances

1 Introduction

The ability to immerse individuals in virtual environments has transformed not only the learning environment but also the mental health of individuals. Virtual reality (VR) is defined as an environment that is generated by a computer and provides three-dimensional images with which users can interact. This interaction feels to the participant as if they are actually in the environment itself, while not exposing them to the potential danger around them. As technology progresses and the VR's reach expands, the comparison of virtual environments with real-time environments is worthy of investigation. Traditional instruction has typically occurred mostly in a face-to-face setting. The use of blended and virtual environments to create or supplement learning outcomes continues to grow in education. These environments include a face-to-face combined with an online component as well as either only face-to-face or the single online delivery environment. This study focuses on the face-to-face only environment.

While much interest exists with virtual reality (VR), the challenges of funding and modality, or the mode in which something exists or is experienced, continue to surround

T.-T. Wu et al. (Eds.): ICITL 2018, LNCS 11003, pp. 215–219, 2018.
https://doi.org/10.1007/978-3-319-99737-7_22

this topic. Fundamental questions appear around cognition and epistemology as users are immersed in such environments. Noted are the advancement in visual technology and its contribution to learning online and at a distance [1]. While the Abrimi study utilizes the distance or online environment for the primary method of instruction, the instructor-student interaction, the student-student interaction, and the student content interaction is vitally important in all types of learning environments. Some of the potential challenges when introducing students to this particular study include immersing them in an environment where there are hazards such as weather, bugs or other animal hazards as compared to a controlled virtual situation where none of these exists, could make a difference to an individual.

2 Theory and Research

Research in both faces to face, distance, and blended environments note that there are challenges when utilizing mixed environments [2]. Boelens, Wever, and Voet indicate that there are challenges when using blended environments. These challenges include the maintaining flexibility in instruction, incorporating interaction that is stimulating for the learner, and facilitation of the learning process by the instructor, all while "fostering an affective learning climate" [2] (p. 2). Distance education can and does happen in a variety of modalities, whether solely online or in a blended environment. The ability of learners to feel engaged in a situation, whether virtually or actually has varied among studies.

Research is well established that being in nature can have restorative effects on humans [3]. With the increasing use of technology, Louv [4] have posited that humans are becoming more disconnected to nature. But, can technology actually help to connect us to nature? This research seeks to understand the possibilities for virtual reality (VR) Nature in creating the same impacts on humans that actual nature does already.

Perrin and Benassi [5] conducted a study that utilized results from previous studies that measured a perceived connectedness to nature. Mayer and Frantz [6] reported that a person's feeling of being connected to nature equates to the emotional nature connection of an individual as related to their perceived relationship. This study by Mayer and Frantz was conducted to determine whether the participants felt more connected to nature and its effect on the feeling of connectedness to the natural world. They performed a confirmatory factor analysis, which showed that the participants did not focus on an emotional connection to nature, but instead felt more of a link to their natural world. Shin [7] discussed the role of affordances concerning virtual environments. The affordances in this study are related to VR as a resource which supports the environment. These affordances depend on the user is actively engaged in the environment rather than recipients who are passively involved. After a ten-year review of mostly empirical research, Mikropoulos and Natsis [8] propose that based on these studies, VR is an opportunity to incorporate multisensory learning and provides a sense of presence that aids the learning and social interaction among students.

3 Method

Participants included 40 students over the age of 18 attending a public university. The participants in this study were all traditional face-to-face students enrolled in courses delivered in forestry and psychology classes. The study utilized an experimental design with the experiment and control group. Students received pre- and post-experimental questionnaire. Each participant was informed that he/she might leave the study at any time without penalty. All research investigators were trained and worked under supervision. Experimental sessions lasted approximately 30 min. At the end of the study, participants completed a post-experimental questionnaire which was the same as the pre-experimental questionnaire.

Participants were recruited using the Psychology Department SONA - the psychology department's online research recruitment portal. If accepted, the participants were randomly assigned the virtual (the experimental group) or the actual nature experience (the control group). The experiment of the exploratory investigation was followed with a questionnaire to assess whether or not five minutes of time spent in Actual Nature is the same in terms of connection to nature and wellbeing as five minutes of VR Nature. Students completed a pre-experimental questionnaire and then spent quietly alone in either VR nature or actual nature. After this time, students took a post-experimental questionnaire to determine whether or not any changes have occurred. The participants completed a questionnaire that sought to measure whether they perceived feelings of the same connectedness to nature when interacting with nature while in an actual outdoor environment as compared to a virtual environment.

The questionnaires consisted of three scales to measure students' perceptions. (1) *The Nature Relatedness Scale (NRS)* measure is a 21-item scale that measures participant's perception of their connectedness to nature [9]. This is a Likert scale which is rated from one to five and measures how connected to nature participants feel at a trait level. (2) *The State Connectedness to Nature Scale (SCNS)* [4] which is a short 14 item questionnaire that contains a five range Likert scale which determines the degree to which the participant feels connected to nature. (3) *The Scale of Positive and Negative Experience (SPANE).* This brief 12-item scale, measures both positive and negative experiences with six items related to each of the experiences. The full range of positive and negative experiences is measured and may include indicators of specific feelings that may be unique with regard to the participant's culture acceptable [10, 11].

4 Results

Significant difference between pre-and post-experimental survey were not found. A marginal significant difference, $p = .053$, change from pre- to post- (post-score minuspre-score) for the Nature Relatedness-Experience subscale was observed. One point of interest were those who were in the VR condition who showed increases in their experience scores from pre- to post- ($M = .1000$), whereas those in the outside condition showed decreases ($M = -.1136$), $t(40) = -1.992$, $p = .053$.

Significant differences between the VR and Outside conditions on State Connectedness to Nature, t (39.070) = 3.318, p = .002 and Satisfaction with Life, t (40) = −2.634, p = .012. For SCwN, Ps reported feeling more connected to nature after being outside (M = 3.5325) as opposed to VR (M = 3.1357; that seems good). However, people in the VR condition (M = 5.4500) felt significantly more satisfied with their lives after experiencing nature than did people in the outside condition (M = 4.509). Of course, the problem with using post-only data is that it doesn't account for preexisting difference, especially with our small sample. Based on excluding participant 102, there is also a marginal difference between VR (M = 7.4) and outside (M = 9.0) on the negative subscale of the SPANE, t (36.593) = 1.819, p = .077.

5 Discussion

Initial data analysis does not indicate a significant difference in the participants' perception and affect in an actual experience in nature as compared to a virtual experience [4]. Mikropoulos and Natsis [8] conducted a review of empirical research spanning a ten-year period from 1999 to 2009. Engagement with nature's beauty as compared to some previous research on the connectedness that individuals feel in nature is important as reported by Zhang, Howell, and Iyer, [12]. Also noted in the aforementioned study is that there is a difference in the connectedness with nature and the perceived well-being while in nature.

Previous research has shown that participation in nature provides a generally positive result on well-being. The ability to feel connected with nature and experience the benefits of being immersed in a natural environment can be enhanced by and could benefit from virtual environments. VR packages range from desktop solutions to fully developed VR labs with sophisticated headsets. Comparing the various types of VR applications for face-to-face, blended or hybrid, as well as online or purely distance-based courses has excellent potential.

6 Conclusion

The research findings identify the effectiveness of VR in a variety of learning environments and disciplines indicating the influence and potential for learning outcomes. The measured efficiency can vary among application and disciplines. There has been much positive research and results conducted in the medical as well as military fields. When broadening the use of VR into diverse disciplinary areas, future research could include categorizing the use of VR with respect to discipline(s). An essential goal in setting instructional context is to provide learning with multiple representations facilitating learning outcomes at cognitive, affective-social and psychomotor learning domains [13]. Respective to this study, repeated research for the connectedness to nature whether actual or in a virtual environment.

Acknowledgments. The IRB was approved for the study providing confidentiality. All study participants were treated within and ethic of respect. All participants were informed about the objectives of the study.

References

1. Abrami, P.C., Bernard, R.M., Bures, E.M., Borokhovski, E., Tamim, R.M.: Interaction in distance education and online learning: using evidence and theory to improve practice. J. Comput. High. Educ. **23**, 82–103 (2011)
2. Boelens, R., De Wever, B., Voet, M.: Four key challenges to the design of blended learning: a systematic literature review. Educ. Res. Rev. **22**, 1–18 (2017)
3. Hartig, T., Van den Berg, A.E., Hagerhall, C.M., Tomalak, M., Bauer, N., Hansmann, R., Bell, S.: Health benefits of nature experience: psychological, social and cultural processes. In: Nilsson, K., et al. (eds.) Forests, Trees and Human Health, pp. 127–168. Springer, Dordrecht (2011). https://doi.org/10.1007/978-90-481-9806-1_5
4. Perrin, J.L., Benassi, V.A.: The connectedness to nature scale: a measure of emotional connection to nature? J. Environ. Psychol. **29**, 434–440 (2009)
5. Louv, R.: Last Child in the Woods: Saving Our Children from Nature-Deficit Disorder. N.C. Algonquin Books of Chapel Hill, Chapel Hill (2005)
6. Mayer, F.S., Frantz, C.M.: The connectedness to nature scale: a measure of individuals' feeling in community with nature. J. Environ. Psychol. **24**, 503–515 (2004)
7. Shin, D.H.: The role of affordance in the experience of virtual reality learning: technological and affective affordances in virtual reality. Telematics Inform. **34**, 1826–1836 (2017)
8. Mikropoulos, T.A., Natsis, A.: Educational virtual environments: a ten-year review of empirical research (1999–2009). Comput. Educ. **56**, 769–780 (2011)
9. Nisbet, E.K., Zelenski, J.M., Murphy, S.A.: The nature relatedness scale: linking individuals' connection with nature to environmental concern and behavior. Environ. Behav. **41**, 715–740 (2009)
10. Diener, E., Emmons, R.A., Larsen, R.J., Griffin, S.: The satisfaction with life scale. J. Pers. Assess. **49**, 71–75 (1985)
11. Diener, E., Wirtz, D., Tov, W., Kim-Prieto, C., Choi, D., Oishi, S., Biswas-Diener, R.: New measures of well-being: flourishing and positive and negative feelings. Soc. Indic. Res. **39**, 247–266 (2009)
12. Zhang, J.W., Howell, R.T., Iyer, R.: Engagement with natural beauty moderates the positive relation between connectedness with nature and psychological well-being. J. Environ. Psychol. **38**, 55–63 (2014)
13. Volk, M., Cotic, M., Zajc, M., Istenic Starcic, A.: Tablet-based cross-curricular maths vs. traditional maths classroom practice for higher-order learning outcomes. Comput. Educ. **114**, 1–23 (2016)

Pedagogies to Innovative Technologies

Developing the Capability Indicators for CNC Machine R&D Staff in Taiwan

Dyi-Cheng Chen(✉) and Tzu-Wen Chen

Department of Industrial Education and Technology,
National Changhua University of Education, Changhua 500, Taiwan
dcchen@cc.ncue.edu.tw

Abstract. The purpose of this paper was to develop the capability indicators for R&D staff of CNC machine industry in Taiwan. In order to improve the effectiveness of developing new CNC machine ability and working skills of R&D staff. In the first parts of this study, three experts in the CNC machine industry field were interviewed, and a list of capability indicator was concluded. In the second part of the study, 10 field experts were invited as subjects. Using the Delphi technique, questionnaires are constructed to assess capability indicators for R&D staff of CNC machine industry. In the third of the study, the data collected from the questionnaires were analyzed using a non-parametric Wilcoxon signed rank test. Finally, this study concluded 31 capability indicators under four dimensions for R&D staff of CNC machine industry in Taiwan.

Keywords: CNC machine · R&D staff · Capability indicators

1 Introduction

In order to strengthen Taiwan's industrial competitiveness and raise GDP per capita, our government is committed to building a New Economic Development Model with the core values of "Innovation, Employment and Distribution" in mind [1]. The competitive CNC machine market and the greater awareness require providing high quality and more efficient, high-tech CNC machine. As is well known, modern CNC machine have become much more complex, both mechanically and electrically [2]. In order to promote intelligent manufacturing technologies, the Taiwan government invested 12 million US$ to build an intelligent manufacturing park, and purchased hardware and software facilities such as intelligent machine tools to provide aerospace components, metal transport tools, hand tools, and 3C et al. Major intelligent industrial manufacturing technologies [3]. 2016 in Taiwan, the total output value of the machine tool global market was 65 billion US$. In the 2017, EMO (Exposition Mondiale de la Machine-Outil. Is a European trade show for the manufacturing industries.) There are 179 Taiwanese machine tool companies take part in EMO exhibition. The total number of Taiwanese machine tool companies is less than the Germany and Italy, ranking third place in EMO exhibition. In Taiwan, CNC machine have long been proven to be reliable, accurate and economical among industrial users from across the globe. The CNC machines embody precision machining suitable for specific shaping and forming applications. Their growing presence in the aerospace industry has caught the

T.-T. Wu et al. (Eds.): ICITL 2018, LNCS 11003, pp. 223–230, 2018.
https://doi.org/10.1007/978-3-319-99737-7_23

attention of quite build an airplane in the U.S. The acquisition of skill through education and training has long been acknowledged as one of the principal forces driving economic growth [4]. Public attention towards a growing manufacturing and an industrial base is rising, especially in the United States. CNC machine manufacturing is becoming ever more important [5]. The CNC machine industry and the school can form a partnership based on the principle of resource sharing. For schools, it helps the CNC machine staff to work immediately after graduation; for the CNC machine industry, it can reduce the cost of pre-service training, which will help achieve their goals and achieve long-term cooperation advantages. It has promoted cooperation between the CNC machine industry and schools to cultivate talents and shorten the gap between "learning" and "skills". This study can be explored through relevant literature, and then analyzed by interviewing methods to unify the CNC machine industry R&D staff, should have the ability to work; and invited experts and scholars in the industry to put forward relevant views, unified the ability to complete and use the relevant research methods to construct the capability indicators of the R&D staff of the CNC machine industry.

2 Literature Review

2.1 Concepts of CNC Machine

CNC machine have long been proven to be reliable in Taiwan, accurate and economical among industrial users from across the globe. These machines embody precision machining suitable for specific shaping and forming applications. Their growing presence in the aerospace industry has caught the attention of quite a few airplane builders in the United Stated [6]. CNC machine is a process used in the manufacturing sector that involves the use of computers to control machine tool, Lathes and milling are typical CNC machines. The goal of the modern manufacturing technologies is to the shortest period of time and in the most cost effective way [7]. For the equipment manufacturers, how to demonstrate the characteristics of the device and to satisfy the needs of the customers is an important factor in determining the customer's motivation to buy [8]. The CNC machine is currently the best production equipment. And, control of CNC machining processes is presently receiving significant attention due to potential economic benefits associated with automated machining [9]. Most countries also develop new features of CNC machines to develop the economy and increase competitiveness (Fig. 1).

2.2 Concepts of R&D Staff

R&D is a knowledge-intensive process existing stock of knowledge is used as an input to develop new knowledge and new applications of existing knowledge [10]. Knowledge and the ability to learn new knowledge are crucial to maintaining a firm's competitiveness in today's world with rapid rates of technological change and technology replacement [11]. Changes in technologies often influence the strategies of R&D entities so significantly that a company, an industry, or even a country may win

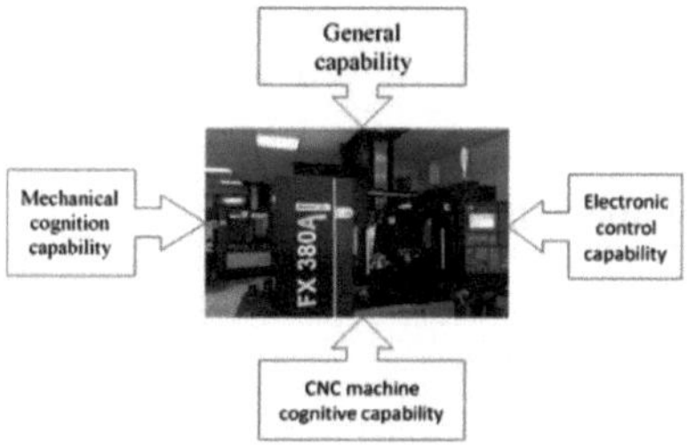

Fig. 1. CNC machines capability dimension

or lose a competitive edge. Correspondingly, researchers in the CNC machine have observed interactions between such technological changes, paying significant attention to "convergence" [12]. The globalization of R&D has made rapid progress in the top R&D investing [13] to promote competitiveness (Fig. 2).

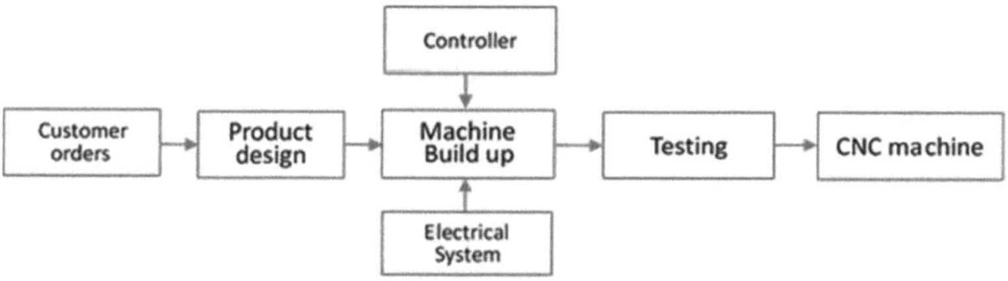

Fig. 2. CNC machines design process

2.3 Concepts of Capability Indicators

Capability Indicators offer potential for defining effective and superior performance and then aligning curriculum and other learning opportunities with individual development goals [14]. In order to achieve the results of this paper, the Delphi technique has been used. The Delphi technique is a widely used and accepted method for gathering data from respondents within their domain of expertise. The technique is designed as a group communication process which aims to achieve a convergence of opinion on a specific real-world issue [15].

3 Research Methods

3.1 Research Design

The research design of this paper includes the following procedures [16].

(1) Identifying desired professional capability required for CNC machine R&D staff education.

The research invitation three experts in the CNC machine industry field were interviewed; the opinion experts interviewed will be form preliminary questionnaire content.

(2) Forming a capability analysis group.

We invite 10 experts in the CNC machine industry field (contains three teachers) forming a Delphi technique group.

(3) Using a professional capability questionnaire to collect research data.

Distributing the questionnaire to 10 field experts and apply three-round Delphi technique questionnaire. The ultimate purpose of expert opinion is to make the opinions of each expert consistent.

(4) Conducting data analysis.

This paper using descriptive statistics, Kendall coefficient of concordance, and nonparametric Wilcoxon signed rank test, can be used to determine whether two dependent samples were selected from populations having the same distribution.

(5) Propose those required professional capability as perceived by field experts.

After experts interviewed, opinion collection, statistical analysis, this paper had proposed capability indicators.

3.2 Questionnaire Design

To fulfill the research objectives, the questionnaire was designed to collect data for CNC machine R&D staff education in 4 dimension: (1) General capability, (2) Mechanical cognitive capability, (3) Electrical control conative capability, (4) Profession capability of CNC machine. Each competency was rated by its importance to job performance in the CNC machine industry. A liker scale was used in this questionnaire. Ten members of the Delphi group were asked to assess each capability according to the following five-point scale: 5-very important, 4-more important, 3-Neutral opinion, 2-less important, and 1-least important in the CNC machine R&D job performance. Capability were classified using cumulative percentages calculated from the importance ratings provided by respondents, as follows: (1) Essential(must have) with 90% of the responses indicating 4 or 5; (2) Important (should have) with 90% of the responses indicating 3, 4, or 5; and (3) Unimportant, as indicated by a failure to meet the above criteria [17, 18].

3.3 Participants

The three-round Delphi technique questionnaire used in this study was distributed to members of the Delphi group in Feb, Mar; 2018. These 10 Delphi group members included 7 field supervisor in CNC machine R&D and 3 scholars at the technology university in Taiwan.

4 Result

After the questionnaires were received, the Kendall coefficient of concordance test was applied to evaluate the relationship between the Chi-square value of 40.528 (see Table 1) and those competencies indicators that the participants considered important. Tables 2, 3, 4 and 5 displays the ranked results, including the mean values of the scores and SD. All mean scores of the 31 competencies were above 3.75, indicating that the Delphi group considered the included competencies as "essential". As seen in Tables 2, 3, 4 and 5, using analysis based on the four dimensions of capability indices proposed, the dimensions deemed to be of greatest importance were General capability dimension (M = 4.21), Mechanical cognitive capability dimension (M = 4.66), Electrical control conative capability dimension (M = 3.93), Profession Capability of CNC Machine dimension (M = 4.58).

Table 1. Kendall coefficient of concordance test

N	10
Kendall's W[a]	0.811
Chi-square	40.528
df	10
Asymp.Sig.	0.000

a Kendall's coefficient of concordance.

Table 2. Analysis of consistency related in general capability

Capability indices	Mean	SD	Wilcoxon signed-rank test
General capability	4.21		
1.1 Industrial analysis	4.21	0.65	–3.31*
1.2 National safety standards	4.15	0.71	–3.25*
1.3 Project management	3.99	0.82	–2.86*
1.4 Quality control	4.05	0.74	–3.01*
1.5 Patent and intellectual property	4.15	0.80	–3.23*
1.6 Office software application	4.01	0.85	–3.01*
1.7 Teamwork	4.39	0.75	–3.22*
1.8 Foreign language communication	4.55	0.60	–3.25*

*$p < 0.05$.

Table 3. Analysis of consistency related in mechanical cognitive capability dimension

Capability indices	Mean	SD	Wilcoxon signed-rank test
Mechanical cognitive capability	4.66		
2.1 Mechanical manufacture	4.66	0.40	–3.31*
2.2 Mechanical design	4.82	0.33	–3.08*

(*continued*)

Table 3. (*continued*)

Capability indices	Mean	SD	Wilcoxon signed-rank test
2.3 CAD/CAE software application	4.79	0.51	–3.27*
2.4 Tolerance selection and decision	4.88	0.38	–3.12*
2.5 The cognitive of mechanical parts	4.52	0.45	–3.23*
2.6 The ISO specification	4.79	0.51	–3.27*
2.7 Mechanical drawing	4.69	0.48	–3.11*
2.8 Mechanical materials	4.43	0.57	–3.16*
2.9 Mechanical treatment	4.39	0.75	–3.14*

*$p < 0.05$.

Table 4. Analysis of consistency related in electrical control conative capability dimension

Capability indices	Mean	SD	Wilcoxon signed-rank test
Electrical control conative capability	3.93		
3.1 Hydraulic pressure	3.75	0.57	–3.33*
3.2 PLC skills	3.93	0.59	–3.01*
3.3 Electromechanical integration	4.11	0.73	–3.25*
3.4 Programming language	3.88	0.38	–2.99*
3.5 Principle of sensor	3.95	0.59	–3.09*
3.6 Electrical drawing	4.25	0.52	–3.13*
3.7 Industrial wiring	3.85	0.34	–3.31*
3.8 Electrical control component	3.76	0.50	–3.31*

*$p < 0.05$.

Table 5. Analysis of consistency related in profession capability of CNC machine dimension

Capability indices	Mean	SD	Wilcoxon signed-rank test
Profession capability of CNC machine	4.58		
4.1 Control system	4.46	0.53	–3.02*
4.2 Transmission system design	4.25	0.52	–3.13*
4.3 Principle of CNC machine	5.00	0.00	–3.08*
4.4 Process analysis	4.71	0.46	–3.22*
4.5 CNC machine structural design	4.88	0.38	–3.12*
4.6 Exterior design of CNC machine	4.21	0.65	–3.31*

*$p < 0.05$.

5 Discussions

Each indicator is given in Tables 2, 3, 4 and 5, and by using the Wilcoxon Signed Rank test the authors evaluated whether there exists a statistically significance difference between the hypothesized mean of 3 (neutral). All of 31 indicators showed a statistically significant difference ($p < 0.05$) through the Wilcoxon Signed Rank test. In Tables 2, 3, 4 and 5, since these p-values were very small, this implies that the mean is sure to be larger than three. Nonparametric tests often are used in conjunction with small samples [19]. In the majority of the applications, the hypothesis is concerned with the value of a median, the difference between medians. This study was limited to a select Delphi group of Taiwanese participants who are well in R&D staff of CNC machine industry.

6 Conclusion

The Tables 2, 3, 4 and 5 shows the results of three rounds of Delphi technique expert questionnaire, including general capability dimension (8 capabilities), Mechanical cognitive capability dimension (9 capabilities), Electrical control conative capability dimension (8 capabilities), and Profession Capability of CNC Machine dimension (7 competencies); and considered essential for the R&D staff of CNC machine industry were proposed. The appropriate non-parametric Wilcoxon signed rank test was used, which was helpful to understand the results. This study aimed to identify the competencies required by university students in CNC machine industry. Based on the literature review, interviews with CNC machine field experts, and the Delphi technique, 31 capacities considered essential for the design of R&D staff of CNC machine industry were identified. Simply put, the results of this paper include the following: (1) Analyzing the practical required for R&D staff of CNC machine industry and (2) those capabilities were considered to be of equal importance; in other words, all essential as perceived by field experts. The implications of the results in this paper are dependent upon the degree to which those findings can be extrapolated. This level of specificity was a requirement of the Delphi procedures to ensure that the competencies identified were an accurate and comprehensive reflection of all aspects of effective performance. This paper was conducted with relatively small samples, especially of the precision measurement experts. This may have caused a sample selection bias problem. The analytic hierarchy process can be applied to future studies on CNC machine education in technology university and election engineer for CNC machine industry.

References

1. Leu, J.H.: Towards a New Industrial Development Model, Industrial Development Bureau, Ministry of Economic Affairs (2016)
2. Hiroyuki, C.: Sources of machine-tool industry leadership in the 1990s: overlooked intrafirm factors. In: Center Discussion Paper, pp. 837–839 (2001)
3. Liu, S.J.: Taiwan government create the capital of intelligence machinery in Taichung, Commercial Times (2017)
4. Lee, W.B., Li, J.G., Cheung, C.F.: Development of a virtual training workshop in ultra-precision machining. Int. J. Eng. Educ. **18**(5), 584–596 (2002)
5. Lamancusa, J.S., Zayas, J.L., Allen, L., Soyster, L.M., Jorgensen, J.: 2006 Bernard M. gordon prize lecture: the learning factory: industry-partnered active learning. J. Eng. Educ. **97**(1), 5–11 (2008)

6. Taiwan Machine Tools Shaping the Future, September 2016. http://www.imis.ncku.edu.tw/ezfiles/398/1398/img/2728/IMTSAgenda_0721.pdf
7. Zoran, P., Andrzej, M., Amadeusz, N.: Virtual modelling and simulation of a CNC machine feed drive system. Trans. FAMENA **39**(4), 37–54 (2015)
8. Kao, Y.C., Lee, C.S., Liu, Z.R., Lin, Y.F.: Case study of virtual reality in CNC machine tool exhibition. In: MATEC Web of Conferences, vol. 123 (2017)
9. Srinivasa Prasad, B., Siva Prasad, D., Sandeep, A., Veeraiah, G.: Condition monitoring of CNC machining using adaptive control. Int. J. Autom. Comput. **10**(3), 202–209 (2013)
10. Parham, D.: Empirical Analysis of the Effects of R&D on Productivity: Implications for Productivity Measurement? vol. 17. OECD Publishing (2009)
11. Zhu, Y.Q.: Why and how knowledge sharing matters for R&D engineers. R&D Manage. **47**(2), 212–223 (2017)
12. Choi, J.Y., Jeong, S.K., Jung, J.K.: Evolution of technology convergence networks in Korea: Characteristics of temporal changes in R&D according to institution type. PLoS ONE **13**(2), 1–23 (2018)
13. Heike, B.: Companies with R&D abroad make Germany a strong research location. DIW Econ. Bull. **7**(46/47), 477–487 (2017)
14. Heather, G.T., Raymond, H., John, N., Chris, S.: Competency model design and assessment: findings and future directions. J. Public Aff. Educ. **19**(1), 141–171 (2013)
15. Hsu, C.C.: The Delphi technique: making sense of consensus. A Peer Rev. Electron. J. **12**(10), 1–8 (2007)
16. Shyr, W.J., Chiou, C.F., Yang, F.C., Li, P.C.: Energy management competency development based on the Internet of Things (IOT)*. Int. J. Eng. Educ. **33**(4), 1380–1385 (2017)
17. Parkes, M., Reading, C., Stein, S.: The competencies required for effective performance in a university e-learning environment. Australas. J. Educ. Technol. **29**(6), 777–791 (2013)
18. Ball, G., Zaugg, H., Davies, R., Tateishi, P.I., Jensen, C., Magleby, P.: Identification and validation of a set of global competencies for engineering students. Int. J. Eng. Educ. **28**(1), 156–168 (2012)
19. Imam, A., Mohammed, U., Abanyam, M.: On consistency and limitation of paired t-test, sign and wilcoxon sign rank test. IOSR J. Math. **10**(1), 1–6 (2014)

Enhancing Student Engagement: One Game at a Time

Sunet Eybers(✉) and Marie Hattingh(✉)

University of Pretoria, Private Bag X20, Hatfield 0028, South Africa
{sunet.eybers,marie.hattingh}@up.ac.za

Abstract. Student engagement is a much-researched topic ranging from the current discourse surrounding a general accepted definition to how student engagement is achieved through specific tools or processes (such as distance education). This study focuses on how game-based learning (GBL) (as a tool) can be used to foster student engagement. The study was conducted during the presentation of a fourth year data science curricula course. During the study students were engaged in playing a customized version of the Monopoly game, labelled 'DWnopoly'. The objective was to investigate the extent to which students prepared course work prior to contact sessions and as a result student engagement to enrich the student learning experience (through collaboration with peers); and lastly to expose students to practical questions on the topic (increase practical curricular relevance).

The interpretive study was conducted based on student course evaluation forms considering six items introduced by Coates [1] investigating student engagement in Australasia. These included the inclusion of challenging academic concepts, active learning, student and staff interaction, enriching educational experiences, supportive learning environment and work integrated learning. The results of the study indicated that the most significant area where student engagement occurred were the opportunity for students and lectures to interact, followed by the presentation of theoretical constructs in an academically challenging way in a supportive learning environment.

The significance of this study lies in the fact that the ubiquity of technology calls for a prepared digital society that includes students that are ready to operate in such an environment.

Keywords: Student engagement · Game-based learning
Data analytics curriculum · Data warehouse

1 Introduction

The need for skilled data scientists has put renewed pressure on academic to deliver theoretical constructs on the topic of data analytics in such a way that students are exposed to practical real world examples [2]. It is therefore more important than ever to satisfy the educational needs of both the student and the industry [3] to develop students into successful data science practitioners. Gone are the days where lecturers 'present' concepts to 'passive' or disengaged students. Research has proven that these methods

T.-T. Wu et al. (Eds.): ICITL 2018, LNCS 11003, pp. 231–240, 2018.
https://doi.org/10.1007/978-3-319-99737-7_24

are simply outdated and that it will hamper learning, and cause low student participation [3, 4]. Instead, in cases where methods have been applied to foster student engagement, a positive correlation between student success and development, including student satisfaction [5, 6] academic persistence and achievement [6, 7], social engagement [3, 8] and practical competence and skills transferability [9].

The successful application of game-based learning (GBL) has been proven to enhance learning [10]. Game based learning, which refers to "the borrowing of certain gaming principles and applying them to real-life settings to engage users" [11], is particularly suitable in instances where students are required to actively engage in learning activities with the objective of 'connecting' or applying theoretical constructs covered. When applied correctly GBL can enhance the student learning experience through the exposure of the student to the real-world examples by means of case studies. GBL furthermore, in the context of this study, offers additional benefits such as a cost-effective, low-risk, highly engaging, immediate feedback, and the active engagement of students in learning activities [12].

Game based learning was adopted in the teaching of fourth year level data science related subjects, in particular the teaching of data warehousing. The adoption of this approach seemed suitable to answer the main research question of this research paper: *How the game based learning approach adopted enhanced student engagement*?

The investigation is based on the six engagement scales as adopted in a study by Coates (1) with the assumption that, should these items or scales be present, a greater level of student engagement will be achieved. The six scales refer to the extent of academic challenging assessments, active learning, student and staff interactions, enriching educational experiences, the creation of supporting learning environments and work integrated learning were achieved. The last 'scale' – the work integrated learning – is of particular importance in achieving the goal of educating data science students that are competent and ready to fulfil their role in the workplace.

The outline of the paper is as follow: the first section focus on the clarification and presentation of generally accepted definition for the concept of student engagement; the second section focus on the description as well as the reason for the adoption of the 'six engagement scales'; the third section describe the research conducted using case study research and contains elements of the game based learning approach adopted with the objective of fostering student engagement followed by a description of the findings of the study. The investigation is concluded by a conclusion section including suggestions for further research opportunities.

2 Defining Student Engagement

Student engagement refers to the 'engaged' student who is actively involved in the learning process with the objective of "develop[ing] his/her knowledge, reflecting on the facts and details presented in the lecture related to their own experiences and 'the big picture'" [13]. The concept of student engagement has evolved over the past couple of decades stemming from student involvement [3]. Kahu [14] proposed that student engagement is a multidimensional construct influenced by the four dominant research perspectives depending on the point of view adopted by the researcher. These perspectives include the behavioural perspective, the psychological perspective, the social-cultural perspective and finally the holistic perspective. The behavioural perspective focuses on student behavior [14] which is similar to behavioural engagement (labelled by Finn 1993 cited in [14]). Behavioural engagement refers to the compliance to behavioural norms, which can include attendance and involvement. It therefore refers to "positive academic and social conduct in the learning activity" [15]. The psychological perspective by Kahu [14] refers to engagement as a "psycho-social" process which can vary in intensity. The psychological perspective is similar to the emotional engagement referring to positive emotional reactions as a result of the learning activity [15]. According to Trowler [3] engagement requires students to experience 'emotions' during the process of sense making or knowledge acquisition during the involvement in activities. Labelled as 'emotional engagement' student engagement can feelings of "interest, enjoyment or sense of belonging" [16]. The socio-cultural perspective [14] refers to the influence of the larger social context on the student experience for example the institution's academic culture. Fredricks [16] has identified cognitive engagement which refer to students' perception of engagement as an investment into their own learning and "go[es] beyond the [academic] requirements, and would relish challenge". The holistic view cater for student engagement as a diverse concept drawing from disciplines such as constructivism and psychology [14] and focus on the central role of student's emotions in the learning process.

Fredricks et al. [16] further indicate that the dimensions (also referred to as perspectives by Kahu [14]) can have positive, non-engagement or negative implications. For example behavioural engagement will be demonstrated by lecture attendance, whilst non-engagement behaviour will be characterised by absence. Negative behavioural engagement will be evidence through the disruption of lectures. Ultimately institutions strive to achieve engagement that fosters positive implications. However students can experience a mix of positive, non-engagement or negative implications amongst the three different dimensions [3]. For example students might attend lectures (positive behavioural engagement) but might get bored with the content (emotional non-engagement) or even reject the content (negative emotional engagement).

For the purpose of this study, the authors have adopted the point of view that student engagement is defined a holistic approach to indicate the extent to which student are actively involved in learning activities which include behavioral, emotional and cognitive engagement with the main objective of achieving positive academic results. This is a valid assumption for the subjects of the study as they are fourth year students that are more mature.

3 Game Based Learning (GBL)

GBL can be perceived as an educational tool or a type of learning activity employed by teachers to expose students to theoretical and/or practical concepts linked to particular learning outcomes with the objective of fostering a learning environment [17]. It is different from gamification in that gamification applies elements of games (such as performance badges) to non-game environments with the main driver of motivation to obtain greater rewards or badges [18]. Plass, Homer and Kinzer [17] summarized four arguments in favor of GBL: (1) the ability of a game to motivate players and keep them engaged through the use of "stars, points, leaderboards, badges, and trophies". (2) engagement on a cognitive, affective, behavioral and sociocultural level (3) the ability of the game to adapt based on the feedback given by the player (4) the ability for students to fail gracefully.

In a study by Groff, McCall, Darvasi and Gilvert [19], the authors distinguish between different types of games including targeted games, linear games, open-ended games and persistent worlds. Each of the type of games had a specific timeframe for completion, a level of open-endedness and a specific manner in which each of the games can be completed.

The game developed for the purpose of this study was a targeted game by means of customized board game based on the game of Monopoly (to be discussed in Sect. 5). The rationale for this type of game is due to the fact that the game was limited to a set period of time at the beginning of the lecture. Also, the aim of the game was to test concepts (in an engaging way) based on work that students had to prepare before coming to class (in a flipped class setup).

The importance and applicability of game based learning is evident through the focus on the application of these technologies to enhance student learning [3], irrespective of the research area.

Evidence of use cases deploying GBL to teach data science is scarce. One element of teaching data science in some institutions is the concept of data warehousing. Khojah and Mannino [20] designed a customized game to expose students to the challenges related to data warehousing by means of role based simulation. Students are exposed during the simulation to select the best possible data warehouse architecture based on the organisational strategy.

4 Theoretical Framework

Coates [1] investigated the extent to which higher educational institutions in Australasia can improve their quality of learning by means of the identification of constraints and opportunities. The author proposed and used six engagement scales to perform his research on student engagement namely:

- [A1] Academic challenge: the extent to which students were exposed to academically challenging concepts that will foster learning.
- [A2] Active learning: the extent to which students were offered the opportunity to create their own knowledge;
- [A3] Student and staff interactions: the quality of contact amongst students and staff;
- [A4] Enriching educational experiences: the opportunity to engage in educational activities with the objective of enriching knowledge;
- [A5] Supportive learning environment: the offering of assistance and support within the broader learning community;

- [A6] Work-integrated learning: the extent to which students are exposed to and activities integrated with real-life environments.

These six 'scales' or elements were adopted for the purpose of this study and included in the questionnaire.

5 The Case of Fourth Year Data Analytic Students

The fourth year semester module focusing on data warehousing as part of the data analytics education stream has limited bi-weekly 90 min contact sessions with students. For this reason, a flipped classroom approach was adopted which required students to complete pre-work prior to contact sessions. Student engagement was also limited due to the limited contact time. It was therefore decided to change the approach with the objective of 'testing' the extent to which students completed the pre-course work which will then subsequently enhance the student's ability to actively engage in class discussion. Figure 1 illustrates the DWnopoly board. The game was played as followed:

Fig. 1. DWnopoly player board

The class was randomly divided into groups of approximately four members each. Thirty-six students registered for the course of which thirty attended the contact session. Each group selected a token representing their group. One team member of each team was allowed to throw a dice. Depending on the number returned, the token was moved by the lecturer on the board projected on an overhead projector. Depending on where the token was placed, an action had to be completed. For example, groups either had to answer a particular question depending on the block landed or had to go to 'jail'.

There were different colour coded blocks on which students could end up after throwing the dice. Each of the colours indicated a particular level of the question to be presented, based on Bloom's taxonomy. Bloom's taxonomy is a classification framework proposing that students should be exposed to different cognitive levels during the acquisition of knowledge [21]. These include - from the lowest to the highest level - the acquisition of knowledge, comprehension of constructs, the application thereof, the ability to analyse and synthesize concepts and finally evaluate constructs (i.e. formulate their own judgements based on the knowledge gained). The higher the level of expertise obtained the deeper the understanding of the theoretical construct. The main focus of fourth year level courses is on the higher level of Bloom's taxonomy, i.e. the analysis and synthesis of concepts although lower levels of the taxonomy could not disregarded.

The questions were directly related to the set of course pre-work that had to be prepared prior to the contact sessions as well as the session course outcomes listed in the course study guide. This is of utmost importance as Bensimon (2009 cited in [3]) and Kuh [5] argue that student engagement activities should correlate with educational outcome in order for students to reap the benefits of these activities. Also the more students are exposed to the subject by means of studying, practicing or feedback, the higher the student engagement positive experience.

Feedback was given to student immediately once they landed on a block with some class interaction allowed through the Quiz section. In this instance the class could ask the group a particular question, normally based on questions they had difficulty in answering or grasping concepts.

6 Research Method

The study aimed to establish to what extent game-based learning can contribute to enhanced student engagement. For this reason, the study followed an interpretive, qualitative approach as the researchers wished to obtain an understanding from the students on their perception of game-based learning. At the beginning of the semester, the ground rules for a flipped classroom was established, as advocated by [22] which ensured that all the students knew what was expected of them in advance. As mentioned in section five, students were instructed to prepare a section of work prior to each lecture. During the lecture, the game questions will cover that specific section of work. The class consisted of thirty fourth year students (out of a total registered of thirty six). Each lecture is one and a half hour long. The customized board game is played during the first thirty minutes of the lecture. This paper reports on the first game played at the beginning of each lecture.

7 Results and Discussion

Table 1 provide a summary of the results obtained from the structured questionnaire using a Likert scale from 1 = Strongly Disagree to 5 = Strongly Agree. Questions were classified and indexed according to the six engagement scales namely [A1] academic challenge, [A2] active learning, [A3] student and staff interactions, [A4] enriching educational experiences, [A5] supportive learning environment, [A6] work-integrated learning. Percentages were calculate by obtaining the mean values of the responses.

The data obtained from the questionnaire is discussed using the six student engagement scales as proposed by Coates [1] as introduced in Sect. 4.

Table 1. Total scores per factor

Index	Description	%
A1	Academic challenge	80.0
A2	Active learning	77.7
A3	Student and staff interactions	87.3
A4	Enriching educational experiences	78.5
A5	Supportive learning environment	80.0
A6	Work-integrated learning	76.5

7.1 Academic Challenge

The results indicated that 80% of the students found that the GBL approach allowed them to be exposed to academically challenging concepts that will foster learning. This is based on 84% indicating that they had a better understanding of theoretical concepts, whilst 76% indicated that they had a better understanding of practical concepts. The lower result for the practical component is not unexpected as the course is practical by nature and the way the game was implemented was in a theoretical manner (none of the questions involved physically implementing/manipulating a data warehouse).

Due to the fact that the game was developed based on the different levels of Bloom's Taxonomy, it ensured that students were exposed to different cognitive process levels [21]. The flipped classroom approach exposed students to the first two levels (remember and understand), whilst the GBL approach catered for the next three levels (apply, analyse and evaluate).

Furthermore, according to the theory of GBL [17] "the learning theory that informed the design of a specific game is reflected in the type of challenge the game provides, the type of responses it facilitates and the kind of feedback it provides". Therefore, due to the fact that the game challenges the students on different levels (according to Bloom's Taxonomy), it will facilitate different responses from the students. Depending on their answers (whether they were correct or not) the feedback from the lecturers will differ. Either elaborating, and thereby providing more richness to the response, or in case of an incorrect or incomplete answer, providing the correct answer.

7.2 Active Learning

The results indicated that 78% of the students felt that the GBL approach allowed them the opportunity to create their own knowledge. This is quite low, and ideally should be higher as one of the advantages associated with GBL is ongoing participatory learning [17]. However, the student feedback explained that although the *"game assisted in understanding, [but] very little [content] covered" (Respondent 37),* which is due to the thirty minute time restriction on playing the game. Furthermore, Respondent 35 indicated that a *"30 s version [to answer the question] of the game would be more interactive and would go faster".*

Therefore, the game design allowed for active learning, however the manner in which the game was played can be optimised.

7.3 Student and Staff Interactions

The results indicated that 87% of the students were content with the quality of contact amongst students and staff. This positive result is important in the context of the students that took part in this game, as the majority of students are already working full time. Therefore, the informal manner in which they can communicate with their lecturers appeals to the professional developmental characteristics of future data scientists [23]. However, the results did indicated that the structure of the game inhibited them from exploiting the full knowledge the lecturers had to offer.

"You have so much knowledge and we only receive bits and pieces of it" (Respondent 23).

Therefore, the structure of the game has an influence on the ultimate success of learning.

7.4 Enriching Educational Experiences

The results indicated that 79% of the students felt that the GBL approach afforded them the opportunity to engage in educational activities with the objective of enriching knowledge. This result is closely aligned with the active learning (Sect. 7.2). It is deduced that the same aspects that inhibited active learning also contributes to the extent of enriching educational experiences. However, due to the fact that students "played" in groups, heard responses from their peers and feedback from the lecturers learning incorporated different points of views. The communication processes that took place within the exchange of the responses and subsequent feedback supported communication the development of communication skills which is a core competency for Data Scientists [24].

7.5 Supportive Learning Environment

The results indicated that 80% of the students experienced a positive and supportive learning environment deriving support from the broader learning community, which included their fellow students. The GBL approach provided an ideal environment in which peer learning could take place. The game allowed students to learn from their peers in two manners: firstly, group discussion when it was their turn to "play the game", secondly, the nature of the game allowed students to formulate a question to another group, this was typically a question they struggled with. Furthermore, the GBL allowed for peer learning within a controlled environment, as lecturers were present to moderate the interactions (in case the question formulated was misunderstood, or if the answers lacks richness).

7.6 Work-Integrated Learning

The results indicated that 77% of the students felt that they were exposed to and activities integrated with real-life environments. As previously mentioned, due to the strong practical component of this course, the theoretical concepts tested in class, through the game, did not address the work-integrated learning criteria. However, it was never the intention of the lecturer for it to be so. The manner in which this component was addressed through the game was through "story telling" based on their own industry experience.

8 Conclusion and Recommendations

The study has shown that a GBL approach within a flipped classroom setting do enhance student engagement. The data was analysed using the six engagement scales as identified and used by Coates [1] - namely academic challenge, active learning, student and staff interactions, enriching educational experiences, supportive learning environment and work-integrated learning. The most significant area where student engagement occurred were the opportunity for students and lectures to interact, followed by the presentation of theoretical constructs in an academically challenging way in a supportive learning environment. Although some enhancements to the game were identified during the administration of the game it did not hamper student engagement. However, a more longitudinal view is required to determine the true impact of GBL in student engagement in order to perform a comparative study. This will be achieved through the continuation of this study is subsequent years.

The significance of this study lies in the fact that the ubiquity of technology calls for a prepared digital society that includes students that are ready to operate in such an environment.

From the results of this game, the following recommendations can be made:

- The pace of the game needs to allow for quick responses. This will allow the optimum learning opportunities for students.
- The 'jail' aspect of the traditional Monopoly game need to be changed, as this was a motivator for students not to answer questions.
- More questions per level of Bloom's Taxonomy needs to be developed as a number of groups picked the same card. In cases where groups picked the same card the lecturers changed the focus of the question in order to enrich the learning experience.
- Because groups could consult their textbooks when answering, they got familiar with the textbook layout, which supported the Open Book exam that will follow later.

References

1. Coates, H.: Engaging students for success Australasian student engagement report australasian survey of student engagement, 1–91 p. Australian Council for Educational Research, Victoria (2009)
2. Hattingh, M.J., Eybers, S.: Towards understanding how game based learning can enhance flipped learning. In: Huang, T.-C., Lau, R., Huang, Y.-M., Spaniol, M., Yuen, C.-H. (eds.) SETE 2017. LNCS, vol. 10676, pp. 106–115. Springer, Cham (2017). https://doi.org/10.1007/978-3-319-71084-6_12
3. Trowler, V.: Student engagement literature review. High Educ. Acad., pp. 1–74, November 2010

4. Meguid, E.A., Collins, M.: Students' perceptions of lecturing approaches: traditional versus interactive teaching, pp. 229–241 (2017)
5. Kuh, G.D., Kinzie, J., Buckley, J.A., Bridges, B.K., Hayek, J.C.: Piecing together the student success puzzle: research, propositions, and recommendations: ASHE higher education report. ASHE Higher Education Report, vol. 32, 200 p. Wiley (2011)
6. Cheong, K.C., Ong, B.: An evaluation of the relationship between student engagement, academic achievement, and satisfaction. In: Tang, S.F., Logonnathan, L. (eds.) Assessment for Learning Within and Beyond the Classroom, pp. 409–416. Springer, Singapore (2016). https://doi.org/10.1007/978-981-10-0908-2_34
7. Hu, S.: Reconsidering the relationship between student engagement and persistence in college, pp. 97–106 (2011)
8. Zobel, E.: The correlation between college student engagement and 1. University of Minnesota Duluth (2016)
9. Smith, M.: Improving student engagement with employability: the project pitch assessment. Planet **26**(1), 2–7 (2012)
10. Pesare, E., Roselli, T., Corriero, N., Rossano, V.: Game-based learning and gamification to promote engagement and motivation in medical learning contexts (2016)
11. Pho, A., Dinscore, A.: Game-based learning. Tips trends, pp. 1–5. Spring (2015)
12. Trybus, J.: Game-based learning: what it is, why it works, and where it's going (2009)
13. Exeter, D.J., Ameratunga, S., Morton, S., Jackson, R.: Student engagement in very large classes: the teachers' perspective, November 2010
14. Kahu, E.R.: Studies in Higher Education Framing student engagement in higher education, 5079, November 2017
15. Pino-James, N.: Evaluation of a pedagogical model for student engagement in learning activities. Educ. Action Res. **792**, 1–24 (2017)
16. Fredricks, J.A., Blumenfeld, P.C., Paris, A.H.: School engagement: potential of the concept, state of the evidence. Rev. Educ. Res. **74**(1), 59–109 (2004)
17. Plass, J.L., Homer, B.D., Kinzer, C.K.: Foundations of game-based learning. Educ. Psychol. **50**(4), 258–283 (2015)
18. Muntean, C.I.: Raising engagement in e-learning through gamification, (1) (2002)
19. Groff, J., McCall, J., Darvasi, P., Gilbert, Z.: Using games in the classroom. In: Schrier. K. (ed.) Learning, Education and Games. Second, 19–42 p. (2016)
20. Khojah, M., Mannino, M.: Experiencing the challenges of data warehouse development: implementation of a serious game (2001), pp. 1–5 (2016)
21. Krathwohl, D.R.: A revision of bloom's taxonomy. Theory Pract. **41**(4), 212–219 (2002)
22. Demski, J.: 6 expert tips for flipping the classroom [Internet]. Tech Enabled Learning (2013). https://campustechnology.com/Articles/2013/01/23/6-Expert-Tips-for-Flipping-the-Classroom.aspx?p=1
23. Saulnier, B.M.: Towards a 21st century information systems education: high impact practices and essential learning outcomes. Issues Inf. Syst. **17**(1), 168–177 (2016)
24. De Veaux, R., et al.: Curriculum guidelines for undergraduate programs in data science. Annu. Rev. Stat. **2016**, 1–26 (2016)

eModeration: The Validation of a User Experience Evaluation Framework

Corne J. van Staden(✉), Judy A. van Biljon, and J. H. Kroeze

School of Computing, University of South Africa,
Science Campus, 28 Pioneer Avenue, Florida Park, Roodepoort 1709, South Africa
vstadcj1@unisa.ac.za

Abstract. The effective, efficient and secure moderation of examination scripts can become challenging when the moderators are geographically dispersed. Despite innovative technological developments and the potential benefits, the use of eModeration (online moderation of examination scripts) in the South African Higher Education Institutions (HEIs) context is limited. Various factors contribute to the adoption of eModeration in HEIs, ranging from human factors to technical issues and organisational resistance to change. The focus of this study is on the human factors involved in eModeration (specifically the user experience) and the research is guided by the following question: *What are the most important constructs in evaluating a user experience evaluation framework for eModeration within the context of Higher Education Institutions in South Africa?* The research uses a design science research methodology, which includes the design, development and testing of a User Experience Evaluation Framework for eModeration, and the focus of this paper is on the validation phase. The data generation methods include interviews with management from two South African HEIs. The contribution of this paper is to propose a validated framework for evaluating eModeration in higher education and demonstrate how that can be used by managers in HEIs to guide the selection and evaluation of eModeration systems towards facilitating more effective learning environments.

Keywords: eModeration · User experience · Usability

1 Introduction

The challenges that Higher Education Institutions (HEIs) face with the implementation and use of electronic moderation systems range from technical obstacles, internet access, file size, infrastructure problems, as well as human factors (user experience). HEIs are also faced with the challenge of finding systems to facilitate moderation of marked examination scripts, which allows an acceptable user experience within the constraints of a developing country such as South Africa. Moderation is an integral part of ensuring standards in developing countries but the problem is that no user experience evaluation framework for eModeration at HEIs exist.

The traditional method of moderation of examination scripts involves the distribution of hard copies of the actual marked examination scripts to moderators using courier

T.-T. Wu et al. (Eds.): ICITL 2018, LNCS 11003, pp. 241–252, 2018.
https://doi.org/10.1007/978-3-319-99737-7_25

delivery or postal services, which is expensive, time consuming and not always effective [1, 2]. Therefore, HEIs, and especially private tertiary institutions (which do not receive government funding), needed to consider other ways of distributing examination scripts to respective moderators. The knowledge gap is that there is no theoretical framework to evaluate the user experience of electronic moderation systems when considering innovative electronic educational technologies as alternative to traditional paper-based moderation approaches.

The way in which eModeration is used in literature is often different to the context in which the concept is used in this paper. For example, eModeration can take place between two entities, such as facilitator and student, where the facilitator acts as an online mentor or 'eModerator' to provide online feedback to the student [3, 4]. Greatorex [5] indicates that, if users (in this case eModerators) encounter negative experiences with eModeration, it can result in low adoption and reluctant use of technology. Within the context of this research, electronic moderation of examination scripts, also referred to as eModeration, involves the use of one or more electronic moderation systems to electronically moderate marked examination scripts [6, 7]. eModeration involves different users in the process of electronic moderation, for example, lecturers (internal examiners), eModerators (external examiners or moderators) and deans (management) involved in the moderation process. The eModerator who electronically moderates examination papers can be described as an external assessor or second examiner. The user experience that is under investigation is that of both the eModerator and management who would be using an eModerate system.

Earlier research [2] described the design and development of the User Experience Evaluation Framework for eModeration in HEIs (UX-FeM). The contribution of the paper is to describe the evaluation and the final, validated UX-FeM that can be used by educators and managers when considering eModeration at Pearson Institute of Higher Education, a private Higher Education Institute (PHEI). Although UX-FeM was developed and tested at a PHEI, all the constructs are relevant to public HEIs as well. However, further research is needed to determine the difference in priorities between public and private Higher Education Institutes (PHEIs) when considering eModeration.

The literature review clarifies the terms and terminology used in the context of the research by focusing attention on moderation, eModeration and user experience, as well as the relationship between user experience and eModeration. This is followed by an explanation of the methodology, the results and discussion including the verified UX-FeM and a conclusion.

2 Literature Review

2.1 eModeration

The concept of eModeration is used in various contexts, for example, social moderation, moderation forums and peer moderation. Social moderation is distinguished from moderation forums because of its focus. A good example of social moderation is the eModeration framework called e-Tivities by Salmon [4]. Salmon's framework [4] can be used by educators, where the lecturer acts as an eModerator (or mentor) and provides feedback to respective students on activities, for example, assessment activities. Authors such as Morgan [8] and Wichmann, Giemza and Hoppe [9] utilise eModeration to moderate eDiscussions between lecturer and student. The e-Tivities framework of Salmon [4] does, however, not cover the user experience of the different users involved in eModeration. Adie's studies [10] on social moderation focus on lecturers acting as eModerators who purposefully develop agreements on standards, quality and consistency of assessment judgement across different programmes. Adie [11, 12] further proposes a theoretical framework for online professional discussions, for example, in an open distance e-learning (ODeL) environment or where a few markers are involved in grading in order to establish a shared understanding of assessment and standards with detailed guidelines to ensure consistency throughout the semester. Grainger et al. [13] use social moderation meetings to discuss the methods which members are supposed to use during assessments. Grainger et al.'s study [13] reaffirms Adie et al.'s typology [11] as a valid and reliable framework for analysis and discussion when used with assessment moderation.

In this paper eModeration does, however, refer to a specific type of peer review, defined as: "the electronic moderation (quality assurance/critical reading) of summative examination scripts by external moderators in a virtual learning environment" [14]. Within the context of peer moderation, electronic moderation of examination scripts involves the use of some electronic moderation systems to electronically moderate examination scripts [6, 15]. Peer electronic moderation involves different users, for example, internal examiners (users who grade the assessment initially) and external examiners (users who grade the assessment externally – eModerators), as well as management who can be deans or examination officers involved in the moderation process. The focus of peer moderation is not between lecturer and student but between lecturers, external examiners and management. External examiners judge the internal examiners' grading using an eModerate system. Management oversees the process of eModeration using the eModerate system to track the progress of the moderation process, to peruse the feedback received from the external moderators and to intervene and take action where necessary.

An eModerate system is supposed to provide the user with an interface that can be used to electronically assess and re-grade marked examination scripts of students at HEIs. The scripts that need to be moderated are scanned from the original, hand-written, internally marked examination scripts. The eModerate system should allow the institution requesting moderation to upload the scanned scripts to, for example, a module site in a virtual learning environment, where the eModerator will have secure access to the documentation. Once the eModerator has finished with the electronic control (confirmation or re-grading) of the marked scripts he/she must be able to upload the documents back onto the same system for the Higher Education Institution (HEI) requesting the moderation to download and view. Some advantages of using an eModerate system are according to [2]: the ability to track the moderation process; cost effectiveness; the fact that it can be done anytime and anywhere; the electronic availability of moderated examination script(s) for future reference. Despite the known advantages eModerate systems are not standard at South African HEIs. There could be many reasons, but the focus of this study is on the user experience which is critical in the decision to adopt and use eModeration. The next section deals with user experience aspects.

2.2 User Experience

According to the International Organization for Standardization's standard 9241-210 (human-centred design for interactive systems), user experience is described as "[a] person's perceptions and responses resulting from the use and/or anticipated use of a product, system or service. User experience includes all the user's emotions, beliefs, preferences, perceptions, physical and psychological responses, behaviours and accomplishments that occur before, during and after use … and the context of use" [16, clause 2.15]. In their definitions of user experience, Hassenzahl and Tractinsky [17] and Roto [18] agree that user experience is the consequence of the following elements:

- Context: The context refers to the environment in which the user operates or interacts with the system. It also refers to how the user is affected by factors such as organisational setting and meaningfulness of the activity.
- System: This refers to the characteristics of a system, e.g. complexity, purpose, usability and functionality.
- User: The user's internal state is based on expectations, needs, motivation, moods and predisposition. It can be said that user experience is a consequence of a user's internal state.

A particular challenge regarding user experience, as formulated by Wimmer, Wöckl, Leitner and Tscheligi [19], relates to how the measurement of all instrumental and non-instrumental aspects or qualities are associated with the design process. The latter provides feedback on the user's use and acceptance of products or services, referred to as the user's emotional reaction to the product or service. Another aspect of user experience concerns the situation in which a product or service is used [5, 20]. While Roto [18] agrees with Hassenzahl and Tractinsky's [17] definition and provides elements (context, system, user) of user experience, Roto [18] extends her definition by including factors under these elements, such as infrastructure, services, people and the technology context that also play a role in user interactions with a product.

The process used to improve the usability of an artifact involves an iterative design cycle, which makes use of "usability-related activities, including goal-setting for usability attributes, operationalizing of attributes, measuring attributes and evaluating measurements to establish goal achievement" [21]. Usability that supports system iterative design promotes effectiveness and efficiency of the task to be performed, as well as the satisfaction of the user [22]. Usability goals are objective [23], while user experience aspects are more subjective.

Preece [23] explains that user experience differs from objective usability goals in that user experience is concerned with how the users experience the product from a personal point of view or perspective, which is in alignment with the ISO definition [16]. User experience aspects are more subjective qualities and are concerned with users' emotions regarding a system, which makes user experience more relevant than usability for this study. As McCarthy and Wright [24] indicate, there has been a shift in determining a product's success from only considering usability aspects to including aspects such as product interaction, individual disposition and context. For the purpose of this paper, usability will be viewed as a concept embedded in user experience [25]. The construct associated with user experience is measured by non-instrumental (non-task-orientated usability) qualities and instrumental (task-orientated user experience) qualities [6]. The constructs associated with user experience identified by different authors [17, 18] were mapped onto eModeration aspects, which guided the design and development of the questionnaire used during the survey. The data gathered during the survey was used to "determine which user experience constructs would be relevant" to a User Experience Evaluation Framework for eModeration [6]. Based on the literature review the following constructs were taken into consideration: system (eModeration web application), context (eModeration in PHEIs) and user (eModerator and management) [6, 15]. To ensure an independent quality assurance the lecturers do not have access to the eModerate system. Concepts and principles fundamental to user experience frameworks were abstracted from diverse studies including users interacting with products in an eCommerce environment [26] and mHealth UX frameworks [27]. The principals abstracted from these UX frameworks, together with the user experience heuristics identified by Hassenzahl [17, 28], as well as Väänänen-Vainio-Mattila and Wäljas [29] guided the design and development of the UX-FeM as described in [2].

3 Research Approach

3.1 Research Design

The Design Science Research approach used in the study is an adaptation of Hevner et al.'s conceptual framework for Design Science Research in Information Systems [30]. This approach was appropriate for the design and development of a User Experience Evaluation Framework for eModeration, given its four evaluation and iteration phases used to construct a validated artifact. The iterative steps of construction and refinement of Design Science Research were followed to ensure the relevance and rigour of the design principles [15, 30–32]. The focus of this paper is on Phases 3 and 4 but we briefly explain Phases 1 and 2 to provide the context.

In this study, each of the four phases (identify problem – design – construct – use) had a specific purpose and contained an evaluation cycle, as well as a construction/refinement cycle (see Fig. 1). During the different iterative phases the collected data was analysed and then used to refine the framework before presenting it into the next phase. In the first phase a literature review was conducted using context analysis to determine the relevance of the field of study (in this case user experience in the environment of eModeration). The initial design and development of a conceptual framework were based on insights gained from this literature study. In the second phase the aim was the formative evaluation of the initial artifact design (*ex ante* evaluation), resulting in a refined artifact. The UX-FeM proposed after Phase 2 is presented in Fig. 2.

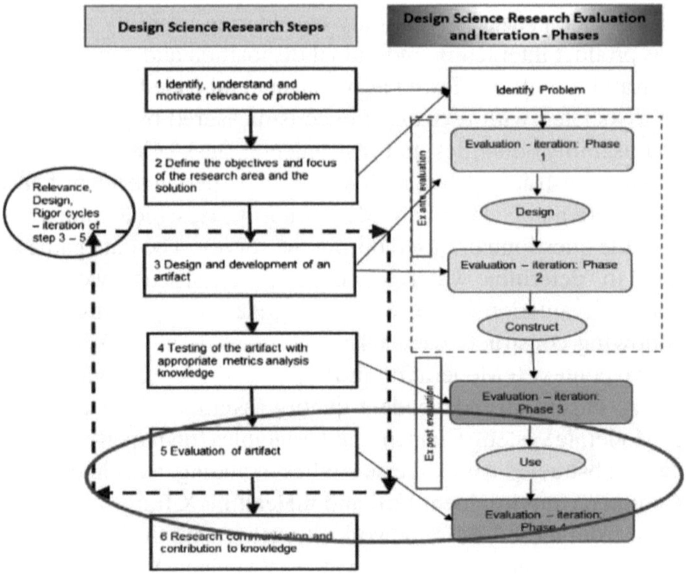

Fig. 1. Information systems research artifact development (adapted from Hevner [30] and Sonnenberg and Vom Brocke [32]) with a specific focus on interviews to determine rigour in Phase 3 (as indicated by the red oval in the figure) (Color figure online)

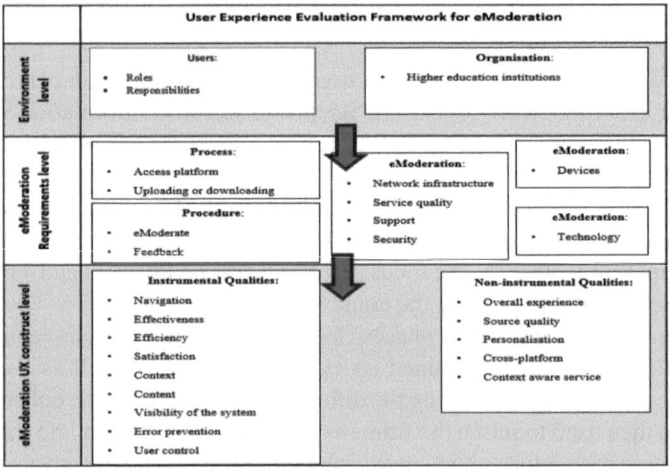

Fig. 2. User experience evaluation framework for eModeration after Phase 2

During the third phase, the second version of the framework (see Fig. 2) was validated, and the results of this *ex post* evaluation were used to refine the artifact before it was validated in the final (fourth) phase. The focus of this paper is on the validation which involves the third and fourth phases. In accordance with the Design Science Research methodology, the evaluation is required to confirm that the artifact solved the identified research problem [34]. Sonnenberg and Vom Brocke [32] argue that it is necessary to structure validation activities with corresponding evaluation criteria. It is recommended to use specific concepts of evaluation patterns associated with Design Science Research artifacts. The researchers adapted the iterative evaluation pattern, with its four cycles (design – evaluate – construct – design), proposed by Sonnenberg and Vom Brocke [32], and incorporated evaluation criteria from literature that relate to artifact evaluation [3]. The questionnaires used in Phase 3 and 4 is available as Appendix A (see https://goo.gl/oq1EP5). The feedback received during Phases 3 and 4 (as described in this paper) was then used to validate and refine the UX-FeM framework again – this improved version is the contribution of this paper (see Fig. 3).

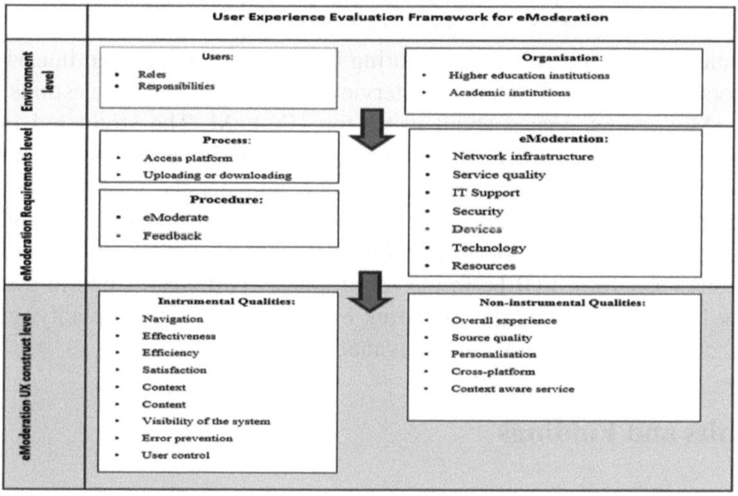

Fig. 3. Final user experience evaluation framework for eModeration (UX-FeM)

3.2 Research in Context

The initial creation of the framework was conducted at Pearson Institute for Higher Education (PIHE), a PHEI in South Africa. The eModerate system was embedded in a learning management system. The electronic moderation system provided users the opportunity to upload or download scanned examination scripts electronically. The eModerate system required the eModerators to download the examination scripts and to mark these either manually on a printout or (preferably) electronically. After completion of the moderation process the eModerator would upload the moderated examination scripts with the moderation report onto the eModerate system in order for the deans to peruse online or download. After three different phases were used to design and develop the framework it was presented to the management of another PHEI (Monash University of South Africa – MSA) to test the viability of using the framework in other PHEIs. The targeted participant population were eModerators at PIHE and managers involved in moderation at MSA. During the third phase ten of the thirty eModerators (from five different faculties) which participated in the development phase were invited and six participated. During the fourth phase an exhaustive approach was followed, i.e. we continued until the last (5th) interview did not add any new information or insights.

3.3 Research Strategy and Data Collection

The interviews were conducted using the telephone and Skype as tools. Notes were made during the interview process and the interviews were transcribed by an independent person. The comments and responses from managers were coded into a structure in which themes emerged across the subset of data using thematic analysis [33, 35]. Common themes were defined, grouped together and named accordingly. The comments, feedback and responses from the participants (managers) were used to refine the User Experience Evaluation Framework for eModeration.

The data generation methods used during the third phase included interviews with eModerators from different faculties. Interviews used open-ended questions to determine the eModerators' views about using the UX-FeM. The structured interviews assisted in informing the refinement of the framework design and to determine whether the user experience constructs were satisfactory, whether the levels were adequate, whether constructs should be added or removed, whether the artifact would be easy enough to use, and whether the framework was general enough to be used at other organizations apart from PHEIs. In the fourth phase, participants had to evaluate the framework holistically, using the following evaluation criteria: simplicity, generality, exactness, clarity, completeness and relevance.

4 Results and Findings

The results are discussed under the criteria of: structure, simplicity, comprehensiveness and overall evaluation, where participants were referred to as: A-F eModerators of PIHE and G-L Managers of MSA.

Structure: Based on the questions related to the adequacy and appropriateness of the three identified levels of the framework, the eModerators of PIHE and managers at MSA agreed that three levels were adequate. Participant D indicated that more levels would make the framework too complex and confusing.

Simplicity: All the participants were in agreement that the constructs, elements and criteria identified in the framework were simple enough to easily comprehend. Participant D commented: "The first solution to remote moderation I encountered that really works well and smoothly." In response to the comprehensiveness of the framework Participant I said that "the system is perfectly integrated [and] that guarantees usability". Under relevance one of the participants said: "Perfect for external moderation! Very useful for internal moderation as well to keep track and record of each semester's examination results and moderation." The participants also agreed that if more information were to be added it would make it difficult to understand.

Comprehensiveness: Participants were required to indicate whether the elements identified under the different levels were comprehensive (detailed) enough. Starting with the *Environment level, category users* the following responses emerged: Participants D, G and H identified an "IT support" person to be added instead of just having an eModerator operator. Overall, the participants were satisfied with the users' roles and responsibilities. The eModerate participants agreed that the users (managers, eModeration system operator, IT support, eModerator) were adequate and indicated that if too many users were added, it "might lead to confusion or slow down the process flow" (Participant D). The researchers then adjusted the roles of the operator and created the roles and responsibilities of the IT support staff member. Participant C was of opinion that the framework is "customised for higher education institutions only", while Participant D identified more potential: "Public HEIs will definitely benefit as well. Colleges, school[s], and any academic institution having access to internet might also benefit, especially where external moderation are needed." Participants G, H and I indicated that the framework could be implemented in various HEIs (not only PHEIs). Participant K and H agreed that the framework could be used by both private and public institutions. Participant I further indicated that the framework could also be used on a "micro level", for example, when moderating assignments during a semester between remote sites. As a result public and other academic institutions were added as evaluation criteria to the framework under the environment level.

Under the *Requirements level of the framework*, Participants A and H were of opinion that IT support should be added as a separate element. Participant H also suggested adding a "resource" element which included cost and cost efficiency, with its respective financial implications, and that suggestion was implemented. The resource requirements for an eModerate system could include internet, bandwidth, scanners, eModeration technology, devices to access the system, and budget to support the implementation. Under the requirements level, Participant K recommended that the elements under eModerate construct be merged, and this was implemented. Participant G expected more detail under "service quality", while participant C and H wanted to include an evaluation criterion for "system maintenance" as part of the support function. Participant H indicated that IT support is not just a person who needs to complete a job but a person that would also need to fulfil a technical function. As a result both "IT support" and "system maintenance" were added as additional evaluation criteria under the support element. None of the participants thought it was necessary to add more elements to the *UX construct level.*

Overall Evaluation: Participants were all satisfied with the framework and the following benefits were identified. Participant G and H indicated that the use of an eModerate system could be useful and valuable for archiving and quality assurance purposes. For example, if a student requests a remark, it would be easy to retrieve the file. eModeration systems also provide a footprint of actions, which could improve quality assurance. Participant H mentioned the flexibility in completing the moderation task offline after downloading the scripts. The eModeration UX construct level was divided into two categories: instrumental and non-instrumental qualities [6, 28, 29]. The participants agreed that the constructs were relevant, clearly explained, complete and comprehensive enough for the eModeration user experience level. Figure 2 represents the initial User Experience Evaluation Framework for eModeration while Fig. 3 represents the updated framework after the feedback from Phases 3 and 4 have been incorporated.

The participants from MSA who mostly consisted of management were satisfied with the instrumental and non-instrumental qualities identified in the artifact. IT support and service maintenance were added to the conceptual framework as extra user roles and responsibilities with a separate IT support element under the eModeration requirements level. The three building blocks namely eModeration (see Fig. 2) were merged into one construct instead of three separate constructs (see Fig. 3).

5 Conclusion

This paper presented the case for eModeration as an innovative technology to support advanced digital learning environments. Despite the known benefits, eModeration is not widely used, specifically not in South African HEIs. While acknowledging the financial, technical and other barriers to the adoption of eModeration, we argue that the user experience of the end-users (moderators and deans) is critical. Therefore, this paper focused on the question: *What are the most important constructs in evaluating a user experience evaluation framework for eModeration within the context of Higher Education Institutions in South Africa?* In response, a User Experience Evaluation Framework for eModeration (UX-FeM) containing the essential constructs was developed [2, 6, 7, 15], and this paper describes the validation thereof. The contribution is the *validated* UX-FeM, which can be used to assess prospective or existing eModeration systems from the user experience perspective.

Acknowledgements. The work is based on the research supported by the South African Research Chairs Initiative of the Department of Science and Technology and National Research Foundation of South Africa (Grant No. 89564). The University of South Africa (UNISA) is acknowledged for granting a period of research and development leave to the third author during which time the paper was completed. Any opinion, finding and conclusion or recommendation expressed in this material is that of the authors, and neither the NRF nor UNISA accepts any liability in this regard.

References

1. Guàrdia, L., Crisp, G., Alsina, I.: Trends and challenges of e-assessment to enhance student learning in higher education. In: Innovative Practices for Higher Education Assessment and Measurement, pp. 295–415. IGI Global Hershey, PA, USA (2017)
2. Van Staden, C.J.: IT moderation going green! In: Proceedings of SAICSIT 2010 Conference, pp. 1–3. UNISA Production Printers, Bela Bela, Limpopo, South Africa (2010)
3. Bridge, P., Appleyard, R.: A comparison of electronic and paper based assignment submission and feedback. Br. J. Educ. Technol. **39**(4), 644–650 (2008)
4. Salmon, G.: E-tivities: The Key to Active Online Learning. Taylor & Francis Group, New York (2013)

5. Greatorex, J.: Moderated e-portfolio evaluation. Evaluation and Validation Assessment Directorate, UCLES (2004)
6. Van Staden, C.J., Van Biljon, J.A., Kroeze, J.H.: eModeration: towards a user experience evaluation framework. In: SAICSIT 2015 Proceedings of the 2015 Annual Research Conference of the South African Institute of Computer Scientists and Information Technologists. ICPS ACM, Article 39, Stellenbosch, Western Cape, South Africa (2015)
7. Van Staden, C.J., Van Biljon, J.A., Kroeze, J.H.: Using a user experience evaluation framework for eModeration. In: Olugbara, O., Millham, R., Heukleman, D. (eds.) Proceedings of IEEE ICTAS 2017, pp. 15–21, Durban, South Africa (2017)
8. Morgan, A.: eModeration: contextualising online learning in undergraduate nurse education. Asian J. Nurs. **11**(1), 48–53 (2008)
9. Wichmann, A., Giemza, A., Hoppe, U., Collide-Group: Effects of awareness support on moderating multiple parallel E-discussions. Computer Supported Collaborative Learning Practices CSCL2009. ISLS, pp. 646–650 (2009)
10. Adie, L.: An investigation into online moderation. Assess. Matters **3**, 5–27 (2011)
11. Adie, L., Lloyd, M., Beutel, D.: Identifying discourses of moderation in higher education. J. Assess. Eval. High. Educ. **38**(8), 968–977 (2013)
12. Adie, L.: Towards a theoretical framework for online professional discussions. J. Learn. Des. JLD **7**(3), 54–66 (2014)
13. Grainger, P., Adie, L., Weir, K.: Quality assurance of assessment and moderation discourses involving sessional staff. J. Assess. Eval. High. Educ. **41**(4), 548–559 (2016)
14. MGI. Assessment Policy, Midrand (2010)
15. Van Staden, C.J., Van Biljon, J.A., Kroeze, J.H.: Adopting eModeration: understanding the user experience in the organisation. In: 8th European Conference on IS Management and Evaluation, ECIME 2014 Conference, pp. 356–365. Ghent, Belgium (2014)
16. ISODIS9241-210. Ergonomics of human systems interaction – Part 210: Human-centred design for interactive systems (formerly known as 13407). ISO (2010)
17. Hassenzahl, M., Tractinsky, N.: User experience – a research agenda. Behav. Inf. Technol. **25**(2), 91–97 (2006)
18. Roto, V.: Web browsing on mobile phones – characteristics of user experience. Doctoral dissertation. University of Technology, Helsinki (2006)
19. Wimmer, B., Wöckl, B., Leitner, M., Tscheligi, M.: Measuring the dynamics of User Experience in short interaction sequences. In: Proceedings of Nordic Computer-Human Interaction CHI 2010, pp. 825–828. ACM, Reykjavik (2010)
20. Law, E.: The measurability and predictability of User Experience. In: Conference Proceedings of EICS 2011, pp. 1–10, Pisa, ACM, New York (2011)
21. Van Schaik, P., Van Aranyi, G.: Research white paper model-based user experience. Teesside University (2014)
22. Van Der Peijl, J., Klein, J., Grass, C., Freudenthal, A.: Design for risk control: the role of usability engineering in the management of use-related risks. J. Biomed. Inform. **45**, 795–812 (2012)
23. Preece, J., Sharp, H., Roger, Y.: Interaction Design. 3rd edn. Wiley, Chichester (2011)
24. McCarthy, J., Wright, J.: Technology as Experience. MIT Press, Massachusetts (2007)
25. Väätäjä, H., Koponen, T., Roto, V.: Developing practical tools for user experience evaluation: a case from Mobile News Journalism. In: Proceedings of ECCE 2009 European Conference on Cognitive Ergonomics beyond the Product – Understanding Activity and User Experience in Ubiquitous Environments, Article 23. ACM, Helsinki (2009)
26. Schulze, K., Krömker, H.A.: A framework to measure User Experience of interactive online products. In: Proceedings of MB 2010 Conference, Article 14. ACM, New York (2010)

27. Ouma, S.: M-health user experience framework for the public healthcare sector. Ph.D. dissertation, Nelson Mandela Metropole University NMMU (2013)
28. Hassenzahl, M.: User experience (UX): towards an experiential perspective on product quality. In: Proceedings of the 20th International Conference of the Association Francophone d'Interaction Homme, pp. 11–15. Machine Metz, Proceedings of IHM (2008)
29. Väänänen-Vainio-Mattila, K., Wäljas, M.: Development of evaluation heuristics for web service User Experience. In: Proceedings of Computer-Human Interaction CHI EA 2009, 27th International Conference on Extended Abstracts on Human Factors in Computing Systems, pp. 3679–3684. ACM, Boston (2009)
30. Hevner, A.R., March, S.T., Ram, S.: Design science in information systems research. MIS Q. **28**(1), 75–105 (2004)
31. Aier, S., Fischer, C.: Criteria for progress of information systems design theories. Inf. Syst. E-Bus. Manage. **9**(1), 133–172 (2011)
32. Sonnenberg, C., Vom Brocke, J.: Evaluations in the science of the artificial – reconsidering the build-evaluate pattern in Design Science Research. Des. Sci. Res. Inf. Syst. Adv. Theory Pract. **7286**, 381–397 (2012)
33. Braun, V., Clarke, V.: Using thematical analysis in psychology. Qual. Res. Psychol. **3**(2), 77–101 (2006)
34. Gregor, S., Jones, D.: The anatomy of a design theory. J. Assoc. Inf. Syst. **8**(5), 312–335 (2007)
35. Cresswell, J.W.: A concise Introduction to Mixed Methods Research. SAGE Publications, London (2015)

Synthesis of Designing Framework for Constructivist Learning Environments Model to Enhancing Programming Problem Solving for Connecting Internet of Thing Devices

Nutthakarn Moeikao and Charuni Samat(✉)

Khon Kaen University, Khon Kaen, Thailand
thaibannok@hotmail.com

Abstract. Internet of Thing (IoT) programming requires a well algorithm design and systematic process of solving the problem, which will lead to efficient production. This research, adopted the principles of problem solving approach are applied problem solving and programming problem solving to encourage students to solve the programming problems for effectively designing new innovation or smart things from internet of thing devices. This research was to synthesis of designing framework for constructivist learning environments model to enhancing programming problem solving for connecting internet of thing devices. The model research: design and development process was employed in this study in phase I: statistic methods are document analysis, and survey. The procedures were as following: (1) synthesizing the theoretical framework and (2) synthesizing the designing framework. The result revealed that: (1) The designing framework comprises of: (1) Problem base, (2) Resources, (3) Cognitive Tools, (4) Collaboration, (5) Programming problem solving center, (6) Scaffolding, and (7) Programming Coaching Room. (2) The efficiency of this theoretical framework and designing framework were evaluated by expert review. They were found the theoretical framework and designing framework of learning environment are appropriate on instructional design.

Keywords: Designing framework · Learning environments · Problem solving Internet of things · Programming

1 Introduction

Nowadays, the world has entered the digital age and directly affect to the people's lifestyle. The development of digital technology bring to create the new innovation, products and services. The smart technology beginning plays an important role in our daily lives. Preparing learners for the digital world and to support the policy Thailand 4.0 and Education 4.0 should be targeted to develop higher order thinking skills and cognitive process rather than teaching to remember information [1]. Therefore, the current study must change the paradigm from "Teaching" to "Learning" that focuses on the learners are most important.

T.-T. Wu et al. (Eds.): ICITL 2018, LNCS 11003, pp. 253–260, 2018.
https://doi.org/10.1007/978-3-319-99737-7_26

IoT programming is an engineering design process that requires multiple skills, especially problem-solving skills [2]. The teaching and learning should focus on thinking skill to create knowledge. Explore knowledge from various sources. Analyze and make decisions correctly [3]. The students are able to solve problems from a situation as a process. Practicing this problem-solving skill will immobilize learners in linking what they have learned in the classroom to real-life. Using the engineering design process, there are tools for teaching and learning to reinforce and develop learners' learning through step-by-step thinking [2], which extends the knowledge to multiple perspective to solve the problem thoroughly and correctly until the development of innovation or how to be competitive in business and increase the intellectual ability of student [3].

Thus, this research was aimed at synthesis of designing framework for constructivist learning environments model to enhancing programming problem solving for connecting internet of thing devices in order to obtain the basis for constructing the appropriate and efficient learning environment model for the learners. Based on the principles of programming problem solving [4, 5] and psychological base theories lead students to develop the intellectual ability to solving the problems.

2 Methodology

This study was aimed to the synthesis of designing framework for constructivist learning environments model to enhancing programming problem solving for connecting internet of thing devices. Research methodology is model research 3 phases including; phase I: Model development, phase II: Model validation and phase III: Model use. In this study used phase I: Model development [6] the procedures were as following: (1) Studying principles and theories, (2) Synthesizing the theoretical framework, (3) Synthesizing the designing framework, and (4) Evaluating the efficiency of the theoretical framework and designing framework to enhance programming problem solving for connecting internet of thing devices.

2.1 Target Group

The target group consisted of 9 experts – 3 experts in content validity by specialized experts in computer programming field, 3 experts in instruction design who evaluated the learning environment model by specialized experts in designing learning environments for enhancing higher order thinking, and 3 experts in evaluation to evaluate the quality of research instruments by specialized experts in learning assessment. So, each experts are selected has specialized expertise in each area.

2.2 Research Instruments

The instruments in this study as following details: (1) the expert review recording for examining the quality in various domains as follows: learning contents validity expert, instructional design experts and media experts, (2) the document examination and analysis recording form, and (3) The recording form for synthesis of designing framework for constructivist learning environments model to enhancing programming problem solving for connecting internet of thing devices. 4) The participant's characteristic survey for designers, developers, and students [6].

2.3 Data Collecting and Analysis

The researchers collected the data in phase I as follows: (1) Synthesis of theoretical framework and components of the learning environment. The data were collected by analyzing principles, theories, related research of the constructivism theory, cognitive theory, media and technology theory, pedagogy, programming problem solving and contextual study. (2) Synthesis of Designing framework of the learning environment: The above synthesized theoretical framework was taken into this process.

The underlined theories base such as, psychological base, pedagogies base, media and technologies base, contextual base and programming problem solving base for the synthesis of the theoretical framework of the learning environment. (3) Evaluate of the learning environment by experts, including 3 experts of the content validity, 3 experts of the instructional design, and 3 experts of evaluation and are revised according to suggestions.

3 Results

The synthesis of designing framework for constructivist learning environments model to enhancing programming problem solving for connecting internet of thing devices are follows:

3.1 The Components of the Learning Environments Model

Synthesis of Theoretical Framework. The synthesis of the theoretical framework of constructivist learning environments model to enhancing programming problem solving for connecting internet of thing devices found 5 crucial bases include: Thailand's learning context base, Psychology base, Pedagogy base, Technology and Media base, and Programming Problem Solving base. (see Fig. 1).

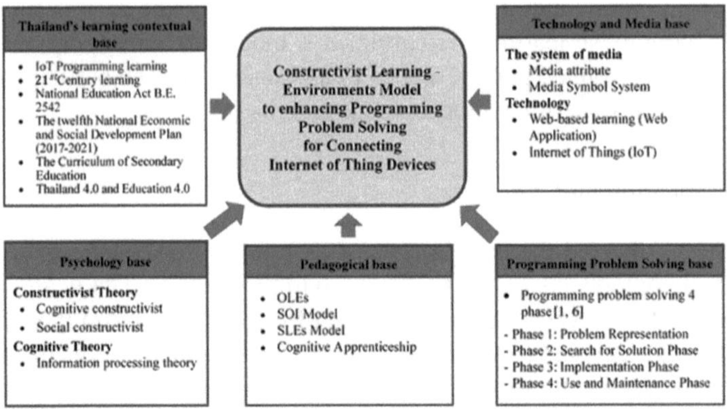

Fig. 1. Theoretical framework of Constructivist Learning Environments Model to enhancing Programming Problem Solving for Connecting Internet of Thing Devices

Synthesis of Designing Framework. According to this study, the findings of synthesis of the theoretical framework which was used as foundation in synthesizing the designing framework of constructivist learning environments model to enhancing programming problem solving for connecting internet of thing devices found that 4 crucial bases which include: *Activating Cognitive Structure, Programming Problem Solving*. Activating cognitive structure, programming problem solving. It illustrated the relationship between the underlined theories and the component as follows: Cognitive constructivism [7]; Cognitive conflict, Situated learning [8]; Authentic context, OLEs [9]; Enabling context, Programming problem solving [4, 5]; 4 phase of programming problem solving: Problem representation, Search for solutions, Implement solutions and Use and Maintenance of the component of which was called Problem base focused on authentic problem to promote programming problem solving, and contextualizing problems.

This may help activating cognitive structure of the students. (see Fig. 2).

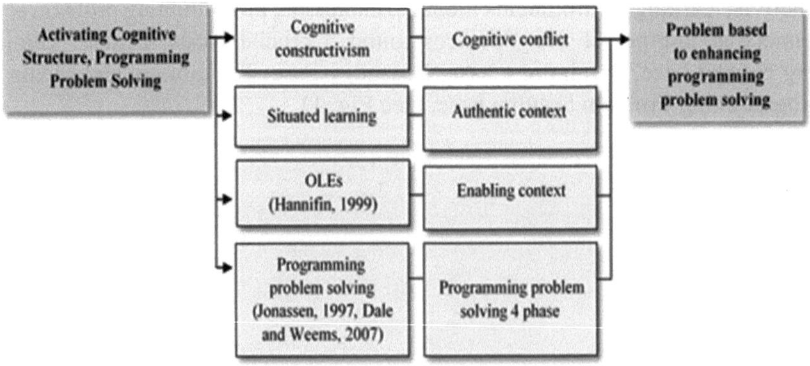

Fig. 2. Activating Cognitive Structure, Programming Problem Solving

Supporting Cognitive Equilibrium. Supporting cognitive equilibrium. It was illustrated the relationship between the underlined theories and the component as follows: Information Processing [10]; Sensory Register, Short-Term Memory, Long-Term Memory, SOI Model [11]; Selection, Organizing, Integrating, OLEs [9];Resource and Cognitive Tools designing of the component of which was called Resource and Cognitive Tools. It focused on how the students process the information effectively. This can help the students understand easily (see Fig. 3).

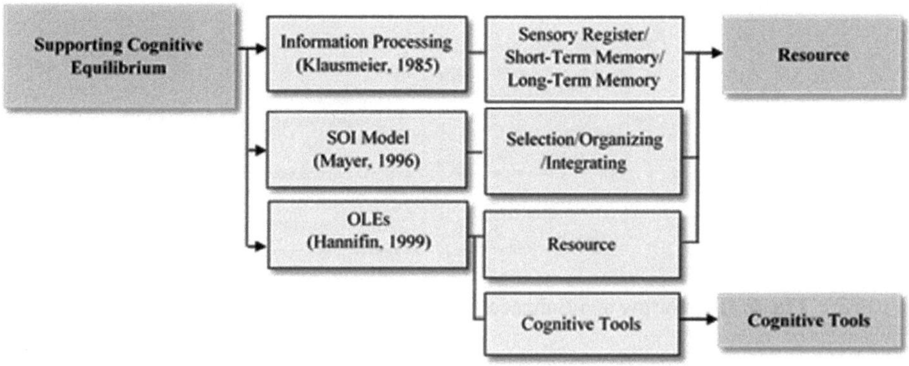

Fig. 3. Supporting cognitive equilibrium

Enhancing Programming Problem Solving. Enhancing programming problem solving. It illustrated the relationship between the underlined theories and the components as follows: Social Constructivism [12]; Social Interaction, The design of the component was called Collaboration, Programming problem solving [4, 5]; 4 phase of programming problem solving: Problem representation, Search for solutions, Implement solutions and Use and Maintenance the design of the component was called Programming Problem Solving Center (see Fig. 4).

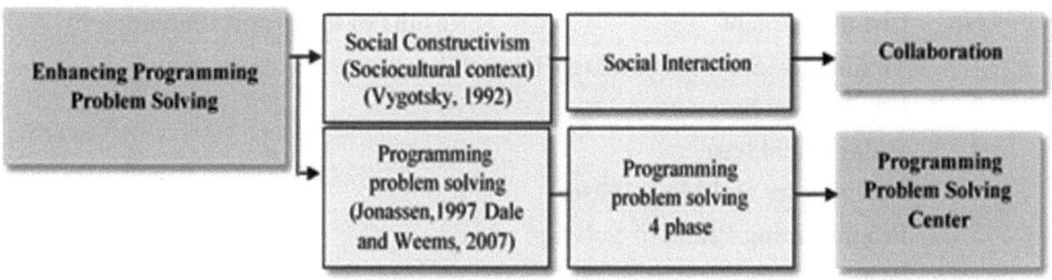

Fig. 4. Enhancing Programming Problem Solving

Supporting and Enhancement for Programming Problem Solving. Supporting and enhancement for constructing knowledge. It illustrated the relationship between the underlined theories and the components, as follows: Social Constructivism [12]; Zone of Proximal Development, OLEs [9]; and Programming problem solving [4, 5]; 4 phase of programming problem solving: Problem representation, Search for solutions,

Implement solutions and Use and Maintenance the design of the component was called 5 scaffolding included Conceptual, Metacognition, Procedural, Strategic and Programming. Cognitive Apprenticeship [8]; Coaching, The design of the component was called Programming Coaching Room (see Fig. 5).

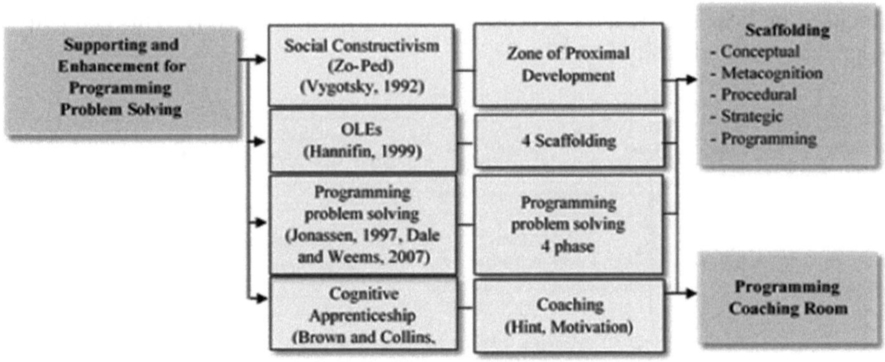

Fig. 5. Supporting and Enhancement for Programming Problem Solving

3.2 The Efficiency of the Learning Environments Model

The efficiency of the synthesis theoretical framework and designing framework for evaluating efficiency [13, 14], were illustrated as the following:

The Experts' Review. Showed that the design of the learning environment model were appropriate and congruent with underlined theories and principles as mentioned above in the theoretical framework and the designing framework, was appropriate detailed in Tables 1 and 2.

Table 1. The efficiency of theoretical framework

No.	List assessment	Results of the expert (Percentage)
1.	Thailand's learning contextual base	83
2.	Psychology base	79
3.	Pedagogical base	78
4.	Technology and Media base	81
5.	Programming Problem Solving base	83
Total		80.80

According to Table 1, the results of the assessment of the experts on the Thailand's learning contextual base (83%), the psychology base (79%), the pedagogical base (78%), the technology and media base (81%), the programming problem solving base (83%) and the total of the assessment of the experts was 80.80%.

Table 2. The efficiency of designing framework

No.	List assessment	Results of the expert (Percentage)
Learning content		
1.	Appropriate learning content	82
		82
The design elements of the learning environments model		
2.	Problem base	79
3.	Resources	78
4.	Cognitive Tools	80
5.	Collaboration	83
6.	Programming Problem Solving Center	85
7.	Scaffolding	73
8.	Programming Coaching Room	84
		80.29
Total		81.15

According to Table 2, the results of the assessment of the expert on the learning content (82%), the design elements of learning environments model (80.29%) and the total of the assessment of the experts was 81.15%.

The experts' review which was found that the elements of constructivist learning environments model to enhancing programming problem solving for connecting internet of thing devices appropriate for support learner to identify problems, create problems space (problem representation) [5], leads learner to search for the solution to solve problem based on the strategies suggestion, Leads learners to effective programming for connecting with IoT devices and know the solution to maintenance when an error occurs.

The Instructional Design of Learning Environment. Exactly consistent with the principles and theories used as a basis for design overall, more appropriate, and providing programming problem solving for connecting internet of thing devices.

4 Conclusion

The synthesis of designing framework confirmed the 7 important components i.e., (1) Problem base, (2) Resources, (3) Cognitive Tools (4) Collaboration, (5) Programming Problem Solving Center, (6) Scaffolding, and (7) Programming Coaching Room. Which will lead to the design and development constructivist learning environments model to enhancing programming problem solving for connecting internet of thing devices in order to support learning internet of things programming and promote the 21st century skills. And guide the development of learning in a context similar to encourage the students to have the skills and knowledge of programming languages. Finish this phase in Phase II the designing framework will be design to learning environment and validation by selected experts including internal validation of model component and external validation of model impact and in Phase III Model Use phase will using the learning environments for explanations about learners' using context, conditions that promote successful model use and success or failures of model use.

Acknowledgement. This work was supported by the Academic and Research Affairs, Innovation and Cognitive Technology Research Group, Faculty of Education, and the Research and Technology Transfers Affairs Division, Faculty of Education, Khon Kaen University.

References

1. Partnership for 21st Century Learning (P 21). Framework for 21st Century Learning (2009). http://www.p21.org/our-work/p21-framework. Accessed 3 Nov 2017
2. Jayavardhana, G., Rajkumar, B., Slaven, M., Marimuthu, P.: Internet of Things(IoT): a vision, architectural elements, and future directions. Fut. Gener. Comput. Syst. **29**(7), 1645–1660 (2013)
3. Madakam, S., Ramaswamy, R., Tripathi, S.: Internet of Things (IoT): a literature review. J. Comput. Commun. **3**, 164–173 (2015)
4. Dale, N.B., Weems, C.: Programming and Problem Solving with Java. Jones & Bartlett Learning (2007)
5. Jonassen, D.H.: Instructional design model for well-structured and ill-structured problem-solving learning outcomes. Educ. Tech. Res. Dev. **45**(1), 65–95 (1997)
6. Richey, R.C., Klein, J.D.: Design and Development Research: Methods, Strategies, and Issues. Routledge, New York (2007)
7. Piaget, J.: The Equilibration of Cognitive Structures: The Central Problem of Intellectual Development. University of Chicago Press, Chicago (1985)
8. Brown, J.S., Collins, A., Duguid, P.: Situated cognition and the culture of learning. Educ. Res. **18**(1), 32–43 (1989)
9. Hannafin, M.: Open Learning Environments: Foundation, Method, and Models. In Charles, New Jersey (1999)
10. Klausmeier, H.J.: (Information Processing Theory) (1985). http://www.oknation.net/blog/print.php?id=132965. Accessed 13 May 2015
11. Mayer, R.E. (ed.): The Cambridge Handbook of Multimedia Learning. Cambridge University Press, New York (2005)
12. Vygotsky, L.: Thinking and Speaking. MIT Press, Cambridge (1962)
13. Chijaroen, S.: Education Technology: Principles, Theories, and Implementation. Anna Ofset, Khon Kaen (2014)
14. Samat, C., Chaijaroen, S., Kanjug, I., Vongtathum, P.: Design and development of constructivist multimedia learning environment enhancing skills in computer programming. In: Proceedings - 2017 6th IIAI International Congress on Advanced Applied Informatics, IIAI-AAI 2017, Japan (2017)

Multidisciplinary Learning Material and Effect in a Technological University – A Case Study of Technology and Life Application in General Education

Kuen-Ming Shu[1] and Chi-Cheng Chang[2(✉)]

[1] Department of Mechanical and Computer-Aided Engineering, National Formosa University, No. 64, Wunhua Road, Huwei, Yunlin, Taiwan
kmshu@nfu.edu.tw

[2] Department of Technology Application and Human Resource Development, National Taiwan Normal University, No. 162, He-Ping East Road Sec1, Taipei, Taiwan
samchang@ntnu.edu.tw

Abstract. The impact of teaching material design for multidisciplinary learning on learning achievement with science and technological university students was examined. The participants were students enrolling in an elective general education course, named Technology and Life Application, at a technological university. The experiment lasted for one semester with a total of 16 weeks. The results revealed that the teaching material design for the four topics, including ultrasonic machining, abrasive jet machining, investment casting, and precision welding machining, significantly enhanced students' learning achievement. However, the teaching material design for the topics of laser beam machining and electrical discharge machining did not have a significant effect on learning achievement. Therefore, the contents of the teaching materials for the topics of laser beam machining and electrical discharge machining required revisions.

Keywords: Multidisciplinary teaching material · Multidisciplinary learning Technology and Life Application

1 Background

Innovations are hard to be done only in a certain field since the world changes rapidly with the continuous development of technology. In the meantime, the ability to create an innovation with multidisciplinary fields is crucial. Cross-domain learning is a process for one's lifetime [1]. It is possible that one incidentally acquires knowledge, which is useless at first but becomes useful after several years. Learning knowledge from an unfamiliar field requires a strong learning motivation that comes from curiosity, not short-term goals.

The key feature for technology universities is practical training programs. Most practical training programs are "learning-by-doing" [2]. However, it has been too early

T.-T. Wu et al. (Eds.): ICITL 2018, LNCS 11003, pp. 261–271, 2018.
https://doi.org/10.1007/978-3-319-99737-7_27

to ask students to choose a major when entering higher education, since it has limited students to focus on only one field. Students can only acquire knowledge and skills from a specific field, which has made them unfamiliar with knowledge and skills in other fields. Consequently, in order to effectively improve the phenomenon, the implementation of general education has been conducted. The main purpose for general education is to cultivate students' cultural literacy, life wisdom, analysis capability, communication skills, and lifelong learning motivation. The intention for general education courses tend to be practicable and entertaining, which is related with daily life. With this intention, the Center for General Education of National Formosa University in Taiwan has opened a course named Technology and Life Application for students to enroll. The paper designed the teaching material for the course and examined self-perceived effect after the implementation of the course with multidisciplinary students. The research question used for this study is accordingly: What is the content of the teaching material of Technology and Life Application course that significantly contribute to the students? How is the student's learning achievement?

2 Literature Review

2.1 Intention of General Education

According to Wikipedia [3], general education has two intentions, which are comprehensive education and holistic education. General education is a recent popular curriculum that is based on the perspective of six arts education in the era of Pre-Qin, or liberal arts in the Western culture. Furthermore, the perspective of general education in recent high schools is according to the 19th century, which was a period that western scholars proposed the viewpoint of general education because they found that academic division has been too narrow and knowledge has been strictly isolated. The purpose of general education is to help students think independently and achieve mastery through a comprehensive study of the subject with knowledge from various majors. In other words, the final aim of general education is to cultivate a complete and perfect person. Since the 20th century, general education has become core courses required to be taken by university students.

2.2 Necessity of General Education

Technology and the New Liberal Arts by DeVore [4] pointed out that educators are responsible for social guidance and direction, as well as hints for the future development. Under the continuous technological development and global industrialization, irretrievable universal nightmares including rapid population growth, malnutrition, and rapid ruining of natural resources, have occurred. Technology educators have perceived the tendency of self-destruction and the outcome of technology development, by pointing out that the mistakes caused by products of the continuous industrialization, and suggested that the enhancement of general education is the only way to facilitate a diverse social development and a correct life style.

Mcdowell [5] thought that thorough education in the 21st century was to integrate the intention of liberal arts into professional and technical courses. An individual with mono-dimensional skill is unable to exist in such a rapid changing technology society. Mcdowell [5] also suggested that one could find a desirable job only with professional knowledge, but general ability is key for one to successfully and continuously stay on the job. Thus, it is important to leave some spaces for students to develop advanced ability and interests after taking general courses, which help students gain a skill for lifelong learning.

2.3 Importance of Multidisciplinary Learning

What is multidisciplinary learning? Multidisciplinary learning includes several elements: multidisciplinary lectures, multidisciplinary text books, multidisciplinary student seminars, multidisciplinary internships, and multidisciplinary theses [6]. With the continuous development of technology, innovations are difficult to complete in a specific field, so ability of cross-domain integration is especially important [7]. When facing the complex and changeable world, governments engage in manpower cultivation plans. For the basis of science learning, the horizontal integration of multidisciplinary learning is the world trend which leads learners to explore various phenomenon in daily life and engage in deep learning on innovations and connections. Finnish National Board of Education [8] proposed a new syllabus which emphasized the cultivation for literacy of horizontal integration and multidisciplinary learning. Schools should create a cooperative learning environment and provide students an opportunity for multidisciplinary learning at least once a year, so that students are able to participate in multidisciplinary phenomenon-based projects. The syllabus also emphasized that a context should be integrated into learning because the integration of multiple disciplines can lead to overall understanding and even problem solving. For the design of teaching materials, teachers from different fields should prepare lessons together and adopt some learning methods including inquiry learning, problem-oriented learning, project learning and portfolio learning. Besides, students need to participate in learning by being encouraged to work with a community of experts. By doing so, students are able to distinguish, analyze, and utilize messages, data, and knowledge, as well as engage in deep learning from practice in their field [9].

Multidisciplinary learning can connect with daily life, social, international affairs, history, literature and philosophy, as well as technology, which enhances learning motivation and broadens one's horizon. Learning with practices or internships is a concept of "learning-by-doing." As long as the goal is to guide students to get rid of routine learning, to integrate knowledge, and to solve problems, any instructional style including problem-oriented, inquiry, or even integrated instructions can probably reach the same effect as multidisciplinary learning.

2.4 Indicators for Assessment of Learning Achievement

For assessment indicators of learning achievement, some studies used test scores [10–12], and some studies used self-assessment or self-perception [13]. Motiwalla and Tello [13] pointed out that learners' learning achievement should be assessed by both objective and subjective methods. Self-assessment, where learners assess their own learning performance subjectively, included self-perceived effect in a questionnaire responded by learners. Self-perceived effect is what students subjectively assess learning achievement, mainly including metacognitive skills and performance, by themselves [14]. Learning achievement need to be assessed, and the assessment should ensure the gap between the knowledge that students hold and the knowledge that students desire to have. The core for learning achievement is to assess learners' behavior changes due to knowledge that they have and their enjoyment with the learning situations. From the viewpoint, students' learning effect can be categorized into formal or standard test.

3 Research Method

3.1 Participant

Participants were 50 students enrolling in an elective general education course, named Technology and Life Application at a national technological university.

3.2 Framework

The study examined the learning achievement subjectively assessed by the students, which differs from the objective assessment, and achievement tests. The framework is shown in Fig. 1.

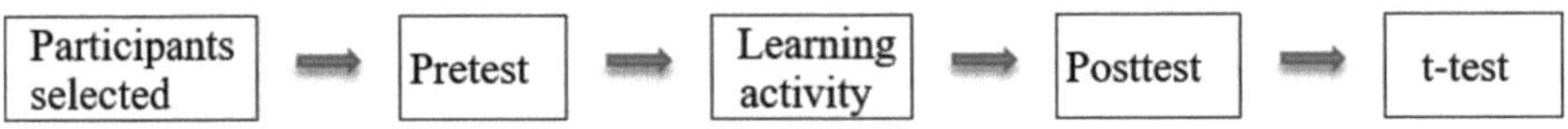

Fig. 1. Research framework

3.3 Procedure

Preparation. For efficiency, instructors summarized and analyzed the relevant technological equipment at special processing laboratories in the school, meticulously listed equipment that could be completed within one semester by multidisciplinary students, and then undertaking the development of teaching materials and assessment rubrics for machining.

Pretest. In order to get to know students' background about technology knowledge before the experiment, students received a pretest including the information about students' gender, department, and technological knowledge on ultrasonic machining, electrical discharge machining, abrasive jet machining, investment casting, laser beam machining, opto-mechatronic machining, and precision welding machining.

Learning Activity. The experiment lasted for 16 weeks, with three hours a week, for a total of 48 h. The instructional contents included ultrasonic machining, electrical discharge machining, abrasive jet machining, investment casting, laser beam machining, opto-mechatronic machining, precision welding machining, and aesthetics. Instructors firstly lectured on self-editing teaching materials for about 30 min, and then students participated in each kind of machining practices.

Posttest. In order to understand students' learning achievement after the experiment, students received a posttest in the last week. The final version of the posttest was revised together by the researcher and instructors.

3.4 Reliability and Validity

Item Analysis. Item analysis was performed for examining the reliability of the pretest and posttest. The top 27% of the total scores were assigned to the high score group, whereas the last 27% were assigned to the low score group. The independent sample t-test was conducted to examine the differences between the high score group and the low score group. The results, as shown in Table 1, revealed that t value for each item was significant, indicating that the tests possessed a good discrimination level. Pearson's correlation was then performed to examine the relationships between each item and the test. The result was consistent, so no item was deleted.

Table 1. Item analysis for pretest and posttest

Questionnaire	Item	Item-total correlation	CR (t)	Retain/delete
Pretest	1	0.532***	−3.165**	Retain
	2	0.487***	−3.616***	Retain
	3	0.699***	−4.611***	Retain
	4	0.778***	−6.450***	Retain
	5	0.642***	−6.495***	Retain
	6	0.399**	−2.590*	Retain
Posttest	1	0.605***	−2.582*	Retain
	2	0.757***	−8.433***	Retain
	3	0.853***	−6.601***	Retain
	4	0.836***	−8.944***	Retain
	5	0.700***	−8.242***	Retain
	6	0.544***	−4.662***	Retain

$^*p < .050$, $^{**}p < .010$, $^{***}p < .001$

Factor Analysis and Reliability. The Kaiser-Meyer-Olkin (KMO) index was greater than 0.5 and the Bartlett test of sphericity was significant (see Table 2), indicating that factor analysis could be performed. Principal factor analysis (PEA) with an orthogonal rotation was conducted to examine the construct validity. The result showed that factor loading for each item in the pretest was greater than 0.390 and posttest was greater than 0.660, indicating that there was no need to delete items. The explained variance of the pretest was greater than 38.000% and posttest was greater than 54%, revealing that the

Table 2. Validity and reliability for pretest and posttest

Scale	KMO	Explained variance	Bartlett test of sphericity		Cronbach's α
			Chi-square	Sig.	
Pretest	0.502	38.174%	65.829	0.000	0.661
Posttest	0.692	54.236%	140.815	0.000	0.812

Table 3. Factor analysis for pretest and posttest

Scale	Item	Eigenvalue	Explained variance	Factor load
Pretest	1	2.290	38.174%	0.796
	2			0.703
	3			0.679
	4			0.593
	5			0.445
	6			0.391
Posttest	1	3.254	54.236%	0.827
	2			0.795
	3			0.731
	4			0.701
	5			0.684
	6			0.666

tests possessed good construct validity, as shown in Table 3. Cronbach's α for the pretest was greater than 0.6, the posttest was greater than 0.8, indicating that the tests had a good reliability.

4 Result and Discussion

4.1 Design of Teaching Material

The teaching materials in the experiment were created according to the course instructors' teaching experiences on nontraditional machining courses for many years in the college of engineering. The knowledge technology adopted for the experiment was appropriate for multidisciplinary students. The contents for nontraditional machining courses include electrical discharge machining, laser beam machining, chemical machining, abrasive jet machining, electrochemical machining, electron beam machining, ion beam machining, plasma beam machining, ultrasonic machining, and water jet machining (Hsu, 2014). For the purpose of the appropriateness of the instructional equipment, ultrasonic machining, electrical discharge machining, abrasive jet machining, and laser beam machining were selected, plus opto-mechatronic machining, precision welding machining, investment casting, and aesthetics, as the teaching materials that could be accepted by multidisciplinary students.

4.2 Student Background

The participants were students enrolling in an elective general education course, named Technology and Life Application, at a national technological university in the year of 2017. There were a total of 50 students from different colleges in the university, which satisfied the features for random sampling. The distributions of gender and college for the participants are shown in Fig. 2.

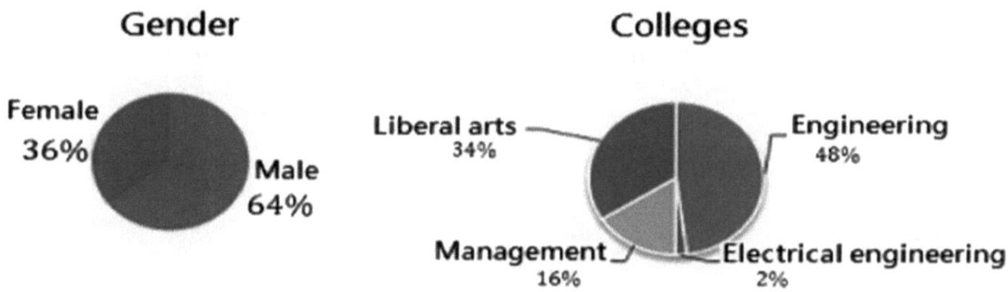

Fig. 2. The distributions of gender and college for the participants

The analysis of the participants' familiarity towards each topic of teaching materials is shown in Table 4. Most of the participants were unfamiliar with the contents of the teaching materials. Students whose family was engaging in the occupation of machining or who worked in the occupation of machining were familiar with the contents. As shown in Fig. 3, 64% of the students never experienced such machining methods.

Table 4. Familiarity towards each topic of teaching materials

Topic	Very familiar	Familiar	Heard before	Never heard before
Ultrasonic machining	0 (0%)	22 (44%)	25 (50%)	3 (6%)
Laser beam machining	1 (2%)	20 (40%)	29 (58%)	0 (0%)
Abrasive jet machining	0 (0%)	12 (24%)	32 (64%)	6 (12%)
Electrical discharge machining	0 (0%)	15 (30%)	30 (70%)	5 (10%)
Investment casting	1 (2%)	17 (34%)	28 (56%)	4 (8%)
Precision welding machining	1 (2%)	18 (36%)	22 (44%)	9 (18%)

4.3 Satisfaction

Students' satisfaction after the experiment is shown in Fig. 4. Sixty-six percent of the students were very satisfied with the general course, 32% felt satisfied, and 2% expressed neutral. The outcome revealed that the course was successfully.

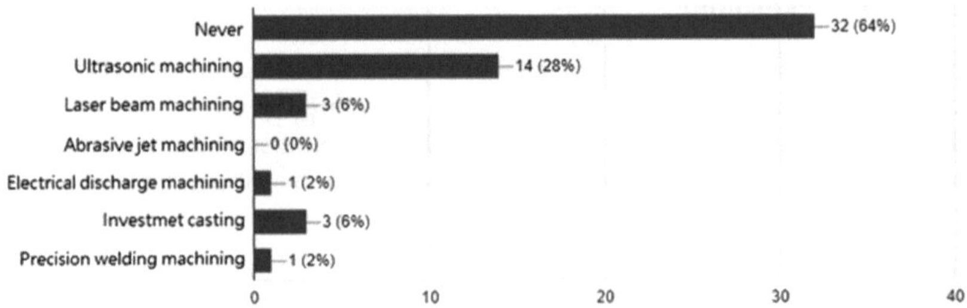

Fig. 3. The distribution for machining methods that students used before the experiment

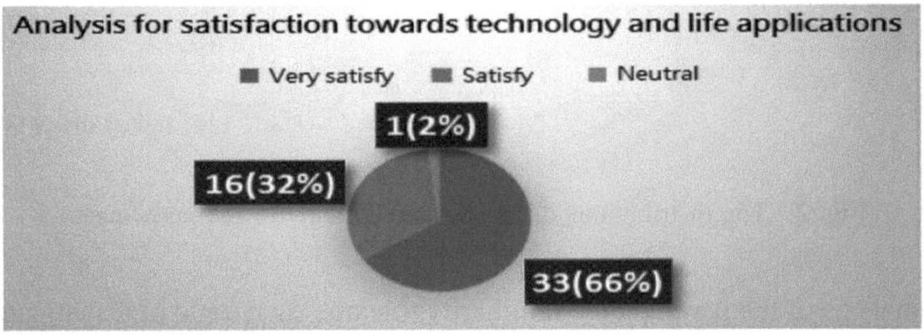

Fig. 4. Satisfaction after taking the course

4.4 Learning Achievement

Students' learning achievement after taking the course is shown in Table 5. The students performed best in ultrasonic machining because about 90% of these students had the ability to guide others to operate the equipment. The reason can be that the machining is safe and fast, and students are able to get a sense of achievement when creating a custom key ring by themselves. The students performed poor in electrical discharge machining since only about 3% of the students had the ability to guide others to operate the equipment, and even about 4% did not like to operate the equipment. In reasoning, there are sparks generated during the process of machining, which is dangerous; the machining is slow, and the smell is unpleasant.

4.5 Differences in Learning Achievement Before and After the Experiment

The scale was a 4-point Likert-type scale with response options from 1 to 4, in order to avoid the bias resulted from neutral option. For the pretest, the participants who were "very familiar with" the teaching material about a specific topic got the highest score (4), followed by "familiar with" (3), "heard before" (2), and the participants who had "never heard of" the teaching material about a specific topic got the lowest score (1). For the posttest, the participants who expressed that "I have ability to guide others to operate the equipment for completing the work" had the highest score (4), followed by "I can operate the equipment to complete the work by myself" (3), "I still need others to

Table 5. Learning achievement for each topic

Topic	I have the ability to guide others to operation the equipment and create a product	I can operate the equipment and create a product by myself	I still need someone to guide me for operating the equipment and creating a product	I do not like to operate the equipment
Ultrasonic machining	45 (90%)	5 (10%)	0 (0%)	0 (0%)
Laser beam machining	5 (10%)	20 (40%)	25 (50%)	0 (0%)
Abrasive jet machining	15 (30)%	32 (64%)	3 (6%)	0 (0%)
Electrical discharge machining	3 (6%)	17 (34%)	28 (56%)	2 (4%)
Investment casting	24 (48%)	17 (34%)	9 (18%)	0 (0%)
Precision welding machining	31 (62%)	18 (36%)	1 (2%)	0 (0%)

guide me to operate the equipment for completing the work" (2), and the participants who expressed that "I do not like to operate the equipment" had the lowest score (1). The four response options in the posttest, including very familiar, familiar, heard before, and never heard, were corresponding to the four response options in the pretest. A paired-samples t test was employed to compare differences in learning achievement for each topic before and after the experiment. For effect sizes, Cohen (1988) mentioned that indicator of effect sizes for the t test is expressed by Cohen's d for distinguishing whether a statistical significance is meaningful.

Table 6. Summary for t test on differences in learning achievement between pretest and posttest

Topic	Pretest		Posttest		t	Effect size	Sig.
	Mean	SD	Mean	SD			
Ultrasonic machining	2.4	0.32	3.9	0.3	16.4	2.625	0***
Laser beam machining	2.46	0.54	2.6	0.67	1.14	0.25	0.25
Abrasive jet machining	2.12	0.59	3.04	0.4	9.07	1.549	0***
Electrical discharge machining	2.2	0.61	2.44	0.68	1.87	0.39	0.06
Investment casting	2.3	0.65	3.3	0.76	7.07	1.55	0***
Precision welding machining	2.22	0.76	3.58	0.57	10.06	1.78	0***

***$p < .001$

In Table 6, the four topics, which were ultrasonic machining, abrasive jet machining, investment casting, and precision welding machining, significantly enhanced students' learning achievement. On the other hand, laser beam machining and electrical discharge machining did not have a significant result, so they required revisions.

5 Conclusion

The study adopted the subjective assessment indicator, self-perceived effect, to examine learning achievement on multidisciplinary learning with the design of teaching materials in the technological university. The result revealed that after the experiment, 98% of students felt satisfied or very satisfying with the general course. Students had significant learning achievement in the four topics including ultrasonic machining, abrasive jet machining, investment casting, and precision welding machining, whereas students did not have significant learning achievement in the two topics including laser beam machining and electrical discharge machining which were required to be revised. There were significant differences in cognition, skill, affection, and overall self-perceived effect before and after the experiment, indicating that the multidisciplinary general course significantly affected students' self-perceived effect.

The course required the participants doing by hands. The participants' designs of works were personalized souvenirs. They came from different departments for the multidisciplinary learning. Therefore, the operation of the equipment was a novelty to them. The materialization of the personalized design also enhanced the satisfaction toward the course. The study results suggested that general education in the future should be delivered by the multidisciplinary method with the instructional strategy of learning-by-doing.

References

1. Weizhi, N., Anan, L., Wenhui, L., Yuting, S.: Cross-view action recognition by cross-domain learning. Image Vis. Comput. **55**(2), 109–118 (2016)
2. Ludovic, B., Pol-Bernard, G., Carl-Philippe, R., Safouana, T.: Learning by doing: A teaching method for active learning in scientific graduate education. J. Eur. J. Eng. Educ. **30**(1), 105–119 (2005)
3. Wikipedia. https://en.wikipedia.org/wiki/General_education
4. DeVore, P.W.: Technology and the new liberal arts. University of Northern Iowa, Washington D.C. (1976)
5. McDowell, J.L.: Increasing the liberal arts content of the professional/technical curriculum. In: Proceedings of Annual Conference of the Association for General and Liberal Studies, Daytona Beach, Florida (1996)
6. Hashimoto, S.: Multidisciplinary learning extends communication skill, and helps cross cultural understandings: biomedical engineering. Syst. Cybern. Inf. **15**(6), 106–112 (2017)
7. Sun, J.: Why is the ability for multidisciplinary learning important? Blog of Common Wealth Magazine (2015). http://blog.cw.com.tw/blog/profile/256/article/2661

8. Finnish National Agency for Education Homepage. http://www.oph.fi/english/curricula_and_qualifications/basic_education
9. Hong, Y.S.: Learning trend: Integrative learning based on multidiscipline and phenomenology. E-Paper about National Academy for Educational Research 134 (2016)
10. Hu, P.J., Hui, W., Clark, T.H.K., Milton, J., Ma, W., Tam, K.Y.: Examining e-learning effectiveness, outcomes and learning style: a longitudinal field experiment. In: Proceedings of Annual Meeting of Pacific Asia Conference on Information System, Bangkok, Thailand (2005)
11. Piccoli, G., Ahmad, R., Ives, B.: Web-based virtual learning environments: a research framework and a preliminary assessment of effectiveness in basic IT skills training. MIS Q. **25**(4), 401–426 (2001)
12. Uribe, D., Klein, J.D., Sullivan, H.: The effect of computer-mediated collaborative learning on solving III-defined problems. Educ. Technol. Res. Dev. **51**(1), 5–19 (2003)
13. Motiwalla, L., Tello, S.: Distance learning on the internet: an exploratory study. Internet High. Educ. **2**(4), 253–264 (2000)
14. Chang, C.C., Peng, S.R.: Use and effects of web-based portfolio assessment on computer course of junior high schools. J. Taiwan Normal Univ. Sci. Educ. **53**(2), 31–57 (2008)

Educational Technology in Resource-Constrained Environments: A Nigerian Case Study

Japari Ngilari(✉)

Department of Learning Technologies, University of North Texas,
3940 N. Elm Suite G150, Denton, TX 76207, USA
japaringilari@my.unt.edu

Abstract. Resource-constrained educational environments are unable to attain optimal pedagogical benefits due to impeding social, economic and cultural factors. This paper is an exploration of learning in these environments, employing Nigeria as the geographical context. The focus is on reported case studies of technological interventions and the associated learning outcomes. Findings reveal a limited number of studies, a sole preference for the quantitative research methodology and software-based educational technology. However, the reviewed studies are unanimous in their verdict of the impact of educational technology on the learning. Accounts of improved confidence, engagement, performance/achievement, retention, participation collaboration were documented.

Keywords: Resource constrained · Learning · Educational technology
Nigeria

1 Introduction

In a modern developed society, access to food, shelter, clothing, primary healthcare and education are all normative. However, even within such societies the degree of access varies. For some, it comes at a higher price, if at all. In populations where such access is limited, they are considered resource-constrained environments. Although there are many discussions in the literature regarding these environments and its inhabitants in a wide variety of disciplines, the focus here is on learning. Basically, this paper seeks to explore the outcomes of educational technology interventions in such environments; their contexts, their nature, their outcomes. This discussion will proceed as follows; a brief literature review and then results of the systematic search will be provided with subsequent analysis on the caveat that this is only preliminary. The wider implications of these findings conclude.

T.-T. Wu et al. (Eds.): ICITL 2018, LNCS 11003, pp. 272–281, 2018.
https://doi.org/10.1007/978-3-319-99737-7_28

2 Literature Review

2.1 Resource Constraints

There are many purported benefits to getting an education; improved welfare, economic prospects and intellectual merits amongst others. It is also true that accessibility to educational resources in any society is seldom ever uniform. Barriers include social, economic and cultural factors. Being born for instance, into a setting where education is not prioritized can set one at a disadvantage. Required support to excel at school will be absent. Evidence has shown that children from disadvantaged backgrounds are more likely to encounter educational detainment through the years [1]. In some cultural settings, there may be a preference for educating boys over girls; this is the case for some northern subcultures in Nigeria. Others may just lack the financial resources to go to school. This begins a consequent trend of disadvantages that may continue from childhood to adulthood. The result is an unfortunate cyclical relationship; though education can break social disadvantages, where it already exists it can reinforce them.

Indeed, it then becomes imperative that mediative strategies in policy, pedagogy or otherwise should be pursued to assuage this. Some interventions that have had some history of success include early childhood intervention schemes, adult literacy programs and policy reforms. Others in the realm of technology, e.g. internet access have had a mixed reception. Though the web can reduce the geographical proximity to educational resources; much reliance on it can also disenfranchise non-users towards digital and consequently, social exclusion [2]. This depicts the conundrum of educational technology in resource-constrained environments; a metaphorical porcupine problem, if you will. For whom it may be the most beneficial, it may also be the least accessible. Thus, designing technology for such educational settings has its own set of concerns; pedagogical and technical. Factors such as literacy, adoption and competency as well as usability, scalability and sustainability will have to be considered, respectively.

2.2 Educational Technology

The definition of educational technology has evolved; often used interchangeably with the terms 'learning technology' and 'instructional design'. Without an undue emphasis on semantics, the perspectives of many acclaimed scholars have been surmised into an all-inclusive definition: "Educational technology is the study and ethical practice of facilitating learning and improving performance by creating, using and managing appropriate technological processes and resources." (p. 1) [3]. This definition is both intentional and justified. Some of the operational elements of interest here are:

- *study*: information gathering, both theoretical and empirical about the applications of technology to learning
- *facilitation*: the role of technology to support not create or cause learning. It includes environmental design, organization and resources allocation
- *appropriate*: this involves ensuring that processes and resources are suitable and compatible with the desired objective

- *technological*: this comprises of hardware and software resources such as audio, video, computer programs, disks et cetera

The research premise here encourages ties to and study of practice; why to proffer an educational technology solution and what happens after it is adopted. The design here also denotes more than a creative process of engineering a new artefact; it encompasses decision making regarding the educational environment, audience, resources, limitations and learning outcomes. In essence, there is an interest of course in how technology is used for learning but also on how it comes into use in learning. This bi-functional view of educational technology is captured succinctly as an approach to: "(1) design, develop and evaluate, human and mechanical resources efficiently and effectively in order to facilitate and leverage all aspects of learning, and (2) guide change agency and transformation of educational systems and practices in order to contribute to influencing change in society" (p. 107) [4].

Both definitions imply then that social, economic and cultural factors influence educational technology. Arguably stated, educational technology itself is not neutral, and discourse thereof is shaped by context; much of which has been presented here [5].

3 Research Design

3.1 Research Motivation

It has been shown that education is universally beneficial but not universally accessible, and that technology is an effective intervention but not without its impediments. The etymology of educational technology provides a basis for its research from a cultural/environmental perspective. In light of this, this study of how educational technology is conceptualized, designed and evaluated in resource-constrained environments is warranted. The Nigerian context considered here is merely illustrative of overarching socioeconomic parallels that exist the world over. Information uncovered can offer insight into optimizing the learning outcomes that are derivative.

3.2 Research Question(s)

This study initially began with an intent to advice on design considerations for resource-constrained environments. A so-titled search of electronic material was carried out that proved abortive. In hindsight, it was highly unlikely that such broad design decisions will be delineated in a solitary publication effort. Narrowing the interests regionally yielded more relevant background material and shaped the ensuing research question; 'what is the impact of technology interventions on learning outcomes in Nigerian educational environments?'

The terms of this research question are employed in their simplest forms. Technology here refers to any artefact, tangible or intangible, that is associated with computing. Intervention is the introduction of any of these artefacts into the instructional process. Learning outcomes refers to the direct or indirect impact on student learning. Educational environment refers to the physical territory where these interactions occur, typically in a classroom or likewise.

4 Methodology

4.1 Systematic Search

This study employs a systematic literature review to address the research above question [6]. A search of an electronic database, Education Resource Information Center (ERIC) at eric.ed.gov was conducted using the keywords ‘design learning technology’. It was restricted to include peer-reviewed articles, and the indicated location was Nigeria. No publication type or date preferences were provided. Subsequently, each abstract was scanned to narrow publications to empirical case studies. Reviews, opinions or synthesis articles were excluded.

4.2 Filtering Criteria

The body of the article was evaluated with particular emphasis on the methodology section. The criteria for inclusion holds that the article must report an actual learning technology (could be any artefact at all; ‘hard’ and/or ‘soft’) deployed in an identified learning environment and for a learning-minded objective. The article must use primary data. Exclusion is made here for studies that are conducted cross-regionally, that is, Nigeria and one or more other countries. Relatedly, this also holds for articles reporting historical data (from studies not conducted by the primary author(s)).

5 Results

The initial results of the search yielded fifty-six articles. When the abstract were scanned, the number was whittled down to twenty-six articles. The application of the other inclusion and exclusion criteria resulted in the elimination of six more articles.

The final set of relevant articles were twenty; these are classified in Table 1 below. The sources are listed in no particular order. The results were classified by academic level of study, the subject in which the student participants were enrolled, the type of technology used and primary impact on learning [3, 4]. Any peculiar or purposive characteristic of the participant population is referenced in the ‘other’ section of the demographic context, but this is not applicable to all reviewed studies.

6 Analysis

The statistical analysis of the results will provide two-fold. First, the descriptive statistics which is categorized by grade level (Fig. 1), discipline (Fig. 2) and technology (Fig. 3). The inferential statistics in Fig. 4 follows after that.

Table 1. Classification of studies in educational technology

Source	Demographic context		Educational technology	Learning outcomes
	Level	Discipline		
[6]	University	Mathematics	Cloud Services	Students confidence in subject matter and behavioral engagement improved
[7]	High School	Environmental Science	Geographic Information System - Envi-Geo Info System (EGIS)	Student learning and retention improved
[8]	Higher Education *Other:* Technical School	Social Studies	Laptop and Mobile Phone	Increased degree of engagement and participation among students
[9]	College	Curriculum Studies	Wordle application	The group that used wordle performed better than those that used lecture method
[10]	Elementary	Mathematics	C++ Application Program	Students preferred using package to manual calculations
[11]	High School	Biology	Video DVD Instructional package	Students using the technology achieved higher scores than other group
[12]	High School *Other:* Hearing Impaired	Economics	Hardware	Improved student achievement from pretest to post test
[13]	High School	Geometry	Computer Assisted Instruction (CAI) - (Animation with Narration)	Learning achievement favor the group exposed to multimedia
[14]	High School	Chemistry	Computer Assisted Instruction (CAI) - Computer Simulation	Increase in student engagement and learning especially towards difficult concepts
[15]	High School	Geometry	Video-based instructional package	Students in co-operative mediated settings performed better than those in individual settings
[16]	University	Educational Technology	Blended Learning (BYOD - Bring Your Own Device)	Students performance was increased in blended learning settings as compared to traditional teaching methods

(*continued*)

Table 1. (*continued*)

Source	Demographic context		Educational technology	Learning outcomes
	Level	Discipline		
[6]	University	Mathematics	Cloud Services	Students confidence in subject matter and behavioral engagement improved
[17]	High School	Physics	Computer Assisted Jigsaw II	Students in computer mediated collaborative settings performed better than those in individual settings
[18]	High School	Physics	Computer Assisted Learning Package	Collaborative learning was preferred to individualised learning; students attitude to learning also improved
[19]	High School	Physics	Computer Assisted Instruction (CAI)	Improvement in student retention and motivation for physics
[20]	High School	Biology	Animated Instructional Resources (AIR)	Improved students learning of subject matter and technology is suitable for in or out of classroom teaching
[21]	University	Mathematics	Advanced Intranet-Internet Pedagogical Package (AIPP)	Students performance improved
[22]	High School	Peace Education	Instructional games	Students had positive attitudes towards instructional games and their achievement improved also
[23]	High School	Agricultural Science	Computer based multimedia maize breeding package	The mean achievement scores of students in computer based setting was better than those taught using conventional methods
[24]	High School	Creative Arts (Drawing & Painting)	Computer-based animated drawing tool	Student performance improved
[25]	High School	Biology	Computer Assisted Instruction (CAI)	Students exposed to CAI performed better than those who weren't

6.1 Descriptive Statistics

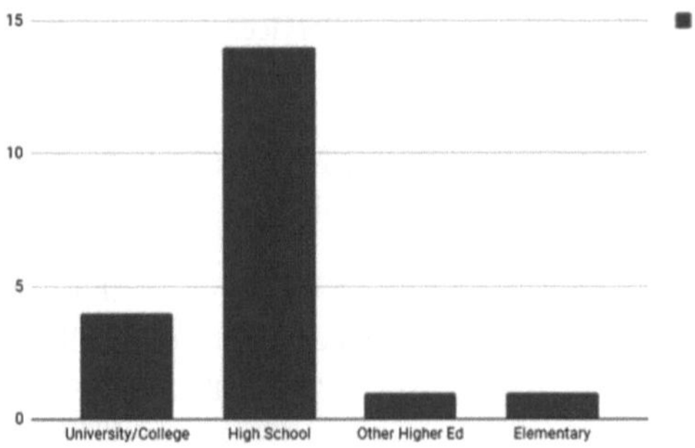

Fig. 1. Reviewed studies by grade level

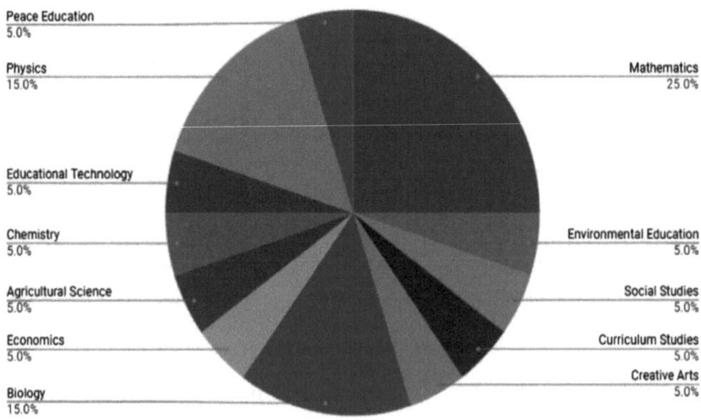

Fig. 2. Reviewed studies by discipline

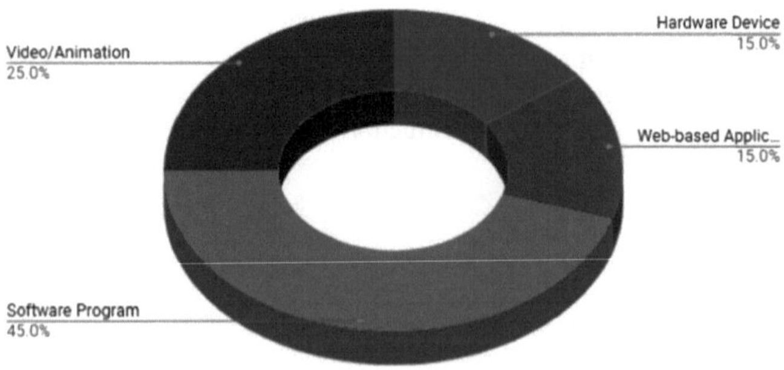

Fig. 3. Reviewed studies by technology

6.2 Inferential Statistics

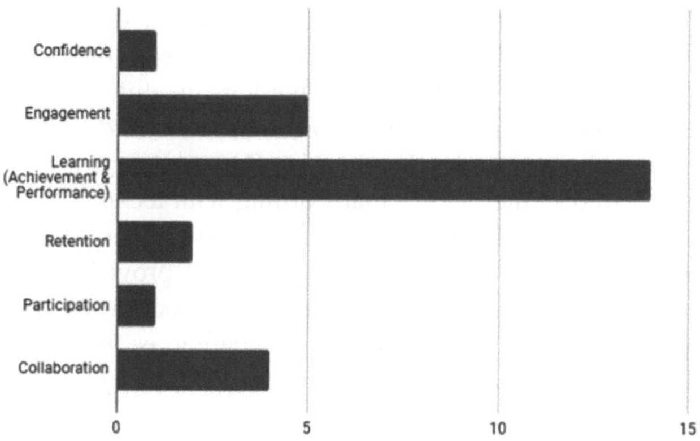

Fig. 4. Reviewed studies by learning outcomes

7 Discussion

This previous analysis shows that most of the studies were conducted at either senior levels of high school or colleges. Only one study was conducted at an elementary school; no lower academic levels were represented. All grade levels were represented though the high school population was the most popular among the reviewed studies. The span of disciplines identified was also broad, STEM being primary. Though no time limit was specifically indicated in the search, all of the studies were published in the last seven years. A large proportion of the technology deployed was software-based. The reviewed studies showed a preference for quasi-experimental design either using: (a) pre-test/post-test approach or (b) control group/experimental group approach. Performance and assessment tests were the primary instruments or measuring learning outcomes

Notably, the effectiveness of using technology in these settings was overwhelmingly positive. The direct influence was reported on students' learning (achievement, performance, retention) as much as indirect influence on students' disposition to learning (confidence, engagement, participation and collaborativeness). What remains to be seen is the degree of impact on respective participants which will require a qualitative research methodology.

The quality of the empirical studies was low; most lacking an explicit reference to an underlying theoretical framework. Sampling methods were always purposive due to concerns about technology literacy and accessibility amongst participants. And the lack of studies predating 2010, makes it difficult to gauge long-term impact of educational technology intervention. These limitations can be attributed to the preliminary nature of the search. Results are restricted to a single though reasonably representative database and thus, may not be generalizable.

8 Conclusion

There are known barriers and challenges to ICT adoption in developing countries, Nigeria inclusive. This study attempts to underlie, not belabour that. Moreso, what it proposes is a nascent positive purview. There needs to be more accounts and reports of successes (as well as failures) of educational technology in different learning environments. This is how knowledge is constructed on what works and what doesn't. The formal term for this is Action research wherein this effort rests.

Analysis of the reviewed studies shows that learning with technology in Nigeria is effective at various academic levels and disciplinary domains. For educational stakeholders, this should implore the research, inclusion of and provision for such technologies. Future research directions can consider the methodology here in a wider range of demographic contexts. The universal implication is the ability to make informed design decisions that are considerate of resource-constrained educational environments.

References

1. Machin, S.: Social disadvantage and education experiences. In: OECD Social, Employment and Migration Working Papers (2006)
2. Warren, M.: The digital vicious cycle: links between social disadvantage and digital exclusion in rural areas. Telecommun. Policy **31**, 374–388 (2007)
3. Januszewski, A., Molenda, M. (eds.): Educational Technology: A Definition with Commentary. Routledge, New York (2013)
4. Luppicini, R.: A systems definition of educational technology in society. Educ. Technol. Soc. **8**, 103–109 (2005)
5. Hlynka, D.: The cultural discourses of educational technology: A Canadian perspective. Educ. Technol. **43**, 41–45 (2003)
6. Istenic Starcic, A., Bagon, S.: ICT-supported learning for inclusion of people with specialneeds: review of seven educational technology journals, 1970–2011. Br. J. Educ. Technol. **45**, 202–230 (2014)
7. Abah, J., Anyor, J.W., Iji, C.O.: Educational cloud services and the mathematics confidence, affective engagement, and behavioral engagement of mathematics education students in public university in Benue State, Nigeria. Int. J. Teach. Learn. High. Educ. **30**, 47–60 (2018)
8. Adeleke, A.G.: Effects of geographic information system on the learning of environmental education concepts in basic computer-mediated classrooms in Nigeria. IAFOR J. Educ. **5**, 125–136 (2017)
9. Adelore, O., Itasanmi, S.A.: The use of two ICT tools in adult literacy. J. Educ. Pract. **7**, 138–144 (2016)
10. Afurobi, A., Izuagba, A., Obiefuna, C., Ifegbo, P.: Effects of the use of lecture method and wordle on the performance of students taught curriculum studies 1: EDU222. J. Educ. Pract. **6**, 142–149 (2015)
11. Bandele, S.O., Adekunle, A.S.: Development of C ++ application program for solving quadratic equation in elementary school in Nigeria. J. Educ. Pract. **6**, 70–77 (2015)
12. Chinna, N.C., Dada, M.G.: Effects of developed electronic instructional medium on students' achievement in biology. J. Educ. Learn. **2**, 1 (2013)

13. Egaga, P.I., Aderigbe, S.A.: Efficacy of information and communication technology in enhancing learning outcomes of students with hearing impairment in Ibadan. J. Educ. Pract. **6**, 202–205 (2015)
14. Gambari, I.A., Ezenwa, V.I., Anyanwu, R.C.: Comparative effects of two modes of computer-assisted instructional package on solid geometry achievement. Conntemporary Educ. Technol. **5**, 110–120 (2014)
15. Gambari, I.A., Gbodi, B.E., Olakanmi, E.U., Abalaka, E.N.: Promoting intrinsic and extrinsic motivation among chemistry students using computer-assisted instruction. Conntemporary Educ. Technol. **7**, 25–46 (2016)
16. Gambari, A.I., Shittu, A.T., Daramola, F.O., James, M.: Effects of video-based cooperative, competitive and individualized instructional strategies on the performance of senior secondary schools students in geometry. Malays. Online J. Educ. Sci. **4**, 31–47 (2016)
17. Gambari, A.I., Shittu, A.T., Ogunlade, O.O., Osunlade, O.R.: Effectiveness of blended learning and elearning modes of instruction on the performance of undergraduates in Kwara State, Nigeria. Malays. Online J. Educ. Sci. **5**, 25–36 (2017)
18. Gambari, I.A., Yusuf, M.O.: Effects of computer-assisted jigsaw ii cooperative learning strategy on physics achievement and retention. Conntemporary Educ. Technol. **7**, 352–367 (2016)
19. Gambari, A.I., Yusuf, M.O.: Relative effectiveness of computer-supported Jigsaw II, STAD and TAI cooperative learning strategies on performance, attitude, and retention of secondary school students in physics. Journal Peer Learn. **10**, 76–94 (2017)
20. Gambari, A.I., Yusuf, M.O., Thomas, D.A.: Effects of computer-assisted STAD, LTM and ICI cooperative learning strategies on nigerian secondary school students' achievement, gender and motivation in physics. Malays. Online J. Educ. Sci. **3**, 11–26 (2015)
21. Kwasu, I.A., Yalams, S.M., Ema, E.: Using design & animation concepts to produce animated instructional resources that can facilitate open distance learning in science and technology education. J. Educ. Pract. **7**, 166–170 (2016)
22. Oginni, O.I.: Effects of mathematics innovation and technology on students performance in open and distance learning. In: Research in Pedagogy, vol. 6 (2016)
23. Okanlawon, A.E., Fakokunde, J.B., Yusuf, F.A., Abanikannda, M.O., Oyelade, A.A.: Attitudes towards instructional games on peace education among second year students in junior secondary schools in South-west Nigeria. Int. J. Educ. Dev. Inf. Commun. Technol. **13**, 98–108 (2017)
24. Olori, A.L., Igbosanu, A.O.: Effect of computer-based multimedia presentation on senior secondary students' achievement in agricultural science. J. Educ. Pract. **7**, 31–38 (2016)
25. Olugbenga, A.E.: Comparative effectiveness of animated drawings and selected instructional strategies on students' performance in creative arts in Nigeria. Malays. Online J. Educ. Sci. **4**, 1–13 (2016)
26. Yusuf, M.O., Afolabi, A.O.: Effects of computer assisted instruction (CAI) on secondary school students' performance in biology. TOJET Turk. Online J. Educ. Technol. **9**, 62–69 (2010)

The Effect of STEAM Course Applied to Science Education on Learners' Self-efficacy

Jan-Pan Hwang[1(✉)], Chun-Yi Lu[2], and Mei-Yao Chang[3]

[1] Department of Information Management, National Chin-Yi University of Technology, Taichung, Taiwan, R.O.C.
jphwang.academic@gmail.com
[2] Department of Information Management, National Penghu University of Science and Technology, Magong, Taiwan, R.O.C.
[3] Center for General Education, Cheng Shiu University, Kaohsiung, Taiwan, R.O.C.

Abstract. In this study, we designed a course based on the STEAM concept. In order to better understand its impact on the learning performance and self-efficacy. The fifty-six participants from six-grade elementary school who voluntary participation in this course period eight weeks. The result points out that STEAM course we design can improve student's self-efficacy and learning performance. Which discusses the improvement of self-efficacy, will give an initial explanation of the impact of the STEAM course on it. The results were discussed and recommends was proposed. It is expected that the design of the STEAM course will be applied in teaching strategies and materials design will be used as a mirror for the future.

Keywords: STEAM · Self-efficacy · Science Education · Maker movement

1 Introduction and Related Work

In recent years, with the development of related technologies and the emphasis placed on science and technology education by advanced countries in the world, the maker movement has become a trend [1]. Based on the scientific basis, unique and innovative thinking to enhance the brand value is no longer a dream. The major companies in the world, such as Google, Microsoft, etc., are known for their innovative services to enhance products that enhance the user experience, at the same time, major technology companies are also actively recruiting technology talents with the spirit of Maker [1, 2]. This trend is reflected in education from elementary school to university, there are corresponding measures.

In Taiwan, Ministry of Education has established a draft of 12-year course outline for the state education, which includes the two main axes of information technology and daily life sciences [3]. The draft has included "programming" as a compulsory subject and has drawn attention from all walks of life.

However, as early as 2012, the small country of the Baltic Sea, Estonia started to be promoted by the first grade of elementary school. Schoolchildren can learn the robot

T.-T. Wu et al. (Eds.): ICITL 2018, LNCS 11003, pp. 282–287, 2018.
https://doi.org/10.1007/978-3-319-99737-7_29

while playing programs. In the UK, programming was incorporated into the course in 2014; the Scratch site developed by the Massachusetts Institute of Technology for children since 2007 has exceeded more than 12 million members and created nearly 20 million works. Programming has become the basic key ability for all countries in the world to create national competitiveness and train the future talents from an early age. And this wave is reflected in the teaching scene, which is an important interdisciplinary integration course.

The core concept is to combine science, technology, engineering, art, and mathematics (STEAM), it's an interdisciplinary teaching method/teaching framework [4–6]. Under this framework, students can focus on specific issues rather than being confined to a single discipline boundary. They can practice thinking from different perspectives and develop cross-border communication under multiple developments [4, 7]. At present, the domestic courses outline of life science and technology are closely related to STEAM. Li et al. also pointed out that the goal of life science and technology courses is mainly to cultivate the ability of students to "do", "use" and "think". At the junior stage, it is the ability to focus on "doing", a common method. It is through Project-Based Learning that students are guided to do practical work.

At Harvard University, the STEAM course gives students the educational meaning. In addition to the operation of equipment, design innovation, and interdisciplinary knowledge, the more important is the learning process through experience and the enhancement of self-efficacy [4, 8, 9].

In contrast, the domestic course of life science and technology often do not have the relevant teachers are not employed according to the structure of the curriculum. All of these will be potential hidden dangers for the STEAM course [5, 7, 9]. This study investment in the STEAM course is to provide the necessary resources for the domestic elementary, to help teachers improve their information skills and technological knowledge, and to understand the impact of the self-efficacy of students.

Therefore, the topic to be explored in this study is the application of the STEAM course to the student's Natural and Life Science course, and how it affects the learning self-efficacy of students. With this as the main axis, the following research questions have been set:

1. Can the STEAM course be conducive to students' learning effectiveness?
2. Can STEAM course help students improve their self-efficacy?
3. What is the impact of STEAM course on self-efficacy?

Today, the design of the STEAM course is more common, and mainly by Dewey, and 'learning by doing' is the main concept [9]. Through the students' active reflection and exploration in the learning situation, they can comprehend the connection between knowledge in different disciplines.

The instructional design of STEAM course established in this study is mainly divided into three aspects: the teaching process and thinking issues and the corresponding STEAM course content. Shown as Table 1.

Table 1. STEAM with teaching content

Thinking issues	STEAM content
• How to capture the attention and interest of students?	• Describe the relevance of course connotation and life in terms of lifestyle
• How to link the past experience of teaching and students?	• Ask students to think about how to use the tools in the course to solve problems in life
• How to make students understand the necessary conditions for success? • How to let students know that success is controlled by their own efforts?	• Ask a question that is moderate and easy. Ask students to do it • What is the improvement of the wrong approach?
• How to provide positive reinforcement to encourage students' achievements? • How to help school children create a positive feeling of success?	• Encourage schoolchildren to try more, while also sharing the experience of others' success • Diversified rewards

(Compiled and revised from: Driscoll, 1994; Keller, 1990; Lin, 2003; Lin, 2014)

2 Research Method

2.1 Participant

The participants were from the sixth grade of an elementary school in southern Taiwan. A total of 56 students (29 males and 27 females) performed this course for an eight-week experiment activity.

2.2 Research Process

In the first week, the pre-test and questionnaire are filled out, and teacher also introduces the STEAM course. Then, pre-class teaching activities will be conducted to understand the use of teaching aids and basic operations. Followed by a total of six weeks of teaching activities. The last, all student completed post-test questionnaires and after-class scales (self-efficacy).

2.3 The Design of STEAM

The content of the STEAM course was mainly organized through two experts and three senior teachers in the focus group, which incorporated the core concepts of STEAM and the experience of senior teachers. The following describes the outline of teaching activities, as well as the focus of each part of the course, as shown in Fig. 1.

2.4 Research Tools

The pre-test assesses the students' basic knowledge of the course subject and the content is the same as post-test, only the order and options were replaced. There are 25 items for single choice questions.

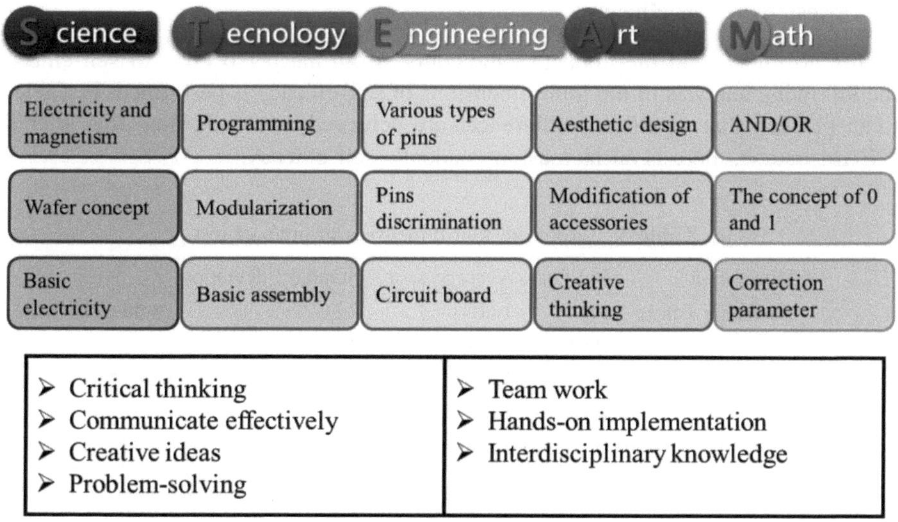

Fig. 1. The structure of STEAM course.

The “self-efficacy scale” referred to the scale compiled by Liang (1998), and Ho, Huang, and Wu (2007). It’s using the Likert 5-point scale, which includes four dimensions, “Persistent Effort,” “Readily Learning,” “Achieving Goals,” and “Physical State.”, and 16 questions in total. The total score as an indicator of self-efficacy, the higher the score means higher self-efficacy, the opposite is lower.

3 Data Analysis

3.1 t-test with Pre/Post Test

As shown in Table 2, the pre-test average score was 66.29, and the post-test average score was 72.44, indicating that there was a significant increase in the post-test of students in terms of learning outcomes, also indicating that after this course, the effectiveness of basic knowledge was improved.

Table 2. t-test with score in pre/post test

	Average score	Standard deviation	*t*
Pre-test	66.29	11.25	28.23*
Post-test	72.44	12.62	

n = 56; * $p < .05$

3.2 t-test with Self-efficacy

Further, to understand the impact of the course from the perspective of self-efficacy. The following analysis of the four dimensions of self-efficacy is performed. In Table 3, it can be seen that significant differences are achieved, and indicating that after the STEAM course, there is an increase in student's self-efficacy.

Table 3. t-test with four dimension in pre/post test

Dimension	Pre/Post	Average score	Standard deviation	*t*
Persistent Effort	Pre	14.04	3.70	3.98*
	Post	15.96	3.17	
Readily Learning	Pre	12.84	2.85	2.84*
	Post	14.08	3.27	
Achieving Goals	Pre	13.36	3.69	0.92
	Post	13.16	3.25	
Physical State	Pre	12.60	2.94	1.09
	Post	13.36	3.26	

n = 56; * $p < .05$

4 Conclusion and Discussion

This study explored the impact of student's self-efficacy through the teaching activities of the STEAM course we design. From the analysis results, the course could improve in the learning effectiveness of students; on the other hand, there has been a significant increase in the self-efficacy of students, especially in the two dimensions, "Persistent effort" and "Readily learning".

In the course of STEAM, the core concept of hands-on implementation can clearly show that student can gain success experience through practice. In addition, the course is organized in groups, during the display and testing of students in each group, they can observe the experience of other groups to gain knowledge transfer; at the same time, the subject knowledge or creative ideas was shared by the students in their group to each other, can inspire and convince themselves.

Acknowledgments. This research is partially supported by the Ministry of Science and Technology (MOST), Taiwan (R.O.C.) under grant no MOST-106-2511-S-268-001, MOST-106-2511-S-216-003.

References

1. Ali, A., Shubra, C.: Efforts to reverse the trend of enrolment decline in computer science programs: issues in informing science and information. Technology **7**, 209–224 (2010)
2. Bandura, A.: Social Learning Theory. Prentice-Hall, Englewood Cliffs (1977)

3. Bandura, A., Adams, N.E., Beyer, J.: Cognitive processes mediating behavioral change. J. Pers. Soc. Psychol. **35**, 125–139 (1977)
4. Corbo, J.C., Reinholz, D.L., Dancy, M.H., Deetz, S., Finkelstein, N.: Sustainable change: a model for transforming departmental culture to support STEM education innovation. Physics Education Research (2014)
5. Hwang, J.P.: Maker movement influence on students' learning motivation and learning achievement: a learning style perspective. Paper Presented at the 2nd International Symposium on Emerging Technologies for Education, SETE 2017, Cape Town, South Africa (2017)
6. Yakman, G.: STEAM education: an overview of creating a model of integrative education. In: Pupils' Attitudes Towards Technology (PATT-19), Research on Technology, Innovation, Design & Engineering Teaching, Salt Lake City, Utah, USA (2008)
7. Hatlevik, O.E., Throndsen, I., Loi, M., Gudmundsdottir, G.B.: Students' ICT self-efficacy and computer and information literacy: determinants and relationships. Comput. Educ. **118**, 107–119 (2018)
8. Gehrke, S., Kezar, A.: The roles of STEM faculty communities of practice in institutional and departmental reform in higher education. Am. Educ. Res. J. **54**(5), 803–833 (2017). https://doi.org/10.3102/0002831217706736
9. Sjøberg, S., Schreiner, C.: How do learners in different cultures relate to science and technology? Results and perspectives from the project ROSE (the Relevance of Science Education). APFSLT **6**(2), 1–17 (2005)

Future Classroom Labs in Norwegian Pre-service Teacher Education

Ann-Thérèse Arstorp(✉)

Directorate of Education and Training, Oslo, Norway
ata@udir.no

Abstract. This paper is aiming at contextualizing the challenges facing teacher education in a societal perspective and how these changes also must change what teaching and learning is to us and how it is practiced. This paper focuses on pre-service teacher education and I will argue that Future Classroom Labs are a viable path for teacher education to move forward in changing the way learning, teaching and competences are conceptualized and put into practice in pre-service teacher education. This is exemplified by Future Classroom Labs in Norwegian pre-service teacher education and the possibilities as well as challenges these examples bring forth.

Keywords: Teacher education · Educational paradigm shift
Future classroom lab · Teachers' professional digital competence

1 Context/Background

There's a global challenge to educate future generations for workplace practices and jobs that do not yet exist [1]. According to OECD globalization and de-industrialisation on the global scene changes the skills and competences we need for the future and therefore this must be integrated into initial education [1]. As more and more functions are automatized and become increasingly complex, we need professionals who can think creatively, as well as critically and who can solve problems they encounter. The argument of this paper is, that when competences needed for the future change, we need to transform teaching and think different about learning in schools as well as in teacher education.

Trilling and Hood [2] as well as Pelgrum and Anderson [3] coined the shifting in pedagogical paradigms from the industrial to the emerging paradigm. The role of the teacher changes from initiator of instruction in whole-class teaching and the teacher as knowledge source in the industrial paradigm to supervisor, facilitator and guide in the emerging paradigm. The same goes for the role of the students moving from passive to active learners [2, 3]. This paradigmatic shift still challenges the way we think of teaching and learning.

Teacher education is where future teachers are shaped and prepared for the teaching profession. Part of getting students ready for the future is instilling in them these skills and competences for the future and professional digital competence is one of them. Newly educated Norwegian teachers report a lack of digital role models and actual

T.-T. Wu et al. (Eds.): ICITL 2018, LNCS 11003, pp. 288–292, 2018.
https://doi.org/10.1007/978-3-319-99737-7_30

pedagogical, digital teaching practice in Norwegian Teacher Education [4]. This has also been reported by the OECD in the country study of Norway [1, 5] and the challenge is the same for many other European countries as well [6–10]. The question remains: How do we make the actual teaching practice change and how do we make sure that students can develop their professional digital competence through their pre-service teacher education? This paper presents specific ideas and experiences of a way to move pre-service teacher education forward.

2 Competences Needed for the Future of Teacher Education

Present day schools were shaped for the industrial age but the skills we need for the digital age, network society, or just in short: the present and future society, are a different set of skills, competences and a different mindset. A way of getting schools and teacher education ready for this is suggested to be through more creativity, more emphasis on critical skills and solving authentic problems such as suggested in the Horizon report [11].

Existing, international frameworks describe the skills needed such as ITL Research's 21st century skills:

(1) Collaboration
(2) Knowledge construction
(3) Self-regulation
(4) Real-world problem-solving and innovation
(5) The use of ICT for learning (use ICT to learn or practice basic skills, knowledge construction, creating ICT products)
(6) Skilled communication [12, p. 2]

Or as ISTEs[1] standards for students:

(1) Empowered Learner
(2) Digital citizen
(3) Knowledge Constructor
(4) Innovative Designer
(5) Computational thinker
(6) Creative communicator
(7) Global Collaborator [13]

These are all oriented towards creating independent learners who can think and act on their own as these are considered the type of skills needed for the future. One could argue, that describing the need for competence for the future is the first step and that we still lack knowledge about how we put this into practice so that it changes the way we teach, and the way students are able to learn. There seems to be a wide consensus, that in the years to come we need teachers with a broad range of skills, including professional digital competence, if we are to change and adapt schooling and teacher education to the future. Particularly if we are to move away from the mindset of "school in the

[1] ISTE is International Society for Technology in Education

industrial age". In this context the Horizon report suggest some changes for schools to consider:

- Progressive learning approaches (e.g. *authentic learning* and *not replacing good teaching but focusing in good guides and mentors*). Students need *"hands-on experiences that enable students to learn by doing cultivate self-awareness and self-reliance while piquing curiosity"*.
- Learners as creators.
- Learning spaces that reflect new approaches in education [11, p. 4].

3 What Is a Future Classroom Lab?

As a way of meeting this challenge, Norwegian teacher education institutions are building Future Classroom Labs. The concept of Future Classroom Labs started with European Schoolnet in Brussels when they created a Future Classroom Lab. The objective with the lab was to create innovative pedagogical approaches in creative learning spaces as a way to build skills and competences for the future[2]. A very central part of the Future Classroom Lab concept are the zones that each specify a different element of the learning and teaching processes such as exploring the subject, researching it, creating/producing, giving and receiving feedback on process or product to presenting the work. This concept has since been adopted around Europe in schools and libraries – and also in teacher education in Norway and Denmark.

Making the zones visible and incorporating them into the didactical practice is done to stimulate independent students who can think and act on their own. It is essential that students are active and engaged while working on authentic problem solving, exploring and producing ideas and projects while integrating technology in the process.

3.1 What Is a Future Classroom in Pre-service Teacher Education?

The Future Classroom Labs in pre-service Teacher Education in Norway have different ways of putting the concept into practice in teacher education, but at the core of them all are:

(1) A place for rethinking the pedagogical practice and teaching in teacher education and schools.
(2) Having a room setup with different zones and flexible furniture allows for teaching experiments that challenge the traditional role of teacher and students.
(3) Working in zones as a way of scaffolding new didactical practices. It seems crucial in creating change that there is some kind of structure or concept to try out, to be inspired from and hence use to create your own changes in your teaching. Different learning zones is a way to visualize and scaffold just this. Zones can be seen as a way to make explicit the pedagogical and didactical ideas. Student assistants are part of running and developing the concept of the lab as well as the practice of the

[2] See more at http://fcl.eun.org

labs. The experience is that having student assistants has been really beneficial as they have a different approach to many areas. One is how they manage to engage their fellow students in using the room and exploring it. A second benefit is how they as staff can take on running courses and workshops that are repeated.

(4) Practice schools are invited in to explore the rooms and get inspired.
The aim of these labs has for the most part been to expand beyond the walls of the lab and involve practice schools, the walls in pull in practice schools, pre-schools in the area and hence to become a resource for the community and not just teacher education.

4 What Are the Key Learnings from These Labs?

The Norwegian labs are for the most part fairly new. The first was established at The Arctic University of Norway in 2012, the second was established at The University of Stavanger in 2017 and the latest at University of South-Eastern Norway in 2018. Although they are new, the potential of these kinds of labs is interesting and promising.

When teachers finish teacher education they should have developed their professional digital competence to a sufficient level and be prepared to teach in ways that support their students' acquisition of these competences. As mentioned before this is quite a challenge in Norway, but the physical labs accentuate this challenge by their mere presence. They make it apparent to everyone on campus that this is something that teacher educators and students need to get involved in and do something about. On the institutional level the labs seem to create awareness and interest around this issue. It seems that the physical labs help make visible that something has to change. The challenge is to make this change actually happen.

A different take away from these labs is that it takes a lot of time and energy to plan and build the labs but most importantly it is time consuming to develop and run these labs. At some of the labs the requests for workshops and peer-to-peer guidance has been difficult to accommodate with the present number of staff. This shows that there is need for support through this process of change and that there is willingness to try out new things and change teaching within teacher education.

References

1. OECD: How technology and globalisation are transforming the labour market. In: OECD Employment Outlook 2017. OECD Publishing, Paris (2017). https://www.oecd-ilibrary.org/employment/oecd-employment-outlook-2017/how-technology-and-globalisation-are-transforming-the-labour-market_empl_outlook-2017-7-en
2. Trilling, B., Hood, P.: Learning, technology, and education reform in the knowledge age or we're wired, webbed and windowed, now what? Educ. Technol. **39**, 5–18 (1999)
3. Pelgrum, W.J., Anderson, R.E.: ICT and the emerging paradigm for life-long learning an IEA educational assessment of infrastructure, goals, and practices in twenty-six countries. IEA & University of Twente (2001)
4. NIFU: Digital competence in Norwegian teacher education, (NIFU report 28-2008) (2008)
5. OECD: ICT in initial teacher training. Country report, Norway (2009)

6. Enochsson, A., Rizza, C.: ICT in Initial Teacher Training: Research Review. OECD Publishing, Paris (2009)
7. Hammond, M., Reynolds, L., Ingram, J.: How and why do student teachers use ICT? J. Comput. Assist. Learn. **27**, 191–203 (2011)
8. Istenic Starcic, A., Cotic, M., Solomonides, I., Volk, M.: Engaging preservice primary and preprimary school teachers in digital storytelling for the teaching and learning of mathematics. Br. J. Educ. Technol. **4**(2016), 29–50 (2016)
9. Røkenes, F.M., Krumsvik, R.J.: Development of student teachers' digital competence in teacher education. Nord. J. Digital Literacy **4**, 250–280 (2014)
10. Tondeur, J., van Braak, J., Sang, G., Voogt, J., Fisser, P., Ottenbreit-Leftwich, A.: Preparing pre-service teachers to integrate technology in education: a synthesis of qualitative evidence. Comput. Educ. **1**, 134–144 (2011)
11. Freeman, A., Adams Becker, S., Cummins, M., Davis, A., Hall Giesinger, C.: NMC/CoSN Horizon Report: 2017 K–12 Edition. The New Media Consortium, Austin (2017)
12. ITL Research: 21st Century Learning Design Rubrics (2012). http://www.kasc.net/2010/21CLD%20Learning%20Activity%20Rubrics%202012.pdf
13. ISTE Standards for students (2016). https://www.iste.org/standards/for-students

Motion Capture Technology Supporting Cognitive, Psychomotor, and Affective-Social Learning

Andreja Istenic Starcic[1,2,3](✉), William Mark Lipsmeyer[3,4], and Lin Lin[3]

[1] Faculty of Education, University of Primorska, Koper, Slovenia
andreja.starcic@gmail.com
[2] Faculty of Civil and Geodetic Engineering, University of Ljubljana, Ljubljana, Slovenia
[3] College of Information, University of North Texas, Denton, Texas, USA
lipsmeyerwm@gmail.com, lin.lin@unt.edu
[4] Zoic Studios, Culver City, CA, USA

Abstract. Human cognition and learning are embodied in socio-cultural contexts and psychomotor activities and are mediated by "tools" on enactive, iconic and symbolic representational levels. Learning technology has been predominantly oriented to manipulatives or tangible objects on an enactive level and with the introduction of computers in education with visual representations. We examine the educational technology and computer-assisted learning that include perceptual-motor activities with a particular focus on whole body motion and learning. We want to explore how the motion capture technology supports the inclusion of sensual knowledge and body motion in the cognitive processes of learning. We focus on the motion capture technology to offer a more natural type of human-computer interaction and immersion into the digital world.

Keywords: Design-based research · Motion capture · Representations · Learning Virtual reality · Instructional design

1 Introduction

Learning involves cognitive, psychomotor and affective-social domains [1]. The three-stage learning model proposed by Bruner involves enactive, visual and abstract levels of representations [2]. Learning technology has been predominantly oriented to manipulatives or tangible objects on an enactive level and with the introduction of computers in education with visual representations. Computer-assisted learning supports the first three levels of geometry reasoning: problem visualization, problem analysis and forecasting solutions [3]. Human-computer interfaces offered possibilities for learning combining cognitive and physical activity in learning. An introduction of tangible user interface (TUI) merges physical and visual representations. A TUI connects the enactive with visual stage when providing learner's fine motor manipulation of tangibles objects with digital objects on the computer screen [3]. We are examining the educational technology and computer-assisted learning that include perceptual-motor activities with a particular focus on whole body motion and learning. We want to study how the motion capture technology supports the inclusion of sensual knowledge and body motion in the cognitive processes of learning.

T.-T. Wu et al. (Eds.): ICITL 2018, LNCS 11003, pp. 293–297, 2018.
https://doi.org/10.1007/978-3-319-99737-7_31

Our discussion is based on the socio-cultural understanding of learning originated from Vygotsky's notion of physical and mental tools for thinking [4]. Cognition is embodied in the socio-cultural context, psychomotor activity and is mediated by "tools" on the enactive, iconic and symbolic representational level [1, 4]. With the development of educational technology and virtual environments, digital visual representations are proliferating in the physical world, and the embodiment of learning in physical activity is challenged. Digital practices, for example, games, are introducing whole body experiences with the motion capture device installed to offer a more natural type of interaction [5]. Virtual reality (VR) applications based on motion capture technology are applied to skills learning. Studies show the impact on learning outcomes and students' motivation for learning [6]. Chan et al. (2011) study examined the advantages of VR for self-directed learning [6]. We are investigating the instructional design and teachers roles in the current landscape of increasingly digitalized social practices. In this paper, we examine the purpose of educational technology in supporting the connection of cognitive, psychomotor and the emotional-social domain.

The embodied cognition researchers are examining the role of perception, action, the body and the environment in the cognitive activity [7]. The connection between body states and cognition is in the focus of theorists of grounded cognition. They are examining the role of sensory-motor representations in cognition [7]. The instructional design for integration of educational technology is considering the creation of learning environment combining traditional activity connected with digital practices [8]. In the search for approaches to utilize educational technology that would provide all domains of learning, we consider mixed as learning environment allowing learners whole body movement and applying physical and virtual representations. The motion capture technology is used to offer a more natural type of human-computer interaction and immersion into the digital world.

1.1 Motion Capture Technology

The need for creating systems capable of interacting well with humans has been identified [9] to recognize the human emotional state and to better communicate expressive – emotional information [2]. A review of studies shows the use of the motion capture technology for the analyses of affective dimensions based on posture features, [9], whole body movement [10], affective aspects based on body gestures [9], the dependency between emotion and movement qualities investigating expressive body movements [9], and the processes of human body movement from "biological movement" [2]. The engagement in activities in digital game play has been examined predicting that involvement of the body can afford the player a stronger affective experience [5].

The motion capture technology is used to offer a more natural type of human-computer interaction. Examples are Wii with a motion capture device installed [5]. The VR application based on motion capture technology facilitates immersion into the digital world. Chan [6] designed virtual reality motion training system for practising dance. The system provides whole body analysis for dancer to improve all body parts movements [6].

2 Methods

Design based research (DBR) in education contributes in four main areas: innovative learning environment design, the design of contextually-based theories about learning and teaching, progressing design knowledge, innovation capacity in education [11]. We have had experiences in DBR in the area of tangible user interfaces in teaching and learning [3].

The first cycle of design-based research (DBR) was conducted in March–May 2018 at the University of North Texas to address the research questions in the process of forming a set of the objective for the application of motion capture technology in instructional design. The research questions addressed were: What is the role of educational technology in supporting the connection of cognitive, psychomotor and the emotional-social domain? How the motion capture technology endorses the inclusion of sensual knowledge and body motion in the cognitive processes of learning? We performed a series of focused discussions between researchers regarding the potentials of using motion capture smart suit technology for instructional design. The first cycle "the design" will be followed during the years 2018 and 2019 by cycles of "performance", "analysis and redesign" which will allow refinement over time [3].

3 The Design Objectives, Conclusions and Future Challenges

The focused discussions were conducted about the role of educational technology supporting the connection of learning domains when introducing the motion capture technology. The discussions' results are indicating the use of motion capture technology for transitioning body movements from a physical into a virtual space to create a mixed reality (Fig. 1).

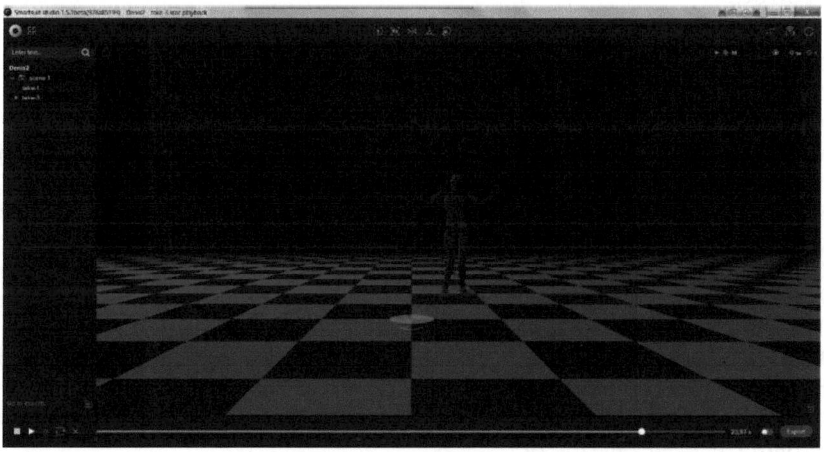

Fig. 1. Motion capture interface in smart suit

The set of objectives identified are:

- motion capture technology for transitioning body movements from a physical into a virtual space and creating a mixed reality;
- to set cross-curricular learning objectives, which will lead a research team to set authentic learning contexts and tasks;
- creating teaching approaches based on the research-based design;
- teacher and students are collaborating and becoming co-creators of the learning environment and learning tasks;

Applying design-based research, we will examine motion capture technology with a particular focus on the role of sensory-motor representations in cognition and collaboration and communication among peers. In the search for scenarios to assist the instructional design for combining traditional activity connected with digital practices and establish cooperation between teachers and students as co-creators of learning environment [8]. We will utilize DBR to create mixed learning environment allowing learners whole body movement and applying physical and virtual representations. The motion capture technology will be used to offer a more natural type of human-computer interaction and immersion into the digital world.

Acknowledgements. This paper is part of a MoCaL research project coordinated by Andreja Istenic Starcic and Lin Lin at the University of North Texas. Andreja Istenic Starcic is a visiting scholar at the University of North Texas, Department of Learning Technologies in 2018. She received funding for teaching mobility from the Republic of Slovenia and European Union under European Social Fund.

References

1. Bruner, J.S.: Toward a theory of instruction. Harvard University Press, Cambridge (1966)
2. Castellano, G., Villalba, Santiago D., Camurri, A.: Recognising human emotions from body movement and gesture dynamics. In: Paiva, A.C.R., Prada, R., Picard, Rosalind W. (eds.) ACII 2007. LNCS, vol. 4738, pp. 71–82. Springer, Heidelberg (2007). https://doi.org/10.1007/978-3-540-74889-2_7
3. Istenic Starcic, A., Cotic, M., Zajc, M.: Design-based research on the use of a tangible user interface for geometry teaching in an inclusive classroom. Br. J. Edu. Technol. **44**, 729–744 (2013)
4. Vygotsky, L.S.: Mind in Society. The Development of Higher Psychological Processes. Harvard University Press, Cambridge (1978)
5. Bianchi-Berthouze, N., Kim, W.W., Patel, D.: Does body movement engage you more in digital game play? and Why? In: Paiva, Ana C.R., Prada, R., Picard, Rosalind W. (eds.) ACII 2007. LNCS, vol. 4738, pp. 102–113. Springer, Heidelberg (2007). https://doi.org/10.1007/978-3-540-74889-2_10
6. Chan, J.C.P., Leung, H., Tang, J.K.T., Komura, T.: A virtual reality dance training system using motion capture technology. IEEE Trans. Learn. Technol. **4**, 187–195 (2011)
7. Barsalou, L.W.: Grounded Cognition. Annu. Rev. Psychol. **59**, 617–645 (2008)

8. Istenic Starcic, A., Cotic, M., Solomonides, I., Volk, M.: Engaging preservice primary and preprimary school teachers in digital storytelling for the teaching and learning of mathematics. Br. J. Edu. Technol. **47**, 29–50 (2016)
9. Kleinsmith, A., Bianchi-Berthouze, N.: Recognizing affective dimensions from body posture. In: Paiva, A.C.R., Prada, R., Picard, Rosalind W. (eds.) ACII 2007. LNCS, vol. 4738, pp. 48–58. Springer, Heidelberg (2007). https://doi.org/10.1007/978-3-540-74889-2_5
10. Crane, E., Gross, M.: Motion capture and emotion: affect detection in whole body movement. In: Paiva, A.C.R., Prada, R., Picard, R.W. (eds.) ACII 2007. LNCS, vol. 4738, pp. 95–101. Springer, Heidelberg (2007). https://doi.org/10.1007/978-3-540-74889-2_9
11. The Design-Based Research Collective: Design-based research: an emerging paradigm for educational inquiry. Educ. Res. **32**, 5–8 (2003)
12. Bernhardt, D., Robinson, P.: Detecting affect from non-stylised body motions. In: Paiva, A.C.R., Prada, R., Picard, R.W. (eds.) ACII 2007. LNCS, vol. 4738, pp. 59–70. Springer, Heidelberg (2007). https://doi.org/10.1007/978-3-540-74889-2_6

Personalized and Adaptive Learning

Teachers' Strategies in Digital and Flexible Online Studies

Synnøve Thomassen Andersen(✉)

The Arctic University of Norway, Alta, Norway
synnove.thomassen.andersen@uit.no

Abstract. The aim of this paper is to highlight how the teachers learning strategies influence students learning outcome. Based on qualitative research we describe a digital online study-project. The results shows that teachers' strategies highly influence students learning outcome. Communication and interaction by use of technology became a key element in the students own learning process. The teachers strategy related to use of technology made the student active include the social and professional environment in their learning process, which contributed to their own competence.

Keywords: Digital · Flexible · Technology · Learning processes Communication

1 Introduction

This paper aims to explore in which way to organize relevant online study for students, based on learning strategies. More specifically, the focus is on the teachers' own learning strategies when planning and organizing online studies.

The world is becoming digital and universities offers updated and relevant education that motivates students learning and use of technology. Online studies have becoming a common form of study all over the world today. In most countries, there is a need to provide lifelong learning, which requires that the learning activities offered are best suited to the students' needs and prerequisites. To realize this, the students themselves, must be able to determine the time, place and progression and working methods largely. However, digitalization has also resulted in a number of challenges [1]. The research question in this paper is; how to organize online study based on the teachers learning strategies, so that the students can get optimal learning outcome? The study program described here is Information Technology in Health Care Services.

2 Theoretical Frame

There are many good examples of online learning activities and assessments methods[1]. NOKUT claim that the use of ICT and digital learning in higher education is a tool for

[1] https://utdanningsforskning.no/.

T.-T. Wu et al. (Eds.): ICITL 2018, LNCS 11003, pp. 301–306, 2018.
https://doi.org/10.1007/978-3-319-99737-7_32

raising the quality of education, focusing especially on the students' learning outcomes. Learning is central, and thoughts and behaviors aimed at obtaining, processing and organizing new material are defines as good learning strategies. Teachers has to include these factors systematic within their own planning of teaching. However, principles of collaborative learning are important for establishing good learning strategies [2]. This include acquiring learning strategies and interest in learning, participate a committed community, get to work, enable opportunities in a constructive manner. Collaborating, coordinating and trusting each other is important to include in studies as factors for teachers, in order for the students to learn something for themselves. Such socio-cultural learning bases on theories by emphasizing that learning takes place in a social context and not in a vacuum [3].

Teacher has to be aware that students can have more control over how they learn, and centered on what they should learn when using technology [4]. However, students need to prepare for online learning to get a better learning effect [1]. One way to do this is use of flipped classroom. Flipped classroom or inverted classroom, is about moving the theoretical learning out of the classroom and the practical learning into the classroom [2]. The principle is that the lecture takes place on video (tutorials) that the students look at home as a lesson, while school time is being used for processing and to communicate about the substance. When students have interest in the subject from the beginning, they will be more motivated to do what is needed to achieve the academic goals. Research [2] highlight that students need to develop their own approaches and ways to solve problems demanding the learning environment where they have time and space to reflect on their own learning process. Further, students must have access to several ways to interact with content outside the classroom. Then they can choose the learning strategy that best suits them and thus increase learning outcomes [2]. Three important factors in organizing these online studies were:

- Give the students the chance to use the most appropriate learning strategy.
- When introducing new subject matter, progression should be carefully structure and efforts must be made to make sense.
- Allow students to reflect on their own learning processes together with other students through a review of each other.

Teachers' must offer a broad teaching repertoire where their own digital skills often becomes critical related to the students' learning outcomes in the digital learning processes, which are used[2].

3 Methodology in the Research

This online study project follows the interpretative and qualitative tradition in pedagogical and information systems research [5, 6]. Qualitative method is characterized by direct contact between the researcher and those studied [7, 8]. The empirical data, were collected in the form of interviews with teachers and observation of students. The data

[2] https://utdanningsforskning.no/artikler/utdanningsledelse-og-digitale-laringsformer-i-hoyere-utdanning/.

collection followed the progress of the study project, since the start in 2013. Data from the teachers, was collected through interviews.

Observation is another important source of data, especially through students online study program. The study also includes analysis of significant amounts of archival data including notes and documentation related to planning and organizing the study. The survey was conducted mainly based on observation of the students during online teaching and teacher supervision. Interpretation is therefore of particular importance. All the students were both students and full time workers, where everyone combined the online study next to their daily work, family and other commitments. The research include dialogue and participation in an active and inclusive learning environment.

3.1 The Case; Information Technology in Health Care Services

UiT, The Arctic University of Norway, (UiT in Alta), offered during the period 2013–2015, an online study program to acquire knowledge and competence in eHealth, named Information Technology in Health Care Services, 30 ECTS credits. The program offered no degree, but considered as part of the MBA. The study aimed at employees in the health and care sector and was an offer in further education.

The admission requirement was that applicants had a bachelor degree in health and social studies or equivalent education. Applicants with different backgrounds and/or practices from the health and care services were considered individually. The study included observation of 30 students in 2013, 25 students in 2014 and 15 students in 2015. In total 60 students completed the study.

The study intended for personnel in health and care services who wish to expand and/or update their ICT skills so that they could use the technology in a safe and efficient way, as well as help to exploit the potential of the technology. The teachers planned the study to cover a number of current topics:

- Premises for ICT in health and care services, health policy objectives, laws and regulations.
- Principles for the treatment of patient information and an understanding of the requirements and rules that were set.
- Ethical and legal issues related to information management in the health and care services.
- Practical solutions to the requirements imposed on users of electronic patient information focusing on electronic patient records.
- Overview of system solutions that were implemented at health institutions focusing on electronic patient records.
- Creation of specific knowledge and skills in system solutions that were used. How to utilize ICT as a tool in your own work situation. Knowledge of change and decision making in the workplace to become an active participant in organizational development.
- Project management and project work.

The teachers structured the theme in the first semester like this: project work, eHealth, health policy, laws and regulations. The second semester included privacy, information security and information quality. The planning was based on the expected learning outcome for the students.

3.2 Planning of the Learning Outcomes

The teacher planned and divided the students' learning outcomes into three different subjects. The argument was that this made it easier to give the students formative and summative assessments in the end of the study

(1) Objectives related to knowledge
Here, the aim was that the students should be able to account for the premises for ICT in the health service, health policy objectives, laws and regulations. Students should also be able to explain the principles for processing patient information and acquire an understanding of the requirements and rules that were set. It was also important to arrange for students to gain knowledge of ethical and legal issues related to information management in the health and care services. Finally yet importantly, a central goal was that the students should acquire an overview of the information system solutions into use at health institutions focusing on electronic patient records.
(2) Goals related to skills
Related to this point, the aim was that students should be able to use online information sources and other electronic interaction systems and services. Another goal was that the students should be able to practice the legal and practical aspects of the storage, retrieval and use of digital patient and client information. To achieve this, the goal was for students to be able to utilize ICT as tools in their work. They also had to be able to initiate practical solutions to the demands made on users of electronic patient information focusing on electronic patient records. Finally, it was a goal of students to be able to carry out project management and project work. It was therefore important that they could develop concrete knowledge and skills in how to use information systems solutions.
(3) Objective of general competence
An important goal of overall compatibility was that the students should understand the relationships between ICT, human and organizational development in the health and care services. Furthermore, the students should use ICT to help to be better utilize to improve service provision in the health and care services, by the use of electronic records and telemedicine, as well as improving the service offering in the health and care services. It was important for the teachers that the students should have knowledge of change and decision-making processes at the workplace to become an active player in organizational development at their own workplace after the study.

4 Analyzing the Planning and Organizing of the Online Study

UiT in Alta used ClassFronter (Fronter) as the communication and learning platform.

ICT was an important tool in the implementation of the study program. It was used e-mail, Internet, e-meetings and use of communication and learning platforms in teaching and counseling and for disseminating information. ICT was an important tool in communication between students, and between students and teachers.

By analyszing the teachers planning and organization of the online study, we found that the students where offered training in and use of computer services at the start of the study. We found that there were used different learning methods and working methods: Lecture, individual or group supervision, group work, project work, discussion boards, wiki, written assignments, etc. An important goal was to involve the students in the teaching themselves. The teaching was put up so that the students could largely come to understanding and insight through independent work. Primarily, the practical side of ICT was by the teachers handled through experience learning, which meant that students could acquire knowledge and skills through use of data processing tools in solving tasks.

Relevant lectures, was introduced as new knowledge for the students. The lectures had have different forms, for example, be lecture sequences presented online and/or on collection. Certainly as introduction to the theme, presentation of the theme/syllabus and factual lectures. It could also be a document, for example a power-point presentation, optionally combined with audio. Finally, there could be lecture at the e-meeting, that is to say direct/synchronous communication over studio or web camera (or audio only). In order to acquire the necessary knowledge, the student received regular assignments in various subjects related to theory and possibly to practice. The work assignments had varied content according to the topics discussed. In the assignments, students could apply for literature in addition to the curriculum. There was guidance and written/oral feedback on some of the tasks.

The teachers pointed out that group and teamwork was an important work and learning activity. UiT in Alta expected students to participate actively in online groups throughout the entire study program. The students had to accommodate each other's opinions and perspectives, and actively participate in academic discussions and reflections. The group processes should help the students learn how to collaborate, by helping and supporting each other as well as professionally and personally. The teachers was responsible for the group composition in cooperation with the students. There was cooperation between learning partners. A learning partner is another online student, usually in the same geographical area, as the student could digitally discuss specific questions, assignments or other questions. The teachers plan activities in use of digital tools that created good learning situations and a good learning environment. The teachers organized the study characterized by individual freedom and collaboration in a collective network. The different tasks required the student to be active, utilizing the social and professional environment both on campus and online, as well as utilizing the flexibility of the online study to develop own skills. In each subject, the students got both formative and summative assessment. The study program was evaluated annually. It is a prerequisite for many motivation and how they create ownership of their own education, and gradually becoming more conscious learning students who see the connection between their own learning processes and their own learning outcomes [9]. Good communication is a prerequisite for good health and social work, and the ability to communicate can be trained and developed [10]. By utilizing student habits and the use of technology, one can facilitate new ways of communicating and learning that can lead to change in their work practices. For example, new opportunities to ensure more student participation. However, use of ICT was important and the students needed more education in order to improve their own skills.

We found that communication and interaction were key elements in the learning process, and students actively use the social and professional environment in the learning process to develop their own skills. Strategies included students the chance to use the most appropriate learning strategy was important. When the teachers introduced new subject, progression was carefully structured and efforts made to make sense. The teachers allowed students to reflect on their own learning processes together with other students through a review of each other.

5 Concluding Remarks

This article argues that teachers learning strategies highly influence students learning outcome in online studies. Digital and flexible online studies offers great opportunities for teachers to plan and organize the learning objects.

The teachers strategy in use of technology made the student active include the social and professional environment in their own learning process, which contributed to their own competence. Communications and interaction based on technology became a central element in the learning process for the students.

References

1. Andersen, S.T.: User-centered innovation in psychiatric healthcare by using mobile technology. Ph.D. thesis, University of Oslo, Oslo (2013)
2. Strayer, J.F.: The effects of the classroom flip on the learning environment: a comparison of learning activity in a traditional classroom and a flip classroom that used an intelligent tutoring system. The Ohio State University (2007)
3. Vygotsky, L.: Tænkning og sprog. København (1982)
4. Krokan, A.: Smart læring: Hvordan IKT og sosiale medier endrer læring? Fagbokforlaget Vigmostad & Bjørke AS (2012)
5. Thagaard, T.: Systematikk og innlevelse. En innføring i kvalitativ metode. 4 utg. Fagbokforlaget (2013). ISBN 9788245014938
6. Walsham, G.: Doing interpretive research. Eur. J. Inf. Syst. **15**(3), 320–330 (2006)
7. Johannessen, A., Tufte, P.A., Kristoffersen, L.: Introduksjon til samfunnsvitenskapelig 1 metode. Abstrakt forlag, Oslo (2004)
8. Kvale, S., Brinkmann, S.: Det kvalitative forskningsintervju, Gyldendal akademisk, Utgave: 2. utg, Oslo (2009). ISBN 9788205385290
9. Hasle, S.: Sammenheng mellom ordforråd og avkodingsferdigheter i teori og forskning. Norsk tidsskrift for logopedi, årgang **59**(2), 6–13 (2013)
10. Eide, H., Eide, T.: Etikk og kommunikasjon, Oslo (2005). ISBN 9788204085146

A Sentence-Wide Collocation Recommendation System with Error Detection for Academic Writing

Yen-Lun Chu and Tzone-I Wang(✉)

Department of Engineering Science,
National Cheng Kung University, Tainan, Taiwan
alanchu29@gmail.com, wti535@mail.ncku.edu.tw

Abstract. Collocation plays an important role in English article writing. This research builds a collocation corpus for academic writings in engineering and science fields. Based on the collocation corpus, this research also establishes a sentence-wide collocation recommendation and error detection system for academic writing. The corpus is built from Science Citation Index (SCI) papers and industry field thesis, which are collected and processed by a formal procedure developed in this research. The first step of the procedure uses the Stanford Parser to parse and retrieve collocations sentence by sentence from those papers and thesis. The second step classifies these collected collocations in different types and gathers their information to establish a collocation corpus specifically for academic article writings. The use of the corpus is through a web-based collocation system built in this study. Distinguished from other collocation systems found on the web nowadays, the system can do full sentence collocation error detections and recommendations. After several conducted experiments, the system is proved capable of giving satisfied feedbacks and recommendations for scientific article authors. Although the collocation corpus now is not complete enough to give the most precise results, the formal procedure can still keep enhancing the corpus and improving the system by automatically collecting articles from various fields.

Keywords: Collocation · Corpus · Sentence-wide · Article writing

1 Introduction

For most of the journals publish their articles in English, ability to write English article in various academic research fields are becoming vital and a must. In recent year, collocation plays an important role in English article writing. More and more researchers are studying how to help English as a Foreign Language (EFL) authors to use accurate collocations to represent their meaning precisely and correctly. The most efficient way to put the soul into an article is to use keywords as many as possible. To use keywords mean that authors use the simpler words and their combinations to describe their thoughts. A keyword combined with another word is a collocation. Appropriate usages of collocations can strength the meaning of keywords and describe an author's thought more clearly. How to use the right keyword combinations, i.e. the

T.-T. Wu et al. (Eds.): ICITL 2018, LNCS 11003, pp. 307–316, 2018.
https://doi.org/10.1007/978-3-319-99737-7_33

collocations, becomes an important issue and is always a hard decision for an author to make. Many researches have yielded so call the collocation system to help authors to use right keyword combinations. Yet, most of the online systems only provide searching results of a keyword's collocation without any recommendation or error detections. Moreover, no collocation systems now can scan a whole sentence and give feedbacks to authors for them to check whether the collocations they write in the sentence are correct or not. This research constructs an online academic English collocation corpus and a web-based collocation recommendation system with error detection for a complete sentence.

2 Establishment of a Collocation Corpus

Definition of a collocation has never come to an agreement in academic researches. Lewis in his research defined it as "certain words co-occur in natural text with greater than random frequency." [1], while the Oxford Collocations Dictionary puts it as "Collocation is the way words combine in a language to produce natural-sounding speech and writing."(Oxford University Press 2002) [2] A general definition may be put as "a collocation is a words combination that, in common language speeches or writings, appears more frequently than others." A collocation consists of a base word and some collocate(s). For a base word found in a collocation dictionary, there would be several words listed as its collocates [3]. For most of the collocation recommendation systems, the interfaces provide a single base word input for search and the results are usually a list of collocations for user to choose. In the BBI dictionary of English word combinations the collocations are divided into two categories, the lexical and the grammatical collocations [4].

2.1 Words Combination Extraction

A common approach used in many collocation recommendation systems to extract collocations from training corpus is the n-gram models. Smadja in his research first used 2-gram to extract a base word and its collocates within a sentence for collocations [5]. To improve precision and variety, in his later researches 2-gram is extended to 5-gram [5, 6]. The approach consists of three steps. In the first step 2-gram combinations are extracted from training articles and whose total appearing frequencies are higher than a predefined threshold are recorded with their combinational distance, i.e. adjacent words has distance 1, and so on. Step 2 uses each of the recorded 2-gram combination as the base and extends the search in the sentences up to 5-grams to find combinations whose appearing frequencies are higher than a predefined threshold. Step 3 chooses an n-gram combination as a collocation by first tagging the Part Of Speech (POS) information on each word of the combination, then, according to the POS tags, judging the possible POS relationship of the word combination (e.g. verb-noun, noun-adjective, and etc.), finally calculating the appearing frequency to see whether it is higher than the pre-determined threshold.

Another commonly used approach uses both Mutual information score (MI-score) and T-score to evaluate the significance, instead of just using frequencies, of an extracted words combination in a training corpus. MI-score is used for measuring the mutual dependence between two random variables, which, in the collocation case, is for measuring the strength of the combination between the words of a collocation [7, 8]. The MI-score formula is as in Eq. (1) where x and y are two discrete random variables, p(x) is the probability of x appearing alone, p(y) is the probability of y appearing alone, and p(x,y) is the probability that x and y appear simultaneously.

$$\mathrm{I(X;Y)} = \sum\nolimits_{\mathrm{x}\in \mathrm{X}} \sum\nolimits_{\mathrm{y}\in \mathrm{Y}} \mathrm{p(x,y)} \log \frac{\mathrm{p(x,y)}}{\mathrm{p(x)p(y)}} \tag{1}$$

If x and y are the words of a combination, the MI(x, y) is then the strength for evaluating if such a combination can be regarded as a collocation [9].

One flaw of using MI-score is that when p(x) and p(y) are low but p(x,y) is high, e.g. the two words in a combination appear only few times in the training corpus, yet when they appear they both appear together, the MI-score will be high and the combination may become a collocation [10]. The statistic T-score is defined as Eq. (2):

$$\mathrm{t} = \frac{\bar{x} - \mu}{\sqrt{\frac{s^2}{N}}} \tag{2}$$

Where $\bar{x}$ is the sample mean, s^2 is the sample variance, N is the sample size, and μ is the mean of the distribution, which generation of words follows. Assuming the bigram distribution in the training corpus is a normal distribution, for a bigram $\boldsymbol{uv}$ the variables can be substituted as: $\bar{\boldsymbol{x}} = \mathbf{p(u,v)}$, $\boldsymbol{\mu} = \mathbf{p(u)p(v)}$, and $s^2 = \mathbf{p(u,v)(1 - p(u,v))} \fallingdotseq \mathbf{p(u, v)}$. For most cases, bigram frequency counts is used to calculate the probability, which makes the t-score become Eq. 3.

$$\mathrm{t(u,v)} = 1 - \frac{f(u)f(v)}{f(uv)} \tag{3}$$

If the t-score is large enough the cases that the high MI-scores due to two words in a combination appearing only few times but always appearing together in the training corpus can be rejected [11].

Yet another approach uses type dependency of words in the sentences of the training corpus to identify possible adequate collocations. A dependency parser is needed for this approach obtain dependency relations of words in a sentence, which is usually the Stanford Parser. In Gao's research, six dependency relation combinations were proposed as the major rules for identifying collocations from training corpus [12]. This research also used POS tags to clear the conflicts between dependency relations. Another research from Wu et al. uses type dependency relations to build a statistical machine learning model. The model uses the Maximum Entropy (ME) as the training algorithm to build an automatic collocation suggestion classifier that can choose the most probable collocation candidates with regard to the given context [13]. The ME algorithm, learning from example sentences, determines both the Head and the Ngram parts in a sentence. The Head is the base of the potential collocation and the Ngram are the possible collocates in the sentence.

2.2 Currently Available Collocation Recommendation Systems

There are currently several collocation search or recommendation systems. Some well-known systems, such as Corpus of Contemporary American English (COCA) [14], Just-the-word (http://www.just-the-word.co, Tango [15], OZDIC(http://www.ozdic.com/), and Collocation Checker (NLPlab) are surveyed here.

COCA is or general writings, which collect corpus material from Internet, books, and academic articles. There are currently 0.45 billion base words all together. It is a popular base used for academic researches. One of the advantage of COCA is the clarity of recommendation results. Recommended collocations are accompanied by their frequencies of usages in the system, which makes user easy in choosing their replacement. Oppose to this advantage is that users, when input their queries, must obey the complicated rules posed by the system, which makes a new user confused.

Just-the-word uses corpus materials from British National Corpus (BNC). It is also famous for its rich search result information. For example, the recommended collocations are displayed with their frequencies of usages in the system. However the system fails to sort the recommended collocations according to their usage frequencies, which makes users inconvenient in searching for their favorite replacements.

Tango has it corpus sources from Sinorama, Voice of America, British National Corpus, Hong Kong News&Laws, Academic collocation from BNC. Users can choose their favorite corpus before making their collocation searches. Tango has a very easy and clear user interface. Users just input the base word and the POSs of the base word and intended collocates. The search results include the recommended collections, their usage frequencies, and several example sentences that use the collocations. The most disadvantage of Tango is that it accepts only *verb+noun* and *adj+noun* search combines, a little bit shortage for the general article writings.

OZDIC searches like traditional dictionaries or collocation dictionaries, with no frequencies of collocations usages displayed in the results. A good feature of OZDIC is instead it gives the actual meanings of the collocations and how they should be used in sentences. But OZDIC gives no priority recommendation on the result collocations.

Collocation Checker is a simpler system that support *verb+noun* collocation check only to see how the base word can be used in other collocation combinations with their usage frequencies.

3 Methodology and Materials

To support a whole sentence collocations detection and recommendation, this research first establishes a methodology to build a collocations corpus and a synonyms corpus from collected SCI indexed journal articles in the specifics fields. A system is then built with interface to allow users to perform a whole sentence collocations recommendation. Figure 1 depicts the architecture of the system.

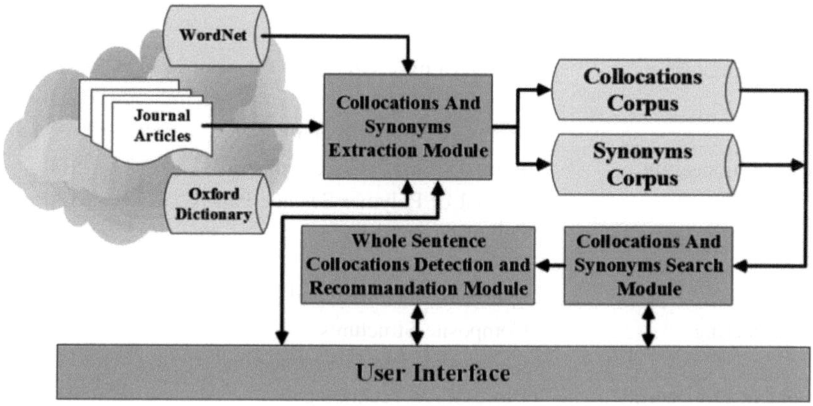

Fig. 1. The system architecture

3.1 Corpus Constructions

Although there are corpuses available, they are not suitable for this research because the target users are only engineering and science fields article authors. Considering that journal articles are peer reviewed and mostly being proofread and collected, this research collects more than three thousand SCI articles in journals of engineering and science fields for training data. The sources of the articles, for the time being, are from those journals listed in Table 1.

Table 1. The sources of the articles for constructing the corpus

Disciplines	Name of the journals	Article numbers
Material Science and Engineering	Journal of polymer science	135
	International Journal of Biological Macromolecules	420
	Polymer	10
Biomedical Engineering	Biomedical Engineering	7
	Physiological Measurement	20
	IEEE Transactions on Biomedical Engineering	10
	IEEE Transactions on Instrumentation Measurement	10
Electronics and Electronics Engineering	IEEE Transactions on Power Electronics	10
	IEEE Transactions on Industrial Electronics	10
	IEEE Transactions on Industry Applications	10
	IEEE Electronic Devices	10

(*continued*)

Table 1. (*continued*)

Mechanical Engineering	Applied Physics A	10
	Thin Solid Films	350
	Surface Coatings Technology	7
Chemistry Engineering	Journal of Materials Chemistry	100
	Journal of Polymer Science Part A Polymer Chemistry	130
	Polymer Chemistry	10
	Materials Chemistry and Physics	650
Civil Engineering	Composite Structures	400
	Composites Part B Engineering	10
Environment Engineering	Bioresource Technology	410
	CEMENT&CONCRETE COMPOSITES	10
	Journal of Hazardous Materials	10
Information Engineering	IEEE Communication Surveys and Tutorial	10
	IEEE Transactions on Communication	10
	IEEE Transactions on Computer	10
	others	185
Optics Engineering	OPTICS EXPRESS	10
	Proceedings of the IEEE conferences on Optics	10
	others	180

Using Natural Language Processing technology, the handling of these articles goes through several steps as shown in Fig. 2. The collected articles, in PDF format, are processed first to extract contents in text format. Each sentence of the articles is parsed by the Stanford Parser to obtain a number of glossaries, their part-of-speech tags, and their dependencies, which indicate the semantic types between the glossaries. By using the WordNet, the glossaries are stemmed before they are paired by the Collocations Identification Algorithm that chooses the collocations, sentence by sentence, which match the collocation type set in the BBI dictionary of English word combinations [4]. Table 2 shows the type dependencies from Stanford Parser used in this study.

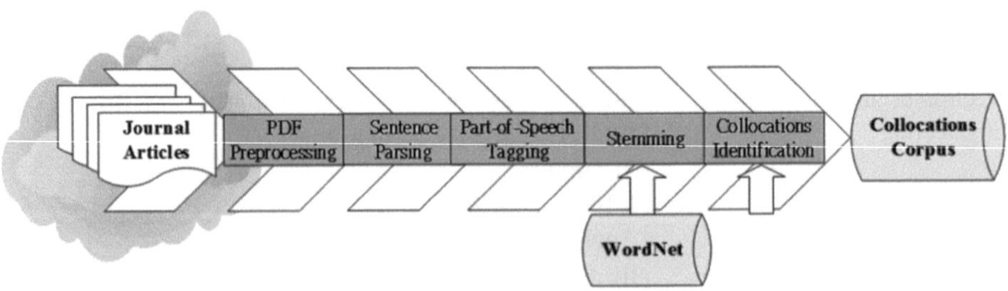

Fig. 2. Steps for constructing the collocations corpus

Table 2. Stanford Parser type dependencies used in this study

Type dependencies	Name	Combinations	Examples
Advmod	adverbial modifier	adv+verb adv+adv adv+adj	Commonly use
Amod	adjectival modifier	adj+noun	High temperature
Dobj	direct object	verb+noun	Use method
Nsubj	nominal subject	noun+verb noun+adj noun+noun	Work show Work point
Pobj	object of a preposition	prep+noun	Sit on the chair
Prep	prepositional modifier	prep+others	I saw a cat with a telescope

On the other hand, a synonym corpus is also needed to provide the synonyms of words to make the collocation system able to recommend alternatives of collocations as many as possible. This research builds the synonym corpus by searching in the Oxford Synonyms Online Dictionary for all the keywords in the collocations corpus and collecting, from the website, their synonyms from the results, as shown in Fig. 3.

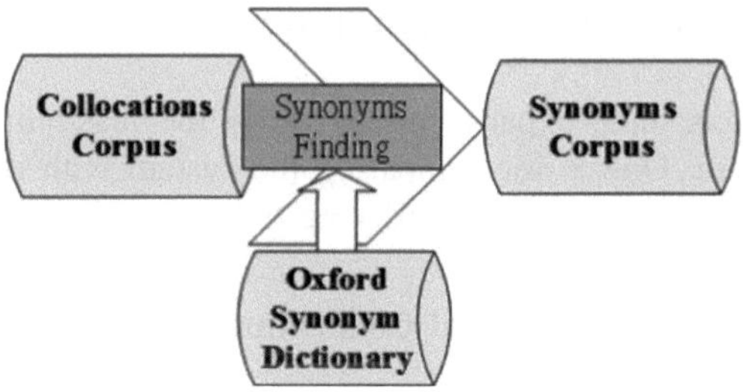

Fig. 3. Constructing the synonyms corpus

3.2 The Collocation Recommendation Interface

For users, the web-based collocation system provides two type of collocation functionalities. One is the key word searching mode, which allows an article author typing in a keyword to search for the collocation combinations that go with the keyword. Along with the collocation combinations, the collocation system provides the relative usage frequency of each collocations to let authors know how often a collocation combination has being used in academic article writings. The other mode allows authors to type in a whole sentence, for which the system will mark all the collocation usages in the sentence. By clicking on a collocation usage, authors can check its alternative combinations recommended by the system and choose one to replace the original usage. In this mode, the system will also mark the uncommon or wrongly used collocations, if any, in a sentence and recommend their proper alternatives. An example is shown in Fig. 4 for the whole sentence collocation recommendation.

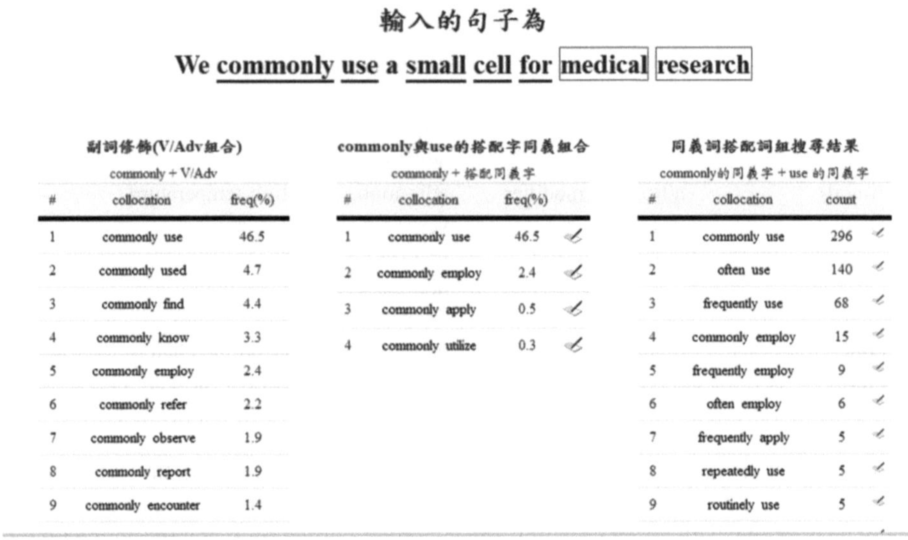

Fig. 4. A whole sentence collocation recommendation example.

4 Experimental Results and Discussions

This research conducts three experiments to verify the feasibility of the collocation corpus and the system. One is for comparing the system with other collocation recommendation system and two are for verifying the performance of the system.

4.1 Uncommon and Wrongly Used Collocations Detections

The first experiment is to evaluate how correct the system can check and mark both the uncommon and wrongly used collocations in a sentence. In other words, to check what is the appearing frequency of the collocations usages in the corpus which can be used as a threshold, below which collocations can be treated as uncommon and wrong. One thousand sentences selected form the same articles for building corpus are modified by replacing some of collocations in each sentence by five experts who have English literature degree. These modified sentences are input to the system for the experiment. The experimental result shows that 73% of the identified uncommon and wrongly used collocations appear no more than three times in the collocation corpus. It's mean that if the system uses the appearing frequency of a collocation usage that is below three times in the corpus as a threshold to indicate a un-common or wrong usage, it will detect most of the error or unsuitable collocation usages by the authors. When the training data get even larger and the appearing frequencies of all the collocations get even higher, the same threshold will filter out almost all the erroneous or unsuitable collocations to make the system's error detection more precise.

4.2 Comparing with Other Collocation Systems

The second experiment is to compare the collocation system built in this study to some other online collocation systems with respect to the recommendation precisions. The online systems chosen for comparisons include the Contemporary American English, the Tango, the Just-the-word, and the OZDIC. After ranking by the Academic Collocation List (ACL), the system built in this study is in the third place of all the five systems. Because the collocation corpus of this study is still in its enfant with its training data and corpus size much smaller than that of the other systems, the shortage of more collocation combinations makes the comparisons somewhat uneven. On the other hand, most of online collocation systems are designed for all kind of general purpose writing, but the system in this study is for academic writing and collects only papers in journals of engineering and science fields as training data. It is well known the collocation usages between daily and academic usages are somewhat different. The collocation corpus and collocation system built in this study can help academic authors using right collocations in academic writing more precisely.

4.3 Performance of the Collocation Recommendation System

The third experiment is to evaluate the performance of the collocation recommendations of the system. Another thousand journal article sentences, selected by the same 5 experts as in the first experiment, are input to the system and, when the system marks the collocations of the sentence, the experts evaluate the adequacy of the replacements recommended by the system for the collocations chosen by the experts. The experiment result shows that the percentage a recommended synonyms of a collocation is the number one candidate is 73.1%, the percentage all the recommended synonyms for the collocations in a sentence are suitable is 60.6%, and percentage all the listed synonyms for the collocations in a sentence are suitable is 51.7%. The low suitable rates of the two latter cases can be improved if the volumes of the corpuses are increased as time goes by. The overall performance of the recommendation and the precision of error detection will be increased if the semantics of the collocation usages in a sentence can be identified via some sentence parsing technologies and semantic information associated to collocation usages are stored in the corpus, which are missing in this study.

5 Conclusion

For English academic article writing in science and engineering fields, this research designs and constructs a collocation corpus, a synonyms corpus, and a web-based collocation system that provides not only traditional keyword search for collocations but also sentence-wide collocation error detection and alternatives recommendations, a distinguished feature not found in other collocation systems. The system can inform authors on how common a collocation are used, and provide alternative synonyms, from which authors can choose to replace the collocation in their own sentences. The system can constantly improve itself by keeping collecting journal papers as training data to update and improve the collocation and synonym corpus. As time goes by, the performance of collocations and synonyms suggestions should improve as the volume of the corpuses increase. Increasing the volume of the corpuses will relatively increase the frequencies of corrected collocations, i.e. the threshold of appearing frequency for judging uncommon or error collocations is increased, the precision of error detection will be increased too.

References

1. Lewis, M.: Implementing the Lexical Approach. Thomson Heinle, Boston (2002)
2. Oxford University Press: Oxford Collocations Dictionary for Students of English (2002)
3. Chen, Y.-C., Yen, T.-X., Chang, J.S.: Associating collocations with WordNet senses using hybrid models. In: Proceedings of the Twenty-Fourth Conference on Computational Linguistics and Speech Processing (2012)
4. Benson, M., Benson, E., Ilson, R.F.: The BBI Combinatory Dictionary of English: A Guide to Word Combinations (1986)
5. Smadja, F.: Lexical Co-occurrence: The Missing Link Journal for Literary and Linguistic Computing (1989)
6. Smadja, F.: Retrieving Collocations from Text: Xtract. Association for Computational Linguistics (1993)
7. Church, K.W., Hanks, P.: Word Association Norms, Mutual Information, And Lexicography (1990)
8. Aji, S., & Kaimal, R. (2012). DOCUMENT SUMMARIZATION USING POSITIVE POINTWISE MUTUAL INFORMATION. International Journal of Computer Science & Information Technology, 4
9. Bouma, G.: Normalized (Pointwise) mutual information in collocation extraction. In: Proceedings of the Biennial GSCL Conference (2009)
10. Clear, J.: T-score and mutual information score from Birmingham Corpus website. http://lingua.mtsu.edu/chinese-computing/docs/tscore.html
11. Thanopoulos, A., Fakotakis, N., Kokkinakis, G.: Comparative evaluation of collocation extraction metrics. In: The International Conference on Language Resources and Evaluation (2002)
12. Gao, Z.-M.: Automatic identification of English collocation errors based on dependency relations. In: 27th Pacific Asia Conference on Language, Information, and Computation, pp. 550–555 (2013)
13. Wu, J.-C., Chang, Y.-C., Mitamura, T., Chang, J.S.: Automatic collocation suggestion in academic writing. In: Proceedings of the ACL 2010 Conference, pp. 115–119 (2010)
14. Davies, M.: The Corpus of Contemporary American English: 450 million words, 1990–present (2008). http://corpus.byu.edu/coca/
15. Jian, J.-Y., Chang, Y.-C., Chang, J.S.: TANGO: bilingual collocational concordancer. In: Annual Conference of the Association for Computational Linguistics (2004)
16. Ackermann, K., Chen, Y.-H.: Developing the Academic Collocation List (ACL) – a corpus driven and expert-judged approach. J. Engl. Acad. Purp. **12**(4), 235–247 (2013)
17. Bahns, J.: Lexical collocations: a contrastive view. ELT J. **47**(1), 56–63 (1993)
18. Peter, H.: Phraseology and second language proficiency. Appl. Linguist. **19**(1), 24–44 (1998)
19. Smadja, F.: From n-grams to collocations an evaluation of Xtract. In: Proceedings of the 29th Annual Meeting on Association for Computational Linguistics (1991)

Features of Personalized Teaching a Foreign Language at Non-linguistic Faculties of the University

Elvira Sabirova, Niyaz Latypov, Agzam Valeev, and Roza Valeeva(✉)

Institute of Psychology and Education, Kazan Federal University, 18 Kremlevskaya Street, 420008 Kazan, Russia
{sabirovaelli,valeykin}@yandex.ru

Abstract. Nowadays there are qualitative changes in the Russian education related to the rapid development of foreign contacts almost in all spheres of life. In this regard, higher education is taking focus on the field of productive practical activity of future specialists. Field-oriented training of the university graduates often depends on the propensities and interests. This provision determines the development of personalized teaching as a purposeful formation of the integrative subjectivity of an individual.

The purpose of this article is to study the problem of personalization in the context of the educational process of teaching foreign languages at non-linguistic faculties of the university. The article elaborates on the conceptual features of personalized teaching a foreign language; it undertakes an experimental study on the provision of conditions for personalization of a student, dwells on the components of the personalized teaching; covers the principles of personalized teaching a foreign language; examines modern technologies of personalized teaching a foreign language; showcases the capacity of implementation of the concept of personalized foreign language teaching. We came to the conclusion that the success of personalized teaching depends not so much on the content of language arts and methods of teaching languages, but on the consistent patterns of student's intellectual activity.

Keywords: Foreign language · Non-linguistic faculty · Personalized teaching
Educational technology · Teaching methods · Intellectual activity of a student
Communicative activity

1 Introduction

Now the sphere of education, as well as the society as a whole witnesses various transformations which recognize the necessity of fulfillment of personal and professional potential of the future specialist. That is why it is so important to understand that the system of university training should be centered around a man or a woman as a personality with all his or her motives, interests and values. This means that a student should be an active participant of the educational process rather than a passive knowledge recipient from the very beginning of his or her studies at the university. It is necessary

T.-T. Wu et al. (Eds.): ICITL 2018, LNCS 11003, pp. 317–328, 2018.
https://doi.org/10.1007/978-3-319-99737-7_34

to recognize that modern pedagogical practice has to bring educational process to the level of interpersonal relations everywhere, which implies organization of productive interaction and dialogue as sources of personal growth of both participants of the process [1]. In this regard, it raises a relevant question of adequate development of a competitive specialist, which is largely determined not only by the high level of his special training, but also by his willingness to carry out professional activities in any multicultural and foreign-language environment. Given this, such subjects as “Foreign Language for Professional Purposes”, “Business and Professional Foreign Language” should become integrative and interdisciplinary in order to promote socialization and individualization of a personality of the future specialist in various fields of his activity.

It should be noted that despite the fact there are quite a few works on personalized teaching in higher education, literature is still missing theoretical, technological and methodological researches. Meanwhile, in order to improve the effectiveness of training, it is necessary to tailor educational programs not only to meet personal needs of a student, but also to fine-tune the social role corresponding to his specialization. Hence, personalized teaching of a foreign language should be aimed at activating the motivation of the teaching. This, in turn, determines the commitment to achieve the desired results. All these create opportunities for university students to more consciously focus on the learning process, be clearly aware of its meaning and benefits, and to perceive language learning as an integral part of everyday life and as an opportunity to overcome specific obstacles.

2 Literature Review

Values system of a person studied by psychologists Buyaks and Zevina [2], Rakovskaya [3], Gavrilyuk and Trikoz [4] are of special interest. The problem of personalized teaching was addressed by the Russian scientists Grachev [5], Kaloshina [6], Petrovsky [7]. Solonina [1], Bespalko [8], Rean et al. [9], Kizesova [10] studied the development of the psychological concept of an individual’s personalization. “Personalization of teaching” concept was substantiated by Barbashova [11], Unt [12], Liver [13]. Problem of the person-oriented teaching of foreign languages at non-linguistic universities was examined by Alunina [14], Yakimanskaya [15], Gabdulkhakov [16], Kolker [17]. The issues of development of students’ learning motivation were addressed by Belykh [18], Latypov and Sabirova [19]. The problems of formation of foreign-language professional communicative competence were studied by Iskandarova [20], Kondratieva and Valeev [21], Golikova [22]. Verbitsky [23], Valeev, Valeeva and Sirazeeva [24] studied contextual learning in their works. Innovative models of training were reviewed by Klarin [25], Aitov [26], Gerasimov, and Loginov [27]. Khuziakhmetov and Valeev [28] did research on the problem of students’ intellectual development. Gardner [29], Rogova and Vereshchagina [30] studied methodological techniques for teaching a foreign language.

3 Materials and Methods

3.1 Research Design

The study was carried out on the premises of the Institute of Psychology and Education and the Institute of Fundamental Medicine and Biology of Kazan (Volga region) Federal University. It was conducted as part of teaching students the "Foreign Language" and "Theory and Technology of Education" subjects. The study was divided into two stages.

At the first stage (1 September–20 December, 2016) the students were introduced to the idea of personalized teaching a foreign language as a possible strategy of professional growth; it was aimed at the development of their intellectual qualities and increasing motivation to learn a foreign language. As part of that stage we analyzed the presence and quality of researches in the scientific literature and educational practice, collected empirical material, studied the nature of the students' approach to the problems of mastering the culture of foreign language; ability to analyze and summarize the study material, etc.

At the second stage (10 January–25 May 2017), there were developed the guiding principles and guidelines for the analysis of a student's subjectivity development; the model of reinforced motivation was experimentally verified to study a foreign language, its potential to actualize and develop the intellectual qualities of students; the study results were recorded.

3.2 Specificity of Personalized Foreign Language Teaching

Personalized foreign language teaching at non-linguistic faculties of the university represents an educational model in which programs, teaching methods and academic strategies are focused on the individual needs, interests and socio-cultural background of a student. In fact, personalized education is an alternative to standard conventional education, which often does not take into account the individual characteristics and priorities of the student [31, 32]. While as for the personalized educational process, methods and styles of teaching are tailored to the personality of a particular student. This defines the main goal of personalized teaching: to prioritize the individual goals of education during preparation of the curriculum and coordination of the educational process. Thus, personalized teaching as a form of training is characterized by the interaction of actors in the process of exploration of the surrounding world, aiming at the transformation of consciousness and behavior of a student, which involves the management of his individual educational trajectory [10].

In this regard, personalized foreign language teaching has the following features:

- creation of an educational profile of a student: evaluation the level of student's knowledge, analysis of his previous training experience and, taking into account the motivation, formulation of his needs and goals in order to choose the most appropriate educational solution;
- selection of a personalized teaching style: plan and style of teaching is chosen for every student taking into account the peculiarities of his personality, motivation and goals;

- creation of a comfortable learning environment: appropriate setting and time of study, as well as the style of the teacher in accordance with the individual needs of the student;
- monitoring of the results: at every stage of the education process there are outlined its intermediate and final goals, the achievement of which is assessed, on the basis of that assessment these goals are further adjusted.

Thus, the personalization of teaching involves the creation of conditions for personalization of a student by means of appropriate forms and educational technologies, as well as the personalization of the learning environment (for example, constant access to training equipment, the Internet; provision of a television set and a video player, multimedia projector and electronic, as well as paper versions of dictionaries; provision of additional space for independent work of small groups or individual training, etc.). The use of various educational technologies is of interest to students, and increases their motivation for learning. However, it should be noted that their use in teaching is different: from full distance learning to partial use in lectures and seminars. In the work with modern educational technologies, the role of the teacher (tutor) as the coordinator and organizer of the learning process is important. Teacher is able to more flexibly guide the learning process, taking into account the individual capabilities of each student [14, 32]. At the same time, personalization of foreign language teaching is possible when the educational activity allows students to use a foreign language to express their own ideas, feelings and thoughts.

Having regard to the above, the concept of "personalized teaching" can be divided into the three components: personalization of a teacher (creation of the original teaching technologies), personalization of interaction (increasing the time of personal communication between the teacher and the student in a classroom and extracurricular time), individualization of the educational process (aligning all its components with the needs of every student).

3.3 The Principles of Personalized Foreign Language Teaching

As university practice shows, the utmost success of personalized foreign language teaching is achieved if the following principles are observed: principle of individualization (focus on the personality of a student and his/her individual capabilities); principle of personality-oriented training (personal experience, interests and needs of every student, as well as the development of all these parameters); principle of considering the educational level of a student (taking into account the current educational level); principle of consciousness (providing targeted perception and understanding of the studied phenomena within the framework of situational conditionality, context, usage of language tools, etc.); principle of personal communication (taking into consideration the cognitive and communicative potential of a student); personal-role principle (considering the motivational side of the teaching process); principle of creative activity (organization of productive activities of students); principle of self-reflection (ensuring the process of self-assessment and self-control of students of their cognitive activity); principle of intensification and concentration (organization of the educational process taking into account the learning of the abundant language material by means of reducing its delivery time); principle of dialogical speech priority (development of communicative competence through the intensification of the communication process); principle of multifunctionality (ensuring the process of simultaneous mastering of language material and formation of speech skills); principle of collective interaction (performance of such tasks that simulate real communication in pairs, in groups and in the "crowd" mode); principle of variability (using multilevel tasks based on students' choice following the 'simple-to-complicated' principle); principle of autonomy (implies a degree of student's personal freedom while choosing his or her educational trajectory). It matters that this system of principles remains open, and these principles should always be interrelated and should not be used in an idealized form.

4 Results

4.1 Modern Technologies of Personalized Foreign Language Teaching

Currently, the following technologies are the most popular in personalized teaching of a foreign language (their most important characteristics are the effectiveness, efficiency, ergonomic effectiveness, high motivation in learning languages):

- technology of collaborative learning: it is based on the idea of collective responsibility for addressing educational problems, when students help each other and are collectively responsible for the success of each of them;
- communicative technology of teaching: it is implemented on the basis of subject-subject relations between the teacher and students and focused on the orderly systematic teaching of a foreign language;
- technology of teaching individualization: it implies the original design of the lesson, when the entire group of students is trained, then it splits up into two parallel processes: independent work of students and individual work of the teacher with every student;
- technology related to computer training: use of training programs designed for individual and unsupervised work with a computer;
- technology of centered learning (student-centered approach): involves student taking maximum initiative in the process of training in order to fully disclose his personal potential;
- technologies of critical thinking development: creating conditions that form the need to find a solution to the educational problem of any complexity (at the beginning it implies motivating a student to develop interest in the topic; then goes the motivation to understand the learned information; then comes reflection, i.e. the formation of their own attitude to the material studied);
- technology of role games: it is a form of recreation of the subject and social content of professional activity, modeling the experience of relations specific to language practice (it implies imitation of activity in the real social system; using the method of collective training; creating emotional state in order to activate the learning process, etc.);

- language portfolio as a teaching technology: it is a database where the recorded achievements of the student and his experience in acquiring the language he learns with the aim of comparing his level of proficiency in the foreign language with the level of other students and also with the European standards);
- expanded-varied technology: it implies creation of conditions under which all students succeed regardless their level of language proficiency (based on the idea of interaction between the "majority" and the "minority" in order to achieve common successful results, when the low-performing minority adjusts to the profile of the majority, for which the teacher is doing everything possible to help those lagging behind adapt to the majority);
- audiovisual method technology: it is a synthesis of sound and visual perception, when a student develops sensuous basis of language skills, which implies the use of the visualization mechanisms: repetition and contrast, i.e. recurrence and contrast of the perceived phenomena of language and speech;
- technology of monitoring and correcting activities: it involves dividing the educational process into units with due consideration of specifically formulated learning objectives; diagnostic test is carried out after studying and working on educational material and all the results are announced immediately after performing the tasks; thus, the only assessment criterion is complete knowledge and skills acquisition.

The use of the latest SMART technologies (webinars, blogs, twitters, video and audio podcasts, asynchronous and online modes) [33] in teaching foreign languages allows to simulate learning situations, increasingly complements traditional teaching methods, helps to build a communicative core or the basic skills of foreign language communication.

Another innovative form, forming the competence of foreign communication and receiving more and more distribution, are webinars. Webinar is an online seminar that provides opportunities for the teacher (tutor) to transmit information, assignments, and participants - to receive information and study using a virtual classroom that is able to hear and see each other anywhere in the world. Webinars help students to show presentations, draw on a virtual board, make active applications, ask questions in the online chat window. The webinar is launched using the web application. This alternative format for building a dialogue with students through the use of modern Smart technologies allows to conduct student learning in a remote format, and organize video conferences online. The use of a new format of communication allows to increase the interest of students to the sessions and seminars held and to increase their attendance, and also to time-shift. Webinars are an effective tool for organizing distance learning of foreign languages with rich demonstration tools. A convenient way to display information in any format, including images and video, makes it possible to hear and see a conversationalist. In this connection, it can be stated that such a technology is a full-fledged alternative to a full-time meeting, which has always been very important in studying foreign languages.

Of particular interest for our students are web journals (blogs). The main content of these websites includes regularly added records or other data forms published in the public domain, to which you can leave a comment. We find the most effective the so-called class blogs in teaching students foreign languages. In a class blog, teachers and students can post information for mainstream auditing. This type of blog acts as an extracurricular classroom and is best suited for an out-of-class collaborative work. Thematic classroom blog as an asynchronous form of communication allows you to extend the time frame of the training course, to enable each student to be accepted active participation in the communication process in a foreign language, realize the principle of an individual approach to teaching.

It is necessary that the teacher wisely chose a technology depending on the group and the individual characteristics of every student in order to support his motivation, which, one way or another, can actively influence the learning process.

4.2 Implementation of Personalized Foreign Language Teaching Concept

The main idea of the concept of personalized foreign language teaching can be summarized as follows: it is a specially organized joint activities of a teacher and a student as part of the educational process, involving the formation of the subjective experience of a young man, as well as his intellectual and moral development based on the socio-psychological content of an individual's personality. In this regard, the implementation of the concept of personalized foreign language teaching can be based on such basic provisions as:

- creation of such conditions of interaction between a teacher and students when purposeful didactic influence is demanded by students, i.e. having personal and social value for them;
- intellectual and moral development of students, involving the development of their intellectual abilities, as well as the formation of social attitudes and moral constructs in order to implement further productive communication in a foreign language, should become the general purpose of personalized teaching (especially development of convergence and creativity);
- personalized training should be aimed not only at the formation of the student's subjective experience, but also at the development of his personal qualities (for example, from the level of egocentrism to altruism);
- it is important to rely not only on the individuality of a student in personalized teaching, but also on the typical features of a teacher and students, taking into account their social status, which is associated with the achievement of integrity in the formation of social identity of young people;
- it is desirable to carry out the personalized teaching in group forms thanks to which it is possible not only to ensure personal growth of students, but also to some extent find the solution to a problem of striking a reasonable balance between the personality and its social onset in the course of their development;
- personalization of teaching should be linked to the content of the learning material so that, for example, as much thematic text material as possible could be personalized (written on behalf of a particular person or persons, having texts based on "case-study" about professional activities of a specialist related to languages, etc.);
- personalized teaching must be associated with the provision of different points of view on a particular problem, which means that students have the right to choose the ways to address it.

- in personalized teaching exercises should be associated with expressing students' own opinion about a particular problem; with writing of various problem-based essays for the organization of group work, etc.

It is important to constantly sustain the urge of students to perform systematic communicative activities, in the process of which their personalities are individualized.

4.3 Experiment Procedure and Results

We sought to implement the most effective transformations during the experiment by aligning students' cognitive process with learning a foreign language and with the due consideration of personalized teaching. As the study results show, it is possible to assess the effectiveness of increasing students' motivation to learn a foreign language only using diagnostic procedures. In this regard, we used operational diagnostics – polls, conversations, questioning of students. It should be noted that the diagnostic stage during the experiment was of particular importance, as it helped to identify current level of student's subjectivity development. We assumed that, apart from high intellectual development, a university graduate should also have a developed individual educational trajectory based on his continuous commitment to acquiring foreign language skills. At the same time, improving the level of foreign language knowledge involves display of social activity by students, for example, in their dedication to practical use of a foreign language.

At the diagnostic stage we used Personal Orientation Inventory by E. Shostrem as a diagnostic technique. It allows to identify the dynamics of the development of students' intellectual potential as part of the pedagogical university practice. Testing of the degree of increasing motivation to learn a foreign language of the future specialists was conducted in 2016–2017 academic year: initially – in September 2016, follow-up – in May 2017 in one experimental and one control groups. The control group consisted of 22 sophomores of the Institute of Fundamental Medicine and Biology of KFU, the experimental group included 24 3rd-year students of the Institute of Psychology and Education of KFU. The results of the diagnostic test are shown in Table 1.

Table 1. Increasing students' motivation to learn a foreign language ("plus" - increase, "minus" - decrease expressed as percentage for the period of September 2016–May 2017).

Increasing students' motivation to learn a foreign language	Control group	Experimental group
Development of student's subjectivity	+4,5%	+42%
Meaningful use of language means	−1%	+22%
Development of communicative competence	+1%	+27%
Practical application of a foreign language	−2%	+38%
Readiness to acquire skills through usage of a foreign language	+11%	+56%
Improving foreign language proficiency	−1%	+35%
Formation of individual educational trajectory	+9%	+40%

The experimental group demonstrated a steady growth in all factors compared to the results of the control group. The dynamics of increasing motivation to learn a foreign language of the students that took part in the experiment exceeds the similar dynamics of the control group. In our opinion, it is quite convincingly prove the effectiveness of personalized foreign language teaching carried out by our team in the course of experimental work in the university. Dynamics of indicators of increasing students' motivation to learn a foreign language within the scope of personalized learning indicates that most students demonstrated increased dynamics of the intellectual parameter of the motivation under consideration. Along with that, there was a decrease in number of students with poor practical experience in foreign language activities.

Taking all the aforesaid into consideration we can argue that the conducted study confirmed the basic provisions of the concept of personalized foreign language teaching. However, this does not exhaust all the issues related to the study of psychological and pedagogical conditions for the effective use of personalized foreign language teaching at non-linguistic faculties of the university. As it seems to us, special research should be carried out in order to analyze the problem of the development of students' ability to actualize language competencies on the basis of personalized learning; problems of pedagogical support of students in the development of their linguistic personality; potential of extracurricular activities (in the field of research work) of students in order to further increase the motivation of students to learn a foreign language.

5 Discussions

One of the main requirements to modern foreign language classes today is to ensure its personalization on the basis of communicative bias, which implies that students can freely express their thoughts and feelings. It should recognize their right to have some violations of language rules and accidental mistakes. Hence, it can be concluded that the personalization of teaching and communicative bias in the field of teaching foreign language are interdependent concepts. Thus, foreign language classes must be organized with the use of tasks that provide natural information imbalance among students of non-linguistic faculties of the university. It creates certain informational advantages for other students, thus contributing to their personalization in the process of authentic communicative activities. For example, when dealing with oral conversation topics as part of the "Business English" course, students are given an "advanced task" associated with the compulsory choice of one or another topic so that they could work on it thoroughly an in-depth; and then they present the results of their work by the time, when this topic is studied by all students.

The personal need to study a particular topic, as well as the need to individualize your personality is the driving force behind that choice. At the same time, the need can be not only pragmatic, but also idealistic in nature, for example, transition from the topic of colloquial genre to the business topic in a foreign language; or when some of the units or topics of the educational program that is being currently studied coincide with the theme of the course work or some questions of the seminars, etc. It is connected, in particular, with ambitious plans of the student concerning his future professional activity involving certain language proficiency that, naturally, sparks his cognitive interest and desire to get additional foreign language skills. Thus, personalized teaching as a system has its own socio-psychological and psychological and pedagogical patterns, which are implemented in the construction of a well-structured teaching methodology, which includes the psychological types of teachers and students, their extraordinary (associated with originality, exclusivity, contingency, uniqueness, authenticity, etc.) pedagogical interaction and the technologies of personalized teaching.

6 Conclusion

This study led us to the conclusion that alignment and fine-tuning of all the components of the educational process should become a necessary requirement for provision of communicative bias in teaching a foreign language at non-linguistic faculties, contributing to the formation of students ‘ worldview, socialization and personalization of an individual as future professionals in the multicultural environment. Personalization is important here for several reasons: it makes a foreign language relevant to students; communication activities acquire its significance for them; teaching can become personalized at any stage of the lesson. Hence, the technology of personalization in the framework of foreign language teaching may consist of the following components: a clear methodology of training related to the analysis of different sources and the creative transformation of ideas into the learning process as a new product; localization of the education content related to the division of the program into separate topics, which are selected and studied in depth by individual students; localized training of students who have studied in depth some subject and further can carry out educational activity and share it with other group mates.

Thus, personalized teaching is different from the traditional holistic approach to the educational process, when the curriculum takes into account the student's capabilities, their innate inquisitiveness, individual goals, etc.

It should be noted that the effectiveness of personalized teaching is largely determined by integrative processes implemented in higher education. Ultimately, the realization of such a paradigm of education determines the construction of polyvalent training (giving a wider basic training), which can be defined as a specially organized socialization of a young man, resulting in his holistic understanding of the world. Educational subjects in this case are modeled not so much on the basis of logic, structure, content of particular language subjects, but on the basis of consistent patterns of student's intellectual activity. His intellectual development in the process of personalized learning involves a consistent "transition" from a lower level to a higher one as a movement from rational to theoretical and practical thinking. All this requires appropriate motivational support, which is provided by personalized teaching. It allows for the development and increased complexity of students' needs for their cognitive activity.

Acknowledgments. The work is performed according to the Russian Government Program of Competitive Growth of Kazan Federal University.

References

1. Solonina, A.G.: The Concept of Personalized Learning. Prometei, Moscow (1997)
2. Buyaks, T.M., Zevina, O.G.: Experience of common human values and cultural symbols affirmation in the individual consciousness. Voporosy psykhologii – Psychol. Issues **5**, 44–56 (1997)
3. Rakovskaya, O.A.: Social Reference Points of Youth: Trends, Problems, Prospects. Nauka, Moscow (1993)
4. Gavrilyuk, V.V., Trikoz, N.A.: Dynamics of values orientations in the period of social transformation (generation approach). Sotsiologicheskoe issledovanie – Soc. Stud. **1**, 96–105 (2002)
5. Grachev, V.V.: Theoretical bases of personalization of educational process in higher education. Doctoral dissertation, Moscow (2007)
6. Kaloshina I.N.: Personalized learning as a factor in the development of students' self-educational activity. Doctoral dissertation, Orenburg (2000)
7. Petrovsky, A.V.: The individual and his need to be a person. Voprosy philosophii – Philos. Issues **3**, 12–18 (1982)
8. Bespalko, V.P.: Personalized education. Schkolnye tekhnologii: Nauchno-prakticheskyi zhurnal schkolnogo tekhnologa – Sch. Technol. Sci. Pract. J. Sch. Technol. (Head Teach.) **4**, 40–55 (2007)
9. Rean, A.A., Bordovskaya, N.B., Rozum, S.I.: Psychology and Pedagogy. Peter, Saint Petersburgh (2002)
10. Kizesova, I.V.: Personalized Teaching of Students in the System of Elective Professional Education. SibGTU, Krasnoyarsk (2007)
11. Barbashova, N.V.: Personalized teaching of senior students with pedagogical aptitude. In: Pedagogical Mastery: Proceedings of the 4th International Scientific Conference, Moscow, pp. 1–3 (2014). https://moluch.ru/conf/ped/archive/100/5005/. Accessed 01 May 2018
12. Unt, I.E.: Individualization and Differentiation of Training. Pedagogika, Moscow (1990)
13. Liver, B.L.: Methods of individualized teaching a foreign language considering the influence of cognitive styles on the process of its assimilation. Doctoral dissertation, Moscow (2002)
14. Alunina, O.G.: Personality-oriented foreign language teaching of students of non-linguistic specialties. Doctoral dissertation, Moscow (2005)
15. Yakimanskaya, I.S.: Personality-Oriented Teaching at Modern School. Director schkoly, Moscow (1996)
16. Gabdulkhakov, V.F.: Elective courses in rhetoric in the system of modern innovative education at school. In: Profil'no-oriyentirovannyye elektivnyye kursy po yazykovym distsiplinam - Profile-oriented elective courses in language disciplines, p. 73. SHKOLA Publishing House, Kazan (2005)
17. Kolker, Y.M., Ustinova, E.S., Ananieva, T.M.: Practical Methods of Teaching A Foreign Language. Academia, Moscow (2004)
18. Belykh, I.L.: Development of student's learning motivation in the process of professionally-oriented elective study of a foreign language. Doctoral dissertation, Krasnoyarsk (2004)
19. Latypov, N.R., Sabirova, D.R.: Exploring motivation patterns in the English-medium academic environment. Int. J. Hum. Cult. Stud. 320–325 (2016). Special Issue
20. Iskandarova O.Yu.: Theory and practice of formation of foreign language professional communicative competence of a specialist. Doctoral dissertation, Orenburg (2000)
21. Kondrateva, I.G., Valeev, A.A.: Technology of students professional competences formation while teaching a foreign language. Procedia Soc. Behav. Sci. **191**, 2250–2253 (2015). http://www.sciencedirect.com/science/article/pii/S1877042815025732

22. Golikova, L.V.: Formation of professional foreign language communicative competence of students at non-linguistic colleges of higher education on the basis of project education technology. Doctoral dissertation, St. Petersburg (2005)
23. Verbitsky, A.A.: New Educational Paradigm and Contextual Learning. Issledovatel'skiy tsentr problem kachestva podgotovki spetsialistov, Moscow (1999)
24. Valeev, A.A., Valeeva, L.A., Sirazeeva, A.F.: Study of university students' foreign language speech activity formation. Rev. Eur. Stud. **7**(5), 38–46 (2015). http://www.ccsenet.org/journal/index.php/res/issue/view/1297
25. Klarin, M.V.: Innovative Models of Teaching in Foreign Pedagogical Science. Arena, Moscow (1994)
26. Aitov, V.F.: Problem and project approach to the formation of foreign-language professional competence of students (case study of non-linguistic faculties of pedagogical universities). Doctoral dissertation, Saint Petersburg (2006)
27. Gerasimov, A.M., Loginov, I.P.: Innovative Approach to Constructing Education (Conceptual and Technological Aspect). MAPKiPRO, Moscow (2001)
28. Khuziakhmetov, A.N., Valeev, A.A.: The development of university students' cognitive capacities. Mod. J. Lang. Teach. Methods (MJLTM) **7**(2), 149–158 (2017). http://mjltm.org/assets/uploads/2016/11/Vol.7,Issue2,February2017.pdf
29. Gardner, R.C.: Learning another language: a true social psychological experiment. J. Lang. Soc. Psychol. **2**, 219–239 (1983)
30. Rogova, G.V., Vereshchagina, I.N.: Methods of Teaching English at the Initial Stage in General Education Institutions. Prosveshcheniye, Moscow (1998)
31. Shakirova, A.A., Valeeva, R.A.: Humanistic educational technologies of teaching foreign languages. Math. Educ. **11**(1), 151–154 (2016)
32. Istenic Starcic, A., Cotic, M., Solomonides, M., Volk, M.: Engaging preservice primary and preprimary school teachers in digital storytelling for the teaching and learning of mathematics. Br. J. Educ. Technol. **47**(1), 29–50 (2016)
33. Lebenicnik, M., Pitt, I., Istenic Starcic, A.: Use of online learning resources in the development of learning environments at the intersection of formal and informal learning: the student as autonomous designer. Ceps J. **5**, 95–113 (2015)

Factors Related to the Use of Online Learning Resources: The Perception of Environmental and Contextual Barriers of Students with Special Educational Needs and Their Peers

Maja Lebenicnik[1] and Andreja Istenic Starcic[1,2,3](✉)

[1] Faculty of Education, University of Primorska, Koper, Slovenia
maja.lebenicnik@pef.upr.si, andreja.starcic@gmail.com
[2] Faculty of Civil and Geodetic Engineering, University of Ljubljana, Ljubljana, Slovenia
[3] College of Information, University of North Texas, Texas, USA

Abstract. Research indicates a diversity of factors that influence the use of online learning resources. Barriers, related to access and accessibility issues are often considered in the literature as inhibiting factors for people with disabilities. Following the established social cognitive theory and the model of digital inclusion, that both highlight interaction between environmental and personal factors, we conceptualise two different types of barriers, named environmental and contextual barriers. This article examines differences between students with SEN and their peers in perceived barriers for OLR use. Our results confirmed as expected that there are no significant differences in perceived contextual obstacles between students with SEN and their peers. However, contrary to our expectations, environmental barriers were not perceived as significantly more or less important in either of the two groups. We discuss possible reasons for such results.

Keywords: Socio-cognitive theory · Special educational needs
Inclusion · Higher education · Online learning resources · Barriers

1 Introduction

The use of information communication technology (ICT) is a complex phenomenon and many theoretical models, explaining it, can be placed in the context of social cognitive perspective [1], that emphasis interaction of numerous factors. In his social cognitive theory Bandura [2, 3] states that personal factors (cognitive and affective), environmental events and individual's behaviour operate interactively as determinants of each other and are highly interdependent. Previous surveys identified numerous factors affecting the usage of ICT for learning. However, there is not enough researching in possible differences between people with and without special needs. In our survey we followed factors emphasized in theoretical conceptualisation by Seale, Draffan and Wald [4]. Their framework is based on qualitative research and provides

T.-T. Wu et al. (Eds.): ICITL 2018, LNCS 11003, pp. 329–336, 2018.
https://doi.org/10.1007/978-3-319-99737-7_35

structure for exploring the digital inclusion of disabled students in higher education. The frame shares many similarities with SCT, indicating that the interaction between three components is central also in explaining the use of ICT among students with special educational needs (SEN). Environmental factors, such as limited access to ICT are often exposed in relation to disabled population [5]. However, some students with SEN decide to reject, not adopt or stop using specialist or mainstream technologies, even though they have access to it [6], which indicates interaction with personal factors.

Personal factors consist of affective and cognitive elements, which cannot be genuinely separated [7] and play an essential role in how someone is receptive for new information about innovations, how someone searches for further information, how someone deals with the uncertainty that new products bring etc. [8]. In the literature, on ICT use the self-efficacy is one of the most important personal factors. Self-efficacy, a central construct of SCT, is a belief in someone's own abilities to perform a specific activity that influences whether someone will act confident or anxious in particular situation [3]. In the framework of the digital inclusion, the concept is named 'high level of confidence in the ability to use technology' [4]. Surveys give inconsistent results regarding differences in self-efficacy between students with SEN and no SEN. No differences in computer self-efficacy were found in a study of Suthakaran and Sedlacek [9]. People with disabilities express lower confidence in digital skills in the survey by Vicente and Jesus Lopez [10]. On the contrary, Paker and Banjaree [11] discovered that students with ADHD express more fluency with ICT than their peers. Other personal factors, often examined in the literature are attitudes, beliefs, anxiety etc.

In the framework of Seale et al. [4], environmental factors consist of technological factors (access to ICT, accessibility of ICT), social factors (family environment, formal, informal support from peers and family) and contextual factors (life-fit, study-fit). According to SCT [2], environmental conditions may serve as facilitating or inhibiting influences of behaviour.

As mentioned before, the interaction between different components, especially between personal and environmental factors, is central to both, the SCT and the model of digital inclusion. SCT distinguishes among three types of environments in which the individual operates: imposed, constructed and selected environments [12]. Imposed environment are physical and socio structural factors that affect individuals whether they like it or not [13]. But Bandura [13] argue that for the most part, the environment is only a potentiality, and people create environments that enable them better control (constructed environment) or choose activities that affect their life's course (selected environment). According to digital inclusion model [4] students with SEN decide whether to use ICT or not on the basis of personal circumstances, on perceptions of affordances and properties of technologies and on concerns being stigmatized through using specialist technologies in public, which all represent involvement of different components.

We tried to capture the mixture of environmental and personal factors that contribute to reducing the use of ICT for learning with measuring perceived barriers. In the literature, inhibiting factors of ICT use by students with SEN are often referred as barriers.

We argue that perceived barriers are a useful concept to measure inhibiting influence of two out of three types of environment that SCT distinguishes: imposed and selected environments. An individual cannot affect the imposed environment. Following Digital inclusion framework [4] we assume student with SEN are affected by imposed technical environment when they have no or limited access to ICT or ICT is inaccessible. Aspects of the social environment that impact negatively and on which student with SEN does not have an impact is stigmatisation by others if using ICT (especially AT) in the classroom. We named those barriers environmental barriers.

In our opinion digital decisions not to use ICT based on personal circumstances and study-fit perceptions on technology reflect the selected environment. According to Bandura [13], a selected environment is an individual's environment, which is shaped on the basis of the selection of activities that an individual acquire during a life course. For example people's activities such as choosing study program, choosing study partner/group, enrolling in a computer course, paying attention to or searching for technology-related information, finding technical support if needed etc. shape individual's environment, which has facilitated or inhibiting effect on the use of ICT for learning. We named barriers, connected to the selected environment, contextual barriers. Someone may not see ICT use for technology relevant in his personal context. Perceived contextual barriers reflect the greatest extent the complex interactions between person, environment and person's behaviour.

Scholars most often examine differences between disabled and non-disabled people in environmental barriers, namely access to ICT and Web. Scholars speculated that barriers to primary online access are still related to inaccessible technologies and extra cost associated to assistive technology [10, 14]. Other reported most often barriers among people with disabilities are the high cost of equipment, lack of information, lack of technical support and lack of training [15].

The present survey was conducted to examine how students use online learning resources. This article discusses finding regarding the perception of environmental and contextual barriers among students with special educational needs and their peers.

Hypothesis 1: Students with SEN perceive more environmental barriers than their peer students without SEN.

A higher degree of environmental barriers indicates some kind of digital divide, originated in students' imposed environment (accessibility issues, unsupportive social environment etc.) and is expected to more negatively affect the OLR use in students with SEN, than their peers.

Hypothesis 2: There will be no differences in contextual barriers between students with and their peer students without SEN.

We expect no significant differences to be found for students with SEN in comparison to their peers, because perceived contextual barriers are more related to personal factors (preferences, attitudes etc.), which are not expected to more negatively affect the OLR use in students with SEN, than their peers.

2 Methods

The survey was conducted to examine university students in Slovenia about the use of online resources. For the purposes of the study we developed an original questionnaire. The initial version of an instrument was tested in 2015 [16].

In this paper, we discuss if there are any significant differences in factors that are connected to online learning resources use, since affecting them may lead to better use of online learning resources for learning among higher education students with SEN. In the online survey participated 1675 university students and 56 university students with special educational needs. Students were from different study programs of the University of Ljubljana and seven students with special needs from University of Primorska, Slovenia. Our research sample is a convenience sample, because only those, willing to participate, are included in the survey. Table 1 presents the structure of special educational needs of participating students.

Table 1. The frequency of different types of special educational needs

Type of special educational needs	*f*	%
Blindness, low vision and other visual impairments	5	8.9
Deafness and hard of hearing	2	3.6
Physical disability	8	14.3
Specific learning disabilities (e.g. Dyslexia, dyscalculia etc.)	10	17.9
Behavioural and emotional difficulties	5	8.9
Other disabilities	13	23.2
Multiple disabilities	13	23.2
Total	56	100.0

For the purpose of the research, the barriers scale was designed by authors. In the analysis of perceived barriers analysed was data for 1487 students (55 with SEN and 1432 mainstream students), who filled out the barriers scale. The exploratory factor analyses was conducted, indicating two-factor structure with adequate reliability (Table 2). Cronbach's alpha for the first factor was 0.812 and for the second factor, the Cronbach's alpha was 0.733.

3 Findings and Discussion

As evident from Table 2, in average students do not perceive any of the barriers as very influential. The most important barrier for more extensive use of ICT for learning lies in the perception that they have different preferences for learning (M = 2.73; SD = 1.19). Students do not perceive their negative beliefs as obstacles for their ICT use (M = 1.99; SD = 0.97).

University students do not agree very highly that environmental (M = 2.17, SD = 0.79) or contextual (M = 2.37, SD = 0.90) barriers represent important obstacles for their more extensive use of ICT for learning.

Table 2. Descriptive statistics and factors of Barriers scale.

	M	SD	1	2
Negative personal beliefs	1,99	0,97	0,207	0,539
Nature of my study program	2,40	1,18		0,680
High prices of ICT	2,25	1,06	0,592	
Different preferences for learning	2,73	1,19		0,758
Insufficient technological equipment	2,07	1,02	0,727	
Because using ICT draw attention to me and makes me feel uncomfortable	2,09	1,01	0,571	
Additional training is needed	2,11	1,06	0,825	–0,111
Because websites and applications are not designed to meet my way of access and usage	2,34	1,09	0,625	
Cronbach's Alpha			0,812	0,733
% of variance			47,84	12,78
No of items			5	3

Principal axis factoring extraction method and Oblimin rotation method was used.
KMO = 0,885
N = 1487
Loadings below 0, 10 are not presented in the table
Factor 1 - Environmental barriers
Factor 2 - Contextual barriers

We analyzed if there are significant mean differences between students with SEN and their peers in perceived barriers to the use of ICT for learning. We anticipated that students with SEN experience more obstacles related to an imposed environment (called environmental barriers) than students without SEN (H1). On the contrary we assumed there would be no differences in barriers, related to selected environment (named contextual barriers) (H2).

Table 3. Homogeneity of variances between two independent samples.

	Levene statistic	df1	df2	Sig.
Environmental barriers	0.27	1	1479	0.60
Contextual barriers	4.30	1	1479	0.04

Both independent samples (students with SEN and no SEN) were checked for assumptions regarding normality of distribution and homogeneity of variances. As in Table 3, on the variable contextual barriers assumption on homogeneity of variance was not met ($F = 4.30$, $df = 1479$, $p = 0.04$).

To test for differences in environmental barriers we used parametric t-test for independent samples and for testing differences in contextual barriers we used Mann-Whitney U test.

As in Fig. 1, scores on factor Environmental barriers did not significantly differ (–0.20, 95% CI [–0.012, 0.414], t = 1.85, df = 1485, p = 0.06) between students with SEN (M = 1.98, SE = 0.10) and students without SEN (M = 2.18, SE = 0.02), d = –0.24. This is completely unexpected because items were selected to reflect barriers, identified in the literature as relevant for students with SEN. In our sample students with SEN do not experience environmental barriers to a significantly higher degree than students without SEN. Both groups do not see this kind of barriers as very important.

Reason for this may lay in the fact that listed environmental barriers in our questionnaire are more relevant for users of AT, as specialised (hardware) assistive technology is more expensive, demand more training and elicits more attention from others

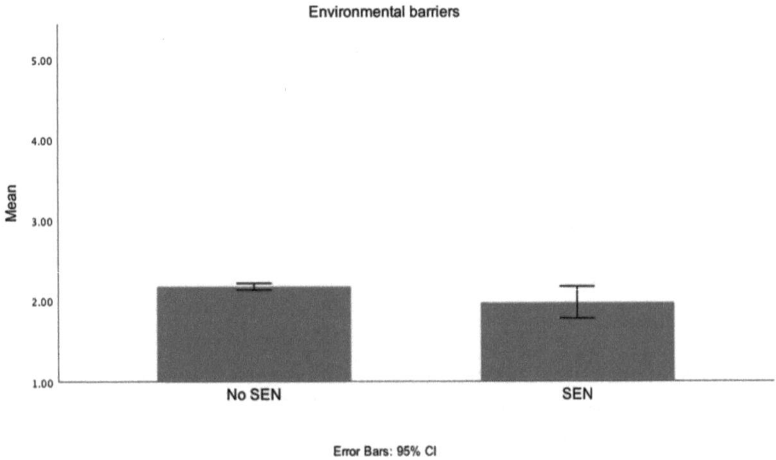

Fig. 1. The comparison of means for Environmental barriers.

while using it than mainstream ICT. Blurring barriers between AT and universally designed ICT with accessibility features may contribute to lower need for specialised AT. Further, results could reflect the nature of SEN participants included in our study. Some disability groups (e.g. blind population, severely physically or cognitively handicapped etc.) need specialised assistive technology to use computers or access the Internet. The majority of students with SEN do not belong to any of those SEN groups. Only 7.1% of students with SEN in our sample reported the use of hardware AT.

We assumed no significant differences between groups would emerge in perceiving contextual barriers (Fig. 2), as they are not assumed to be related to disability but to other personality (learning preferences, positive orientation towards ICT) and social factors (e.g. study-fit). Results indeed show that students with SEN (M = 2.38, Mdn = 2.33) and their peers (M = 2.37 Mdn = 2.33) did not significantly differ in perception of Contextual barriers, U = 38.50, z = –0.28, p = 0.77, r = –0.01.

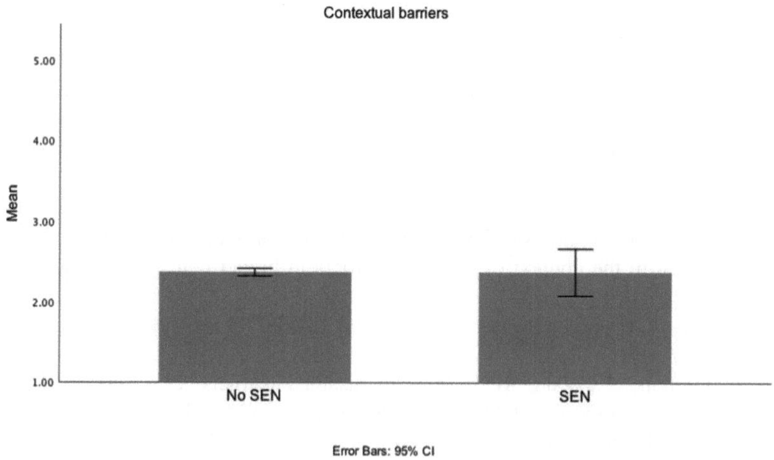

Fig. 2. The comparison of means for Contextual barriers.

4 Conclusions

In this article, we conceptualized two different types of barriers. Environmental barriers reflect 'pure' environmental inhibiting effect on OLR. Contextual barriers reflect the interaction between person's characteristics and the environment he/she selects and can have an inhibiting effect on OLR use. University students with SEN in our sample did not differ from their peers in any type of the perceived barriers. This was not expected for environmental obstacles. One of the possible explanations is that the universally designed ICT, that is inexpensive, easier to use and not as stigmatizing is reducing barriers for students with SEN.

Acknowledgements. The study was financed by young researcher for acquiring a PhD scheme of Slovenian Research Agency (ARRS) as a part of PhD study. Andreja Istenic Starcic was nominated as mentor of young researcher in 2011 (6316-3/2011-784). Maja Lebenicnik was selected as a young researcher in 2012. A survey among students of the University of Ljubljana was conducted without additional financing within a project: «The integration of information and communication technology in the higher education pedagogical process» led by University of Ljubljana in June and early July 2017. The project «The integration of information and communication technology in the higher education pedagogical process» is co-financed by the European Union from the European Social Fund and the Republic of Slovenia. Authors would like to thank participating students and vice-rector of the University of Ljubljana, prof. Goran Turk for promoting a survey among students.

References

1. Straub, E.T.: Understanding technology adoption: theory and future directions for informal learning. Rev. Educ. Res. **79**, 625–649 (2009)
2. Bandura, A.: Social Foundations of Thought and Action. Prentice-Hall, Upper Saddle River (1986)
3. Bandura, A.: Human agency in social cognitive theory. Am. Psychol. **44**, 1175–1184 (1989)
4. Seale, J., Draffan, E., Wald, M.: Digital agility and digital decision making: conceptualising digital inclusion in the context of disabled learners in higher education. Stud. High. Educ. **35**, 445–461 (2010)
5. Cruz-Jesus, F., Oliveira, T., Bacao, F.: Digital divide across the European Union. Inf. Manag. **49**, 278–291 (2012)
6. Seale, J., Draffan, E., Wald, M.: Exploring disabled learners' experiences of e-learning. LEXDIS Poject report (2008). http://www.jisc.ac.uk/media/documents/programmes/elearningcapital/lexdis_projectreport_dec08final.pdf. Accessed 20 Mar 2013
7. Mischel, W., Shoda, Y., Mendoza-Denton, R.: Situation-behavior profiles as a locus of consistency in personality. Curr. Dir. Psychol. Sci. **11**, 50–54 (2002)
8. Rogers, E.: Diffusion of Innovations, 5th edn. The Free Press, New York (2003)
9. Suthakaran, V., Sedlacek, W.E.: Computer aversion among students with and without learning disabilities. J. Coll. Student Dev. **40**, 428–431 (1999)
10. Vicente, M.R., Jesus Lopez, A.: A multidimensional analysis of the disability digital divide: some evidence for internet use. Inf. Soc. **26**, 48–64 (2010)
11. Parker, D.R., Banerjee, M.: Leveling the digital playing field. Assess. Effect. Interv. **33**, 5–14 (2007)
12. Bandura, A.: Reconstrual of 'Free Will' from the agentic perspective of social cognitive theory. In: Baer, J., Kaufman, J.C., Baumeister, R.F. (eds.) Are We Free? Psychology and Free Will, pp. 86–127. Oxford University Press, Oxford (2008)
13. Bandura, A.: On the functional properties of the perceived self-efficacy revisited. J. Manag. **38**, 9–44 (2012)
14. Dobransky, K., Hargittai, E.: Unrealized potential: exploring the digital disability divide. Poetics **58**, 18–28 (2016)
15. Alper, S., Raharinirina, S.: Assistive technology for individuals with disabilities: a review and synthesis of the literature. J. Spec. Educ. Technol. **21**, 47–64 (2006)
16. Lebeničnik, M., Pitt, I., Istenič Starčič, A.: Use of online learning resources in the development of learning environments at the intersection of formal and informal learning: the student as autonomous designer. CEPS J. Center Educ. Policy Stud. J. **5**, 95–113 (2015)

Development of Videos for Flipped Classroom. Using Self-study as Methodology to Improve the Quality

Presentation of a Work in Progress

Tove Leming(✉)

UiT the Arctic University of Norway, Postbox 6050, Langnes, 9037 Tromsø, Norway
tove.leming@uit.no

Abstract. This paper presents an action research project in its first phase, where technology is used as a tool to strengthen the teacher student's active role in the learning-process. Using self-study methods, I focus on two different issues in this paper. First, I show and discuss how the students reacted to the use of video. Secondly, I use my own reflection log, and discuss how I as a teacher reacted to the video, and how this reaction directed the project in a different direction. In the last part, I discuss how the project can be developed further by using self-study as methodological approach, and the importance of doing research on teaching practice and technology.

Keywords: Teacher education · Flipped classroom · Self-studies
Student active learning methods · Action research

1 Introduction

This paper presents an action research project in an early phase. The objective of the project is to improve the learning processes for teacher students, by developing videos of good quality to be used as a part of a "Flipped Classroom"-project. The technology is here used as a tool to strengthen the teacher student's active role in the learning-process. The methodology used is within the frame of *practitioner research*, with elements of *self-study*. In the self-study tradition, the identity as teacher is highlighted. Some will argue that this type of study is one of the most important tools for development of research on teacher education [1–3]. However, the results of self-study research projects must be discussed and articulated in a broader context. This can be national and international communities of research and practice, and will then contribute to the development of research based teaching. I will, using self-study methods, focus on two different issues in this paper. First, I will show and discuss how the students reacted to the use of video. Secondly, I will by using my own reflection log, discuss how I as a teacher reacted to the video, and how this reaction developed my pedagogical agenda in another direction. In this discussion, I use an auto-ethnographic perspective; focusing on my emotional and professional reaction to the learning material I had produced. In

T.-T. Wu et al. (Eds.): ICITL 2018, LNCS 11003, pp. 337–341, 2018.
https://doi.org/10.1007/978-3-319-99737-7_36

the last part, I discuss the project development further, and the importance of doing research on teaching practice and technology.

2 The Project "Flipped Classroom in Social Science in the Teacher Education"

2.1 Background of the Project

In 2017, my colleague and I developed a project called *Flipped classroom in social science in the teacher education.* A flipped classroom is a pedagogical model in which the typical lecture and homework elements of a course are reversed [4], and the model is based on the work of the teachers Bergman and Sams [5]. The overall objective of our project was to improve the learning processes amongst the student teachers in social science, by developing small teaching videos, and thus give more time to student initiated activities in the schedule. The focus on more student active learning processes in higher education is strong, both on a national and international level. In addition, the focus on use of innovative technology to develop teaching methods in higher education, and especially in teacher education programs, is also considerable in Norway *(White paper no. 16 (2016–2017) Quality Culture in Higher Education.)* [6].

In the project, we will develop small videos as introduction to different parts of the course in social science, and in the development of videos, we will use our own professional specialties, and also invite other professional specialists to participate in dialogues in videos on various issues within social science. Examples can be the use of historians to focus on special historical periods, political scientists to focus on issues like democracy and citizenship, and social anthropologists to focus on cultural varieties. The curriculum of the social science course in teacher education in Norway is quite wide, and contains issues like "The multicultural society", "citizenship", "critical thinking", "migration processes", to mention a few. By including professional specialists we're able to use technology to apply the high competence within various academic fields to teacher education programs. The videos will then be distributed to the student teachers, and the student teachers are supposed to watch them before the real-life learning sessions at the university. This gives us the opportunity to start the sessions with various student active working methods; like role-plays, writing texts, group work, etc. Furthermore, we will systematically reflect together with the student teachers on what kind of student initiated working methods that will be suitable for the different videos.

2.2 Implementing the First Phase in the Project

In the first phase of the project, spring term 2018, we developed a first video as an introduction to the issue "The multicultural school". My colleague gave a brief introduction to history of immigration and multi-culture in Norway, and my contribution was a session in which I outlined the current state of immigration in Norway, various categories of immigrants, Norwegian official policy regarding immigration, and so on. The video lasted 20 min, my contribution was 10 min. We had qualified assistance from a technical staff in the studio at the university, and discussed the layout beforehand, the use of slides and pictures to illustrate and to serve as background. We had to make some adjustments from what we originally had prepared, and the session in the studio was a fruitful learning process for us.

The following week, I used the video as planned, for a group of first year student teachers in social science. This was the introduction for a new part in the course, with focus on *The school in a multicultural context.* The video was distributed through the learning platform Fronter, and the student teachers were asked to watch it before next day. When the classes started, they started straight on group-based work, where they worked on various methods for handling multicultural issues as a teacher. This was an important objective in the project; giving more time to student active work methods. My role as a teacher was to participate in the various groups, supervise, and to give small lessons in plenary sessions when necessary. We worked with a role-play where the case was a formal meeting between a teacher and two parents with immigrant background. In the case, the discussion was on diverging perspectives on values and child raising, and how to be able to handle this cultural variation as a teacher.

3 Reactions and Feed-Back on the Use of Video

3.1 How the Student Teachers Reacted

My colleague and I had prepared a survey when we met the student teachers. There were 11 student teachers present when we made the survey. 8 of them had seen the video, 3 had not seen the video, but answered some of the questions. We first asked them to what degree they experienced the video as relevant for the subject, and thereafter whether the flip seemed like a professional production. The answers from the student teachers on these two questions showed that most of them saw this as a relevant video for the subject, and they thought the video was made professionally. On the next question where we asked to what degree they did experience the flip as motivating and engaging related to the theme, the answers were more negative. From what we could read out of the answers, this was given a medium score. The next three questions were on a more general level; focusing on their opinion regarding the use of flipped classroom in the program. In general, they liked the idea that they could use more time on student active learning methods, and that they could watch the video whenever they wanted. One interesting objection, however, mentioned by several of the student teachers, was that they would not have the possibility to ask questions to the teacher if they passively watched videos.

3.2 My Own Reaction to the Video

I kept a meticulous log during the first phase, since I wanted to use my own observations and my own reactions as data in the project. I noted, among other things, what kind of methodical choices we made during the work with the video, and how to work with the visual aspect of the video: using pictures, background, etc. When I received the final product, I sat down in my office and watched my contribution to the video at my PC. This is what I wrote: *"It was a shock to see the video, and my first reaction was that this video must be deleted. I appeared as boring, monotonic, lifeless and without involvement."* I was disappointed with my performance in the video, and it reminded me of how I used to teach when I started as young teacher at the university. Several years of experience and professional development has hopefully made me into another type of teacher, not the one I saw in the video. This emotional reaction to the video is an important part of the project. In inquiries based on auto-ethnographic approaches, the researcher's emotions are also part of the empirical basis, and the episode mentioned above, is a good example of how the emotional reaction made a change in how the project was developed further [7, 8].

4 To Improve the Quality in Learning Processes

4.1 The Self-study Approach as Methodology in the Project

By using self-study methodology, observing and reflecting on my own appearance in the video, combined with student's reactions, I will articulate a knowledge of practice that one often takes for granted. It is important that teacher educators discuss and develop their professional practice, and in this way contribute to research based knowledge about teacher education methods. Since teacher educators have an additional commitment in their professional work, that is giving the student teachers knowledge about teaching methods, they must be able to articulate their own perspectives on teaching and learning. In my case, I became even more aware of the importance of teaching as a dialogical process; involving student teachers or dialogues between me as a teacher and another professional. Watching the video, seeing myself as a teacher with the student's eye, gave me important information and motivated me to improve and further develop my teaching. This has consequences for my next video production, which will be more dialogue based. Loughran argues that outcomes of self-studies should "genuinely affect the work of teacher education beyond the individual…" (Loughran 2007). A systematic and disciplined inquiry will contribute to qualitative development of teaching practice, and I do hope that the next phases in my project will support this development.

4.2 Further Development of the Project

This paper presents a project in progress, and in its very first phase. It also presents the methodological approach to the inquiry, by using self-study methods. The experiences from the first phase suggest that it will be necessary for me to develop the videos to a more visual medium; it is not sufficient to make a boring version of yourself as a teacher when this is supposed to inspire students to come to your classes. Even though this experience is based solely on my own performance, I must say that I have observed some quite boring videos aimed at inspiring students. Only if we study our own teaching practices, using self-studies or other methodological approaches, will we be able to improve and develop the quality of teaching. The outcome must be shared and distributed amongst teacher educators, to secure a professional development, and a good integration of technology in teacher education.

References

1. Zeichner, K.: Accumulating knowledge across self-studies in teacher education. J. Teach. Educ. **58**(1), 36–46 (2007)
2. Loughran, J.J.: Researching teacher education practices: responding to the challenges, demands, and expectations of self-study. J. Teach. Educ. **58**(12), 12–20 (2007)
3. Smith, K.: Selvstudier – verktøy for profesjonell utvikling for lærerutdannere. In: Ulvik, M., Riese, H., Roness, D. (red.) Å forske på egen praksis- aksjonsforskning og andre tilnærminger til profesjonell utvikling i utdanningsfeltet. Fagbokforlaget. (2016)
4. Educause: Flipped classroom (2012). https://www.library.educause.edu/topics/teaching-and-learning/flipped-classroom
5. Bergman, J., Sams, A.: Flip Your Classroom: Reach Every Student in Every Class every Day. ISTE, ASCD (2012)
6. Ministry of Education & Research: White paper no. 16 (2016–2017) Quality Culture in Higher Education. Oslo, Kunnskapsdepartementet (2017)
7. Bochner, A.P., Ellis, C.: Autoethnography, personal narrative, reflexivity. Researcher as a subject. In: Densin, N., Lincoln, Y. (eds.) Handbook of Qualitative research. Sage, Thousand Oaks (2000)
8. Leming, T.: Hvor ble JEG av? In: Jakhelln, R.E., Leming, T., Tiller, T. (red.) Emosjoner i forskning og læring. Eureka Forlag, Tromsø (2009)

Social Media and Online Learning

Exploring Influence of Cultural Constructs and Social Network on Cross-Cultural Learning

Rustam Shadiev[1(✉)], Narzikul Shadiev[2], and Mirzaali Fayziev[2]

[1] Nanjing Normal University, No. 122, Ninghai Road, Nanjing, China
rustamsh@gmail.com

[2] Samarkand State University, No. 15, University Boulevard, Samarkand, Uzbekistan

Abstract. In this study, we designed an online cross-cultural learning activity for participants from different countries, representing various cultures and speaking diverse languages. The participants interacted and exchanged culture-related information with each other in their native languages. We employed a speech-enabled language translation technology to support participant interaction and information exchange in order to facilitate their cross-cultural learning. We analyzed a social network of participants of cross-cultural learning activity and measured their perceptions related to cultural constructs. Finally, we investigated the relationship between cross-cultural learning and social network characteristics and between cross-cultural learning and cultural constructs. According to our results, first, cross-cultural learning of participants was facilitated in terms of declarative and procedural knowledge of foreign traditions and related culture. Second, Group II had better social network characteristics compared to Group I. Third, our results revealed that there is no relationship exist between cross-cultural learning and cultural constructs. We make several implications based on our results in this paper.

Keywords: Cultural constructs · Social network · Cross-cultural understanding Speech-enabled language translation

1 Introduction

Cross-cultural understanding is the basic ability of individuals to understand the different cultures [1]. Due to globalization, cross-cultural understanding has become a very important issue because people are in close proximity, exposed to an increasing variety of culturally diverse people, and are fostered to have a range of different relationships [2]. As a result, there is an increasing demand for competence in communicating and living peacefully with people of different cultural backgrounds. Scholars argued that communication and information exchange are the main component of cross-cultural learning process; they help people reach a mutual understanding of each other's culture [1]. People communicate and share among themselves experiences of and insights into other cultures which lead to the expansion of their cultural awareness and behavior [3]. Cross-cultural communication and information exchange among people from different cultures can be supported by various technologies [4]. Çiftçi [5] found that social

T.-T. Wu et al. (Eds.): ICITL 2018, LNCS 11003, pp. 345–350, 2018.
https://doi.org/10.1007/978-3-319-99737-7_37

networking services such as online discussion boards, text-based chatting, blogs, etc. were frequently used technologies to aid cross-cultural learning. The main reason is because social network services facilitate communication, social interactions, and coordination among distributed learners [9].

Scholars warned that some issues exist and may hinder cross-cultural learning; the most challenging one is the language gap [7]. When learners do not have a common language, it is difficult and even impossible to communicate and exchange information with others and so achieve cross-cultural understanding [8]. Application of speech-enabled language translation (SELT) technology was proposed to overcome this issue. According to [9], SELT receives speech input in one language and simultaneously translates it into different language making interaction among representatives of different cultures without common language possible.

One important aspect of cross-cultural learning is cultural constructs. Several studies claimed that various cultural factors lay behind different people's behavior. Cultural constructs theory describes the effects of specific culture on the values of its representatives and how these values relate to their behavior [10]. That is, the theory can explain observed differences between cultures on the following constructs: (1) power distance – the extent to which the less powerful members of organizations and institutions accept and expect that power is distributed unequally; (2) individualism – degree to which people in a society are integrated into groups; (3) uncertainty avoidance – a society's tolerance for ambiguity; and (4) masculinity – a preference in society for achievement, heroism, assertiveness and material rewards for success [10]. For example, the scores for the power distance construct are very high for Asian countries whereas they are very low for western European countries.

Our review revealed some issues in related studies. First, several studies were carried out in which participants were engaged in cross-cultural learning activities. However, only two nationalities were involved in such activities. That is, the participants had very limited choice of a foreign culture (only one) to learn about. Second, learning activities were designed for participants to communicate in a common language only. This approach limited communication to be in one language, i.e. participants either spoke to those who understood their native language or spoke to those whose language they understood. Third, not much attention was paid on analysis of social network and/or cultural constructs. It is important to analyze social networks and cultural constructs because there are several characteristics of a social network and cultural perceptions and they may affect participant cross-cultural learning differently. Findings in this aspect can be useful for educators and researchers in designing appropriate learning activities to foster cross-cultural understanding. Therefore, we aimed to address these limitations. To this end, informed by earlier research, we designed cross-cultural learning activity based on communication and information exchange. Our participants, representatives of thirteen nationalities, communicated and exchanged culture-related information with each other on their native language using a social network service. We employed SELT so that the participants could speak in their native language, SELT translated the speech input into language which others understood, and so communicated content could be understandable and useful for cross-cultural learning. We explored whether application of SELT facilitated cross-cultural understanding. We also analyzed a social network of participants and measured their perceptions related to cultural constructs. Finally, we investigated the relationship between cross-cultural learning and social network characteristics and between cross-cultural learning and cultural constructs.

2 Method

Twenty one university students representing thirteen nationalities participated in our study. We divided participants into two groups: (Group 1) the participants had interaction with those members of their group whose tradition/culture they wanted to learn and experience and communication was limited to discussion of a tradition/culture of interest; (Group 2) the participants had interaction with every member of their group and their interaction was not limited to a tradition/culture they wanted to learn and experience. Our cross-cultural learning activity included the following steps: *Self-introduction* - we asked the participants to introduce themselves; *Introducing local traditions* - we asked the participants to introduce their local traditions and related culture; *Experiencing foreign traditions* - we asked participants to select one tradition, to experience it, and then to share his/her personal experience of a foreign tradition and related culture with other participants; *Sharing experiences* - we asked the participants to communicate with each other about themselves, their traditions, and their experiences of foreign traditions and related cultures. The participants communicated in a closed Facebook group during the first three steps and via Skype during the fourth step.

We used the following instruments: *evaluation of cross-cultural understanding* – we evaluated cross-cultural understanding in terms of procedural (knowing how to perform certain activities) and declarative (factual knowledge and information that a person knows) knowledge on a five-point scale ("5" is Excellent and "1" is Unacceptable); *social network analysis* – we employed "Gephi," an open-source network analysis and visualization software package; *Hofstede's model* – we used this model to measure cultural constructs.

3 Results

According to results, the participants had cross-cultural understanding in terms of procedural and declarative knowledge. That is, the participants were able to explain foreign traditions and related cultures (declarative knowledge) as well as how the traditions can be carried out (procedural knowledge). When we compared procedural and declarative knowledge of the participants in the two groups, our statistical results showed that Group I ($M = 4.82$; $SD = 0.60$) outperformed Group II ($M = 4.00$; $SD = 0.67$) on the procedural knowledge, $t = 2.954$, $p < 0.05$ and Group I ($M = 4.45$; $SD = 0.69$) outperformed Group II ($M = 3.70$; $SD = 0.67$) on the declarative knowledge, $t = 2.534$, $p > 0.05$.

Results of the social network analysis for two groups are presented as follows. The social network of Group I had 12 nodes and 248 edges. This network had average degree 20.667 and diameter was 3. The average path length of the network was 1.36 and the density was 1.879. The social network of Group II had 11 nodes and 397 edges. The average degree of the network was 36.091 and the diameter was 2. The network had the average path length 1.12 and the density as 3.609. The nodes in two networks showed the number of participants. The edges showed the number of communication instances among the nodes; Group I had less edges compared to Group II. We explored the number of edges related to social and cognitive categories in two social networks and found that the participants in Group I had more edges related to cognitive category whereas Group II had more edges related to social category. Average degree showed higher average number of links per node; that is, each participant in Group II had more communication instances (i.e. sent or received) compared to participants in Group I. Network diameter reveled the maximum distance between any pair of nodes in the graph and it was higher in Group I than in Group II. Average path length is the average number of steps along the shortest paths for all possible pairs of network nodes; it measures the efficiency of information on a network. Group 1 had longer average path length compared to group II. Social network density is defined as the ratio of the number of edges and the number of possible edges; it shows how well connected a network is. Results showed that network density of Group II was higher compared to Group I.

Results of cultural construct evaluation are presented in Table 1. According to the table, the participants ID14,21,11,2 had the highest power distance whereas the participants ID4,16 had the lowest. The participants ID17,19,10 had higher level of individualism and he participants ID4,14 had lowest level. The participants ID21,5,9,20 had higher level of uncertainty avoidance whereas the participants ID2,11,12 had the lowest level. The participants ID11,14,21 had highest masculinity and the participants ID1,16,19 had the lowest. We could not find any significant correlation between cultural constructs and cross-cultural learning.

Table 1. Cultural constructs

ID/Country	Power distance	ID/Country	Individualism	ID/Country	Uncertainty avoidance	ID/Country	Masculinity
14 Paraguay	4.33	17 Mexico	4.33	21 Uzbekistan	4.00	11 Indonesia	3.25
21 Uzbekistan	4.00	19 Mongolia	4.00	5 Taiwan	3.67	14 Paraguay	3.00
11 Indonesia	3.67	10 Indonesia	3.67	9 India	3.67	21 Uzbekistan	3.00
2 Taiwan	3.33	1 Taiwan	3.33	20 Philippines	3.67	6 Burkina Faso	2.75
- -	- -	- -	- -	- -	- -	- -	- -
17 Mexico	2.00	18 Belize	2.33	2 Taiwan	2.67	1 Taiwan	1.00
4 Taiwan	1.33	4 Taiwan	2.00	11 Indonesia	2.67	16 Honduras	1.00
16 Honduras	1.00	14 Paraguay	2.00	12 Vietnam	2.00	19 Mongolia	1.00

4 Discussion and Conclusion

Results of cross-cultural learning evaluation showed that the participants had procedural and declarative knowledge; i.e. the participants were able to explain foreign tradition and how it can be carried out. This suggests that our activity supported by SELT was beneficial for cross-cultural learning. Similar results were reported in other related studies. The participants in [9] communicated and exchanged culture-related information with each other using SELT and so their cross-cultural learning was promoted.

However, this present study is different from earlier research in that the participants in our study were from multiple nationalities and spoke in multiple languages whereas the participants from two nationalities speaking in two languages only were involved in earlier studies [9].

Social network for Group II was much better compared to Group I. Group II had higher number of edges compared to Group I. In addition, Group II had higher average degree compared to Group I; however, cross-cultural understanding of Group II in terms of procedural and declarative knowledge was lower compared to Group I. The network diameter was higher in Group I than in Group II. This suggests that if participants interact with a few members but focus on a specific culture, their cross-cultural understanding will be better. On the other hand, if participants interact with more members and do not focus on a specific culture, their social network will be stronger. This finding needs to be considered by educators and researchers, specifically, how to facilitate cross-cultural understanding and improve social network.

Our results are contradictory to those from earlier research. Hofstede et al. [10] ranked representatives of different countries according to power distance, individualism, uncertainty avoidance and masculinity. If we compare the results of [10] with ours, our results showed that representatives from the same culture had the highest and lowest values for some constructs; e.g. the participant ID 2 had the highest power distance and the participant ID 4 had the lowest power distance - both are from the same country. In addition, representatives from countries which were ranked to have the highest values for some constructs in [10] had the lowest value in this present study or vice versa. Similar findings were reported elsewhere; Viberg and Grönlund [11] argued that Hofstede's factors couldn't explain the differences in student attitudes in the chosen sample and thus, the Hofstede's model must be questioned.

Cultural constructs had no relationship with cross-cultural learning. This findings draws on the globalization over the past few decades; i.e. proposed cultural differences are not the same as before. Due to modern communication tools, media and travel, cultural ideas, meanings, and values transmit around the world; therefore, different nationalities and cultures become increasingly interconnected and people form shared norms and knowledge. So people had stronger power distance/masculinity a few decades ago compared to the present. That is, people perceptions related to cultural constructs can be shaped by globalization processes.

References

1. Yamazaki, Y., Kayes, D.C.: An experiential approach to cross-cultural learning: a review and integration of competencies for successful expatriate adaptation. Acad. Manag. Learn. Educ. **3**(4), 362–379 (2004)
2. Aparicio, M., Bacao, F., Oliveira, T.: Cultural impacts on e-learning systems' success. Internet High. Educ. **31**, 58–70 (2016)
3. Gudykunst, W.B., Ting-Toomey, S., Chua, E.: Culture and Interpersonal Communication. Sage Publications, Thousand Oaks (1988)

4. Shadiev, R., Wu, T.T., Sun, A., Huang, Y.M.: Applications of speech-to-text recognition and computer-aided translation for enhancing cross-cultural learning: issues and their solutions. Educ. Tech. Res. Dev. **66**(1), 191–214 (2018)
5. Çiftçi, E.Y.: A review of research on intercultural learning through computer-based digital technologies. J. Educ. Technol. Soc. **19**(2), 313–327 (2016)
6. Shadiev, R., Hwang, W.Y., Huang, Y.M.: A pilot study: facilitating cross-cultural understanding with project-based collaborative learning in an online environment. Australas. J. Educ. Technol. **31**(2), 123–139 (2015)
7. Rienties, B., Johan, N., Jindal-Snape, D.: Bridge building potential in cross-cultural learning: a mixed method study. Asia Pac. Educ. Rev. **16**(1), 37–48 (2015)
8. Shadiev, R., Sun, A., Huang, Y.M.: A study of the facilitation of cross-cultural understanding and intercultural sensitivity using speech-enabled language translation technology. Br. J. Educ. Technol. (2018). https://doi.org/10.1111/bjet.12648
9. Shadiev, R., Huang, Y.M.: Facilitating cross-cultural understanding with learning activities supported by speech-to-text recognition and computer-aided translation. Comput. Educ. **98**, 130–141 (2016)
10. Hofstede, G., Hofstede, G.J., Minkov, M.: Cultures and Organisations: Software of the Mind. McGrawHill, London (2010)
11. Viberg, O., Grönlund, Å.: Cross-cultural analysis of users' attitudes toward the use of mobile devices in second and foreign language learning in higher education: a case from Sweden and China. Comput. Educ. **69**, 169–180 (2013)

Understanding the Extent of and Factors Involved in the Use of YouTube as an Informal Learning Tool by 11- to 13-Year-Old Children

Neliswa Dyosi(✉) and Marie Hattingh(✉)

University of Pretoria, Private Bag X20, Hatfield 0028, South Africa
neliswa.dyosi@investec.com, marie.hattingh@up.ac.za

Abstract. Web 2.0 technology has changed the way and setting where learning takes place. This study has attempted to contribute to the understanding of how children, aged 11 to 13 can use YouTube as an informal learning tool. This was accomplished by conducting four focused groups consisting of children aged 11 to 13. Thematic content analysis was used to analyse the interview data. The data has revealed that children use YouTube as home and at school (limited). They had multiple methods of access, although was constrained by parental control and limited by restricted data. The children further experienced two types of informal learning, self-directed and incidental. Interestingly, they did distinguish between appropriate and inappropriate content. Cognitively, they displayed low levels of self-regulation but were extremely self-efficient. Children had high expectations that there is entertainment on YouTube, and that resulted in them constantly using YouTube to entertain themselves. Finally, through observational learning, the children not only learnt how to use YouTube but they also acquired different skills from watching YouTube videos. These findings enhance the current understanding of the role YouTube can play in learning.

Keywords: YouTube · Children · Informal learning · Social cognitive theory

1 Introduction

Learning "is no longer about providing materials for people to learn and be tested on like parrots as our entire ecosystem of working, learning and developing have evolved" and are still evolving daily [1]. However, the first thing that comes to mind when the word "learning" is mentioned is school or some sort of formalized learning environment [2]. The problem with this kind of thinking is that at times the other type of learning which takes place as part of our normal day-to-day duties gets overlooked [2]. Technology has changed the manner and setting in which learning takes place. In a study conducted by Sefton-Green [2], she concluded that "Computers and other aspects of Information and Communication Technologies (ICTs) allow children and young people a wide variety of activities and experiences that can support learning, yet many of these transactions do not take place in traditional educational settings".

Learning in non-traditional educational settings are described as informal learning. Researchers described informal learning as something unavoidable [3]; spontaneous [4]

T.-T. Wu et al. (Eds.): ICITL 2018, LNCS 11003, pp. 351–361, 2018.
https://doi.org/10.1007/978-3-319-99737-7_38

and most influenced by interactions with people, our hobbies, like the TV programs we watch, searching the internet and social life [3, 4]. You do not have to have intentions to learn in order to learn, by virtue of individuals having interactions with each other whether be it through face to face or through the internet as a medium of communication, you are bound to learn [3, 5].

Sharples et al. [6] and Hattingh [7] showed that there are many learning opportunities offered by Web 2.0 for people of all ages as social media provides rich and rewarding learning experiences. However, there is currently under representation in the literature about the benefits of using social media as a learning tool for children, especially as an informal learning tool. According to Mao [8], most studies have investigated use and benefits of social media ("either as individual tools or as a general category") in higher education, with only a fewer studies choosing to focus on secondary education. Greenhow and Lewin [9] concurs with Mao [8], saying that, this area is currently under-theorized. Amongst the most popular reasons cited for this lack of research is "students' age and schools' responsibility and protection awareness" [8]. Although informal learning has been studied as a concept, there is a gap in current literature about how parents, teachers and children can take advantage of the informal learning opportunities presented by the world of social media. Thus, this exploratory study seeks to examine what informal learning opportunities, and the factors that influence it for children aged 11–13 years on YouTube.

The paper is structured as follows. Firstly, the social cognitive theory will be discussed in Sect. 2 followed by literature on informal learning and social media and informal learning in Sect. 3. Section 4 will explain how the study was conducted. The results will be presented and discussed in Sect. 5. The study concludes in Sect. 6.

2 Theoretical Underpinning: Social Cognitive Theory

The main purpose of this study is to understand informal learning opportunities available for children in social media and the factors that influences it. The Social Cognitive Theory (SCT) has been employed as the theoretical underpinning for this study. "Social cognitive theory is rooted in the notion of human agency, which suggests that individuals are proactively engaged in their own development and that they are able to exercise a measure of control over their thoughts, feelings, and actions" [10, 11]. SCT consist of three main elements, environment, behavior and cognitive factors. Each of these factors influence one another in a triadic fashion [10, 12]. In terms of this study the environment includes the use of YouTube in the child's informal environment, behavior includes the extent to which informal learning takes place and cognitive factors include the child's ability to use, regulate and learn (informally) from YouTube.

By adopting social cognitive theory, the researcher is able to explain how and why people acquire and maintain certain behavioural patterns [10]. In light of this, the researcher will be able to understand why and how children use YouTube and what informal learning benefits they derive from their use.

3 Learning: Formal and Informal

Learning is an integral element of human existence. According to Marsick and Watkins [5] "learning is the way in which individuals or groups acquire, interpret, reorganize, change or assimilate a related cluster of information, skills, and feelings. It is mainly the way in which humans construct meaning in their lives". While the term "learning" is usually associated with schooling [2], research has shown that learning happens even outside of the structured schooling system [13], after all, we do not spend all our time in a classroom setup and there is no sudden switch off on learning once one leaves the classroom. Learning is continuous.

For the purposes of this study, the researchers focused on the "unstructured" informal learning. According to Yoo and Kim [14] eighty percent of learning is informal. Most of what people learn in the course of their lives is learnt outside the classroom environment integrated mostly to the day to day activities that people engage in [15].

A large proportion of what we do every day constitutes informal learning. Even though there may be concerns about the definition of informal learning, one thing that researchers seem to agree on is that this type of learning is an integral part of our daily lives. Informal learning is so embedded in our daily activities to an extent that the learner does not necessary have to have objectives of learning in order for it to happen. In fact, Pilz and Wilmshöfer [16] suggest that it is even easy for the learners themselves to not recognize that learning is taking place because it is mostly unintentional. According to Siemens [17], informal learning is the engine and an integral part of human learning experiences. Pilz and Wilmshöfer [16] agrees with Siemens [17] and refers to informal learning as a "natural accompaniment to everyday life". As learners progress through the different learning stages i.e. from K12 through to university it is, becoming evident that informal learning has a crucial role as learning can happen anywhere at any time [18].

3.1 Types of Informal Learning

Rogers [19] and Schugurensky [20] propose that informal learning takes on three forms. He says that if we were to look at informal learning as a single process we would probably be making mistakes. Rogers [19] lists the following as the three forms of informal learning: (1) "Self-directed" learning which include activities that are both organized and controlled from the learner's side. The learner decides to learn something without being assisted by another person i.e. teacher, parent etc. [20]. Furthermore, the learner has an intention to learn something; because there was an intention to learn, success of learning would have to be measured. The learner takes what and how much they have learnt and use it to measure success – the learner is conscious about what they have learnt. Gikas and Grant [21] suggest that although there is usually an intention to learn, the methods and ways to learn are usually "unstructured and contextualized". (2) "Incidental" learning where the learner is engaged in a task, there is no intention to learn, however as they complete the task they pick up that they have actually learnt something although that was not the intention. Marsick and Watkins [5], Schugurensky [20] Rogers [19] agree that incidental learning is a "sub-category" of informal learning. They further go on to say that, incidental learning is actually a "by-product of another activity". Schugurensky [20] uses a very simple example yet something that many people can relate to; the example is that of a toddler touching a hot iron while they are playing without knowing that it is hot. The intent is obviously not to test if the iron is hot and will burn them – they are involved in a task of playing but in that process learn that touching hot iron burns and will probably not do it again. (3) "Unintentional" learning is a form of learning which tests "false" for both intention and awareness. It is difficult to measure success with this kind of learning. According to Schugurensky [20] "The awareness that an unintentional and unconscious learning experience took place (through socialization) could occur immediately after the learning experience or many years after it, and the process of retrospective recognition can be internally generated or externally led". In explaining this type of learning, Gikas and Grant [21] concluded that it is often "unanticipated, unorganized" and at times even unacknowledged by the learner. Yakin and Gencel [22] concluded that informal learning takes place whenever "Conversations, reading, watching TV, observing the world, experiencing an accident, or embarrassing situation, observation, trial and error, asking for help, listening to stories, reflecting on a day's events, or stimulated by general interest" are present.

3.2 Social Media as an Informal Learning Tool

Unintentional and self-directed learning form a big element of learning when it comes to social media [23]. As suggested by Dabbagh and Kitsantas [23] not only is informal learning becoming a critical element of education for learners at all stages, but there is also substantial evidence that confirms, "Social media is increasingly supporting informal learning at home and in the community". Yoo and Kim [14] agree with Dabbagh and Kitsantas [23] view, suggesting that social media is increasingly being used as a tool for developing both formal and informal learning spaces and experiences. According to [24] "technology-enhanced informal learning is an integral part of children's education because it not only develops technical knowledge and skills but is constructivist (enabling them to reflect upon and construct their own understanding of the world), experiential (involving behavioural and affective as well as cognitive dimensions) and situated (joining and learning from online communities through social media)". Whether the need is to address a problem at school, work or home, or even to just satisfy their curiosity, it is evident that learners are in a constant search for information and to find the solutions, they take advantage of the social media world [23]. In literature, informal learning is often linked to ICT, Web 2.0 and social software [22]. Informal learning according to Yakin and Gencel [22] is a buy-product of social activities and these could be anything from families, communities, leisure activities and even the web as it has transformed into a social platform. Latchem [24] agrees, stating that "most people's learning throughout their lifespans is informal, occurring in family, community and work settings". Many young people regard social media as a learning tool outside of school [25].

There is also evidence in literature that YouTube has a potential to be used as informal learning tool with some people already exploring the benefits. As suggested by Clifton and Mann [26], "YouTube is an established social software and has millions of users and is already being used as both an informal and formal learning tool by many". Latchem [24], Clifton and Mann [26] agree that "YouTube has matured into one of the biggest resources for educational content ever". Baumer [27] refers to YouTube as "multi-voiced and multifarious tool for informal learning." According to Tan [28] an informal learning environment is characterized by attributes such as "Open-ended, non-threatening, enjoyable and explorative" and the nature of the YouTube environment fits these attributes. Another key feature of an informal learning environment is that it should be both "educational and enjoyable" [28]. Furthermore, the freedom to express yourself, in an uncontrolled, unvetted environment with little or no editorial process on the uploaded content, makes YouTube an appealing medium for informal learning [15]. The ability to create and view content with minimal barriers is another feature that makes YouTube a resource for informal learning [15]. However, although social media provides many benefits as a learning tool for all age groups, it is also important to note that it does have some limitations and poses certain risks and security concerns to its users, with children being the most vulnerable [37]. The risk, and associated controls are discussed in Sect. 5.

4 Research Methodology

The aim of this research project is to understand how children use YouTube for informal learning. This study follows a qualitative research approach, based on an interpretive epistemology, which analyses responses from four focus groups conducted with children aged 11 to 13.

"The purpose of a focus group interview is to get collective views on a certain defined topic of interest from a group of people who are known to have had certain experiences" [29]. A focus group is defined as "a technique involving the use of in-depth group interviews in which participants are selected because they are purposive, although not necessarily representative, the sampling of a specific population, this group being 'focused' on a given topic" [30]. The decision to use focus groups as a data collection technique for this study was motivated by a number of factors including the age of the participants and the type of data the researcher aims to get out of the participants. In addition, because social media use by children carries a bad stigma around adults, by using focus groups the researcher sought to avoid a situation where the participants would be uncomfortable with one-on-one interviews and would have ended up telling the researcher what they believe she wanted to hear as opposed to what is actually happening.

The researchers employed thematic content analysis as the data analysis technique for this study. Thematic Content Analysis (TCA) is a data analysis method used to analyse written, verbal or visual messages. It will therefore be ideally suited to analyse focus groups interviews [31].

The following section will describe how the data was analysed.

5 Analysis and Discussion

Interview data was analysed based on the interpretation of the researcher. In Sect. 2, the researcher presented the notion that, cognitive theorists believe that there is an "on-going reciprocal interaction" [12] between behaviour, environment and cognitive factors [10]. In addressing the objectives of the study, the Social Cognitive Theory framework was used as an underlying framework from which the themes were derived. By following the thematic analysis six-phase approach suggested by Braun and Clarke [31] the researcher was able to identify initial codes from the data by going through the audio recordings of the interviews. The initial codes identified together with the raw data from the interview extracts are presented in Table 1 below:

Table 1. Main themes and sub-themes identified from the data mapped on to SCT elements

SCT element	Theme	Sub-themes	Example Codes
Environment	Home environment	Ease of Access	"Yes, we use our playstations, phones, laptops, TV, ipads"
		Parental control	"Not really, but my dad checks my history"
		Monetary constraints	"Yeeessss! I only watch videos when I am connected to Wi-Fi"
	School environment	Access	"Well, no. And again what will the children use to access YouTube, the free Wi-Fi here at school doesn't work that well"
Behaviour	Informal learning	Self-directed learning	"I like watching videos where they show you stuff like skills and videos that show you how to make stuff"
		Incidental learning	"Since I have been watching the music videos, I now know lyrics to the songs"
		Evaluation of inappropriate content	"No, children should not be allowed open access then it will be easy for them to go to any kind of videos"
Cognitive factors	Role of cognitive factors on YouTube use	Role of self-regulation	"My brother is addicted, it's really not funny. He got a playstation for his birthday and ever since then he gained a lot of weight because he is using the playstation 24/7, he refuses even to go for a walk with my parents"
		Role of Self - efficacy	"I was eaves dropping on my brother and he was watching YouTube, that how I learnt"
		Role of Outcome expectations	"If I didn't know how to use YouTube I would search on YouTube for videos on how to use YouTube
		Role of observational learning	"I like looking at DIY videos"

Due to page restrictions, each of the themes will now be briefly discussed next.

5.1 Environment

From this theme, it was evident that the children understood the addictive nature of YouTube. There was a consensus amongst all four groups, with eighteen 18 out of the 22 children agreeing that YouTube should not be allowed during school hours. The other six children were undecided on this matter saying that maybe it can be allowed "sometimes".

Bloom and Johnston [36] however suggested that instead of abolishing YouTube from the school environment, teachers and learners should rather be taught how to use YouTube as a valuable tool. Furthermore, they emphasize that blocking YouTube access during school hours results in educators isolating themselves from the spaces in "which students are spending tremendous time and energy and in which much informal learning is taking place".

Children are not in control enough to be able to stay away from YouTube during class time and hence their preference was that YouTube remains blocked. In the study conducted by Ferguson [32] the participants had a similar view to the findings of this study, children thought it was good that schools block certain social media sites and YouTube was one of the sites children thought should blocked. They cited inappropriate content and some things that can come up which they should not be looking at during school hours.

5.2 Behaviour

From the analysis of the results, it was evident that informal learning is taking place amongst children on YouTube. Two types of informal learning were evidently taking place – self-directed learning and incidental learning. The responses are in line with the findings of Downes [33] as he suggested that "educational videos are widely popular within YouTube proper". In a study done by KKMAdmin [34] to understand the top 12 categories of YouTube videos, the "How-to-Videos" came in second place after "product review" videos. The popularity of "How-to-videos" is motivated by the fact that these type of videos help their viewers to understand how to perform specific tasks. When the children were asked why they preferred watching the videos on DIY rather than reading the instructions in a book. What the children did not realise was that they were actually learning and acquiring skills unintentional so. The children defined entertainment as things like (1) "watching soccer game highlights", (2) "watching music videos", (3) "playing games" and (4) "watching funny or comedy videos". Whilst the key activity was entertainment, unconsciously, they were learning soccer tricks, lyrics of songs, dancing skills and new tricks on how to excel in computer games. In a study conducted by Sefton-Green [2] there are two particular findings that are of interest to the current study. Firstly, she concluded that "the 'culture' of games playing (the contexts, peers and surrounding texts) creates a productive background allowing for complex intellectual engagements". Secondly, when children are engaged in playing games, they have a distinct, demanding learning environment. During the interviews, the children admitted that they were actually not aware that they were learning. One of the learners, who was interested in watching music videos, thought the fact that now she knows how to dance better from the videos was just a coincidence and not something that could be defined as learning. It was also evident that with the use of YouTube, children have learnt that there is inappropriate content on YouTube. The analysis also revealed that even with the tightest measures in place, there are still no guarantees that children cannot be exposed to inappropriate content on YouTube. Ways to filter out inappropriate content and ensuring that children continue to enjoy the informal learning benefits on YouTube were discussed in detail as part of this theme.

5.3 Cognitive Factors

In this theme, the researcher sought to understand the role played by cognitive factors on how children learn on YouTube and their use of YouTube. From the analysis of the results, it was evident that cognitive factors play a significant role on the children's use of YouTube. Self-regulation plays a significance role on controlling the intensity of use. It was evident that, the lower the levels of self-regulation, the higher the intensity of use and vice versa. According to O'Keeffe and Clarke-Pearson [35], a low level of self-regulation and susceptibility to peer pressure exposes children to certain risks as they navigate social media. Self-efficacy plays a crucial role in the confidence of the children in terms of their abilities to use and navigate on YouTube. The results revealed that the children had high levels of self-efficacy. Outcome expectations was another factor of SCT that played a role on the use of YouTube. Children had high expectations that there is entertainment on YouTube, and that resulted in them constantly using YouTube to entertain themselves. Finally, through observational learning, the children not only learnt how to use YouTube but they also acquired different skills from watching YouTube videos.

6 Conclusion

The study indicated that both access to a device and ownership of a google account are environmental factors that influence behaviour – use of social media which in turn would influence informal learning on YouTube. Furthermore, parental restrictions also have an impact on whether children use YouTube or not and how much time they spend on YouTube. Lastly, monetary resources are seen as another environmental factor that influence the use of YouTube. Due to limited monetary resources, children are not using YouTube as much as they would prefer. There was a consensus amongst all four groups, with eighteen out of the 22 children agreeing that YouTube should not be allowed during school hours. The other six children were undecided on this matter saying that maybe it can be allowed "sometimes".

It was evident that informal learning is taking place amongst children on YouTube. Two types of informal learning were evidently taking place – self-directed learning and incidental learning. It was also evident that with the use of YouTube, children have learnt that there is inappropriate content on YouTube. The analysis also revealed that even with the tightest measures in place, there are still no guarantees that children cannot be exposed to inappropriate content on YouTube. Ways to filter out inappropriate content and ensuring that children continue to enjoy the informal learning benefits on YouTube were discussed in detail as part of this theme.

Cognitive factors play a significant role on the children's use of YouTube. Self-regulation plays a significance role on controlling the intensity of use. It was evident that, the lower the levels of self-regulation, the higher the intensity of use and vice versa. Self-efficacy plays a crucial role in the confidence of the children in terms of their abilities to use and navigate on YouTube. The results revealed that the children had high levels of self-efficacy. Outcome expectations were another factor of SCT that played a role on the use of YouTube. Children had high expectations that there is entertainment on YouTube, and that resulted in them constantly using YouTube to entertain themselves. Finally, through observational learning, the children not only learnt how to use YouTube but they also acquired different skills from watching YouTube videos.

In this study, the researchers used a very small, significant purposive sample and in turn, this posed a limitation on the generalisation and transferability of the findings of the study. The limitations on the transferability of the research findings are a justification for future study that would include a larger sample as the current study focuses on a very small significant purposive sample only.

References

1. Stodd, J.: Exploring the Social Age and the New Culture of Learning, UK, September 2014
2. Sefton-Green, J.: Literature Review in Informal Learning with Technology. futurelab series, Bristol (2004)
3. Yaşar, Ö., Karadeniz, Ş.: The power of social media in informal learning. Education in a technological world: communicating current and emerging research and technological efforts, pp. 531–538 (2011)
4. Eshach, H.: Bridging in-school and out-of-school learning: formal, non-formal, and informal education. J. Sci. Educ. Technol. **16**(2), 171–189 (2007)
5. Marsick, V.J., Watkins, K.: Informal and Incidental Learning in the Workplace. Routledge, Oxon (2015)
6. Sharples, M., Graber, R., Harrison, C., Logan, K.: E-Safety and Web2.0 for children aged 11–16. J. Comput. Assist. Learn. **25**, 70–84 (2009)
7. Hattingh, M.: A preliminary investigation of the appropriateness of youtube as an informal learning platform for pre-teens. In: Xie, H., Popescu, E., Hancke, G., Fernández Manjón, B. (eds.) ICWL 2017. LNCS, vol. 10473, pp. 101–110. Springer, Cham (2017). https://doi.org/10.1007/978-3-319-66733-1_11
8. Mao, J.: Social media for learning: a mixed methods study on high school students' technology affordances and perspectives. Comput. Hum. Behav. **33**, 213–223 (2014)
9. Greenhow, C., Lewin, C.: Social media and education: reconceptualizing the boundaries of formal and informal learning. Learn. Media Technol. **41**(1), 6–30 (2016)
10. Bandura, A.: Social cognitive theory: an agentic perspective. Asian J. Psychol. **52**(1), 21–41 (1999)
11. Stefanone, M.A., Lackaff, D., Rosen, D.: The relationship between traditional mass media and "Social Media": reality television as a model for social network site behavior. J. Broadcast. Electron. Media **54**(3), 508–525 (2010)
12. Compeau, D.R., Higgins, C.A.: A social cognitive theory perspective on individual reactions to computing technology. In: International Conference on Information Systems (1991)

13. Song, D., Lee, J.: Has Web 2.0 revitalized informal learning? The relationship between Web 2.0 and informal learning. J. Comput. Assist. Learn. **30**, 511–533 (2014)
14. Yoo, S.J., Kim, S.: How and why college students use Web 2.0 applications. Int. J. Web Based Communities **9**(2), 174–186 (2013)
15. Burlington, C.: How Does Digital Literacy Mediate Informal Learning on YouTube? (2016)
16. Pilz, M., Wilmshöfer, S.: Formal, nonformal, and informal learning in rural India: The case of fishing families on the Chilika Lagoon (2015)
17. Siemens, G.: Connectivism: a learning theory for the digital age. Int. J. Instr. Technol. Dist. Learn., 1–100 (2005)
18. Chen, B., Bryer, T.: Investigating instructional strategies for using social media in formal and informal learning. Int. Rev. Res. Open Distrib. Learn. **13**(1), 87–104 (2012)
19. Rogers, A.: The classroom and the everyday: the importance of informal learning for formal learning. Investigar em Educação (2014)
20. Schugurensky, D.: The forms of informal learning: towards a conceptualization of the field (2000)
21. Gikas, J., Grant, M.M.: Mobile computing devices in higher education: student perspectives on learning with cellphones, smartphones & social media. Internet High. Educ. **19**, 18–26 (2013)
22. Yakin, I., Gencel, I.E.: The utilization of social media tools for informal learning activities: a survey study. Mevlana Int. J. Educ. **3**(4), 108–117 (2013)
23. Dabbagh, N., Kitsantas, A.: Personal learning environments, social media, and self-regulated learning: a natural formula for connecting formal and informal learning. Internet High. Educ. **15**(1), 3–8 (2011)
24. Latchem, C.: Informal learning and non-formal education for development. J. Learn. Dev. (2014)
25. Greenhow, C., Robelia, B.: Old communication, new literacies: social network sites as social learning resources. J. Comput. Mediated Commun. **14**, 1130–1161 (2009)
26. Clifton, A., Mann, C.: Can YouTube enhance student nurse learning? Nurse Educ. Today **31**(4), 311–313 (2011)
27. Baumer, S.: Digital Youth Research, 06 February 2018. http://digitalyouth.ischool.berkeley.edu/node/49
28. Tan, E.: Informal learning on YouTube: exploring digital literacy in independent online learning. Learn. Media Technol. J. **38**(4), 463–477 (2013)
29. Myers, M.D.: Qualitative Research in Business & Management. Sage, London (2013)
30. Rabiee, F.: Focus-group interview and data analysis. In: Proceedings of the Nutrition Society, pp. 655–660 (2004)
31. Braun, V., Clarke, V.: Using thematic analysis in psychology. Qual. Res. Psychol. **3**(2), 77–101 (2006)
32. Ferguson, C.J.: Do angry birds make for angry children? A meta-analysis of video game influences on children's and adolescents' aggression, mental health, prosocial behavior, and academic performance. Perspect. Psychol. Sci. **5**(10), 646–666 (2015)
33. Downes, S.: Places to go: YouTube. Innovate J. Online Educ. **4**(5) (2008)
34. KnockKnockMargeting. 12 Popular types of Video Content on YouTube (2017). https://knockknockmarketing.com/2017/08/04/12-popular-types-of-video-content-on-youtube/. Accessed 23 Mar 2018
35. O'Keeffe, G.S., Clarke-Pearson, K.: The impact of social media on children, adolescents, and families. Pediatrics (2011)

36. Bloom, K., Johnston, K.M.: Digging into YouTube videos: using media literacy and participatory culture to promote cross-cultural understanding. J. Media Literacy Educ. **2**(2), 113–123 (2010)
37. Kritzinger, E.: Online safety in South Africa - A Cause for Growing Concern. IEEE (2014)

Social Media and the High School Environment

Morgan Carter[1(✉)] and Andreja Istenic Starcic[1,2,3]

[1] College of Information, University of North Texas, Denton, TX, USA
MorganCarter4@my.unt.edu, andreja.starcic@gmail.com
[2] Faculty of Civil and Geodetic Engineering, University of Ljubljana, Ljubljana, Slovenia
[3] Faculty of Education, University of Primorska, Koper, Slovenia

Abstract. The growth of social media over the past five years is staggering with around 1 in 3 people globally on some form of social media. Seventy-five percent of US high school students are on some social media and educators are starting to use the technology in the learning process. However, recent reports are beginning to question the benefits of social media on one's well-being. The purpose of this study is to see how social media sites are being used in the high school environment and what is the impact on the learning process and social well-being of students. A review of four educational technology journals will guide the discussion to answering the research questions. Outcomes of this study include an analysis of how these technologies are being used in the classroom and what are the perceptions of using these technologies on learning and well-being.

Keywords: Social media · Social network sites · High school
Learning · Well-being

1 Introduction

Social network sites (SNSs) and the phenomenon of "Internet addiction" or "problematic Internet use" have been in the news recently. Several articles [1–3] have cautioned the use of social media and activities in Silicon Valley in programming apps to keep us both physically and mentally connected. To be continuously connected can be incredibly exhaustive in a developing child's brain [4, 5]. Educators are introducing these platforms in teaching and learning capitalising benefits of social media potentials for connecting formal and informal learning [6, 7] and the contribution of social media for experiential learning [8]. Educators need support in instructional design for social media platforms in the classroom and decision making between varied opinions in designing learning activities.

Hawi and Samaha [9] state that as of January 2016 a third of the world's population is on some social media platform. They go on to provide the following number of users for the most popular applications at the time (March 2016). Facebook had more than 1.09 billion daily active users, Instagram had more than 400 million monthly active users, Twitter had more than 310 million active monthly users, and LinkedIn had more

T.-T. Wu et al. (Eds.): ICITL 2018, LNCS 11003, pp. 362–370, 2018.
https://doi.org/10.1007/978-3-319-99737-7_39

than 433 million active users (p. 1). Statistics surrounding high school students use of social media sites are varied, but estimates, according to NORC [10], indicate 75% or higher of American teens age 13–17 are on some kind of social media with Instagram and Snapchat leading the way. Due to the fact that so many high school students are on some form of social media, it makes sense to try and meet them where they are at in the 21st century.

Research in the area of social media use for learning with this population is limited. According to Khan, Wohn, and Ellison [11], "studies about academic uses of Facebook by high school students are scant" (p. 138). This references Facebook and academic uses in particular, but the need for new research with other platforms and the effects on learning and social well-being are in demand [12–14]. Also, the novelty effect keeps the social media landscape continually changing with new platforms emerging every few years (think MySpace and Vine). There are plenty of opportunities in this area so that this paper will look at the following research questions in selected educational technology journals:

1. How is social media being used in high school environments and what are the effects on learning and social well-being?
2. What are high school students' and teachers' perspectives of using social networking sites for instruction?

2 Theory and Research

Why are so many people spending time on social media sites and what are they doing? A study by Cabral [15] poses the question "is Generation Y addicted to social media"? That study concludes Generation Y "has made social media their top priority and continues to need more usage in order to feel satisfied" (p. 11). The study by Cabral did not look at Snapchat but rather Facebook, Twitter, MySpace and LinkedIn, or the popular applications in the early 2010's. In a more recent study of well-being and problematic Facebook use, Satici and Uysal [16] found their prediction to be true in that "results demonstrated that problematic Facebook use has predicted determinants of human well-being negatively", and that "problematic Facebook use is associated with a lower well-being" (p. 188). The authors noted that users are spending much more time on social network sites in general.

Moreover, prominent news organisations have also picked up on the internet addiction and social well-being discussion. Cooper [1], in a 60 min interview, discusses how tech insiders are programming applications and social media sites to keep users "addicted" and coming back for more. They are trying to get people hooked by hacking their brain and making them think they might be missing out on something or more recently referred to as the 'Fear of Missing Out' or FoMO. To help curb FoMo, Brodwin [17] reports that Google is unveiling an initiative called "Digital Wellbeing" that aims to focus on the "JOMO" or the joy of missing out. These efforts are intended to help users keep track of their digital time and focus on balancing social well-being within all areas of their life.

Cyberbullying has also been linked to social media use. Watts, Wagner, Velasquez, and Behrens [18] cite *"bullying is a major problem in today's society and occurs at many different ages and in many different forms"* (p. 269). They go on to say that this harassment can go on 24 h a day, seven days a week. Ho, Chen, and Ng [19] report that cyberbullying has been increasing worldwide and that 40% of American adolescents were victims of some form of cyberbullying. This increase coincides with the rapid expansion of social media use, but the results are not necessarily causational.

Not all studies and media downplay the harmful effects of social sites [20]. O'Keeffe and Clarke-Pearson [21] cite benefits to children using social media in that they can enhance their learning opportunities and learn social skills at a younger age. A study by Chu, Capio, van Aalst and Cheng [22] concluded that *"wikis supported group writing and performance by promoting collaboration"* (p. 179). Another study by Wohn, Ellison, Khan, Fewins-Bliss, and Gray [23] showed how social media could help shape first-generation high school students by providing them information on the college admissions process they might not receive elsewhere. With increased proliferation of social media in the personal, academic and professional sphere, the attention in all levels of education is needed to integrate advanced levels of media use and examine attitudes towards media. Integration in teaching and learning will influence its use in bridging academic and professional life [7] and balance personal sphere with other spheres.

Social media sites also foster sharing experiences and the notion of social constructivism [24, 25]. For experiential and social learners, social media sites can provide an environment where a picture is worth a thousand words. It allows sharing and possibly experiencing it alongside the person who posted almost simultaneously. This was possible not too long ago with camcorders and disposable cameras, but today the person can experience it live with them through many social media platforms that accommodate live streaming.

3 Method

There were two separate searches for literature and resources related to this paper. The initial search was for the Theory and Research section to get an idea what has been looked at broadly while the second search focused on the research questions and will be analysed in the Discussion section. The intent was to get a narrower scope of the high school population with a focus on education technology journals as the search progressed.

The following databases were searched for the Theory and Research section of this paper to identify recent literature and empirical studies relating to social media in the high school environment: University of North Texas library, Learn Tech Lib, and Google Scholar. The following keywords and combinations thereof were used: social media, social network sites, high school, teen, learning, and well-being. Each search engine returned several pages of results of which a wide range of articles was chosen for review based on titles and abstracts. These articles did not have to be in the field of educational technology and included areas such as industry and psychology among others. In addition, recent news articles using the keyword 'social media' were searched from several respected organizations including Time, New York Times, and 60 min. Close to 20 were used for the Introduction and Theory and Research sections of this paper.

From those results, the second search focused more on the research questions in the following educational technology journals: Computers and Education, Tech Trends, Educational Technology Research & Development, and the British Journal of Educational Technology. These journals were chosen with the objective to examine the field of learning technologies and due to their recurrence in the first results set. The same keywords were used to get the initial list of articles from within those journals, although this search was restricted to the last five years of publications. That list yielded 320 articles. Based on manual search and reading abstracts, the eleven were chosen for in-depth analysis and theme building. The words high school, teen, or secondary had to be in the title or abstract of those selected articles. The careful review was taken not to include post-secondary in the chosen items. Table 1 shows each journal and the total articles returned based on the search criteria and also the number of pieces selected.

Table 1. Educational Technology Journals

Journals	Total articles	Articles selected
Computers & Education	33	6
TechTrends	144	3
Educational Technology Research & Development	37	1
British Journal of Educational Technology	106	1

Table 2 further provides themes of the articles in addition to authors, title, year of publication, and keywords. Eight pieces were empirical while three were reviews of existing literature. Close to half focused on the cautions of using social media while the others were more focused on how social media platforms enhance the learning process. Each article was analyzed to provide answers to the research questions.

Table 2. Themes of articles

Title of the article	Year	Keywords	Themes
Evaluating the use of a social media tool for collaborative group writing of secondary school students in Hong Kong [10]	2017	Social media; PBworks; Collaborative writing; Cooperative writing; Secondary education; Wikis	Collaboration; Engagement
The role of social media in shaping first-generation high school students' college aspirations: A social capital lens [35]	2013	Post-secondary education; Secondary education; Computer-mediated communication; Media in education;	Information access; Efficacy

(*continued*)

Table 2. (*continued*)

Title of the article	Year	Keywords	Themes
Social networking sites and cognitive abilities: Do they make you smarter? [1]	2013	Working memory; IQ; Facebook; YouTube; Academic performance	Engagement; Connectedness
Actual friends matter: An internet skills perspective on teens' informal academic collaboration on Facebook [21]	2014	Academic collaboration; Facebook; Internet skills; Instrumental support; Social capital	Collaboration; Information efficacy
Comparing cyberbullying perpetration on social media between primary and secondary school students [17]	2017	Computer-mediated communication; Secondary education; Elementary education; Cyberbullying; Social media	Cyberbullying; Well-being
The promise, reality and dilemmas of a secondary school teacher-student interactions in Facebook: The teacher perspective [4]	2015	Teacher-student communication; Facebook; Social network sites	Collaboration; Well-being
Social Networking: Boundaries and Limits Part 1: Ethics [2]	2014	Social Networking, Faculty Member, Ethical Principle, Social Networking Site, Social Role Theory	Ethics; Well-being
Social Networking: Boundaries and Limitations Part 2: Policy [19]	2014	Social Networking, Public School, School District, Social Networking Site, Instructional Technology	Ethics; Policy
Digital Citizenship: You Can't Go Home Again [18]	2017	Digital citizenship, BYOT, BYOD, Mobile-based learning, Digital etiquette, Digital safety, Technology	Cyberbullying; Well-being
Does recreational computer use affect high school achievement? [6]	2013	Secondary education, High school, Computer attitudes, Video games, Computer-based communication, Computer access, Achievement, Reading, Mathematics, Television, Internet, Extracurricular activities, Homework	Achievement; Engagement
Engaging students in school participatory practice through Facebook: The story of a failure [23]	2017	Social media, Civic engagement, Facebook, Student voice	Engagement; Well-being

4 Discussion

While sorting through the second set of search results, it became reasonably evident that the high school population was not as well studied as those in higher education. In the journals under examination in the field of educational technology, there were significantly higher numbers of articles dealing with post-teens and college students as there were for the teenage group. Table 1 backs this claim up in that only 11 out of 320 articles in the four researched journals discussed high school aged students. Although the high school studies were limited in nature, themes to the research questions did start to emerge.

The review of four EdTech journals indicated that social media use for instruction in the high school classroom and its effects on learning and well-being are not yet widely examined. This may be due to some factors which include, but are not limited to, a lack of use/acceptance by teachers [26], how to efficiently use the technology [27], and access issues for students who do not have the means to communicate through these sites. Most social networking is conducted from mobile devices but not every student has a mobile device and not every student is on social media.

Privacy and ethical issues emerged from the literature [28]. Aragon, AlDoubi, Kaminski, Anderson, and Isaacs [29] mention that we are in "unchartered territory" (p. 29) with educator/student relationships. These social media tools allow educators to message and stay in touch with their students outside the typical school day and vice versa. This increases the chances for an inappropriate student/teacher relationship to form, though research in this study did not cite specific examples. A Principles of Ethical Guidelines framework has been proposed to help teachers learn about ethical uses of social media. Student's also expressed privacy concerns. They did not want their teachers "monitoring" them and their personal/social lives outside of school. However, the literature indicated [29–31] that the ethical and privacy worry was more on the educator side but that the concern does go both ways.

Cyberbullying and digital awareness were discussed throughout the literature. Hollands worth, Donovan, and Welch [32] conclude "the dramatic increase in technology use and the increased accountability for misuse and abuse of technology denotes the need for more awareness of digital citizenship for all key stakeholders" (p. 529). These stakeholders include everybody from parents, faculty, administrators, friends, and the students themselves. It is indeed a collaborative effort to be respectful of one another in an anonymous digital world. The earlier students can be aware and practice digital citizenship; the better social well-being will be for everyone.

Surprisingly, no studies cited using social media with specific, measurable learning outcomes. There were studies involving informal or other non-critical type learning, but none of the studies concluded that the use of social media improved learning significantly or had a big enough effect size. Alloway, Horton, Alloway, and Dawson [33] did conclude that the duration of using social media in a particular learning environment did have a significant effect on cognitive abilities and some aspects of academic attainment, though this is not generalizable. For the most part, social media was not perceived as an accepted or highly valuable tool in the learning process. This is due to a number of factors stated earlier in this section.

A theme of the majority of articles suggests that social media is growing rapidly and not going anywhere anytime soon. Though it is not as widely used in the learning process at the high school level than the college level, there is potential for expanded use. Chu et al. [22] recommend *"pedagogical practices may need to be aimed at improving students' attitudes and competencies in using social media tools"* (p. 178). This could be said about high school faculty as well.

5 Conclusion

There are many limitations of this study. The most obvious is the inclusion of only four educational technology journals over a five-year period. Social media has been around a little longer than five years, so the additional years before that five-year period could have expanded the results of the high school population. Also, there are many other peer-reviewed journals that could have been included. The first search was not limited to educational technology journals and the inclusion of those journals outside our field, in addition to several other educational technology journals, could have provided additional references to the discussion and research questions. Though the search intended to narrow the results from the Theory and Research section to the Discussion section, indirect references to social media in the high school environment might have emerged, though none were visibly present during the first search.

Another limitation of the study and results was the lack of other major social media platforms. Facebook was almost exclusively studied, though usage of other social media platforms like Snapchat and Instagram is just as popular among high school students. Due to the fact that social media platforms come and go, this might be a constant moving target. Facebook is the most stable and longest tenured social media site [34] but the study of other platforms with regard to the learning process and well-being would have made this study more comprehensive. Additionally, foreign social media sites like China's WeChat was not included in this study.

The last limitation of the study is the lack of empirical, direct reference to learning outcomes with social media in the high school environment. Informal and casual use of social media sites in the learning process was mostly documented. The research and literature seem to be scarce to non-existent in this area, so it is hard to give a well understood, holistic view of the learning effectiveness of social media use in the learning process.

Limitations of any study give way to future research opportunities. Possibly the most pressing future research opportunity is the need for direct, measurable learning outcome assessment and social media use in the learning process with high school students. This could help educators better understand how valid and useful such platforms could be. Another possible research opportunity is the inclusion and collaboration among researchers outside the field of educational technology. Since social media does involve social well-being and psychological component, studies from both domain areas could prove useful to educators looking to find that balance between social media use in the classroom and how could this contribute to its use in all spheres of life for well-being.

In conclusion, social media sites do not appear to be going away anytime soon. Even as researchers and the tech titans start to focus on the potential issues of social media sites, there are many questions that need to be answered with regards to social networking sites being a help or hindrance within the learning process. This research is still in its infancy, and there are many unknown variables that need to be addressed before we can classify social media use as truly beneficial to our learning and well-being. The hope is that this study provides recent insight into social media and the high school environment.

References

1. Cooper, A.: What is "brain hacking"? Tech insiders on why you should care. CBS News (2017). https://www.cbsnews.com/news/what-is-brain-hacking-tech-insiders-on-why-you-should-care/
2. Langone, A.: Ex Google and Facebook employees are banding together to protect kids from social media addiction. Time (2018). http://time.com/5133185/ex-facebook-google-fight-tech-addiction/
3. Manjoo, F.: Even the tech elite are worrying about tech addiction. The New York Times (2018). https://www.nytimes.com/interactive/2018/02/09/technology/the-addiction-wrought-by-techies.html
4. Cook, L., Lin, L.: Your brain on tech: promises & perils of technology use in the developing brain [PowerPoint Slides] (2018). https://www.youtube.com/watch?v=vn3d2OxgH4o
5. Pugh, S.: Investigating the relationship between smartphone addiction, social anxiety, self-esteem, age & gender (2017). https://esource.dbs.ie/handle/10788/3329
6. Dabbagh, N., Kitsantas, A.: Personal learning environments, social media, and self-regulated learning: a natural formula for connecting formal and informal learning. Internet High. Educ. **15**, 3–8 (2012)
7. Istenic Starcic, A., Barrow, M., Zajc, M., Lebenicnik, M.: Students' attitudes on social network sites and their actual use for career management competences and professional identity development. Int. J. Emerg. Technol. Learn. **12**, 65–81 (2017)
8. Arnold, N., Paulus, T.: Using a social networking site for experiential learning: appropriating, lurking, modeling and community building. Internet High. Educ. **13**, 188–196 (2010)
9. Hawi, N.S., Samaha, M.: The relations among social media addiction, self-esteem, and life satisfaction in university students. Soc. Sci. Comput. Rev. 1–11 (2016)
10. NORC at the University of Chicago: New survey: Snapchat and Instagram are most popular social media platforms among American teens: Black teens are the most active on social media and messaging apps. ScienceDaily (2017). www.sciencedaily.com/releases/2017/04/170421113306.htm. Accessed 10 May 2018
11. Khan, M.L., Wohn, D.Y., Ellison, N.B.: Actual friends matter: an internet skills perspective on teens' informal academic collaboration on Facebook. Comput. Educ. **79**, 138–147 (2014)
12. Bányai, F., Zsila, Á., Király, O., Maraz, A., Elekes, Z., Griffiths, M.D., Demetrovics, Z.: Problematic social media use: results from a large-scale nationally representative adolescent sample. PLoS One **12**, 1–13 (2017)
13. Cela, K.L., Sicilia, M.Á., Sánchez, S.: Social network analysis in e-learning environments: a preliminary systematic review. Educ. Psychol. Rev. **27**, 219–246 (2015)

14. Gikas, J., Grant, M.: Mobile computing devices in higher education: Student perspectives on learning with cellphones, smartphones & social media. Internet High. Educ. **19**, 18–26 (2013)
15. Cabral, J.: Is generation Y addicted to social media. Future Child. **18**, 5–14 (2011)
16. Satici, S.A., Uysal, R.: Well-being and problematic Facebook use. Comput. Hum. Behav. **49**, 185–190 (2015)
17. Brodwin, E.: Google has announced it's taking major steps to curb 'tech addiction' – here's the reality. Business Insider (2018). http://www.businessinsider.com/google-io-tech-addiction-privacy-reality-2018-5
18. Watts, L.K., Wagner, J., Velasquez, B., Behrens, P.I.: Cyberbullying in higher education: a literature review. Comput. Hum. Behav. **69**, 268–274 (2017)
19. Ho, S.S., Chen, L., Ng, A.P.: Comparing cyberbullying perpetration on social media between primary and secondary school students. Comput. Educ. **109**, 74–84 (2017)
20. Bowers, A.J., Berland, M.: Does recreational computer use affect high school achievement? Educ. Technol. Res. Dev. **61**, 51–69 (2013)
21. O'Keeffe, G.S., Clarke-Pearson, K.: The impact of social media on children, adolescents, and families. Pediatrics **127**, 800–804 (2011)
22. Chu, S.K., Capio, C.M., van Aalst, J.C., Cheng, E.W.: Evaluating the use of a social media tool for collaborative group writing of secondary school students in Hong Kong. Comput. Educ. **110**, 170–180 (2017)
23. Wohn, D.Y., Ellison, N.B., Khan, M.L., Fewins-Bliss, R., Gray, R.: The role of social media in shaping first-generation high school students' college aspirations: a social capital lens. Comput. Educ. **63**, 424–436 (2013)
24. Greenhow, C., Lewin, C.: Social media and education: Reconceptualizing the boundaries of formal and informal learning. Learn. Media Technol. **41**, 6–30 (2016)
25. Tess, P.A.: The role of social media in higher education classes (real and virtual) - a literature review. Comput. Hum. Behav. **29**, A60–A68 (2013)
26. O'bannon, B.W., Thomas, K.: Teacher perceptions of using mobile phones in the classroom: age matters! Comput. Educ. **74**, 15–25 (2014)
27. Mao, J.: Social media for learning: a mixed methods study on high school students' technology affordances and perspectives. Comput. Hum. Behav. **33**, 213–223 (2014)
28. Manca, S., Grion, V.: Engaging students in school participatory practice through Facebook: the story of a failure. Br. J. Educ. Technol. **48**, 1153–1163 (2017)
29. Aragon, A., AlDoubi, S., Kaminski, K., Anderson, S.K., Isaacs, N.: Social networking: Boundaries and limits Part 1: ethics. TechTrends **58**, 25–31 (2014)
30. Asterhan, C.S., Rosenberg, H.: The promise, reality and dilemmas of secondary school teacher–student interactions in Facebook: the teacher perspective. Comput. Educ. **85**, 134–148 (2015)
31. Isaacs, N., Kaminski, K., Aragon, A., Anderson, S.K.: Social networking: boundaries and limitations Part 2: policy. TechTrends **58**, 10–15 (2014)
32. Hollandsworth, R., Donovan, J., Welch, M.: Digital citizenship: you can't go home again. TechTrends **61**, 524–530 (2017)
33. Alloway, T.P., Horton, J., Alloway, R.G., Dawson, C.: Social networking sites and cognitive abilities: do they make you smarter? Comput. Educ. **63**, 10–16 (2013)
34. Voivonta, T., Avraamidou, L.: Facebook: a potentially valuable educational tool? Educ. Media Int. **55**, 34–48 (2018)
35. Sung, Y.T., Chang, K.E., Liu, T.C.: The effects of integrating mobile devices with teaching and learning on students' learning performance: a meta-analysis and research synthesis. Comput. Educ. **94**, 252–275 (2016)

The Online Learning Resources Definition and Students' Use in Higher Education Across Disciplines

Maja Lebenicnik[1] and Andreja Istenic Starcic[1,2,3(✉)]

[1] Faculty of Education, University of Primorska, Koper, Slovenia
maja.lebenicnik@pef.upr.si, andreja.starcic@gmail.com
[2] Faculty of Civil and Geodetic Engineering, University of Ljubljana, Ljubljana, Slovenia
[3] College of Information, University of North Texas, Texas, USA

Abstract. The definitions of online learning resources are discussed within two approaches for classifying existing learning technology, the pedagogical and the functional approach. The findings of a survey about online learning resources use among 1667 students are presented with a focus on differences among study disciplines. Average mean for a total sample and the differences according to disciplines are presented in five subsections: The Online learning content, Interactive technology, Social network sites, Communication and collaboration technology, Information organising technology.

Keywords: Higher education · Educational technology
Online learning resources · Slovenia · E-learning
Information communication technology

1 Introduction

In the literature review, we discovered two approaches for classifying existing learning technology, the pedagogical and the functional approach. Within the first authors highlight the pedagogical component, which is learning experience or educational function or learning technology. Examples of such classifications are the classification of educational media by Laurillard [1], the classification of learning objects by Churchill [2], and the classification of social software tools by Dabbagh and Reo [3]. The second group of authors classifies learning technology on the basis of a similar functionality [4–6]. In recent times authors have developed numerous taxonomies of Web 2.0 learning technology [4].

The classification by Laurillard [1], which is among most established classifications, differentiates between five different forms, depending on different kinds of learning experiences they represent for the learner. Their rating is the classification of learning media, and so includes also other devices (e.g. television), not purely information communication technology (ICT). Descriptions of classes are based on Conole and Fill [7] and Laurillard [1]: the narrative media, the interactive media, the communicative media, the adaptive media and the productive media. Churchill [2] developed the

T.-T. Wu et al. (Eds.): ICITL 2018, LNCS 11003, pp. 371–480, 2018.
https://doi.org/10.1007/978-3-319-99737-7_40

classification of learning objects. Learning objects are digital resources, designed for use in different educational contexts. Churchill's grouping consists of presentation objects, practice objects, simulation objects, conceptual models, information objects, contextual representations [2]. The classification of social tools by Dabbagh and Kitsantas [8] (and its earlier version by [3]) is based on the level of interactivity that social media usage enables [8].

In this study, we examine the online learning content, Interactive technologies, Communicative and collaborative technologies, and Information organisation technology.

Class I: Online learning content

This class can be found in different classifications under different names such as narrative media, presentation and information learning objects, multimedia [1, 2, 6], Online learning content can be delivered through different presentation modes (verbal, pictorial), sensory modalities (auditory, visual), and delivery media (text, video, simulations) [6]. It can be found in media repositories [5], on learning websites and portals, educational blogs or integrated into online learning courses and in learning management systems. Consuming online learning resources (reading, listening, viewing) is considered as a passive [9], 'sit back' [1] learning activity. Regarding technology, the underpinning technology for a presentation of diverse learning content consists of media players, web browsers, etc.

Class II: Interactive technologies

This class includes the usage of interactive tools to interact with online learning content (search engines, databases search tools, hypertext and hypermedia, inquiry-based information retrieval etc.) and the usage of simple interactive tools such as tutorials, online quizzes.

Class III: Communicative and collaborative technologies

Communicative media facilitates exchanges between people. This class includes tools for synchronous communication (chats/instant messaging, video or audio conference) and asynchronous communication (e.g. online forums). The connection can be video, audio or text-based. Tools, allowing communication, are standalone tools or integrated into more complex technologies such as social network sites, learning management systems, online courses, games etc. Also features allowing comments on websites, blogs and online learning environments can be classified under communicative technologies. Thompson [10] discovered that communication through social network sites, texting, making voice calls and computer chatting belong to the same latent factor of ICT use. A study by Arkilic et al. [11] found out that among most preferred communication tools are instant messaging, followed by video/audio conference, private discussion groups and least preferred voice mail.

Cooperative technologies allow a learner to produce joint digital products with others and to exchange ideas with others [1]. Class, therefore, includes technologies for producing joint digital products as well as tools and features for sharing thoughts. Both types of devices belong to the same latent factor of the technology use [10]. Cooperative technologies are derived from several authors [8, 11–13].

Class VI: Information organisation technology

In this class are tools used to organise online (learning) information and content. An online user is a today exposed to a significant amount of data, whether looking actively for it (visiting websites) or being just a recipient of it through various channels (social network sites, e-mail etc.). For a more optimal flow of information, related to learning content, a learner can use multiple tools such as: republishing, aggregators, social feed aggregators, (social) bookmarking tools, digital pinboards [4], A learner can subscribe to a digital content (e.g. subscribing to channels and people on social networking sites, digital newsletters etc.). Computer recommendation systems integrated into online platforms filter and suggest information for the user.

The survey was conducted to examine how students use OLR end engage in online formal and informal learning. In this paper, we present the OLR use.

Hypothesis: There is the difference how university students of different disciplines use online learning resources.

2 Methods

The survey was conducted to examine university students in Slovenia about the use of online learning resources. For the study, we developed an original questionnaire. The initial version of an instrument was tested in 2015 [14]. In this paper, we discuss if there are any significant differences between students' OLR use across study disciplines.

In the survey participated 2325 students of the University of Ljubljana, which decided to fill in the online survey received at their e-mail address. Data collection took place in June and early July 2017. The number of students, in total 292 students filled-in only the demographic data and were therefore not included in the statistical analysis presented in this report. The size of the sample analyzed is 1667 participants who filled-in the question about online learning resources. The sample is heterogeneous according to study program. Participants are students of all study degrees and study fields according to the KLASIUS classification. Most students from the field of Natural sciences, mathematics and computer science (N = 404) followed by students from the fields of Social sciences, business, administrative and legal sciences (N = 315), technology, production technology and construction (N = 255) Arts and Humanities (N = 232) and Health and Social Affairs (N = 196). There are fewest participants in the field of Education and Teacher Education (N = 170). For the analysis Agriculture, Forestry, Fisheries and Veterinary and Services (N = 95) were merged.

For the purpose of this study, the OLR scale was developed. Students were asked to indicate how often they perform each of 31 ICT activities, related to their formal or informal learning. Items are assessed on 5 point scale (1 – never, 2 – rarely, 3 – sometimes, 4 – often, 5 – very often). Cronbach's alpha of the total scale with 31 items is 0.926, indicating high reliability of the scale.

For comparison between the study disciplines, a one-way analysis of variance was applied, previously verified the assumption of the normal distribution with Shapiro-Wilk's test and histograms, and the assumption of the homogeneity of the variance with the Leven test. In the case of violation of the assumptions, a nonparametric form of a one-way variance analysis - Kruskal-Wallis test was used. For significant p-values, the Games-Howell test, otherwise the Tukey test was applied. Tables with statistical results are available on a request to authors' emails.

3 Findings and Discussion

Presented are findings about OLR use and specifically in activities outside the classroom for formal or informal learning connected with study field. Results are presented in five sections:

- Online learning content
- Interactive technology
- Social network sites
- Communication and collaboration technology
- Information organizing technology

In the paper, the acronyms for KLASIUS study field will be applied:

- Education – Education science and teacher education
- AH - Arts and Humanities
- SS - Social sciences, business, administrative and legal sciences
- NS - Natural sciences, mathematics and computer science
- TP - Technology, production technology and construction
- AFVS - Agriculture, Forestry, Fisheries and Veterinary and Services
- HS - Health and Social Affairs

3.1 Online Learning Content

The set Online learning content provides an insight into the use of different forms of digital learning materials and content (e-books, web portals, educational videos, online guides, images) and identifies the sources of educational material/content (e.g. web portals, social media, home university, foreign university, asynchronous communication tools, online courses).

As can be seen from Fig. 1, the students most frequently mention resources of their home faculty (M = 3.88; SD = 1.17), followed by social media (M = 3.22; SD = 1.23), while the most commonly reported are participation in online courses (M = 1.58; SD = 0.92).

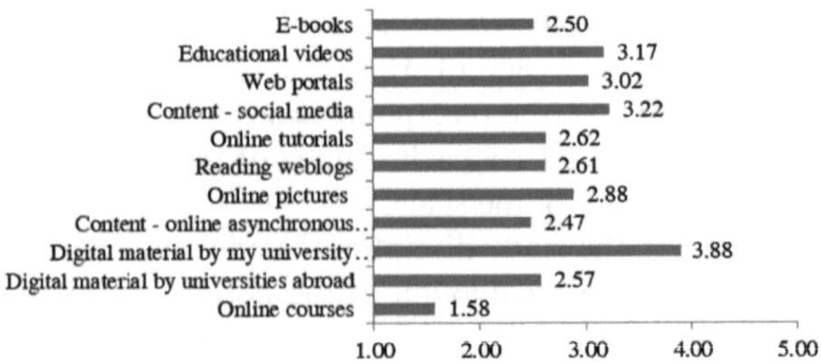

Fig. 1. Online learning contents – average mean.

The differences among KLASIUS fields are the following:

Social media (e.g. YouTube, Slideshare, etc.) as the source of educational materials mostly indicate NS, TP and HS students. Significantly less than the listed ones, social media as a source of educational materials is mentioned by students in education. The difference between NS and AH students is also essential.

Similarly to social media, asynchronous online communication (e.g. forum posts, questioning websites, comments) as a source of learning content are mainly indicated by SS and NS students as students of education, HS and AH.

Students SS, NRM and AFVS significantly more use material from their faculty as their peers from the fields of Education and AH. TP students also use materials from their home faculties more often than AH students.

Students of NS and TP mostly use materials from foreign faculties as AH students. SS students use foreign materials to a lesser degree than NRM.

SS students participate more often in online courses than students of Education and HS. NRM students also participate more frequently in online courses than HS students.

Of the various forms of materials and content, students are on average the most frequently used educational videos. This applies for the whole sample ($M = 3.17$, $SD = 1.20$), as for all subgroups. At least on average, e-books ($M = 2.50$; $SD = 1.23$), weblogs (blogs, social network announcements) ($M = 2.61$; $SD = 1.17$) and online guides ($M = 2.62$; $SD = 1.32$) are used on average less frequently. Here we mention that all other subgroups, with the exception of TP and NS students, use online guides as often or less often as e-books.

When analysing the differences between KLASIUS groups, we found differences in the items:

Students of NS, SS and HS report on reading e-books to a greater extent than students of TP and AFVS.

Learners considerably less often watch educational videos than their colleagues in the field of NS, SS and TP.

NS and TP students are more likely to use online tutorials than others in learning.

Web-based materials in the image format (for example, thought patterns, diagrams) are mostly used by NS and HS students than AH students.

SS and AH students have the highest average when reading online records from the field of study. The differences between SS and TP, AFVS and HS, are essential. The least often webcasts are read by AFVS, but this group differs significantly only from SS and AH.

Students the most commonly used materials for learning are from their home faculties, followed by contents that they access through social media, Less often students use materials from foreign faculties and universities. Scarce students participate in online courses. The students of the Education and the AH are most reserved for social media materials. Part of the differences in the use of online learning resources can undoubtedly be attributed to the nature of the various study programs (for example, NRM and TP students use web guides to a greater extent than their peers, HS and NS students are increasingly using the use of diagrams and mind maps as AH students). The results of the survey showed the importance of educational videos compared to some other online resources, such as onscreen text-based web feeds (e-books, online records).

3.2 Interactive Technology

The interactive technology contains items on the use of interactive tools and search tools. As shown in Fig. 2, the most commonly used are web search engines (M = 4.19; SD = 0.96) and the least used web tools for self-assessment (M = 1.71; SD = 0.97).

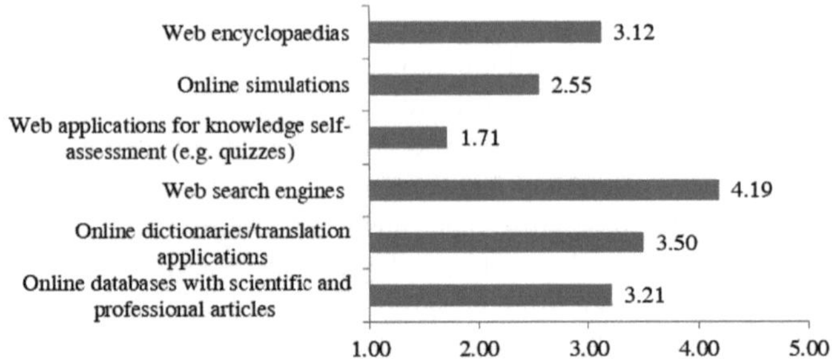

Fig. 2. Interactive technology – average mean.

The specific differences between KLASIUS groups are as follows:

Online encyclopedias are less by students of AFVS. The frequency of their use differs significantly from NS, SS, AH and HS students. NS students use online encyclopedias to a greater extent than students of TP and TP students.

Web simulations are more commonly used by students of NS, TP and HS, and to lesser extent students of education. The use of students from AH, AFVS and SS. NS significantly differs from all four of the subgroups above, HS is different from the three subgroups, and TP differs from AH students.

SS students are more likely to use the application for self-assessment of knowledge compared to students of education, TGTP and AFVS.

There are fewer differences between students when using search engines. Significantly more frequently use of search engines students from NS in comparison with students of education.

Web dictionaries are most commonly used by AH students, much more frequently than NS, TP, AFVS and HS students.

The databases with professional and scientific articles are mostly used by HS and SS students. These students use bases significantly more often than students of Education, NS and TP. The least commonly used databases are TP students, differences are essential in all peers except with Education and AFVS.

Throughout the sample, interactive technologies are among the most commonly used, with the exception of online self-assessment applications and web simulations. The downward deviation was evident in the case of the use of online encyclopaedias in students of the AFVS and the use of databases in TP students. The more common use of specific tools in specific groups is consistent with the nature of the study (for example, AH students use web dictionaries more often; students of HS, NS and TP use web simulations to a greater extent).

3.3 Social Network Sites

This section presents the items describing individual engagement in social network sites. The two issues are included in other subsections, "access to learning content via social network sites" is contained in a subsection Online learning content, "searching for help and discussion through online networks" is included in Communication and collaboration technology.

All of the above activities are relatively widespread among students (M < 3); the exception is participation in the online community, where students know the majority of participants (e.g. class FB communities) (M = 3.49; SD = 1.36) (Fig. 3).

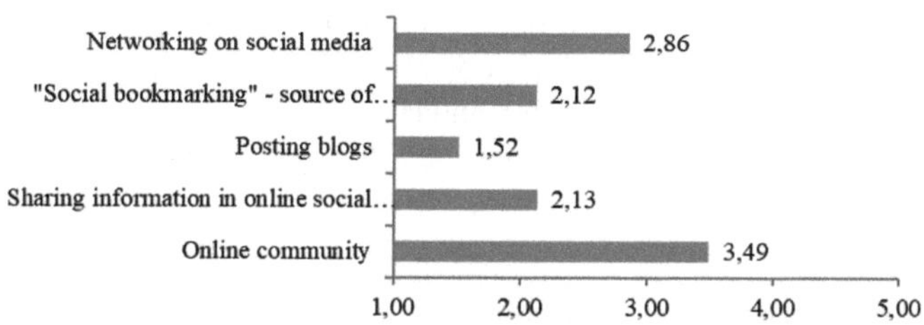

Fig. 3. Social network sites – average mean.

We have identified the following differences between the study fields:

AH, students considerably refer to the creation of social networks as students of Education, NS, TP and AFVS.

Students of education and AH report the much more frequent use of "social bookmarking pages" (e.g. reddit.com, pinterest.com, del.icio.us) through which of the others they find for exciting web sources as their peers on SS, AFVS and HS.

The smallest differences occur when participating in a narrower online community, where the student knows most of the participants (for example, the class group Facebook, etc.). Significantly more frequently, such activities are carried out by HS students compared to SS students.

The differences between students in the use of social network sites are not numerous. Creating networks and using social bookmarking sites is more common in the students of Education and AH. Significant differences occur only at the level of networking (networks, others are a source of information of web resources, participating in the web community). There is no significant difference in a more active form of engagement in social network sites (for example, sharing information, writing records).

3.4 Communication and Collaboration Technology

When using ICT for communication and collaboration, the most common use of tools for synchronous communication between students (e.g. Skype, Facebook Messages, gTalk, Viber, etc.) (M = 3.44; SD = 1.36), and less frequently students use tools to participate in online discussions (e.g. on social network sites, on-line forums and chat rooms) related to their field of study (M = 2.20; SD = 1.23) (Fig. 4).

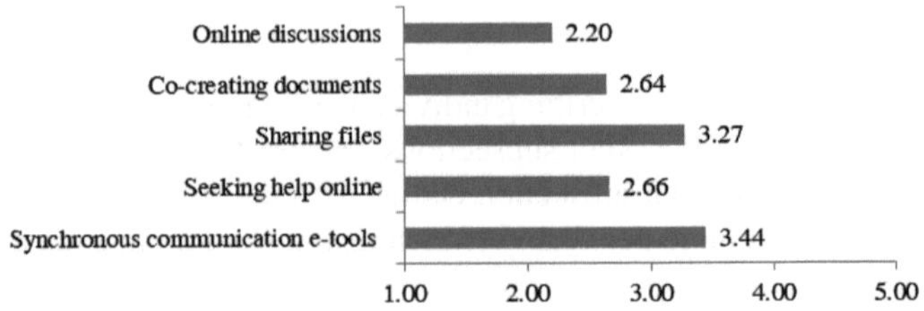

Fig. 4. Communication and collaboration technology – average mean.

Significant differences between KLASIUS fields are identified only with the "I co-create collaborative documents with others for study purposes (e.g. in Google Docs, wikis, brainstorming tools)". For this subject, AFVS students report a statistically significantly lower frequency than SS, NS and HS students. SS students have the highest average for this item, considerably higher than their peers with education, AFVS, TP and NS.

3.5 Information Organising Technology

All of the above activities are relatively low among students (M < 3), indicating that on average students are less likely to use ICT for organising information (Fig. 5).

Fig. 5. Information organising technology – average mean.

Differences between study fields are as follows:

AH, students use bookmarks more often than other subgroups.

When subscribing to electronic newsletters and updates, AH and SS students report higher activity than TP students.

Among students, ICT is the most widely used method for organizing information by creating bookmarks M = 2.65; SD = 1.38), followed by the use of computer recommendation systems (M = 2.25; SD = 1.11). AH, students, in this case, stand out by using bookmarks and subscribing to electronic newsletters.

4 Conclusions

From the trends, the authors would point out social media as they are indicated as an important online learning resource. Given the frequency of using social media contents, students need to be encouraged to critically evaluate the use of such materials.

The survey showed low usage of online courses, which should be further verified.

Based on the findings it was established, that students should be encouraged and educated towards the use of online tools and resources also for the purpose of organising information and planning and monitoring their learning process.

Among the KLASIUS fields, there are differences in the use of ICT in teaching and learning. Although, due to the nature of the study programs and the differences between them, differences are also expected in the actual use of ICT in teaching and learning, however, this fact needs to be studied in detail.

Acknowledgements. The study was financed by a young researcher for acquiring a PhD scheme of Slovenian Research Agency (ARRS) as a part of PhD study. Andreja Istenic Starcic was nominated as a mentor of a young researcher in 2011 (6316-3/2011-784). Maja Lebenicnik was selected as a young researcher in 2012. A survey among students of the University of Ljubljana was conducted without additional financing within a project: «The integration of information and communication technology in the higher education pedagogical process» led by University of Ljubljana in June and early July 2017. The project» «The integration of information and communication technology in the higher education pedagogical process» is co-financed by the European Union from the European Social Fund and the Republic of Slovenia. Authors would like to thank participating students and vice-rector of the University of Ljubljana, prof. Goran Turk for promoting a survey among students. Tables with statistical results are available on a request to authors' emails.

References

1. Laurillard, D.: Rethinking University Teaching: A Conversational Framework for the Effective Use of Learning Technologies, 2nd edn. Routledge, London (2002)
2. Churchill, D.: Towards a useful classification of learning objects. Educ. Technol. Res. Dev. **55**, 479–497 (2007)
3. Dabbagh, N., Reo, R.: Back to the future: tracing the roots and learning affordances of social software. In: Lee, M.J.W., McLoughlin, C. (eds.) Web 2.0-Based E-learning: Applying Social Informatics for Tertiary Teaching. Information Science Reference, Hershey, New York, pp. 1–20 (2011)
4. Bower, M.: Deriving a typology of Web 2.0 learning technologies. Br. J. Edu. Technol. **47**, 763–777 (2016)
5. Culatta, R., Leavitt, M.: Classification based on similar functionality. Innovative learning, Mind map (2010). http://innovativelearning.com/instructional_technology/categories.html. Accessed 1 Mar 2018
6. Graesser, A.C., Chipman, P., King, B.G.: Computer - mediated technologies. In: Spector, J.M., Merril, M.D., van Marrienboer, J., Driscoll, M.P. (eds.) Handbook of Research on Educational Communications and Technology, pp. 211–224. Taylor & Francis Group, New York, London (2008)

7. Conole, G., Fill, K.: A learning design toolkit to create pedagogically effective learning activities. J. Interact. Media Educ. **8**, 1–16 (2005)
8. Dabbagh, N., Kitsantas, A.: Personal learning environments, social media, and self-regulated learning: a natural formula for connecting formal and informal learning. Int. High. Educ. **15**, 3–8 (2012)
9. Levy, Y.: An empirical development of Critical Value Factors (CVF) of online learning activities: an application of activity theory and cognitive value theory. Comput. Educ. **51**, 1664–1675 (2008)
10. Thompson, P.: The digital natives as learners: technology use patterns and approaches to learning. Comput. Educ. **65**, 12–33 (2013)
11. Arkilic, I.G., Peker, S., Uyar, M.E.: Students preferences of communication tools for group projects in a computer-supported collaborative learning environment: a survey. Procedia – Soc. Behav. Sci. **83**, 1121–1125 (2013)
12. Bennett, S., Bishop, A., Dalgarno, B., Waycott, J., Kennedy, J.: Implementing Web 2.0 technologies in higher education: a collective case study. Comput. Educ. **59**, 524–534 (2012)
13. Calvo, R., Arbiol, A., Iglesias, A.: Are all Chats suitable for learning purposes? a study of the required characteristics. Procedia Comput. Sci. **27**, 251–260 (2014)
14. Lebeničnik, M., Pitt, I., Istenič Starčič, A.: Use of online learning resources in the development of learning environments at the intersection of formal and informal learning: the student as autonomous designer. CEPS J. Center Educ. Policy Stud. J. **5**, 95–113 (2015)

Technologies Enhanced Language Learning

WASS: Web-Based Annotation and Search System to Facilitate English Vocabulary Learning in Vocational High School

Yu-Suan Ji[1], Nguyen-Thi Huyen[1(✉)], Wu-Yuin Hwang[1], and George Ghinea[2]

[1] Graduate Institute of Network Learning Technology, National Central University, Taoyuan, Taiwan
yuhsuan716@gmail.com, joynguyen7@gmail.com, wyhwang1206@gmail.com

[2] United Kingdom Brunel University, London, UK
george.ghinea@brunel.ac.uk

Abstract. In this study, we proposed a web-based annotation and search system named WASS, which not only provides annotation making but also peers' annotation searching and reviewing for vocabulary learning. Four-week experiment was conducted among 75 vocational high school students, divided into experimental group and control group. The student learning behavior and their influence on learning achievement were explored, the results showed that experimental group outperformed control group in vocabulary post-test. Further investigation in experimental group showed low achievement students made more text annotation than the high achievement students and obtained more significant score gain, thereby indicating that our system is capable to motivate the low achievement students to make more text annotation, this is because through searching and learning peers' annotation, low achievement students can make more annotation and acquire more vocabulary. Those findings may confirm that searching and reviewing peers' annotation plays an important role in fostering vocabulary learning, especially for those low achievement students in vocational high school. Therefore, designing the supported powerful function to utilize annotations completely is vital (like searching tool for peers' annotation in this study) and encouraging students to learn through their own annotation and peers' by searching tool.

Keywords: Annotation system · Vocational education · Vocabulary learning

1 Introduction

Recently, there were great emphases on vocational education in Asian Pacific. One of the emphases is to strengthen the English ability for vocational students. However, the effort appears to be ineffective since teaching strategies have failed to motivate student interests and enthusiasm, which has led to poor learning outcome in English. One possible reason for that is due to strong desires to enter regular universities and over emphases on academic performance in Asian pacific. So most of the students who enter

T.-T. Wu et al. (Eds.): ICITL 2018, LNCS 11003, pp. 383–392, 2018.
https://doi.org/10.1007/978-3-319-99737-7_41

technological and vocational colleges usually are those who do not perform well in academic [1]. In the meanwhile English teachers also feel frustrated about when and how to incorporate new vocabulary into their literature curricula [2]. This is because students have low motivation and lack of support from peers' help.

Annotation systems have become increasingly attractive to EFL students in educational settings. Several studies have further demonstrated benefits provided by digital annotations for peers' learning through collaborative annotation making and sharing [3–5]. However, those studies tended mainly focus on learning interaction aspect like how beneficial of annotation making and sharing is, but less on how to utilize annotation benefits through technical aspects, for example, adding functionality or supported tools for annotation making and sharing. There was much less research, which investigated how those technical aspects influence on students with different ability, such as high and low ability of, especially, vocational high school EFL students who often pose low confidence and motivation in learning. Thus, there is pressing need for the research, which concerns on this matter.

To this end, we proposed a web-based annotation and search system named WASS, which not only provide annotation making on vocabularies but also support peers' annotations searching and viewing through a searching tool. We would like to investigate the learning behaviors of vocational high school students when they use our proposed system WASS. Participants typically were divided (base on Post-test score) into low achievement students and high achievement students, and their learning behaviors have been recorded to find out the difference of using pattern (on WASS) between them. Our research questions are:

1. What are relationships between learning behaviors and posttest-score as well as score gain? (Including making text annotation, seeing vocabulary video, searching peers' annotation and using google translator described at Sect. 3.1). How do the learning behaviors predict the post-test scores?
2. What are the differences of learning behaviors between high and low achievement students and their influences on learning?

2 Methodology

2.1 The WASS System

In this study, Web-based Annotation and Search System (WASS) present students with a sort of learning materials including lecture videos topics. They are structured via tree map. The lecture videos contain two parts: the first part is call main lesson video (MLV) and the second one is vocabulary definition (VDV) (see Fig. 1). Additionally, video scripts were also provided for helping students understanding as well as annotation making. Furthermore, WASS allows students to make Annotation, for example, highlighting and adding text notes, directly on the scripts (Fig. 3). During learning session, if students encounters any unfamiliar vocabulary WASS provides three ways to look up suitable definition for a given word, as below:

Fig. 1. Video of materials (Left), Vocabulary definition (Right)

Vocabulary Definition Video: As abovementioned, each MLV comes along with one VPV where vocabularies found in MLV are explained. In particular, students watch the VPV to learn about that word. As the result, student may use text Annotation function to creating notes to express what they learned. For instance, they may show their understanding about that vocabulary like its meaning or how to use the word in particular context.

Peers' Annotation: WASS works like an online classroom where students' profiles are tracked. In one hand, WASS provides Annotation searching tool as shown in the right side of Fig. 3 where students input the unfamiliar vocabulary, and system responses completed list of related peers' Annotation created for the vocabulary (Fig. 2). Those Annotations might be made after obtain knowledge from VPV, or simply their prior understanding.

原作者(Author)	上傳日期(Date)	註記內容
[redacted]	11/12/14 07:56	apartment公寓
[redacted]	11/10/14 16:36	apartment n. 公寓(房間)
[redacted]	11/07/14 07:50	apartment 公寓
[redacted]	11/05/14 08:01	apartment building 公寓大樓
[redacted]	11/03/14 16:42	apartment公寓
[redacted]	11/03/14 16:39	apartment公寓(房間)
[redacted]	11/03/14 16:16	apartment n. 公寓(套房)
[redacted]	11/03/14 16:15	apartment n. 公寓(套房)
[redacted]	11/03/14 16:13	apartment n.公寓(套房)
[redacted]	11/03/14 16:09	apartment N.公寓(套房)
[redacted]	11/03/14 08:04	apartment 公寓
[redacted]	11/03/14 08:04	apartment 公寓
[redacted]	11/03/14 08:04	apartment n. 公寓(房間)
[redacted]	11/03/14 08:03	apartment 公寓
[redacted]	[illegible]	[illegible]

Fig. 2. List of all annotations marked on "Apartment" word.

Therefore, for those who are looking up for any unfamiliar words, this function is the option for acquiring new word usage from other class peers' Annotation. On the other hand, all students are able to reach other peers via name list, as shown on the left top of Fig. 3. In particular, Name list contains ID of whole students in the class. Whenever students select their mate in the list, the system shows entire Annotation made by that peer on a certain lesson.

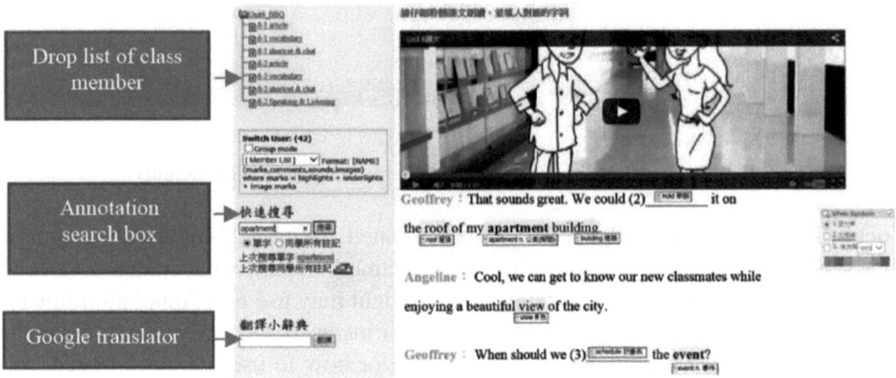

Fig. 3. Basic functions of WASS

Google Translator: To provide convenient searching, Google translator was integrated into WASS and located right beside the script as shown in left bottom of Fig. 3. The new word definition is returned instantly below the search box. This design aims to minimize the effort of switching to other windows, thus it might reduce extraneous cognitive load by this action.

2.2 Experiment Procedures

A total of 75 tenth-grade students in one female vocational high school participated into the study. The students were randomly divided to two groups. More specifically, half of sample (N = 38) was assigned to the experimental group while the other half (N = 37) were allocated to the control group. Before the treatments, all participants were required to take the pre-test to identify their prior knowledge of the tested subject. Subsequently, both groups received two phases of treatments namely "Learning Activity one" and "Learning Activity two." Each activity took a half of total four-week experiment.

Learning Activity One Which Focuses on Looking Up Unfamiliar Vocabulary via VPV: students in both groups were delivered the same video lesson MVL that related to Health and Art on WASS. However, during and after the lesson, for any unfamiliar vocabulary, the experimental groups were asked to highlight and create the text note directly on WASS. Besides that, they were also asked to use VPV and integrated Google translator. In contrast, control group was asked to create paperbased text note and traditional dictionary for any unfamiliar word.

Learning Activity Two, Which Focus on Looking Up Unfamiliar Vocabulary via Peers' Annotation: students in both groups were delivered the same video lesson MVL, which related to Food, and News on WASS. Similarly, during and after the lesson, for any unfamiliar vocabularies, the experimental group was asked to highlight and create the text note directly on WASS. However, unlike the activity one, they were asked to use peer Annotation searching and integrated Google translator. In contrast, control group were asked to create paper-based text note and use traditional English-Chinese dictionary for any new vocabulary.

Finally, after the treatment in each activity, the participants were requested to take the post-test to evaluate their learning performance. In addition, questionnaires were also provided to evaluate students' perception on system usage.

2.3 Data Analysis

In this study, we collect three variables: First, *Post-test score*. Second, *score gain*, which shows how well a student improves his or her learning performance after the treatments by calculating pretest and protest score. Third, learning behavior variables include seven attributes extracted from the log file of those who in experimental condition, namely (1) the total number of text Annotation, (2) the total number of searched unfamiliar vocabulary via VPV, (3) the total number of searched unfamiliar vocabulary via peers' Annotation (4) the total number of searched unfamiliar vocabulary via the built-in Google translator. In parallel, attributes of control groups were collected via quantity of paper-based text Annotation, and number of searched word via traditional vocabulary. Methods of statistics were employed for data analyses is Pearson's correlation, which is typically used for analysis correlation between any variables. In this study, Pearson's correlation was used to analyze the relationships between variables related learning behaviors and post-test score as well as score gain. We also use stepwise regression to investigate the explanation of variance and to determine whether either the text Annotation, VPV, searching peers' Annotation or searching Google translate corresponded to the grades of Score gain and Post-test score.

3 Results and Discussion

The relationships between learning behavior and post-test score as well as score gain of the experimental group were analyzed using Pearson's correlation. The results were shown in Table 1 and some findings were discussed below.

Table 1. Correlation statistics of learning behaviors and learning achievement

Learning behavior attributes	Post-test score		Gain-score	
	Activity one	Activity two	Activity one	Activity two
Total number of text Annotations	−0.356* p = 0.031	−0.329* p = 0.047	0.329* p = 0.047	0.326* p = 0.049
Total number of watching VPV	0.069 p = 0.680	N/A	0.680 p = 0.069	N/A
Total number of using Google translator	−0.328* p = 0.048	−0.238 p = 0.156	0.212 p = 0.207	0.146 p = 0.309
Total number of seeking peers Annotation	N/A	−0.328* p = 0.048	N/A	0.211 p = 0.209

**p < 0.001, *p < 0.05,

Finding 1: text Annotation has significant correlation with Post-test score and Gain-score in both activities.

Easy seen on the Table 1, total number of text Annotation has significant correlation with learning performance and score gain. Interestingly, the results were not consistent in activity one and activity two on two variables post-test score and score gain. More specifically, total number of text Annotation appeared positive correlation with score gain in activity one (0.039, $p = 0.047 > 0.05$) and activity two (0.326, $p = 0.049 < 0.05$) while it showed negative correlation with post-test score in both activity one (-0.356, $p = 0.031 < 0.05$) and activity two (−0.329, $p = 0.047 < 0.05$). About positive correlation between quantity of text Annotation and score gain, it can be explained via study of [6] that showed students who have more score gain generated more text annotations than students who have less score gain did.

Concerning about negative correlation between quantities of text Annotation and post-test score, to clarify the symptom, the researchers interviewed students who obtained high achievement and low achievement on the posttest. The result revealed that students who performed lower achievement score usually found a lot of unfamiliar vocabularies in main lesson. In comparison, low achievement students normally found more unfamiliar vocabulary than high achievement students did. Consequently, students in the low achievement group expressed that they spent more time to do highlight text and wrote more text Annotation on these marks. As the result, total number of text Annotation belongs to these students are typically higher than other peers. The followings are from the interviews:

High achievement: "*Because I have remembered these vocabularies before, so I just highlighted incomprehension of the vocabulary.*";" *I have remembered many vocabularies (in textbook) before, so my incomprehension of vocabulary is less, that Annotation is less*".

Low achievement: "*Because I don't know a lot of vocabulary, so I need to write a lot of text Annotation.*" "*My English is not good, there have a lot of vocabulary I don't know it, so I need to write lots of text Annotation.*"

Further investigation using Stepwise regression analysis was conducted to study the explanation of variance and to determine whether either the text Annotation, VPV, searching peers' Annotation or searching Google Translate corresponded to the grades of Score gain. The result showed that VPV, searching peers' Annotation or searching Google Translate were eliminated in both activities. However, text Annotation revealed the explanatory power of 8.3% F = 4.237 and p = .047 (Activity 1) and 8.1%, F = 4.161and p = .049 (Activity 2) from which the differences were significant. Thus, only text Annotation could effectively predict the score gain.

Finding 2: (Activity one) the total number of surfer VPV has no signification correlation with Post-test score but the total number of searched word from Google translator.

The total number of surfer VPV has no signification correlation with post-test score 0.069 ($p = 0.680 > 0.05$). The interview revealed students using WASS for the activity one was encouraged to spend time with it in order: If they found any unfamiliar vocabulary, they should learn the target word via VPV firstly. In case they still cannot acquire the meaning of the target word, they possibly will use the built-in Google translator. Another notice is that VPV was recorded in English language. Therefore, for higher achievement students, if they do not get the meaning of the target word via VPV at the first time, they might repeat the VPV several times until they really get well on the target word. However, unlike the high achievement students, the low achievement students might ignore the VPV, so that they turned directly to Google translator to learn the word. It might results in another interesting phenomenon found was post-test score from activity one appeared in negative correlation with the total number of searched word from Google translator on correlation coefficient −0.328 ($p = 0.048 < 0.05$). Further study would be needed to find out the reason. Some of the high and low achievement students were interviewed, and the possible explanation for found phenomenon is because VPV contains a limited of new words. Therefore, VPV contents were not sufficient for those who had a lot of unfamiliar words. As abovementioned, students might switch to Google translator if VPV could not satisfy theirs need. As the result, students used Google translator to translate the unfamiliar words, thus they gained the knowledge. Few students' opinions on this master are listed below:

High achievement: *"Because I have less vocabulary which I don't know, so I seldom use Google translate to find definition." "Because I know a lot of vocabulary."*

Low achievement: *"Because video provide less vocabulary, so the quantity which I watch video is less." "Because I don't know a lot of vocabularies, so I need to use Google translate to find definition."*

Finding 3: (Activity two) Post-test score appeared in negative correlation with total number of seeking peers' Annotation but no significant correlation with the total number of searched word via Google translator.

The Pearson's correlation analysis from the activity two showed that post-test score appeared in negative correlation with a total number of seeking peers' Annotation. The further interview revealed that high achievement students typically knew more vocabulary than low achievement students did. Therefore, high achievement students were likely to devote their time for this function less than other peers. This result is somehow in harmony with those from finding 1, which shows that high achievement students who are familiar with a lot of vocabulary were probable to create fewer notes than other does. Similarly, because of their sufficient prior knowledge on tested subject, high achievement students might not need much to search for peers' Annotation for obtaining word knowledge. It might lead to the insignificant correlation phenomenon found between post-test score and the total number of searched word from Google translator. The interview revealed that students using WASS for the activity two were inspirited to use functions of WASS in order: If they found any unfamiliar vocabulary, they should learn the target word from peer Annotation firstly. In case they still cannot acquire the meaning of the target word from other peers' Annotation or the target word is not annotated yet, they possibly will use the built-in Google translator. However, from the finding three, that shown the post-test score has significant correlation with the number of times searching peers' Annotation, explained that searching peers' Annotation is helpful for learning. So that student might stay with this strategy but not switching to Google translator. Some of the interviews are listed below:

High achievement: *"Because I know a lot of vocabularies, so I seldom use search (peers; annotation) function." "Use searching teacher or classmate's Annotation to find the answer can faster than" "Google translate. And sometime use the Google Translate found a lot of meaning.*

Low achievement: *"Because I don't know lot of vocabulary, so I need to spend more time to use search (peers' annotation) function." "I need to find a lot of vocabulary definition." "Use searching teacher or classmate's Annotation to find the answer can faster than Google translate. And sometime I got confused because Google translate provide a lot of similar words and meaning".*

Finding 4: Text annotation is not only for self- learning but also for helping peers' learning, if learning system is capable of providing an useful tool to utilize annotation completely, like search box for annotation database in this study, it significantly can improve learning outcome.

Many studies showed that text annotation is useful for learning in many ways. From our finding 1, we once again double confirmed this statement. Combine with finding two and finding three, we revealed that text annotation do not benefit for selflearning only, but it could also support for peers' learning. In other words, learning from peers' annotation can be potential way to obtain knowledge. Therefore we might have to pay more attention on this potential then support related function (like searching tool for annotation database in this study), which can promote the advantages of learning annotation for both selflearning and peers' learning. In addition, it may be a way to exchange the idea among students, thus it also can have a great impact on those low learning ability students in which they benefit from the good quality annotation of high learning ability student.

4 Discussion and Conclusion

In this study, we investigated the influence of WASS on students learning performance and differences of learning behaviors between high and low achievement students. The experimental results showed that, the experimental group performed better than the control group on the post-test. Especially low achievement students created more text notes and gained more knowledge than high achievement students did. Low achievement students also utilize WASS more often to search for peers annotation as well as using built-in translator. We revealed that text annotation do not benefit for self-learning only, but it could also supports for peers' learning. In other words, learning from peers' annotation can be potential way to obtain knowledge. Therefore, we might have to pay more attention on this potential then support related function (like searching tool for annotation database in this study), which can promote the advantages of learning annotation for both selflearning and peers' learning. In addition, it may be the way to exchange the idea among students, thus it also can have a great impact on those low learning ability students in which they benefit from the good quality annotation of high learning ability student.

Limitation and Future Study: Our study was conducted in female vocational high school, therefore the finding its self might cannot generalize to male students since gender differences also influences on learning behaviors. The primary target of WASS was to facilitate the vocabulary learning. However, besides vocabulary learning, making sentence and phrase is also essential. Therefore, focusing on sentence making still is our next target. Moreover, future studies could pivot on different English skills such as listening and speaking, and expand the research variables.

Acknowledgements. Our thanks to National Science Council of the R.O.C. for funding us conducting this research. We also want to thank to those who participated the system design and experiment.

References

1. Barton, J.: Teaching vocabulary in the literature classroom. English J. **90**(4), 82–88 (2001)
2. Bilal, D., Kirby, J.: Differences and similarities in information seeking: children and adults as Web users. Inf. Process. Manage. **38**(5), 649–670 (2002)
3. Brown, A.L., Smiley, S.S.: The development of strategies for studying texts. Child Dev., 1076–1088 (1978)
4. Carter, R., McCarthy, M.: Vocabulary and Language Teaching. Routledge, London (2014)
5. Chang, C.-C., Tseng, K.-H., Liang, C.: Is reflection performance correlated to the learning effect in a web-based portfolio assessment environment for middle school students? Asia-Pacific Educ. Res. **23**(1), 73–82 (2014)
6. Chen, J.-M., Chen, M.-C., Sun, Y.S.: A novel approach for enhancing student reading comprehension and assisting teacher assessment of literacy. Comput. Educ. **55**(3), 1367–1382 (2010)
7. Chen, Y.-C., Hwang, R.-H., Wang, C.-Y.: Development and evaluation of a Web 2.0 annotation system as a learning tool in an e-learning environment. Comput. Educ. **58**(4), 1094–1105 (2012)
8. Chiang, W.-L. Technological & Vocational Education in Taiwan, ROC (2012). http://www.studyintaiwan.org/album/v4_publications/5254f7bd7b0ec.pdf
9. ChinaTimes. Taiwan's vocational education must be reformed (2013)., http://www.taiwantoday.tw/ct.asp?xItem=206123&ctNode=426. Accessed 12 Dec 2015
10. Dochy, F., Segers, M., Sluijsmans, D.: The use of self-, peer and co-assessment in higher education: a review. Stud. High. Educ. **24**(3), 331–350 (1999)
11. Feng, H.-Y., Fan, J.-J.: A study on students' learning motivation of EFL in Taiwanese vocational college. Int. J. Learn. Dev. **2**(3), 260–269 (2012)

12. Gardner, R.C.: Attitudes and motivation in second language learning. In: Paper presented at the Bilingualism, Multiculturalism, and Second Language Learning: The McGill Conference in Honour of Wallace E. Lambert (1991)
13. Grabinger, R.S., Dunlap, J.C.: Rich environments for active learning: a definition. Research in learning Technology **3**(2), 5–34 (1995)
14. Hidi, S., Anderson, V.: Producing written summaries: Task demands, cognitive operations, and implications for instruction. Rev. Educ. Res. **56**(4), 473–493 (1986)
15. Hwang, W.-Y., Hsu, J.-L., Shadiev, R., Chang, C.-L., Huang, Y.-M.: Employing self-assessment, journaling, and peer sharing to enhance learning from an online course. J. Comput. High. Educ. **27**(2), 114–133 (2015)
16. Hwang, W.-Y., Liu, Y.-F., Chen, H.-R., Huang, J.-W., Li, J.-Y.: Role of parents and annotation sharing in children's learning behavior and achievement using e-readers. J. Educ. Technol. Soc. **18**(1), 292–307 (2015)
17. Hwang, W.Y., Chen, N.S., Shadiev, R., Li, J.S.: Effects of reviewing annotations and homework solutions on math learning achievement. Br. J. Edu. Technol. **42**(6), 1016–1028 (2011)
18. Kulik, J.A., Kulik, C.-L.C.: Timing of feedback and verbal learning. Rev. Educ. Res. **58**(1), 79–97 (1988)
19. Laufer, B.: The lexical plight in second language reading: words you don't know, words you think you know and words you can't guess Second language vocabulary acquisition: a rationale for pedagogy, pp. 20–34 (1997)
20. MacAlpine, J.: Improving and encouraging peer assessment of student presentations. Assess. Eval. High. Educ. **24**(1), 15–25 (1999)
21. Marshall, C.C.: Annotation: from paper books to the digital library. In: Paper Presented at the Proceedings of the Second ACM International Conference on Digital Libraries (1997)
22. Nokelainen, P., Miettinen, M., Kurhila, J., Floréen, P., Tirri, H.: A shared document-based annotation tool to support learner-centred collaborative learning. Br. J. Edu. Technol. **36**(5), 757–770 (2005)
23. Orsmond, P., Merry, S., Reiling, K.: The use of student derived marking criteria in peer and self-assessment. Assess. Eval. High. Educ. **25**(1), 23–38 (2000)
24. Read, J.: Assessing Vocabulary. Cambridge Language Assessment Series. Cambridge University Press, Cambridge (2000)
25. Shadiev, R., et al.: Effects of unidirectional vs. reciprocal teaching strategies on web-based computer programming learning. J. Educ. Comput. Res. **50**(1), 67–95 (2014)
26. Slotte, V., Lonka, K.: Note-taking review-practical value for Learners (2003). Accessed 17 March 2007
27. Su, M.-H.M.: A study of EFL technological and vocational college students' language learning strategies and their self-perceived English proficiency. Electron. J. Foreign Lang. Teach. **2**(1), 44–56 (2005)
28. Towler, L., Broadfoot, P.: Self-assessment in the primary school. Educ. Rev. **44**(2), 137–151 (1992)

A Study on the Effect of Using Digital Games for Self-learning of English in Elementary School

Ching-I Cheng[1(✉)], Shih-Wei Wang[1], and Ling-Wei Lin[2]

[1] Taipei University of Marine Technology, New Taipei City, Taiwan, R.O.C.
chingi720@gmail.com

[2] Haishan Elementary School, New Taipei City, Taiwan, R.O.C.

Abstract. Compared with traditional learning, self-learning has supplemented it and with some great results. Additionally, digital game-based learning is an effective way to motivate the students and increase their learning performance. The purpose of the study is to examine the effects of the designed digital game on third-grade students' English vocabulary learning. The data was collected by questionnaires that were given before and after using the designed digital game, observation sheet, and interview. It also investigated the relationship between learning styles and English vocabulary learning achievements using a digital game approach. The data showed that the overall gained scores of the experimental class were improved. The students' attitudes toward English were significantly higher than before. This indicated that joyful learning approach of using digital games can enhance elementary school students' attitudes toward English. The results show that using digital games motivates students to learn after school.

Keywords: Game-based learning · Game · Joyful learning · Self-learning Unity · English tutor

1 Introduction

Why is English such a difficult language to learn? It is always the question when non-native speakers start to learn English as their second language. Learning a second language is clearly a challenge that requires much motivation, as described in [1]. Traditionally, especially in Asia, teachers teach English word-by-word in the classroom, and students force themselves to follow the instructions. Most students want to quit English learning because it is generally boring in the classroom.

In order to improve the shortcomings of traditional teaching methods, educators constantly develop new teaching innovations. With information technology rapidly growing, researchers and educators keep working hard on cooperating computer techniques to motivate the students and increase their learning performance. In the past decades, traditional, instructional learning ways have been changed by the development and progress of digital technology. The use of information technology in the classroom has increasingly been the object of study. eLearning has become a new teaching model that improves the shortcomings of traditional teaching methods. The media/video

T.-T. Wu et al. (Eds.): ICITL 2018, LNCS 11003, pp. 393–402, 2018.
https://doi.org/10.1007/978-3-319-99737-7_42

sharing data recorded with streaming format has been widely accepted by most people including the information in YouTube and the open courses proposed by MIT [2–5].

Additionally, digital game-based learning has proved to be an effective way to motivate students and improve learning results. As indicated in [6], when using computer games for educational purposes, learners are encouraged to combine knowledge from different areas to choose a solution or to make a decision at a certain point, and they can test how the outcome of the game changes based on their decisions and actions. Hence, the purpose of this study was to determine if using situated learning with digital games would improve the effectiveness of learning English vocabulary for non-native speakers in elementary education. More specifically, this study was undertaken in order to understand how third-grade students can enhance their motivation and the effectiveness of self-learning without instructions, and to suggest some theoretical as well as practical implications of this process. The practicality of the proposed methodology is demonstrated through an experimental method. The data was collected by questionnaires that were given before and after using the designed digital game, observation sheet, and interview.

This study has taken the issue of game-based learning into consideration. The specialized areas such as self-learning effectiveness, learning performance and learning styles have all been taken into account.

2 Literature Review

Traditional, instructional learning ways have been changed by the development and progress of digital technology. There has been much research focusing on how to enhance motivation and learning effectiveness in the past years. There is a review of relevant literatures in this section.

2.1 Game-Based Learning

The interaction of playing games is usually fulfilled with joy and fun, so that people are always attracted to them. In recent years, much research proposed that using computer games, or games in general, for educational purpose motivates the learners and further enhances the learning effectiveness and improves the performance. As indicated in [6], game-based learning has been widely adopted for children's learning and has a proven success in the improvement of learning as well as in children's acceptance. Gaming becomes a new form of interactive content, worthy of exploration for learning purposes. Many studies have investigated the effects of digital game-based learning on learning and motivation in different areas, such as computer science education, business education and advanced training [6–8]. Additionally, [9] Liu et al. reported a positive relationship between the level of intrinsic motivation and learning scores in a digital learning game. Intrinsic motivation refers to the inner desire to engage in a task out of interest or amusement, or even because of the challenge it offers [10, 11]. Furthermore, Erhel and Jamet systematically demonstrated the benefits of digital game-based learning in their publication [12]. The benefits of digital game-based learning are often attributed to its entertainment aspect.

Generally, learning English as a second language is difficult for Asians, especially Chinese. The reason that Chinese learners find English tough to master is that there is no connection between English and Chinese. Educators found that pupils who have high motivation and concentration have high learning effectiveness. Hence this study exploited computer games to motivate pupils to learn English vocabulary without instructions.

2.2 Learning Styles

The term *learning styles* refers to the view that different people learn information in different ways [13]. It was first proposed by Thelen in 1954, but it was applied to the discussion activities of group dynamics at that time [14]. *Learning styles* is one of the topics of psychology, initially only focused on explaining some of the characteristics of individuals in terms of cognition. It has now been widely applied in various fields, including medical personnel training, business management, professional training, and so on. In recent decades, educators have recognized that each person has his preferred learning ways and techniques. When the pedagogy and the teaching materials that are matched to the learning style of students, anxiety will be reduced and higher learning performance will be achieved. The study of Hsu was to understand the preferences of learning styles among elementary school students, and trying to figure out the relationship between different learning styles and Chinese/English learning achievements in Taiwan [15]. The researcher adopted the questionnaire survey and then compared the results with their Chinese/English learning achievements through statistical analysis. It found that students' Chinese and English learning achievements were highly correlated.

As mentioned previously, digital game-based learning has been proved to be an effective way to improve the learning performance. This study also explores the relationship between learning styles and English vocabulary learning using digital games.

2.3 Self-learning

Situated learning is essentially a matter of creating meaning from the real activities of daily living, where learning occurs relative to the teaching environment [16]. Anderson and his colleagues provided a review of claims that situated learning has an increasing influence on education generally and mathematics education particularly [17]. They reviewed the four central claims of situated learning with respect to education: (1) action is grounded in the concrete situation in which it occurs; (2) knowledge does not transfer between tasks; (3) training by abstraction is of little use; and (4) instruction must be done in complex, social environments. Key to situated learning is the authenticity of the learning context—be it simulated as in PBL (problem-based learning) discussions in university or applied as in patient diagnosis and treatment in clinical settings [18]. Situated learning is an effective way to learn English. Using things of daily life as the materials for learning English is the most natural and direct way for effective learning. With computer technology and instructional design, an interactive, cooperative and real learning situation can be simulated in virtual environment so that participants can interact with situations to stimulate the ability to think and solve problems and to get better learning achievements.

3 Methods

As mentioned in the previous section, digital game-based learning generally improves the motivation and performance while learning. This study is to prove digital game-based learning is also effective for pupils, who have different learning styles, and enhances pupils' interests on learning English vocabulary without instructions. In the following subsections, the processes of situated digital content design and the entire experimental procedure are given.

3.1 Participant

This study investigated the effects of a digital game-based learning approach on Taiwanese elementary school students' attitudes toward English. Thirty-three third-grade students in Haishan Elementary School were used for this study. Most students in the class were active and working hard on every fresh thing, but a few were careless in learning. There was no relevant course taken before using the digital game, and the participants explored the game by themselves after school.

3.2 Situational Game Design

For providing learners a directly life-oriented English learning situation, this study designs a 3D virtual kitchen that contains all the kitchen objects in real life, and four life events as interactive game mission for learning English, as shown in Fig. 1. "Mom is the best cook," "Dad is willing to help," "Let's make pizza," and "We'll have a party" are the four missions for participants to learn English vocabulary through situated life events. The illustration of the scenario game is shown as Fig. 2. The participant has to choose one of the missions as the first step, and the related life event comes out with the conversation. The participants can interact with the scenarios to learn English directly by pressing "A", "W", "S", "D", and mouse moving. They can get a point of what to gather by clicking on the question mark. The scenarios used in the digital game were provided by the CoolEnglish production team led by Professor Chen of National Taiwan Normal University. The whole procedure of the game is shown as Fig. 3. In the context of life-oriented learning, students actively participate in learning activities and interact with situations to build their own cognitive structure and model, which then stimulates the learners' ability to think and solve problems.

3.3 Procedure

This study was to understand how the third-grade elementary students can enhance the motivation and the effectiveness of self-learning using a digital game without instructions, and to further explore the relationship between learning styles and English vocabulary learning achievements. The participants of this study were 33 third-grade

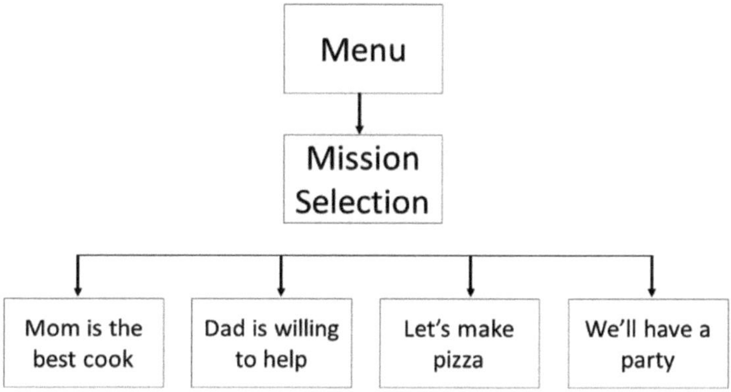

Fig. 1. The structure of the game used in this study.

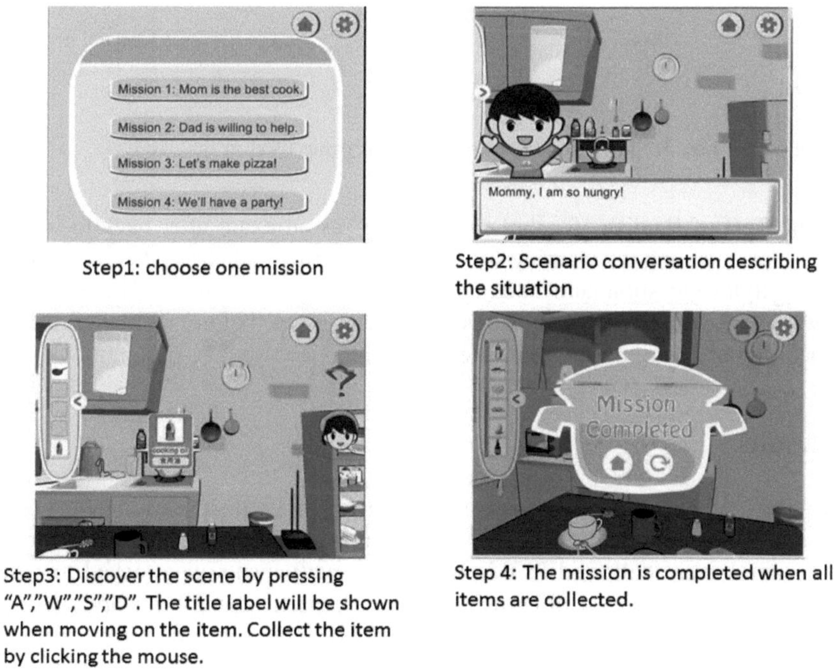

Fig. 2. The illustration of the scenario game.

students of Haishan Elementary School in New Taipei City. The tools used in this study are: "Felder & Soloman Learning Styles Questionnaire" [19], "The Test of English Vocabulary Learning", and "Learners' Feedbacks Questionnaire." In order to know the participants' familiarity with the English vocabulary appearing in the virtual scene, "The Test of English Vocabulary Learning" was first applied. Then the participants were asked to use the digital game at home during a one-week vacation, and

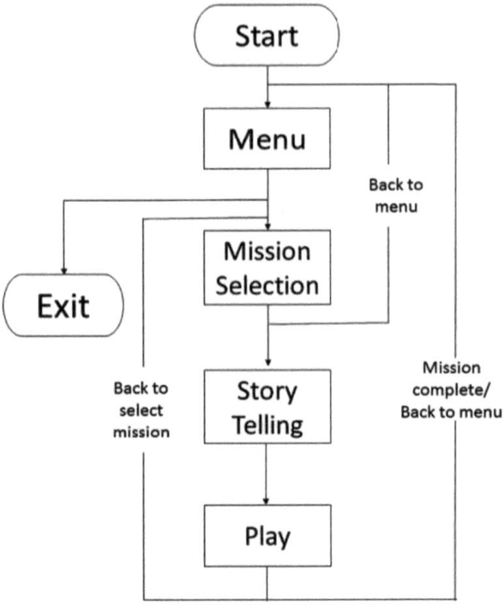

Fig. 3. The overall procedure of the game used in this study.

had "The Test of English Vocabulary Learning" as an exam after back-to-school. In addition, for obtaining the learning styles of the experimental class, "Felder & Soloman Learning Styles Questionnaire" was applied before the experiment. The experimental data was collected by questionnaires that were given before and after using the designed digital game, observation sheet, and interview.

4 Results

We carried out experiments to assess the impact of English learning on cognitive information processing in digital game-based learning. A total of 33 valid learning style questionnaires were collected in this study. The participants were asked to take the vocabulary test before and after using virtual scenario game for learning English. Description of the achievement toward English vocabulary learning score before and after using the virtual game is shown in Fig. 4. In general, the learning achievement of the participants was significantly improved. Before using the game-based situated learning, about 36% of the participants received failing grades, and the number of participants who gained the score of 30 were 2. After using the virtual game, the failure rate was reduced to 6%, and the lowest score was 50. Additionally, there were 4 participants got a perfect score of 100 after using the virtual game.

Moreover, participants were asked to do "Learners' Feedbacks Questionnaire" after using the situated game. There were 58.8% participants agreed that the game is easy to use without any instructions and less than 20% participants disagreed, as shown in Fig. 5. Figure 6 shows that there were 61.7% participants agreed that using the game to

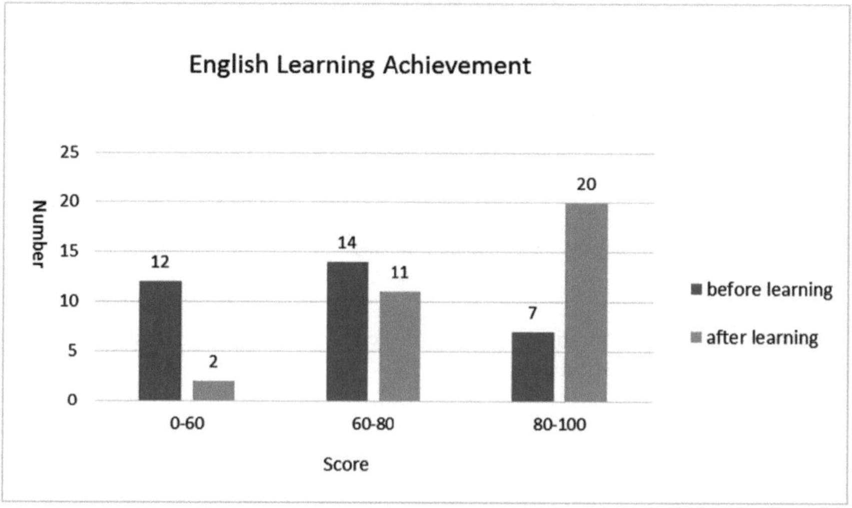

Fig. 4. Description of English Learning achievement before and after using the virtual game.

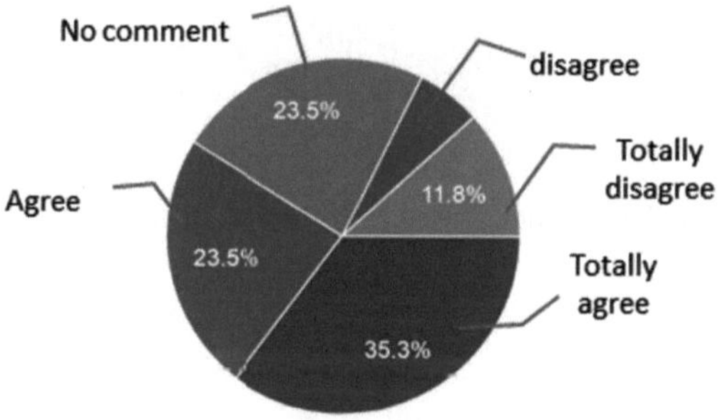

Fig. 5. The feedback of the question, "I don't need an instruction and I can do it by myself."

learn English can lead them to think individually. And more than 40% participants increased their confidence in learning English by exploiting the situated game, as shown in Fig. 7. However, the efficiency of remembering English vocabulary is not relevant to the use of situated game according to the feedback shown in Fig. 8.

Further, according to the interviews, most participants indicated that they were passive on English vocabulary learning. They used to force themselves to make efforts every day on English vocabulary learning. As mentioned in the previous section, using things of daily life as the materials for learning English is the most natural and direct way to learn. With the virtual game, the participants became active to English because they were interested in the scenario. Through the virtual objects and the interactive process of the game, English vocabulary learning became easy to remember. Students reviewed that they had learned through the game-based learning. However, learning style and English vocabulary learning using the situated game were not much related through the results of learning style questionnaires.

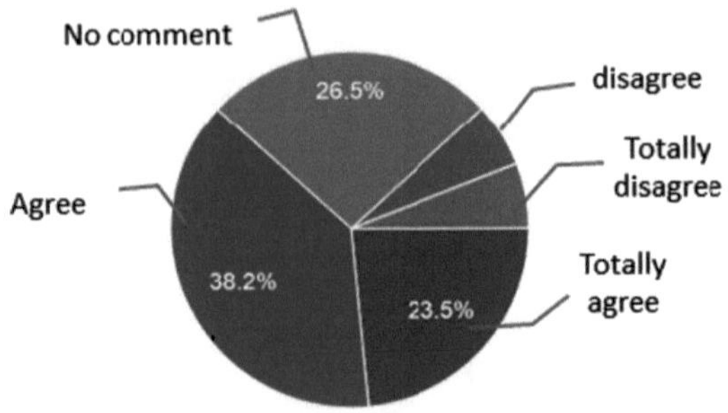

Fig. 6. The feedback of the question, "Using a situated life mission, I can think for myself what to take and to learn English vocabulary."

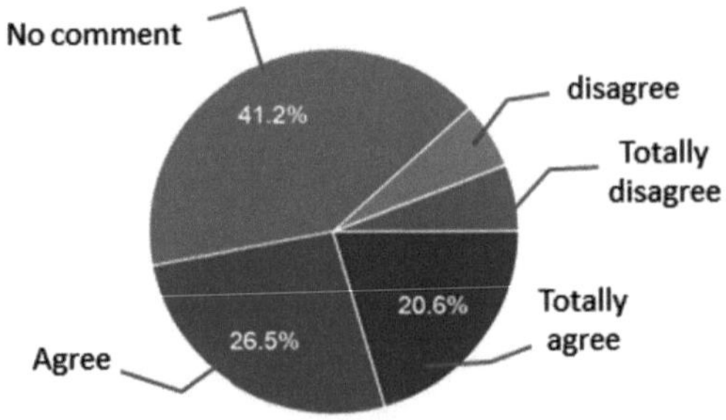

Fig. 7. The feedback of the question, "Using this game, I have more confidence in learning English vocabulary."

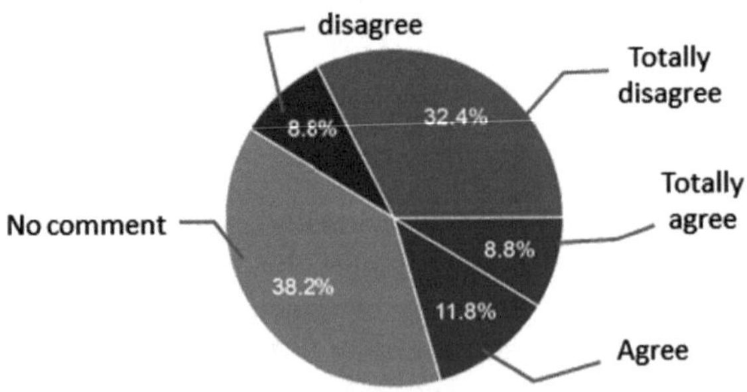

Fig. 8. The feedback of the question, "Using this game, I can remember the relevant English vocabulary faster."

5 Conclusions and Future Works

Based on observations in the experimental class, it can be concluded that digital game-based learning is effective for third-grade pupils, who have different learning styles, and enhances pupils' interests in learning English vocabulary without instructions. If it is supported through the affective experience, interesting subject matter, methods as well as enthusiasm and fun, it will make students have a positive desire or inclination to learn English vocabulary for non-native speakers. The results show that the learning achievements of the participants have been significantly improved using game-based learning. Students who have an opinion that English learning is beneficial to themselves, engaging, and fun in the learning process have a tendency to study harder. Further, the participants indicate that they become active and having higher concentration on learning English vocabulary when using situational virtual game. Therefore, creating situational virtual game helps Taiwanese elementary students to overcome the barriers towards English.

Moreover, learning style and the impact of English vocabulary learning using the situational virtual game do not have obvious correlations in this study. It means that game-based learning has no significant effect on students with different learning styles in this study. This is because digital games are exciting and appealing to children in modern society. The participants were third-grade elementary students whose ages were around 10 years old, and felt a situational virtual game is more interesting than instructions. Hence, participants were willing to spend time on playing the game in short time so that the achievements are higher after using the game regardless of the learning style. In the future, senior students will be involved as study subjects to explore whether game-based learning of English vocabulary is suitable for different kinds of learning styles.

References

1. Wold, J.B.: Difficulties in learning english as a second or foreign language. All Regis University theses, Paper 333 (2006)
2. Abelson, H., Long, P.D.: MIT's strategy for educational technology innovation, 1999–2003. Proc. IEEE **96**(6), 1012–1034 (2008)
3. Carson, S., Forward, M.L.: Development of the OCW consortium. Paper presented at the Education Engineering (EDUCON). IEEE (2010)
4. Lerman, S., Potts, J.P.: Unlocking knowledge, empowering minds: MIT's OpenCourseWare project. IEEE Sig. Process. Mag. **23**(5), 11–15 (2006)
5. Tovar, E.: OCW consortium: learning through the worldwide sharing and use of free, open, high-quality education materials organized as courses: special session. Paper presented at the Education Engineering (EDUCON). IEEE (2010)
6. Pivec, M., Dziabenko, O., Schinnerl, I.: Aspects of game-based learning. In: Proceedings of I-KNOW 2003, Austria, pp. 216–225 (2003)
7. Chandel, P., Dutta, D., Tekta, P., Dutta, K., Gupta, V.: Digital game based learning in computer science education. CPUH Res. J. **1**(2), 33–37 (2015)
8. Garris, R., Ahlers, R., Driskell, J.E.: Games, motivation and learning: a research and practice model. Simul. Gaming **33**(4), 441–467 (2002)
9. Liu, M., Horto, L., Olmanson, J., Toprac, P.: A study of learning and motivation in a new media enriched environment for middle school science. Educ. Technol. Res. Dev. **59**, 249–265 (2011)
10. Deci, E.L., Ryan, R.M.: The, "what" and "why" of goal pursuits: human needs and the self-determination of a behavior. Psychol. Inq. **11**(4), 227–268 (2000)

11. Martens, R.L., Gulikers, J., Bastiaens, T.: The impact of intrinsic motivation on e-learning in authentic computer tasks. J. Comput. Assist. Learn. **20**, 368–376 (2004)
12. Erthel, S., Jamet, E.: Digital game-based learning: Impact of instructions and feedback on motivation and learning effectiveness. Comput. Educ. **67**, 156–167 (2013)
13. Pashler, H., McDaniel, M., Bjork, R.: Learning styles: concepts and evidence. Psychol. Sci. Public Interest **9**(3), 105–119 (2008)
14. Ehrman, M.E., Leaver, B.L.: Cognitive styles in the service of language learning. System **31**, 393–415 (2003)
15. Hsu, Y.-C.: Research on the Relationship between learning styles and Chinese/English learning achievements in the elementary school. Master thesis (2000)
16. Stein, D.: Situated learning in adult education. https://www.ericdigests.org/1998–3/adult-education.html. Accessed15 Mar 2018
17. Anderson, J.R., Reder, L.M., Simon, H.A.: Situated learning and education. Educ. Rese. **25**(4), 5–11 (1996)
18. Bridges, S., Chan, L.K., Hmelo-Silver, E.C.: Situated learning and educational technologies: theory and practice. In: Bridges, S., Chan, L., Hmelo-Silver, C. (eds.) Educational Technologies in Medical and Health Sciences Education, Chap. 1, pp. 1–6. Springer, Cham (2011). https://doi.org/10.1007/978-3-319-08275-2_1
19. Solomon, B.A., Felder, R.M.: Index of learning styles questionnaire. North Carolina State University. https://www.researchgate.net/publication/228403640_Index_of_Learning_Styles_Questionnaire. Accessed 05 Mar 2017

Mobile Applications for English Learning Performance Upgrade

Liliia A. Latypova(✉), Oksana V. Polyakova, and Dilyana D. Sungatullina

Institute of Management, Economics and Finance, Kazan Federal University, 18 Kremlevskaya Street, 420008 Kazan, Russia
melilek@yandex.ru

Abstract. The rapid growth of the Internet has significantly changed the way English teachers transfer knowledge to their students. It is obvious that nothing is comparable with teacher-student interaction, but there is no doubt mobile applications have aggressively penetrated into the learning process and even proved their effectiveness, especially with Generation Z, for they facilitate meaningful learning environment. Mobile Assisted Language Learning (MALL) is the use of mobile devices to improve language acquisition. Authors of the research investigated the shift from teacher-led learning to student-led one studying the way under-graduates use the mobile application ELEVATE. The aim of this experimental study has been to find out the potential of using the interactive mobile application ELEVATE with Z-learners to upgrade their skills in English learning performance such as vocabulary, pronunciation, listening and comprehension of the ESL learners without teacher's help as well as to develop critical thinking skills along the way. The results of the post-test showed that students in the focus group significantly outperformed those in the standard group, which means students' learning performance considerably enhanced. Interview data showed that students have positive attitudes towards the creative ways of language learning. Meaningful learning paradigm can remarkably improve English learning effectiveness. There are some limitations in MALL approaches though they have high potential for further development and improvement. Enhancing mobile devices are sure to make MALL-based technology more efficient both for teachers and students.

Keywords: Mobile application · Mobile Assisted Language Learning (MALL) Mobile devices · Mobile learning · On-line education · Critical thinking ICT (Information and Communication Technologies) · Generation Z Learning performance · Meaningful learning · ESL students

1 Introduction

Mobile Assisted Language Learning (MALL) is a subset of Mobile Learning (m-learning) and Computer-assisted language learning (CALL). Mobile Assisted Language Learning describes an approach to language learning that is interactive and assisted or enhanced through the use of a handheld mobile device [6, 25]. "ICT (Information and Communication Technologies) has been brought into educational environments as a

T.-T. Wu et al. (Eds.): ICITL 2018, LNCS 11003, pp. 403–411, 2018.
https://doi.org/10.1007/978-3-319-99737-7_43

useful supplement to existing resources" [22]. Mobile devices are not substitute for existing learning devices, but they serve as extension for learning in new environment having new capabilities, though, not all learning content and activities are appropriate for mobile devices [10, 27]. Mobile devices draw a new path to learn and teach outside the classroom with little or no direction from a teacher and mobile learning arose as the next generation of electronic learning (e-learning) [3, 5, 9, 19]. Mobile apps as well as social networks serve as useful tools to foster students' employability and build social media skills [12]. Klopfer et al. note "the following benefits of mobile devices: (1) portability: such devices can be taken to different places due to small size and weight; (2) social interactivity: exchanging data and collaboration with other learners is possible through mobile devices; (3) context sensitivity: the data on the mobile devices can be gathered and responded uniquely to the current location and time; (4) connectivity: mobile devices can be connected to other devices, data collection devices, or a common network by creating a shared network; (5) individuality: activities platform can be customized for individual learner" [14].

In the recent studies on pedagogy and psychology "it is highly recommended to use interactive technologies, which involves giving students the opportunity to individually expand and deepen their language skills, as well as forming their subject position in determining their educational path". Valeev et al. advocate the importance of applying interactive technologies as they "upgrade learning efficiency, increase the speed of assimilation of the material, encourage the active participation of each student in the learning process, awake students' interest in learning a foreign language; provide multi-faceted impact on them" [26]. In fact, MALL can be considered as an ideal solution to language learning barriers in terms of time and place [19].

The most popular currently used mobile applications are Duolingo, LangBook, LinguaLeo, Grammar Up, Memrise and Elevate [21]. By means of freely available Duolingo application one can learn English, Italian, French, Spanish, German and Portuguese. It can be used as an additional manual with interactive exercises. Duolingo trains such skills as written and spoken language (you will be offered to pronounce the learned phrases), reading and listening [7]. The educational mobile application Memrise is aimed at effective assimilation of vocabulary [18]. The Grammar Up application is intended for those facing difficulties in constructing foreign language sentences, using articles and other grammar difficulties. This app contains rules and examples of usage [11]. The LangBook application can be used for traditional translation as well as for training. This educational application offers users thesaurus, explanatory, encyclopedic, geographic, engineering and many other dictionaries. For example, the application contains a dictionary, tools for learning and remembering difficult words and helps to learn a foreign language using interactive cards with the tasks, competently structured and broken down into educational topics. The main purpose of the program is to perform the functions of the dictionary. The benefit of the program is that it can work off-line [15]. The program for memorizing words LinguaLeo is integrated with the site, allowing to learn foreign words, read, listen to educational texts, do crossword puzzles. All words to be studied on the site become available in the mobile version [8, 21].

Elevate is an app where users take part in a series of fast-paced tests and quizzes targeted specifically at improving memory, focus, reading comprehension, and writing.

Users give their age and choose the areas which they believe they need most upgrade in. Then Elevate offers a series of questions that are suited to users' needs. The app is supposed to be used every day, so users can keep practicing and improving their skills. After each round of testing, users receive a score and are ranked among other users. This helps users to track their progress, allowing them to see where they have improved as well as subject areas where they still need training. Elevate has a specific focus on communication. With the games, you'll be challenged to enrich your vocabulary, improve your grammar and writing, and shore up your reading comprehension. Elevate also says that through its writing- and reading-based games, you'll also improve your memory and attention. The idea is to improve your overall communication skills, and help you process information easier [20].

2 Literature Review

The pervasive use of interactive technology and mobile applications serves as the intellectual basis for teaching creativity in a new generation. It is common knowledge that Generation Z "can quickly and efficiently shift between work and play, with multiple distractions going on in the background…working on multiple tasks at once. Generation Z was born into a world overrun with technology. What was taken as amazing and inspiring inventions, are now taken as a given for teens" [2]. For this reason, "there is actual development of methodological approaches to the use of interactive learning technologies for realization of the ideas of personality-oriented and adaptive training for the purpose of development of the student's personality" [26]. Recently, researchers "have become interested in the affordance of tablets in the learning process and its effects on students' achievements" [27].

As learning English is considered to be one of the leading factors for professional development, providing more convenient environment for people to learn English is the strategic educational goal towards increasing students' achievements and facilitating differentiation of learning requirements. Learning English by means of using mobile applications improves the quality and intensity of training as it stimulates students' cognitive activity. Latypova et al. state that "students' autonomy in choosing their way to build education is essential to promote lifelong learning practice". New approaches are required to build Z-learners' independence of mind. Mobile applications undoubtedly serve as the tool to stimulate meaningful learning process that has "crucial value for University students' success in mastering the English language and maintaining learners' continued engagement in the process of acquiring linguistic competence" [16]. Mayer notes that in meaningful learning students seek to make sense of their experiences and mentally integrate incoming information with existing knowledge [17].

Considering the educational value of technology usage in a language classroom, Saranya indicates that technology would make teaching lessons more student-centered and foster thinking skills and learner autonomy [23]. In contrast to the traditional classroom learning that centers on teachers, MALL "offers a learner-centered self-paced learning environment" [28]. As Miangah and Nezarat specify, MALL has "the potential for learning process to be personalized, spontaneous, informal and ubiquitous. Although learning through mobile phones may take longer time compared to computers, the learners feel a greater sense of freedom of time and place, so that they can take the advantage of spare time to learn a second language when and where they are" [19]. Moreover, according to Starcic et al., "mobile technology providing instant information access and connectivity supports new types of learning relationships, connecting students outside the immediate classroom context. Mobile technology is transforming social practices and facilitates learning embedded in them. Students are engaged in cross-cultural learning and thus develop knowledge, skills and attitudes from within the context meeting other cultures" [13].

It is crucial to emphasize that a mobile language class supports a great diversity of learning styles in a timely and interactive mode. It is a paradigm shift from e-learning to m-learning. Valarmathi believes that "the influence of technology on current academics is such that in near future the whole context of learning will come under single umbrella of m-learning" [25].

3 The Aim of the Study

The aim of the study has been to define the efficiency of interactive mobile application ELEVATE for ESL students and to find out the potential of using the ELEVATE to assist critical thinking formation. To reach this aim authors have come to the following research questions:

(1) Does the mobile application ELEVATE have the potential to develop critical thinking skills in Z-learners?
(2) Are there any significant differences between the pre- and post-test results of focus and standard groups?
(3) If yes, how can the implications of these finding improve practice of ESL learners at the tertiary level?

4 Materials and Methods

The research was carried out during 18 months period (fall 2015 – winter 2017) at the Institute of Management, Economics and Finance (Kazan Federal University, Russia), namely, the Foreign Languages Department for Economics, Business and Finance. The department specializes in Business English teaching or teaching English for specific purposes (ESP), whereby developing the Four Cs (4Cs – communication, collaboration, critical thinking and creativity) of the 21st century learning is of primary importance [4]. The research focuses on the development of critical thinking skills through various English teaching tools. The tools implemented in the study include Unlock 4 Cambridge University Press academic skills course [24] and the ELEVATE application installed by the students before the experimental period started [20].

The research involved 27 students, 18 female and 9 male aged 18–19 (first-year undergraduates) at the C1 level in English in accordance with Common European Framework of References (CEFR). All the participants represented two autonomous academic groups. A binary variable was subsequently created to distinguish between students who were developing their critical thinking skills via Unlock 4 and ELEVATE combined (focus group) and those who were studying without mobile application but with Unlock 4 authentic book course (standard group).

The first phase of the research (9 months) focused on developing critical thinking skills in the framework of Benjamin Bloom's classification of learning objectives (Bloom's Taxonomy) [1] through Unlock 4 authentic course. The Unlock series is remarkable for the comprehensive approach to critical thinking. The tasks in the book are tailored in a way that students need to analyze information, formulate main challenges, generate their own solutions and present them in written and oral forms.

The second phase of the research (9 months) started when the focus group was exposed to ELEVATE mobile application along with the Unlock 4 learning materials, whereas the standard group was deprived of this technological opportunity. Predominantly, the focus group was practicing all the basic elements of the game – Writing, Listening, Reading, Speaking (Maths was excluded from the list due to its irrelevance towards the subject the authors teach) in accordance with their level of English proficiency. Gradually, as students advanced in their achievements, playing options diversified in their range and totaled the amount of thirty one games. Eventually, only eight were selected for the constant practice due to the fact that they were aimed at developing critical thinking skills: Brevity and Expression (Writing), Sequences (Listening), Eloquence and Precision (Speaking), and Agility, Comprehension and Context (Reading). Brevity is the type of task which enhances the ability of thoughts' concise articulation, whereas Expression acts as common phrases facilitator. Sequences in Listening enhance brain work as it is connected with short-term memory tasks. Eloquence assists in more rigorous word and tone choice along with Precision which recognizes errors in speech to advance clear and accurate speaking. Reading has got broader range of games, while Agility expands the vocabulary list; Comprehension stimulates written text understanding and analysis; Context encourages semantic context clues usage. The Focus group was exposed to ELEVATE mobile app during nine months' period.

To analyze the difference in critical thinking skills level in the participants of both groups the authors of the research gave the students an obligatory case study. The authors implemented a complex variety of methods: theoretical (study and generalization of innovative teaching experience) and empirical (participants observation, stating and forming experiment, survey, testing, interviews, statistical treatment of data; interpretation and evaluation of the results of experimental work).

5 Results

During the first phase of the research students' 9 months immersion into the Unlock learning materials facilitated the development of their critical thinking skills. The participants both in the standard group and the focus group demonstrated identical results in their achievements of various activities shown in Table 1:

Table 1. Students' achievements in critical thinking activities after phase 1 (M – Means, SD – Standard Deviation)

Type of activity	Standard group		Focus group	
	M	SD	M	SD
Remembering previously learned information	4.844	1.087	4.789	1.069
Grasping the meaning of information	4.594	1.055	4.645	1.08
Applying the knowledge in the real life	4.397	1.069	4.415	1.034
Breaking the information down into its componential parts	3.951	1.088	4.018	1.104
Making judgments of the information received	3.534	1.208	3.489	1.312
Creating or composing new input	3.187	1.103	3.195	1.204

During the second phase of the experiment the students in the Focus group were offered to install the ELEVATE App on their mobile phones and were required to assess progress regularly. The application itself opened advanced options only after less demanding ones were successfully completed. The first two weeks of using the App were under teacher's scrutiny. Students consistently provided short reports about their progress, discussed difficulties that arose while playing the App. All these actions stimulated some culture of having the App as the part of the studying process.

In the classroom of generation Z that view technology as their everyday reality teacher should admit that students tend to learn more effectively if they are left to solve problems and find solutions. Gamification fosters desire to achieve progress, consequently there is a strong eagerness to advance in achievements among the group members. At the same time, students are given rewards from the App in the form of short stimulating appraisals that assist in maintaining the interest to proceed playing the game.

Representatives of generation Z are greatly dependent on their social connections and use them as learning tools. This generation is accustomed to intense relationships that are not limited to a classroom. They have 24/7 access to all possible social networks. This characteristic feature of Zers was used to foster collaboration among peers through technology. To a Generation Z learner, no single source of knowledge can become an expert one. Their expertise lies in the collective knowledge. Additionally, one can be self-taught on the desired topic through the network.

The Fig. 1 clearly represents all the benefits ELEVATE has as the tool to boost self-regulatory processes among students. The prerequisite of the experiment to play the App every day with the inevitability of this process conclusively triggered students' motivation, improved self-assessment and encouraged self-organisation. Being real Zers they promptly join the process of sharing their success with peers via all forms of social networks.

Another unique feature of this generation is the social focus of the learning process. The content they are learning should have relevance on a global scale. These learners are practical, savvy, and thrive on a good challenge, especially when it reflects their personal interests and is accompanied by instant gratification. The content of the Unlock course is perfectly structured to meet the needs of Z-learners. It nurtures collaborative learning, enhances reflection and support social engagement.

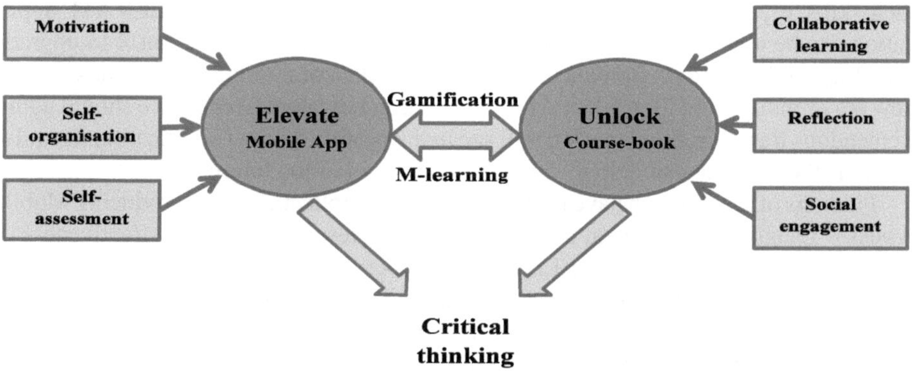

Fig. 1. Critical thinking enhancement via M-learning (Elevate app).

As the post-test assessment, students in the standard and the focus groups were offered to be engaged in the project on "Ageing" [24]. By scaffolding critical thinking skills the students were targeted upon the final essay on population pyramid in their home countries and the ways society can be affected by the changes they describe. The results of students' achievements are displayed in Table 2.

Table 2. Students' achievements in critical thinking activities after phase 2 (M–Means, SD – Standard Deviation)

Type of activity	Standard group		Focus group	
	M	SD	M	SD
Remembering previously learned information	4.93	1.072	4.912	1.097
Grasping the meaning of information	4.72	1.039	4.753	1.049
Applying the knowledge in the real life	4.519	1.081	4.613	1.052
Breaking the information down into its componential parts	4.037	1.046	4.257	1.154
Making judgments of the information received	3.786	1.245	3.954	1.497
Creating or composing new input	3.648	1.213	4.016	1.247

As it is seen from Tables 1 and 2, students from the focus group demonstrated exceptional performance in comparison with students from the standard group. The students in the focus group exposed better understanding of fact-opinion correlation, deeper and more structured reasoning, more profound examples from vocabulary perspective. The focus group students also made no loose implications. Alternatives were critically reviewed and predictions were made on data rather than on their subjective opinions.

6 Discussion and Conclusions

The results indicated that learning skills of ESL students had higher statistically significant improvements as a result of using the ELEVATE application in the focus group and most learners from focus groups gave positive feedback that ELEVATE upgraded their skills, especially vocabulary. Thus, it can be concluded that the ELEVATE application can be used as an educational tool by ESL students of generation Z to upgrade their English learning performance. Facing the problem of training the specialist for the new era of industrialization when AI is not a fiction but rather a reality we should admit tremendous transformation that we will see in the nearest future. Gamification unequivocally is the tool that can help to shape the classroom of the future.

Findings of the research have important positive implications for introducing Mobile Assisted Language Learning at a tertiary level. The results proved the effectiveness of interactive mobile application ELEVATE to upgrade the skills in English learning performance. The materials applied facilitated the development of students' critical thinking skills, which constitutes one of the Four Cs (4Cs – communication, collaboration, critical thinking and creativity) of the 21st century defined by the United Nations.

Acknowledgments. The work is performed according to the Russian Government Program of Competitive Growth of Kazan Federal University.

References

1. Anderson, L.W., et al.: A Taxonomy for Learning, Teaching, and Assessing: A revision of Bloom's Taxonomy of Educational Objectives. Pearson, Allyn & Bacon, New York (2001)
2. Beall, G.: 8 Key Differences between Gen Z and Millennials. Huffpost (2017). https://www.huffingtonpost.com/george-beall/8-key-differences-between_b_12814200.html
3. Beatty, K.: Mobile language learning: the world in our hands, no. 17. Anaheim University, USA (2015). www.anaheim.edu/schools-and-institutes/graduate-school-of-education/diploma-in-tesol/243-about/faculty-and-staff/tesol-faculty/886-ken-beatty-phd-ken-beatty-phd
4. Bell, D.V.J.: Twenty first Century Education: Transformative Education for Sustainability and Responsible Citizenship (2016). http://lsf-lst.ca/media/Twenty_First_Century_Education_FINAL_2016.pdf
5. Cavus, N., Ibrahim, D.: M-Learning: an experiment in using SMS to support learning new English language words. Br. J. Educ. Technol. **40**(1), 78–91 (2009). https://doi.org/10.1111/j.1467-8535.2007.00801.x
6. Cavus, N., Ibrahim, D.: Learning English using children's stories in mobile devices. Br. J. Educ. Technol. **48**(2), 625–641 (2017). https://doi.org/10.1111/bjet.12427
7. Duolingo: Learn languages for free (2016). https://play.google.com/store/apps/details?id=com.duolingo&hl=ru
8. English with Lingualeo (2016). https://play.google.com/store/apps/details?id=com.lingualeo.android&hl=ru
9. Frank, V.M., Freynik, S., Richardson, D.L.: Technologies for foreign language learning: a review of technology types and their effectiveness, vol. 1(27). Center for Advanced Study of Language, University of Maryland, College Park, MD (2014). https://www.learntechlib.org/p/153571
10. Gay, G., Stefanone, M., Grace-Martin, M., Hembrooke, H.: The effects of wireless computing in collaborative learning environments. Int. J. Hum. Comput. Interact. **13**(2), 257–276 (2001)
11. Grammar Up (2016). https://play.google.com/store/apps/details?id=com.eknathkadam.grammarup&hl=ru

12. Istenic Starcic, A.I., Barrow, M., Zajc, M., Lebenicnik, M.: Students' attitudes on social network sites and their actual use for career management competences and professional identity development. Int. J. Emerg. Technol. Learn. **12**, 65–81 (2017)
13. Starcic, Andreja Istenic, Huang, Po-Sen, Valeeva, Roza Alexeyevna, Latypova, Liliia Agzamovna, Huang, Yueh-Min: Digital storytelling and mobile learning: potentials for internationalization of higher education curriculum. In: Huang, Tien-Chi, Lau, Rynson, Huang, Yueh-Min, Spaniol, Marc, Yuen, Chun-Hung (eds.) SETE 2017. LNCS, vol. 10676, pp. 400–406. Springer, Cham (2017). https://doi.org/10.1007/978-3-319-71084-6_45
14. Klopfer, E., Squire, K., Jenkins, H.: Environmental detectives: PDAs as a window into a virtual simulated world. In: Proceedings of IEEE International Workshop on Wireless and Mobile Technologies in Education, pp. 95–98. IEEE Computer Society, Vaxjo (2002)
15. LangBook (2016). https://itunes.apple.com/ru/app/langbook-oflajn-slovari-+/id357766149?mt=8
16. Latypova, L.A., Polyakova, O.V., Latypov, N.R.: University students' peer assessment in the language environment: from rote to meaningful learning. IEJME Math. Educ. **11**(6), 1911–1917 (2016)
17. Mayer, R.E.: Teaching and testing for problem solving. In: Anderson, L.W. (ed.) International Encyclopedia of Teaching and Teacher Education. Pergamon, Oxford (1995)
18. Memrise – learning languages (2016). https://play.google.com/store/apps/details?id=com.memrise.android.memrisecompanion&hl=ru
19. Miangah, T.M., Nezarat, A.: Mobile-assisted language learning. Int. J. Distrib. Parallel Syst. (IJDPS) **3**(1), 309–319 (2012). https://pdfs.semanticscholar.org/2902/cf4ef0284cb407e986ec2cbed96c7ddbfeb8.pdf
20. Mitroff, S.: Lumosity vs. Elevate: Battle of the brain-training apps (2014). https://www.cnet.com/news/lumosity-vs-elevate-brain-training-apps
21. Odinokaya, M.A., Kollerova, M.V.: The role of educational mobile applications in the study of English. Interact. Sci. **2**(12), 100–102 (2017). https://doi.org/10.21661/r-117419
22. Plowman, L., Stephen, C.: A 'benign addition'? Res. ICT Pre-school Child. J. Comput. Assist. Learn. **19**, 149–164 (2003)
23. Saranya, P:. Incorporating technology in the language classrooms. J. Technol. ELT **7**(2) (2017). https://sites.google.com/site/journaloftechnologyforelt/archive/v7-n2/2
24. Sowton, C.: Unlock. Level 4. Reading and Writing Skills. Student's Book and Online Workbook. Cambridge University Press (2014)
25. Valarmathi, K.E.: Mobile assisted language learning. J. Technol. ELT **1**(2) (2011). https://sites.google.com/site/journaloftechnologyforelt/archive/april2011/mobileassistedlanguagelearning
26. Valeev, A.A., Latypova, L.A., Latypov, N.R.: The use of interactive learning technologies in teaching a Foreign language in high school. IEJME-Math. Educ. **11**(6), 1773–1785 (2016). http://iejme.com/makale/809
27. Volk, M., Cotič, M., Zajc, M., Starcic, A.I.: Tablet-based cross-curricular maths vs. traditional maths classroom practice for higher-order learning outcomes. Comput. Educ. **114**, 1–23 (2017)
28. Zhang, D., Zhao, J.L., Zhou, L., Nunamaker, Jr., J.F.: Can e-learning replace classroom learning? In: International Conference on Information Technology and Systems, ICITS 2018, vol. 721 pp. 631–639 (2018)

Exploring the Relationships Between EFL Learners' Usage of Technology and Their Approaches to Learning English

Ching-Fang Juan[1(✉)], Hsin-I She[1], Chia-Yin Hung[2], Silvia Wen-Yu Lee[3], Jyh-Chong Liang[4,5(✉)], Kuo-En Chang[1], and Chin-Chung Tsai[4,5]

[1] Graduate Institute of Information and Computer Education, National Taiwan Normal University, Taipei, Taiwan
chingfang@ntnu.edu.tw
[2] Wenzao Chinese Language Center, Kaohsiung, Taiwan
[3] Graduate Institute of Science Education, National Changhua University of Education, Changhua, Taiwan
[4] Program of Learning Science, National Taiwan Normal University, Taipei, Taiwan
[5] Institute for Research Excellence in Learning Sciences, National Taiwan Normal University, Taipei, Taiwan

Abstract. Objective: Nowadays, technology plays an important role in learning; hence, it is important to explore the relationships between EFL learners' usage of technology and their approaches to learning English. **Method:** This study involved 186 English department undergraduates in Taiwan and utilized two questionnaires to respectively survey EFL learners' usage of technology and their approaches to learning English. In particular, the approaches to learning English survey used in this study is a newly designed questionnaire which includes eight factors: Intrinsic Interest, Commitment to Work, Relating Ideas, Understanding, Fear of Failure, Aim for Qualification, Minimizing Scope of Study, and Memorization. **Results and findings:** Exploratory factor analysis revealed adequate validity of the new questionnaire. The regression analyses indicated that EFL learners' approaches to learning English were associated with their technology usage for learning English such as recommendation, usefulness, and ease of use. **Discussion:** This study will contribute to our understanding of EFL learners using technology for learning in the future.

Keywords: EFL learners · Technology · Approaches to learning English

1 Introduction

In past studies, most of the literature shows that technology-assisted learning is the current trend of learning. It also pointed out that using technology in the classroom was positive for learning and teaching. The innovation of technology with various types of

T.-T. Wu et al. (Eds.): ICITL 2018, LNCS 11003, pp. 412–420, 2018.
https://doi.org/10.1007/978-3-319-99737-7_44

learning includes the use of a variety of hardware and software such as pads, e-books, applications (apps), and websites. Technology plays an important role in learning.

However, many teachers also integrate technology into their teaching to enhance students' learning motivation and to provide more diversified teaching [1], while learners use technology to learn, make learning more flexible, and have choices according to their learning needs. Moreover, they can test their learning effectiveness through technological feedback. In order to motivate learners' requirements for self-learning and to understand the ease of use and usefulness of technology for learners [2], these factors should be considered while designing learning software. Learning by technology also leads to increased learning motivation and confidence [1].

This study had two main objectives: to understand the learners' usage of technology and to understand the relationship between learners' approaches to learning English and their use of technology.

2 Literature Review

2.1 The Technology Acceptance Model

The Technology Acceptance Model (TAM) was developed by the American scholar [3] based on the Theory of Reasoned Action (TRA) in information systems. The technical field has evolved to explain and predict people's acceptance of information technology [4]. The Technology Acceptance Model (TAM) claims that the use of information technology by people is influenced by their behavioral intentions to explore the influence of external factors on users' internal beliefs, attitudes, and intentions, which in turn affects information [3].

The theory consists of two factors. One is perceived usefulness (PU), which refers to how users subjectively consider the degree of improvement in their work performance when they face a new technology. The second is perceived ease-of-use (PEOU), which refers to the degree to which users consider that they can reduce their efforts when using a particular system. Therefore, the higher the users' perceived ease of use, the more positive their attitude toward its use. At the same time, the higher the users' perceived ease of use, the greater their perceived usefulness.

This study aimed to reveal the usage of technology by EFL learners based on TAM.

2.2 Approaches to Learning

The approaches to learning refer to the learner's learning motivation and strategies. Learning motivation can be divided into internal interest and external interest. Internal interest means that learners have a deep understanding of basic knowledge, and use strategies to learn. On the contrary, external learning motivation is dependent on learning content and involves "rote learning," "memorizing," and "reproducing" [5–7].

However, in the cognitive theory of learning, it was defined that learners use different learning methods to learn in different environments and learning tasks. Learning through doing practical tasks, they will have a deeper understanding of the learning content [8–10].

In this study, the use of technology-assisted language learning provided learners with more realistic language tasks and feedback, and more possible ways of learning.

2.3 Relationships Between the Technology Acceptance Model and Approaches to Learning

The aim of this study was to explore the relationships between EFL learners' approaches to learning English and their usage of technology. The usage of technology will enhance learning effect and provide multiple learning environments for learners. [11]. It will help us learn about the learning situation of the learner and what factors they are most concerned about when they engage in technology-assisted learning.

2.4 Purpose

As mentioned previously, to understand the relationship between EFL learners' approach to learning and the use of technology, in this study we developed an English questionnaire about learning approaches to investigate the learners' learning situation, and to measure their learning methods. Second, through the stepwise regression and correlations of statistical methods, we can better understand the relationship between technology and learning methods, and predict which factors in science and technology affect learners' learning.

3 Methodology

3.1 Participants

The participants in this study included 186 undergraduates (33 males and 153 females) from a university in Taiwan. All of the students in this study were majoring in English. Their ages ranged from 19 to 23 years (mean = 22.81 years); 79 were freshman and sophomore students, while 107 were junior and senior students.

3.2 Usage of Technology

According to Usage of Technology questionnaire (Perceptions of Price, Ease of use, Recommendation, Content, and Usefulness) measured with a 5-point Likert scale ranging from 1 (strongly disagree) to 5 (strongly agree) was adopted as the survey instrument.

3.3 Approaches to Learning English

The EFL learners' Approaches to Learning English questionnaire (ALEQ) is a self-report instrument for measuring how EFL learners learn English (Eight factors: Intrinsic Interest, Commitment to Work, Relating Ideas, Understanding, Fear of Failure, Aim for Qualification, Minimizing Scope of Study, and Memorization). The questionnaire is primarily targeted at Taiwanese university students. This questionnaire includes 37 items from eight factors measured with a 5-point Likert scale ranging from 1 (strongly disagree) to 5 (strongly agree).

3.4 Data Analysis

Data screening and analysis were conducted using SPSS version 23.0. The aim of this study was to explore the relationships between EFL learners' usage of technology and their approaches to learning English. The alpha coefficient for each factor of the survey was computed to ensure its reliability. Pearson's correlation was utilized to explore the relationships between EFL learners' usage of technology and their approaches to learning English. The correlations between EFL learners' usage of technology in language learning and the ALEQ factors were then analyzed. Finally, stepwise regression analyses were conducted, in which the usage of technology was considered as the predictors, while their approaches to learning English were the outcome variables.

4 Results

We firstly performed EFA to establish the factor structure of the ALEQ. Principal component analysis was used as the extraction method with the rotation method of varimax with Kaiser normalization (Kaiser, 1958). Following the principle stated by Stevens (1996), items weighted higher than 0.50 on the relevance factor and lower than 0.50 on all other factors were maintained. The results of the rotated factor analyses of the EFL learners' approach to learning questionnaire are shown in Table 1. The factor loading of each item weighed greater than 0.5 on the relevant factor. Therefore, a total of 37 items were kept in the final version, under seven main factors as follows: "Intrinsic Interest" (II), alpha: .94 (six items), "Commitment to Work" (CW), alpha: .86 (four items), "Relating Ideas" (R), alpha: .92 (seven items), "Understanding" (U), alpha: .74 (three items), "Fear of Failure" (FF), alpha: .91 (three items), "Aim for Qualification" (AQ), alpha: .84 (four items), "Minimizing Scope of Study" (MSS), alpha: .84 (five items), and "Memorization" (MEMO), alpha: .87 (five items), with an overall alpha coefficient of .90.

In addition, the total variance explained is 72.51%, and it was also proved that internal consistency was achieved.

Intrinsic Interest (II), alpha: .94; Commitment for Work (CW), alpha: .86; Relating Ideas (R), alpha: .92; Understanding (U), alpha: .74; Fear of Failure (FF), alpha: .91; Aim for Qualification (AQ), alpha: .84; Minimizing Scope of Study (MSS), alpha: .84; Memorization (MEMO), alpha: .87; Overall alpha: .90; Total variance explained: 72.51%.

Table 2 presents the mean scores and the standard deviations of students' use of technology for each item of students' use technology. According to Table 2, all the mean scores were over 4 points on the 5-point scale except for recommendation. The highest score is usefulness (mean = 4.60, SD = .57) and the lowest is recommendation (mean = 3.88, SD = .90). This result indicates that students (N = 186) most care about usefulness when they use technology to learn English.

Table 1. Rotated factor loadings, descriptions and Cronbach's alpha values for the EFL learners' approaches to learning

Item	Factor loading	Mean	S.D.	Range
II1	.72	3.87	.84	1.0–5.0
II2	.75			
II3	.79			
II4	.81			
II5	.84			
II6	.82			
CW1	.60	3.48	.94	1.0–5.0
CW2	.72			
CW3	.66			
CW4	.55			
R1	.71	3.87	.78	1.0–5.0
R2	.81			
R3	.87			
R4	.85			
R5	.74			
R6	.74			
R7	.57			
U1	.79	3.58	.92	1.0–5.0
U2	.70			
U3	.69			
FF1	.88	2.56	1.16	1.0–5.0
FF2	.87			
FF3	.87			
AQ1	.70	3.98	.93	1.0–5.0
AQ2	.86			
AQ3	.62			
AQ4	.77			
MSS1	.78	2.69	1.1	1.0–5.0
MSS2	.80			
MSS3	.82			
MSS4	.69			
MSS5	.69			
MEMO1	.71	2.65	1.10	1.0–5.0
MEMO2	.88			
MEMO3	.83			
MEMO4	.74			
MEMO5	.76			

In order to explore the relationships between EFL learners' usage of technology and their approaches to learning English, the Pearson's correlation coefficients were calculated and are listed in Table 3. It was found that "price," "ease of use,"

Table 2. Students' use technology survey (N = 186)

Factor	Mean	S.D.	Range
Price	4.26	.75	1.0–5.0
Ease of use	4.26	.72	1.0–5.0
Recommendation	3.88	.90	1.0–5.0
Content	4.33	.73	2.0–5.0
Usefulness	4.60	.57	3.0–5.0

Table 3. The correlations between the scales of the students' approach to learning and using technology survey (n = 186)

	Price	Ease of use	Recommendation	Content	Usefulness
Intrinsic interest	.06	.08	.15*	.20**	.22**
Commitment to work	.07	.22**	.17*	.19	.19**
Relating ideas	.15*	.13	.21**	.16*	.22**
Understanding	.06	.14	.16*	.12	−.01
Fear of failure	.09	.22**	.11	.10	.12
Aim for qualification	.16*	.12	.28**	.21**	.19**
Minimizing scope of study	.12	.05	.05	.08	−.02
Memorization	.15*	.03	.16*	.11	−.04

Notes: *$p < .05$; **$p < .01$

"recommendation," "content," and "usefulness" were correlated to their approaches to learning English.

In other words, the item of "price" was related to relating ideas ($r = 0.14$, $p < .05$) and aiming for qualification ($r = 0.16$, $p < .05$); the item of "ease of use" was related to commitment to work ($r = 0.22$, $p < .01$) and fear of failure ($r = 0.22$, $p < .01$); the item of "recommendation" was related to intrinsic interest ($r = 0.15$, $p < .05$), commitment to work ($r = 0.17$, $p < .05$), relating ideas ($r = 0.21$, $p < .01$), aim for qualification ($r = 0.28$, $p < .05$), and memorization ($r = 0.16$, $p < .05$); the item of "content" was related to intrinsic interest ($r = 0.20$, $p < .01$), relating ideas ($r = 0.16$, $p < .05$), and aim for qualification ($r = 0.21$, $p < .01$); the item of "usefulness" was related to intrinsic interest ($r = 0.22$, $p < .01$), relating ideas ($r = 0.22$, $p < .01$), and aim for qualification ($r = 0.19$, $p < .01$).

This result indicated that the three factors of "recommendation," "content," and "usefulness" seemed to be the more important factors related to students' approaches to learning English.

Stepwise regression analyses were used to examine the predictions among EFL learners' usage of technology and their approaches to learning English. Table 4 presents the stepwise regression model of predicting EFL learners' approaches to learning English. The results indicated that EFL learners' "Recommendation" of technology usage significantly predicted their approaches to learning English such as Relating ideas ($\beta = .17$, $T = 2.25$, $p < .05$), Understanding ($\beta = .16$, $T = 2.14$, $p < .05$), Aim for qualification (β = .28, T = 4.02, $p < .001$), and Memorization (β = .16, T = 2.22, $p < .05$). In addition, EFL learners' "Usefulness" of technology usage significantly predicted their approaches to learning English such as Intrinsic Interest (β = .22, T = 3.02, $p < .01$) and Relating ideas (β = .18, T = 2.41, $p < .05$). Furthermore, EFL learners' "Ease of use" of technology usage significantly predicted their approaches to learning English such as Commitment to Work (β = .22, T = 3.09, $p < .01$) and Fear of Failure (β = .22, T = 3.03, $p < .01$).

Table 4. Stepwise regression model of predicting students' approaches to learning English (n = 186)

Approaches to learning English	Predictor	B	S.E.	Beta	T	R
Intrinsic interest						.22
	Constant	2.60	.43		6.12***	
	Usefulness	.28	.09	.22	3.02**	
Commitment to work						.22
	Constant	2.43	.34		7.08***	
	Ease of use	.25	.08	.22	3.09**	
Relating ideas						.27
	Constant	2.53	.38		6.66***	
	Usefulness	.20	.08	.18	2.41*	
	Recommendation	.12	.05	.17	2.25*	
Understanding						.16
	Constant	3.08	.24		12.87***	
	Recommendation	.13	.06	.16	2.14*	
Fear of failure						.22
	Constant	1.19	.46		2.60*	
	Ease of use	.32	.11	.22	3.03**	
Aim for qualification						.28
	Constant	3.05	.24		12.81***	
	Recommendation	.24	.06	.28	4.02***	
Minimizing scope of study	None					
Memorization						.16
	Constant	2.03	.29		7.10***	
	Recommendation	.16	.07	.16	2.22*	

Notes: *$p < .05$, **$p < .01$, ***$p < .001$

Firstly, both internal interest ("Relating ideas" and "Understanding") and external interest ("Aim for qualification" and "Memorization") are shown in the importance of "Recommendation." Secondly, "Usefulness" was associated with "Intrinsic Interest" and "Relating Ideas." Thirdly, the factor "ease of use" was associated with "Commitment to Work" and "Fear of Failure." Therefore, the factor "Recommendation" seemed to play the most important role in learning English by using technology.

5 Conclusion

In this study, we found two phenomena. The first is about the learners' usage of technology for learning English. The most important factor was "recommendation"; if many peers recommended using a certain technology to get good learning results, it would arouse learners' interest and make them download it as a learning tool. On the other hand, the EFL learners will consider the factors of "ease of use" and "usefulness" of technology for learning. This finding is consistent with the previous studies [2].

The second phenomenon was to understand the relationship between EFL learners' approaches to learning and technology. Approaches to learning can be divided into surface motivation and deep motivation [12]. We can see that, regardless of whether they had surface or deep motivation, learners believed that "recommendation" associated with them. Good learning tools were recommended by people who had used them. It is an important factor for learning a language. In addition, for deeper motivation, it is necessary to maintain interest in learning language for a long time. Therefore, the approach to learning will be more focused on "usefulness" because language learning is not only for communication, but also for maintaining interest of learning.

Therefore, EFL learners have a high degree of acceptance of learning English by using technology. At the same time, they consider that technology-assisted learning is a viable learning method and can be selected according to their own learning needs. It is expected that more samples will be available in the future to understand whether using technology would improve their language skills.

References

1. Hussein, G.: A content analysis evaluation of The Journal of Teaching English with Technology (TEwT) between the years of 2008 & 2013. Procedia Soc. Behav. Sci. **191**, 31–36 (2015)
2. Wu, B., Chen, X.: Continuance intention to use MOOCs: integrating the technology acceptance model (TAM) and task technology fit (TTF) model. Comput. Hum. Behav. **67**, 221–232 (2017)
3. Davis, F.D.: Perceived usefulness, perceived ease of use, and user acceptance of information technology. MIS Q. **13**, 319–340 (1989)
4. Legris, P., Ingham, J., Collerette, P.: Why do people use information technology? A critical review of the technology acceptance model. Inf. Manag. **40**(3), 191–204 (2003)
5. Biggs, J.B., Kember, D., Leung, D.Y.P.: The revised two-factor study process questionnaire: R-SPQ-2F. Br. J. Educ. Psychol. **71**, 133–149 (2001)
6. Entwistle, N., McCune, V., Walker, P.: Conceptions, styles, and approaches within higher education: analytical abstractions and everyday experience. In: Sternberg, R.J., Zhang, L.-F. (eds.) Perspectives on Cognitive, Learning and Thinking Styles, pp. 103–136. Lawrence Erlbaum Associates, Mahwah (2001)
7. Trigwell, K., Prosser, M.: Improving the quality of student learning: the influence of learning context and student approaches to learning on learning outcomes. High. Educ. **22**, 251–266 (1991)

8. Baeten, M., Kyndt, E., Struyven, K., Dochy, F.: Using student-centered learning environments to stimulate deep approaches to learning: factors encouraging or discouraging their effectiveness. Educ. Res. Rev. **5**(3), 243–260 (2010)
9. Entwistle, N., McCune, V.: The conceptual bases of study strategy inventories. Educ. Psychol. Rev. **16**(4), 325–345 (2004)
10. Huang, W.L., Liang, J.C., Tsai, C.C.: Exploring the relationship between university students' conceptions of and approaches to learning mass communication in Taiwan. Asia Pac. Educ. Res. **27**(1), 43–54 (2018)
11. Jeng, Y.L., Wu, T.T., Huang, Y.M., Tan, Q., Yang, S.J.: The add-on impact of mobile applications in learning strategies: a review study. Educ. Technol. Soc. **13**(3), 3–11 (2010)
12. Kember, D., Biggs, J., Leung, D.Y.: Examining the multidimensionality of approaches to learning through the development of a revised version of the Learning Process Questionnaire. Br. J. Educ. Psychol. **74**(2), 261–279 (2004)

Application and Design of Innovative Learning Software

Exploration of Learning Effectiveness and Cognitive Load on Interactive and Non-interactive E-book Introducing into Nursing Education

Lei Chang[1], Ting-Ting Wu[1(✉)], and Chen-Ying Su[2]

[1] Graduate School of Technological and Vocational Education, National Yunlin University of Science and Technology, Yunlin 64002, Taiwan, R.O.C.
zegxiazhang@gmail.com, danytingting@gmail.com
[2] Department of Nursing, National Quemoy University, Kinmen 892, Taiwan, R.O.C.
cysu1209@gmail.com

Abstract. The purpose of this study is to investigate the use of e-books, as well as interactive and non-interactive elements, as a way to present learning content, and the effect of application of e-books to nursing education on learning effectiveness and cognitive load of students in Department of Nursing. This study used quasi-experiment research method to conduct an experiment on two classes of different students receiving instruction from the same teacher and using the same teaching materials. The research results showed that e-books had a significant effect on the improvement of learning effectiveness in both classes. Compared with students using non-interactive e-books, the improvement of learning effectiveness of students using interactive e-books was more significant. In terms of cognitive load, cognitive load was gradually decreased during learning process. However, a certain extent of cognitive load still existed.

Keywords: Nursing education · E-books · Cognitive load

1 Introduction

The progress of information technologies and prosperous development of internet technology have contributed to the transformation and diversification of learning methods, as well as enriched learning content. In recent years, with the updates of devices and technologies of e-learning models, e-learning has advanced to mobile learning, which has advanced to ubiquitous Learning (u-learning) through the progresses and advances of internet technologies. Due to these changes, learners also have to engage in various types of learning by learning different technologies and devices. Brown, Collins, and Duguid [1] indicated that the construction of knowledge is dependent upon the interactions between environments and learners. Therefore, students' construction of knowledge may be limited if they only engage in learning in a single situation.

T.-T. Wu et al. (Eds.): ICITL 2018, LNCS 11003, pp. 423–432, 2018.
https://doi.org/10.1007/978-3-319-99737-7_45

Although e-learning has been rapidly developed, the main teaching method of current nursing education is still traditional classroom instruction. However, in recent years, increasing information technologies have been integrated with medical and nursing education. The introduction and integration of information technologies can create innovative applications of resources and services of medical and nursing education for medical and nursing personnel [2]. The literature review performed in recent years showed that the scholars in various countries around the world have constantly studied the introduction of information technologies into nursing education. Many of these studies analyzed students' preference for and acceptance of information technologies. In terms of the research results, the attitude towards the introduction of information technologies into nursing education of most of the students in nursing-related departments is aggressive and positive. Besides, these students are highly interested in the application of information technologies to teaching and are fond of witnessing the introduction of more similar technologies into other courses in the future. This trend reveals that the introduction of mobile technologies into nursing education is under development and is extremely promising [3–5].

The rise of e-books enables many books to be presented in a digital manner. Shelbume [6] mentioned that e-books possess many characteristics that are absent in many traditional books, including search function, individualization, real-time updates, multiple presentations, and portability. In addition to text and images, e-books are also able to present the content using multimedia to increase learners' interest in book content and even add interactive elements to enhance memory and learning effect.

The studies concerning the introduction of information technologies into education conducted in recent years mainly performed a comparison between e-teaching materials and traditional teaching, and fewer of them performed a comparison on the effect and difference of the use of different presentation methods of the same e-teaching materials on learners. Therefore, this study used e-books as the media of information technologies, and attempted to introduce e-books of different levels of interaction into nursing education and observe the effect of e-books of different levels of interaction on students' learning effectiveness and cognitive load after their learning.

2 Literature Review

2.1 E-Book Integrate Education

The rise of e-books has redefined people's past concept of "books." In educational circles, e-books have also been gradually used in schools of all levels. According to the studies by domestic and foreign scholars, the integration of multimedia and video and audio presentation of e-textbooks can better achieve high interactivity, which can effectively improve students' learning effectiveness and enable them to more concentrate on course learning to increase their problem-solving ability. The researcher investigated the papers in foreign journals [7, 8], and summarized the main characteristics and advantages of e-textbooks, including affordability, proximity, functionality, individuality, initiative, diversity, interactivity, editability, and timeliness. E-textbooks have a lot of advantages. Based on the above, e-books possess many characteristics that are suitable to be used as a learning tool. The studies where e-books were used as a device conducted in recent years [9, 10] have proved that e-books have a positive effect on learning effectiveness.

2.2 Multimedia Introduced in Nursing Education

In recent years, an increasing number of studies associated with the introduction of multimedia into nursing education have been conducted. The studies conducted in recent years have also gradually integrated multimedia-combined technological tools with the medical systems of nursing.

Relevant studies can be divided into two major types. Type 1 is pilot studies where the research dimensions are interest, perception, preference, etc. This type of studies mainly investigates the ideas about and opinions on such a teaching material or device of students and teachers during the use of multimedia technologies to engage in learning and teaching. The review on the studies conducted in recent years discovered that most of the studies used smart phones and tablet PCs as the study device. Because these two products are highly popular, researchers did not have to additionally provide the device or teach users to use them [11, 12]. The results of relevant studies showed that students' acceptance of and preference for multimedia technologies are positive, they show strong interest in related teaching, and they are fond of seeing more similar teaching materials being introduced into other courses in the future. Therefore, the studies in this field are still at development stage and are promising.

Type 2 is the studies used the effect of teaching designed by multimedia education on students' learning effectiveness. Because many subjects and themes are involved in nursing education, it is less likely to categorize such studies. Besides, the teaching strategies and methods using multimedia teaching are also extremely diversified, including the use of existing online media and community websites to provide students with discussions and interactions [4], the use of videos as a review method [3], and to introduce problem-based learning into courses [5], etc. These courses can be divided into theoretical courses and practical courses. The introduction of mobile technologies into theoretical courses can increase students' learning interest and provide them with teaching media other than textbook, which helps students get rid of the learning method of single environment and improve their learning in different learning environments. In theoretical courses, teachers use a mobile device to enable students to engage in learning through the designed teaching materials. In these courses, pre- and post-tests of and questionnaire survey, etc. of teaching intervention are mainly used to evaluate learning effectiveness. Besides, qualitative interviews are performed after the courses to understand students' attitude towards and opinions on the introduction of mobile technologies into courses. In the courses of clinical internship, system simulation is mainly used to overcome the limitations of insufficient equipment and uneven use in school laboratories to enable every student to engage in clinical operation through system simulation. Because system simulation still cannot replace clinical internship courses, it can only be used as an assistant teaching method.

In terms of research results, the learning effectiveness of most of the experimental group was significantly improved. Learners' attitude towards the introduction of mobile technologies into teaching was aggressive and positive, and they looked forward to participating in similar courses in the future. As for research subjects, most of the studies in various countries around the world enrolled nursing students as the subjects, and the major difference was educational level: junior college vs. university.

2.3 Cognitive Load

Pass and Vanmerrienboer [13] suggested that the so-called cognitive load refers to the load imposed on cognitive system of learners during their execution of a specific task, namely, the mental and cognitive resources spent by learners. They also indicated that the sources of cognitive load include learning task, learning environment, and interaction among learners. Relevant factors used to evaluate cognitive load include mental load, mental effort, and work effectiveness. Mental load refers to the level of load imposed on learners by the demand of learning task itself; mental effort refers to the level of effort required to be paid by learners to complete a learning task; work effectiveness refers to the overall evaluation or effect of a task completed by learners. According to cognitive load theory, there are 3 types of cognitive load in learning, including intrinsic cognitive load, extraneous cognitive load, and germane cognitive load, of which the sources and effects are different. The former two will have a negative effect on students and increase students' learning burden. The latter one will help students engage in learning and improve their concentration. This experiment intends to investigate whether the addition of interactive elements to teaching materials to strengthen learners' impression and connection with teaching materials during interactions has a positive effect on learners' learning effectiveness.

3 Methodology

3.1 Participants

This study enrolled the juniors in Department of Nursing of a certain university in Taiwan as the experiment subjects for a total of 2 academic years. The students were divided into the experimental group and control group. This study introduced e-book teaching material into the obligatory course "Community Health and Nursing" for juniors in the Department. The instructor was a senior associate professor in Department of Nursing. The course is also an obligatory course in national examination of nurses in Taiwan. The teaching units in this study included a total of 7 sections, and 3 classes per week and 50 min per class were given. The experiment lasted for 9 weeks. There were a total of 32 subjects in the control group and 35 subjects in the experimental group. The teaching materials used by the 2 groups were the same, and the difference was the interaction presentation method of e-book teaching materials.

3.2 Research Process

At week 1 of the experiment, the researcher performed a pretest on the subjects in the university. 1 tablet PC with inbuilt e-book reading App and course e-book to be used in the experiment was distributed to all of the subjects. The experimental group used the interactive e-book to receive teaching, while the control group used general e-book to receive teaching. The difference was the presentation method. Interactive e-book provided users with interface interaction functions. From week 2 to week 8, this study conducted the experiment where the e-book was introduced into nursing education. The instructor used a wireless projector to project the tablet content on the screen in a real-time manner, and used the note system of e-book to mark the key points and provide reminders. At week 9, this study performed a post-test. The research flowchart is as shown in Fig. 1:

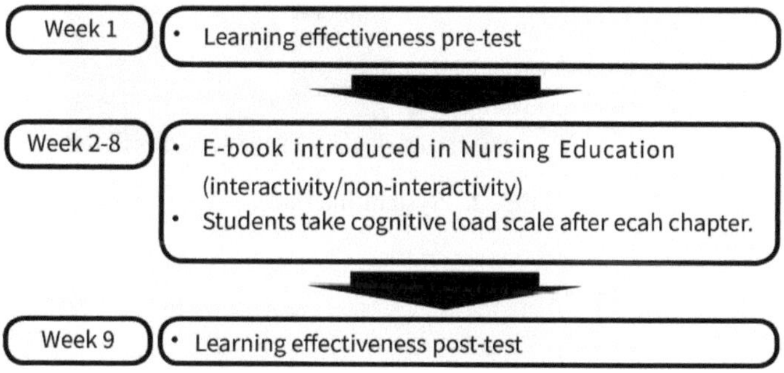

Fig. 1. Experiment procedure.

The e-book software used in this study was the product of HAMASTAR Technology: SimMagic eBook interactive e-book editing software. Raw materials, such as PDF and PPT, can be imported into the editing software through simple steps, and a variety of multimedia components, including images, pictures, and text, can be integrated.

3.3 System Introduction

The e-book used in the course in this study included a total of 7 chapters and was compiled using the contents and course PPT files of Community Health and Nursing newly edited by Yong-da Books.

The practice questions of a chapter were provided at the end of each chapter for the students to practice. The system interface is shown in Fig. 2. The differences between interactive and non-interactive e-books were text masks, scratch cards, cloze questions, matching questions, etc. The objective of e-books is to increased students' impression of focuses to improve learning effectiveness. The comparison diagram between interactive and non-interactive interfaces is shown in Fig. 3.

3.4 Evaluation Tools

Learning Effectiveness Test. The researcher requested the instructor to formulate the questions of the learning effectiveness test. The scope was chapters 1 to 7 involved in

Fig. 2. System interface.

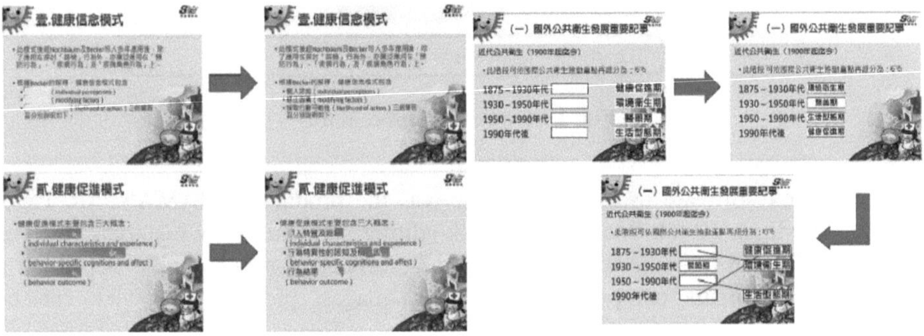

Fig. 3. Text masks, scratch cards and matching questions.

this study. Because the subjects had taken nursing-related courses before this course, they possessed the prior knowledge to a certain extent. The question type was multiple choice questions, and the test included a total of 40 questions. Google Forms was used to enable the students to answer the questions and give a score through tablet PC. The questions of the same level of difficulty were included in the post-test of learning effectiveness, which was performed at midterm examination week.

Cognitive Load Scale. The researcher referred to the dimensions of cognitive load summarized by Paas, Vanmerrienboer, and Adam [14] to develop the E-book Cognitive Load Scale used in this study. The scale included a total of 4 items, aiming to measure students' mental load and mental effort. Item 2 was a reverse coded item that could be used to screen valid scales. A 5-point Likert scale was applied to this scale for scoring. This experiment used Google Forms to enable students to provide feedbacks. Both the web link and QR code were provided on the last page of each chapter of e-book to enable students to immediately answer questions upon termination of learning.

4 Results and Findings

After the experiment of introduction of e-book into nursing education was completed, this study performed the post-test on the learners to evaluate the learning effectiveness, evaluate the cognitive load after the termination of each unit, and collect the data for statistical analysis.

4.1 Learning Effectiveness Test

In terms of learning effectiveness, this study performed an independent sample t test on the pre-test of two groups of students. The statistical results are shown in Table 1:

Table 1. Independent sample t-test for learning effectiveness pre-test.

	M(SD)		df	t	*p*	d
	E-Group (*N* = 35)	C-Group (*N* = 32)				
Pre-test	60.36(8.51)	60.23(9.11)	65	.057	.96	0.015

Note. E-Group = Experimental group; C-Group = Control group

As shown in Table, the results showed that there was no significant difference in performance between the two groups of students before the experiment.

After proving that there was no significant difference in pre-class score between two groups of students, this study then performed a dependent sample t test to analyze the learning effectiveness of the two groups in the pre-test and post-test. The test results are shown in Table 2:

Table 2. Dependent sample t-test for learning effectiveness pre-test and post-test.

	M(SD)		df	t	*p*	d
	Pre-test	Post-test				
E-Group (N = 35)	60.36(8.51)	84.57(7.15)	34	−12.94	$.000^{***}$	3.21
C-Group (N = 32)	60.23(9.11)	79.84(8.96)	31	−14.31	$.000^{***}$	2.17

$^{*}p < .05$ $^{***}p < .001$

The dependent sample t test results in the Table showed that there were significant differences in both the pre-test and post-test of learning effectiveness between the experimental group and control group. Experimental group was a significant difference between pre-test score and post-test score of students in the experimental group. There was a significant difference between pre-test score and post-test score of students in the control group. Therefore, the introduction of e-book into nursing education had a significant effect on learning effectiveness of students in Department of Nursing. After proving that the use of e-book had a significant effect on students' learning effectiveness, this study then continued to investigate whether there was any difference in learning effectiveness after students received the teaching of interactive and non-interactive e-books. This study performed an independent sample t test on the post-test scores of the two groups. The statistical results are shown in Table 3.

Table 3. Independent sample t-test for learning effectiveness post-test.

	M(SD)		df	t	*p*	d
	E-Group ($N = 35$)	C-Group ($N = 32$)				
Post-test	85.57(7.15)	79.84(8.96)	65	2.91	.005**	0.73

$^{*}p < .05$ $^{***}p < .001$

As shown in the table, the independent sample t test on the post-test of learning effectiveness of the experimental group and control group showed that there was a significant difference between two groups of students. There was a significant difference between post-class score of the students in the experimental group and pre-class score of students in the control group, suggesting that although both groups received the same teaching of e-book, interactive e-book more significantly improved students' learning effectiveness than non-interactive e-book did. Moreover, the standard deviation of score of students in the experimental group was lower than that of those in the control group, suggesting that after the teaching of course of interactive e-book, the students' difference in scores was decreased and the gap in learning performance was reduced.

4.2 Cognitive Load Scale

In terms of cognitive load scale, the learners were requested to complete the scale after the termination of each chapter of the course. As shown in Figs. 4 and 5, the scores were mainly between neutral and satisfied (3–4 points). Therefore, e-book teaching tool still created a certain extent of cognitive load to students. Moreover, the figures also showed that the cognitive load of the experimental group was gradually decreased over time. Although the cognitive load of the control group was also gradually decreased, the change in the experimental group was still more significant.

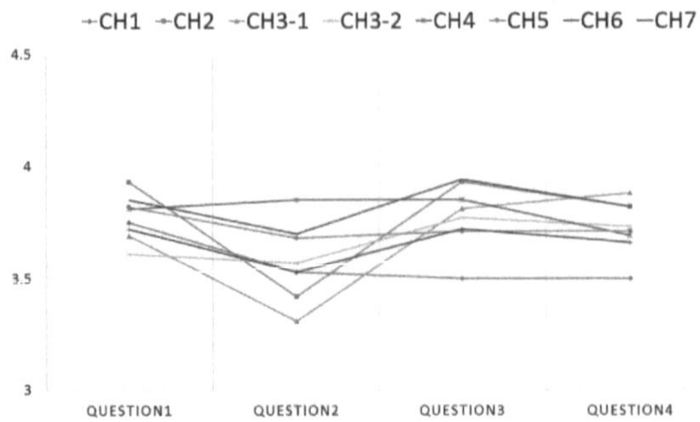

Fig. 4. Experimental group cognitive load line chart.

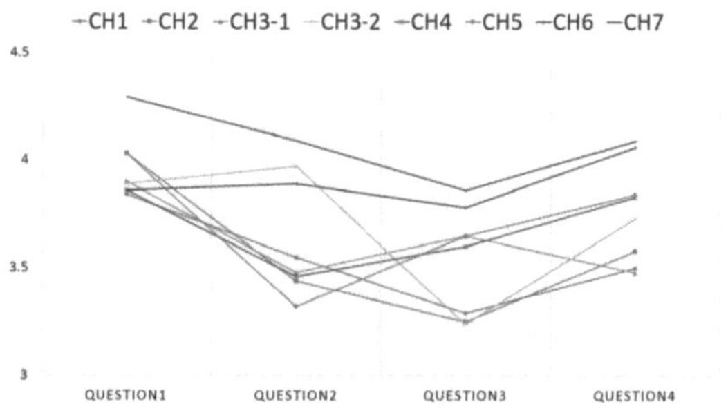

Fig. 5. Control group cognitive load chapters line chart.

The difference in standard deviation between the two groups could also be investigated. The standard deviation of the experimental group was slightly higher than that of the control group, suggesting that although, on average, the use of interactive e-book to engage in teaching could decrease students' cognitive load, cognitive load could not be decreased in all the students. There were still students perceiving the burden of this learning method. Although the cognitive load of the control group was slightly higher than that of the experimental group, the standard deviation deceased over time, suggesting that the burden perceived by students was more consistent.

5 Conclusions

This study introduced e-book into nursing education, and investigated the effect of different presentation methods of e-book on learning effectiveness and cognitive load. The comprehensive observation on the overall experiment showed that after the teaching of e-book, the overall learning effectiveness of both the control group and experimental group significantly improved. Apparently, the use of e-book as a device for introducing multimedia teaching into nursing education was very effective. The addition of interactive elements also more significantly improved students' learning effectiveness than non-interactive e-book did. However, the teaching material still created cognitive load to a few learners. Future studies will continue to investigate the teaching material elements creating load to students and improve teaching materials according to the results. Hopefully, the learning achievement of learners can be more significantly improved. Hopefully, in the near future, there will be more opportunities to apply e-learning to the field of nursing education and more novel research results can be obtained.

Acknowledgments. This work was supported in part by the Ministry of Science and Technology (MOST), Taiwan, ROC, under Grant MOST 104-2511-S-224-003-MY3, and MOST 105-2628-S-224-001-MY3.

References

1. Brown, J.S., Collins, A., Duguid, P.: Situated cognition and the cultural of learning. Educ. Res. **18**(1), 32–42 (1989)
2. Demircelik, M.B., et al.: Effects of multimedia nursing education on disease-related depression and anxiety in patients staying in a coronary intensive care unit. Appl. Nurs. Res. **29**, 5–8 (2016)
3. Lee, N.J., Chae, S.M., Kim, H., Lee, J.H., Min, H.J., Park, D.E.: Mobile-based video learning outcomes in clinical nursing skill education: a randomized controlled trial. CIN Comput. Inform. Nurs. **34**(1), 8–16 (2016)
4. Wu, T.T.: The use of a mobile assistant learning system for health education based on project-based learning. CIN Comput. Inform. Nurs. **32**(10), 497–503 (2014)
5. Lin, Y.T., Lin, Y.C.: Effects of mental process integrated nursing training using mobile device on students' cognitive load, learning attitudes, acceptance, and achievements. Comput. Hum. Behav. **55**, 1213–1221 (2016)
6. Shelburne, W.A.: E-book usage in an academic library: user attitudes and behaviors. Libr. Collections Acquisitions Tech. Serv. **33**(2), 59–72 (2009)
7. Miles, M.L., Cooper, B.S.: Reimagining the textbook. Educ. Week **29**(11), 24–25 (2009)
8. Nicholas, D., Rowlands, I., Jamali, H.R.: E-textbook use, information seeking behavior and its impact: case study business and management. J. Inf. Sci. **36**(2), 263–280 (2010)
9. Miller, M.D., Valenti, M., Schettler, T., Tencza, B.: A multimedia e-Book - a story of health: filling a gap in environmental health literacy for health professionals. Environ. Health Perspect. **124**(8), A133–A136 (2016)
10. Sung, T.W., Wu, T.T.: Learning with e-books and project-based strategy in a community health nursing course. CIN-Comput. Inform. Nurs. **36**(3), 140–146 (2018)
11. Secco, M.L., Furlong, K.E., Doyle, G., Bailey, J.: Validation of the Mobile Information Software Evaluation Tool (MISET) with nursing students. J. Nurs. Educ. **55**(7), 385–390 (2016)
12. Zayim, N., Ozel, D.: Factors affecting nursing students' readiness and perceptions toward the use of mobile technologies for learning. CIN-Comput. Inform. Nurs. **33**(10), 456–464 (2015)
13. Paas, F., Vanmerrienboer, J.J.G.: Instructional-control of cognitive load in the training of complex cognitive tasks. Educ. Psychol. Rev. **6**(4), 351–371 (1994)
14. Paas, F., Vanmerrienboer, J.J.G., Adam, J.J.: Measurement of cognitive load in instructional-research. Percept. Mot. Skills **79**(1), 419–430 (1994)

Exploring Learning Behavior Transformation Patterns in an AR English System: A Study of Gender Differences

Yu-Che Huang[1(✉)], Ting-Ting Wu[2], Yueh-Ming Huang[1], and Frode Eika Sandnes[3]

[1] National Cheng Kung University, Tainan 701, Taiwan ROC
featherflew@gmail.com
[2] National Yunlin University, Yunlin 64002, Taiwan ROC
[3] Oslo Metropolitan University, Oslo, Norway

Abstract. The aim of this research is to explore learners' learning behavior differences in a customized augmented reality (AR) English learning system (CARELS) by analyzing the learners' behavioral history. The results show that male learners lost the scan directions of AR learning targets more often than female learners, while female learners learning in one AR target was more careful and detailed compared to male learners. One implication of these results is that researchers should consider the gender difference, and give adaptive feedback or teaching materials when designing this type of AR English learning system.

Keywords: Learning behavior · Augmented reality · English learning Lag sequential analysis

1 Introduction

Language is the most essential medium of interpersonal communication. In the era of globalization, English has become the most common language of international communication [1]. English is also the mainstream language of the world today [2], there is no doubt that English proficiency is an important communication skill. Taiwan is an EFL (English as Foreign Language) English learning environment. According to the education curriculum outline published by the Ministry of Education of Taiwan, children start taking formal English courses from 3rd grade [3]. However, in the traditional English teaching environments, teachers usually explain the static contents of the textbooks in a passive learning process [4]. This way of learning makes it hard for learners to effectively apply what they have learnt to real life, and this situation still needs to change. In recent studies many scholars have pointed out that it is important to change the teaching methods and strategies to increase the motivation and interest of learners to learn English [5, 6]. Moreover, it is crucial that different types of knowledge become meaningful and better connected to real life during the learning process [7]. In other words, the influences of learning scenarios are of vital importance for EFL learners [8]. According the Spatial Contiguity Principle and Temporal Contiguity

T.-T. Wu et al. (Eds.): ICITL 2018, LNCS 11003, pp. 433–442, 2018.
https://doi.org/10.1007/978-3-319-99737-7_46

Principle of 12 multimedia design principles proposed by Mayer [9] corresponding and associated information can be generated immediately besides the learning object. Augmented reality (AR) is a technology that combines virtual information with the real-world image [10]. This technology allows the learning process to better meet the principles proposed by Mayer [9].

2 Literature Review

2.1 AR Applied to Education

AR involves importing the images, objects, and scenes generated by computers to the real environment. Its purpose is to enhance the effect of perception. That is, the virtual objects are added to the real environment. This technology must have three characteristics: (a) combine the virtual and the real world, (b) be able to interact immediately, (c) be necessary in 3D space [10]. Milgram, Takemura, Utsumi, and Kishino [11] regarded real and virtual environments as a closed set as shown in Fig. 1. The left represents a purely real environment and the right represents a purely virtual environment. Virtual reality attempts to replace the real world, while augmented reality involves augmenting the virtual picture generated by computers into the real environment.

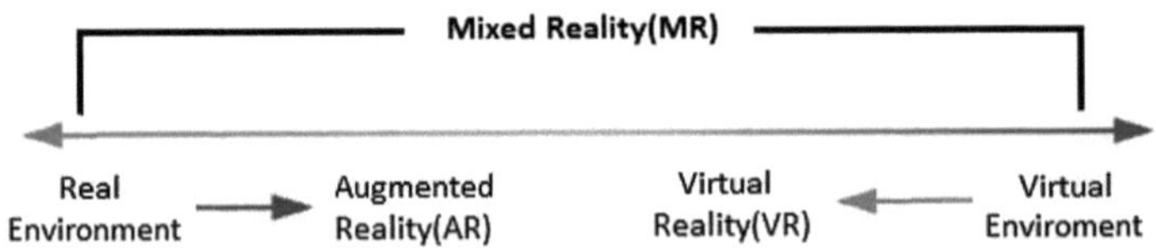

Fig. 1. The definition of AR proposed by Milgram et al. [11].

There are many applications of AR technology to language learning. For example, Hsieh and Lin designed an AR system for English vocabulary learning which had immersive learning outcomes. The experimental results showed that the learners were willing to use the system. Chang, Chen, Huang and Huang also built an AR game-based English vocabulary learning system. The above two English vocabulary learning systems are both based on AR technology, but the methods are different. The former used English vocabulary magic books so that learners could scan the learning objects in the books while the latter scanned the 3D learning objects directly to conduct learning. The advantage of the latter is that it can scan real objects in a real environment. It does not need extra teaching objects. However, the above teaching systems are all only for simple English words or vocabulary. The applications of related words or example sentences are lacking. In addition, it is inconvenient as additional objects are required. Therefore, we developed a customized English learning system based on AR technology. It is hoped that through the combination of the real situation and the virtual information, the learning motivation and effectiveness of learners can be enhanced.

2.2 The Influence of Human Factors in Learning

It has been pointed out that important human factors include: gender differences, prior knowledge and cognitive style [12]. The results of the experimental analysis show: female learners more often and easily lose the direction of the problem than male learners. Expert learners like to learn with flexible learning paths, while structured content is more conducive among novice learners. In addition, people with different cognitive styles like to use different search strategies [17]. Thus, the aim of this study was to explore learners' learning behavior through the lag sequential analysis (LSA) method, with particular focus on gender differences.

2.3 Learners' Behavioral Patterns

Cheng and Tsai [13] pointed out that analysis of learners' learning behaviors is considered as an effective method for understanding how students behave in detail. It ha been suggested to explore and analyze learning behaviors with different learning performance of learners, to understand what the key points cause the difference between high and low achieving learners [14–16]. Lag sequential analysis (LSA) can helps researchers to examine the statistical significance of a certain behavior being followed by another behavior, and a visualized diagram of behavioral patterns can be rendered using this method [17]. Behavior transform patterns refers to the sequential relationships between each types of coded topics. It can be determined by calculating the statistical significance of a behavioral sequence of a certain behavior followed instantly by another. Interestingly, there is much research that explore learners' behavioral patterns in different types of learning systems, but usually they focus on the relationship of learning effectiveness between control groups and experiment groups, which is only learning using different learning strategies. That is to say, most studies usually discusses the differences of learner's behavior on the learning strategies topic in kinds of learning system.

However, if educators only teach students and analyze their behaviors with some learning strategies but did not consider students' personal differences, it may not achieve the best teaching improvement. This study therefore explored learners' behavioral transform patterns with a particular focus on gender difference.

3 Research Method

3.1 Customized AR English Learning System

To start learning English, students need to scan the learning target which is a real object in the class or a picture in the English books content. When the identification is completed, the interactive learning in the real object and the virtual teaching material will be conducted. The operating procedures of the AR English learning system is shown in Fig. 2.

As stated above, after students scan the AR learning target, the system will show the main learning object material (a real object in the class) and related learning object material (a virtual object which is combining through AR) on the screen with shining

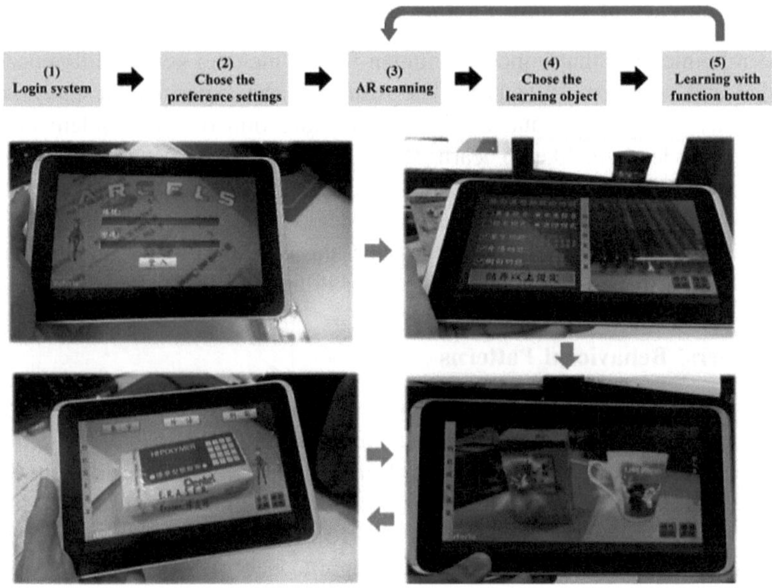

Fig. 2. The operating procedures of the AR English learning system.

effects. Then, students can click the object they want to learn, and the word, phrase or sentence function button will appear on the top center of the screen, the process of operation as shown in Fig. 3.

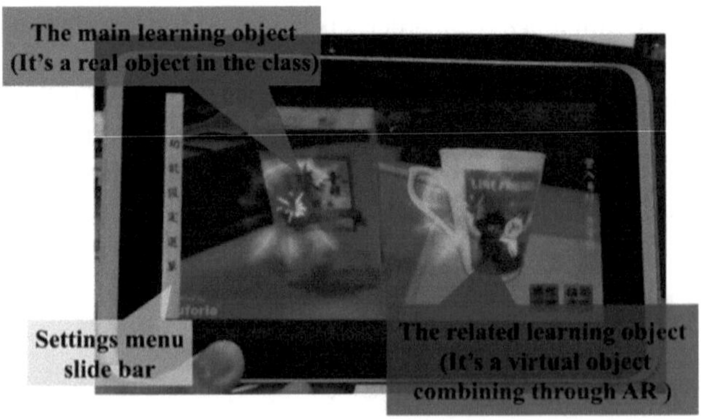

Fig. 3. Learning object selection.

When learners click the "word" button, the system will first split the word into letters and read out each letter. Then, the word will be read out once. Next, the Chinese meaning will be explained using a Chinese voice. If learners click the "phrase" button, the teaching material of phrases will appear on the screen. The phrase will be read out loud using English and the Chinese meaning will be explained using Chinese.

In addition, the system gives simple phrases in the easy mode and give more difficult phrases in the advanced mode. Finally, while learners click the "sentence" button, the teaching material of sentences will appear on the screen. Then, the sentence will be read out using English and the Chinese meaning will be explained using Chinese voice. According the easy or advanced mode, the degree of difficulty of the sentence is also different. Such design is to meet the Modality Principle of 12 multimedia design principles proposed by Mayer [9]. The design allows the learners to use auditory and visual senses to receive a single message. This interface is shown in Fig. 4.

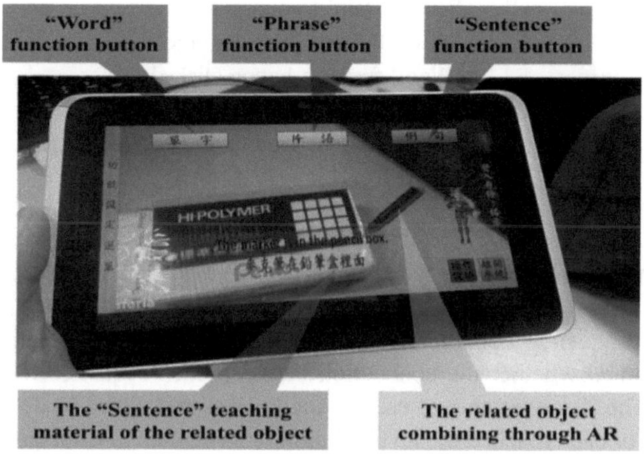

Fig. 4. The illustration of sentence function button.

3.2 Coding Scheme and Behavioral Data Collection

During the learning activity, the students' learning behaviors were all automatically coded and recorded in the system. The definition of the code, and examples are presented in Table 1.

3.3 Experiment Participants

There were a total of 4 classes with about 82 fifth grade elementary school pupils whose average age was 11 who participated in this study. Of these 44 were male and 38 were female. In addition, they were learning English as a Foreign Language (i.e., EFL) and studied English for three hours per week in central Taiwan. The four classes were taught by the same English teacher, a female teacher with more than ten years of elementary school teaching experience. All students had previous experience of using a Tablet Personal Computer and were familiar with using their fingers to draw on a tablet.

Table 1. The coding scheme and the definition for learning behaviors in the system.

Code	Behavior
M	Change learning mode
V	Change pronunciation voice
W	Open or close ‘Word’ function
P	Open or close ‘Phrase function
S	Open or close ‘Sentence’ function
H	Read explanation document
SH	Open or close ‘Explanation UI’
C1	Select ‘Main’ learning object
C2	Select ‘Related’ learning object
B1	‘Word’ function button clicked
B2	‘Phrase’ function button clicked
B3	‘Sentence’ function button clicked
X	Other

4 Experiment Results

Based on the frequency transition tables, we then conducted sequential analysis and further determined whether the connection between each sequence reached statistical significance. The Z-score value of each sequence was calculated to determine whether the continuity of each reached the level of significance and a Z-value greater than +1.96 indicates that a sequence reaches the level of significance ($p < .05$) [17, 18]. In that case, the codes obtained from the male students and female students yielded the adjusted residuals tables (see Tables 2 and 3).

Furthermore, we deduced the behavior-transfer diagrams between male and female students, which are presented in Fig. 5, respectively. This figure illustrates all sequences that have reached significance and the numerical values in the figures are the sequences’ Z-scores and the arrow indicates the direction of transfer for each sequence.

According to the behavioral transition diagram, we found male and female students demonstrated similar behavior sequences in the learning procedure, where → indicates a unidirectional sequence and ⇆ indicates bio-directionality. However, 4 unidirectional sequences were different for male students (blue line) and female students (pink line), i.e., SH → SH, S → SH, S → C1, S → X and C2 → B2. These behavior sequences demonstrate some interesting trends.

5 Discussion and Conclusions

In the students’ learning achievement, no significant difference be-tween the two genders were found. At first, by observing the behavior pattern associated graphs, we found that male students were more active than female students when searching for the next AR targets (S → C1, $Z = 9.92$). Then, according to the unidirectional sequences S → X ($Z = 3.73$), it was found that male students do something unrelated to learning

Table 2. The results of sequential analysis of behaviors with male users.

Z-score	M	V	W	P	S	H	SH	C1	C2	B1	B2	B3	X
M	−7.81	−7.81	124.56*	−7.8	−7.8	−2.37	−7.29	−8.56	−9.86	−21.29	−13.02	0	−4.5
V	124.56*	−7.81	−7.81	−7.8	−7.8	−2.37	−7.29	−8.56	−9.86	−21.29	−13.02	0	−4.5
W	−7.81	−7.81	−7.81	124.48*	−7.8	−2.37	−7.29	−8.43	−9.86	−21.29	−13.02	0	−4.5
P	−7.8	−7.8	−7.8	−7.8	124.56*	−2.37	−7.28	−8.55	−9.85	−21.28	−13.01	0	−4.49
S	−7.79	21.78*	−7.79	−7.78	−7.78	−2.36	51.92*	9.92*	7.87*	−21.17	-12.89	0	3.73*
H	−2.37	−2.37	−2.37	−2.37	−2.37	21.8*	31.38*	−2.6	−2.99	−6.46	−3.95	0	0.89
SH	−7.46	98.62*	−7.46	−7.45	−7.45	32.05*	2.34*	−7.76	−9.42	−20.34	−12.43	0	−4.04
C1	−8.57	−7.77	−8.57	−8.57	−8.57	−2.6	−5.73	8.69*	−5.8	27.62*	−4.14	0	−4.05
C2	−9.9	−9.78	−9.9	−9.89	−9.89	−3	−3.58	−1.36	22.85*	19.34*	−6.25	0	−2.55
B1	−21.28	−21.28	−21.28	−21.26	−21.26	−6.46	−8.1	14.51*	13.87*	53.66*	−12.35	0	−6.76
B2	−13.02	−13.02	−13.02	−13.01	−13.01	−3.95	−8.78	−2.24	−5.05	−16.83	78.6*	0	−3.66
B3	0	0	0	0	0	0	0	0	0	0	0	0	0
X	−4.2	−4.2	−4.2	−4.19	−4.19	−1.27	8.69	−1.03	0.19	−11.45	−7	0	78.85*

*$p < 0.05$.

Table 3. The results of sequential analysis of behaviors with female users.

Z-score	M	V	W	P	S	H	SH	C1	C2	B1	B2	B3	X
M	−6.23	−6.23	91.44*	−6.23	−6.22	−1.87	−5.76	−8.77	−9.07	−13.69	−7.97	0	−3.95
V	91.44*	−6.23	−6.23	−6.23	−6.22	−1.87	−5.76	−8.77	−9.07	−13.69	−7.97	0	−3.95
W	−6.23	−6.23	−6.23	91.44*	−6.22	−1.87	−5.76	−8.77	−9.07	−13.69	−7.97	0	−3.95
P	−6.23	−6.23	−6.23	−6.23	91.35*	−1.87	−5.57	−8.77	−9.07	−13.69	−7.97	0	−3.95
S	−6.21	16*	−6.21	−6.21	−6.21	−1.87	32.95*	1.07	8.09*	−13.66	−7.95	0	0.23
H	−1.87	−1.87	−1.87	−1.87	−1.87	13.87*	21.65*	−1.77	−2.3	−4.11	−2.39	0	0.56
SH	−5.92	72.02*	−5.92	−5.92	−5.91	24.06*	1.28	−8.34	−8.63	−13.02	−7.58	0	−3.18
C1	−8.79	−8.51	−8.79	−8.79	−8.78	−2.64	−6.66	2.5*	−9.15	36.36*	−0.81	0	−5.16
C2	9.13	−8.86	−9.13	−9.13	−9.12	−2.74	−3.57	−6.6	7.8*	25.38*	4.34*	0	−3.76
B1	−13.68	−13.58	−13.68	−13.68	−13.67	−4.11	−2.34	27.74*	20.5*	10.48*	−8.15	0	−2.07
B2	−7.96	−7.96	−7.96	−7.96	−7.96	−2.39	−1.79	0.02	1.77	−11.77	48.96*	0	0.6
B3	0	0	0	0	0	0	0	0	0	0	0	0	0
X	−3.62	−3.62	−3.62	−3.62	−3.62	−1.09	3.11*	−1.23	0.5	−7.96	−4.63	0	54.93*

*$p < 0.05$.

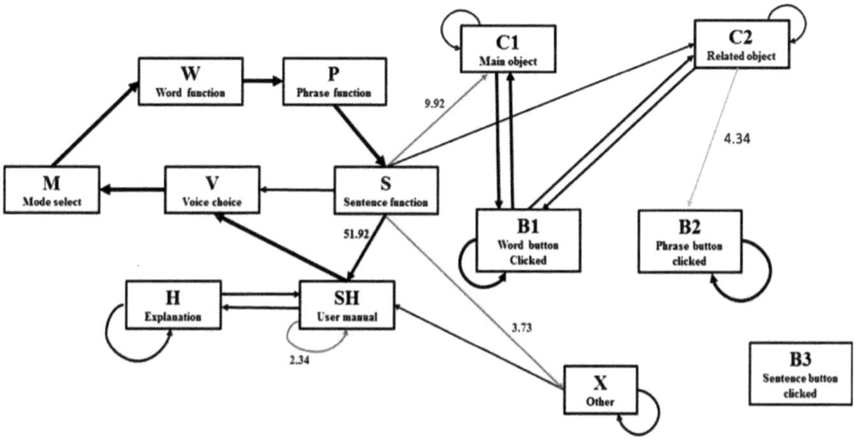

Fig. 5. The behavioral transition diagram between male and female students. (Color figure online)

activities more often than female students after opening or closing the "sentences function". In other words, male students stray from AR learning activity easier than female students. So, for the male students, it is suggested to add a correction method or function in this type of AR English learning system, to help learners return to the correct learning process during the learning activities. In addition, according to the unidirectional sequences C2 → B2 (Z = 4.34), we can observe that female students click the phrase button more often than male students after selecting related object actions. From this result, female students' concentration of attention is higher than males' in this kind of AR English learning activity, because female students were more likely to read extra related learning materials. Therefore, one could design some suggested learning tips for the male students in this type of AR English learning system to improve the level of detail in their learning process. It is also suggested to provide extra learning contents in the system for the female students.

Acknowledgements. This research is partially supported by the Ministry of Science and Technology, Taiwan, R.O.C. under Grant no. MOST 106-2511-S-006-006-MY3 and MOST 106-2511-S-006-001-MY3.

References

1. Spolsky, B., Shohamy, E.G.: The languages of Israel: Policy, Ideology, and Practice, vol. 17. Multilingual Matters (1999)
2. Smith, R.: Global English: gift or curse? English Today **21**(2), 56–62 (2005)
3. Hwang, G.J., Wang, S.-Y.: Single loop or double loop learning: English vocabulary learning performance and behavior of students in situated computer games with different guiding strategies. Comput. Educ. **102**, 188–201 (2016)

4. Savignon, S.J.: In Second Language Acquisition/Foreign Language Learning, Nothing Is More Practical than a Good Theory. Issues Dev. Eng. Appl. Linguist. (IDEAL), **3**, 83–98 (1988)
5. Chang, C.C., et al.: The impact of college students' intrinsic and extrinsic motivation on continuance intention to use English mobile learning systems. Asia-Pacific Educ. Res. **22**(2), 181–192 (2013)
6. Jong, B.S., et al.: Using game-based cooperative learning to improve learning motivation: a study of online game use in an operating systems course. IEEE Trans. Educ. **56**(2), 183–190 (2013)
7. Knobelsdorf, Maria: The theory behind theory - computer science education research through the lenses of situated learning. In: Brodnik, Andrej, Vahrenhold, Jan (eds.) ISSEP 2015. LNCS, vol. 9378, pp. 12–21. Springer, Cham (2015). https://doi.org/10.1007/978-3-319-25396-1_2
8. Golonka, E.M., et al.: Technologies for foreign language learning: a review of technology types and their effectiveness. Comput. Assist. Lang. Learn. **27**(1), 70–105 (2014)
9. Mayer, R.E.: Multimedia Learning, in Psychology of Learning and Motivation, pp. 85–139. Elsevier (2002)
10. Azuma, R.T.: A survey of augmented reality. Presence Teleoperators Virtual Environ. **6**(4), 355–385 (1997)
11. Milgram, P., et al.: Augmented reality: a class of displays on the reality-virtuality continuum. In: Telemanipulator and Telepresence Technologies. International Society for Optics and Photonics (1995)
12. Bremner, S.: Language learning strategies and language proficiency: investigating the relationship in Hong Kong. Can. Modern Lang. Rev. **55**(4), 490–514 (1999)
13. Cheng, K.H., Tsai, C.C.: The interaction of child–parent shared reading with an augmented reality (AR) picture book and parents' conceptions of AR learning. Br. J. Edu. Technol. **47** (1), 203–222 (2016)
14. Hou, H.T.: Exploring the behavioral patterns of learners in an educational massively multiple online role-playing game (MMORPG). Comput. Educ. **58**(4), 1225–1233 (2012)
15. Hwang, G.J., et al.: Interaction of problem-based gaming and learning anxiety in language students' English listening performance and progressive behavioral patterns. Comput. Educ. **106**, 26–42 (2017)
16. Lai, C.L., Hwang, G.-J.: A spreadsheet-based visualized Mindtool for improving students' learning performance in identifying relationships between numerical variables. Interact. Learn. Environ. **23**(2), 230–249 (2015)
17. Bakeman, R., Gottman, J.M.: Observing Interaction: An Introduction to Sequential Analysis. Cambridge University Press (1997)
18. Bakeman, R., Quera, V.: Sequential Analysis and Observational Methods for the Behavioral Sciences. Cambridge University Press (2011)

Exploration of Computational Thinking Based on Bebras Performance in Webduino Programming by High School Students

Jian-Ming Chen[1], Ting-Ting Wu[1(✉)], and Frode Eika Sandnes[2]

[1] School of Technological and Vocational Education, National Yunlin University of Science and Technology, Yunlin 64002, Taiwan, R.O.C.
n10543007@yuntech.org.tw, danytingting@gmail.com
[2] Oslo Metropolitan University, Oslo, Norway
frodes@oslomet.no

Abstract. The 12-year Basic Education Curriculum Guidelines by the Ministry of Education in Taiwan includes learning performances related to computational thinking and programming languages in technology courses. The students will develop other important competence through programming. Learning a programming language should not only involve focus on writing the programs, but should also stimulate students' computational thinking competence and allow them to solve daily problems through information techniques. Situated learning emphasizes students' learning in real scenarios where knowledge is applied as the tool in these real situations. Without such scenarios, the tool has limited value. Likewise, computational thinking competence can be translated as effective problem-solving by the means of information technology. Hence, the thinking process involves analyzing the problems resulting in answers. In addition, the Bebras learning model is based on a concept of informatics which supports comprehension of information science phenomenon and development of computational thinking. This study explored the effects of computational thinking competence on the Bebras test performance. The study targeted senior high school students' who learned program design using a situated learning strategy.

The results confirm the importance of the situated learning strategy when cultivating students' computational thinking competence. Based on homogeneity of two groups of students, the experimental group's posttest score of computational thinking is higher than that of control group. The experimental group were exposed to a situated learning strategy and the control group was not. Significant difference between the two groups shows that the situated learning strategy reinforces computational thinking competence.

Keywords: Situated learning · Computational thinking · Bebras

1 Introduction

The year 2014 was the "Year of Code" in the UK. According to regulation of Department of Education of Britain, children must start learning programming language from five

T.-T. Wu et al. (Eds.): ICITL 2018, LNCS 11003, pp. 443–452, 2018.
https://doi.org/10.1007/978-3-319-99737-7_47

years of age. Besides, program design courses have been included as one of obligatory subjects in junior high schools and elementary schools. Implementation of the policy influences the future competitiveness of a country. In Taiwan, the 12-year Basic Education Curriculum Guidelines list computational thinking and programming languages as competences for technology courses. It is a signal that students should enhance other important abilities through programming. Learning programming languages does not simply refer to superficial writing of programs. The goal is to stimulate students' computational thinking allowing them to solve daily problems by the means of information techniques. By learning program design, young people can master new technology which is highly important in this digital era as they do more than simply interact with the new technology. Through technology, they express their creativity and thoughts to further develop computational thinking competences [1].

Computational thinking is a type of core structure of conceptual evaluation. Programming teaches students to write programs and accomplish tasks through program design instructional tools. At the beginning and the end of the course, students' computational thinking competence is examined [2]. Bebras is an international competition of informatics and computer literacy. In the second Bebras international conference in 2006, there was one brainstorming meeting which proposed different types of questions of tasks that can be applied in the competition. In the conference, more than 120 tasks were developed and around 90 of these were accepted and elaborated further [3]. The Bebras learning model is based on concept of informatics which supports comprehension of information science and development of computational thinking.

Situated learning can effectively lead to knowledge construction. Brown, Collins, and Duguid stated the definitions and importance of situated cognition and situated learning. Thus, situated learning is gradually valued. Knoweldge should be constructed in real activities and learning activities should be combined with culture. Students thus interact with scenarios and result in knowledge. Situated learning emphasizes students' learning in real scenarios. Knowledge is treated as a tool in real scenarios. Without scenarios, these tools have limited value [4]. Likewise, computational thinking competences implies the ability to effectively solve problems using information technology. Thus, the thinking process involves analysis of problems that result in solutions.

Hence, explored effects of computational thinking competences on the Bebras test performance by senior high school students' that learned program design using a situated learning strategy.

2 Literature Review

2.1 Computational Thinking

In 2011, Wing broadly elaborated that question and solution are not simply a matter of mathematical problems. Solution must be analyzed and proved. It can be real problems in daily life which are solved by large-scale complex software system. Therefore, computational thinking, logic thinking and system thinking overlap. Wing thus re-defined "computational thinking as reflection process to develop problem and solution and the method to present solution by message processing in problem-solving planning" [5].

Computational thinking resembles core objectives of basic education, reading, writing and arithmetic which should be included as one of core objectives required by computational thinking. In the field of computer science in the U.S. and the UK, computational thinking has been specifically listed as important core competences. Chen studied students' computational thinking competences through robot programming. Based on the computational thinking standard of the computer science teachers' association, he developed one computational thinking tool to evaluate grade 5 students. According to the above research, programming language instruction by robots leads to students' learning challenge and enhances their computational thinking competences [2]. In Leonard's study of robots and game design, the said researcher enhanced students' self-efficacy, STEM attitude and computational thinking competences. A study involving 124 secondary school students demonstrated that game design by robots significantly influenced students' computational thinking competences [6]. Chaudhary et al. explored the effects of LEGO robots on program design and computational thinking experience. They demonstrated that program design instruction reinforced students' comprehension of skill and knowledge and problem-solving [7]. Yindi analyzed cultivation of students' computational thinking competences though Visual Basic programming and realized that students' learning became more active and students were capable of solving real problems with professional knowledge [8]. Parmar implemented program design instruction in virtual environment to evaluate students' computational thinking competences. According to the findings, learning computer science concept and programming language in context of virtual environment can effectively trigger students' motivation and interest [9].

According to previous literature, computational thinking is not a type of programming language. It can be applied to explain and describe calculation, abstraction and information terms. Hemmendinger argued that the objective of computational thinking is to teach students to as economists, physicists and artists and realize how to solve, create and discover problems by arithmetic [10].

2.2 Situated Learning

The cultivation of situated learning has become more important in recent years. Professional talents should cooperate with each other and solve problems in different environments and situations [11, 12]. Lave and Wenger defined situated learning as follows: "direct observation in the field and learning of various operations in exchange and interaction" [13]. Situated learning was first proposed by Brown, Collins and Duguid in 1989. It is an instructional model developed upon theory of modern cognitive psychology. The basic assumption is to allow students to learn in real, or simulated, situations. They simulate real environment in the instruction of course to allow students to be engaged in instructional situations and learn more efficiently.

Stein defined four key factors of situated learning environments, namely Content: task and process which learners must execute; Scenario: situated and environmental clues which surround the learners and meaningful support in creative process;

Community: learners will create and negotiate the situations with them; and Participation: learners work together and with experts and in one social group, they solve problems related to daily life environments. Learning becomes a social process. It depends on interaction with others in the same situation. The interactions should be similar to those of a practical environment [14]. Chen and Lin applied situated learning of a digital game to instruction of Chinese poetry. Using Chinese poetry of the Tang Dynasty as an example, they developed animations to simulate poets' obstacles in writing and assisted with Chinese poetry learning of junior high school students in Taiwan [15]. According to the above research, situated learning positively influenced students' perception. In College of Education of University of Zaragoza, Bravo-Alvarez et al. applied situated learning in two obligatory Early Childhood Education subjects. According to the experiment, students were highly satisfied with the learning experience of situated learning and it enhanced students' judgement competences [16]. Lin et al. introduced situated learning in research on English drama education of 5th graders in elementary school. Interviews with teachers and analysis of in-class video recording showed that the instruction reinforced students' motivation to participate in group learning activities [17].

According to the previous literature, situated learning is an effective instructional tool for students to comprehend concepts in school. By situated learning, students recognize correlation and importance of course content and more actively participate in learning. More importantly, they apply knowledge in reality. Hence, computer science education should break through the past boundary on information technology use, emphasize content of computer science, strengthen students' comprehension of computer science content, cultivate their logic thinking and problem-solving competence, introduce learning in daily lives to trigger students' learning interest and satisfy basic living needs of the digital era.

2.3 Computational Thinking and Bebras

Bebras is an international competition of informatics and computer literacy. It was launched in Lithuania in 2003. Early planning of task construction and preparation of implementation of Bebras lasted for nearly one year. The first competition was in held in October 2004. Objective of this organization is to turn Bebras into one international competition. In May, 2005, Olympiad of informatics was held in Lithuania [18]. During the spring of 2006, Lithuania held two international Bebras conferences and founded the Bebras international organization committee [19]. The main purpose of the conference is to construct a series of questions for future Bebras competitions.

Students use computer and technology every day. Though the assistance of technology, some students further develop their problem-solving comprehension. However, when applying technology, students need thinking skills to solve daily problems. The best measure is to develop the computational thinking competences. Students' daily problem-solving competences is the most significant issue according to educators and decision makers [20, 21]. When teaching informatics and computer science literacy through problem solving, it is important to stimulate students' learning through interesting questions. Therefore, one should propose questions from by various fields of science and daily life. The most common questions of computer science are application of daily lives and general questions of history, language, art and even mathematics. It is extremely important to select questions that students can solve with the same opportunities using different operating systems or computers.

In the second international Bebras conference in 2006, a brainstorming meeting was held to propose ideas on different types of questions applied in the competition. More than 120 tasks were developed at the conference and around 90 of these were accepted and elaborated further. The issues are categorized below [3], including general logic thinking, information and communication technology in daily lives, real and technology problems, information comprehension, calculation and program design, basic mathematics of computer science, history, to mention a few.

According to previous literature, the Bebras learning model focuses on concept of informatics which supports comprehension of information science phenomenon and development of computational thinking. Therefore, this study cultivates students' computational thinking competence through situated learning regarding students' competence of technology, logic thinking and problem solving. Among others, students' computational thinking competence is evaluated through the Bebras questions.

3 Methodology

This study explored effects of computational thinking competences on Bebras test performance by senior high school students' who learned program design using a situated learning strategy.

3.1 Participants

The participants comprised second-year students who were in the Life technology course in one senior high school in Taiwan. These students had not yet been taught computational thinking. Hence, they were beginners in computational thinking. Two second-year classes were selected. The experimental group included 20 students and the control group included 19 students. There were a total of 39 students. Each student was given one computer and one Webduino instructional tool.

3.2 Procedure

The experiment lasted 10 weeks. There were 50 min in one session. Week 1 of the experiment included the international computational thinking competence pretest; Week 2 and 3 covered basic operation instruction of Webduino instructional tool and the purpose was to allow students to be familiar with operation of the Webduino instructional tool to successfully proceed with experimentation. Week 4 to 9 covered the Webduino instructional tool. The experimental group learned using a situated learning strategy, while the control group followed a traditional course. The experiment lasted for 6 weeks. During week 10 the international computational thinking competence posttest was conducted. After the course, the data was analyzed and documented (see Fig. 1).

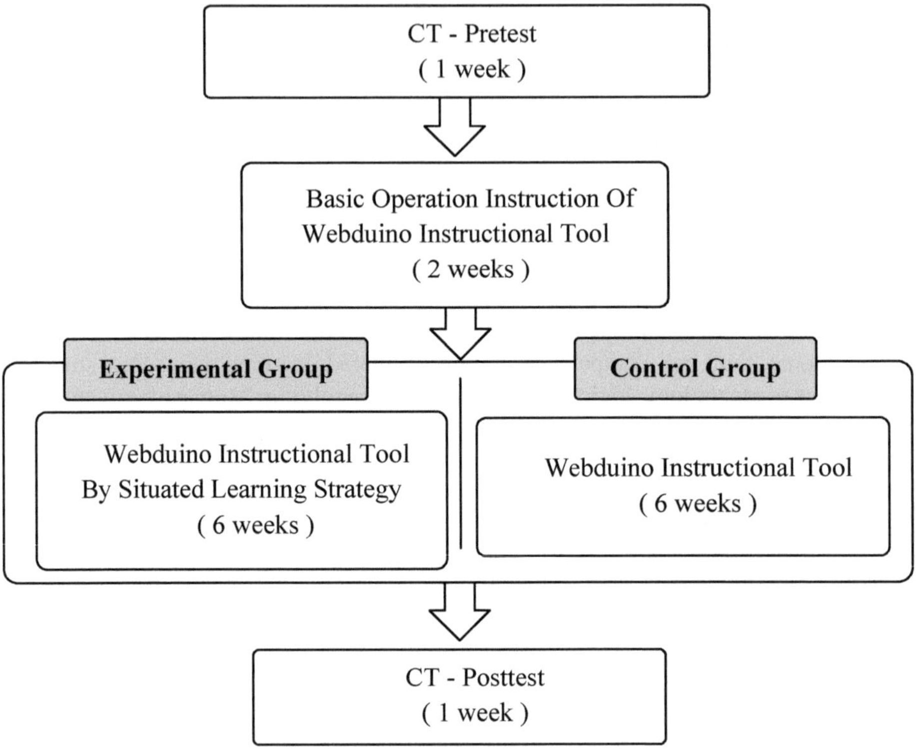

Fig. 1. Experimental procedure

3.3 Research Tool

3.3.1 Examination Questions of International on Informatics and Computational Thinking

To recognize students' computational thinking competence before the instructional experiment, this study conducted computational thinking competence tests to avoid effects of learners' prior knowledge. Pretest items were those of Senior (grade 11 and 12) group of the 2015 international computational thinking competence test; posttest items were those of Senior (grade 11 and 12) group of the 2016 international computational thinking competence test. The purpose of the test was to trigger students' learning interest in information science, reinforce students' competence to solve problems through information measures and avoid students' fear of information science. The test was scored by difficulty degree of items. Scores of correct answers were added and wrong answers were deducted. The omitted answers were not scored. To avoid negative scores, the starting point of the test was the total of deduction of items. There were totally

15 items. Five items were equally distributed at different degrees of difficulty. The starting point was 60, the lowest was 0 and the highest was 300, as shown in Table 1.

Table 1. The scoring rules of examination questions

Group	Difficulty						Questions	Starting score	Highest score
	C		B		A				
	Correct	InCorrect	Correct	InCorrect	Correct	InCorrect			
Senior	12	−3	16	−4	20	−5	15	60	300

3.3.2 Webduino Fly Microcontroller

This study adopted a Webduino Fly microcontroller unit developed by KING JIH of Taiwan in 2015. It was cloud extension board of Arduino UNO. By assistance of Webduino Fly, users could possess complete Webduino development function through Wifi. Without complicated hardware techniques, they could control Arduino compatible sensor modules. In addition, this study also adopted the Webduino electronic component package with a learning sheet. The Webduino electronic component package includes 13 electronic component modules and 7 sensors. The components and sensors makes the course more diverse and interesting.

3.3.3 Worksheet

This study expected that students can recognize important relationship between subjects and lives thorough computational thinking learning in the course. It constructs knowledge in real activities and combines activity and culture to allow learners to develop knowledge by interacting with scenarios. It emphasizes that learners make progress in situated context of life and use knowledge as a tool in the scenarios. Likewise, the Ministry of Education repetitively emphasizes that life related practice learning activities and course instruction should be combined with life situations with significance. The learning sheet of the experimental group included three parts. Part 1 scenario, Part 2 practice of examples and Part 3 extended questions; The control group had the same apart from Part 1 scenario.

4 Results

A one-way ANOVA were performed with IBM SPSS. According to the homogeneity test results shown in Table 2, two groups' *p* value of computational thinking competence is 0.638 and higher than the significance level of .05. The null hypothesis is thus accepted. It shows that the slope of two groups' regression lines are the same. In other words, the relationship between covariance (pretest score of computational thinking competence) and dependent variable (posttest score of computational thinking competence) are not different because of different processing levels of independent variable. It meets the hypothesis of homogeneity of in-group regression coefficient in analysis of covariance. Analysis of covariance can be further conducted.

Table 2. Two groups of regression coefficient homogeneity test summary

Item	F	df	*P*
Computational thinking skill	.225	38	.638

Table 3 shows the analysis of the covariance of two groups' computational thinking competence. According to the results, after eliminating the effect of covariance (pretest score of computational thinking competence) on the dependent variable (posttest score of computational thinking competence), it shows that experimental effect of two groups' learning of independent variable (experimental group and control group) on total score of computational thinking competence is significant. ($F(1,38) = 84.705$, $p < .001$). It reveals that after receiving situated learning strategy, experimental group's overall computational thinking competence is superior to that of control group.

Table 3. Two Groups one-way ANCOVA summary

Item	SS	df	MS	F	*p*
Computational thinking skill	51717.093	38	51717.093	84.705	.000***

***p<0.001

5 Conclusion

The results confirm the importance of situated learning strategy on the cultivation of students' computational thinking competences. The experimental group's posttest score of computational thinking is significantly larger than that of the control group..

There are several possible factors that have resulted in the experimental group's higher posttest score of computational thinking. First, learning sheet items are simulation of realistic situations. Teachers simulate real environments in class to allow students to be involved in the instructional scenario which lead to more efficient learning. The classroom resembles a learning community and teachers and students collectively create and discuss real daily situations to solve problems. Situated learning can effectively result in knowledge construction. Brown et al. stated the importance of situated learning. Situated learning should be established in real situations and students develop knowledge by interacting with situations. Situated learning emphasizes that students are in real situational context and use knowledge as tool in realistic scenarios [4]. Likewise, computational thinking competences implies effective problem solving using information technology. Thus, the thinking process is needed to analyze problems that result in answers. Computer science education should break through the past boundary of information technology use, emphasize content of computer science, reinforce students' comprehension of computer science content, cultivate their logic thinking and problem-solving competence, introduce learning in daily lives to trigger students' learning interest and satisfy their basic life needs in digital era.

This study is limited to Second-year senior high school students. Thus, it is necessary to expand the scope of the study to include other student groups. Future research will validate various advantages to apply situated learning strategy.

Acknowledgments. This research is partially supported by the Ministry of Science and Technology (MOST), Taiwan, R.O.C. under Grant MOST 104-2511-S-224-003-MY3, MOST 105-2628-S-224-001-MY3.

References

1. Resnick, M.: Learn to code, code to learn. EdSurge, May 2013
2. Chen, G., Shen, J., Barth-Cohen, L., Jiang, S., Huang, X., Eltoukhy, M.: Assessing elementary students' computational thinking in everyday reasoning and robotics programming. Comput. Educ. **109**, 162–175 (2017)
3. Opmanis, M., Dagiene, V., Truu, A.: Task types at "Beaver" contests. Inf. Technol. Sch. 509–519 (2006)
4. Brown, J.S., Collins, A., Duguid, P.: Situated cognition and the culture of learning. Educ. Res. **18**, 32–42 (1989)
5. Wing, J.: Research notebook: computational thinking—what and why? The Link Magazine, Spring. Carnegie Mellon University, Pittsburgh (2011)
6. Leonard, J., Buss, A., Gamboa, R., Mitchell, M., Fashola, O.S., Hubert, T., Almughyirah, S.: Using robotics and game design to enhance children's self-efficacy, STEM attitudes, and computational thinking skills. J. Sci. Educ. Technol. **25**, 860–876 (2016)
7. Chaudhary, V., Agrawal, V., Sureka, P., Sureka, A.: An experience report on teaching programming and computational thinking to elementary level children using lego robotics education kit. In: 2016 IEEE 8th International Conference on Technology for Education (T4E 2016), pp. 38–41 (2016)
8. Yindi, D.: Visual basic program designing based on computational thinking capabilities training. In: Proceedings of the 2nd Information Technology and Mechatronics Engineering Conference (ITOEC 2016), vol. 24, pp. 175–178 (2016)
9. Parmar, D., Isaac, J., Babu, S.V., D'Souza, N., Leonard, A.E., Jorg, S., Gundersen, K., Daily, S.B.: Programming moves: design and evaluation of applying embodied interaction in virtual environments to enhance computational thinking in middle school students. In: 2016 IEEE Virtual Reality Conference (VR), pp. 131–140 (2016)
10. Hemmendinger, D.: A plea for modesty. ACM Inroads **1**, 4–7 (2010)
11. Gardiner, L.R., Corbitt, G., Adams, S.J.: Program assessment: Getting to a practical how-to model. J. Educ. Bus. **85**, 139–144 (2009)
12. Meyers, S., Lester, D.: The effects of situated learning through a community partnership in a teacher preparation program. SAGE Open **3**(3) (2013). https://doi.org/10.1177/2158244013497025
13. Lave, J., Wenger, E.: Situated Learning: Legitimate Peripheral Participation. Cambridge University Press, Cambridge (1991)
14. Stein, D.: Situated Learning in Adult Education. ERIC Digest No. 195 (1998)
15. Chen, H.-R., Lin, Y.-S.: An examination of digital game-based situated learning applied to Chinese language poetry education. Technol. Pedagog. Educ. **25**, 171–186 (2016)
16. Angeles Bravo-Alvarez, M., Escolano-Perez, E., Navas-Macho, P., Luisa Herrero-Nivela, M., Eguinoa-Zaborras, F., Acero-Ferrero, M.: A situated learning experience: student satisfaction and improvement of their assessment skills in joint reference disorder. In: ICERI 2015: 8th International Conference of Education, Research and Innovation, pp. 7819–7825 (2015)

17. Lin, W.-C., Huang, D.-Y., Huang, C.-W., Liu, Y.-C., Chen, G.-D.: A video comic for group situated learning in the classroom. In: Edulearn15: 7th International Conference On Education and New Learning Technologies, pp. 4264–4271 (2015)
18. Dagienė, V., Futschek, G.: Bebras international contest on informatics and computer literacy: criteria for good tasks. In: Mittermeir, R.T., Sysło, M.M. (eds.) ISSEP 2008. LNCS, vol. 5090, pp. 19–30. Springer, Heidelberg (2008). https://doi.org/10.1007/978-3-540-69924-8_2
19. Verhoeff, T., Horváth, G., Diks, K., Cormack, G.: A proposal for an IOI syllabus. Teach. Math. Comput. Sci. **4**, 193–216 (2006)
20. Dagiene, V., Skupiene, J.: Learning by competitions: olympiads in informatics as a tool for training high-grade skills in programming. In: ITRE 2004: 2nd International Conference on Information Technology: Research and Education 2004, pp. 79–83 (2004)
21. Dagiene, V.: Information technology contests-introduction to computer science in an attractive way. Inform. Educ. **5**, 37 (2006)

Effects of Problem-Solving Strategy Based Interactive E-Book on Measurement Concepts

Yu-Hsien Huang[1], Po-Han Wu[2(✉)], and Hsu-Cheng Chiang[3]

[1] National Taiwan University of Science and Technology, Taipei, Taiwan
[2] National Taipei University of Education, Taipei, Taiwan
phwu.academic@gmail.com
[3] National Taiwan Normal University, Taipei, Taiwan

Abstract. Being a critical stage for mathematics enlightenment, the establishment of quantity conservation in lower grades of elementary schools is the key in learning various measurements. Assisting students in establishing strong problem-solving strategy is an important task for teachers. Aiming at the length measurement concept of students, a problem-solving strategy based interactive e-book learning system is developed for the length measurement instruction in this study. The research findings show that applying the problem-solving strategy based interactive e-book to the length measurement instruction could enhance students' learning outcome and help them learn good problem-solving strategy and establish correct measurement concepts.

Keywords: Problem-solving strategy · Interactive e-book
Measurement concept

1 Introduction

In elementary mathematics, "quantity and measurement" aims to cultivate students' numerical concepts. Quantity covers length, weight, capacity, time, angle, area, and volume, where properly establishing the length concept allows continuously establishing the measurement concepts of area and volume. Apparently, the length measurement concept presents the primary status. In lower grades of elementary schools, students compare the lengths of two objects by perception and operating experience. Research revealed several myths in students' "measurement concept" learning [14], including wrong use of measuring tools, intuitive myths, and comprehension difficulty in individual units. It therefore relies on teachers posing and establishing good problem-solving strategy to help students deal with problems gradually and think completely. With different levels, each student requires different problem-solving strategy. The assistance of technology in the learning process could help teachers efficiently enhance students' learning outcome. Research also revealed that the practice exercises of technological virtual teaching aids could actually enhance students' learning standard [4].

Along with the development and popularity of cloud computing and mobile technology, schools have developed the integration of digital technology with instruction into mobile learning curricula. Highly interactive e-books with images, sound, and films

T.-T. Wu et al. (Eds.): ICITL 2018, LNCS 11003, pp. 453–462, 2018.
https://doi.org/10.1007/978-3-319-99737-7_48

become one of the best teaching material development tools. E-books present the characteristics of contextualization and personalization and allow students learning according to teaching materials designed by teachers [7]. The interactive characteristic also attracts students' interests in the active learning and enhances the learning outcome.

Based on problem-solving strategy, an interactive e-book system is developed in this study, allowing each student presenting the correspondent problem-solving strategy prompts, according to their level, for problem solving. It is expected that students could learn the real meaning of length measurement to solve various mathematical problems. This study aims to discuss the effects of the problem-solving strategy based interactive e-book and a generally designed e-book on elementary students' length measurement concept. According to the research objectives, the research questions are listed as followings.

1. To discuss different learning outcome of students learning with "problem-solving strategy based interactive e-book" and "general interactive e-book".
2. To discuss the learning motivation of students learning with "problem-solving strategy based interactive e-book" and "general interactive e-book".
3. To discuss the establishment of length measurement concept of students learning with "problem-solving strategy based interactive e-book" and "general interactive e-book".

2 Literature Review

2.1 Problem-Solving Strategy

Problem-solving strategy, proposed by [11], was a problem-solving method attempting to simplify or systemizing problems to propose solutions; the goal of strategy, in the entire problem-solving stage, contained understanding the problem, drawing up plans, carrying out the plan, and looking back. It stressed on the changes of students' inner thinking systems and delivering message to stimulate students' logic thinking through the teaching situations designed by teachers and to seek for the roots of problems to further assume, reason, and propose possible solutions [17].

Problem-solving strategy has been broadly applied to instruction and extended several patterns in various academic areas, such as the application to mathematics to discuss various problem-solving strategy [1, 2, 6, 15], the application to physics to discuss the problem-solving capability [3], the application to chemistry to discuss the relationship with metacognition [13], or the application to children's construction of analog concepts [12].

Problem-solving strategy used to be guided by teachers in big classes, but seldom discussed individual student's problem-solving strategy, because it was rather difficult to take care of individual student's development level in a classroom with numerous students. The combination of information technology in the digital era with tablet PC and teaching materials designed by teachers to timely assist students in the individual development would help students' learning and enhance the learning interests.

2.2 Interactive E-Book

Along with the advance of technology, e-books have changed traditional learning methods. With the multimedia characteristics of images, films, and sound, it is no longer one-way learning from paper-based textbooks, but is able to interact with learning contents to visualize more difficult, complicated, and dynamic contents [7, 9, 19]. The application of multimedia of e-books is more advantageous than paper-based books, and the application of multimedia could more easily enhance students' learning motivation. Such different experiences could better enhance students' learning interests.

In past research, e-book has been broadly applied to education, e.g. the combination with mathematics [5], art [7], and nursing [16], and has been proven the effectiveness. Interactive e-books, specially designed for learning, could enhance interests as well as be integrated into teaching and learning processes to reinforce learning [8].

From above research, interactive e-books could enhance learners' learning motivation and learning outcome, but it still depends on teachers considering the relationship among problem-solving strategies, including types of questions and known or unknown conditions, suitable for students, as well as designing teaching materials based on students' prior knowledge of mathematics. A problem-solving strategy based interactive e-book is therefore developed in this study, based on the strategies of understanding the problem, devising a plan, carrying out the plan, and looking back [11], to deeply discuss the effects on students' length measurement concept and expect to help students.

3 Problem-Solving Strategy Based Interactive E-Book

To allow students learning according to the capability development level, a problem-solving strategy based interactive e-book is developed in this study for students, according to the levels, proceeding learning and clarifying myth concepts through the problem-solving strategy prompts designed by teachers.

SimMAGIC eBook, interactive multimedia e-book editing software, is used for developing teaching materials in this study. It provides students with the interactive learning environment. The system is divided into "length measurement question library", "teaching material library", and "problem-solving strategy module". Length measurement question library contains questions for elementary length measurement concepts, from easy to difficult. Teaching material library includes the functions of situational pictures, sound, films, notes, and real-time feedback to help students establish correct measurement concepts with images. Problem-solving strategy module is designed, based on "understanding the problem", "devising a plan", "carrying out the plan", and "looking back" to guide students solving problems [11], give different modules with problem-solving strategy, and allow students following the strategy to learn step by step.

For instance, to compare the lengths of a button and a paper clip, the question in e-books would display images and texts and has students answer the question according to the question meaning. When students do not understand the question, the system would guide them into the problem-solving strategy step 1 "understanding the problem" (Fig. 1), where key words in the text are marked with different colors and the pictures are marked with guide lines for the length comparison to guide the students reading the question again to understand the question.

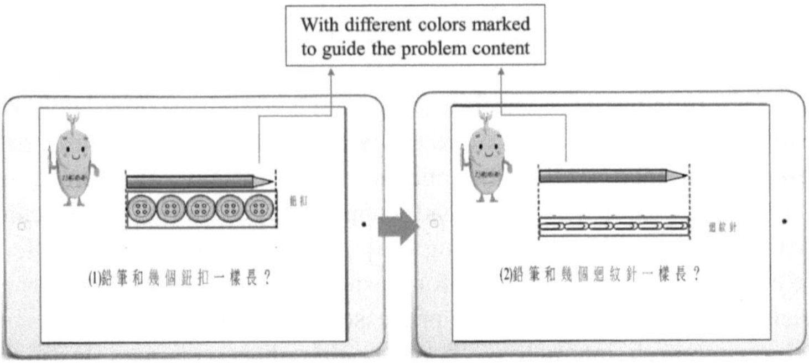

Fig. 1. Understanding the problem

In step 2 "devising a plan" (Fig. 2), the key points are marked with images and texts, and prompts are given for students thinking how to find out the relationship between known numbers and unknown numbers according to known conditions.

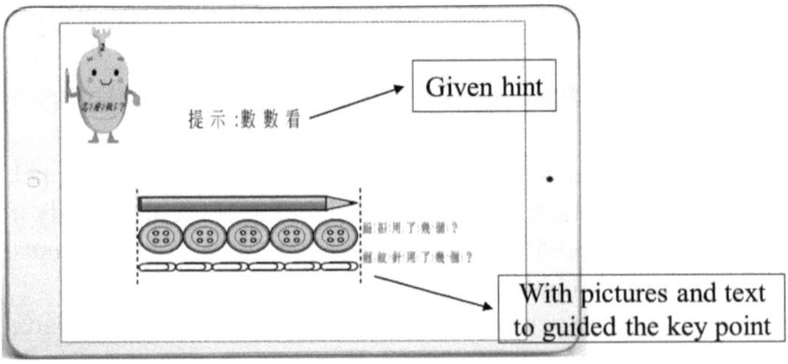

Fig. 2. Devising a plan

Step 3, "carrying out the plan" allows students learning how to precede problem-solving strategy, gives relevant prompts, and has students solve the question again (Fig. 3).

If students still make mistakes, an image informing the mistake is given, and the previous steps are repeated for students continuing answering the question after learning. An award is given for a correct answer and the system skips to step 4 "looking back" (Fig. 4) to guide students reviewing the question concept again and checking the problem-solving strategy and method to help students establish correct cognition structure and strategy.

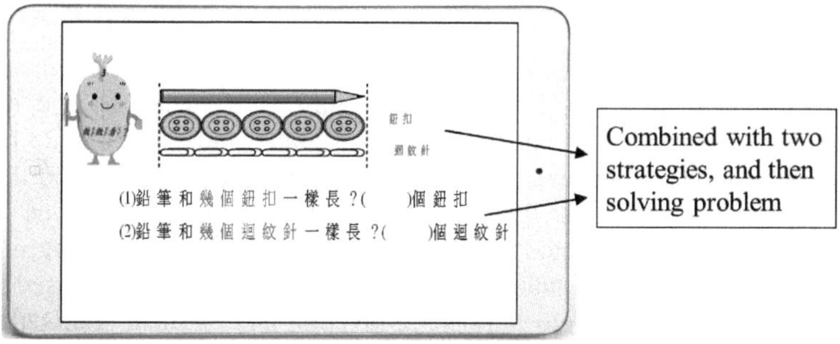

Fig. 3. Carrying out the plan

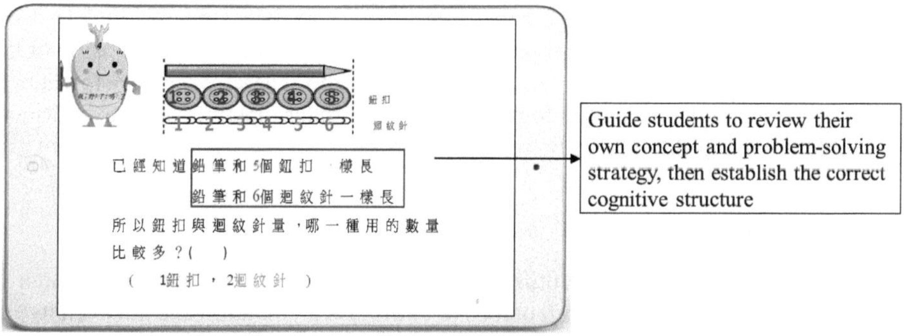

Fig. 4. Looking back

4 Research Design

This study aims to discuss the effect of the problem-solving strategy based interactive e-book on second-grade students' learning achievement and motivation as well as analyze the establishment of problem-solving concepts on length measurement in order to help students solve the myth problem in length measurement.

4.1 Research Subject

Total 56 second-grade students in two classes, with similar pretest performance on mathematics achievement test, of an elementary school in Taiwan are selected as the research subjects. A class (n = 28), as the experimental group, applies the problem-solving strategy based interactive e-book learning model and the other class (n = 28), as the control group, utilizes a generally designed interactive e-book learning model. Both classes are taught by the same teacher to prevent the results from being affected by different teaching styles.

4.2 Research Tool

The prior knowledge of length measurement concept is applied to the mathematics achievement pretest, and the achievement posttest is designed by the researcher according to the instruction objectives for second-grade students. Total 25 questions, including 13 basic questions and 12 advanced questions, are revised according to the opinions of two senior teachers with more than 12-year teaching experience.

The learning motivation scale in this study is referred to the learning motivation scale, proposed by Pintrich, Smith, Garcia and McKeachie [10] and revised by Wang and Chen [18]. It is divided into intrinsic motivation and extrinsic motivation and is proceeded with Likert 5-point scale, where "5" stands for extremely agree and "1" represents extremely disagree.

Furthermore, students in lower grades can hardly express the opinions with texts that interviews are preceded after the e-book experiment to analyze students' length measurement concept development and problem-solving process after the application of the problem-solving strategy based interactive e-book and the generally designed interactive e-book learning model as well as to present learners' inner thoughts. It aims to discuss the problem-solving differences between two groups.

4.3 Experiment Process

Quasi-experimental research is utilized in this study. The experimental research is preceded according to the research objective to discuss the relationship between two e-book learning models and mathematics learning achievement. The instructional experiment is preceded 4 sessions for total 160 min, including the instruction and class exercise

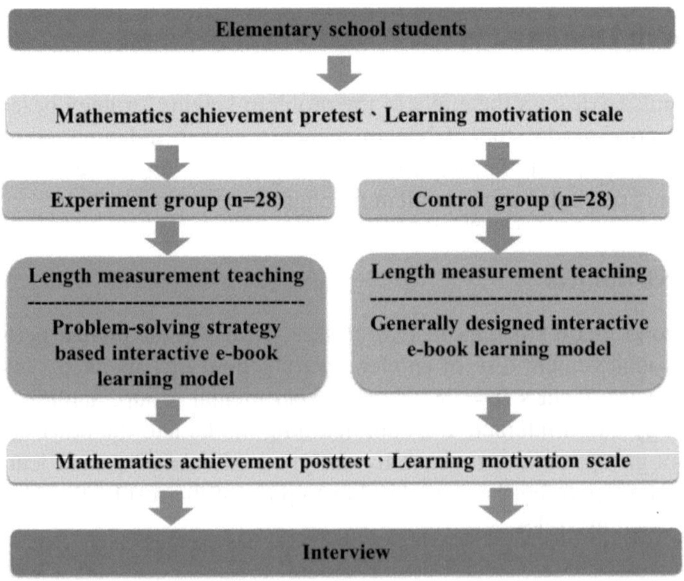

Fig. 5. Experiment process

of length measurement. The experimental group and the control group learn with different models of e-book. The design model is shown in Fig. 5.

The experimental group uses the problem-solving strategy based interactive e-book learning model. When students make mistakes in the learning, the system would automatically guide to the four-step problem-solving strategy to understand the problem solving gradually. The control group uses a generally designed interactive e-book learning model. Similar to the experimental group, a real-time feedback would be acquired for correct answers, while the students are requested to read the book again when making mistakes. The correct answer would be given after making mistakes for three times, and the system skips to the next question.

5 Experimental Result

With quasi-experimental research, 28 students in the experimental group apply the problem-solving strategy based interactive e-book learning model, and another 28 students in the control group utilize a generally designed interactive e-book learning model. Both groups use tablet PC for the learning, and length measurement concepts for second-grade students are instructed. The test results are analyzed with SPSS 21.

5.1 Mathematics Achievement Test

Two kinds of e-book learning models for the experimental group and the control group are compared to discuss the differences in second-grade students' length measurement achievement test. The pretest performance of mathematics achievement test is regarded as the covariate, and the posttest results are preceded One-way Analysis of Covariance (ANCOVA). To conform to the basic assumption of Analysis of Covariance, the students in two groups are proceeded in-group regression coefficient homogeneity test. The homogeneity test of pretest does not achieve the significance ($F = 0.128$, $p = .722 > .05$) that it satisfies the assumption of in-group regression coefficient homogeneity.

The learning models (groups) are further regarded as the constant factor, mathematics achievement pretest as the covariate, and mathematics achievement posttest as the covariance for Independent Sample One-way Analysis of Covariance to analyze the learning differences between two groups of students under distinct learning models. The ANCOVA results, Table 1, show the variance of the experimental group and the control group achieving the significance ($F = 23.364$, $p = 0.000 < 0.05$), revealing that the posttest performance of both groups changes with learning models. The mean of the experimental group 83.00 and the mean of the control group 66.86 present the higher learning achievement with the problem-solving strategy based interactive e-book learning model than with a general interactive e-book learning model. In other words, the problem-solving strategy based interactive e-book learning model could enhance second-grade students' learning achievement on length measurement.

Table 1. The one-way AVCOVA of the learning achievement

Group	N	Mean	SD	Adjusted mean	SE	F	p
Experiment group	28	83.00	14.053	82.889	2.329	23.364	.000
Control group	28	66.86	16.648	66.968	2.329		

5.2 Learning Motivation

To conform to the basic assumption of Analysis of Covariance, the learning motivation pretest of both groups is proceeded in-group regression coefficient homogeneity test for the comparison. The results show that the homogeneity test of the pretest satisfies the variance homogeneity assumption ($F = .363$, $p = .549 > .05$).

The motivation pretest/posttest is further analyzed, Table 2. The variance of both the experimental group and the control group does not achieve the significance ($F = 1.507$, $p = .225 > 0.05$), revealing that the learning motivation, with the problem-solving strategy based interactive e-book learning model and the general interactive e-book learning model, does not appear significant differences before and after the experiment.

Table 2. The one-way AVCOVA of the learning motivation

Group	N	Mean	SD	Adjusted mean	SE	F	p
Experiment group	28	27.1429	3.40712	26.990	.502	1.507	.225
Control group	28	25.9643	3.28275	26.117	.502		

It is assumed that using tablets for mathematics learning might be a fresh experience for students in lower grades and presents attraction on both groups. It is also observed that students in both groups are particularly happy and concentrated when using tablets in the classes. In spite of different learning models, both groups use tablets for the learning and are induced the curiosity to promote the learning motivation.

6 Conclusion and Suggestion

6.1 Conclusion

With quasi-experimental research, second-grade students in an elementary school in Taiwan are studied. The problem-solving strategy based interactive e-book developed by the researcher and a generally designed interactive e-book are utilized for the length measurement instruction to discuss elementary students' mathematics learning outcome.

Regarding mathematics learning achievement, students using the problem-solving strategy based interactive e-book learning model present remarkably higher learning achievement than those using the generally designed interactive e-book. It reveals that the problem-solving strategy based interactive e-book could better enhance second-grade students' multiplication learning outcome. The interviews with students after the experiment also show that students in the experimental group would re-read the questions and mark points as well as simplify questions with tables or pictures when encountering difficult questions. For instance, student S2 in the experimental group said, "I would re-read the question and make points as well as draw pictures." Student S4 in the experimental group said, "I recall that the e-book teaches me to do so. I therefore draw a table to answer questions." It is therefore guessed that the problem-solving strategy based e-book learning model could assist students in the complete thinking of problem-solving strategy and solving problems so that they have better performance on mathematics achievement posttest.

In terms of learning motivation, the experimental results reveal no significant difference in learning motivation between two groups. It is assumed that the use of tablets for mathematics learning is rare and novel for students in lower grades and could attract students so that the students in both groups are attracted. Although there is no remarkable difference between two groups, the statistical results present the higher motivation after learning, revealing that both groups enhance the motivation.

From above analyses, the problem-solving strategy based interactive e-book learning model is helpful for students. The problem-solving strategies of understanding the problem, devising a plan, carrying out the plan, and looking back guide students to establish good problem-solving strategy, solve myth concepts, and establish stable measurement concepts to become the successive mathematics basis and further help students develop to the higher level.

6.2 Suggestion for Future

This study integrates problem-solving strategy based interactive e-book to help second-grade students establish length measurement concepts in the enlightenment stage. The problem-solving strategy gradually guides students to analyze question meanings and simplify questions to promote the learning achievement. It is suggested that the system could be augmented to real-time record learners' learning processes in order to provide the researcher with richer research data. Besides, abstract mathematics instruction could be combined with different emerging technology to enhance students' learning interests and promote the learning outcome.

References

1. Alibali, M.W., Phillips, K.M., Fischer, A.D.: Learning new problem-solving strategies leads to changes in problem representation. Cogn. Dev. **24**(2), 89–101 (2009)
2. Attali, Y., van der Kleij, F.: Effects of feedback elaboration and feedback timing during computer-based practice in mathematics problem solving. Comput. Educ. **110**, 154–169 (2017)
3. Çalışkan, S., Selçuk, G.S., Erol, M.: Effects of the problem solving strategies instruction on the students' physics problem solving performances and strategy usage. Procedia Soc. Behav. Sci. **2**(2), 2239–2243 (2010)
4. Crompton, H., Burke, D., Gregory, K.H.: The use of mobile learning in PK-12 education: a systematic review. Comput. Educ. **110**, 51–63 (2017)
5. Hwang, G.J., Lai, C.L.: Facilitating and bridging out-of-class and in-class learning: an interactive e-book-based flipped learning approach for math courses. Educ. Technol. Soc. **20**(1), 184–197 (2017)

6. Intaros, P., Inprasitha, M., Srisawadi, N.: Students' problem solving strategies in problem solving-mathematics classroom. Procedia Soc. Behav. Sci. **116**, 4119–4123 (2014)
7. Kao, G.Y.M., Tsai, C.C., Liu, C.Y., Yang, C.H.: The effects of high/low interactive electronic storybooks on elementary school students' reading motivation, story comprehension and chromatics concepts. Comput. Educ. **100**, 56–70 (2016)
8. Liu, C.C., Chen, W.C., Lin, H.M., Huang, Y.Y.: A remix-oriented approach to promoting student engagement in a long-term participatory learning program. Comput. Educ. **110**, 1–15 (2017)
9. Liu, C.C., Chen, Y.C., Tai, S.J.D.: A social network analysis on elementary student engagement in the networked creation community. Comput. Educ. **115**, 114–125 (2017)
10. Pintrich, P.R., Smith, D.A.F., Garcia, T., McKeachie, W.J.: A Manual for the Use of the Motivated Strategies for Learning Questionnaire (MSLQ). National Center for Research to Improve Postsecondary Teaching and Learning, MI (1991)
11. Polya, G.: How to Solve It: A New Aspect of Mathematical Method. Princeton University Press (1945)
12. Resing, W.C., Bakker, M., Pronk, C.M., Elliott, J.G.: Dynamic testing and transfer: An examination of children's problem-solving strategies. Learn. Individ. Differ. **49**, 110–119 (2016)
13. Scherer, R., Tiemann, R.: Factors of problem-solving competency in a virtual chemistry environment: The role of metacognitive knowledge about strategies. Comput. Educ. **59**(4), 1199–1214 (2012)
14. Stavy, R., Tirosh, D., Tsamir, P., Ronen, H.: The role of intuitive rules in science and mathematics education. Eur. J. Teach. Educ. **19**(2), 109–119 (1996)
15. Sulak, S.: Effect of problem solving strategies on problem solving achievement in primary school mathematics. Procedia Soc. Behav. Sci. **9**, 468–472 (2010)
16. Sung, H.Y., Hwang, G.J., Yen, Y.F.: Development of a contextual decision-making game for improving students' learning performance in a health education course. Comput. Educ. **82**, 179–190 (2015)
17. Van MerriëNboer, J.J.: Perspectives on problem solving and instruction. Comput. Educ. **64**, 153–160 (2013)
18. Wang, L.C., Chen, M.P.: The effects of game strategy and preference-matching on flow experience and programming performance in game-based learning. Innovations Educ. Teach. Int. **47**(1), 39–52 (2010)
19. Yang, C.C., Hwang, G.J., Hung, C.M., Tseng, S.S.: An Evaluation of the learning effectiveness of concept map-based science book reading via mobile devices. Educ. Technol. Soc. **16**(3), 167–178 (2013)

Usability Evaluation of the Game Based E-Book System on Natural Science Teaching System

Meng-Chun Tsai[1(✉)], Hao-Chiang Koong Lin[1], and Chad Lin[2]

[1] Department of Information and Learning Technology, National University of Tainan, Tainan, Taiwan (R.O.C.)
cherrybearpipi@gmail.com
[2] Faculty of Health Sciences, Curtin University, Perth, Australia
elin123au@yahoo.com.au

Abstract. The purpose of this research is to design a digital-based e-book "Plant World View", it combines the diversity of multimedia and natural science, which meets different personal needs in learning method. The research sample are fifth grade students from an elementary school in Tainan, they usually divide students into two classes, 20 students with normal teaching style, and 20 students used tablets as learning tool in class. The way they divide students into two different classes made it easy to study and analyze the interaction satisfaction and the system's usability. As a result, as for system's usability, students with the multimedia tablet teaching method picked up faster than the students of normal teaching method. For the user interaction satisfaction, the student with tablet's subjective feeling is better than the students of normal teaching method.

Keywords: Digital Game-Based Learning (DGBL)
A cognitive theory of multimedia learning · System Usability Scale (SUS)
Questionnaire for User Interaction Satisfaction (QUIS) · Usability

1 Introduction

In an era of information and developing technology, Taiwan education begin enforcing the "E-Learning Advocacy Program" in 2014 in order to keep up with the technology and the future education trend, and to promote digital learning in hope to create a customized learning method to meet each individual's need, therefore realize the open, independent and convenient education and learning environment. Many educators have already started to bring digital technology and efficient instructional strategies into courses to improve and enhance student's learning efficiency [1].

Interdisciplinarity is a tool to consider technology as a curriculum operation with the main function to help students solve problem, let students have a deeper understanding of the knowledge and improve their motivation to learn [2]. Gamification is to use game design techniques and game elements in a non-gaming environment to attract

T.-T. Wu et al. (Eds.): ICITL 2018, LNCS 11003, pp. 463–472, 2018.
https://doi.org/10.1007/978-3-319-99737-7_49

learners to develop problem-solving skills, digital game-based learning have already shown potentials, it can make education and teaching easier [3, 4]. Different from the traditional teaching style, this can improve the zero-interaction problem [5]. As for today, many educators has efficiently used games to enhance student's learning motivation and results [6].

This research uses digital multimedia technology, combining digital game-based learning to design a natural science's teaching material "Plants World View". After the fifth grade students in a Tainan's elementary school use the system, then evaluate tablet teaching and normal teaching method and see the overall feedback and satisfaction rating of system usage and interaction. The research questions are below:

1. What are the overall satisfaction ratings of the usability and interaction satisfaction?
2. In terms of usability, what's the difference between normal teaching method and digital tablet method?
3. In terms of interaction satisfaction, what's the difference between normal teaching method and digital tablet method?

2 Literature Review

2.1 Digital Game-Based Learning (DGBL)

Digital Game- Based Learning (DGBL) is a competitive learning method, the design of the user interface is mainly by using situation stimulation as academic environment, and it contains two key factors: entertainment and education [7]. Recently, DGBL has been widely applied in learning, it has a significant impact on strengthening and encouraging learning motivation and knowledge construction. One of the key factor is the "coming together" of studying hard and interactive entertainment, in other words, digital game-based learning can be considered as a learning method, its purpose is to lead the gamer's cognitive changes while using the system, which is different from traditional learning methods (non-game based learning). In comparison, gaming-based learning is more efficient in knowledge accommodation and development [8]. Since game-based learning's developed system and application have already brought interest to many field of education [9], Raybourn and Bos [10] points out that a game-based learning environment can allow learners to experience abstract conception and enhance learning opportunities. According to researches, DGBL can be an effective teaching tool for teachers, especially when it comes to encourage learner's learning motivation and fulfil the lower learning objective in Bloom's taxonomy, therefore, learning motivation and interaction are related [7], mostly used in serious gaming environment, the main target of developing the system is to enhance student's ability to absorb knowledge and develop cognitive skills, so the learner can practice those skills in a stimulated environment, pushing the learner to initiatively process the contents that he is learning, which can induce active learning and improve learning motivation.

2.2 Cognitive Theory of Multimedia Learning

Selecting text and images from learning materials, organize them into coherent mental representation, then integrate the language produced with visual presentation [11]. From a teaching perspective, multimedia is already an important factor when it comes to combining technology into teaching, teachers can use multimedia in teaching, so the learners can learn in an interactive multimedia environment. Mayer and Moreno [12] presented a frame diagram of Cognitive Theory of Multimedia Learning, learners mainly receives information such as images and words through visual and hearing, they will integrate these information and find the relevance between them, then it will then internalize into a meaningful learning content. So, when combining teaching materials with technology, the way that it is presented will affect the integration process of the learner.

2.3 Usability

Usability is a user-centered design concept, which is used to evaluate if the multimedia interactive tool contains the traits of easy-to-learn and bring a fun experience for the users. With this in mind, the user-centered idea will have to be included while developing the system. In the book Interaction Design [13] states that there are two main category when it comes to designing interaction, first is usage goals, which includes: effectiveness, efficiency, safety, utility, learnability and memorability; the second is user's experience goal, it can fulfill mind-level needs, which includes: satisfying, enjoyable, fun, entertaining, helpful, motivating, aesthetically pleasing, supportive of creativity, rewarding, emotionally fulfilling. Users are willing to accept digital multimedia learning system is due to its usefulness, easy to use and the self-efficacy and satisfaction that it can ring to the user itself [14].

3 Methodology

3.1 Instructional Design

Game base E-book System "Plant World View". According to the IFLA (International Federation of Library Associations) Guide-lines for Audiovisual and Multimedia Materials in Libraries and other Institutions [15], it points out that multimedia includes two or more visual and hearings convey, for example: sounds and image, words and animations…etc. Game based learning utilizes various different learning methods while presenting the information in many visual and hearing method [16]. Mayer's [17] empirical research shows that the presentation of integrated text and corresponding images results in better learning performance comparing to the presentation of separated text and corresponding images. Based on the "Grade 1–9 Curriculum Guideline" released by Taiwan's Ministry of Education, the "All about Plants" section of natural science and life technology and technical knowledge's third stage (Fifth, Sixth Grade) is the core material used in designing game-based E-book system "Plant-World View". By using the richness of digital multimedia, and the features of animation, music, sounds and interaction to blend with the teaching material. In this way, the students can switch from traditional books to game based E-book system, abandon the old rote memorization learning, experience the two-way interaction that the one-way books can't bring, leading the students can learn about plants from multiple perspective. The teaching material is "Water Movement inside Plant", as shown in Fig. 1.

Fig. 1. Screenshot of "Plant World View" system.

3.2 Research Tools

System Usability Scale (SUS). This scale's prototype was developed by Digital Equipment Co Ltd in 1986, with a total of ten questions to evaluate the system's usability, from Strongly Agree to Strongly Disagree, with the Likert Five Point Scale as the questionnaire, with the cross interrogate technique to evaluate the subject's re-view, then use formula transformation to convert the choices made by each subject on the questions into data information, the higher the score means higher usage. This scale is a trustworthy, fast and low-cost method [18], the higher the score, the easier it is for the users to interact with the system. Below are the 10 questions: Q1. I think that I would like to use this system frequently, Q2. I found the sys-tem unnecessarily complex, Q3. I thought the system was easy to use, Q4. I think that I would need the support of a technical person to be able to use this system, Q5. I found the various functions in this system were well integrated, Q6. I thought there was too much inconsistency in this system, Q7. I would imagine that most people would learn to use this system very quickly, Q8. I found the system very cumbersome to use, Q9. I felt very confident using the system, Q10. I needed to learn a lot of things before I could get going with this system.

Questionnaire for User Interaction Satisfaction (QUIS). This is presented by America's Maryland University Human Computer Interaction Lab (HCIL), the questionnaire method is to use the human-computer user interface as point of view to evaluate the human-computer user interface and the user's satisfactory rating [19], it is a reliable satisfaction measurement By using Likert Scale and ask the user to rate according to its own perspective, from a score 1–7. This research modifies the questionnaire, the questionnaire contains the following 7 categories: the overall system interface, the presentation of the system interface, word choice and information, system control panel, system function, system's user interface and user's experience, with the total of 25 questions.

4 Results

The research samples of this research came from the fifth grade students of an elementary school, the 40-people grade is originally divided into two classes with different teaching method. The teaching style was separated into two: tablet and normal teaching style. 20 students was assigned to each style. The survey is against how the subjects of each teaching style feels about the game-based E-book system, there are 40 valid surveys.

4.1 System Usability Scale (SUS)

SUS Reliability Analysis. The system evaluation used for this research is the SUS, to analyze 40 valid survey with ten question on each of them, the Cronbach's Alpha value is 0.813, reaching the reliability score of 0.7 or above, which shoes that the "System Usability Scale" has high credibility.

SUS Descriptive Statistic Analysis. This research analyzes the statistical data collected, by taking the sum of the percentage of the two highest number in the five-point scale, it will show the positive reviews from the users. From Table 1 it is shown that the overall subjective feeling is 55.91%. In Q1, 45% of the users think will keep using the system. In Q2, 55% thinks the system is not complicated. In Q3, 55% thinks the system is easy to use. In Q4, 52.5% of the users won't need technical assistance while using the system. In Q5, 57.5% thinks that all the system features are integrated well. In Q6, 60% of the users thinks that the system doesn't have inconsistency. In Q7, 72.5% of the users think that majority can learn how to use the system quickly. In Q8, 62.5% thinks that the system is not hard to use. In Q9, 60% of the users are confident that they can use the system. In Q10, 27.5% of the users thinks that no knowledge is required before using this system.

Table 1. The overall SUS descriptive statistic analysis

Sample size	Q1	Q2	Q3	Q4	Q5	Q6	Q7	Q8	Q9	Q10	Overall
40	45	55	55	52.5	57.5	60	72.5	62.5	60	27.5	55.91

From Table 2, it is shown that the subjective feeling for tablet teaching method is 71.5% and the overall subjective feeling of the normal teaching method is 38%. In Q1, 70% and 20% of the users think will keep using the system. In Q2, 80% and 30% thinks the sys-tem is not complicated. In Q3, 75% and 35% thinks the system is easy to use. In Q4, 70% and 35% of the users won't need technical assistance while using the system. In Q5, 70% and 45% thinks that all the system features are integrated well. In Q6, 65% and 55% of the users thinks that the system doesn't have inconsistency. In Q7, 85% and 60% of the users think that majority can learn how to use the system quickly. In Q8, 85% and 40% thinks that the system is not hard to use. In Q9, 75% and 45% of the users are confident that they can use the system. In Q10, 40% and 15% of the users thinks that no knowledge is required before using this system. Comes to

Table 2. The comparative SUS of tablet teaching method and normal teaching method

Type	Sample size	Q1	Q2	Q3	Q4	Q5	Q6	Q7	Q8	Q9	Q10	Overall
Tablet (%)	20	70	80	75	70	70	65	85	85	75	40	71.5
Normal (%)	20	20	30	35	35	45	55	60	40	45	15	38

system usability, the tablet teaching method subjects learns faster than the normal teaching method subjects.

SUS Point Conversion. Table 3 shows the points of the system usability, overall is 64.06, when viewed separately, the tablet teaching style's average score for the sys-tem usability is 73.25, median 75, standard deviation of 15.58, the maximum and minimum values are 98 and 28. For the normal teaching style, the average score for the system usability is 54.88, median 53.75, standard deviation of 16.83, the maxi-mum and minimum values are 90 and 30. The average system usability for this sys-tem is 73.25 and 54.88, and it is noticeable from Fig. 2 that the score given by the subjects of the tablet teaching method falls into the "Good" range, and for normal teaching method is "Ok".

Table 3. The overall SUS descriptive statistic analysis

Type	Sample number	Median	Minimum	Maximum	Mean	Standard deviation
Tablet	20	75.00	28	98	73.25	15.58
Normal	20	53.75	30	90	54.88	16.83
Total	40	70	28	98	64.06	18.516

Independent Sample T Test. The Independent Sample T Test is used to compare the average difference between the two populations. Table 4 shows that in Q5, Q6, Q7 the statistical significance of the two teaching methods (double-tail) >=0.05, so it can't deny null hypothesis. The subjects of the tablet teaching method and normal teaching method did not have a significant difference, the statistical significance of the rest of the questions (double-tail) <0.05, so it denies null hypotheses, accepts alternative hypotheses. The subjects of the tablet teaching method and normal teaching method have a significant difference, the users of the tablet teaching method in system usability is more outstanding than the users of normal teaching method.

4.2 Questionnaire for User Interaction Satisfaction, QUIS

QUIS Reliability Analysis. Analyze 40 valid surveys. The questionnaire contains 25 questions, the QUIS Cronbach's Alpha value is 0.969, proving that it is reliable. According to the statistical analysis of the overall interaction satisfaction of the seven categories, it is shown in Table 5 that all 40 subjects gave a score of 5 or above on the overall satisfaction for the game based E-Book, with an average of 5.52, standard deviation of 1.51. Table 6 shows that all the subject from tablet teaching method have an overall satisfaction score of 6 and above, with an average of 6.26, standard deviation

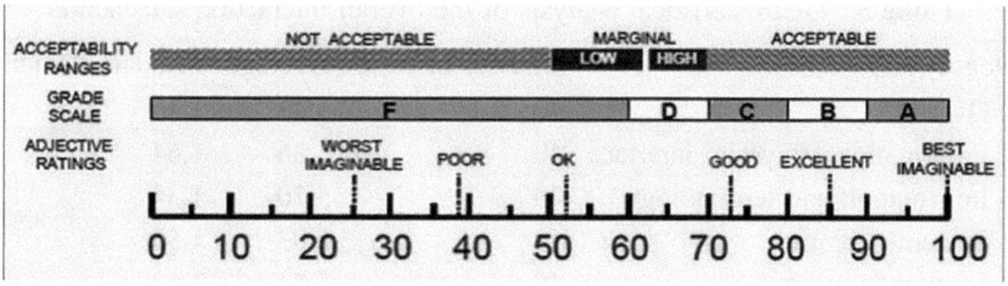

Fig. 2. SUS score

Table 4. The result of the SUS independent sample T Test of tablet teaching style and normal teaching style.

Question	Type	Type	Standard deviation	T	Statistical significance (double-tail)
Q1	Tablet	3.80	1.20	2.83	.007**
	Normal	2.70	1.26		
Q2	Tablet	2.00	1.08	2.39	.022*
	Normal	2.90	1.29		
Q3	Tablet	4.15	1.09	2.28	.028*
	Normal	3.30	1.26		
Q4	Tablet	2.20	1.36	2.17	.036*
	Normal	3.20	1.54		
Q5	Tablet	4.10	0.85	1.83	.075
	Normal	3.50	1.19		
Q6	Tablet	2.45	1.23	−0.75	.457
	Normal	2.20	0.83		
Q7	Tablet	4.30	1.03	1.89	.067
	Normal	3.70	0.98		
Q8	Tablet	1.70	1.03	3.09	.004**
	Normal	2.85	1.31		
Q9	Tablet	4.10	0.79	2.04	.048*
	Normal	3.50	1.05		
Q10	Tablet	2.80	1.20	2.12	.040*
	Normal	3.60	1.19		

*p < .05, **p < .01, ***p < .001

of 0.85. Subjects of the normal teaching method gave a score of 5.03 in system terminology, the rest had a score of above 4.5 but under 5, with an average of 4.78, standard deviation of 1.66. This demonstrates that the participants of the tablet teaching method have better subjective feeling than the normal teaching method participants.

Furthermore, the Independent Sample T Test is used to analyze and see whether the overall satisfaction between Tablet teaching method and Normal teaching method demonstrated difference. Table 6 shoes that from the 7 different categories, the

Table 5. QUIS statistical analysis of the overall interaction satisfaction

Category	Number of entry	Average	Standard deviation
(1) Overall	40	5.43	1.40
(2) Presentation of system interface	40	5.36	1.64
(3) Information and terminology	40	5.70	1.34
(4) System operation	40	5.83	1.55
(5) System function	40	5.44	1.62
(6) User's interface	40	5.46	1.46
(7) User's experience	40	5.42	1.56
Average	40	5.52	1.51

Table 6. Statistical analysis of the overall interaction satisfaction of the two teaching method and independent sample T Test

Category	Type	Entry	Average	Standard deviation	T	Statistical significance (double-tail)
(1) Overall	Tablet	20	6.17	0.74	3.85	.001**
	Normal	20	4.70	1.54		
(2) Presentation of system interface	Tablet	20	6.14	1.05	3.40	.002**
	Normal	20	4.58	1.77		
(3) Information and terminology	Tablet	20	6.38	0.70	3.66	.001**
	Normal	20	5.03	1.49		
(4) System operation	Tablet	20	6.70	0.41	4.28	.000***
	Normal	20	4.95	1.78		
(5) System function	Tablet	20	6.13	1.16	2.93	.006**
	Normal	20	4.75	1.75		
(6) User's interface	Tablet	20	6.19	0.80	3.64	.001**
	Normal	20	4.73	1.61		
(7) User's experience	Tablet	20	6.11	1.12	3.10	.004**
	Normal	20	4.73	1.66		
Average	Tablet	20	6.26	0.85		
	Normal	20	4.78	1.66		

*p < .05, **p < .01, ***p < .001

statistical significance (double-tail) <0.05, so it deny null hypothesis, accepts alternative hypotheses. There is a statistical significance in the average score between the two methods, with the users of the tablet teaching method showing a higher score in the system interaction satisfaction.

5 Conclusion

This section will conclude this research as below:

What are the overall satisfaction rating of the usability and interaction satisfaction?

The SUS of subject's subjective feeling is 55.91%. The overall score for SUS is 64.06, falls between "Ok" and "Good", the acceptability ranges is acceptable. As for interaction satisfaction, 40 participants gave a 5 or above for the game based E-book, the average is 5.52, standard deviation 1.51, overall is satisfactory.

In terms of usability, what's the difference between normal teaching method and digital tablet method?

The subjective feeling for tablet teaching method is 71.5% and the overall subjective feeling of the normal teaching method is 38%. It is easier for the Tablet teaching method participants will learn faster than the normal teaching participant. When analyzing the two teaching method's average difference, it is shown on Table 4 that the statistical significance (double-tail) of the two groups in Q5, Q6, Q7 >0.05, stating that the two presents no significant difference, the rest of the other questions shows significant difference.

The Tablet-teaching method participant did not show lack of interest just because they were already using tablets as learning tool. In contrary, they have higher score in usability and interaction satisfaction than normal teaching method participants. In the other hand, the normal teaching method participants who usually learn by the traditional teaching style, 60% of the users thought that the majority can easily learn how to use the system after using "Plant-World View", but only 20% of the user will continuously use the system, the rest of them were not attracted because of the newly introduced game-based E-book system.

In terms of interaction satisfaction, what's the difference between normal teaching method and digital tablet method?

Table 6 shows that the Tablet teaching method participants gave a score of 6 or higher on the seven categories satisfaction, the average is 6.26, standard deviation 0.85. Participants of the Normal teaching method gave a 5.03 in system terminology and information, the other categories were all around a score of 4, and the average is 4.78, standard deviation 1.66. This demonstrates that the subjective feeling of the participants of the Tablet teaching method is better than the participants of Normal teaching method. Independent Sample T Test is used to analyze the difference between the two groups to see if there is statistical significance on interaction satisfaction. Table 6 shows that the statistical significance (double-tail) of the seven categories is <0.05, which indicates that the result of the user interaction satisfaction is the Tablet teaching method participants is greater than the Normal teaching method participants.

References

1. Levine, J.: Planning strategically for technology integration. In: McNeil, S., Price, J., Boger-MeHall S., Robon, B., Willis, J. (eds.) Technology and Teacher Education Annual, pp.293–295. Charlottesville (1998). Association for the Advancement of Computing on Education
2. Sprague, D., Dede, C.: Constructivism in the classroom: if i teach this way, am i doing my job? Learn. Lead. Technol. **27**(1), 6–9 (1999)
3. Kam, M., Agarwal, A., Kumar, A., Lal, S., Mathur, A., Tewari, A., Canny, J.: Designing e-learning games for rural children in India: a format for balancing learning with fun. In: Proceedings of the 7th ACM Conference on Designing Interactive Systems, pp. 58–67. ACM (2008)
4. Schmitz, B., Czauderna, A., Klemke, R., Specht, M.: Game based learning for computer science education. In: Computer Science Education Research Conference, pp. 81–86. Open Universiteit, Heerlen (2011)
5. De-Marcos, L., Domínguez, A., Saenz-de-Navarrete, J., Pagés, C.: An empirical study comparing gamification and social networking on e-learning. Comput. Educ. **75**, 82–91 (2014)
6. Stott, A., Neustaedter, C.: Analysis of gamification in education, Surrey, BC, Canada, p. 8 (2013)
7. Bellotti, F., Kapralos, B., Lee, K., Moreno-Ger, P., Berta, R.: Assessment in and of serious games: an overview. Adv. Hum. Comput. Interact. **2013**, 1 (2013)
8. Papastergiou, M.: Digital game-based learning in high school computer science education: Impact on educational effectiveness and student motivation. Comput. Educat. **52**(1), 1–12 (2009)
9. Kim, B., Park, H., Baek, Y.: Not just fun, but serious strategies: using meta-cognitive strategies in game-based learning. Comput. Educ. **52**(4), 800–810 (2009)
10. Raybourn, E.M., Bos, N.: Design and evaluation challenges of serious games. In: CHI 2005 Extended Abstracts on Human Factors in Computing Systems, pp. 2049–2050. ACM (2005)
11. Mayer, R.E.: Multimedia learning: are we asking the right questions? Educ. Psychol. **32**(1), 1–19 (1997)
12. Mayer, R.E., Moreno, R.: Nine ways to reduce cognitive load in multimedia learning. Educ. Psychol. **38**(1), 43–52 (2003)
13. Rogers, Y., Sharp, H., Preece, J.: Interaction Design: Beyond Human-Computer Interaction. Wiley, New York (2011)
14. Lee, D.Y., Lehto, M.R.: User acceptance of YouTube for procedural learning: an extension of the Technology Acceptance Model. Comput. Educ. **61**, 193–208 (2013)
15. Royan, B., Cremer, M.: Guidelines for Audiovisual and Multimedia Materials in Libraries and Other Institutions. International Federation of Library Associations and Institutions (2004)
16. Prensky, M.: "Engage me or enrage me": what today's learners demand? Educause Rev. **40**(5), 60 (2005)
17. Mayer, R.E.: Multimedia Learning. Cambridge University Press, New York (2001)
18. Brooke, J.: SUS-a quick and dirty usability scale. Usability Eval. Ind. **189**(194), 4–7 (1996)
19. Chin, J.P., Diehl, V.A., Norman, K.L.: Development of an instrument measuring user satisfaction of the human-computer interface. In: Proceedings of the SIGCHI Conference on Human Factors in Computing Systems, pp. 213–218. ACM (1988)

Augmented Reality Applied to Smartphones and Wearable Devices - Virtual Furniture Simulation System

Yi-Cheng Liao[1(✉)], Tao-Hua Wang[2], Hao-Chiang Koong Lin[1], and Kuan-Yu Lin[1]

[1] National University of Tainan, Tainan 70005, Taiwan
edcr@mail.nutn.edu.tw
[2] National Cheng Kung University, Tainan 70101, Taiwan

Abstract. The purposes of this research is to solve the problem we may face in buying new furniture. For instance, in judging the size of furniture and the choice of decoration, it would be helpful through replacing real objects with augmented reality. This measure can greatly reduce effort and time consumption. In the study, we combine the augmented reality technology with smartphones; tablet PCs and wearable devices to build a simulation system of virtual furniture system. Users of this system can use a variety of virtual furniture model to simulate the display in virtual world. In this study, we tested 55 subjects. After brief instruction about how to operating system, our subjects would be asked to experience our system through the smartphones, tablet PCs and wearable glasses. The result shows that the subjects have a positive assessment of the usability and interactivity of the system. Therefore, the system is of practical help to help the selection and arrangement of furniture in the real world.

Keywords: Augmented reality · Android · Mobile device
Wearable device furniture · Furnishing

1 Introduction

According to the eMarketer 2016 survey, the Asia-Pacific region is the region with the highest percentage usage of smartphones globally. Among them, Taiwanese use the smartphone with a population ratio of 73.4%, ranking the highest in the world. In addition, according to a survey conducted by the NCC in 2016, 64.4% of Taiwan's population now use 4G services in Taiwan. The Android platform occupy 84.31% of the Taiwan smartphone market in 2016 [5], so this study uses Android as the development platform. Furthermore, we add AR glasses in this study in order to compare the differences in user's perceptions with different presentation modes (Fig. 1).

The purpose of this study is to develop the "True scale virtual furniture display simulation system". Via the photography function of the smartphone, this system combines the 3D model of the real furniture in proportion with the augmented reality technology. Thus the furniture model can be physically simulated and placed in the

T.-T. Wu et al. (Eds.): ICITL 2018, LNCS 11003, pp. 473–481, 2018.
https://doi.org/10.1007/978-3-319-99737-7_50

Mobile Phone* and Smartphone Users in Taiwan, 2015-2020**

	2015	2016	2017	2018	2019	2020
Mobile phone users*	**19.7**	**19.8**	**19.9**	**20.0**	**20.1**	**20.2**
—% of population	84.1%	84.5%	84.8%	85.0%	85.3%	85.5%
—% change	1.0%	0.7%	0.5%	0.4%	0.5%	0.3%
Smartphone users**	**16.4**	**17.2**	**17.8**	**18.3**	**18.6**	**18.8**
—% of population	69.9%	73.4%	75.8%	77.6%	78.9%	79.9%
—% of mobile phone users	83.1%	86.8%	89.3%	91.3%	92.5%	93.4%
—% change	8.3%	5.2%	3.4%	2.6%	1.8%	1.4%

*Note: *individuals of any age who own at least one mobile phone and use the phone(s) at least once per month; **individuals of any age who own at least one smartphone and use the smartphone(s) at least once per month*
Source: eMarketer, Sep 2016

215560 www.eMarketer.com

Fig. 1. Mobile Phone* and Smartphone** Users in Taiwan, 2015–2020

virtual space. Due to the furniture model is presented in a 1:1 ratio in real environment, user can experience the entity of the virtual furniture correctly. The value of this study is to provide users a reference before them purchase the furniture. In the study, we integrate this system into three different devices: smartphones, tablet PCs and wearable devices. The topics in this study are as follows: (1) The usefulness and user satisfaction of this system. (2) User satisfaction toward the interactivity of this system. Moreover, how user feels differ from using smartphones, tablet PCs, and wearable glasses.

1.1 A Subsection Sample

Augmented Reality is the technology that combines and mix virtual digital information with the real world. To mix the visual entities and reality at the same time in the same place. AR is considered a technical evolution of Virtual Reality. In 1997, Azuma [1] proposed three definitions of augmented reality: 1. Combines real and virtual 2. Interactive in real time 3. Registered in 3-D. Augmented Reality breaks the limit of virtual reality which builds itself on purely virtual scenes. AR cross the real and virtual boundaries, and bring the virtual objects into the real world [8].

1.2 A Subsection Sample

At present, there are three main types that can be used to augment the content of virtual reality. The first one is Marker-based augmented reality produce a result only when the marker is sensed by a reader [2, 3, 9]. The second is Location based augmented reality either partially or fully replaces the original view of an object with a newly augmented view of that same object [7]. The last one is GPS augmented reality use a GPS, digital compass, velocity meter, or Geotagged information which is embedded in the device [6]. The entities will be projected in relative position and resize according to different distances. Augmented reality combined with mobile devices will significantly increase their flexibility in application. Only need to use the camera lens on the mobile device as the main medium for augmented reality, users can collect more markers using mobile device everywhere.

1.3 Wearable Devices

Wearable devices reflect the maneuver and mobility of mobile devices. BT-200 smart 3D glasses launched by EPSON are selected in this study (Fig. 2).

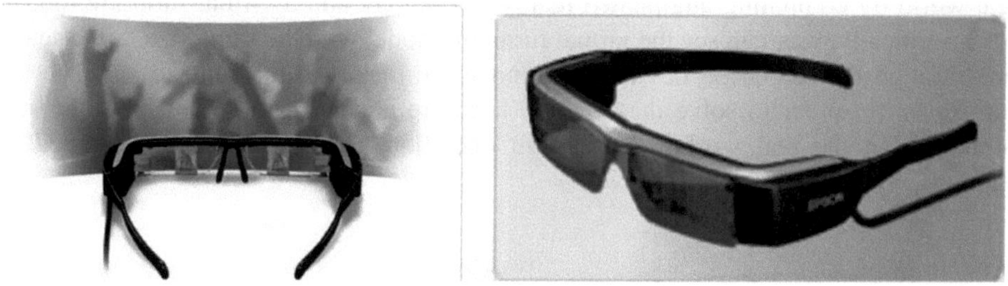

Fig. 2. EPSON BT200

1.4 Markerless Augmented Reality

The current identification mechanism of augmented reality is using marker as the primary method. The use of marker is considered the bridge between reality and virtual world. Specifically, recognize the patterns presented on the marker card as the identification bases, and then the camera takes the marker card to generate corresponding virtual information and pictures. Those kinds of technology are mainly divided into two presentation methods; one is marker while the other is markerless augmented reality. The markerless do not have obvious outlines like marker, while they are mainly based on the recognition of "natural features" in the images. It also supports full-color images and is more beautiful and humanized than traditional marker. Therefore, we choose markerless technology in this study.

2 System Development

2.1 The Software and Resources

The software and resources used in this study are: 3ds MAX 2016: 3D Model Furniture Modeling, Unity (Development software), Vuforia sdk (Augmented reality development kit), Android operating system (Operating system), Smartphones and Tablets (Research tools), and Eps Epson BT200 smart glasses (Wearable research tools).

2.2 Furniture Modeling

The virtual furniture model of this study is built by 3ds MAX. The actual dimensions of furniture are measured and modeled, and then we adjust the dimensional parametric of virtual furniture the same as the real one. So that the virtual furniture displayed through the lens can exhibit 1:1 state. Moreover, it can be combined with the surrounding environment.

2.3 A Subsection Sample

This study develops a "True scale virtual furniture display simulation system", which is developed by Unity. The system allows users to sense virtual furniture simulation in real world by combining augmented reality technology and a virtual furniture model.

Specifically, user can see the virtual furniture model with the same size as the actual one through the screen on devices, and move the maker of furniture to simulate the furnishings in order to solve the how the furniture is shaped to complement the surroundings in the real world. The system operation and interface are illustrated as follows (Figs. 3 and 4):

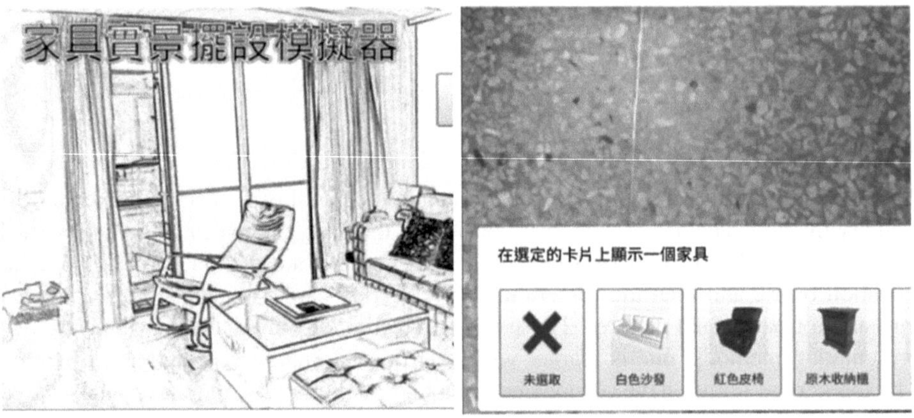

Fig. 3. System interface

3 First Section

3.1 System Usability Scale

System Usability Scale (SUS) is used to understand the user's post-use assessment of the research system. The higher the score indicates the higher the satisfaction of the subject with the usability of the system.

3.2 Questionnaire for User Interaction Satisfaction

Questionnaire for User Interaction Satisfaction (QUIS) is to understand the user's perception of interaction with the system. Specifically, QUIS evaluate the user's satisfaction with the research system in the Man Machine interface view. This study uses this questionnaire to investigate the user's interactive satisfaction with the system and

Fig. 4. A variety of furniture screen

the use of the system in different devices such as smartphones, tablet PCs, and wearable glasses.

4 Results

A total of 55 questionnaires were collected. Among them, 52 were valid while the other 3 invalid. Tables 1 and 2 below are the questionnaires for SUS and QUIS.

Table 1. System Usability Scale (SUS) results

	Items	Mean	SD
1.	I think that I would like to use this system frequently	3.58	0.87
2.	I found the system unnecessarily complex	3.83	0.88
3.	I thought the system was easy to use	4.00	0.89
4.	I think that I would need the support of a technical person to be able to use this system	3.33	1.06
5.	I found the various functions in this system were well integrated	3.79	0.64
6.	I thought there was too much inconsistency in this system	3.87	0.63
7.	I would imagine that most people would learn to use this system very quickly	4.27	0.74
8.	I found the system very cumbersome to use	4.21	0.64
9.	I felt very confident using the system	4.31	0.78
10.	I needed to learn a lot of things before I could get going with this system	3.81	0.93
	Average	3.90	0.81

Table 2. Questionnaire for User Interaction Satisfaction (QUIS) results

	Items	Mean	SD
1.	Overall view of interface	5.35	1.13
2.	System Information	5.83	1.13
3.	User experience	5.69	1.06
4.	User interface	5.22	1.18
5.	System availability	5.60	1.11
6.	Screen Rendering and System Performance (Smartphones)	5.73	1.07
7.	Screen Rendering and System Performance (Tablet PCs)	5.83	0.93
8.	Screen rendering and system performance (wearable glasses)	5.37	1.11
	Average	5.58	1.09

Tables 3, 4 and 5 below show the screen rendering and system performance of three different devices (Fig. 5).

Table 3. Screen rendering and system performance (Smartphones)

	Items	Mean	SD
1.	The text on the screen is easy to read	5.81	1.01
2.	The overall layout of the screen is clear	5.83	0.98
3.	The screen presents a clear style	5.63	1.12
4.	System execution speed and fluency	5.58	1.24
5.	Device convenience	5.83	1.00
	Average	5.73	1.07

5 Conclusion

5.1 Usability Satisfaction of the Research System

The results of System Usability Scale (SUS) show that except for Q4 “I think that I would need the support of a technical person to be able to use this system.” there are positive evaluation (3.58–4.31). The score of the system’s usability after conversion calculation was 72.45 points, showing that the subject’s usability for this system was good.

5.2 Questionnaire for User Interaction Satisfaction (QUIS) of the Research System

Users’ satisfaction with the system’s interactivity and the experience of the research system in using smartphones, tablet PCs, and wearable glasses are slightly different. The average number were 5.83, 5.73, and 5.37, respectively. Of which the satisfaction of tablet PCs received the highest rating. And the score of wearable glasses in “System execution speed and fluency” is significantly lower than those of tablet PCs and

Table 4. Screen rendering and system performance (Tablet PCs)

	Items	Mean	SD
1.	The text on the screen is easy to read	6.00	0.95
2.	The overall layout of the screen is clear	5.87	0.79
3.	The screen presents a clear style	5.75	0.88
4.	System execution speed and fluency	5.71	1.00
5.	Device convenience	5.83	1.00
	Average	5.83	0.93

Table 5. Screen rendering and system performance (wearable glasses)

	Items	Mean	SD
1.	The text on the screen is easy to read	5.38	1.11
2.	The overall layout of the screen is clear	5.50	0.90
3.	The screen presents a clear style	5.48	1.13
4.	System execution speed and fluency	5.40	1.09
5.	Device convenience	5.10	1.35
	Average	5.37	1.11

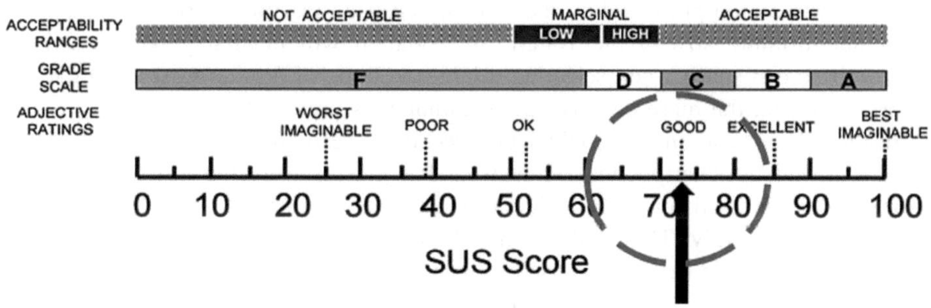

Fig. 5. Score of System Usability Scale (SUS)

smartphones. Finally, the scores of the three devices in the "Device Convenience" item are all low.

Comprehensively analyze the results of the SUS and QUIS. We can conclude the advantages and disadvantages of the three mobile devices using in this study as follows:

5.3 Smartphones

The advantages of smartphones are excellent portability, convenience, and excellent lens elements (with more than 5 million pixels). The disadvantages of smartphones are small screen size and large processor performance gap (this system is less able to operate smoothly in the cheaper smartphone).

5.4 Tablet PCs

The advantages of Tablet PCs are having a generally large-size screen and higher specifications. The disadvantages are the camera lens is poor (the universal tablet refers to a camera with 3 to 5 million pixels), and tablet PC is bulky and inconvenient to carry.

5.5 Wearable Glasses

The advantages of wearable glasses are novelty (freshness), wide field of view (synchronized with binocular vision), and market potential. The disadvantages are he camera lens is extremely poor (only 300,000 pixels), the Android version is old and there is no driver updateable, the product design is poor (because most users cannot adapt to its operating mode), and the processor performance is ordinary.

There are three main factors affecting the perception of the system presented to the user: the lens pixel of the device, the processor performance, and the screen size. The lens pixel. will directly affect the presentation of the system screen. The better the pixel, the better the device can display the system screen. A more elegant presentation to the user's eyes, while the lens pixel also indirectly affects the efficiency of the maker. The processor. performance directly affects the speed of the maker recognition and the smoothness of the overall system operation. The screen size. directly affects the virtual furniture. The screen presented on the screen, because the virtual furniture model and the actual furniture size of the system are equal, it will inevitably occupy a large amount of screen space when selecting a larger volume of furniture. At this time, the larger the screen, the more effective the simultaneous presentation.

In the QUIS scale analysis, tablet PCs received the highest rating in all competitions, followed by smartphones, while wearable glasses were the last. As the technology continues to advance, the technology and specifications of technology products have improved rapidly. This study is only based on the current situation. The representative three mobile devices are used as research tools. In the future, mobile devices will continue to progress and change, and users will have different and better feelings.

References

1. Azuma, R.T.: A survey of augmented reality. Presence-Teleoperators Virtual Environ. **6**(4), 355–385 (1997)
2. Billinghurst, M.: The future of augmented reality in our everyday life. In: 19th International Display Workshops, Nagoya, Japan, p. 1975 (2011)
3. Cawood, S., Fiala, M.: Augmented Reality: A Practical Guide. Pragmatic Bookshelf, Dallas (2007)
4. Seo, D.W., Lee, J.Y.: Direct hand touchable interactions in augmented reality environments for natural and intuitive user experiences. Expert Syst. Appl. **40**, 3784–3793 (2013)
5. eMarketer Homepage. https://www.emarketer.com/Article/Mobile-Taiwan-Look-Highly-Mobile-Market/1014877?ecid=NL1007. Accessed 01 May 2018

6. Lee, R., Sumiya, K.: Measuring geographical regularities of crowd behaviors for Twitter-based geo-social event detection. In: 2nd ACM SIGSPATIAL International Workshop on Location Based Social Networks, pp. 1–10 (2010)
7. Liarokapis, F., Brujic-Okretic, V., Papakonstantinou, S.: Exploring urban environments using virtual and augmented reality. J. Virtual Reality Broadcast. **3**(5), 1–13 (2006)
8. Milgram, P., Kishino, F.: A taxonomy of mixed reality visual displays. IEICE Trans. Inf. Syst. **77**(12), 1321–1329 (1994)
9. Wagner, D., Schmalstieg, D.: Making augmented reality practical on mobile phones, part 1. IEEE Comput. Graph. Appl. **29**(3), 12–15 (2009)
10. Wagner, D., Schmalstieg, D.: Making augmented reality practical on mobile phones, part 2. IEEE Comput. Graph. Appl. **29**(4), 6–9 (2009)

A Board Game Designing of Serious Mini Game in Complementary Colors

Ya-Lun Yu and Ting-Ting Wu(✉)

Graduate School of Technological and Vocational Education,
National Yunlin University of Science and Technology, Douliu, Yunlin 64002, Taiwan R.O.C.
r9745210@gmail.com, danytingting@gmail.com

Abstract. With the advent of the era of multiple learning, the game-based teaching provided has also being increasingly diversified. However, in game-based learning, there may be fewer games concerning complementary colors. Nevertheless, the basic knowledge about colors is associated with students' development. Therefore, this study mainly investigated, developed, and designed the game based on the concept of complementary colors in chromatics. This study attempted to integrate game concepts with teaching. In particular, the features of Serious Mini games are simple and easy-to-learn. This study used the basic knowledge of complementary colors as the rules, and integrated them with Serious Mini game, which was divided into 5 stages: definition, testing & modification, modification & game rule setting, second testing, and completion. This study explained each stage phase by phase, and predicted the effect after the actual future introduction.

Keywords: Serious Mini game · Board games · Complementary colors

1 Introduction

There are fewer existing studies investigating students' views and feelings about colors [1]. Besides, many students or event adults may not necessarily be aware of complementary colors or analogous colors, and they will not particularly intend to understand and investigate chromatics unless required by art-related departments or art class. However, as a matter of fact, ordinary people can see colors as long as they open their eyes, and colors may even affect an individual's emotions and reactions in a day. Nevertheless, not everyone will particularly intend to understand the relationships between colors. Children's emotions about colors tend to be more intense; however, such emotions are merely limited to color matching and feelings. They cannot further understand colors until they attended relevant courses. In Taiwan, chromatics is mentioned in relevant courses. Unfortunately, chromatics is usually introduced shallowly or students cannot further apply it after the courses, which is actually a shame. In particular, colors are important to the development of every student because colors may affect their interest in and understanding of other relevant subjects. The importance of colors to learning cannot be overlooked. Therefore, the purpose of this study is to design a set of Serious Mini game integrated with the basic knowledge of complementary colors basic

T.-T. Wu et al. (Eds.): ICITL 2018, LNCS 11003, pp. 482–489, 2018.
https://doi.org/10.1007/978-3-319-99737-7_51

knowledge, as well as to develop an adequate and suitable mini table game based on the game design process proposed by De Jans et al. [2] to facilitate the application of games to future chromatic education.

2 Literature Review

2.1 Serious Mini Game

Game-based teaching is frequently used in education circles, and it tends to demonstrate significant effects. With the introduction of information education, game-based teaching has also been increasingly diversified and its scope of application has been relatively expanded. As a result, many students are able to benefit from and utilize game-based learning to create a chance to change individual's psychological behaviors, and Serious game is a part of it.

There are increasing studies using Serious game to assess the learning effect of subjects. The main design is used for specific teaching purpose other than entertainment [3]. However, current games are increasingly complicated and players need to spend more time to understand the operating rules. Serious Mini games are extended from Serious games. Therefore, players can spend less time to understand games and operate games more easily [2]. To teachers, in particular, Serious Mini games can be easily integrated as a unit in class. After the course where a simple Serious Mini game was used, the students could find it easy to play the game, as well as achieve the learning objectives in class during the operation of the game. Therefore, Serious Mini games are not merely funny; they are also able to convey knowledge [2].

2.2 Board Games

Table games, games on the table, a.k.a. board games, firstly appeared in the Europe in early days. Chess, Chinese chess, Go, etc. all are table games. Table games mainly refer to games that are played on a table. The main functions are to train players' logical thinking ability or to provide entertainment [4, 5]. However, table games generally mentioned in Taiwan mainly refer to Board Games, which are more refined compared with table games. The rules of board games are also more complicated. Because the types and complexity of Board Games are diverse, each type of Board Game has unique styles and offers different fun. Due to the diversified features of Board Games, board games are usually used as relevant educational tools to achieve educational objectives [6–8]. Adults and children both will be fond of table games or Board Games. Because there are commonalities between table games and board games, in addition to providing entertainment, table games and board games can also enhance social relationships to improve interactions among people.

Due to the advent of information era, many table games or Board Games have started to change. To meet the demand for games, information technologies, such as AR and VR, have been properly integrated to enrich games.

Also, table games are adequate educational tools integrated with the concept of Serious Mini game to become game-based teaching with educational objectives. Table games not only provide entertainment but also strengthen education, which enables students to integrate basic knowledge with long-term memories more rapidly.

In order to provide more complete basic knowledge of complementary colors, this study developed a game of complementary colors to facilitate students' rapid storage of basic knowledge of complementary colors in their memories, as well as flexible application.

3 Methodology

This study used the basic concepts of most important complementary colors in chromatics to develop a Serious Mini game. This study designed the game mainly using the matching of primary color systems (red and green, yellow and purple, blue and orange, and black and white) where players can obtain scores based on accurate primary color matching. Complementary colors refer to two colors that are opposite each other, namely, hues that are 120° apart from each other on the color wheel are the complementary colors. This study mainly applied 4 sets of simple complementary colors to the designed game as the most preliminary basic knowledge for beginners of chromatics. This study referred to the method published by Steffi De Jans in 2017 to divide the designing process of the complementary colors game into 5 stages. [3]. Stage 1 of the design process was implemented from May 2017 to August 2017. Stages 2 and 3 were both completed within one month (August 2017). Stage 4 was implemented from September 2017 to October 2017. It took 1 month to complete the last stage (March 2018).

3.1 Stage 1 Definition

This study mainly used primary color matches, red and green, yellow and purple, blue and orange, and black and white as the major game rules. Players cannot obtain scores unless they match the colors accurately. This study referred to the game rules, elements of cards themselves, and the relationships among cards of the table game "Pick-a-Dog Pick-a-Pig Pick-a-Polar Bear" released by Yawan Stationery Co., LTD. to develop the game in this study.

This study adopted the concept of complementary colors in chromatics to design the game.

- Complementary colors play an important role in color matching, painting, or other color-related studies.
- In painting, complementary colors are used for processing shadows, and they are much more natural than the pure use of black.
- The understanding of the knowledge of complementary colors can improve students' understanding and application of complementary colors.
- Recently, there have been fewer games associated with complementary colors. Therefore, this study designed this game of complementary colors (as shown in Fig. 1).

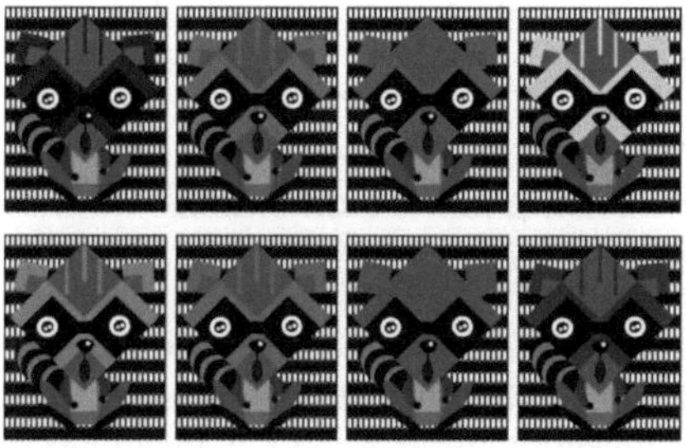

Fig. 1. First draft of card. (Color figure online)

3.2 Stage 2 the First Testing and Car Modified

There were too many colors in the game itself. There were at least 4 sets of complementary colors; however, the hues of 2 sets of them were so close to those of pure colors that visual fatigue might be easily caused and colors could not be easily identified, either. Therefore, improvements were recommended.

- The background of the cards was so complicated that the game-playing was indirectly affected.
- The colors of the color blocks were not recommended to be too fine, which might easily blur the focus.
- The front and back sides of cards could be utilized to enrich the game.

Modified cards (as shown in Fig. 2)

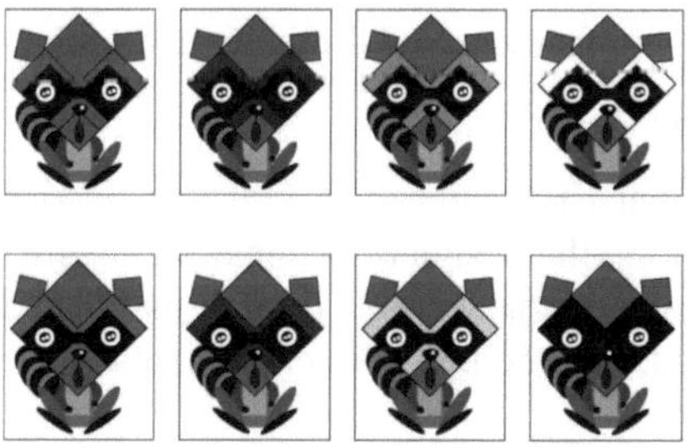

Fig. 2. Second draft of card. (Color figure online)

- The background was removed.
- The color blocks were simplified and redundant color blocks and stripes were completely removed.
- The main body was reduced. The bright colors were changed to 4 set of complementary colors: red and green, purple and yellow, blue and orange, and black and white
- Contour lines were added to color blocks to facilitate color identification.

- The utilization of front and back sides interfered with the game-playing instead, and could not be adopted.

3.3 Stage 3 Game Rule Setting and Modification

- The game rules were set up and explained.
- The difficulty of the game could be increased. For example, more background colors could be added to change the number of background colors of 1 card from 2 background colors to 3 background colors as an advanced card.

After the modification

- The game rules were re-modified.

The number of cards was re-considered because the additional increase of one color would increase the number of cards from 64 cards to 512 cards. How the modification should be made had to be thought over.

However, after the modification, this study discovered difficulties in implementation. The difficulties were as follows: because the colors were so complicated that it was difficult to identify them and too much time was wasted on the calculation of scores. There were so many cards that the overall time spent on the game was increased. Besides, it was difficult to operate the game. Therefore, the number of cards was decreased to 64 cards.

3.4 Stage 4 the Second Testing

- Time limit could be added to increase the excitement and fun of activities.
- The game rules were re-set because the scoring method was so complicated that adding or subtracting points increased difficulty and took a lot of time.

After the modification

- The time limit was set at 1 min.
- To easily identify colors, the design of original pictures was changed (as shown in Fig. 3). For example, objects that were not directly associated with color identification were directly removed, and the most direct elements were retained to facilitate the scoring.

Fig. 3. Second draft of card. (Color figure online)

Therefore, the body, limbs, and tail of characters were removed, while the simplest head was retained. Besides, the head was zoomed in properly to facilitate color identification.

- Scoring method: 1 point would be added to the total score for successful matching of each pair of complementary colors. The total score would be neither deducted nor added for a mismatch. For the advanced version of the game, 1 point would be deducted from the total score for a mismatch.

3.5 Complete the Game Setting

Game rules (after the modification); the advanced version was removed.

Number of players: 2–4 players.

Game time: after all of the cards were completely played, the host said, “Start.” The time calculation started and ended at 1 min.

(The game time could be adjusted to 2–3 min for the first trial)

Game rules

1. Every player picked a card and covered it on the table near him/her (without looking at the card or letting other players look at it).
2. Turning over the rest of the cards and putting them on the table with front side (picture side) facing up.
3. When the host said, “Start,” the players turned over the covered card and put it on the hand to start to look for the match.
   Players looked for the card with complementary colors. There were at least 1–2 colors in a card, so players were able to find a card with complementary colors on the Table.
4. After finding out a card with complementary colors, players stacked it with the card originally put on the hand to become a new card, and then find out the card with complementary colors of the new card.
5. The game continued until the time was up or there wasn’t any card on the Table.
6. Scoring of cards

The students in the team checked the cards of each other to find out whether the matches were accurate.

Only the cards on the hand were included in the score calculation. However, the card (covered) originally on the hand was not included in the score calculation.

1 point was added to the total score for successful matching of each pair of cards. The total score would be neither deducted nor added for a mismatch.

Precautions: The order of cards checked should not be messed up during the calculation.

4 Analysis

This study found that the combination of table games and courses needs full coordination. Besides, time should be properly controlled to ensure the implementation of experiment. The analysis on the advantages and disadvantages is as follows:

- Advantage
  1. Increasing students' concentration. During game-playing, students would concentrate on the game and their operating speed would increase, especially when they were familiar with game rules.
  2. Increasing students' interest. During game-playing, students would look forward to obtaining joy and excitement from the game and intend to achieve something in the game performance.
  3. Improving students' color learning. During game-playing, the concept of complementary colors would be continuously and imperceptibly implanted into students' mind. Due to the need of the game, students had no choice but to memorize the basic knowledge of complementary colors to avoid making mistakes in the game.
- Disadvantage
  1. Students' excessive expectation towards the game. Students would hold a high expectation due to the game, and constantly urge the teacher to start the game sooner. The game part might easily distract students in class.
  2. Students' sense of helplessness after the game. After game-playing, students tended to lose confidence or expect another game and lose learning focus in the next unit in next class.

5 Conclusion

Based on the above, this study found that a Serious Mini game can assist students in learning to a certain extent. A serious mini game is different from the past serious game that cannot be played unless players fully understand the rules and spend a large amount of time, which causes the overall learning strategies to be adjusted. However, students are interested in games to a certain extent. In order to trigger students' interest, teaching strategies must be properly used to enable students to fully concentrate on both the course and game. Students' game performance is associated with the fact that whether they can identify the complementary colors intuitively. One of the advantages of Serious Mini game used in this course was that students could fully utilize the knowledge of chromatics when facing colors in life, as well as apply it to the implementation of color-related learning or work. To students, color learning plays an important role in any future learning. As a result, colors can fully assist students in learning and are beneficial to their future achievements and development.

Acknowledgments. This research is partially supported by the Ministry of Science and Technology (MOST), Taiwan, R.O.C. under Grant MOST 104-2511-S-224-003-MY3, MOST 105-2628-S-224-001-MY3.

References

1. Huang, Y.M.: Reason and emotion: how they drive students to play a color game. Eurasia J. Math. Sci. Technol. Educ. **14**(5), 1911–1924 (2018)
2. De Jans, S., Van Geit, K., Cauberghe, V., Hudders, L., De Veirman, M.: Using games to raise awareness: How to co-design serious mini-games? Comput. Educ. **110**, 77–87 (2017)
3. Tong, T., Chignell, M., Tierney, M.C., Lee, J.S.: Test-Retest reliability of a serious game for delirium screening in the emergency department. Front. Aging Neurosci. **8**, 11 (2016)
4. Sala, G., Foley, J.P., Gobet, F.: The effects of chess instruction on pupils' cognitive and academic skills: state of the art and theoretical challenges. Front. Psychol. **8**, 4 (2017)
5. Sala, G., Gobet, F.: Does far transfer exist? Negative evidence from chess, music, and working memory training. Curr. Dir. Psychol. Sci. **26**(6), 515–520 (2017)
6. Laurens, T., Batlolona, F.A., Batlolona, J.R., Leasa, M.: How does Realistic Mathematics Education (RME) improve students' mathematics cognitive achievement? Eurasia J. Math. Sci. Technol. Educ. **14**(2), 569–578 (2018)
7. Ladur, A.N., van Teijlingen, E., Hundley, V.: 'Whose Shoes?' Can an educational board game engage Ugandan men in pregnancy and childbirth? BMC Pregnancy Childbirth **18**, 8 (2018)
8. Rogerson, M.J., Gibbs, M.: Finding time for tabletop: board game play and parenting. Games Cult. **13**(3), 280–300 (2018)

The Study of Creativity, Creativity Style, Creativity Climate Applying Creativity Learning Strategies - An Example of Engineering Education

Wei-Shan Liu, Yu-Tzu Wu, and Ting-Ting Wu(✉)

Graduate School of Technological and Vocational Education,
National Yunlin University of Science and Technology, Yunlin, Taiwan
judyjudy12334@gmail.com, hae88019@gmail.com,
ttwu@yuntech.edu.tw

Abstract. Creativity is currently regarded as one of the critical competence in numerous learning theories. With cultivation of positive creativity, the reinforcement of critical ability and thinking will be advantages in the era. At present, many evaluations on creativity result are mainly based on students' finished work. As to the analysis, the discussion mostly focuses on single dimension. However, there are various factors of creativity and it lacks the study on correlation among creative style, creative climate and creativity. Thus, based on creativity learning, this study applies PBL, Project-Based Learning, in information engineering project and conducts pretest and posttest of Torrance Tests of Creative Thinking (TTCT) and the indicators of creativity. In the course of project, it introduces SCAMPER creative thinking strategy in learning platform and learners fill in questionnaires of creative style and creative climate after the class. According to analytical result, pretest and posttest of the TTCT show significant difference. In questionnaire of creative style, learners' creative core characteristics and creative assistance habit reveal significant and positive feedback; as to questionnaire of creative climate, it is significant. Students recognize the importance of atmosphere and positive creative climate reinforces development of creative competence.

Keywords: Creativity · Creativity style · Creativity climate
Engineering education · SCAMPER

1 Introduction

Time changes and technology makes progress. In constantly innovative and changing competitive market structure, manpower needed by industrial circle successively refers to talents with interdisciplinary experience and innovative thinking competence. Thus, various educational objectives aim to cultivate the students with capacity to solve problems by innovative measures. Engineering education is no exception. By creative thinking, design and integrated course, it cultivates students' creative thinking, critique and reflection and technique to adapt to change. Nowadays, creativity is regarded as

T.-T. Wu et al. (Eds.): ICITL 2018, LNCS 11003, pp. 490–499, 2018.
https://doi.org/10.1007/978-3-319-99737-7_52

one of the important competence in numerous learning theories. Definitions on creativity are different according to perspectives or fields. During the time of study, if a person can cultivate positive creativity, in this era, he (she) can reinforce critical competence and thinking. It not only enhances the performance of creativity in education, but also avoids the constraints of others or society. Some people argue that creativity is the competence of invention, some suggest that it is divergent thinking and even some scholars treat it as imagination [1]. In short, creativity is the competence of initiation and creative people's characteristics and abilities [2].

In process of creativity learning, to find if creative climate and creative style enhance learners' creativity is critical. According to some past studies, in learning process, learners' mental feelings and change influence playfulness, humor, creative attitude and environmental factor in development of creativity learning [3]. It is effect of creative climate on creativity learning; in addition, individuals' creative style influences and judges strategy or belief to practice creative work. Sternberg argued that creative style is the preference of thinking, practice and problem solving. Characteristics of creative style influence outcome of creativity learning performance [4]. However, at present, most of creativity evaluations are based on students' finished work and they rarely explore and analyze style and climate of creativity and students' feelings. Even in analysis of record, they tend to define or probe into characteristics of creativity by single dimension.

Hence, in course of information engineering project, this study applies strategy of PBL (Project-Based Learning) and based on SCAMPER creative thinking strategy, it introduces Moodle learning platform. By objectives of five activities on learning platform and proper guidance of SCAMPER creative thinking strategy, it successively communicates, discusses and interacts in the group. By teachers' problem-solving and divergent to convergent thinking, it solves creative problems in the group and by questionnaire record of the platform, it attempts to find if engineering department students' creative thinking competence is enhanced after experiencing PBL and SCAMPER creative thinking strategy. In the course of information engineering project, this study explores perception of creative style and creative climate to allow teachers to provide appropriate instructional resources, instructional guidance and counseling. Total analytical result can serve as reference for teachers' following assistance instruction and instant feedback in order to enhance students' innovative and creative thinking, lead to connection between creativity and imagination and upgrade innovative application of engineering education.

2 Literature Review

2.1 Creativity

Key factor of creation is based on individuals' passion at work and the pleasure resulted from work. In other words, high-level motivation can result in creative behavior. Creativity is complicated and multi-dimensional phenomenon [5]. It is the interaction among various individual, process and environmental factors. Ghiselin stated that creation is the process of change, development and progress of subjective life and it results in new, useful and acceptable outcome [6]. Hallman argued that creation is a kind of life style rather than individuals' possible production of new things [7]. Torrance suggested that creation means to develop new hypothesis on problem and modify or re-test the hypothesis in order to solve the problem. The competence to solve unknown problems is called creativity [8].

2.2 Creativity Style

Style is a complicated concept. According to Sternberg, various styles play different roles in message processing. For instance, cognitive style is the preference of individuals to cope with messages. Learning style is individuals' preferred learning method regarding the message. Thinking style is individuals' preferred thinking method regarding the message [9]. Kumar et al. argued that style of creativity is based on the concern of individuals' performance of creative style in daily creative practice. Creativity is not a single concept and with creative style, different individuals might practice their creative work by different beliefs and different strategies [10]. Therefore, creative style theory of this study is based on Kumar et al. and the dimensions include final product positioning, technique use, belief of unconscious process, dependency on others, superstitious behavior, environmental control and self-regulation of behavior and sensory use [10]. In addition, creative style is derived from creativity theory and 7 beliefs of creative style emphasized are closely associated with creativity individuals' strategies. Creative style shows that many scholars pay attention to relationship between social work environment factors and individuals' creativity and they argue that environment is critical to result in and restrain individuals' creative performance [11].

2.3 Creativity Climate

Tesluk, Farr and Klein stated that climate is the key factor in the organizations to enhance creativity. Climate is defined as organizational leaders' behavior and their support and encouragement to individuals' self-efficacy. Climate means perception and behavior. It is individuals' feelings to various attributes of organizations. Creative climate includes individual-level psychological process, including individuals' learning, problem-solving, motivation of creativity and commitment to organization; organizational process is the total of individuals of the organizations, including problem-solving of group, policy construction, communication and negotiation [12]; some scholar argued that learners' creativity is influenced by mutual learning from teachers and peers and inferred that learners' creativity performance is directly and indirectly influenced by creative climate [13]. Individuals' cognition of some events, activities and programs at work and the possible behavior rewarded, supported and expected can be regarded as all members' common recognition in the same organization [14]. According to perspective of Csikzenmihyli, people's cognition of creativity influences creative climate and people's attitude toward creativity. Importance of creative climate in the society determines creative performance. Climate is a kind of ambience which can be perceived by learners through daily affairs of business, rules of business and reward system. People are the most critical factor in the environment and positive creative climate is created by human [15].

2.4 Scamper

SCAMPER was proposed by American psychologist, Robert Eberle. It is aimed at improving products or executive process of projects, and modifying the characteristics. Through 7 thinking dimensions, it enhances the thoughts and triggers new ideas to adjust current situations. The 7 thinking dimensions are substitution, integration, adjustment, modification, other usage, elimination, reconstruction and reorganize current product structure, production and manufacturing or executive process or re-arrangement of the order [16].

2.5 Project-Based Learning

Project-Based Learning was proposed by American educator, John Dewey. It values experiment, practice and situation of learning in doing to lead to learning outcome. The key of project making learning is to actively probe into themes in learning process and explore, interpret, create and construct new knowledge by knowledge to demonstrate collaborative learning, integrated planning, problem-solving competence. It emphasizes that teachers should cultivate students' abilities of exploration and problem-solving by designing instructional activities [17]. "Project-oriented learning" is based on statement of constructionism. It argues that acquisition of knowledge is not by communication. Hence, Project-Based Learning is construction-oriented learning. It provides learners with highly complicated and realistic projects. Students recognize the themes, design the questions, plan action projects, collect data, solve problems, construct decision-making action, accomplish exploration and present the work.

3 Methodology

3.1 Participants

Subjects of this study were juniors of college of engineering in one national university of Taiwan who studied course of information engineering project (1) and (2). There were 45 students in one class. One group included 4 to 5 students and there were 10 groups. By successive guidance instruction on Moodle learning platform, each student experienced systematic project-oriented learning and activity learning of SCAMPER creative thinking strategy.

3.2 Learning Platform

Moodle learning platform includes various types of insert module. In order to meet the requirement of instructional design of this study and comply with PBL (Project-Based Learning) and SCAMPER creative thinking strategy, on the platform of this system, it adopted insert module of Activity Module and added functions required by Project-Based Learning and SCAMPER creative thinking strategy to Moodle learning platform system. Users' interface is shown by webpage.

System interface is shown in Fig. 1. Design of the system includes bulletin board of course, reminder of calendar, forum (non-simultaneous), video conference (simultaneous), submission of assignments, feedback evaluation, the basic functions provided by most of learning platforms. The special design of system interface is below: by introduction of Project-Based Learning and SCAMPER creative thinking strategy, the system of learning platform includes five phases: Preparation (P)-Implementation (I)-Presentation (P)-Evaluation (E)-Revision (R). By project learning participation and engagement in platform activities, it encourages in-group and between-group discussion, expands thinking competence, stimulates diverse view development and further guides learners to experience higher level of cognitive skill learning.

Fig. 1. System interface.

3.3 Research Instrument

Torrance Tests of Creative Thinking (TTCT). According to learners' simultaneous and non-simultaneous questionnaires of scales and discussion record on the platform, this study analyzes creative style scale and teachers' and students' analysis of creative climate scale and conducts and explores pretest and posttest of TTCT in order to recognize difference before and after learning of learners with high and low degrees of creativity.

Creativity Style Questionnaire. In order to probe into learners' enhancement of creative style after project learning, this study adopts questionnaire of path model of effects of university students' hope, constructive thoughts and emotional creativity on creative style developed by Yeh to evaluate effect on students' creative style learning; there are 34 items in the questionnaire, including two dimensions: creative core characteristics and creative assistance habit. Creative core characteristics are classified into technique use, dependency on others, final product positioning and belief of unconscious process; creative assistance habit is divided into superstitious behavior, sensory use, environmental control and self-regulation of behavior. There is a total of 7 items for analysis and discussion [18].

Creativity Climate Questionnaire. Scale of creative climate is based on generalized relationship among teachers' teaching style, creative climate of class and creativity. It is revised as creative climate scale of this study. The objective is organizational members' perceived climate which enhances organizational creative outcome. There are 70 items, including 10 categories: support of concept, liveliness and freedom, teachers' encouragement, challenge participation, active learning, dialogue communication, support of thoughts and new concept, conflict, activeness and humor, engagement and autonomy. 45 students fill in the questionnaires. Through questionnaire analysis, it shows teachers' perception of environment and climate in learners' learning and explores learners' perception of creative climate when executing assignments of project course [19].

3.4 Experimental Process

Courses of information engineering project (1) and (2) are respectively in the first and second semesters. Each semester includes 18 weeks and there are two sections in every week. Assignment distribution of the course is shown in Fig. 2; in the first week of the first semester, the teacher explained the objectives of project course to all students and elaborated the process and content of different phases in project activity. In the course of the first week, all learners must fill in pretest of TTCT. By evaluation of test, this study recognized the learners' creativity competence; in the second week of the first semester, according to result of TTCT, it divided the learners into groups by heterogeneity and allowed learners to practice learning platform webpages and be familiar with functions and rules of the system; from Week 3 to Week 9 of the first semester, it conducted preparation of PBL (Project-Based Learning). At this phase, learners could apply various assistance functions on the platform, discuss project direction and scope, construct topic and theme and plan project schedule and objectives. During these 7 weeks, they learned to use 7 thinking dimensions of SCAMPER to properly adjust project objectives and apply creative thinking and change habitual thinking perspective and direction. From Week 10 of the first semester to Week 8 of the second semester, it conducted the phase of implementation. At this stage, the groups continued applying functions on learning platform and practiced the system constructed for the project. From Week 9 to Week 12 of the second semester, it was the phase of presentation. Before formal project presentation, group members could interact and exchange with each other by online discussion function, practice project report by simultaneous video function and submit documents by uploading data. After one group presents the project, other groups must provide instant feedback and suggestion. By sharing of project result, they learned from each other and exchanged knowledge. From Week 13 to Week 14 of the second semester, it was the phase of evaluation. According to learning result and learning process, the teacher showed evaluation and suggestion and uploaded the suggested content and evaluation on learning platform; from Week 15 to Week 16, it was the phase of revision. According to feedback obtained from teacher and peers, learners would practice reflection, self-examination, negotiation, communication, modify project report according to feedback content and adjust personal learning capability. In Week 17 of the second semester, learners must upload revised project report to learning platform and conduct posttest of TTCT; finally, in Week 18 of the second semester, learners filled in creative style scale and creative climate questionnaire to review the learning and acquisition of creativity training in two semesters.

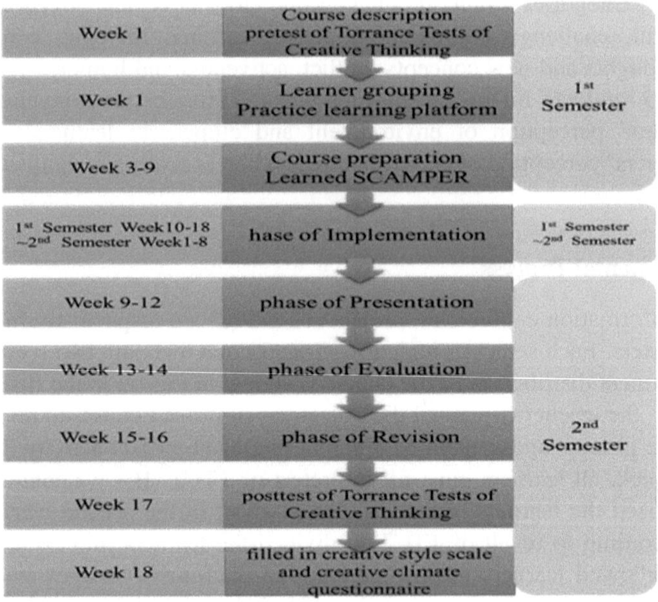

Fig. 2. Experimental procedure.

4 Results

4.1 TTCT

This study integrates PBL and SCAMPER creative thinking strategy in engineering education to find if learners' creative thinking competence is enhanced after participating in the course. It conducts paired sample t test to analyze learners' pretest and posttest grades of TTCT. Analytical result is shown in Table 1. p value = .000 < 0.05 and learners' performance in pretest and posttest of TTCT is significantly different. The result reveals that after course learning of SCAMPER creative thinking strategy and PBL, learners' creative thinking performance is strengthened.

Table 1. TTCT results.

TTCT	Mean	SD	N	t	df	p
Pretest	64.46	7.17	45	−11.467	44	.000*
Posttest	73.91	4.40				

*$p < .05$

4.2 Creativity Style Questionnaire

There are 34 items in creative style scale which is mainly classified into creative core characteristics and creative assistance habit. Creative core characteristics includes technique use, dependency on others, final product positioning and belief of unconscious process. Creative assistance habit includes superstitious behavior, sensory use, environmental control and self-regulation of behavior. This study adopts single sample t test to analyze the previous 8 items. According to Table 2, p values of all items are <.05 and it is significant. Subsequently, it further explores the items and it shows that in project learning process, learners tend to reveal daily life habit and learn in specific and comfortable environment and habit to lead to more significant project learning and creative ideas and enhance creative competence.

Table 2. Creativity style questionnaire results.

Categories	N	M	SD	p
Technique use	45	3.33	.46	.000*
Dependency on others	45	3.56	.72	.000*
Final product positioning	45	3.60	.72	.000*
Belief of unconscious process	45	3.44	.59	.000*
Superstitious behavior	45	2.40	1.04	.000*
Sensory use	45	2.48	.93	.000*
Environmental control and self-regulation of behavior	45	2.72	.81	.000*

*$p < .05$

4.3 Creativity Climate Questionnaire

Questionnaire of students' creative climate scale includes 70 items and 10 categories: support of concept, liveliness and freedom, teachers' encouragement, challenge participation, active learning, dialogue communication, support of thinking and new ideas, conflict, activeness and humor, engagement and autonomy. In order to find learners' perception of environment and atmosphere when conducting project assignment and their perception of positive creative climate, this study conducts single sample t test on the items. Analytical result is shown in Table 3. According to the table, p values of the items are <0.5 and it is significant. Thus, in project learning process, learners experience positive learning climate which reinforces creativity learning and positively influences autonomic learning or collaboration.

Table 3. Creativity climate questionnaire results.

Categories	N	M	SD	*p*
Support of concept	45	3.99	.41	.000*
Liveliness and freedom	45	3.89	.49	.000*
Teachers' encouragement	45	3.96	.56	.000*
Challenge participation	45	3.79	.43	.000*
Active learning	45	3.45	.80	.000*
Dialogue communication	45	3.87	.51	.000*
Support of thinking and new ideas	45	3.78	.45	.000*
Conflict	45	2.29	1.14	.000*
Activeness and humor	45	3.85	.50	.000*
Engagement and autonomy	45	3.95	.44	.000*

*$p < .05$

5 Discussion

This study focuses on learners and after PBL and SCAMPER instructional activity on the platform, it clarifies and recognizes the effects of creative style and creative climate on factors of creativity; after learners experience project creativity training, from pretest and posttest of result of TTCT, this study realizes that learners' creative thinking is reinforced. In other words, project course upon thinking dimensions of SCAMPER significantly reinforces learners' creative thinking. Items of creative style scale are all significant. Thus, learners all agree that group members' friendly cooperation can strengthen creativity and result in positive ideas. They also recognize that PBL behavioral process results in more knowledge and ideas; in the scale of creative climate, all items are significant. It means that learners recognize the importance of climate. All learners state that mutual learning is one of the key factors to upgrade learning motivation and direction.

This study generalizes pretest and posttest of TTCT result and exploration on creative style and creative climate scale. In creative style scale, mean of learners' creativity performance is around 3. However, according to pretest and posttest grades of TTCT, learners' performance is upgraded. Thus, with positive creative climate in learning, as to students' perception of teachers or group members' mutual learning, although the feeling of creativity learning is not profound, the test result shows that the effect is positive.

In the future, it can conduct in-depth study and analysis on correlation among dimensions, such as learners' learning behavior, personal motivation, cognitive style and cognitive loading to evaluate and recognize this study.

Acknowledgments. This work is partially supported by Ministry of Science and Technology, Taiwan under grant MOST 104-2511-S-224-003-MY3 and MOST 105-2628-S-224-001-MY3.

References

1. Torrance, E.P.: Education and the Creative Potential. University of Minnesota Press, Minneapolis (1963)
2. Guilford, J.P.: Creativity. Am. Psychol. **5**(9), 444–454 (1950)
3. Chang, J.H., Chen, H.C., Hsu, C.C., et al.: Flexible humor styles and the creative mind: using a typological approach to investigate the relationship between humor styles and creativity. Psychol. Aesthet. Creat. Arts **9**(3), 306–312 (2015)
4. Sternberg, R.J.: Thinking Styles. Cambridge University Press, New York (1997)
5. Henle, M.: The birth and death of ideas. In: Gruber, H.E., Terrell, G., Wertheimer, M. (eds.) Contemporary Approaches to Creative Thinking, pp. 31–62. Atherton Press, New York (1962)
6. Ghiselin, B.: The Creative Process. University of California Press, Berkeley (1952)
7. Hallman, R.J.: The commonness of creativity. Educ. Theor. **13**(2), 132–136 (1963)
8. Torrance, E.P.: Guiding Creative Talent. Prentice-Hall, Inc., Englewood Cliffs (1962)
9. Sternberg, R.J., Grigorenko, E.L.: Styles of thinking in school. Eur. J. High Abil. **6**(2), 201–219 (1995)
10. Kumar, V.K., Kemmler, D., Holman, E.R.: The creativity styles questionnaire revised. Creat. Res. J. **10**, 51–58 (1997)
11. Csikszentmihalyi, M.: Creativity: Flow and the Psychology of Discovery and Invention. HarperCollins Publishers, New York (1996)
12. Tesluk, P.E., Faar, J.L., Klein, S.R.: Influences of organisational culture and climate on individual creativity. J. Creat. Behav. **31**(1), 21–44 (1997)
13. O'Neil, B.: Improving learning for underachievers. Clear. House **74**(5), 236–237 (2001)
14. Reichers, A.E., Schneider, B.: Climate and culture: an evolution of constructs. In: Schneider, B. (ed.) Organizational Climate and Culture, pp. 5–39. Jossey-Bass, San Francisco (1990)
15. Csikszentmihalyi, M.: Implications of a systems perspective for the study of creativity. In: Sternberg, R.J. (ed.) Handbook of Creativity, pp. 313–335. Cambridge University Press, New York (1999)
16. Eberle, R.F.: Scamper: Games for Imagination Development. D.O.K., New York (1971)
17. Trop, L., Sage, S.: Problems as Possibilities: Problem-Based Learning for K-12 Education. Association for Supervision and Curriculum Development, Alexandria (2002)
18. Yeh, Y.C.: Seventh graders' academic achievement, creativity, and their ability to construct a cross-domain concept map—a brain function perspective. J. Creat. Behav. **38**(2), 125–144 (2004)
19. Isaksen, S.G., Lauer, K.J., Ekvall, G., Britz, A.: Perceptions of the best and worst climates for creativity: preliminary validation evidence for the situational outlook questionnaire. Creat. Res. J. **13**(2), 171–184 (2001)

The Effectiveness of Health Communication for Implement Multimedia E-Book into Large and Small Groups

Yi-Chen Lu[1], Ting-Ting Wu[1(✉)], and Chen-Ying Su[2]

[1] Graduate School of Technological and Vocational Education, National Yunlin University of Science and Technology, Douliou, Taiwan
luangel0520@hamil.com, ttwu@yuntech.edu.tw
[2] Departments of Nursing, National Quemoy University, Quemoy, Taiwan
cysu@nqu.edu.tw

Abstract. This study investigated the use of multimedia e-book by nursing interns to promote health communication. The characteristics of e-book were utilized to facilitate the health communication. It aimed to explore the outcomes of health communication in a group setting, for both large and small groups, in order to determine whether nursing interns could use e-book to enhance the outcome of health communication and strengthen their literacy of nursing informatics. Comparison was conducted. This study selected 32 junior nursing students that are about to enter their senior year from a national university of Taiwan. Questionnaire survey was based on Likert 5-point scale. The results showed that in either large or small group, outcome of nursing students' personal communication by multimedia e-book and cultivation of personal nursing informatics literacy are significant. Field feedback is also positive. Hence, multimedia e-book can effectively assist with nursing students' community health communication.

Keywords: Multimedia e-book · Nursing informatics · Health communication

1 Introduction

It makes progress in the times, people's life styles are thus different and types of communication also change. With the advancement of technology, medical system and medical personnel provide people with medical knowledge different from the past. Upon the progress of information technology, "information assisted instruction" is successively introduced in nursing education curriculum [1]. Integration of e-book system can enhance nursing students' attention and interest. Nevertheless, "Good craftsmanship depends on use of the right tools". Introduction of new technology results in soft declaration in nursing education and properly applies technology media in promotion of health education. Hence, nursing students introduce health education by innovative learning method and interactive model and reinforce effectiveness of internship.

With the progress and prevalence of information technology and internet, digital technology imperceptibly penetrates in our world. Unconsciously, our living culture

T.-T. Wu et al. (Eds.): ICITL 2018, LNCS 11003, pp. 500–509, 2018.
https://doi.org/10.1007/978-3-319-99737-7_53

changes. Likewise, medical system also becomes different. As to nursing, it turns into electronic, non-paper and mobile information system era. E-learning is rapidly blended in medical education system [2, 3]. Through expansion and communication of daily digital platforms, people show different views on communication of health knowledge.

The number and scale of group members considerably influence degree of interaction and practice model of group activity. As to the number of group members, large group includes at least 35 members, such as class, group counseling or conference. The number of medium group members is 20–35, including seminar and workshop. The number of small group members is below 20. Based on definition of Encyclopedia of Social Work of the U.S. [4], the number of small group members is generally 2–15 and the number of large group members is 20–50. Thus, this study treats definitions of number of members in large and small groups in Encyclopedia of Social Work as scope in experiment in order to differentiate and explore nursing students' health education subjects.

In nursing students' internship of community health nursing, this study allows them to practice health communication by multimedia e-book and probes into outcomes of the communication implemented in large and small groups. With communication characteristics of e-book, this study assists with promotion of health education and classifies it into two research dimensions to find if nursing students' health education promotion by multimedia e-book can enhance effectiveness of their practice of health communication and if their cultivation of nursing informatics literacy is strengthened by using multimedia e-book.

2 Literatures

2.1 Health Communication

Health communication research is derived from theories such as communication, psychology and sociology [5]. In terms of essence, health communication is one branch of communication. In 1994, Rogers Everett M proposed the definition below, "health communication is the behavior to transform medical research finding into public health knowledge and by change of attitude and behavior, it lowers occurrence rate and death rate of illness to effectively upgrade life quality and health level of one community or country."

In 1996, Rogers Everett M. proposed new interpretation on health communication in the article: "all categories of human communication associated with health are called health communication." Since the definition is simple and clear, it is adopted and cited by the majority [6].

With the development of health communication, it shows that people pay more attention to their health and health issues are important. With the continuous progress of technology and communication, health communication not only conveys health information, but also reflects social context. The receivers are not simply the active agents. They can construct their comprehension of health information and they are more likely to decide the possible health information conveyed to other receivers through change of sharing, comments and permission [5].

2.2 Nursing Informatics

Objective of nursing education aims to cultivate nursing students' core literacy of sharp exploration, active thinking and professional affection and attitude and develop the proper nurses for workplace. Hence, learner-centered instructional design and strategy can lead to students' reflection on nursing knowledge and competence and experience literacy to show lifelong learning capacity of self-growth and continuing education [7].

The earliest historical discussion on nursing informatics can be traced back to early 19th century. The first nursing informatics scholar was Florence Nightingale who was regarded as the mother of modern nursing and the safety advocate of patients at early phases. Florence Nightingale presented figures by collection, tables, explanation and diagrams in order to improve patient care during the period of Crimean War and implement statistical analysis of hospital reform [8].

Graves and Corcoran defined nursing informatics as one science subject which combines nursing science, information science and computer science [7]. It is mainly applied to processing and management of nursing data, information and knowledge in order to assist with nursing practice and provide nursing care.

2.3 Multimedia E-Book

Digital presentation of books refers to e-book which can be read by e-devices such as computer or mobile devices [9].

Online educational resources thus increase. More and more teachers are putting away traditional textbook instruction and introduce multimedia and interactive e-textbooks to create more personalized learning methods for students [10]. By different devices, it enhances instruction, strengthens various interactive learning and provides multimedia learning environment such as video image, animation text and virtual reality and allows students to work according to their situations. Therefore, traditional textbooks are no longer the single measures of instructional information [11].

In recent years, by creation of active learning opportunity, personalized experience and immediate feedback, it significantly increases students who use e-book [11]. The examples include interactive simulation, social interaction, test with immediate feedback and other widget application [11].

Nowadays, in e-book, paper and books are digitalized and it is different from physical books with fixed texts or paper. It also includes interactive functions such as full-text index, hyperlink and multimedia. It saves files and information by codes. Regarding full text or specific chapters, readers can download the content they are interested in or need from internet to computers or personal reading devices to read and share at any time and in any place. It reveals brand-new and convenient reading model. In short, e-book is not simply presented by devices. It shows abundant and multiple interactive functions.

3 Method

3.1 Participants

Subjects of this study were future senior students of nursing department in one national university of Taiwan. They practiced internship after studying the course of community health nursing, obtained editing of e-book in class and applied it to the field of internship. There was a total of 32 students. One group included 8 members and there were 4 groups. Group health education was based on local community and nursing home. Health education subjects were community residents or students in different levels of schools. Group health education was implemented by large group (more than 20 members) and small group (less than 15 members). Each student promoted health education to two groups.

In the process, nursing students applied self-edited and self-designed multimedia e-book, produced proper e-book for individual group health education content and input it in tablet as the mobile device and content to promote health education. Teaching materials of health education communication can be decided by discussion between nursing students and registered nurses, or directly by registered nurses. In Fig. 1, it shows the process in which nursing students promote health education by multimedia e-book in large and small groups. Through e-book, it conducted group health education and attempted to find if nursing students' application of multimedia e-book can enhance the effect of their implementation of health communication and if the process in which nursing students learn and apply multimedia e-book can upgrade their cultivation of nursing informatics literacy.

Fig. 1. The process in which nursing students promote health education by multimedia e-book in large and small groups.

3.2 E-Book Communication Health Education Interface

In the experiment, this study adopts e-book system of interactive e-book editing program of SimMAGIC eBook of Hamastar Technology. The interface is simple and it does not require any programming language and design background. Users can re-construct module and can directly input and edit original materials such as PPT briefing and PDF documents as e-book and further integrate various multimedia components, including images, pictures, sound and words. In addition, SimMAGIC eBook also provides various simulated operation, such as interactive process, mouse dragging (such as drag-and-match and jigsaw puzzle), screen selection (such as post-it and scratch), pop-up window of messages, hyperlink and sharing; as to multimedia file integration, users can input multimedia materials such as videos, images, online sound recording and reading to enrich reading process of communication; besides direct presentation, image setting also includes the functions such as 360° image rotation and carousel of images. Users can even select and share the images by email or social network (such as Line and facebook).

Readers can not only read, but also interact with e-book and practice simulated test to enhance reading and learning participation intention [12]. With multiple interactive functions and design, receivers pay more attention to messages and it results in feasibility of health communication, as shown in Fig. 2.

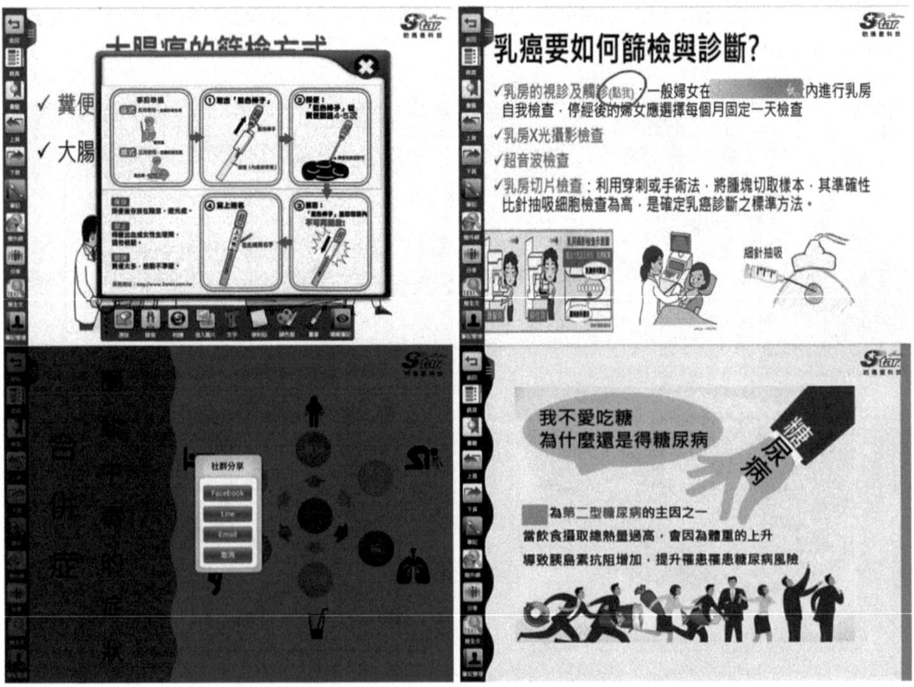

Fig. 2. Multimedia e-book interface of health education.

3.3 Experimental Process

Before operation of experiment, this study explained the experimental process and objectives to the subjects in detail and thus the subjects could thoroughly recognize the research. Nursing students independently edited and designed multimedia health education e-book of health communication in internship. The experiment included three phases. Each phase lasted for three weeks. Period of internship was 15 days, from Monday to Friday. In the process, nursing students implemented health communication in large and small groups.

After internship, nursing students filled in questionnaire according to personal experience. Before the subjects filled in questionnaire, this study informed and promised that the information filled only served for the statistical survey. It did not influence teachers' attitude, academic grades and peers. It also protected their personal information to meet research ethics. Thus, the subjects responded to the questionnaire comfortably and honestly for the precision of figures. Experimental process is shown in Fig. 3.

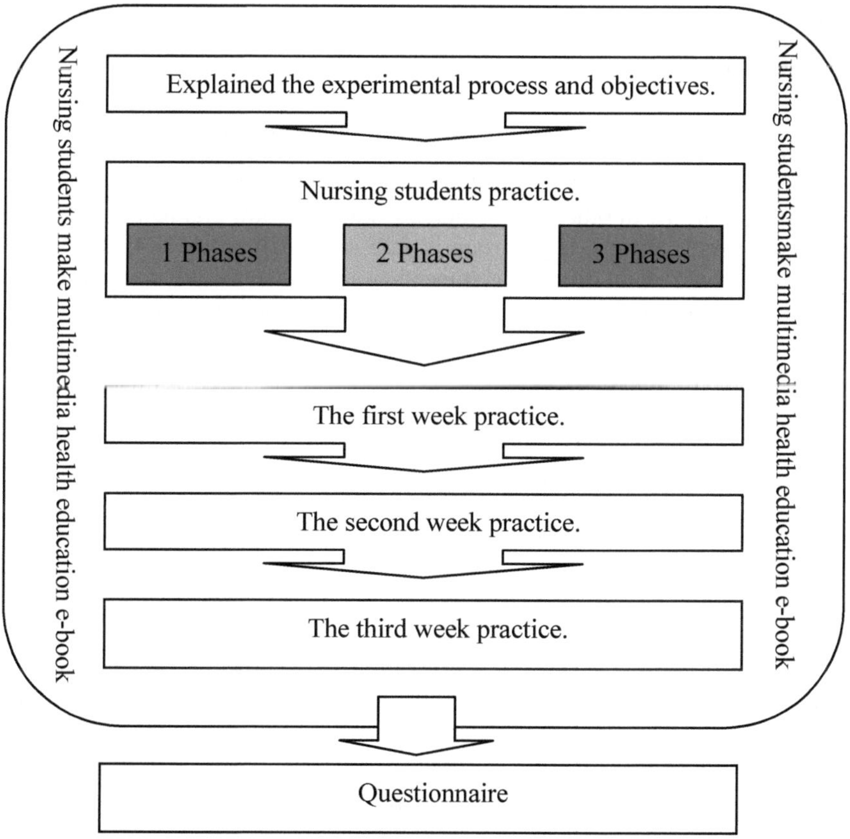

Fig. 3. Experimental process.

3.4 Research Instrument

Questionnaire of this study includes 15 items, based on usage of practice of health communication by multimedia e-book. It was further classified into 2 dimensions in order to explore effect of nursing students' execution of health communication on cases by multimedia e-book and nursing students' nursing informatics literacy in internship. The former included 7 items and the latter included 8 items. Questionnaire design was the revision of evaluation and feedback questionnaire designed by Miller et al. [13]. The analysis was based on Likert 5-point scale (Strongly agree 1, Strongly disagree 5) to meet the requirement of research direction. Questionnaire aims to explore effect of personal health communication of nursing students on small and large groups to convey health education by e-book during the internship of community health nursing and personal nursing informatics literacy. By evaluation of expert validity, this study treated revised questionnaire as the criterion of practice.

In the questionnaire of this study, single sample t test was conducted to analyze the previous outcomes. In addition, this study also probed into analytical result.

4 Results and Discussion

4.1 Self-effect of Implementation of Health Communication

Analytical result of single sample t-test is shown in Table 1. P = .000 < .05. It means to reject null hypothesis. In other words, nursing students show significant difference by using e-book. As to means, large group is 4.22 and small group is 4.23. The figures reveal that personal effect of nursing students to implement health communication by e-book in large and small groups is positive. Besides, most of nursing students suggest that by practicing health communication upon e-book, health education content becomes interesting and it considerably upgrades the effect of communication.

Table 1. Analytical result of self-effect of implementation of health communication.

Group	N	M	SD	*p*
Large	32	4.22	0.34	.000*
Small	32	4.23	0.38	.000*

*$p < .05$

In addition, according to teachers' observation, in the process of internship, nursing students reinforce interaction of group health education by multiple tools of multimedia e-book and further strengthen their personal expertise and knowledge.

4.2 Cultivation of Nursing Informatics Literacy

According to figures of statistical analysis of Table 2, P = .000 < .05. Thus, nursing students' nursing informatics literacy shows significant difference in the process to execute health communication by multimedia e-book; as to means of samples, large group is 4.18; small group is 4.25. Hence, nursing students' cultivation of nursing informatics literacy is significantly reinforced. Most of nursing students suggest that execution of health communication by e-book considerably enhances the effect of communication.

Table 2. Analytical result of cultivation of nursing informatics literacy.

Group	N	M	SD	*p*
Large	32	4.18	0.43	.000*
Small	32	4.25	0.41	.000*

*$p < .05$

From teachers' perspective, by applying characteristics and advantages of multimedia e-book on group health education, nursing students can enhance learning quality in process of internship and strengthen interaction with peers and group health education subjects. Because of introduction of new technology, students must practice health education by innovative learning and interaction. Thus, it indirectly reinforces nursing students' information operation and information literacy.

4.3 Comparison Between Large Group and Small Group

In this section, this study further adopts paired sample t test to compare the difference between large and small groups on nursing students' self-effect of health communication and cultivation of nursing informatics literacy. As to self-effect of health communication, according to figures of Table 3, t value of self-effect of health communication of large and small groups is .000 and p value = 0.05 which is not below 0.05 and it is insignificant. However, means of large group or small group are above 4. It means that according to most of nursing students, in large or small group, they are satisfied with self-effect result of health communication by multimedia e-book. Nursing students mention that by multimedia e-book, they can re-draw the attention of health education subjects and obtain positive responses in interaction. They become more confident in the process of practice of health communication.

Table 3. Analytical result of compare the difference between large and small groups on nursing students' self-effect of health communication.

Group	M	SD	N	t	df	*p*
Large	4.22	.34	32	.000	31	.05
Small	4.23	.38				

*$p < .05$

As to cultivation of nursing informatics literacy, according to figures of Table 4, t value of nursing informatics literacy cultivation of large and small groups is −2.829 and p value = 0.008 < 0.05. It shows that according to nursing students, in health education promotion by multimedia e-book, their cultivation of nursing informatics literacy in large and small groups show significant difference. Besides, nursing informatics cultivation in small group is superior to large group. Nursing students suggest that in comparison to small group, it is more difficult to control number of people and time of large group. Thus, in large group, they cannot present functions of multimedia e-book in detail for health education subjects. In addition, in interaction in small group, they can more easily take care of all. By enhancing interaction, they can present in-depth health education content of multimedia e-book.

Table 4. Analytical result of compare the difference between large and small groups on nursing students' cultivation of nursing informatics literacy.

Group	M	SD	N	t	df	*p*
Large	4.14	.43	32	−2.829	31	.004
Small	4.25	.41				

*$p < .05$

5 Conclusions and Recommendations for Future Work

According to Cognitive Theory of Multimedia Learning proposed by Clark and Mayer [14], when learners are provided with terms and pictures, they can begin constructing mental representation to lead to meaningful learning. By multimedia such as pictures, maps and tables or dynamic media such as videos and simulation, learners practice active learning. The innovation reveals great impact on instruction and learning.

Learning is social and collective outcome realized by dialogue, knowledge communication and social network [15]. In recent years, e-book becomes popular with the continuous progress of technological devices and it considerably influences people's reading habit. Instruction and learning of communication show more possibilities. By tablet, this study adopts multimedia e-book as mobile device to assist with nursing students' community health education and upgrade their self-effect of health communication execution and nursing informatics literacy. According to the analytical result, the figures are significant. It reveals that multimedia e-book can effectively allow nursing students to realize self-effect of health communication and enhance cultivation of nursing informatics literacy. Nursing informatics literacy cultivation in small group is superior to large group.

Since mobile devices are portable, interactive and instant, the development can break through the boundary of traditional instruction and it reveals various applications in educational field [16]. Application of mobile devices becomes more prevailing and it results in the trend of learning methods [16]. Mobile devices are not only used in general hospitals, but also successively introduced in nursing practice courses, such as clinical practice course, tracing and management of medicine, outpatient service and nursing home and even children department [15]. "Good tools are prerequisite to the successful execution of a job." In the future, this study will further introduce multimedia e-book in various medical and nursing fields and analyze execution of health communication and group health education in different fields and explore the fields in which nursing students obtain the optimal effect of health communication by multimedia e-book, and try to combine with nursing staff to meet the medical needs.

Acknowledgments. This work is partially supported by Ministry of Science and Technology, Taiwan under grant MOST 104-2511-S-224-003-MY3 and MOST 105-2628-S-224-001-MY3.

References

1. Sung, T.W., Wu, T.T.: Learning with e-books and project-based strategy in a community health nursing course. CIN Comput. Inform. Nurs. **36**(3), 140–146 (2018)
2. Beam, E.L., Gibbs, S.G., Hewlett, A.L., Iwen, P.C., Nuss, S.L., Smith, P.W.: Evaluating isolation behaviors by nurses using mobile computer workstations at the bedside. CIN Comput. Inform. Nurs. **34**(9), 387–392 (2016)
3. Lee, E., Daugherty, J.: An educational plan for nursing staff in the procedural treatment unit of the Sulpizio Cardiovascular Center. J. PeriAnesthesia Nurs. **31**(2), 134–145 (2016)
4. Mizrahi, T., Davis, L. (eds): The Encyclopedia of Social Work, no. 4, pp. 297–308. Oxford University Press, New York (2008)
5. Cameron, K.A., de Haes, H., Visser, A.: A Theories in health communication research. Patient Educ. Couns. **74**(3), 279–281 (2009)
6. Rogers, E.M.: the field of health communication today: an up-to-date report. J. Health Commun. **1**, 15–23 (1996)
7. Fan, J.Y., Wang, Y.H., Chao, L.F., Jane, S.W., Hsu, L.L.: Performance evaluation of nursing students following competency-based education. Nurse Educ. Today **35**(1), 97–103 (2015)
8. Collen, M.F., Walker, P.H.: Nursing informatics: past, present, and future. In: Collen, M.F., Ball, M.J. (eds.) The History of Medical Informatics in the United States. HI, pp. 385–406. Springer, London (2015). https://doi.org/10.1007/978-1-4471-6732-7_7
9. Tang, Y.Q., Barnett-Ellis, P.: Nursing students' learning experience with e-books. J. Acad. Librarianship **43**(1), 67–71 (2017)
10. Gu, X., Wu, B., Xu, X.: Design, development, and learning in e-Textbooks: what we learned and where we are going. J. Comput. Educ. **2**(1), 25–41 (2015)
11. Weng, C., Otanga, S., Weng, A., Cox, J.: Effects of interactivity in E-textbooks on 7th graders science learning and cognitive load. Comput. Educ. **120**, 172–184 (2018)
12. Hsiao, C.C., Tiao, M.M., Chen, C.C.: Using interactive multimedia e-Books for learning blood cell morphology in pediatric hematology. BMC Med. Educ. **16**, 290–298 (2016)
13. Miller, M.D., Valenti, M., Schettler, T., Tencza, B.: A multimedia e-book a story of health: filling a gap in environmental health literacy for health professionals. Environ. Health Perspect. **124**(8), 133–136 (2016)
14. Clark, R.C., Mayer, R.E.: E-learning and the Science of Instruction: Proven Guidelines for Consumers and Designers of Multimedia Learning. Wiley, Hoboken (2016)
15. Wu, T.T.: Using smart mobile devices in social-network-based health education practice: a learning behavior analysis. Nurse Educ. Today **34**(6), 958–963 (2014)
16. Wu, T.T., Chen, A.C.: Combining e-books with mind mapping in a reciprocal teaching strategy for a classical Chinese course. Comput. Educ. **116**, 64–80 (2018)

Exploring Perceived Value Creation of MOOCs Service Systems - A Preliminary Investigation

Tonny Meng-Lun Kuo(✉) and Jyun-Cheng Wang

Institute of Service Science, National Tsing Hua University, Hsinchu 300, Taiwan
kuo@mx.nthu.edu.tw

Abstract. Massive Open Online Courses (MOOCs) have been considered disruptive innovative service that potentially pose threats to traditional higher education. However, few people carefully consider how MOOCs services support and co-create values for post-secondary institutes, on-campus students, and working professions from the perspective of value co-creation and service system. Through the analysis of in-depth interviews of nine cases, five qualitative categories of perceived values with structural hierarchy were profiled and analyzed: (1) learning new knowledge, skills, and perspectives, (2) verifying learning process using certificates, (3) supporting on-campus learning and teaching, (4) solving real-world problems at work, and (5) co-learning with world-wide learners. Implications will be presented and discussed in the paper.

Keywords: Massive Open Online Courses (MOOCs) · Value creation Service system · Value co-creation · Higher education

1 Introduction

Massive Open Online Courses (MOOCs) have been seen as efficient and potential learning resources of free and high-quality through multiple integrated resources in terms of the videos, webpages, podcasts, e-textbook, blogs. Applying MOOCs into different learning contexts have been studied for years, such as on-job training [1], lifelong learning [2], programing [3], and teacher education [4]. Even though MOOCs were considered "open educational resources (OER)", the freemium model of MOOCs is, in some sense, disruptive innovative service targeted at users worldwide to create a brand-new area of learning service in higher education [5–7].

The success of MOOCs brings a MOOCs movement since 2012, which encourages higher education institutes all over the world to generate MOOCs content. However, does the success of MOOCs guarantee learning quality in online learning environment? Can learners acquire knowledge, skills, and competences that traditional post-secondary institutes offer only through online platform? We found several arguments that challenge the service operation of MOOCs in terms of low completion rate (or high dropout rate), inadequate assessment mechanism, online cheating, lack of collaborative learning and embodied cognition [8–10]. From educational perspective, it seems

T.-T. Wu et al. (Eds.): ICITL 2018, LNCS 11003, pp. 510–517, 2018.
https://doi.org/10.1007/978-3-319-99737-7_54

natural to scholars of education/learning sciences that the weakness of MOOCs stems primarily from inadequate theoretical foundation of large-scale online learning. However, in service system view, we care more about how service system creates values for customers and what are underlying mechanisms that leads to resistance of service operation.

Unfortunately, to our knowledge, limited studies evaluate the values co-creation of MOOCs service in a systematic and holistic way. In view of the considerable investment from both prestigious and residential universities as well as large number of learners on MOOCs, it is of significant importance to investigate what are values that MOOCs service create for different stakeholders. Understanding the created values not only help evaluate the value propositions of MOOCs service but also serve as a compass to give clear direction to research and development of more valuable educational service.

This preliminary study aims to investigate the value co-creation process of customers. To capture the divergent customers' experiences of using MOOCs, we conducted in-depth interviews of nine cases, including six online learners and three teaching faculty. The thematic analysis of conceptions of value co-creation on MOOCs were profiled and concluded. To make our study more concrete, the following question drives this study: In the current MOOCs service system, what are perceived values of MOOCs through integration of different resources?

2 Method

To explore customers' authentic experiences of using MOOCs and the value co-creation process, the in-depth interview method was used. In this exploratory study, nine cases in Taiwan and China serve as empirical investigations of contemporary phenomena within real-life contexts [11]. By conducting individual interview with nine cases in Chinese-speaking society, customers' value co-creation process was profiled and analyzed to find variations in their experiences.

2.1 Participants

There are two sources of participants in the current study. The sample of MOOCs learners in this study included six undergraduate and graduate students (5 males and 1 female) in Taiwan and China, aged from 21 to 32. These participants came from five different universities. Most of the them from engineering school (four of them) including Industrial Engineering and Computer Science; one from science school and one from business school. The participants were chosen because they had prior experience of using the massive open online courses. All the participants had enrolled at least three MOOCs courses and three of them had completed the courses and got the certificates (see Table 1 for details).

To investigate instructor's view of value co-creation of MOOCs service, three instructors with experiences of teaching MOOC(s) are identified and interviewed (see Table 2). The three cases (two male and one female) come from different academic backgrounds and have rich experience of teaching. The average years of teaching is

Table 1. Demographic description of six MOOCs learners.

Case	Gender	Education	Age	Nationality	MOOCs experiences
S1	Male	Undergraduate Industrial Engineering	21	China	Enrolled: 20–30 Completed: 15
S2	Male	Undergraduate Computer Science	21	China	Enrolled: 4 Completed: 3
S3	Male	Undergraduate Industrial Engineering	21	China	Enrolled: 15 Completed: 9
S4	Male	Graduate student Computer Science	32	Taiwan	Enrolled: 6–8 Completed: 0
S5	Female	Undergraduate Management	24	Taiwan	Enrolled: 4 Completed: 0
S6	Male	Undergraduate Applied Mathematics	21	Taiwan	Enrolled: 3 Completed: 0

Table 2. Demographic description of three MOOCs instructors.

Case	Gender	Education	Years of teaching	Position	Online teaching experiences
T1	Male	PhD in Management Information System	21	Professor	Teaching one MOOC Course on two platforms
T2	Male	PhD in Life Science	15	Professor	Teaching three MOOCs Courses on multiple platforms; Three OpenCourseWares; Blended teaching
T3	Female	PhD in Statistics	17	Professor	Teaching one MOOC; Blended teaching; Have taught several online Statistic courses

17.6 years. Among the three instructors, T1 is the most junior to teaching a MOOCs. He had teaching one MOOC in two different platforms. T2 is the most experienced MOOCs instructor who had taught three MOOCs in several platforms and adopted MOOCs in on-campus blended instruction. T3 is a female instructor who has great experiences of online teaching and had taught a MOOC and blended course.

2.2 Data Collection and Analysis

The research data were collected by semi-structured interviews via online voice calls as well as face-to-face interviews. Each participant was interviewed individually by a trained researcher. The interview time ranged from approximately 30 to 60 min.

The semi-structured interview was administrated following pre-determined open questions. Example guided questions used to probe the customers' ideas about value co-creation on MOOCs are as follows:

- What is your experience of using MOOCs?
- What motivates you to use MOOCs?
- What do you expect to achieve in MOOCs? (such as obtain certificate, learn new skills)
- Are there any communities that support your learning/teaching on MOOCs?
- Do you perceive any underlying rules/regulation/social norm when using MOOCs service?
- Please describe a scenario that you are learning a MOOC.
- In your view, what values do you think of that MOOCs bring you?

In order to help the participants to express their neutral and authentic experiences, our interview begins with informal talks to lower anxiety. The interviews are conducted in Mandarin Chinese with the focus on MOOCs experiences and value co-creation. All the individual interviews were audio-recorded and transcribed for further data analysis. The transcripts of the interviews were the primary data for analyzing the customers' conceptions of value co-creation. The transcripts of the participants were main ideas used and translated by the researcher to explore their views toward MOOCs.

The analysis of the transcripts of the interviewed was conducted by the thematic clustering based on the components of activity theory and value co-creation process [12]. The researcher first reviewed each participant's ideas expressed in the interview. Then, the researcher underlined some important sentences and categorized into different meaningful clusters. For instance, the researcher categorized the following sentences into "instrument" category in activity theory:

> *"(Q: Except the MOOC platform, what other tools or service do you use while learning in MOOCs?) S3: Oh! I also used QQ circles to interact with other learners in China when I have a question. Sometimes people will share course resources, such as lecture notes, or ask for help."*

The researcher highlighted the keyword "QQ circle", "interact", and "lecture notes" and sorted them into the analytical table for further analysis.

By comparing the different categories from the interview transcripts, the content-specific commonalities and distinctions among different participants were explored and summarized. Finally, the categories based on the interview transcripts were double-reviewed and coded into sub-categories in accordance with participants' different perception to exemplify their differences. To ensure the credible research design, the researcher orally asked for informed consent explaining participants' rights and how researcher analyze the data. The setting and the participants would be anonymous and cannot be identified in print.

3 Results: Value Co-creation Using MOOCs Service

Five qualitatively different categories of users' perceived values of MOOCs service were identified. The participating online learners and teachers viewed MOOCs service as (1) learning new knowledge, skills, and perspectives, (2) verifying learning process using certificates, (3) supporting on-campus learning and teaching, (4) solving real-world problems at work, and (5) co-learning with world-wide learners. These five qualitatively different ways of experiencing MOOCs could be marked by five key aspects: (1) value driver, (2) value creator, (3) process of value creation, (4) measurement of value, and (5) role of customers to illustrate their structural relationship. In the following sections, we first report on the five categories and then present their structural hierarchy.

3.1 MOOCs Service as Learning New Knowledge, Skills, and Perspectives

In this category, MOOCs service was described as a means of learning new knowledge, skills, and perspectives. Some learners reported that some courses offered in MOOCs are unique and they cannot find such courses in school catalogs. The use of such courses helps them explore their personal interests and empower knowledge building process through MOOCs service. Some learners also indicated that MOOCs offer them autonomy to choose high-quality course that they will never take in engineering school without the costs. The heavy loads in school differ them choosing courses from other college. Therefore, the affordances of diverse courses make them plausible to take a closer look into the fields.

3.2 MOOCs Service as Verifying Learning Process Using Certificates

This category encapsulates learners' view of considering obtaining learning certificate as goal to verify their learning outcome. They believe that the MOOCs service provide such way to increase their motivation of learning MOOCs course. Those certificates can be used for both working (job finding) and academic purpose (applying for graduate school).

3.3 MOOCs Service as Supporting on-Campus Learning and Teaching

In on-campus setting, two of our interviewed instructors used MOOCs to support the on-campus learning in terms of flipped classroom and blended instruction. They believe the use of the videos improve the learning readiness before the class so that students have more discussion in real classroom on projects or related issues. From learners' perspective, they indicate the use of MOOCs resources on the Internet to understand difficult concepts and knowledge. They used MOOCs as online resources to review and preview the learning content.

3.4 MOOCs Service as Solving Real-World Problems at Work

Category 1–3 put more emphasis on individual value creation, meaning that the created value is primarily used to improve individual needs. This category described the experiences of a working profession using MOOCs to solve problems he encountered in a company. The value of MOOCs is co-created with the value in this working context. This category reflects significant values of MOOCs for working professions who can keep up with latest trend and technology through current MOOCs services.

3.5 MOOCs Service as Co-learning with World-Wide Learners

This category centers on using MOOCs as co-learning on the Internet with world-wide learners. Co-learning on MOOCs refers to the value of learning at scale. After learners watching the videos on MOOCs, learners of diverse backgrounds (academic or professional) might hold different perspectives to the same issue. The ideas exchange and knowledge building at scale increase the co-learning values of MOOCs. The peer interaction based on the same group of people with similar interest might also form a special interest group worldwide and potentially inspire more great ideas.

3.6 Key Aspects to Illustrate Structural Relationship and Conclusion

Our five categories reveal variance of different values provided by MOOCs service system. Six key aspects were identified to reflect different value creation. Table 3 offer a comprehensive view of the values. The difference between individual and collective values is determined by creating values in use and in new context. We found co-learning with world-wide learners the most difficult collective values in MOOCs service systems while learning new knowledge, skills, and perspectives creates easiest values. Based on the current analysis of the value creation, we match plausible measures for assessing and measuring the value (co-)creation in MOOCs service system. For example, to measure the value of "verifying learning process using certificates", number of certificates, perceived values of certificates, or learning engagement could be utilized to measure the created values. Future work can focus on antecedents or mechanisms of such values (as outcome valuable) to understand how MOOCs services create values for worldwide users and thus design successful educational services for all kinds of learners.

Additionally, the complexity of resource integration increases when the level of values increases. Compared with individual values, we found the creators of values involve multiple actors and actants in the highest level of collective values including MOOCs service providers, knowledge network, instructors and online learners. For measurement of values, although learning engagement was widely seen as important KPI in MOOCs to determine success of MOOCs. We tend to hesitate to accept single measurement. With the level of value increases, different and diverse measures could be identified to better evaluate the effectiveness of MOOCs' value. Therefore, we argue that collective value creation may require multiple constructs in MOOCs service sys-

Table 3. Key aspects of perceived value creation.

Key aspects	Individual value			Collective value	
	1 Learning new knowledge, skills, and perspectives	2 Verifying learning process using certificates	3 Supporting on-campus learning and teaching	4 Solving real-world problems at work	5 Co-learning with world-wide learners
Value driver	Value-in-exchange	Value-in-exchange	Value-in-exchange Value-in-context	Value-in-use Value-in-context	Value-in-use Value-in-context
Creator of value	MOOCs service providers	MOOCs service providers	MOOCs service providers Universities: Teachers, classmates	MOOCs service providers Firms: Project managers, colleagues	MOOCs service providers, knowledge network, instructors, online learners
Process of value creation	Value-added	Value-added	Value in use	Value in use	Value in use
Measurement of value	Perceived values, learning engagement	Number of certificates Perceived values of certificates Learning engagement	Academic learning performance (at school), engagement Teaching and learning quality	Working performance (Problem solving, project quality, working efficiency) Dynamic capability	Knowledge creation Idea generation Group-based discussion Cross-disciplinary learning
Role of customers	Consuming resources provided by MOOCs service	Consuming resources provided by MOOCs service and universities	Co-creating values through integration of values of teachers, local learners, and MOOCs service	Co-creating values through integration of values of MOOCs service, firms, and co-workers	Co-creating values through integration of MOOCs service and value network
Knowledge representation	Surface	Surface	Sophisticated	Sophisticated	Sophisticated

tem to represent the co-learning values. We also encourage further investigation into measures of collective value creation from perspective of knowledge management, human resource management and service science.

4 Conclusion

The purpose of this study to depict the perceived values of MOOCs service in terms of online learners and instructors behind the current MOOCs service system. This preliminary work found different kinds of value creation in MOOCs service system and conclude five structural categories, including (1) learning new knowledge, skills, and perspectives, (2) verifying learning process using certificates, (3) supporting on-campus learning and teaching, (4) solving real-world problems at work, and (5) co-learning with world-wide learners. Due to the limitation of number of interviewees, there might be other sophisticated categories underlying in MOOCs service. However, our current categories illustrate an overall picture of perceived value creation, enabling future researchers to explore value creation of MOOCs services. Our future work will focus on (1) successful drives and mechanisms among MOOCs service, (2) sustainable MOOCs service for higher education, and (3) service design/innovations to foster MOOCs services.

References

1. Hajkowicz, S., Reeson, A., Rudd, L., Bratanova, A., Hodgers, L., Mason, C., Boughen, N.: Tomorrow's digitally enabled workforce: megatrends and scenarios for jobs and employment in Australia over the coming twenty years. Australian Policy Online (2016)
2. Kay, J., Reimann, P., Diebold, E., Kummerfeld, B.: MOOCs: so many learners, so much potential. IEEE Intell. Syst. **28**, 70–77 (2013)
3. McKinsey, J., Joseph, S., Fox, A., Garcia, D.D.: Remote pair programming (RPP) in massively open online courses (MOOCs). In: Proceedings of the 2014 Conference on Innovation and Technology in Computer Science Education, p. 340. ACM (2014)
4. Fyle, C.O.: Teacher education MOOCs for developing world contexts: issues and design considerations. In: Proceedings of the Sixth Conference of MIT's Learning International Networks Consortium (LINC) (2013)
5. Christensen, C.M., Eyring, H.J.: The Innovative University: Changing the DNA of Higher Education from the Inside Out. Wiley, New York (2011)
6. Harker, P.T.: Commentary—making sense of higher education's future: an economics and operations perspective. Serv. Sci. **6**, 207–216 (2014)
7. Qiu, R.G.: Service Science: The Foundations of Service Engineering and Management. Wiley, Hoboken (2014)
8. Eisenberg, M., Fischer, G.: MOOCs: a perspective from the learning sciences. In: Learning and Becoming in Practice: 11th International Conference of the Learning Sciences (ICLS), pp. 190–197 (2014)
9. Liyanagunawardena, T.R., Adams, A.A., Williams, S.A.: MOOCs: a systematic study of the published literature 2008–2012. Int. Rev. Res. Open Distrib. Learn. **14**, 202–227 (2013)
10. Liyanagunawardena, T.R., Lundqvist, K.Ø., Williams, S.A.: Who are with us: MOOC learners on a FutureLearn course. Br. J. Educ. Technol. **46**, 557–569 (2015)
11. Yin, R.K.: Case Study Research: Design and Methods. Sage Publications, Thousand Oaks (2013)
12. Fereday, J., Muir-Cochrane, E.: Demonstrating rigor using thematic analysis: a hybrid approach of inductive and deductive coding and theme development. Int. J. Qual. Methods **5**, 80–92 (2006)

The Creation of Interactive Visual Music with Kandinsky Abstract Arts

Yu-Hsuan Lin[1(✉)], Chad Lin[2], Chia-Wei Chang[1], and Hao-Chiang Koong Lin[1]

[1] Department of Information and Learning Technology, National University of Tainan, Tainan, Taiwan
m10455004@gm2.nutn.edu.tw

[2] Faculty of Health Sciences, Curtin University, Perth, Australia
elin123au@yahoo.com.au

Abstract. Sounds are invisible, though they surround our lives, we cannot realize the form of sounds. However, visualization of sounds can be produced using Digital Arts to make sounds visible or even interact with people. This study created a voice-based composition of digital art in the form of joint exhibition.

During the joint art exhibition, details such as light effects and the design of exhibition area help to promote the quality of the exhibition. After the exhibition, spectators were asked to fill out a questionnaire designed by [18], the results of which were later analyzed with descriptive and inferential statistics to account for satisfaction and procedures of the exhibition, reception aesthetic, playability of substantial device and spectator's feeling from the composition in exhibition. The analytics of this research helped to account for key elements of the overall exhibit, including satisfaction, receptional aesthetic, playability of substantial devices, and spectator's perceptions, as well as the correlations among them.

Keywords: Digital art · Interactive art · Aesthetic acceptance

1 Introduction

1.1 Motivation of the Research

Multimedia, whether in the form of texts, pictures, or film animation, has become an indispensable part of human lives. The existence of multimedia is witnessed in a variety of art or design exhibitions. The multimedia in the exhibition could increase the audience's interest and allow the audience to interact in real time with the exhibits. While traditional works of art could only be appreciated, modern artists' have tried to enable the audience to participate in the art display [5]. Many art exhibitions are in the modern time are interactive with the hope attract the audience, increase their learning motivation, or help them stay focused [9]. With such goals in mind, this research combines music and visualization to attract the audience to explore the exhibit and

T.-T. Wu et al. (Eds.): ICITL 2018, LNCS 11003, pp. 518–527, 2018.
https://doi.org/10.1007/978-3-319-99737-7_55

engage in physical interaction with the artwork for a different kind of art exhibition experience.

The creation of this work employed the basic shape of the circle and lively colors to combine with music. Because the circles are able to move and change with the music, the digital artworks appear as the beating notes found in musical scores.

2 Literature Review

2.1 Kandinsky's Abstract Art

Kandinsky is a pioneer of Abstract Art. [20] pointed out that Kandinsky is widely regarded as an abstract painter who has influenced several generations of abstract artists. His painting style varied from the early realistic copy to impressionist and expressionist works After 1920, Kandinsky's work combined his earlier style with geometry to describe relationships among colors, geometrical shapes, sounds, and music (see Fig. 1).

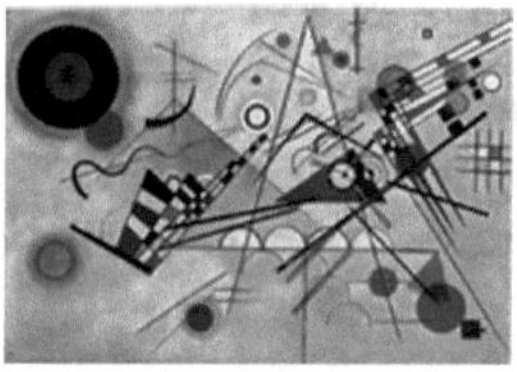

Fig. 1. Wassily Kandinsky, 1923, Composition VIII From: Guggenheim

2.2 Receptional Aesthetic

Receptional Aesthetic, a concept proposed by in 1960s [3]. Jauss pinpointed the flaw in previous aesthetic research that focused on the artist instead of the audience, such ignorance of the receiver led Jauss to focus on the audience thus naming the concept Receptional Aesthetic. Jauss argued that an aesthetic experience included three aspects – production, acceptance, and communication. These three aspects of an aesthetic experience corresponded to the three areas of aesthetic pleasure, which were creation, beauty, and purification. At the same time he also proposed five modes of aesthetic identification, which were association, admiration, compassion, purity, and irony.

Barthes [1], one of the founders of the Deconstructivism, proposed "The death of author," as he believed that the relationship between the author and the work ended at the moment of the completion of the artwork. Thus, the idea of the creator is not as important as the focus on audience, since the audience are the beholders who come to appreciate and interpret the works, and create a new meaning to the work. The interpreter of the work is therefore the audience, not the author.

2.3 Interactive Art

Interactive art refers to the artwork that enables the audience to participate in it. It includes many kinds of interactions which can be visual or tactile. In the digital age today, more and more artists use computing tools to generate works of art [10]. Many artists not only use paper and pens, they also begin to use digital tools such as computers to form their ideas and create art works in the digital era [13].

After the rise of post-modern art, there was a new mode of interaction between the artist, the viewer, and the work. Artworks were no longer confined to static physical patterns, but involved interactions between the works and the audience to form the true core value for works of art. When "interaction" gradually replaced simple "look" or "hearing" and became a way to appreciate the contemporary works, the meaning of the interaction process also changed for the artist and the audience. Unique aesthetic concepts also came into being [15].

3 Research Methods

3.1 Creation Process

The researchers first identified the artwork types, then began to review literature for the research methods while planning the exhibition process. After the planning, data were collected using the questionnaire. Finally, the results of the questionnaire were analyzed and discussed (see Fig. 2).

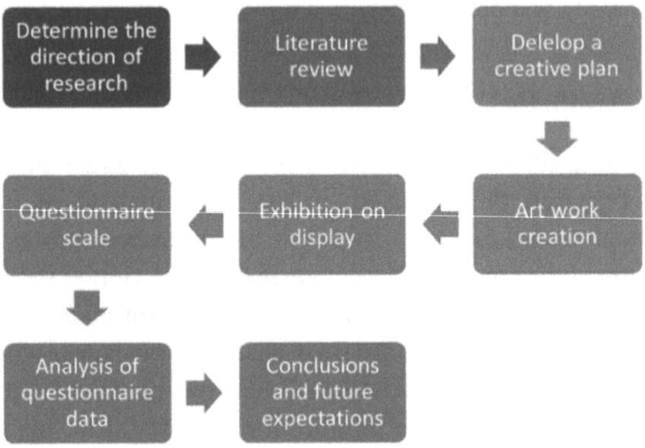

Fig. 2. Research flow chart

3.2 The Concept for the Artwork Creation

Kandinsky is one of the pioneer of abstractionism, when he had listened the music, he drew the melody into an artwork. His work in the later period combined many geometries to elaborate the relationship among color, geometry, shape, sound and music.

In addition, many of the early art works still have a profound influence on contemporary design or artistic creation. Many works now use points, lines, faces, and geometries to produce lively images through different shapes and colors. Therefore, the researchers used geometry to create the digital art composition.

3.3 The Concept for the Artwork Creation

Motivation for the Creation. The researcher converted sounds into a visual images, which could in turn interact with the audience. The audience thus were able to experience the visualization of sounds and interact with these visual effects.

People encounter sound visualization images occasionally in daily life. The most common example is the music player's visual effects, the particles shown on the screen usually change their size as the musical frequency changes. When music is different, then visual effects are also different, giving the audience a variety of visual experiences.

The researchers hoped to allow the audience to operate somatosensory devices to interact with the artwork in real time.

The Process of Artwork Creation. With the proliferation of somatosensory devices, many art or design exhibitions have also added somatosensory devices to allow viewers to interact with the artworks and enhance the quality of such interactions. The artwork in the current study was equipped with somatosensory devices so that the audience could experience the visualization of the sounds and interact with the artwork.

In this work "Rhythm", the researchers used "Processing" and somatosensory device "Leap Motion" to form the basic design for the interactive artwork (see Fig. 3). The "Leap Motion" infrared lens was able to catch body movements above it as an example of real-time sensing [12]. As the audience operated the somatosensory devices, real-time interactive works were created. In this exhibit, the sounds went through "Processing" on the Minim library and were further analyzed in terms of frequencies in order to be transformed into visual images. The music chosen for this artwork was Rameses B's "Every Cloud" on the Sound Cloud music platform, which is licensed under Creative Commons (CC).

Fig. 3. Processing; leap motion

The creation of the main object of this exhibit consisted of circular objects with changing t colors and positions. The researchers used "Processing" to set the maximum number of circles on the scene to randomly generate circular objects which could change in size and color along with the changing melodies of the music. The circular objects also engaged in random movements following the dynamics of the music. When the somatosensory device detected hand movements, the circular objects would centralize and move along with the audience's fingers. As for the effects of the colors, a number of bright colors were preset using Chromatics color matching in "Processing" to produce pleasant feelings among the audience with the lively Orange-Yellow color system (see Fig. 4).

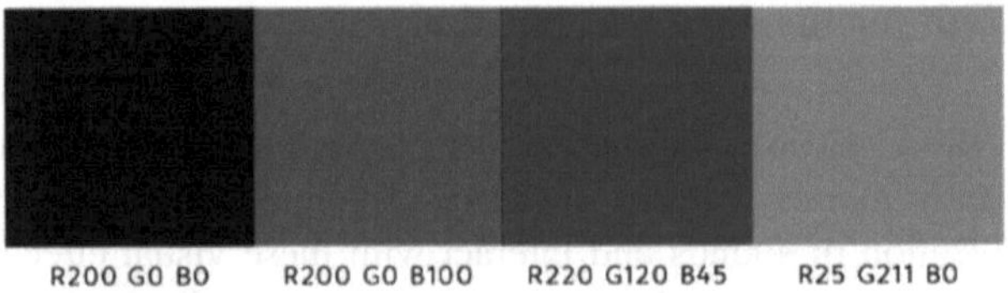

Fig. 4. System color application (Color figure online)

The images produced by the music visualization consisted mainly of circular objects. In "Processing", the number of objects in the scene were limited to fifty. This was because too many objects on the scene would cause delay in the operating system and result in displeasure among the audience (see Fig. 5).

Fig. 5. The image after sound visualized

3.4 Plan and Layout of the Exhibition

The space planning, layout of the exhibition, and the exhibition route were the most important elements of exhibitions in general. A good movement plan and layout of the display will help to improve the quality of the entire exhibition. Even lighting effect of the exhibition will create an experience for the audience.

3.5 Design Evaluation

Design Tool. The study employed a 7-point Likert scale questionnaire developed by [18], which considered the attributes of receptional aesthetic, audience, experiment equipment, process, playability, satisfaction, and loyalty.

Statistical Analysis. This study used the Statistical Product and Service Solution software (SPSS) 20.0 to carry out descriptive statistics and the Pearson correlation coefficient analysis.

4 Results

4.1 Questionnaire Collection

The research used a questionnaire based on a 7-point Likert scale [18] to collect the audience's responses about the attributes summarized in Table 1. The "Zone Echo" exhibition was held at a national university for 7 days. 99 valid questionnaires were collected from 64 man and 35 women ranging from 19–22 years in age, all of whom had received university education.

Table 1. Operating definitions of the research variables.

Research variables	Definition
Receptional aesthetic	The interpretation of the work is the audience
Audience	Users and other users of feeling in the process
Experiment equipment	The device can improve the speed and performance of the service. In process, a part of the satisfaction is from the equipment
Process	Good program management to ensure service quality
Playability	The interface of the work itself with the use of the operation, control, interactive intensity, and increase the work's attractiveness of the fun
Satisfaction	The degree of satisfaction of the whole process
Loyalty	A product or service forms a preference degree

4.2 Statistical Analyses

Each of the facets was encoded in numerical sequence. Respectively, the sequences were Receptional Aesthetic (A1, A2, A3), Audience (B1, B2, B3, B4), Process (C1, C2, C3, C4), Experiment Equipment (D1, D2, D3), Playability (E1, E2, E3, E4), Satisfaction (F1, F2) and Loyalty (G1, G2, G3). The researchers then developed the questions for each facet.

Receptional Aesthetic. The overall average was 5.42, with a standard deviation of 0.9, showing that the works cloud was perceived to be good work and was accepted by the audience. The value of the work was also considered positive (Table 2).

Table 2. Descriptive statistics on receptional aesthetic.

	Min	Max	Avg	SD
A1	1.00	7.00	5.25	1.10
A2	3.00	7.00	5.50	1.15
A3	3.00	7.00	5.50	1.14
Overall	3.67	7.00	5.42	0.90

Audience. The overall average was 5.91, with a standard deviation of 0.83, indicating that the audience interacted well with other audience. The audience's interaction with the artwork attracted the others who were curious (Table 3).

Table 3. Descriptive statistics on audience

	Min	Max	Avg	SD
B1	4.00	7.00	6.08	0.91
B2	4.00	7.00	5.77	1.04
B3	3.00	7.00	5.86	0.99
B4	3.00	7.00	5.92	1.00
Overall	3.75	7.00	5.91	0.83

Process. The overall average was 6.08, with a standard deviation of 0.74, indicating that the exhibition line planning and the artwork's operation process were smooth and contributed to promoting the exhibition quality (Table 4).

Table 4. Descriptive statistics on process

	Min	Max	Avg	SD
C1	3.00	7.00	6.08	0.97
C2	3.00	7.00	6.07	0.91
C3	3.00	7.00	6.19	0.92
C4	4.00	7.00	5.98	0.93
Overall	3.50	7.00	6.08	0.74

Experiment Equipment. The overall average was 6.05, with a standard deviation of 0.76, reflecting satisfactory feedback from the audience about the exhibition's layout, the hardware equipment, and the sound quality of the artwork (Table 5).

Playability. The overall average was 5.97 with a standard deviation of 0.77. The average of E1, E2, and E3 in the playability items were greater than 6, indicating that the audience who interacted the artwork had a pleasant experience and satisfaction (Table 6).

Table 5. Descriptive statistics on experiment equipment

	Min	Max	Avg	SD
D1	4.00	7.00	5.97	0.97
D2	3.00	7.00	6.15	0.89
D3	3.00	7.00	6.04	0.95
Overall	4.33	7.00	6.05	0.76

Table 6. Descriptive statistics on playability

	Min	Max	Avg	SD
E1	4.00	7.00	6.11	0.87
E2	2.00	7.00	6.02	0.94
E3	3.00	7.00	6.02	0.90
E4	3.00	7.00	5.74	1.03
Overall	3.75	7.00	5.97	0.77

Satisfaction. The overall average was 5.78, and the standard deviation was 0.92, indicating that most of the audience was satisfied with the exhibition (Table 7).

Table 7. Descriptive statistics on satisfaction

	Min	Max	Avg	SD
F1	3.00	7.00	5.74	0.99
F2	4.00	7.00	5.81	0.94
Overall	3.50	7.00	5.78	0.92

Loyalty. The overall average was 5.85, and the standard deviation was 0.91, indicating that most of the audience would like to make a visit to the exhibition again and recommend this exhibition to others (Table 8).

Table 8. Descriptive statistics of loyalty

	Min	Max	Avg	SD
G1	4.00	7.00	5.92	0.95
G2	4.00	7.00	5.93	0.96
G3	3.00	7.00	5.68	1.05
Overall	4.00	7.00	5.85	0.91

4.3 Correlation Coefficient Analysis

Through the correlation coefficient analysis, results showed the highest correlation was found for H5, proving that the more interaction between the artwork and the audience, the higher the satisfaction of the audience (Table 9).

Table 9. Statistic result of the usability scale of holistic and serial cognitive styles displayed as figures.

Hypothesis	Pearson correlation coefficient	Influence direction
H1 There is a positive correlation between Receptional Aesthetic and Audience	0.622**	Significantly: Moderate correlation
H2 There is a positive correlation between Audience and Satisfaction	0.619**	Significantly: Moderate correlation
H3 There is a positive correlation between Experiment equipment and Satisfaction	0.671**	Significantly: Moderate correlation
H4 There is a positive correlation between Process and Satisfaction	0.662**	Significantly: Moderate correlation
H5 There is a positive correlation between Playability and Satisfaction	0.725**	Significantly: Highly correlation
H6 There is a positive correlation between Satisfaction and Loyalty	0.717**	Significantly: Highly correlation
H7 There is a positive correlation between Interactive satisfaction and Receptional Aesthetic	0.678**	Significantly: Moderate correlation

** At significant levels of 0.01 (two tails), the correlation was significant.

5 Conclusion

According to analytics of this research, all seven hypotheses were found to show correlation between the proposed attributes respectively with moderate correlation; however, the highest correlations were found for H5 on "Playability and Satisfaction" and H6 on "Satisfaction and Loyalty." Since the highest correlation was found for H5, the researchers considered playability to be the key indicator for satisfaction. It was also reasonable to infer that satisfaction due to playability could lead to loyalty, according to the second highest correlation result. The current study had some limitations related to the software and hardware during the creation of the exhibit. It is hoped that in future research, this limitation could be overcome. It is hoped that this research could shed light on the research space related to digital artworks for sound visualization.

References

1. Barthes, R.: The death of author (1977)
2. Chao, Y.K., Yang, X.R., Zhang, H.Y., Xu, C.Y.: The author is dead - Barth and postmodernism. J. Int. Sociol. (2003). http://mail.nhu.edu.tw/society/ej/29/29-26.htm
3. Jauss, R.: Aesthetic Experience and Literary Hermeneutics Hans (1982)
4. Chiu, C.Y.: Depicting the Subjectivity of Taiwanese Digital Art History via Creations (2010). http://www.dac.tw/event/stream/files/articles3.pdf
5. Chiu, C.Y.: On the Interactivity of Digital Art Taiwan Digital Art and Information Centre (2014). http://goo.gl/MqNXb7
6. Dai, M.: Modern Color Science: Color Theory. Perception and Application, New Taipei City (2011)
7. David, H.: Interaction Design Fundamentals (2012)
8. Düchting, H.: Wassily Kandinsky, 1866–1944: A Revolution in Painting. Taschen, Germany (2000)
9. Huang, Y.M., Hsu, C.C., Su, Y.N., Liu, C.J.: Empowering classroom observation with an e-book reading behavior monitoring system using sensing technologies. Interact. Comput. **26** (4), 372–387 (2014)
10. Jochum, E.A., Putnam, L.: Computation as medium: agency and motion in interactive art. Akademisk Kvarter **16**, 9–21 (2017)
11. Kandinsky, W., Rebay, H.: Point and Line to Plane. Courier Corporation, North Chelmsford (1947)
12. Leap Motion (2016). https://www.leapmotion.com
13. Hao, L., Yinxia, F.: A study of interactive concept medium and aesthetics of digital arts. J. Chin. Art (74), 99–111 (2004)
14. Lin, C.H.: The study of geometric shapes applying to form design. J. Donghai Univ. **44**, 87–96 (2003)
15. Lin, P.C.: Taiwan Digital Art e-Files. Artist Publisher, Taipei (2012)
16. Lin, Y., Chuang, H.: Aesthetics of digital art. Aesthetic Educ., 62–71 (2002)
17. Saffer, D.: Designing for Interaction: Creating Innovative Applications and Devices. New Riders, USA (2010)
18. Sie, Z.Y.: The influence of aesthetic acceptance, service quality, and playability on visitors' satisfaction toward digital art exhibitions (Master's thesis). National University of Tainan (2012)
19. Whittaker, S.: Interaction design: what we know and what we need to know. Interactions **20** (4), 38–42 (2013)
20. Zhang, K., Yu, J.: Generation of Kandinsky art. Leonardo **49**(1), 48–54 (2016)

Robot Assisted Reading: A Preliminary Study on the Robotic Storytelling Service to Children in the Library

Wei-Wei Shen[1] and Jim-Min Lin[2](✉)

[1] Department of Foreign Languages and Literature, Feng Chia University, Taichung City, Taiwan
wwshen@fcu.edu.tw

[2] Department of Information Engineering and Computer Science, Feng Chia University, Taichung City, Taiwan
jimmy@fcu.edu.tw

Abstract. It is important for the modern library to cultivate the public's information literacy and reading literacy. When these two important tasks can be rooted in the children's readers, the function of the library can be even more meaningful and demanded. Therefore, all public libraries try their best to attract more children to come to the library, and naturally parents come together with children to enjoy reading in the library. Because children have only limited vocabulary ability, reading plain written books is very difficult for them and it is not even effective. As a result, various digital children's readings have been developed over the years, such as pictures (picture books), audio (CD audio books), and video (multimedia e-books). However, the interaction between these materials and children is limited to 2D flat touches, such as texts, pictures, and audios/videos. Children would not feel touched and interactive when listening to the stories read by adults who have no training for reading aloud skills. Therefore, this study intends to combine the robot with the existing digital picture books of the library to complete a "robotic storytelling service for children." In this study, we designed a scenario that combined a digital picture book with added robot voices and body postures/movements that match the mood of stories. This allows the robot to tell a story and perform a story like a human being with body movements to attract children's interest and attention. And the robot can also draw the children's attention to the story and increase the listening effects. This service has received a very enthusiastic response from the children readers. It also enabled the children to be close to the robots and listened to the robots to tell stories for them in a very focused and exciting manner. Furthermore, they seem to be motivated to go to the library to find the corresponding story books to read. Therefore, robotic storytelling approach may have a potential to promote children's reading interests and can be widely implemented in the future.

Keywords: Robot assisted reading · Robotic storytelling service
Digital picture books

T.-T. Wu et al. (Eds.): ICITL 2018, LNCS 11003, pp. 528–535, 2018.
https://doi.org/10.1007/978-3-319-99737-7_56

1 Introduction

What many people may miss so much in their lives is that parents read story books for them during their childhood because it can be really warm, enjoyable, and memorable. Such experience also greatly influences whether children can get close to books in the future, be willing to read, be able to read for their life, and even achieve the ideal state of a scholarly society. This is why many countries aim at promoting literacy for the preliminary and primary education.

In a society, the library has the functions of education, information provision, culture, and leisure. It is also dedicated to playing the life and knowledge center. Moreover, with the development of science and technology and the great changes made by the advent of the digital era, the means of disseminating knowledge is no longer only via papers, but e-books, e-journals, electronic databases, and digital audio and video resources. The digitization of science and technology has caused changes in people's reading behaviors, affecting the ways reading materials can be presented, and transforming the original library services.

With the booming development of information technology and the growing maturity of digital communication applications, there is also a trend to upgrade from a digital library to an intelligent one [1]. Therefore, libraries are currently actively researching robot-related applications [2]. They hope to introduce robot services into libraries and use robots to attract more people to come to libraries or make people enjoy reading.

In addition, since reading is a basic function of the libraries, it is facing the challenge of digitalization. In recent years, in response to the advent of the digital age, libraries have purchased diversified electronic resources especially for the needs of children's picture books. Generally, there are three types of the database for children's electronic picture books: procurement, collecting public resources, and self-built sharing. Among them, self-built sharing is made by National Library of Public Information (NLPI), Taiwan assets. Since 2011, a "Digital Collection Project for Students Created Picture Books" funded by NLPI has been established. The content of picture books was created by students. And then, NLPI selected the qualified vendors to carry out the digital works on the electronic picture books and then formed the "collection" and "circulation" of a "Picture Book Database (PBD) [3]". Although it is an original resource consisting of different students' works, the library has maintained the copyright of the created online reading/picture books for the public. The purpose of PBD mainly aims at making students' dreams come true when they create their own picture books!" [4].

This article will first introduce the NLPI service of humanoid robot storytelling for children by using the stories of children's picture books in the PBD. It further describes the creativity and imagination of the robot engineers to form robots' various performances and functions depending on the users' requirements. So far, we have decided to select a humanoid robot, NAO [5] because of its human-like appearance, behavioral actions, thinking, and emotional expressions. Moreover, this article will depict how to design a humanoid robot program to perform audio storytelling in conjunction with body movements and expressions, so that it will be easier to attract readers' attention and affection.

2 The Design Process of Robotic Storytelling Using an NAO Robot

In the robot storytelling service, the robot is not only a system platform showing the content of the story, but its more important role is to tell a story that can attract children. This section will refer to the process of how to design the robot storytelling service.

Step 1: Selecting the story and get its voice file (.mp3)

As indicated, the story source of the e-book is from the PBD of NLPI. A target story would have the features of interesting and emotional content from the database. Since a story will be told by a robot, the story selection is based on the style of the storyteller as the first person. In this way, the robot can express actions and sounds in the way of the first person. That is, a robot is talking about its own experience/story, so that the story can be more direct, vivid and real.

Step 2: Matching the segmented voice files with the story content and time sequence

The idea of robotic storytelling service is that the robot's action can associate with the meaning of the children's story. It can be achieved by adding a human body gesture or movement that is consistent with the meaning or symbolic expression of a specific storyline. The human body gesture or movement is then designed as an robotic action. Afterwards, voice files are fit into each storylines. This study uses the e-book "A talking hole" as an example for the robotic to tell this story (see Fig. 1).

Step 3: Designing body gestures/movements that meet the storyline

A robot motion designer must firstly listen to a story in order to understand this story. Then, he or she will design a body movement either matching the story or focusing on certain keywords in the plot. For example, the protagonist, Dongdong, has an "exhaustively pondering about …" statement in the "A talking hole 005.mp3". A robot motion designer may design a matching movement in which a robot repeatedly grabs its head by its hand several times so that the listeners can easily associate and figure out the story situation- "thinking over again and again" (see Fig. 2).

Step 4: Combining the story's voice files and matching robot's body movements

In this step, the designer will use Choregraphe [6], an NAO robot application development tool, to combine its body movements with the voice files of the story. Choregraphe can help designers to edit NAO's actions and behaviors that are linked together with events and time sequence. The timeline is used to express the time sequence accordingly. NAO's body movements can be edited to be the multimedia data, such as voice files, text-to-speech files, etc. can match with the movements. Through the management of timing and triggering, NAO's events, actions, behaviors, and voice files can be activated to allow NAO to have conversations with users. As a result, this allows robots to tell stories with interesting effects of actions.

Sequence of story paragraphs	Segmented voice file	The text of each storyline
1	A talking hole 001.mp3	"A talking hole"
2	A talking hole 002.mp3	"A cub, Dongdong, is very annoying."
3	A talking hole 003.mp3	"Because the Lion King makes an order"
4	A talking hole 004.mp3	"all the animals have to write their own dream cards."
5	A talking hole 005.mp3	"Dongdong exhaustively thinks about that, but he does not know what to write on his own dream card."
6	A talking hole 006.mp3	"It's the best job to be a doctor because you can make much money."
7	A talking hole 007.mp3	"A tiger Pangpang said that in a very confident manner."
8	A talking hole 008.mp3	"However, Dongdong does not want to make much money."
9	A talking hole 009.mp3	"A rabbit Meimei said:"
10	A talking hole 010.mp3	"being a pianist is the best dream,"
11	A talking hole 011.mp3	"so that you can look beautiful."
…	…	…

Fig. 1. Example of segmented voice files from an original e-book

Fig. 2. NAO repeatedly grabs its head by its hand to express "exhaustively thinking"

3 Results and Discussions

As aforementioned, a robotic storytelling service has been implemented and opened to the NLPI readers, so there was a need to explore the degree of reader acceptance for this service by using a questionnaire investigation.

There were 52 children (31 boys and 21 girls) from an Elementary School nearby the library in Taichung City. They were first invited to come to NLPI to get involved in the robotic storytelling service. Then, they were guided to answer the questionnaire.

The experimental process is as follows:

1. The moderator made a welcome speech and gave a brief introduction to the robot NAO.
2. NAO introduced itself.
3. NAO began to tell stories with the story slides behind it (the two stories were: "A Talking Hole!" 4 min and 26 s, "Pippi Adventure" 2 min and 57 s). Instead of using an overhead projector, a large-sized (55 inches) computer screen is used behind Nao to show an e-book story in order to make it easier for listeners to get involved in the visual background of the story.
4. After the two stories had been heard, the children were grouped with five people each. The assistant researchers helped the children to complete the questionnaire by verbally reading the questionnaire.
5. Before leaving the robotic storytelling room, children were awarded to watch NAO dancing for 3 min and 30 s. By observation, they were so excited and left the room happily

It can be seen from the records that many children were so engaged and very focused during the robot's storytelling time. From time to time, their facial expressions changed.

After the robotic story time was over, a questionnaire was used to collect children's opinions of the robot's storytelling. The Likert scale 1 to 5 was designed to indicate the level of their preferences. As the children were little, the assistant researchers had to explain the meaning of the topic to the students so that this could increase and assure their understanding of the questionnaire items.

The basic information was obtained from Part A. The two classes have similar proportions of gender and age. They are students of about 7 to 9 years of age and live in the school district around NLPI, i.e. in the southern district of Taichung City. The result shows that the majority of these children had never or rarely visited this library (nearly 68%) before this robotic storytelling experience.

This can be compared with the follow-up question "Have you ever come to NLPI Children Learning Center to listen to stories?" The answer to "No" (80%) was much more than the one of to "Yes" (20%).

The data analysis for the part B of the questionnaire was analyzed by SPSS statistical software. The reliability level reached a high confidence of 0.898. Table 1 shows the means and standard deviations of the 9 questions.

Similar to what the researchers observed during the robot's presence, all items have the average score at least 4 points. Regarding Question 8, when children were asked if

Table 1. Statistical results of Part B of the questionnaire

	Average	SD
Part I. The system acceptance Q1. I can see the movement of the robot clearly	4.49	1.023
Q2. I can hear what the robot talked clearly	4.78	0.685
Part II. Content acceptance Q3. I like the story that robots told	4.59	0.840
Q4. I agree that robot gestures/moves in the storytelling are very appealing	4.53	0.793
Part III. Learning Pace Q5. I agree that the speed of the robot's storytelling is just right	4.65	0.830
Part IV. Comparison with traditional law Q6. I agree that robots are more attractive than listening to the audio materials	4.51	0.938
Part V. Motivation improvement Q7. After listening to the robotic storytelling, I am willing to read this story book	4.08	1.336
Part VI. Future promotion Q8. I would like to hear robots telling stories next time	4.80	0.577
Q9. I would like to have my friends to listen to robots to tell stories	4.39	1.239

they would like to hear robots telling stories next time", their agreement was the highest among all. In addition, reading the result of Question 6 to know if they agree that robots are more attractive than other audio storytelling materials, we can see a high score of 4.51, indicating that children feel that robots' three-dimensional, real, and touchable may be more interesting when comparing to the monotonous flat audiobook story CD (auditory only). So the interaction between humans and robots can be applied to teaching because this will not only improve teaching efficiency but also increase learning motivation. This also echoes the study of a scholar [7]: if the learning process can make students feel less anxious and happy, it can effectively improve students' learning motivation and teacher's teaching effectiveness. Obviously, this service is consistently and eagerly anticipated by these children.

However, the lowest mean score and the highest standard deviation was found in Question 7, "After listening to the robot storytelling, I am willing to find out this story book". Perhaps partly because these children were not interested in this particular story, or children usually do not often read or borrow books in the library. Thus, the future study may have to consider the selection of the story, such as action story for the robot to make more interesting actions. Moreover, some children's favorite background music may be used to attract the attention of children.

In addition, this study further explored the difference between male and female students' preference and acceptance of robot storytelling by the analysis of a single sample t-test. Surprisingly, most people may have a stereotype that boys' acceptability and preference of robots should be higher than that of girls. However, from Table 2, it can be found that girls' preference for robot storytelling is even higher. The average number of opinions on each issue is higher than that of boys, and the analysis of standard deviations shows that the views of girls are more consistent. At the same time, from the analysis of the Q7 and Q9 questions, we can find that compared with boys, girls have a more positive attitude towards the use of robot storytelling services. Furthermore, from the p-value result, it can be found that the gender factor is indeed a significant and important difference factor for the robot storytelling service ($p < 0.05$, as indicated by the p-value in Table 2 '*'mark). Except Q2 and Q8, the p values of other questionnaires are less than 0.05. In terms of Q7, girls are more likely to use library resources to find out and understand the original content of the story. The results can be provided to the library if they wish to attract children readers to use robot-related services.

Table 2. Differences in opinion of the questionnaire between boys and girls

	Gender	Average	SD	p value
Part I. The system acceptance Q1. I can see the movement of the robot clearly	Boy	4.21	1.236	0.007*
	Girl	4.90	0.308	
Q2. I can hear what the robot talked clearly	Boy	4.66	0.857	0.086
	Girl	4.95	0.224	
Part II. Content acceptance Q3. I like the story that robots told	Boy	4.38	1.015	0.014*
	Girl	4.90	0.308	
Q4. I agree that robot gestures/moves in the storytelling are very appealing	Boy	4.34	0.897	0.030*
	Girl	4.80	0.523	
Part III. Learning Pace Q5. I agree that the speed of the robot's storytelling is just right	Boy	4.48	1.022	0.046*
	Girl	4.90	0.308	
Part IV. Comparison with traditional law Q6. I agree that robots are more attractive than listening to the audio materials	Boy	4.31	1.105	0.044*
	Girl	4.80	0.523	
Part V. Motivation improvement Q7. After listening to the robotic storytelling, I am willing to read this story book	Boy	3.66	1.542	0.002*
	Girl	4.70	0.571	
Part VI. Future promotion Q8. I would like to hear robots telling stories next time	Boy	4.69	0.712	0.074
	Girl	4.95	0.224	
Q9. I would like to have my friends to listen to robots to tell stories	Boy	4.07	1.510	0.012*
	Girl	4.85	0.366	

4 Conclusions and Future Studies

As the development and application technologies of robots become more and more mature, the development of "humanity" for humanoid robots will become more and more real. The focus of this research is to share experience in narrating services for children with NAO robots. The preliminary results have already received a very enthusiastic response from children's readers.

Although the robot storytelling service for children was proved to be greatly welcomed by children in this study, the main difficulty in practicing this type of service is not the technical problem of robot programming but the issue of how the robot can do more interesting but not simple performances. The robot's gestures and motions may need to combine with sound and light, as well as the artistic design on the stage or platform. Therefore, the robot performance designer is likely to be a very important market-based emerging work and talent demand areas in the future when the governments in different countries vigorously develop robot applications.

Looking ahead, it may be worthwhile pondering whether the use of robots can lead and accompany these children to enhance their reading habits and long-term interest in reading, and even to enhance reading concentration. In addition to the storytelling performed by NAO humanoid robots in this study, more different types of robots can be used in the future. For example, a Pepper robot with a human appearance but a larger body and a tablet capable of displaying information. The Zenbo robot, as well as being cute and compact, has a tablet that can show the expression and slide, to develop more intelligent robotic services for library users. In the future, the library-provided robot services may need to know how such a technology can let readers enjoy various functions and tasks.

Acknowledgment. 1. This research was supported in part by the Ministry of Education, Taiwan, R.O.C. under the project number and category B04 "2016 University's Digital Humanities Project based on Social Education Institutions".

2. The authors would like to thank the National Library of Public Information and the Taiwan Public Library Journal for the permission of rewriting and updating in English according to our previous paper written in Chinese [8].

References

1. Ouyang, H.J.: Sharing the experience of planning picture book databases. Taiwan Public Libr. J. **5**, 5-1–5-14 (2017)
2. Tsai, M.-F., Lin, J.-M., Shen, W.W., Lai, C.-C.: Exploring the feasibility of applying robots to library services. Nat. Central Libr. Bull. **1**, 153–180 (2017)
3. Picture Book Database. http://storybook.nlpi.edu.tw/. Accessed 31 May 2018
4. Lan, M.-K., Jhang, W.-J.: The service of picture books in public library: a case of the picture book database. Public Libr. J. **3**, 1–21 (2016)
5. Product introduction to Robot NAO. http://www.nao.com.tw/product. Accessed 18 Dec 2017
6. Choregraphe. http://ii.tudelft.nl/naodoc/site_ch/greendoc/choregraphe/choregraphe.html. Accessed 5 Feb 2018
7. Papert, S.: Mindstorms: Children, Computers, and Powerful Ideas, 2nd edn. Basic Books, New York (1993)
8. Tsai, M.-F., Shen, W.W., Lin, J.-M., Lai, C.-C., Syu, Y.J., Lin, S.T.: Applying humanity robot to the storytelling service for children in a library–a case study on national library of public information. Taiwan Public Libr. J. **7**, 1–33 (2018)

An Extensive Reading System Built on the Basis of Comprehensible Input Principles - A Key to Rescuing the Lower-Level EFL University Students' Vocabulary Ability

Wei-Wei Shen[1(✉)], Jim-Min Lin[2], and Zeng-Wei Hong[3]

[1] Department of Foreign Languages and Literature, Feng Chia University, Taichung, Taiwan
wwshen@fcu.edu.tw

[2] Department of Information Engineering and Computer Science, Feng Chia University, Taichung, Taiwan

[3] Department of Computer Science, Faculty of Information and Communication Technology, Universiti Tunku Abdul Rahman, Kampar, Malaysia

Abstract. Although scholars of extensive reading and vocabulary pedagogy confirm that the two research fields have a strong connection to improve one's language competence, little seems to be implemented on students who are studying English as a foreign language (EFL) in the reading courses. This paper, first, used a case study in an EFL university context such as Taiwan to show that there is a need to examine the facts behind the deficient training of extensive reading. We then proposed a possible solution via some help of technology and created a mobile reading system. During the system implementation period, we observed one selected subject who might not be seen as an active or motivated EFL learner in reading classrooms and had a very low level of English proficiency, but our preliminary finding shows that his vocabulary ability can be enhanced because of the extensive reading opportunities guided by the system. Suggestions and future development of the system are finally indicated.

Keywords: Vocabulary learning · Extensive reading · Vocabulary levels
Computer-assisted reading · Computer-assisted vocabulary learning
English as a foreign language

1 Introduction

Stephen Krashen has best known for his theory regarding comprehensible input since the 1980s, and his innovative teaching approach has been a fashion for the English language teaching community [14–19]. There was a time that his theory was under attacked because there was no sufficient research evidence to support such a reasonable assumption [16, 17]. For example, it might be difficult to control or measure the teaching that may or may not follow the rule of comprehensible input (i + 1). In other words, it seemed to be a perfect hypothesis that teaching can take a step further (+1) of learners' current knowledge (i) but may not be easy to prove.

T.-T. Wu et al. (Eds.): ICITL 2018, LNCS 11003, pp. 536–545, 2018.
https://doi.org/10.1007/978-3-319-99737-7_57

However, such criticisms no longer exist nowadays because of the abundant studies in extensive reading connecting to the advancement of language abilities and lower degree of negative feelings [15–18, 24, 25]. In addition, it was also proved that general reading skills can be improved obviously and quickly through extensive reading [33]. Therefore, Krashen's theory has not only become a core concept of second/foreign language (L2) acquisition but one of the frequently cited references in extensive reading research.

On the other hand, in the field of vocabulary research, scholars also confirm that extensive reading is a way to rapidly expand the vocabulary size. Thus, the two factors, extensive reading and vocabulary growth, can form a good foundation of developing L2 learners' abilities at least in terms of the early development of language acquisition.

Perhaps unlike the natural process of first language acquisition that most children like to read, sometimes L2 reading is a burden and stress for many learners who are not using English in their daily life. Then how can it be possible to get into the higher-level of vocabulary proficiency without a large number of readings in the current or conventional L2 reading classrooms? Moreover, in terms of teaching methods, as Nation [25] noticed that although there are extensive reading courses offered, it is still difficult to implement extensive nature in the end because when learners are doing the silent reading in the classrooms, teachers may feel strange of not doing any teaching in the classrooms.

Another reality in L2 classrooms is that those low achievers who are supposed to do more of extensive reading may not even have the motivation to take any additional or optional English lessons in the conventional classrooms. Somehow they do not even feel comfortable to sit in the classrooms learning something that might be beyond their abilities. For example, many L2 university students in Taiwan, especially with regard to the non-English majors, normally have no reading habits and their vocabulary size is small. This can form the worst cycle of reading English because these learners cannot easily read to improve their low level of vocabulary size, and then too many unknown words hinder them to enjoy reading more. Eventually, their confidence or motivation to read English texts and learn vocabulary could be crushed altogether.

This paper intends to report a possible solution to lift up L2 learners' vocabulary level through reading more via the help of technology, as scholars have identified about the benefit of technology to make learning personal and effective without the confinement of space [2, 32]. It first mentions such a need through a case study and then describes the background of the self-made reading system. Finally, the implementation and future development will be mentioned.

2 A Case Study

The paper uses a university in Taiwan as a learning context because it has similar and major features of Chinese cultural learning and teaching style mentioned in, for example, Jin and Cortazzi's long-term research [13]. To name just a few, using books and relying on teachers can be the pattern in the classroom; memorization can be the main learning strategy.

One student called Howard as a pseudonym studying in a technology field as a graduate student at this university in Taiwan. That is, the student is real but not his name, and there are plenty of such graduate and undergraduate students studying in this university setting labeled as a low-level of English language learner. As English is his foreign language (EFL) and not his majoring subject, he does not need to perform English well to graduate from his first degree and can continue his further education without many obstacles because the enrollment of quite a few universities does not take his English ability into account. Meanwhile, in recent years, partly because the birth rate is low in Taiwan and partly because the number of universities is more than needed, it is easy to get the enrollment permission of many, if not all, universities.

However, such a low English level student may encounter a lot of the difficulties reading English papers or texts because he does not know many words in English. The photo (Fig. 1) shows that the habitual style Howard manages to study English materials is to write down a lot of Chinese equivalents on the paper. But the problem is that he not only takes a lot of time to look up the dictionary but eventually cannot put all pieces together to understand the text meaning. Undoubtedly, Howard is normally labeled as a low EFL achiever with little motivation of attending English courses if he is not required to do so.

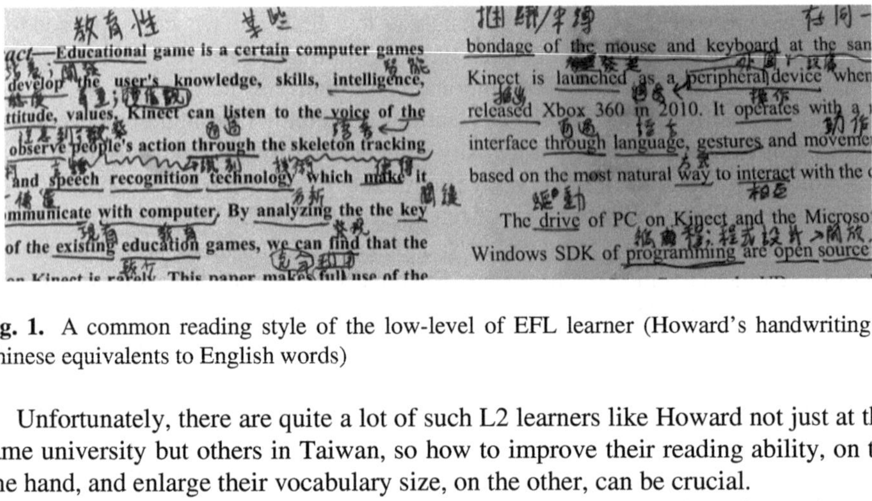
act—Educational game is a certain computer games
develop the user's knowledge, skills, intelligence,
ttitude, values, Kinect can listen to the voice of the
observe people's action through the skeleton tracking
and speech recognition technology which make it
mmunicate with computer, By analyzing the the key
of the existing education games, we can find that the

bondage of the mouse and keyboard at the san
Kinect is launched as a peripheral device when
released Xbox 360 in 2010. It operates with a
interface through language, gestures and moveme
based on the most natural way to interact with the
The drive of PC on Kinect and the Microso
Windows SDK of programming are open source

Fig. 1. A common reading style of the low-level of EFL learner (Howard's handwriting of Chinese equivalents to English words)

Unfortunately, there are quite a lot of such L2 learners like Howard not just at this same university but others in Taiwan, so how to improve their reading ability, on the one hand, and enlarge their vocabulary size, on the other, can be crucial.

When extensive reading can be a solution to help Howard or others, it may be more effective to start this training from a younger age. But then, in fact, students like Howard have already missed out this critical period, as innate theorists may proclaim to be an important time before teenage to develop a language easily [21], some remedial teaching may be needed for these low-level EFL university students. Thus, to use a modern technology to flip the conventional design of the extensive reading course may be a realistic solution for university students like Howard.

3 Design Principles of the Extensive Reading System

As mentioned, the enhancement of extensive reading and vocabulary size can be like two sides of the same coin [15, 25], but this does not mean that L2 learners can be left on their own without any guidance or instruction when reading more or widely [26]. That is, the training of reading more and vocabulary growth must be well controlled in order to be effective.

Based on some features of the comprehensible input via the extensive reading and the development of vocabulary size, we recruited an Information Technology program trainee studying for his Master's Degree to write the software we needed. We then created a platform suitable to guide students to do the extensive reading work based on individual needs, interests, and abilities. The system can be used on the Samsung Samsung Galaxy S3 (i9300) mobile phone and used the Android 4.1 or later system to set up a personalized reading English learning article recommendation system. It is a paper-based augmentation mobile device to make article recommendations based on the functions of vocabulary testing and topic interest, and it can record all individual profiles [10].

The following will present some relevant background information to explain the background we attempted to design this extensive reading system.

3.1 Comprehensible Reading and Appropriate Vocabulary Size

There is a consensus that vocabulary is the key to success of language learning, and one best way of learning words quickly is through extensive or pleasure reading. This means that reading without destroying learners' confidence in reading, so that reading becomes a pleasure activity. In order to get some understanding of which vocabulary size can help learners to cope with reading comprehension without difficult hurdles, scholars have proposed some estimation of the comprehension abilities. For example, if the intention is to have a survival index of 95% comprehension ability, then 2,000 to 3,000-word families may be enough [7, 30]. When getting to the higher level of knowing 8,000 to 9,000-word families, learners may be able to understand up to 98% of the encountering contents [25].

Although it is hard to get a precise indication of the vocabulary size and reading comprehension, it is obvious EFL learners who have less than 2000 or 3000 frequently seen vocabulary may need more help when learning to read and to increase vocabulary.

3.2 A Hybrid Approach to Design the System

In recent years, information technology has been fast developed in extensive reading and proved its effectiveness of motivation, self-confidence and positive growth of affection [1, 6, 11, 12].

However, some scholars such as O'Hara and Sellen [28] and Chu [5] have warned that reading paper version may not be easily abolished because on the one hand, reading from the prints can still be read anywhere without being limited by machines, electricity, or batteries. On the other hand, for some non-technical users or lovers, complete technology-based reading may not be favored. Thus, as many textbooks for English reading courses are still paper format, it was then found that a hybrid approach, i.e. using the system to guide extensive reading can effectively co-exist with traditional printing materials [3, 4, 20].

3.3 Recommended and Graded Nature

Although the recommended and graded nature of designing an extensive reading course is nothing new because some well-known publishers, like Oxford University Press, have devoted to creating this type of materials [29]. Besides, more e-books are also gradually established. Another example is that Macmillan [23] has many story sets and has a special culture category [23]. Readers' language levels are classified into five-phase abilities: Starter and Beginner (A1), Elementary (A2), Pre-intermediate (A2–B1), Intermediate (B1), and Upper Intermediate (B2). Quiz questions are also designed to test readers' present abilities. Meanwhile, there were also attempts in Taiwan to design recommendation system [8, 9].

However, students like Howard in this case study may not be willing to buy or borrow such materials due to the following reasons. First, university students' living allowance may be tight, and quite a few of them may have a loan to study in the higher education, so more often than not, the last thing they would want to do is buy more books or pay for APPs. Second, even if Howard's university can buy a set of the graded readers and store them in the library, students might be in the cue to wait for one particular or popular book item to be available because there are around 20000 students in total at Howard's university; therefore, the waiting time for one popular book to be returned may be needed. Under such circumstances, it is not always easy for learners to read extensively any time or anywhere via the help of the library. Besides, even if a university can buy a collection of graded readers for students, it is quite difficult for the same book to be borrowed by different learners at the same time. For example, a compulsory English reading class in the freshman year at Howard's university may have about 30 to 50 students in one class [22]. Therefore, in this EFL setting, the class teacher follows up a unified English curriculum and may require all students of the same class to use one single textbook. Nevertheless, one printed reading textbook used for a whole class may ignore various individual needs or interests [31].

Therefore, before we created the reading system, we took these hurdles of the current learning and teaching environment into account. Then we approached a book author, Neil Anderson, who designed one reading program, ACTIVE: Skills for Reading, for EFL learners, and this set was used as the main reading source. We obtained his consent to allow us to install, modify, re-order, and research one particular set of his reading texts.

After the calculation of the reading difficulty of the 96 articles, we then formed a recommendation mechanism to assist students choosing their favored reading texts and completing vocabulary tests.

4 System Implementation: The Low-Level Learner's Process and Progress

This section is to show how we may use the extensive reading system and provide some preliminary result of the system implementation. Using a case study, Howard's English ability is first described and the methods used to deal with his problems in reading and vocabulary size are presented here.

4.1 The Subject's Initial Vocabulary Ability

As English language learning was not Howard's compulsory course indicated above, we could only ask Howard to do this extensive reading system in his free time. So actually this fulfills one main advantage of doing reading activities based on one's own time and comfortable space.

Before Howard started his extensive reading program guided by the system, we tested his vocabulary level according to the levels tests on the website designed by Nation and Beglar [27]. Howard did not pass the first thousand recognition test, which means that he was not able to recognize 1000 words in the test easily. This result actually matches with our original assumptions about low his initial vocabulary competence was before he used the system.

4.2 The Subject's Learning Process Guided by the System and Teacher

We gave him one pre-training session of using the system so that he could run the system smoothly. As his major is in information technology, he seems happier to accept the idea of using technology to assist him reading and learning words than studying in regular reading classes. He followed the flow of the system steps below:

- The reader registers the system;
- The reader tests and types in the current vocabulary recognition level;
- The reader completes the topic interest questionnaire;
- The reader notices that there is a topic list suggested by the system;
- The reader can decide which article to read first;
- The reader can do the vocabulary test related to each reading. But the same reading article may be suggested again if there are less than 60% of the words which cannot be recognized.

The above flow is not a strictly linear process without the flexibility to go backward. For example, when the reader finds that the reading list may not match with his/her interests completely, he/she can re-do the questionnaire, and then the system can come up with another alternative list with another set of the suitable articles. Or the reader can choose to do all vocabulary tests after he/she finishes several different articles. Besides, the vocabulary recognition level does not have to be tested all the time because it will be so unbelievable to have a fast improvement only with few readings. Most importantly, the system will not give them a score, but if the article is not recommended again, this will show that most words can be comprehended. But as indicated earlier, if the reader finds the same article recommended two times or more, this may mean that he/she cannot understand quite a few of words in the article. Therefore, in this way, the reader does not necessarily get anxious when thinking about the score all the time.

Howard's reading process was monitored through the sector in the management system, which can be used by the technician or teacher. Howard's login/logout dates and time, topics, and vocabulary tests during the use of the system can be found in the management record. If we found that Howard did not proceed to read through the help of the system for several days, and then we contacted him through Facebook to confirm if he had any difficulties proceeding. We asked him occasionally in the process to see if he progressed to next level of the recognition vocabulary, and then the time he progressed, we stopped this extensive reading.

4.3 The Subject's Learning Outcome

After Howard read the quantity of about 20 different topics in two months, he increased one vocabulary level higher. That is, originally he had less than 1000 vocabulary level, but he had a breakthrough to move to 2000 words.

We kept communicating with Howard for another 6 months without any further guidance of extensive reading via the help of technology and confirmed that he did not attend any reading course and did not try to study English systematically by himself. We tested him again of his vocabulary level and found that Howard did not lower down his level but he did not proceed to next level either. In other words, he more or less stayed at the same vocabulary level as the one when we left him alone.

5 Conclusion

Our study aimed at EFL low level of learners to design an English recommendation system based on one's reading interests and vocabulary abilities to ensure learners' readability or comprehension. To begin with, we mentioned some requirements and proposed solutions to assist such learners' needs. We then referred to the past related work and designed a system that may help this targeting population to read with little supervision or teaching in classrooms. In the system, articles in a three-level reading textbook can be recommended to each learner.

At the stage of the implementation, we analyzed a low-achieving EFL university student who did not attend English course elsewhere, did not know what to do to make his English better, and was afraid of learning English at first, but was delighted to see his development of vocabulary ability to be one level higher after he read 20 different articles in about two months of his free time. It is encouraging at this initial stage of system implementation that using it to guide a low-level EFL learner to read more may be possible to help his vocabulary growth. Therefore, this pilot finding is in the line of the past discussions on the benefits of using extensive reading and vocabulary learning to enhance acquisition.

Although there was only one EFL student's profile examined in the paper, he actually might represent quite a few of the university students who are waiting for a modern solution to enhance their poor vocabulary size to understand English reading texts because they have little chances to study or survive in the current reading classrooms or programs.

Hopefully, in the future, we may keep finding more of Howard's learning achievement. We will also be able to expand the use of the system into a real learning curriculum and involve more students. Furthermore, it is also useful to check learners' reading comprehension through writing and to see the correlation between reading and writing.

Acknowledgments. 1. This study is supported in part by the Ministry of Science and Technology of the Republic of China under contract number MOST 105-2511-S-035-002-MY2.

2. We are very grateful for Mr. Chun-Po Huang's assistance in drafting a software program to materialize our initial teaching ideas.

3. We thank for Howard's agreement to allow us to show his handwriting and observe his learning process.

References

1. Arnold, N.: Online extensive reading for advanced foreign language learners: an evaluation study. Foreign Lang. Ann. **42**(2), 340–662 (2009). https://doi.org/10.1111/j.1944-9720.2009.01024.x
2. Chen, C.M., Hsu, S.H.: Personalized intelligent mobile learning system for supporting effective English learning. Educ. Technol. Soc. **11**(3), 153–180 (2008)
3. Chen, G.D., Chao, P.Y.: Augmenting paper-based learning with mobile phones. Interact. Comput. **21**(3), 173–185 (2009). https://doi.org/10.1016/j.intcom.2009.01.001
4. Chen, N.S., Teng, D.C.E., Lee, C.H.: Augmenting paper-based reading activity with direct access to digital materials and scaffolded questioning. Comput. Educ. **57**, 1705–1715 (2011). https://doi.org/10.1016/j.compedu.2011.03.013
5. Chu, H.C.: Potential negative effects of mobile learning on students' learning achievement and cognitive load—a format assessment perspective. Educ. Technol. Soc. **17**(1), 332–344 (2014)
6. Chung, H.H., Chen, S.C., Kuo, M.H.: A study of EFL college students' acceptance of mobile learning. Procedia Soc. Behav. Sci. **176**, 333–339 (2015). https://doi.org/10.1016/j.sbspro.2015.01.479
7. Cobb, T.: Computing the vocabulary demands of L2 reading. Lang. Learn. Technol. **11**(3), 38–63 (2007)
8. Hsu, C.K., Hwang, G.J., Chang, C.K.: Development of a reading material recommendation system based on a knowledge engineering approach. Comput. Educ. **55**, 76–83 (2010). https://doi.org/10.1016/j.compedu.2009.12.004
9. Hsu, C.K., Hwang, G.J., Chang, C.K.: A personalized recommendation-based mobile learning approach to improving the reading performance of EFL students. Comput. Educ. **63**(1), 327–336 (2013). https://doi.org/10.1016/j.compedu.2012.12.004
10. Huang, C.P.: An individual mobile learning tool for scaffolding paper-based EFL extensive reading. Master's thesis, Feng Chia University, Taichung, Taiwan (2016). (in Chinese). http://ndltd.ncl.edu.tw/cgi-bin/gs32/gsweb.cgi?o=dnclcdr&s=id=%22104FCU05392007%22.&searchmode=basic#XXX

11. Huang, K.L., Huang, K.H., Ho, C.H.: Users' behavior patterns and the interactive interface design of tablet readers. Enhanc. Read. Exp. **32**(3), 509–528 (2014). https://doi.org/10.1108/LHT-01-2014-0002
12. Hwang, G.J., Wu, P.H.: Applications, impacts and trends of mobile technology-enhanced learning: a review of 2008–2012 publications in selected SSCI journals. Int. J. Mob. Learn. Organ. **8**(2), 83–95 (2014). https://doi.org/10.1504/IJMLO.2014.062346
13. Jin, L., Cortazzi, M. (eds.): Researching Chinese Learners: Skills, Perceptions and Intercultural Adaptations. Palgrave Macmillan, Basingstoke (2011)
14. Krashen, S.: Principles and Practice in Second Language Acquisition. Prentice Hall, Englewood Cliffs (1982). https://doi.org/10.1093/elt/37.3.283
15. Krashen, S.D.: We acquire vocabulary and spelling by reading: additional evidence for the input hypothesis. Mod. Lang. J. **73**, 440–464 (1989). https://doi.org/10.1111/j.1540-4781.1989.tb05325.x
16. Krashen, S.: The input hypothesis and its rivals. In: Ellis, N. (ed.) Implicit and Explicit Learning of Languages, pp. 45–77. Academic Press, London (1994)
17. Krashen, S.: Explorations in Language Acquisition and Use: The Taipei Lectures. Heinemann, Portsmouth (2003)
18. Krashen, S.: The Comprehension hypothesis extended. In: Piske, T., Young-Scholten, M. (eds.) Input Matters in SLA, pp. 81–94. Multilingual Matters, Bristol (2009)
19. Krashen, S.: Who invented comprehension input? Int. J. Lang. Teach. **12**(2), 32–33 (2017)
20. Leone, S., Leo, T.: The synergy of paper-based and digital material for ubiquitous foreign language learners. Knowl. Manag. E-Learn. Int. J. **3**(3), 319–341 (2011)
21. Lightbown, P.M., Spada, N.: How Languages Are Learned. Oxford University Press, Oxford (2013)
22. Luo, B., Shen, W.W.: Repeated reading: a practical approach when using an ESL textbook? Feng Chia J. Hum. Soc. Sci. **30**, 77–103 (2015)
23. Macmillan Education: Using graded readers in the classroom (2014). http://www.macmillanreaders.com/wp-content/uploads/2010/07/UGRIC-web-2014-Macmillan.pdf. Accessed 14 Apr 2018
24. Mason, B., Krashen, S.D.: Can extensive reading help unmotivated students of EFL improve? ITL Int. J. Appl. Linguist. **117**(1), 79–84 (1997). https://doi.org/10.1075/itl.117-118.04mas
25. Nation, I.S.P.: How large a vocabulary is needed for reading and listening? Can. Mod. Lang. Rev. **63**(1), 59–82 (2006)
26. Nation, P.: Principles guiding vocabulary learning through extensive reading. Read. Foreign Lang. **27**(1), 136–145 (2015)
27. Nation, P., Beglar, D.: A vocabulary size test. Lang. Teach. **31**(7), 9–13 (2007)
28. O'Hara, K., Sellen, A.: A comparison of reading paper and online documents. In: Proceedings of the SIGCHI Conference on Human Factors in Computing Systems (CHI 1997), pp. 335–342 (1997)
29. Oxford Bookworms Library (n.d.). https://elt.oup.com/catalogue/items/global/graded_readers/oxford_bookworms_library/?cc = tw&selLanguage = zh. Accessed 14 Apr 2018
30. Schmitt, N., Jiang, X., Rabe, W.: The percentage of words known in a text and reading comprehension. Mod. Lang. J. **95**, 26 (2011)
31. Shen, W.W.: Approaches to designing a mobile-Assisted reading programme. In: 51st Annual International IATEFL Conference and Exhibition, Glasgow, UK (2017)

32. Wu, T.T., Sung, T.W., Huang, Y.M., Yang, C.S., Yang, J.T.: Ubiquitous English learning system with dynamic personalized guidance of learning portfolio. Educ. Technol. Soc. **14**(4), 164–180 (2011)
33. Yamashita, J.: Extensive reading and development of different aspects of L2 proficiency. System **36**(4), 661–672 (2008)

Educational Data Analytics Techniques and Adaptive Learning Applications

Research on Instructional Design Strategies for Training Students' Problem Solving Ability

Zengzhao Chen, Ting Qian(✉), Jing Zhang, Qianfan Yu, and Guilin Liu

National Engineering Research Center for E-learning, Central China Normal University, Wuhan, China
953151091@qq.com

Abstract. With the proposal of "China's students' development core qualities", the new period puts forward higher requirements for students' innovative spirit and practical ability. Problem solving, as one of the qualities needed for practical innovation, occupies an important position, and there is very little research on instructional design to improve student problem-solving skills from the perspective of teachers. At the same time, with the continuous development of new technologies such as big data and internet of things, teacher education must also follow the trend. Teachers need to think about how to reshape and grow professionally in the wave of education reform. This article selects a junior high school geography teacher as the research object and tries to construct a teaching design strategy that aims at the cultivation of students' problem solving skills. There are situation-constructed strategy, task-driven strategy, and thinking-inspired strategy, and based on these strategies we create an aided analysis table and an teaching design evaluation scale, so as to provide valuable reference for teachers' teaching design, and improve students' problem-solving abilities.

Keywords: Practical innovation · Problem solving · Educational data
Instructional design strategy

1 Introduction

"Chinese students' development core qualities" pointed out that students in new era should have practical innovation ability, and ability to solve problems as one of the core competences of practical innovation, they play an important role in cultivating students' creative thinking and are necessary skills for students to learn. At present, the research on problem solving or problem solving ability focuses on the evaluation methods of problem solving capabilities, the influencing factors of problem solving capabilities, the process of problem solving, and the evaluation of problem solving capabilities. Based on the internationally shaped PISA students' problem solving ability test, scholar Yang Bin used a combination of qualitative and quantitative research methods to construct a Q-C-Q comprehensive evaluation system and data integration analysis model [1]. Yuan, a scholar, used PISA's test data to examine the impact of problem-solving persistence, problem-solving openness, and simple use of students ICTs on problem-solving ability

T.-T. Wu et al. (Eds.): ICITL 2018, LNCS 11003, pp. 549–560, 2018.
https://doi.org/10.1007/978-3-319-99737-7_58

[2]. According to the perspective of metacognition, Schoenfeld divided the problem-solving process into six stages: questions reading, analysis and exploration. Hu believes that the problem-solving ability evaluation model integrates cognitive and non-cognitive factors based on the fusion of implicit cognition and thinking content [4]. Throughout these existing studies, it was found that most of the students explained or improved their problem-solving skills from the perspective of the students, but teachers played a crucial role in improving the problem-solving ability of students throughout the class. The Central People's Government and the State Council's "Opinions on Comprehensively Deepening the Reform and Development of the Teaching Staff in the New Era" proposed that we should create high-quality, professional and innovative teachers and implement the basic tasks of moral education. This shows that teachers' professionalism and innovation are of great significance. The innovativeness of teachers has been improved, and students' thinking has room for improvement, so as to promote student problem solving.

However, in terms of the professionalism and innovation of teachers, in terms of teacher's most basic professional skills—teaching design, the following issues are currently faced. First of all, studies have shown that teachers spend less time on instructional design, lacking innovative awareness in teaching materials, focusing on teaching and learning, and thinking lightly, making the students' thinking stay on the surface of understanding teaching content, and it is difficult to diverge and innovate, which is not conducive to students' problem solving ability. Second, teachers emphasize teaching methods and light learning methods. Teachers and students interact in a single form. If teachers interact with learners in the form of questions, they can stimulate students' interest and thinking. Students can seek happiness in the process of solving problems and constantly challenge themselves. Based on the above analysis, this paper proposes teaching design strategies for the cultivation of students' problem-solving abilities, namely situation-constructed strategy, task-driven strategy, and thinking-inspired strategy. Based on these strategies, we design aided analysis table and teaching design evaluation scale. The rating scale is designed to improve the overall level of teachers' teaching design and promote student problem solving.

2 Problem Solving Related Research

Based on the existing research, we can find the theoretical foundations that affect students' problem-solving abilities are contextual cognitive theory, task-driven teaching, and heuristic teaching.

Situational cognitive theory holds that the ultimate goal of learning is to place yourself in a particular situation and gain knowledge, construct meaning, and solve problems by actively participating in social practices in specific situations. A large number of studies have shown that an appropriate problem situation can promote learner problem solving. The cognitive grammarians Godden and Baddeley proposed in 1975 that when learning content in the same or similar context in the future, knowledge and skills are more easily remembered and retained [5]. Torp and Sage (1998) pointed out that the situational information of the problem helps learners to connect the constructed knowledge and acquired skills with relevant situations in real life. The lack of situational knowledge may make it difficult for students to Knowledge is transferred to real life scenarios [6]. Wei, a scholar, believes that the problem situation helps students identify problem goals and choose problem solving strategies. Similar problem situations can help learners recall certain special rules from previous studies and find a suitable rule for this situation [7]. Zhang, a scholar, expounded the four characteristics of problem solving and put situationality as the primary feature. He believed that the proper teaching situation can promote student problem solving [8].

The situation runs through the entire teaching content. The teacher that chooses which teaching method to teach the new lesson content plays an important role in the cultivation of students' thinking. Task-driven teaching, as an important teaching method, takes the task as the main line, advocates the task's goal and creation of teaching situations, builds tasks around the teaching goals, and provides students with practical situations and situational issues. Some studies have shown that teaching content is divided into different task modules according to different focuses and teaching objectives, which is conducive to the cultivation of learner reproducibility and creative problem solving skills. Guo Xinyue, a scholar, expounded the design of inquiry tasks as the first key point in expounding the key points of inquiry-based instructional design. He believed that the tasks and traditional teaching were different in their features and meanings. They were closely linked to the learning objectives and were disciplinary, open, and extensible. specialty. Scholar Jay J.G. Van Meinenbour believes that the sorting of learning tasks will have an impact on the cognitive load of learners. Expected value theory believes that the motivation of learners for accomplishing tasks depends on the learners' expectation of the task's success. The greater the possibility of accomplishing tasks, the greater the learners' motivation for learning. Learners should start with relatively simple but still complete learning tasks, and then gradually transition to more complex tasks so as to stimulate learner motivation.

This learning based on problem solving starts with the problem and ends with the problem. There is a mutual transformation between knowledge and problem. The problem design is the basis of knowledge construction in problem solving learning, and it is a prerequisite for problem solving learning [9]. Heuristic teaching is an important teaching method. The key to teaching lies in setting problem situations, inspiring students' thinking as the core, and fully mobilizing the students' initiative and enthusiasm for learning. If we can combine the above two aspects, that is, to guide the problem and conduct heuristic teaching, we can not only improve students' ability to solve problems, but also inspire students' thinking. The scholar Song Weina proposed a heuristic teaching method focusing on problem solving. He advocated designing corresponding heuristic questions according to the student's thinking process, inspiring students to think and complete learning tasks, and improving students' ability to solve problems on their own [10]. Scholar Yang proposed a hegemonic frustration design that suits flipping classroom teaching forms. It also emphasizes problem-based learning and teaching to develop problem solving and innovation capabilities [11].

From above analysis, it seems not difficult for us to see that situation-constructed, task- driven, and thinking-inspired are not unrelated to each other. Situation-constructed is the foundation for improving problem solving capabilities. Task-driven is the hub.

Tasks are solved in a way of solving problems so that students thinking are inspired and its practical innovation ability are cultivated.

3 Teaching Design Strategy Related Research

Influenced by learning theories and various media technologies at different periods, the theoretical research of instructional design has mainly experienced three generations of instructional design guided by behaviorism, cognitivism, and constructivism. The new curriculum teaching design emphasizes the theory of constructivism as guidance, that is learner-centered, takes the initiative to construct meaning. The word "strategy" is interpreted in the Chinese dictionary as "a collection of programs or methods that can achieve a goal." At present, there are not many researches related to instructional design strategies. Scholar Chai Shaoming builds a theoretical framework based on dialogue and collaborative knowledge construction, constructs instructional design strategies, and proposes that the core of instructional design is to provide space and tools for the creation and development of the three dialogues and design appropriate themes and activities, and create social and cultural contexts for dialogue, and promote knowledge building within the group [12]. Based on the theory of cognitive flexibility, Pang Kun proposes the following teaching design strategies for teaching training for primary and secondary school teachers: (1) multi-view representation of concepts, multi-dimensional analysis of design concepts, (2) case teaching using concepts, and implementation of concepts and cases cross design (3) create a real learning situation and implement the teaching situation design of the learning task (4) apply the cognitive elastic hypertext to implement the three-dimensional mesh structure design of the teaching content [13]. The famous education technologist C.M. Reigeluth proposed four kinds of teaching design strategies: teaching organization strategies, teaching delivery strategies, teaching management strategies, and motivating students' motivation strategies. Based on the theory of constructivism, the scholar Wu Fati divided instructional design strategies into learning environment designs: active strategies, social strategies, and situational strategies. On the basis of the above two factors, the scholar Luo proposed a web-based subjective classroom instruction design strategy: teaching organization strategy, learning environment design strategy and learning support strategy [14].

4 Three-Dimensional Teaching Design Strategy Model

Based on the above analysis, we believe that the problem-solving abilities of students can adopt three-dimensional instructional design strategies, namely situation-constructed, task-driven, and thinking-inspired three-dimensional strategy models. It consists of three parts: situation construction strategy, task-driven strategy, Thinking inspired strategy. Three strategies will be described in detail below.

4.1 Situation-Constructed Strategy

The situation studied in this paper includes not only a scenario thread but also a problem situation throughout the instructional design. The situation of instructional design needs to be created based on the cognitive level of students of different ages. For example, primary school students have limited cognitive abilities. Therefore, it is possible to select a story, game, and other situations that meet the student's cognition at this stage to implement teaching. All teaching content is centered on the situation, fully attracting students' attention and helping them smoothly realize the transfer and use of knowledge. Liu proposed situational simulation-based instructional design style, that is, contextual experience as the center [15], learners apply the learned knowledge in the experience in the simulated or virtual situation through the theory of the teacher in the experience or the role-playing method under the guidance of the teacher., and promote the completion of deep learning goals in the development of the plot.

Then teachers should design what characteristics of the situation to promote teaching? The characteristics of the situation are nothing more than the following two points: authenticity and livingness. Where authenticity means that the situation of the design is real or virtual, a large number of studies have shown that if students can participate in more realistic situations, they will learn more in complex tasks and perform better [16]. The nature of life refers to the fact that teaching situations must focus on the real life of students, and discover and tap the resources for learning situations in the students' daily living environment. Fang Li summed up the situational features of mathematics problems as familiarity and specificity. Familiarity refers to the degree of distance from real life [17]. She pointed out that the higher the familiarity is, the closer the situation is to real life, thereby enhancing students' ability to solve creative problems.

Based on the above analysis combined with expert opinions, we believe that the ideological nature of the situation and the degree of integration of the situation and content are also of great significance. Ideology refers to whether the design situation has risen to a higher level of ideology, and whether it will give us a valuable reference value in life learning. For example, given a video of Wuhan City's waterlogging, the author analyzes the natural causes and human-induced causes of waterlogging, and draws inspiration from humans. The situation is thus sublimated. The integration of situation and content emphasizes that the creation of situation should reflect the characteristics of the discipline, closely follow the content of the study, and avoid the creation of teaching situations that are not related to the content of the teaching.

4.2 Task-Driven Strategy

The task-driven strategy advocates the concept of "teacher-oriented, student-centered" curriculum reform, which fully mobilizes students' initiative in inquiry learning and emphasizes that students are in a meaningful "task" situation that is closely related to study, life, and society. Learn knowledge, acquire skills, develop skills, and internalize ethics by completing tasks. Liu believes that only teaching centered on complete teaching tasks can effectively promote the learning of learners [18]. When designing a task, it should be noted that the goal of the task is guided clearly and clearly. It will be even more challenging for students to complete tasks with their goals. Xiong et al. proposed learning task modules to organize teaching content during the implementation of personalized instructional design [19]. He divided the teaching content into several learning task modules, and presented task goals and available learning in each module. Method etc. Therefore, we believe that the teaching content will be divided into different task modules according to teaching objectives to carry out teaching will help improve the classroom teaching effect, and the task is output in the form of problems. The main problem of each module is the task, and the students complete the problem solving. The task thus achieves a sense of accomplishment and enables the student to maintain a positive learning state. At the same time, Hu adopts the idea of integrated design to ensure the pertinence and extensibility of each module task. According to the complexity of the task, the main problem is decomposed into multiple operable sub-questions to attract students' continuous attention and encouragement. Students think about ways to solve problems from multiple perspectives [20].

The task goals mentioned above are also three-dimensional teaching goals: knowledge and processes, skills and methods, emotional attitudes and values. From these three aspects, we examine the achievement of the goal of teachers' teaching design. Different types of classes have different teaching objectives, and teaching methods are different. For example, the commonly used teaching methods include lecture method, discussion method, and intuitive demonstration method. No matter what teaching methods teachers use to teach, their purpose is to promote the transfer and application of students' knowledge. Many front-line practitioners believe that choosing, organizing and presenting good teaching content in the teaching process can better focus the attention of students and mobilize their initiative in learning. Teachers should clarify the status of teaching content in the entire course of teaching, and have any connection with the learning of other contents. Using the systematic viewpoints and methods, analyze the status and role of specific teaching content.

4.3 Thinking-Inspired Strategy

The enlightening strategy emphasizes that students are the main body of learning. Teachers should guide students to think independently and actively explore and improve their ability to analyze problems and solve problems. We use the problem as a bridge. Teachers design different types of teaching problems to guide students' thinking and inspire students' thinking. The relatively mature question classification model is the dimension of cognitive process in Bloom's educational target classification system—remember, understanding, apply, analyze, evaluate, and create. These six categories again contain two or more specific cognitive processes (a total of 19) [21]. Jiang Wantong believes that memory is a kind of mechanical learning, but understanding, application, analysis, evaluation, and creation are meaningful learning [22]. Meaningful learning promotes students' transfer ability, mechanical learning promotes students maintain abilities, and problem solving requires maintaining and migrating together. Therefore, these six cognitive dimensions are all important in solving problems.

In terms of problematic levels of thinking, teachers should consider the types of problems when designing problems and design as many high-level problems as possible in analysis, evaluation, and creation. This will not only help students consolidate their old knowledge, but also help students develop their thinking. In terms of problem structure, each issue should be related to each other, including the link between the main issue and the sub- question, and the relatedness of the front-to-back issues in the sub-question, to form a gradual gradient, and to form a problem chain so that students can step on the problem ladder to construct knowledge. At the same time, we should use as many of the 19 verbs or synonyms that are involved in these cognitive processes as possible to indicate students' direction of thinking and to try to figure out students' thinking. What are their possible answers? From what perspective do they think about the question? In the design process, students' response presets are fully considered so that the teacher can adjust the classroom teaching in time and further inspire students' thinking after the students give answers beyond the preset.

5 Research Design

Based on the above analysis of the three-dimensional teaching design strategy, combined with expert advice, we designed a teaching design aided analysis table (see Fig. 1) and a teaching design evaluation scale (see Fig. 2), as shown in the following table. The instructional design aid analysis form is designed to help teachers to fill in all aspects of instructional design before writing a lesson plan. The instructional design implementation evaluation scale is an objective and fair evaluation by the expert teacher according to the teacher's instructional design. Follow-up instructional design provides a reference to promote teachers' teaching reflection.

situation construction strategy	task-driven strategy			thinking-inspired strategy					
situation Line	design goals	modules		memory	understanding	application	analysis	evaluation	creation
		module one	main questions						
			subquestions						
		module two	main questions						
			subquestions						
		module three	main questions						
			subquestions						

Fig. 1. Teaching design aid analysis table

First-level indicators	Secondary indicators		Before intervention (Out of 10 points)	The reason	After intervention (Out of 10 points)	The reason
Situation-constructed strategy	Authenticity					
	Ideological					
	Living					
	Situation and content integration					
Task-driven strategy	Achievement of teaching goals	Knowledge and skills				
		Processes and methods				
		Emotional attitudes and values				
	Targeting teaching content	Teaching method				
		Student				
		Content				
Thinking-inspired strategy	Problematic thinking level					
	Problem structure	Before and after the problem associated				
		Main question and sub question related				
		Students answer presets				

Fig. 2. Teaching design evaluation scale

5.1 Research Objectives

To analyze the effect of the three-dimensional instructional design strategy on teacher's teaching design ability and the improvement of students' problem-solving ability, this research adopts a quasi-experimental research method to select an expert teacher with rich teaching experience H, and use the teaching design evaluation scale to target Teacher teaching design evaluates.

5.2 Research Object

The subjects of this study were from a secondary school junior high school geography teacher M (with an average of 4 years or less).

5.3 Research Process

The main flow of this study is shown in Fig. 3.

Step 1: Teacher M chooses a class for teaching design (Teaching Design 1.0) and class A;
Step 2: Expert Teacher H uses the Instructional Design Rating Scale and combines the interview with teacher to score Teacher M's Instructional Design 1.0 and explain why.
Step 3: Use the three-dimensional instructional design strategy to intervene the teacher M. The teacher M completes the teaching design aid analysis table according to the strategy and completes the teaching design (Teaching Design 2.0), and class B;

Step 4: Expert teacher H uses the Instructional Design Rating Scale and scores the teacher's teaching design 2.0 combined with the interview and explains the reason for the score.

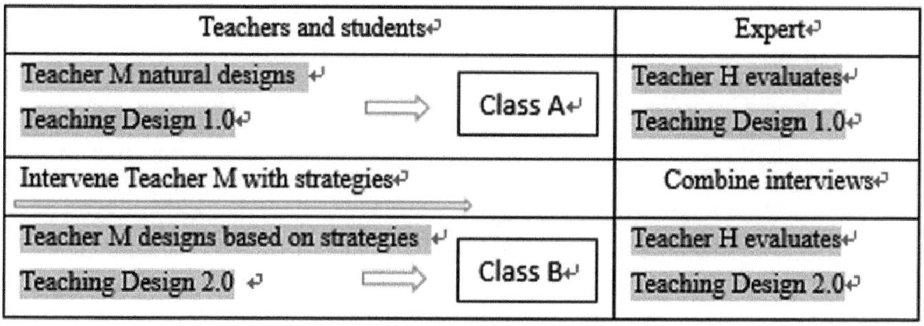

Fig. 3. Research process

In order to prevent the difference between the levels of A and B students in the two classes from affecting the experimental results, the experiment was conducted in two parallel classes and two classes were recorded throughout the course. At the same time, That in order to avoid different choices of lesson design content in instructional design will bring greater error to the experimental results. So in order to enhance the persuasiveness of the experiment, before and after the strategic intervention, the content of the instructional content selected by the teacher M's instructional design was taken from the same lesson time.

5.4 Data Collection

At the time of this study, the author conducted experiments in multiple secondary schools and multiple teachers, intervened during the process of instructing teachers, and urged the experimental teachers to improve the supplementary analysis tables for teaching design. The author, the experimental teacher, and the expert teacher communicated with each other so as to point out the deficiencies in the experimental teacher's instructional design. The results show that teachers' teaching design after strategic intervention has been improved. However, due to the limited space of this article, only the scores of teachers M before and after the intervention are shown here.

The scores of the teaching design of Teacher H before and after the intervention of Teacher M are as follows (Figs. 4 and 5):

First-level indicators	Secondary indicators		Before intervention (Out of 10 points)	the reason
situation construction strategy	Authenticity		6	The main situation of this lesson is to establish a WeChat group for the EU. Each member country is equivalent to a friend of a circle of friends. Although this situation is not true, it can help students understand the meaning of the EU through analogy.
	Ideological		7	The dairy and livestock industry in western Europe contains the concept of sustainable development. In classroom teaching, the conditions for the development of the dairy industry are emphatically explored, so that students can understand the importance of developing agriculture according to local conditions.
	Living		6	You can contact the Europeans' food on the table and the European scenic spots, and have a certain basis for life cognition. However, teachers did not contact the students' own catering in the event design. In fact, the catering structure of the modern family in China has also been increasingly affected by the West. Milk products have increased and there are also dairy farms in the suburbs of large cities.
	Situation and content integration		8	The degree of integration of situation and content is high.
task-driven strategy	Achievement of teaching goals	Knowledge and skills processes and methods emotional attitudes and values	7	There is a lot of attention in the teaching of knowledge, teaching design is not enough to focus on the process, lack of complete, relatively independent problem design, serious problem fragmentation, is not conducive to the cultivation of student ability. Emotions, attitudes and values are implemented in context and are relatively good.
	Targeting teaching content	teaching method student content	6	Mainly in lectures, the teacher-student interaction mode is relatively monotonous, and is mainly based on the "one-question-one-answer" approach. It lacks interaction between students and students and human-computer interaction. The content of the teaching is book-based, lacking in contact, activating the geography around them, and associating students with less real life.
thinking inspired strategy	Problematic thinking level		6	Judging from the 5W principle of the question, there are many factual questions about what is there and what is it. There are few procedural questions such as "why? How to do it?". Thinking training is not enough.
	Problem structure	Before and after the problem associated Main question and sub question related Students answer presets	6	Before and after the problem is not relevant, the main problem and the sub-question have a certain relevance, the student's answer is basically in the teacher's preset range.

Fig. 4. Pre-intervention score results

First-level indicators	Secondary indicators		After intervention (Out of 10 points)	the reason
situation construction strategy	Authenticity		6	Little change
	Ideological		8	The design of the activities of the "European industrial revolution's birthplace" was added to guide students to pay attention to the process of human civilization, highlighting the importance of Europe in modern industrial civilization and embodying the importance of human-land relations.
	Living		7	The design of tourism activities has been increased. Tourism and life are closely linked. Europe's natural tourism resources and humanistic tourism resources are abundant, which can stimulate students' aesthetic interest in the geographical environment. Through understanding the culture and traditions of various countries in the world, they can help students form a global awareness
	Situation and content integration		8	Through adjustments, we further explored the geographical features of the EU in terms of industry and tourism.
task-driven strategy	Achievement of teaching goals	Knowledge and skills processes and methods emotional attitudes and values	8	The main changes are: the time for students to think about is increasing, which is conducive to internalized learning content. From the knowledge structure chart on the blackboard, the construction is more complete.
	Targeting teaching content	teaching method student content	7	Compared with the pre-preset, part of the content has been added, but it is still not good enough to contact student life.
thinking inspired strategy	Problematic thinking level		6	Taking the problem of "seeing the scenery of Western Europe and designing tourist routes." As an example, the lack of theme design should be clear whether it is a natural landscape or a humanistic feature? Vibrant themes are more conducive to operations and more prominent geographical significance. Second, the teacher gave the tourist route on the blackboard, which was not designed by the students. The openness of the problem was not enough, which limited the students' ideas. Taking the problem of "seeing the scenery of Western Europe and designing tourist routes." As an example, the lack of theme design should be clear whether it is a natural landscape or a humanistic feature? Vibrant themes are more conducive to operations and more prominent geographical significance. Second, the teacher gave the tourist route on the blackboard, which was not designed by the students. The openness of the problem was not enough, which limited the students' ideas.
	Problem structure	Before and after the problem associated Main question and sub question related Students answer presets	7	The number of problems has increased, and the main problems in this part of the dairy and livestock industry have been associated with sub-problems, and the information given is also sufficient. Teachers in the process of students to answer questions, according to the appropriate guidance

Fig. 5. Post-intervention score results

As can be seen from the figure, there has been a significant change before and after the intervention in instructional design. Situation-building modules, both ideological and life-enhancing, are mainly reflected in the increased number of event designs. In the task-driven module, although there are more time for students to think about, it is still not good enough to connect with student life, and we need to make persistent efforts. In the heuristic module of thinking, compared with the pre-intervention, although open problems were designed, the openness is not enough, which is not conducive to the development of student thinking. In short, the novice teachers have made progress before and after the strategic intervention. Although the progress is not obvious, but also from the side that the novice teacher has room for improvement in the teaching design, they need to continue to accumulate, summarize and improve the future of teaching design to improve their professional level to improve student problem solving skills.

6 Summary

This article takes a junior geography teacher in junior high school as the research object, and scores the teaching design before and after the three-dimensional strategy intervention. The research results show that the three-dimensional teaching design strategy has a positive effect on the teaching design of teachers. At the same time, our teaching design aided analysis table and teaching design evaluation scale based on strategy construction provide important basis and reference for the teaching design of the majority of frontline teachers. However, due to my limited research experience and theoretical knowledge, I have personal opinions when giving instruction to the novice teachers, subjectivity is strong and needs to be improved. In the future research, we hope to consider the design principles of teaching objectives, the classification of teaching objectives, etc., and further improve the teaching design aid analysis table and the implementation of the evaluation scale, and put the teaching design into classroom teaching practice, and discover the problem that the teaching design exists. The aim is to promote teacher's teaching reflection and improvement, and provide valuable reference for more teachers' teaching design, and improve students' problem solving ability.

References

1. Yang, B., Zhang, B.L.: Study on the comprehensive evaluation method of student problem solving capacity. E-education Res. **8**, 24–30 (2017)
2. Yuan, J.L., Liu, H.Y., Zhang, S.: Analysis of influencing factors of students' problem solving ability in digital test environment—a case study of PISA 2012. China Educ. Technol. **08**, 74–81 (2016)
3. Hu, Y.L.: Research on Problem Solving Ability Evaluation Based on Learning Analysis Technology. East China Normal University (2016)
4. Godden, D., Baddeley, A.: Context-dependent memory in two natural environments: on land and underwater. Br. J. Psychol. **66**, 325–332 (1975)
5. Torp, L., Sage, S.: Problems as Possibilities: Problem-Based Learning for K-16 Education, 2nd edn. Association for Supervision & Curriculum Development (2002)
6. Wei, X.F., Cui, G.Z.: Cognitive model of problem solving in primary school mathematical problem solving. E-education Res. **11**, 79–85 (2012)
7. Zhang, L.G., Xie, J.R., Wang, G.H.: Deep learning model based on problem solving. Dist. Educ. China **08**, 27–33 (2017)
8. Song, W.N.: Application and thinking of process heuristic teaching method in information technology curriculum. China Educ. Technol. **04**, 88–90 (2009)
9. Yang, Y.Q.: Design study of heuristic frustration—fulfillment classroom implementation strategy. China Educ. Technol. **11**, 111–115 (2014)
10. Chai, S.M.: Strategies for promoting collaborative knowledge construction in CSCL. Mod. Dist. Educ. Res. **04**, 35–40 (2012)
11. Pang, K., Li, M.Z.: Primary and secondary school teachers training under the guidance of cognitive flexibility theory. Curriculum Teach. Mater. Method **04**, 73–76 (2007)
12. Luo, D.J., Li, M.: Study on the classroom teaching strategies based on network. E-education Res. **12**, 52–56 (2004)
13. Liu, M.Z., Zhu, Z.T.: Research on teaching design style of MOOCs. China Educ. Technol. **07**, 19–24 (2014)

14. Feng, R.: A review of the design model of 3C3R problem-oriented learning. J. Dist. Educ. **01**, 70–74 (2010)
15. Fang, L.: The Effect of the Situational Features of Mathematics Problems on the Solution of the Creative Problems of Junior Students. East China Normal University (2014)
16. Liu, X.J., Zhang, J.P., Du, W.F.: Research on teaching design of micro-class based on five-star teaching principle. Mod. Dist. Educ. Res. **01**, 82–89 (2015)
17. Xiong, M., Wang, Y.L., Ai, Q.H.: Personalized teaching design and implementation strategies. Curriculum Teach. Mater. Method **08**, 18–23 (2011)
18. Hu, X.Y., Li, L.J., Zheng, X.D.: Strategic research on learners' collaborative problem-solving in online environment. China Educ. Technol. **01**, 44–50 (2015)
19. Lorin, W.A.: Bloom's Taxonomy of Educational Objectives. Foreign Language Teaching and Research Press (2009)
20. Jiang, W.T.: Micro-course Design and Organization Research Based on prOblem Solving. Northeast Normal University (2017)

Research on Collaborative Filtering Recommendation of Learning Resource Based on Knowledge Association

Hao Li(✉), Fanfan Du(✉), Mingyan Zhang(✉), Libin Wang(✉), and Xue Yu(✉)

National Engineering Research Center for E-learning Central China Normal University, Wuhan, China
lihao205@mail.ccnu.edu.cn, 2294634272@qq.com, newmingyan@126.com, 2297725187@qq.com, 1351462450@qq.com

Abstract. With the development of Internet communication equipment, educational resources are rapidly accumulating on the Internet. While learners enjoy the convenience of the information age, they often face problems such as "resource disorientation" and "learning theme drift". As the most effective personalized recommendation technology, collaborative filtering is mainly based on the dual relationship between learners and resources. This paper utilizes the association of learners, knowledge points, and learning resources to construct associated matrix of the learners, knowledge points and learning resources. It introduces the related knowledge information into user similarity calculation and scoring prediction of traditional collaborative filtering algorithm, which can make the recommendation results conform to learners' learning needs and improve the recommendation quality of personalized recommendation.

Keywords: Knowledge-Association · Collaborative filtering

1 Introduction

Collaborative filtering uses group intelligence to provide users with recommendation services and rapidly grows into one of the most widely used technologies for personalized recommendation services. However, with the increasing number of learners and resources, the problem of "data sparseness" [1] and "cold start" [2] of the collaborative filtering algorithm have gradually emerged. In order to improve the recommendation quality of the recommendation system, many researchers have conducted a series of research work. Salehi [3] utilized the attributes of resources and learners as well as the sequential mode of learner accessing resources, and also introduced learning tree (LT), sequential pattern mining algorithms (BIDE) and matrix decomposition technique to provide learners with resources which meet their actual learning preferences. Yang [4] used ant colony algorithm and Kolb learning style model to design AACS learning resource recommendation system, which provides personalized service for learners based on learners' characteristics. Wang [5] used content filtering and

T.-T. Wu et al. (Eds.): ICITL 2018, LNCS 11003, pp. 561–567, 2018.
https://doi.org/10.1007/978-3-319-99737-7_59

implicit scoring methods respectively to solve the "cold start" problem and "data sparseness" problem of the traditional collaborative filtering. The above research is mainly based on the dual relationship between learners and resources to find learners similar to the target learner, and then recommendations are generated based on learning records and preferences of similar user groups. This paper proposed a learning resources collaborative filtering recommendation algorithm based on knowledge-association. It utilizes the association of learners, knowledge points, and learning resources to construct associated matrix of the learners, knowledge points and learning resources as well as introducing the related knowledge information into the user similarity calculation and scoring prediction in traditional collaborative filtering algorithm. The research shows that it is more conducive to make the recommendation results meet learners' actual needs and improve the recommendation quality of personalized recommendation of learning resources.

2 Learner-Knowledge-Resource Association Model

Recommendation of learning resources based on knowledge association is different from the traditional collaborative filtering recommendation. It does not only consider the dual relationship between learners and learning resources, but also fully exploits the intrinsic relationship between learners and knowledge points. Firstly, get the set of knowledge points which is related to learners. Secondly, according to the association weight between knowledge point and learning resource we can summarize that between knowledge point and learner. Finally, once learner's knowledge attributes information changed or learner has learned new resources, system will execute above two steps to obtain the latest knowledge points set and association weight (Fig. 1).

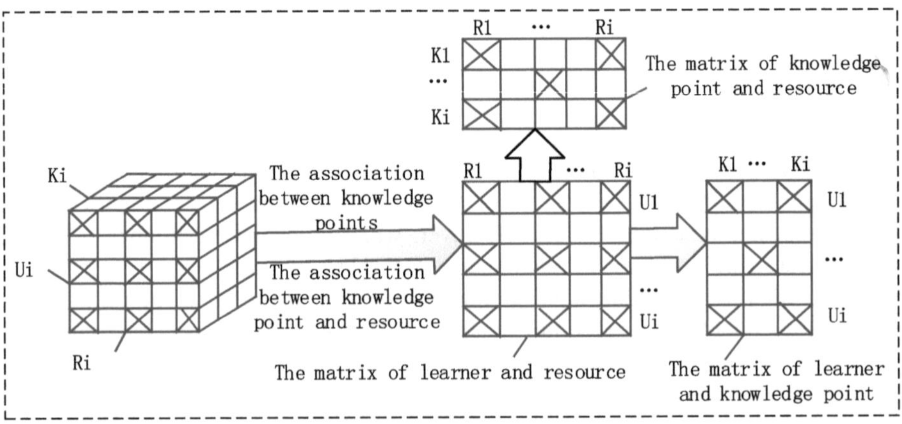

Fig. 1. The association matrix model of learner-knowledge-learning resource

3 Collaborative Filtering Recommendation Based on Knowledge Association

Firstly, a learner-knowledge-resource association model is established based on the association among learners, knowledge points and learning resources. Secondly, introducing the related knowledge information into the calculation of user similarity and scoring prediction so as to obtain the nearest neighbor learners and the score matrix. Thirdly, system uses the preferences of similar users to predict the current learner's interest score for resources which he may be interested in. Finally, the recommended sequence results are presented to learners by Top-N recommendation (Fig. 2).

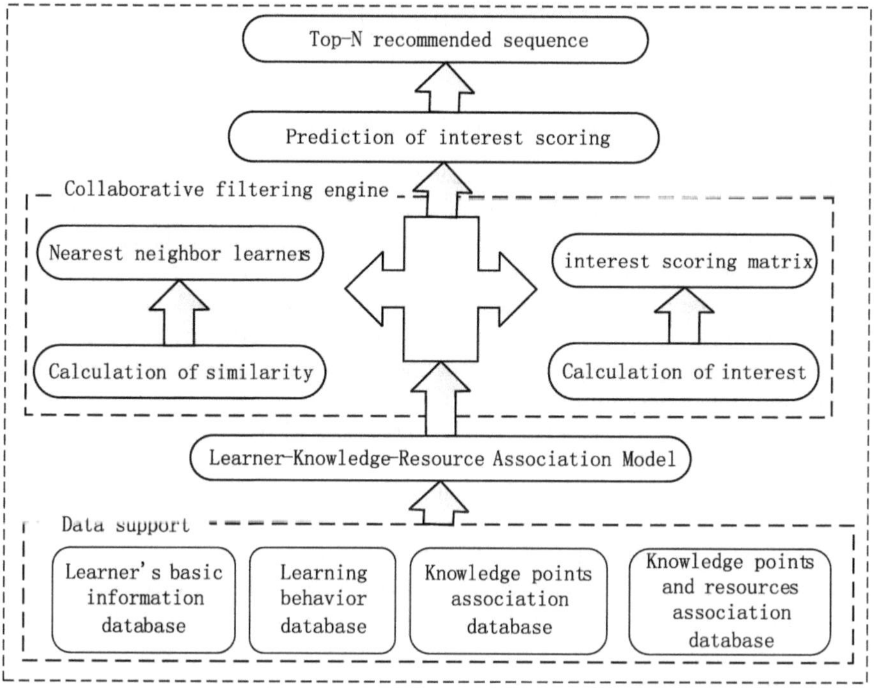

Fig. 2. Learning resources recommendation strategy based on knowledge association.

3.1 Calculation of User Similarity

Knowledge-Association CF introduced the association weight between learner and knowledge points and the relationship between knowledge points into the traditional similarity measure method.

Firstly, from the learner-knowledge-resource association model, we can get u_i's and u_j's related knowledge points set and corresponding association weight.

Secondly, obtain the common parent knowledge points set F_G of u_i and u_j, then calculate u_i's and u_j's association weight with each parent knowledge point.

$$W_{u_i,F_i} = \sum\nolimits_{k_i \in F_G} w_{u_i,k} \tag{1}$$

F_G is the set of all sub knowledge points learned by learner u_i under knowledge point F_i; $w_{u_i,k}$ is the association weight of learner u_i and the sub knowledge point k. The weight vector matrix of learner and parent knowledge point is constructed.

$$UF_{u_i} = \left[\left(F_1,\ W_{u_i,F_1}\right)\cdots\left(F_i,\ W_{u_i,F_i}\right)\right] \tag{2}$$

Finally, it will calculate the similarity between learners based on Formula 3.

$$S(u_i, u_j) = \frac{UF_{u_i}\ .\ UF_{u_j}}{\left|UF_{u_i}\right|.\left|UF_{u_j}\right|} \tag{3}$$

3.2 Calculation of "Learner-Resource" Interest

To provide learners with learning resources that meet their actual needs, the relationship between learners and knowledge points is introduced into implicit scoring method [5]. System will track and record learners' learning behavior. Those behaviors (such as learning duration, collection, and download) which can express learners' preferences for resources will be translated into learners' implicit scoring. D, C, and T are used to indicate download, collection, and learning durations (> 10 min) respectively. The resource score uses a 5-point scale. We define the correspondence between behavior and score in implicit scoring just as:

{D:3.5; C:3.5; T:3.5; D+C+T:5; D+C:4; D+T:4; C+T:4}

$$M_{u_iI} = w_{u_iI}.Mark \tag{4}$$

M_{u_iI} indicates the interest score of learner u_i for resource I, w_{u_iI} represents the association weight between resource I and knowledge points which learner u_i has learned; *Mark* represents the implicit score of learner u_i for learning resource I.

3.3 The Process of Recommended Algorithm

The collaborative filtering recommendation of learning resources based on knowledge association is summarized as follows:

Input: the matrix of learner's interest score

Output: Top-N recommended resources with higher scores

1. generate K nearest learners with the highest similarity to the target learner;
2. predict the score of resources that the current user may be interested in based the follow formula:

$$R_{u_i,c} = \overline{M_{u_i}} + \frac{\sum_{u_j \in N_u} S(u_i, u_j)\left(M_{u_j,c} - \overline{M_{u_j}}\right)}{\sum_{u_j \in N_u} |S(u_i, u_j)|};$$

3. recommend N resources with higher scores.

$R_{u_i,c}$ is the prediction score of learner u_i for the recommended resource c, and $S(u_i, u_j)$ represents the similarity between u_i and u_j, and $M_{u_j,c}$ represents the learner's actual score, and N_u expresses the nearest neighbor users of learner u_i. $\overline{M_{u_i}}$ and $\overline{M_{u_j}}$ respectively indicate the average score of learner u_i and u_j.

4 Experimental Design and Result Analysis

This experiment used the size of 100k Movie Lens dataset [6], including 943 learners, 1682 video resources and 1 million scoring data. The whole dataset was divided into five parts according to the 80% training set and 20% test set. Each experiment used four of them as a training set to generate recommendation results; and the other set was used as test set to verify the recommendation effect. The average value of five cross-validations were compared with the traditional User-Based collaborative filtering (Table 1).

Table 1. Knowledge category

Knowledge category	Number	Knowledge category	Number	Knowledge category	Number
Film-Noir	26	Horror	110	Fantasy	81
Action	254	War	68	Animation	44
Children	127	Romance	299	IMAX	3
Western	29	Documentary	51	Comedy	
Sci-Fi	105	Drama	839	Mystery	
Musical	65	Thriller	303	Crime	

RMSE and Precision are two common methods [7] to evaluate the recommended quality. The smaller the value of RMSE, and the bigger the value of Precision, the higher the recommended quality.

$$RMSE = \sqrt{\frac{\sum_{u_i \in U} \left(m_{u_i,c} - M_{u_i,c}\right)^2}{|T|}} \tag{5}$$

|T| is the length of test dataset, $m_{u_i,c}$ indicates $u_i^{'}s$ actual score for resource c; $M_{u_i,c}$ represents the learner's predicted score for resource c by the algorithm. $R(u_i)$ is the recommended list, $T(u_i)$ indicates user's behavior list on the test set.

$$Precision = \frac{\sum_{u_i \in U} |R(u_i) \cap T(u_i)|}{\sum_{u_i \in U} |R(u_i)|} \tag{6}$$

K represents the number of nearest neighbors and Top-N represents the recommended number of resources. We get the precision and RMSE in the case where K is

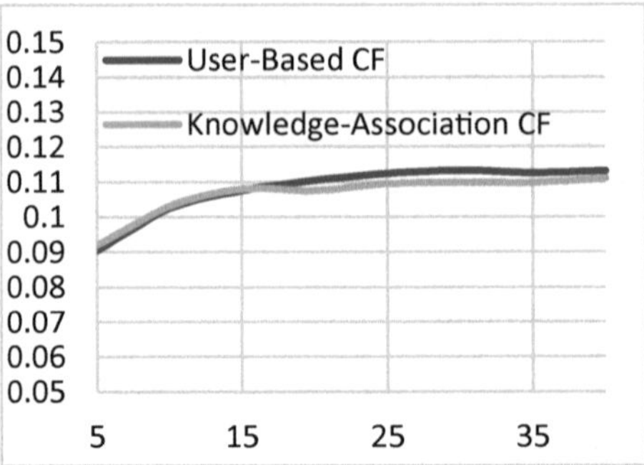

Fig. 3. Precision under different training.

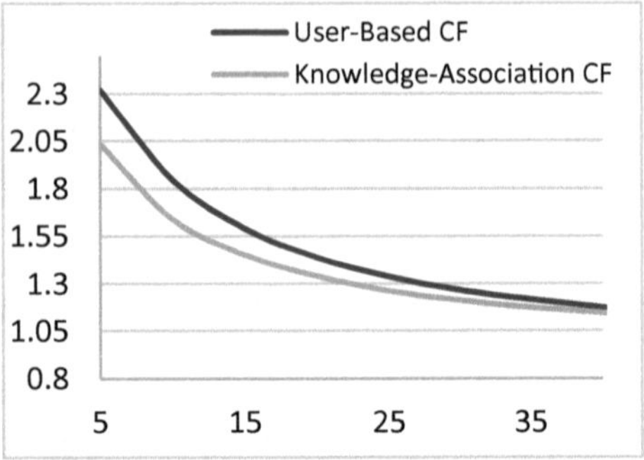

Fig. 4. RMSE under different k neighbors.

from 5 to 40 and N is 10. Compared with the traditional User-Based collaborative filtering, the precision of Knowledge-Association collaborative filtering is higher before K = 15, and the RMSE based on Knowledge-Association collaborative filtering is smaller than that of the traditional User-Based collaborative filtering (Figs. 3 and 4).

5 Conclusions and Future Works

This paper established a learner-knowledge-resource association model and improved the calculation of user similarity and interest scoring, which not only effectively alleviated the problem of "data sparseness" and "cold start", but also improved the recommendation quality of traditional collaborative filtering. As different learners always have held different learning styles, if the recommendation system can intelligently recommend learning resources according to different styles of learners, it will be more conducive to improve learners' learning quality. The above problem will be improved in the follow-up work.

Acknowledgements. This paper was supported by selfdetermined research funds of CCNU from the colleges' basic research and operation of MOE (CCNU15A02050, CCNU16A05036).

References

1. Sarwar, B.M., Karypis, G., Konstan, J.A., John, T.: Application of dimensionality reduction in recommender system – a case study. In: ACM WEBKDD Workshop (2000)
2. Massa, P., Avesani, P.: Trust-aware collaborative filtering for recommender systems. In: Meersman, R., Tari, Z. (eds.) OTM 2004. LNCS, vol. 3290, pp. 492–508. Springer, Heidelberg (2004). https://doi.org/10.1007/978-3-540-30468-5_31
3. Salehi, M.: Application of implicit and explicit attribute based collaborative filtering and BIDE for learning resource recommendation. Data Knowl. Eng. **87**, 130–145 (2013)
4. Yang, Y.J., Wu, C.: An attribute-based ant colony system for adaptive learning object recommendation. Exp. Syst. Appl. **36**(2), 3034–3047 (2009)

5. Wang, Y., Qiu, F., Zhao, J. A., Liu, H.: Research on personalized recommendation of learning resources based on collaborative filtering recommendation technology. J. Distance Educ. **14**, 21–33 (2011)
6. Grouplens Homepage (2018). https://grouplens.org/datasets/movielens
7. Park, Y.J., Tuzhilin, A.: The long tail of recommender systems and how to leverage it. In: ACM Conference on Recommend System, pp. 11–18 (2008)

Research on Result Integration Mechanism Based on Crowd Wisdom to Achieve the Correlation of Resources and Knowledge Points

Xu Du(✉), Fan Zhang(✉), Mingyan Zhang(✉), Shuai Xu(✉), and Mengjin Liu(✉)

National Engineering Research Center for E-Learning Central China Normal University, Wuhan, China
duxu@mail.ccnu.edu.cn, 734278852@qq.com, newmingyan@126.com, 1024434368@qq.com, 972707581@qq.com

Abstract. Correlating massive resources with knowledge points can help to achieve effective aggregation of resources and to improve learners learning efficiency and learning experience. This paper proposes a result integration mechanism based on the crowd wisdom to determine the association of learning resources and knowledge points, and ensure the final annotation result has certain credibility. Accordingly, we propose a user confidence to evaluate the user's ability to complete the tasks. The experimental results show that the proposed algorithms improve the accuracy and efficiency comparing with the majority voting method, and algorithm to estimate user's confidence can converge to actual value efficiently.

Keywords: The result integration mechanism · The crowd wisdom Task result confidence · User confidence

1 Introduction

The correlation between learning resources and knowledge points is the basis for learning resources to rapid iteration, and dynamic integration. It also provides the conditions for in-depth knowledge sharing, aggregation, and the construction of learners' personalized learning service. Correlating massive resources with knowledge points can achieve effective aggregation of resources and help resolve issues such as resource silos, knowledge evasion, and theme drift, thereby improving learners' learning efficiency and learning experience. In the face of massive knowledge services, how to efficiently and accurately represent the relevance of learning resources in the knowledge structure system, and mark them with knowledge points, so that learners can quickly and efficiently acquire personalized learning resources and services are the current research hot spot.

At present, semantic analysis uses natural language processing algorithms to extract the core concepts of knowledge and the relationship between concepts conveyed by learning resources [1]. It has been widely applied in information retrieval, information clustering, and text classification [2]. It is difficult to ensure the accuracy of the results

T.-T. Wu et al. (Eds.): ICITL 2018, LNCS 11003, pp. 568–577, 2018.
https://doi.org/10.1007/978-3-319-99737-7_60

only relying on semantic analysis to label large-scale resources for correlation because learning resources have knowledge characteristics. Compared with manual annotation, the overall accuracy rate is still relatively low, and it still cannot provide enough credible markup services. For issues that marking massive resources, Wikipedia, Google Translation and other applications are based on the concept of co-creation, co-construction and co-share. They collect the power of the masses to complete the labeling, translation and they have achieved remarkable results through the crowd wisdom mechanism.

However, due to the different knowledge backgrounds, ages, and identities of the users participating in the tasks, it is difficult to evaluate the credibility of the annotation results. For the integration of public intelligence results, most of the existing researches adopt the method of filtering out noise data and learn the final annotation results of a certain task from the annotation results of multiple people through relevant algorithms [3]. There are also studies using the majority voting method to achieve labeling tasks. The annotation tasks of learning resources have strict requirements on the professional background of users, so the annotation accuracy still needs to be confirmed by the above method.

This paper studies the key issues in the mechanism to achieve correlation of learning resources and knowledge points based on the crowd wisdom and to improve the accuracy of the association. Among them, how to integrate annotation results to form final integration result with high credibility is the focus of this study.

2 Related Work

The concept of crowdsourcing was first proposed by Howe [4]. It means that, a company or organization outsources the tasks to a non-specific public network in a free and voluntary manner which should be performed by its employees in the past. In recent years, crowdsourcing has received extensive attention in the industry and academia. In the research of user's reliability, the user's reputation value is usually regarded as an important index for the public platform to judge the quality of the task. Zhang et al. [5] proposed a task distribution mechanism based on the user's reputation value. For question-and-answer tasks, due to the differences in knowledge reserves and age backgrounds of public users, integration of crowd wisdom results by the majority voting method is often not accurate enough. Liu et al. [6] calculated the accuracy of the user's answer and used Bayesian theory to combine the user's answer accuracy rate with the answer and integrated the final crowd wisdom results. Demartini et al. [7] proposed a probabilistic model based on a factor graph which obtained the results by integrating the workers' answers, the accuracy of the workers' answers and other factors. However, both methods assume that the accuracy rate of the user's answer is a fixed value; Yan et al. [8] based on the EM algorithm to integrate the crowd wisdom results and used the confusion matrix to reflect the accuracy of the user's answer. However, it is difficult to achieve a balance between accuracy and real-time for the calculation of the answer accuracy.

This paper focuses on the result integration mechanism of crowd wisdom, specifically addressing the following three issues:

(1) How to choose the best time for annotation result integration.
Due to the users who participate in the tasks have a chronological order and the number of users involved may increase over time, the labeling results may be gradually diversified. To reduce human resources and the amount of calculation, and ensure the accuracy of labeling, it is necessary to study the optimal integration timing for different labeling tasks.
(2) How to choose the best integration method.
Due to the difference in the quality of the annotation of different users, the majority voting method tends to ignore this difference, resulting in a decrease in the accuracy of the final integration result. Therefore, the result integration mechanism should fully consider the ability of the participating users.
(3) How to ensure the credibility of the integration result.
To ensure the credibility of the final integration result, the final integration result needs to be evaluated because the labeling tasks often have no preset answers. when the evaluation result reaches a certain expectation, the integration result can be used as the result of the task. Otherwise, the mechanism should be used to adjust and increase the credibility of the integration result until it reaches the expected standard.

For the problem of the result integration timing, this paper proposes the user confidence to evaluate the user credibility, and it is determined by the user's historical annotation behavior. And the cumulative confidence in the task determines the result integration timing of crowd wisdom. For the method of labeling results integration, this paper adopts the task result confidence and EM algorithm to calculate crowd annotation results to generate final integration result for a labeling task. In addition, the task results confidence can ensure the credibility of the final integration result.

3 Result Integration Based on Crowd Wisdom

Correlating the learning resources and knowledge points based on crowd wisdom gave full play to the crowd wisdom created by interaction and solved the problem of hidden knowledge semantics that the machine has difficulty to understand. To achieve effective integration of annotation results, this paper introduces the concepts of user confidence and task results confidence, the former is a quantitative indicator for the user's ability to complete labeling tasks, and the latter is used to initialize the value as the input value of the EM algorithm.

The process of the knowledge-resource correlation model can be divided into three parts: task assignment, result integration, and user confidence evaluation. Firstly, the user label the task which is pushed by the platform considering the user's activity on the platform and user confidence. In the way, execution efficiency of the task will be improved and the user submission rate about the task is higher in the specified time. Secondly, after the task is completed by the most users, the cumulative confidence of the task is calculated. If the value is higher than the preset threshold, the confidence degree of each user's annotation result is calculated, and these values will be integrated by the EM algorithm. The final integration result can be output until the algorithm converges. Finally, the user confidence can be updated by comparing his annotation result with the final integration result. The process of correlating the learning resources and knowledge points based on crowd wisdom is shown in Fig. 1.

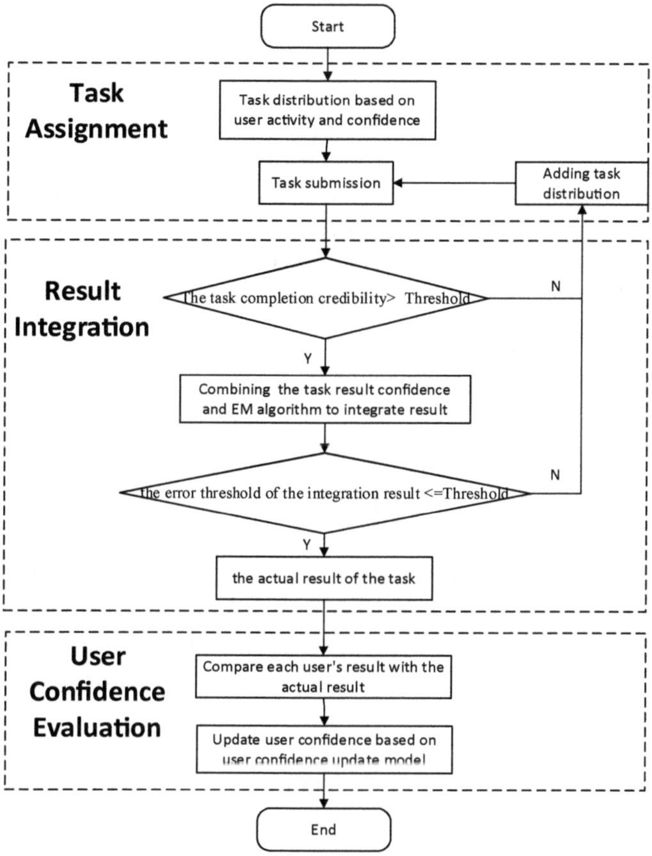

Fig. 1. The process of correlating the learning resources and knowledge points based on crowd wisdom.

3.1 The Integration Mechanism of Crowd Wisdom Result

According to the user activity and the user confidence, the platform calculates the distribution expectation for the task. The purpose is to predict the completion of the task within a specified time. The larger the distribution expectation, the better the task is accomplished.

Distribution Expectation. The user activity on the platform is denoted as A_k. The user confidence in the platform is denoted as C_k. The formula of distribution expectation is

$$E = \sum\nolimits_{k=1}^{N} A_k * C_k \tag{1}$$

Cumulative Confidence. The optimal integration timing is determined by calculating the cumulative confidence of users participating in an annotation task. When it is greater than the set threshold, the integration of annotation results begins. The user confidence of user k is denoted as C_k, N means that N users with known confidence have completed the task, and the cumulative confidence is denoted as C_c. The formula of cumulative confidence is

$$C_c = \sum\nolimits_{k=1}^{N} C_k \tag{2}$$

When N is too small, or the cumulative confidence does not exceed the threshold, the task labeling results will not be integrated and the platform will continue to send this task to users. If the cumulative confidence exceeds the threshold, the result will be integrated. It can effectively reduce the integration of computing work.

Task Result Confidence. Task result confidence is a parameter which characterizes the effectiveness of each result annotating by users. The user confidence of user k is denoted as C_k, and the confidence that a task is marked as a result is denoted as T. The formula of the task result confidence is

$$T = 1 - \prod\nolimits_{k=1}^{N} (1 - C_k) \tag{3}$$

EM Algorithm. when the confidence T of a certain result exceeds the set threshold, and this result is taken as the initial result of the task. Taking task i as an example, the confidence that users mark the result of task i as j is T_{ij}. When the confidence T_{ij} exceeds the set threshold, then $t_{ij} = 1$, It means result j is the real result of the task i. otherwise $t_{ij} = 0$. The initial result of task i is

$$t_{ij} = \begin{cases} 1, \ if\ T_{ij} \geq \text{threshold} \\ 0, \ if\ T_{ij} < \text{threshold} \end{cases} \tag{4}$$

When the task is randomly selected, $\sum_i t_{ij}$ indicates the number of tasks per result, r_j means the probability that j is the true result of this task. The total number of tasks is expressed as TaskNums. The estimation method is

$$r_j = \frac{\sum_i t_{ij}}{TaskNums} \tag{5}$$

In the case of knowing the true classification of the task (the value t_{ij} obtained by initialization for the first time), n_{ij}^k means that user k labels task i as j and it will be calculated. Using R to represent the number of times that user k marks a task that real result is j as result l. Using S to represent the number of tasks that real result is j and are labeled by user k. And the confusion matrix for each user can be calculated as shown.

$$e_{jl}^{\widehat{(w)}} = \frac{R}{S} = \frac{\sum_i t_{ij} \times n_{il}^{(k)}}{\sum_l \sum_i t_{ij} \times n_{il}^{(k)}} \tag{6}$$

Then the probability of task i on result j can be calculated by the model proposed by Dawid [9].

$$\mathrm{D}(j) = \frac{\prod_{w=1}^{W} \prod_{l=1}^{J} (e_{jl}^{(w)})^{n_{il}^{(w)}} r_j}{\sum_{q=1}^{J} \prod_{w=1}^{W} \prod_{l=1}^{J} (e_{ql}^{(w)})^{n_{il}^{(w)}} r_q} \tag{7}$$

Formula 6 gives the probability that each task corresponds to each result. And the maximum probability of the corresponding result is the true result of the task.

3.2 The User Confidence Update Mechanism

As the differences in the user's knowledge background, work attitude and other attributes, there will be some noise and error in the labeling results. This paper quantifies the ability of the user by comparing the result annotated by the user and the true result of the task.

User Confidence. User confidence is a parameter to measure user annotation capabilities and reflect the quality of the user's history annotation task. High user confidence indicates the high credibility of the task labeling results. The initial user confidence is set the same in the mechanism, and the user confidence will update after the user completes the task. The update algorithm is

$$C_u = \alpha \times PC + \beta \times UC \tag{8}$$

The user confidence before participating this labeling task is denoted as PC and the credibility of this labeling task is denoted as UC. α is the change step of the user's previous confidence, β is the change step of this annotation result. α and β are parameters that control the weight of PC and UC.

If a user's confidence is initialized by the platform, α is very small and β is large in a task annotation. This means that the result of this annotation has a great influence on the user confidence. As the number of tasks increases, α gradually increases and β gradually decreases. If the user continuously gives incorrect answers, α will decrease and β will increase.

Algorithm Steps. The algorithm steps of annotating the correlation of knowledge and resources based on crowd wisdom is shown in Table 1.

Table 1. Algorithm steps.

Input:	The set for each user's result; User confidence (C_u); the threshold
Output:	Updated User confidence (C_u); The integration result of labeling tasks (T_{final}).

1. Initialize T.
2. Obtain estimates of the prior probability and the confusion matrix.
3. Calculate new estimates of T.
4. Repeat steps 2 and 3 until the results converge.
5. Update user confidence according to compare T_{final} with user's result.

4 Experimental Design and Result Analysis

4.1 Methodology

This paper uses open datasets to conduct related experiments to achieve the following objectives:

(1) Verify the effectiveness of the integration mechanism based on crowd wisdom proposed in this article. By selecting the relevant data sets, we adopt the annotation results integration mechanism based on confidence and the majority voting method to integrate the annotation results submitted by the crowd and compares the accuracy of the integration results. Since the actual category of each task in the data set is known, the number of tasks marked correctly is $\sum_{i=1}^{n} Correct\_label$, and the total number of tasks is n. The accuracy of the algorithm can be calculated.

$$Accuracy = \frac{\sum_{i=1}^{n} Correct\_label}{n} \times 100\% \tag{9}$$

(2) Explore the relationship between the accuracy of the annotation results and the number of participating users. And analyze user confidence with the number of labeling tasks.

4.2 Data Collection and Result Analysis

The dataset used in the experiment is BlueBirds, a real experimental data collected by Peter Welinder et al. [10]. The data set contains a total of 108 tasks, 39 participating users. The number of marking is 4212. The users have completed the annotation task on the pictures to simulate the correlation between the knowledge points and picture-based learning resources under the learning resource annotation environment.

Two methods are used to implement the labeling experiment on the above dataset. The relationship between the accuracy of two methods and the number of users is shown in Fig. 2. The conclusions are as follows:

(1) When the number of users reaches a certain number, the accuracy rate of the result integration mechanism based on crowd wisdom is higher than that of the majority voting method.

(2) When the number of users is small, the accuracy of two methods is similar and is not high. With the increase in the number of participants, the both accuracy rate have increased, and the advantage of the result integration mechanism is more obvious.

(3) In terms of stability, the accuracy of the majority voting method is not stable, because the method sets the confidence of all users to be the same. When some users label errors, it will affect the final calculation results. The result integration mechanism based on crowd wisdom, giving the user different weights based on the accuracy of the user previous annotation. In the computation of the model confidence, the annotation results with lower user confidence will not be integrated. In this way, the result integration mechanism is superior to the majority voting method in stability.

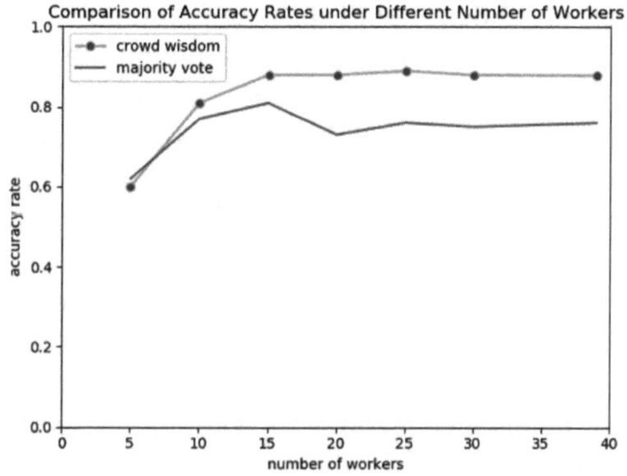

Fig. 2. Comparison of accuracy rates under different number of works.

The convergence processes of confidence estimation of typical users are shown as Fig. 3. The actual confidence value of user1 is 0.72 and that of user2 is 0.37. At the beginning, the initial confidence of each is set as 0.2. With the number of tasks annotated by the users increases, the user's confidence level gradually stabilizes and converges to

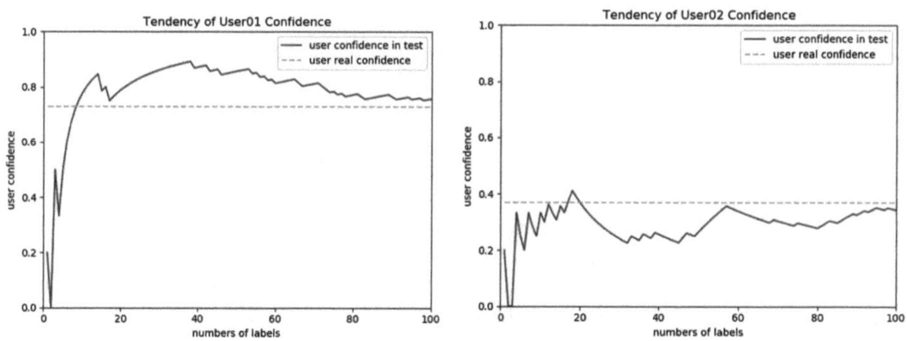

Fig. 3. Tendency of two-user confidence values.

the actual confidence rapidly. Shown as Fig. 3, the confidence of user1 converges to 0.72 and the confidence of user2 converges to 0.37.

In the platform, to ensure the effectiveness and reliability of the integration results, the results that the user with unknown confidence annotate will not be calculated into the cumulative confidence until his confidence have been converged. Therefore, in this process, his annotation results are only used to update his confidence.

5 Conclusions and Future Works

This paper proposes a mechanism which correlating the learning resources and knowledge points based on crowd wisdom, mainly focus on annotation result integration and user confidence update mechanism. As for the selection of optimal timing of integration, by calculating each user's confidence of the task, when cumulative confidence is greater than our setting threshold value, annotation results integration begins. As for the selection of the results integration, the user's annotation ability should be fully considered. As for the evaluation of the credibility of the mark results, this paper introduces cumulative confidence to calculate. The analysis of our experiment proves that the proposed method has higher accuracy and tends to be stable when the number of users increases. It is in line with general expectations.

There are some problems in the study of this paper, such as the optimal integration timing depends on the cumulative confidence, and the selection of threshold needs further study. For the results integration method can try to consider other probability classification algorithms in machine learning. In addition, the evaluation mechanism for users is not perfect. How to evaluate the relative annotation capabilities of users according to different types of tasks, and how to properly handle the results with low user confidence, these will be the problems to be solved in the next step.

Acknowledgments. This paper was supported by the specific funding for education science research by self-determined research funds of CCNU from the colleges' basic research and operation of MOE (CCNU16JYKX004).

References

1. Wu, D., Li, B.: Research on the aggregation of topic model based learning resources in big data environment. E-education Res. **9**, 69–75 (2016)
2. Qin, C., Zhu, T., Zhao, P., Zhang, Y.: Research review on semantics analysis of natural language. Libr. Inf. Serv. **58**(22), 130–137 (2014)
3. Sun, H.: Study of Crowdsourced Learning Algorithm for Crowdsourced Labeling. Zhejiang University, Master (2015)
4. Howe, J.: Crowdsourcing: why the power of the crowd is driving the future of business. Crown Publishing Group. **67**(4), 1565–1566 (2010)
5. Zhang, Y., Schaar, M.V.D.: Reputation-based incentive protocols in crowdsourcing applications. In: IEEE INFOCOM 2012, pp. 2140–2148. IEEE (2012)
6. Liu, X., Lu, M., Ooi, B.C., Shen, Y., Wu, S., Zhang, M.: CDAS: a crowdsourcing data analytics system. Proc. VLDB Endow. **5**(10), 1040–1051 (2012)

7. Demartini, G., Difallah, D.E., Cudr, & Mauroux, P.: ZenCrowd: leveraging probabilistic reasoning and crowdsourcing techniques for large-scale entity linking. In: International Conference on World Wide Web, pp. 469–478. ACM (2012)
8. Yan, Y., Rosales, R., Fung, G., & Dy, J.G.: Active learning from crowds. In: International Conference on Machine Learning, DBLP, pp. 1161–1168 (2012)
9. Dawid, A.P., Skene, A.M.: Maximum likelihood estimation of observer error-rates using the EM algorithm. J. Roy. Stat. Soc. **28**(1), 20–28 (1979)
10. Welinder, P., Branson, S., Belongie, S., Perona, P.: The multidimensional wisdom of crowds. In: International Conference on Neural Information Processing Systems, pp. 2424–2432. Curran Associates Inc. (2010)

Two-Stage Predictive Modeling for Identifying At-Risk Students

Brett E. Shelton[1], Juan Yang[2], Jui-Long Hung[1(✉)], and Xu Du[2]

[1] Boise State University, Boise, ID 83725, USA
andyhung@boisestate.edu
[2] National Engineering Research Center for E-Learning, Central China Normal University, Wuhan 430079, China

Abstract. This study proposes an analytic approach which combines two predictive models (the predictive model of successful students and the predictive model of at-risk students) to enhance prediction performance for use under the constraints of limited data collection. A case study was conducted to examine the effects of the model combination approach. Eight variables were collected from a data warehouse and the Learning Management System. The best model was selected based on the lowest misclassification rate in the validation dataset. The confusion matrix compares the model's performance with the following parameters: accuracy, misclassification, and sensitivity. The results show the new combination approach can capture more at-risk students than the singular predictive model, and is only suitable for the ensemble predictive algorithms.

Keywords: Learning analytics · Academic at-risk factors
Academic success factors · Ensemble model

1 Introduction

1.1 Background

According to a recent report of enrollments in higher education [1], 30% of all students in higher education institutions are taking at least one online course. Furthermore, 65% of higher education institutions now claim that online learning is a critical part of their long-term strategy [2]. No matter in the face-to-face or online learning settings, retention is an area which attracts lots of research attentions as well as efforts. Due to the natural format of online education, issues of retention arise. Researchers, instructors, and administrators attempt to identify significant and key success or at-risk factors via quantitative or qualitative approaches. However, based on most recent research literature, the success or at-risk factors were influenced by factors that include sociological, psychological, organizational, economical, and behavioral. Without a systematic, long-term data collection plan, it is often difficult to acquire necessary data to support related predictive model training, especially prediction accuracy as the most important attribute during the model construction. Ideally, higher education institutions should investigate what key variables should be collected in order to support all kinds of data-driven

T.-T. Wu et al. (Eds.): ICITL 2018, LNCS 11003, pp. 578–583, 2018.
https://doi.org/10.1007/978-3-319-99737-7_61

applications. However, such data collection efforts can be very labor-intensive and costly. Therefore, in practice, model training usually utilizes what have been collected instead of what should be collected. Data scientists should explore solutions to improve prediction accuracy using the available data.

1.2 Purpose of the Study

The purpose of this study is to propose an analytic approach which combines two predictive models (the predictive model of successful students and the predictive model of at-risk students) to enhance prediction accuracy. The primary research aim is to investigate whether or not the new combination approach can capture more at-risk students under the constraints of having a limited amount of data available.

2 Literature Review

2.1 Adoption Level of Academic Analytics

Data driven decision-making is a trend for educational administration at all levels. Goldstein [3] proposed a framework to define levels of academic analytics implementation. The framework is useful because it can be used to measure the adoption level of academic analytics in educational institutions.

- Stage 1: Extraction and reporting of transaction-level data
- Stage 2 Analysis and monitoring of operational performance
- Stage 3 What-if decision support (scenarios building)
- Stage 4 Predictive modeling and simulation
- Stage 5 Automatic triggers of businesses (alerts)

A survey of analytics implementation conducted in 2005 found that 70 percent of 380 US higher education institutions were at "Stage 1" of the five stage implementation process. Other studies have reported that while 70 percent of surveyed institutions agreed that analytics is a major priority for their school, the majority had yet to move beyond basic reporting [4–6]. Although most of the higher education institutions still stay in the lower level of academic analytics adoption, a large portion of higher education institutions agree that data driven decision making is a major priority and look to create action plans to deploy a data warehouse to store their educational data.

2.2 Key Factors of Student Retention

Retention is a key indicator of academic success [14]. The topic has attracted research efforts to identify key factors which influence student's retention. Due to the nature format of online education, the issue of retention rate is even more important than the F2F educational environments. The authors of this article categorized these factors into sociological [8, 20, 21], psychological [9, 12, 13, 18, 19, 22, 24, 26], organizational [7, 10, 17, 22, 23, 25], economical [15, 16], and behavioral [11, 19].

3 Research Method

3.1 Data Source

In this case study, data were collected from a higher education institution in the United States. Data sources include student demographic data and student behavioral data stored in the university's data warehouse and Learning Management System, respectively. A fully online graduate program was selected as the target. The program offers approximately 20 graduate-level courses hosted in Moodle. The datasets contain all master-level courses in the semesters of spring and fall 2016. Behavioral logs were extracted from 13 courses with 25 sections (418 enrollments) in the spring and 18 courses with 26 sections (566 enrollments) in the fall. Unique course activities, such as Blog, Glossary, and Wiki, were excluded. The following four common course behaviors were collected for analysis (1) frequency of course material accessed, (2) frequency of forum read, (3) number of discussions posted, and (4) number of replies posted. After initial cleaning, the dataset contained 818,122 logs over both semesters, both in a time period covering 16 weeks. Students' final grades were consolidated into a binary variable (pass or fail). To simulate a situation of limited available data as a common constraint, four course behaviors and three demographic factors, including gender, ethnicity and Academic_Load, were selected as input variables and student's final grade was considered as output variable in the following predictive modelling.

3.2 Data Analysis

SAS Enterprise Miner 13.1 was utilized to construct predictive models. Two models were constructed. One aims to predict successful students (Ms, hereafter) and the other aims to predict at-risk students (Mr, hereafter). The following modeling algorithms were selected to compete with each other: Logistic Regression, Random Forest, Support Vector Machines, Neural Network, and Decision Tree. Stratified sampling was applied to randomly select 65% of data for training and the rest of data for validation. To avoid overfitting, the best model was selected by the lowest misclassification rate in the validation dataset. After model training and validation, the best models in Ms and Mr were generated by the Neural Network algorithm. Results are revealed later in the confusion matrix as Table 1.

Figure 1 shows the distribution of successful probabilities (Ps), at-risk probabilities (Pr), and the sum of Ps and Pr (Pt). Ideally, Pt should be close to 1 (a high Ps student should obtain low Pr and vice versa).

However, based on the results of Fig. 1, the range of Pt is from 0.53 to 1.54. Only about 78.5% of Pt are between 0.95 to 1.05. Therefore, the authors constructed another predictive model using Ps and Pr as inputs. The combined approach can identify more at-risk students with the following rules: $Ps < 0.5$ and $Pr > 0.9547$. Table 1 lists three parameters, accuracy, misclassification, and sensitivity, to compare models' performances.

- True positive (TP): a student whose status is positive and the model also correctly predicts the student as positive. In this study, positive means passed in Ms and failed in Mr.

- True negative (TN): a student whose status is negative and the model also correctly predicts the student as negative. In this study, negative means failed in Ms and passed in Mr.
- False positive (FP): a student whose status is negative but the model predicts the student as positive.
- False negative (FN): a student whose status is positive but the model predicts the student as negative.

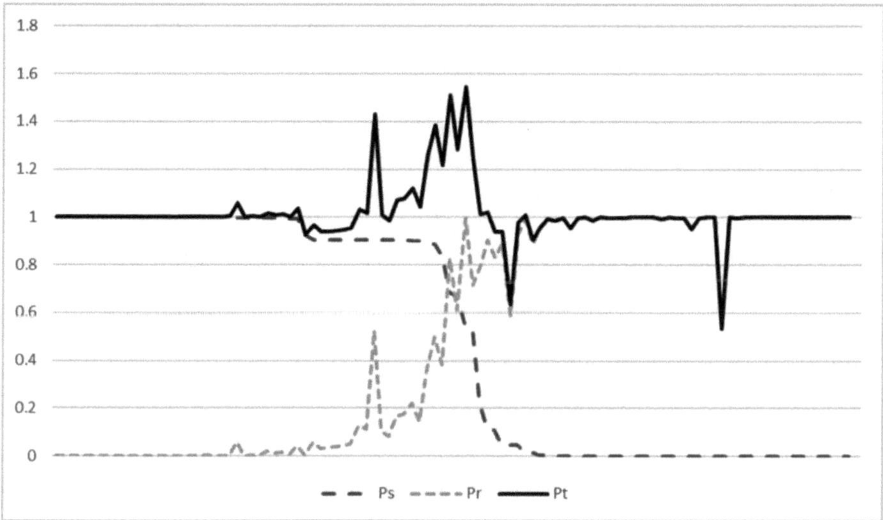

Fig. 1. The Distributions of Ps, Pr, and Pt

Table 1. The Confusion Matrix

Model	Accuracy	Misclassification	Sensitivity
Ms (Neural Network)	0.773373984	0.226626016	0.863636364
Mr (Neural Network)	0.759146341	0.240853659	0.766917293
Model_Combined (Ms + Mr)	0.906976744	0.093023256	0.954545455

Definitions for accuracy, misclassification, and sensitivity are listed below:

$$\text{Accuracy} = \frac{TP + TN}{TP + FP + TN + FN}$$

$$\text{Misclassification} = \frac{FP + FN}{TP + FP + TN + FN}$$

$$\text{Sensitivity} = \frac{TP}{TP + FN}$$

In Table 1, the values of sensitivity represent the proportion of target students captured by models. The target students are successful students in Msm at-risk students in Mr, and in Model_Combined. The combined approach improves sensitivity from 0.767 to 0.955. Therefore, the results show the combined approach can effectively improve model's performance under the constraints of data collection.

4 Discussion

The students whose prediction values calculated beyond the range of 0.95 and 1.05 can be regarded as subjects who cannot be explained by neither Ms nor Mr (nor both). These unexplained subjects might be resulted from the model's inherent errors or by not accounting for additional, uncollected factors. This study demonstrates an alternative approach to improve predictive performance. However, predictive algorithms like Logistic Regression is not applicable for this kind of approach because the generated probabilities of Pt are always equal to one. Therefore, the model combination approach should use ensemble methods like Neural Network or Random Forest.

References

1. Babson Survey Research Group: Digital learning compass: distance education enrollment report (2017). http://digitallearningcompass.org/. Accessed 13 May 2017
2. Floyd, C., Schultz, T., Fulton, S.: Proceedings of the 16th Colloquium for Information Systems Security Education. Colloquium for Information Systems Security Education, Lake Buena Vista, Florida (2012)
3. Goldstein, P. J.: Academic analytics: the use of management information and technology in higher education. Educause (2005)
4. Bichsel, J.: Analytics in higher education: benefits, barriers, progress, and recommendations. Educause (2012)
5. Norris, D., Baer, L.L.: Building organizational capacity for analytics. Educause (2013)
6. Yanosky, R.: Institutional data management in higher education. Educause (2009)
7. Giesbers, B., Rienties, B., Tempelaar, D., Gijselaers, W.: Investigating the relations between motivation, tool use, participation, and performance in an e-learning course using web-videoconferencing. Comput. Hum. Behav. **29**(1), 285–292 (2013)
8. Nora, Amaury, & Gloria, C.: Hispanic student participation and success in developmental education. Hispanic Association of Colleges and Universities (2012)
9. Freitas, S., Gibson, D., Du Plessis, C., Halloran, P., Williams, E., Ambrose, M., Dunwell, I., Arnab, S.: Foundations of dynamic learning analytics: using university student data to increase retention. Br. J. Educ. Technol. **46**(6), 1175–1188 (2015)
10. Ivankova, N.V., Stick, S.L.: Students' persistence in a distributed doctoral program in educational leadership in higher education: a mixed methods study. Res. High. Educ. **48**(1), 93 (2007)
11. Jo, I.-H., Yu, T., Lee, H., Kim, Y.: Relations between student online learning behavior and academic achievement in higher education: a learning analytics approach. In: Chen, G., Kumar, V., Kinshuk, Huang, R., Kong, S.C. (eds.) Emerging Issues in Smart Learning. LNET, pp. 275–287. Springer, Heidelberg (2015). https://doi.org/10.1007/978-3-662-44188-6_38

12. Aragon, S.R., Johnson, E.S.: Factors influencing completion and noncompletion of community college online courses. Am. J. Distance Educ. **22**(3), 146–158 (2008)
13. Bowen, W.G., Chingos, M.M., McPherson, M.S.: Crossing the Finish Line: Completing College at America's Public Universities. Princeton University Press, Princeton (2009)
14. Campbell, J.P., deBlois, P., Oblinger, D.G.: Academic analytics: a new tool for a new era. Educause **42**(4), 40–57 (2007)
15. Campbell, J.P., Oblinger, D.G.: Academic analytics. Educause **42**, 1–24 (2007)
16. Choy, S.: Students whose parents did not go to college: postsecondary access, persistence, and attainment. NCES Publication no. 2001–126 (2001)
17. Colorado, J.T., Eberle, J.: Student demographics and success in online learning environments. Emporia State Res. Stud. **46**(1), 4–10 (2010)
18. Cortes, C.M.: Profile in action: linking admission and retention. New Dir. High. Educ. **2013**(161), 59–69 (2013)
19. Demetriou, C., Schmitz-Sciborski, A.: Integration, motivation, strengths, and optimism: Retention theories past, present, and future. In: Hayes, R. (ed.) Proceedings of the 7th National Symposium on Student Retention, Charleston, pp. 300–312. The University of Oklahoma, Norman (2011)
20. Falcon, L.: Breaking down barriers: first-generation college students and college success. Innovation **10**(6). https://www.league.org/innovation-showcase/breaking-down-barriers-first-generation-college-students-and-college-success. Accessed 16 Apr 2017
21. Holder, B.: An investigation of hope, academics, environment, and motivation as predictors of persistence in higher education online programs. Internet High. Educ. **10**, 245–260 (2007)
22. Hung, J.L., Hsu, Y.C., Rice, K.: Integrating data mining in program evaluation of K-12 online education. Educ. Technol. Soc. **15**(3), 27–41 (2012)
23. Levy, Y.: Comparing dropouts and persistence in e-learning courses. Comput. Educ. **48**(2), 185–204 (2007)
24. Morris, L.V., Wu, S.-S., Finnegan, C.L.: Predicting retention in online general education courses. Am. J. Distance Educ. **19**(1), 23–26 (2005)
25. Tello, S.F.: An analysis of student persistence in online education. Int. J. Inf. Commun. Technol. Educ. **3**(3), 47–62 (2007)
26. Yasmin, I.: Application of the classification tree model in predicting learner dropout behavior in open and distance learning. Distance Educ. **34**(2), 218–231 (2013)

Behavior Data Analysis for Physical Exercise Through Sports Bracelets

Chuan-Yi Chang[1(✉)], Jun-Ming Su[2], and Jia-Sheng Heh[1]

[1] Department of Information and Computer Engineering, Chung Yuan Christian University, Taoyuan City, Taiwan
jsheh@ice.cycu.edu.tw

[2] Department of Information and Learning Technology, National University of Tainan, Tainan, Taiwan

Abstract. This paper proposes a systematic approach to analyze the learners' behavior equipped with sports bracelets. The study begins with the step counts retrieved from the mobile database, transformed to behavior events and behavior states, which then are represented by consecutive strings of discretized step counts. Such behavior state strings are then decomposed and clustered to get behavior parameters: behavior lengths and behavior strengths.

An integrated flow chart with behavior decomposition and behavior clustering algorithms are illustrated. The approach is implemented and verified by a five-month pilot experiment, through which 153379 step counts of 19 learners' mobile sports bracelets are obtained. Henceforth, 2833 person-days behavior states with 72 time-periods are derived. Finally, these 19 learners are clustered into four groups: 9 for no exercise, 7 for average exercise, 2 for long-term exercise and 1 for very long-term exercise. Such behavior models may give more precise exercise planning in physical education.

Keywords: Mobile devices · Sports bracelet · Step count · Behavior analysis
Behavior states

1 Introduction

After the vast development of mobile devices, an Internet of Things (IoT) brings a world of connecting network with almost all physical devices, including vehicles and home, are interconnected through embedded hardware, software, and sensors. [1] The fast development of IoTs show several characteristics of future Internet: the ambient intelligence by the autonomous control of devices [2], the event-driven multi-agent system [3], and big-data analysis for behavior analysis [4].

Physical education (PE) is an educational course to keep the human body through physical exercises, which maintains person's fitness and health through bodily activities. [5] Such activities and behaviors can be detected by some wearable technologies, embedded sensors and big data analysis to measure analyze different parameters of such exercise environment to provide useful information [6].

In additional to standard voices and photograph of nowadays mobile phone, mobile devices are equipped with more and more sensors, including GPS (Global Positioning

T.-T. Wu et al. (Eds.): ICITL 2018, LNCS 11003, pp. 584–593, 2018.
https://doi.org/10.1007/978-3-319-99737-7_62

Systems), accelerometer to 3D gyroscope sensors, and so on. [7] Although GPS provides the real geographic positions to some degree, such information is still not detectable for most mobile devices. For this moment, the most popular sports data available in mobile devices are the vibrations, which comes from the accelerometer and can be used to represent the movement of the user.

Different kinds of sports bracelets have different kinds of recording forms; for examples, some bracelet can watch the sleeping temperature and some can monitor the burned calories. However, a common recording for sports bracelets is *step count*. From the measurement point of view, such recording is not very accurate [8], but it is still very useful as a sports measure.

For physical exercises with sports bracelets, this paper proposes a systematic approach to analyze the learners' behaviors. Section 2 describes the mobile behavior analysis problem. As the step counts from sports bracelets are transformed into behavior states in Sect. 3, Sect. 4 continues to carry out the user behavior analysis. These analysis results are collected in the flow chart of Sect. 5, which also held a pilot experiment to prove our idea. Finally, Sect. 6 gives a conclusion.

2 Mobile Behavior Analysis Problems

2.1 Data Collected from Sports Bracelets

For the purpose of sporting, the formal description of *step count* c_k can be formulated as:

$$c_k = \boldsymbol{SC}(u_k, t_k) \quad (1)$$

where $\boldsymbol{c_k}$ represents user u_k generates step count $c_k = \boldsymbol{SC}(u_k, t_k)$ at time t_k. For example, $c_k = \boldsymbol{SC}(u_k =$ "148640", $t_k =$ "20170101,06:20") = 356 means that $u_k =$ "148640" have a period of motion with step count $c_k = 356$ in the time period (say, $\Delta\mathbf{T}$) at time $t_k =$ "20170101,06:20". Here, a parameter time period ($\Delta\mathbf{T}$) is the time duration for accumulating step count c_k from the accelerometer and the time t_k may be the beginning time point or the ending time point of the time period $\Delta\mathbf{T}$. The time period $\Delta\mathbf{T}$ of step recording is designed by the sports bracelet hardware and its software. Given a time period $\Delta\mathbf{T}$, the sports bracelet hardware will count the vibration from the accelerometer then store the count number in its storage and reset for a new counting.

2.2 The Problem for Mobile Behavior Models

As learners are equipped with mobile sports bracelets, it is possible to collect the daily step counts $\{c_k\}$ of learners, then the data analysis of these step counts can be carried out to look into the daily activities and the implementation of physical education can be adjusted by personal conditions. Thereupon, a set of concrete research objectives can be formulated accordingly:

(1) Given the step counts of a set of learners with sports bracelets, how to find out their behaviors?

(2) As the behavior models of these learners are found, how to analyze the categories of these behaviors?

As the categories of the behavior models of learners are obtained, it is possible to design different implementation strategies of physical education for different behavior categories. And the following sections will begin to make a sophisticated analysis about the step count data first.

3 From Step Counts to Behavior States

3.1 Step Counts of a User

A step count vector $c_k = \boldsymbol{SC}(u_k, t_k)$ in Eq. (1) just records a single motion c_k of user u_k at time t_k; however, such formula $\boldsymbol{SC}(u_k, t_k)$ can be re-written as

$$\boldsymbol{SC}(u_k) = \boldsymbol{SC}(t_k; u_k) \tag{2}$$

thus all the step counts of a specific user u_{kO} in a duration $\boldsymbol{T}$ are collected in a *step count vector*:

$$\boldsymbol{SC}(u_{k0}) = [\boldsymbol{SC}(u_{k0}) = \boldsymbol{SC}(t_k; u_{k0}) : t_k \text{ in } \boldsymbol{T}], \text{ where } \boldsymbol{T} = [t_k] \tag{3}$$

Moreover, a series of step counts of all the users u_k in $\boldsymbol{U}$ within $\boldsymbol{T}$ contain all the motions within this duration $\boldsymbol{T}$. For all users, the motions within the duration $\boldsymbol{T}$ can be collected in a *step count collection* $\boldsymbol{SC}_U$:

$$\boldsymbol{SC}_U = \{\boldsymbol{SC}(u_{k0}) : u_{k0} \text{ in } \boldsymbol{U}\} \tag{4}$$

For example, $\boldsymbol{SC}_U$ = {$\boldsymbol{SC}(u_1$ = "148640") = [(t_{k1}; u_1)] = [("20170101,06:20", 356), ("20170101,06:40", 528), …], $\boldsymbol{SC}(u_2$ = "148941") = [(t_{k2}; u_2)] = [("20170301, 11:00", 242), ("20170301,11:20", 84), …], …}.

Note that even a person sit/lie with almost no movement, the bracelet would still generate some values with small quantities, like [8, 10]. The all-zero values [0, 0, …, 0] in a behavior events means the take-off of the bracelet. Furthermore, a person may generate more than one behavior events in a day; these behavior events need to be segmented by some methods. This brings out the discretization of step count values, which means the transformation from step counts to behavior events.

3.2 Behavior Events

As mentioned above, the measured values of step counts are not very correct for a measurement device; however, these values depict a vague picture of a person's activities. Under such applications, a precise measurement of motions is not so important; on the contrary, a fuzzy description of the person's motions is more suitable. Such requirement is the so-called *continuous-to-discrete* data transformation, which is one methodology of big data analysis.

The continuous-to-discrete transformation from step counts to behavior events is a typical mechanical perception, which always follow the Weber-Fechner law then the (motion) behavior events (the perceived intensity of mechanical stimulus in the law) is proportional to the logarithm of the stimulus strength (step counts). [9] Thereby, the *behavior events* $\boldsymbol{BE}(t_k; u_{kO})$ of the step count $\boldsymbol{SC}(t_k; u_{kO})$ is formally defined as:

$$\boldsymbol{BE}(t_k; u_{k0}) = floor(log_a(\boldsymbol{c}(t_k; u_{k0}) + 1)) = floor(log_a(c_k + 1)) \tag{5}$$

in which the one-increment of c_k + 1 is to avoid the vanishing of c_k (which makes the logarithm illegal) and the floor function *floor*(z) takes the least integer of z. Moreover, the determination of radix a is dependent on the upper limit of the measurement and the discrete values of behavior events (between 1 and N, says 5 in general); for example, a maximum of step count of 6000 and gives a choice of radix a:

$$a = floor(exp(log(6000 + 1)/5)) = floor(5.69698) = 5,$$

then the previous example of the step count 356 can have a behavior events coding:

$$\boldsymbol{BE}(c_k = 356) = floor(log_{a=5}(356 + 1)) = floor(3.652) = 3,$$

and the step count 20 possesses the behavior events

$$\boldsymbol{BE}(c_k = 20) = floor(log_{a=5}(84 + 1)) = floor(2.76) = 2.$$

3.3 Behavior States

As researched in social science for a long time, behaviors can be represented as events or as states. The former are instantaneous events, as the previous subsection discussed, representing a coding of the step counts during a time period ΔT. The latter are described within some amount of time, which accumulates (behavior) events to makes states meaning behaviors. [10]

As sports bracelet is wearing, user motions will be collected as step counts (in about 20 min). With the recorded step counts, though the actual user activity is not easily identified, its exercise capacities of the behavior events can be detected by its step counts. For examples, a 40-min walk may possess a behavior events of $\boldsymbol{SC_1}$= [356. 528], a 1.5-h work $\boldsymbol{SC_2}$= [120, 76, 103, 23, 96], and 7-h sleep $\boldsymbol{SC_3}$= [0, 0, 0, 0, 0, 0, 0, 0, 0, 0, 0, 0, 0, 0, 0, 0, 0, 0, 0, 0, 0].

Take the first $\boldsymbol{SC_1}$ as the example, the step counts 356/528 of 40-min walk can be coded as behavior events 3/3, which makes a behavior state "33". Formally in this paper, a *behavior state* is defined as a series of consecutive behavior events:

$$\boldsymbol{BS}(\boldsymbol{SC}_i, u_{k0}) = \left[\boldsymbol{BE}(t_k; u_{k0}) : t_k'\text{s are consecutive in a time duration } \boldsymbol{T}_i \text{ of } \boldsymbol{SC}_i\right] \tag{6}$$

Briefly, the aforementioned other two examples make $\boldsymbol{BS}(\boldsymbol{SC}_2)/\boldsymbol{BS}(\boldsymbol{SC}_3)$ equal to "22212"/"000000000000000000000", which are the behavior states (coding) of a 1.5-h work and 7-h sleep.

It is notable that string notations is used as behavior representations instead of vectors for abbreviation, then each digit denotes a 20-min motion (behavior event) and a N-digit string means N/3-h behavior state. The following will extend such notations to daily behaviors.

4 User Behavior Analysis

4.1 Day-Hour Step-Count Matrix

Even the step count vector $\boldsymbol{C}_U$ encircles all the motions of sports bracelet, a more explicit data structure is needed for the development of user behaviors. As is known to all, human habit is a 24-h cycle: a person eats about 3 meals in a day, everybody has to sleep 8 h for a day, and so on. Hence, a time record t_k can be transformed into a format of two-element (day, hour) pair ($d_k = day(t_k)$, $h_k = hour(t_k)$), e.g., "20170101,06:20" can be described as (d_k = "20170101", h_k ="06:20"). And then $\boldsymbol{SC}_U = \{\boldsymbol{SC}(t_k; u_{kO})\}$ can be further rewritten as $\boldsymbol{SC}_U = \{\boldsymbol{SC}(d_k, h_k; u_{kO})\}$

The (day, hour) time-format gives step-count a *day-hour step-count matrix* (or *step-count matrix*, concisely) for a single user u_{kO}:

$$\boldsymbol{SCM}(u_{k0}) = [\boldsymbol{SC}(d_k, h_k; u_{k0}) : d_k = day(t_k) \text{ in } \boldsymbol{D}, h_k = hour(t_k) \text{ in } \boldsymbol{H}] \quad (7)$$

Take the previous example, the corresponding day-hour step-count matrix (partial) is

$$\boldsymbol{SCM}(u_{k0}) = \begin{array}{c} \\ 20170101 \\ 20170102 \\ \vdots \end{array} \begin{array}{c} \begin{array}{ccc} 06:20 & 06:40 & \cdots \end{array} \\ \begin{bmatrix} 356 & 528 & \cdots \\ 0 & 20 & \vdots \\ \vdots & \vdots & \ddots \end{bmatrix} \end{array}$$

where d_k in the *day vector* $\boldsymbol{D}$ = [20170101, 20170102, …] and h_k in the *hour vector* $\boldsymbol{H}$ = [06:20, 06:40, …].

Each row of step-count matrix denotes the motions of a person in a day. In the previous example, the time period (Δ**T**) is taken as 20 min and then there are 72 elements (from 00:00, 00:20, to 23:40) in a row. The day-hour step-count matrix gives a interpretative representation of a user's motions, which are possibly used to find out the real user behavior model in the following.

4.2 Observation of Real Step-Count Matrix

Applying the continuous-to-discrete transformation in Eq. (5) to step counts in the previous Step-Count Matrix (SCM), a more compact form can be obtained. The above-mentioned behavior states can be deeply investigated with the kinds of SCM

	00:00	00:20	00:40	01:00	01:20	01:40	02:00	02:20	02:40	03:00	03:20	03:40	04:00	04:20	04:40	05:00	05:20	05:40	06:00	06:20	06:40	07:00	07:20	07:40
[1,]	0	0	0	0	0	0	0	0	0	0	0	0	0	0	0	0	0	0	0	0	0	0	0	0
[2,]	0	0	0	0	0	0	0	0	0	0	0	0	0	0	0	0	0	0	0	0	0	0	0	0
[3,]	0	0	0	0	0	0	0	0	0	0	0	0	0	0	0	0	0	0	0	0	0	0	0	0
[4,]	0	0	0	0	0	0	0	0	0	0	0	0	0	0	0	0	0	0	0	0	0	0	0	548

	08:00	08:20	08:40	09:00	09:20	09:40	10:00	10:20	10:40	11:00	11:20	11:40	12:00	12:20	12:40	13:00	13:20	13:40	14:00	14:20	14:40	15:00	15:20	15:40
[1,]	0	0	0	0	0	0	0	0	0	0	0	0	0	0	0	0	0	0	0	0	0	0	0	0
[2,]	0	0	0	0	0	0	0	0	0	0	0	0	0	0	0	0	0	0	0	0	0	0	0	0
[3,]	0	0	466	220	534	190	294	0	0	70	72	0	42	0	0	0	0	0	26	0	0	0	0	0
[4,]	136	948	188	276	0	22	0	0	464	0	0	0	0	94	88	748	234	26	154	722	0	0	34	300

	16:00	16:20	16:40	17:00	17:20	17:40	18:00	18:20	18:40	19:00	19:20	19:40	20:00	20:20	20:40	21:00	21:20	21:40	22:00	22:20	22:40	23:00	23:20	23:40
[1,]	0	0	0	0	0	0	0	0	0	0	0	0	0	0	0	0	0	0	0	0	0	0	0	0
[2,]	0	0	0	0	0	0	0	0	0	0	0	0	0	0	0	0	0	0	0	0	0	0	0	0
[3,]	516	538	0	34	0	210	370	464	702	66	110	80	0	232	626	546	54	446	1020	0	0	0	0	0
[4,]	106	0	112	480	20	0	154	10	0	0	54	0	0	0	918	0	0	0	0	0	0	0	0	0

Fig. 1. A real step-count matrix (SCM)

representation. Figure 1 shows a real such SCM of a user, in which the actual dates is neglected. As expected, four rows represent four-day step counts, and every row include 72 elements (shown as column labels), each of which represents an accumulation of 20-min step counts.

Notably, the first two rows are all-zero rows, which give a hint that the user did not wear sport bracelet in these two days. And the third day (fourth day, respectively), the user begins to move (maybe get up or put on the bracelet) at 8:40 (7:40, respectively) and finally to rest (may go to bed or take off the bracelet) at 22:00 (20:40, respectively).

With the derivation in the above section, it is easy to derive the whole behavior states of the third day(row) as "000000000000000000000000000333330022020000 0200000330203334222034323400000" and the states of the fourth day(row) as " 000000000000000000000003343301003000022432340023202310310020004000000 000". As consecutive behavior events as behavior states, this case gives the following a set of behavior states:

$$\boldsymbol{BS}(u_{k0}) = \{33333,\ 22,\ 2,\ 2,\ 33,\ 2,\ 3334222,\ 343234,\ 33433,\ 1,\ 3,\ 2243234,\ 232,\ 231,\ 31,\ 2,\ 4\}$$

4.3 Behavior Sub-states and Behavior Clustering

The behavior set $\boldsymbol{BS}(u_{k0})$ is just an example with less than twenty behavior states; nevertheless, a practical behavior state set

$$\boldsymbol{BS}_U = \{\boldsymbol{BS}(u_k) : u_k \text{ in } \boldsymbol{U}\} \tag{8}$$

will come from more than one person and decades of days, thus thousands and tens of thousands behavior states will be generated. From the above actual behavior states, two phenomena can be observed:

(1) A behavior state perhaps consists of several Behavior Sub-States (called ***BSS***); for example, 343234 can be composed of 343 and 34/234.
(2) More than one behavior states can be very similar, e.g., 33333 is similar to 33433, and 232 is similar to 231.

The first observation proposes a **behavior decomposition problem**, which means the behavior states should be further decomposed into more basic components. One the other hand, the second one suggests a **behavior clustering problem**, which may help condense thousand behavior states into decades of behavior categories. These two problems can be transformed into standard algorithm in data science.

Since all the behavior states have been coded as a string with digits 1–5, e.g., "3343234" and then the behavior state bank $\boldsymbol{BS_U}$ is a set of *Behavior Sub-State* (***BSS***) strings. Thereupon, the behavior composition problem can be easily transformed into a substring search problem, which can be solved by standard string search algorithm. [11] Here, only a functional formation is described here:

$$\boldsymbol{BSS_U} = SubstringSearchAlgorithm(\boldsymbol{BS_U}) \tag{9}$$

In the same way, behavior clustering problem is still one of the clustering problems because a behavior state is a digit-string, like [2–4]. Of course, the direct application of step counts, e.g., [232, 626, 546, 54, 446, 1020], for clustering is also possible. On the other hand, behavior states can be transformed into a set of behavior parameters, such as the *behavior length* (the time periods of the behavior, e.g., 6 (2 h) for "343234") or the *behavior strength* (the average behavior events, e.g., (3 + 4 + 3 + 2 + 4 + 3)/ 6 = 3.167). The in-depth study of these transformation is out of the scope of this paper and will be investigated in the future research. On this spot, a general data clustering algorithm is enough to deal with the above behavior clustering problem. [9] The aim of such clustering is to get the corresponding *Behavior Cluster* (***BC***):

$$\boldsymbol{BC_U} = DataClusteringAlgorithm(\boldsymbol{BSS_U}) \tag{10}$$

The presentation of these two algorithms needs the process of a whole data set, which will be shown after the introduction of the integrated algorithm in the next section.

5 User Behavior Analysis

5.1 Integrated Flow Chart for Behavior Analysis

Incorporated with the derivation of behavior states, an integrated flow chart with the substring search algorithm for behavior decomposition and data clustering algorithm for behavior clustering can be described in Fig. 2.

This behavior analysis flow chart satisfies the objectives of this paper: given the step counts of sports bracelets, to find the behaviors and then the behavior categories of users. With such behavior categories, the users' behavior histories and behavior models can be easily drawn. The following will show a real implementation.

5.2 A Real Pilot Experiment

To prove the idea of behavior analysis flow chart in Fig. 2, a real pilot experiment is carried out during 2017/01/01 to 2017/05/31. For 19 learners with the sports bracelets,

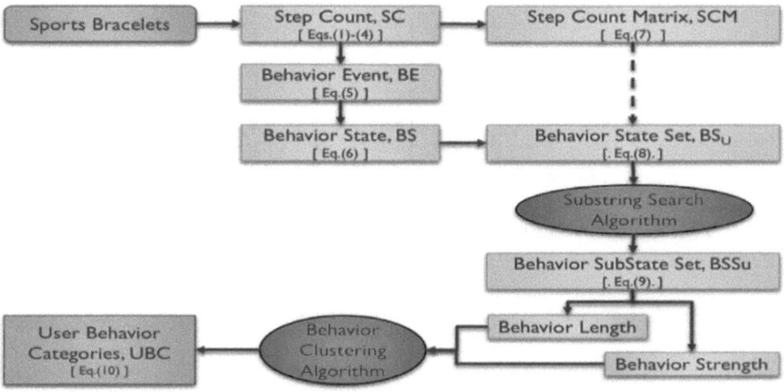

Fig. 2. Integrated flow chart for behavior analysis

then all their motions are recorded and transferred/stored in a cloud database to construct 19 ***SCMs*** (Step Count Matrices), which contain 153379 step counts with the following characteristics in Fig. 3. It can be seen out that more than 96% step counts are zeroes, which is very normal since many persons are not used to ware bracelets and even he/she will wear, the wearing time is not very long. However, the rest nonzero (153379–147660 =) 5719 step counts expose the human behaviors.

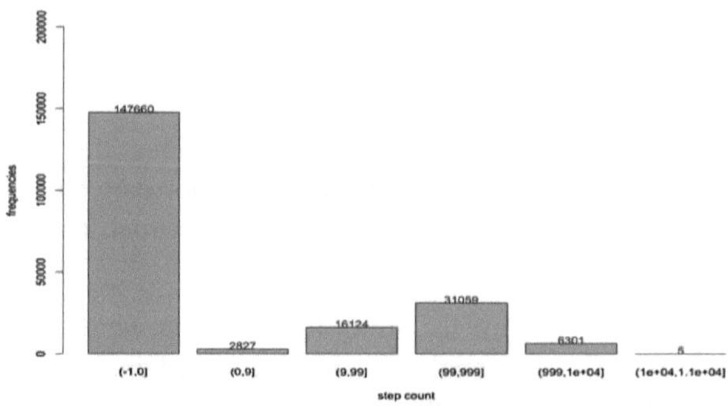

Fig. 3. Distribution of step counts

5.3 Behavior States and User Clustering

After filtering zero step counts, the resultant 19 $\boldsymbol{BS(u_k)}$s are aggregated and transformed to get a 2833 (rows/days) × 72 (time periods in a day) $\boldsymbol{BS_U}$ (Behavior State Set) of all users. The distribution of all the corresponding behavior lengths and behavior strength are depicted in Fig. 4.

In Fig. 4, almost all the behavior strengths are less than 1, the interpretation of behaviors depends on the behavior lengths, which are mostly distributed from 1–6 h. On the other hand, there are only 20 (= 17 + 1 + 1 + 1) behaviors with more than one behavior strengths. These 20 behaviors are not too many but very important.

	(-1,0]	(0,1]	(1,2]	(2,3]	(3,4]
(0,1]	0	1	1	1	1
(1,3]	0	19	17	0	0
(3,6]	0	207	0	0	0
(6,9]	0	183	0	0	0
(9,18]	0	195	0	0	0
(18,48]	0	85	0	0	0

Fig. 4. Distribution of behavior lengths and behavior strengths

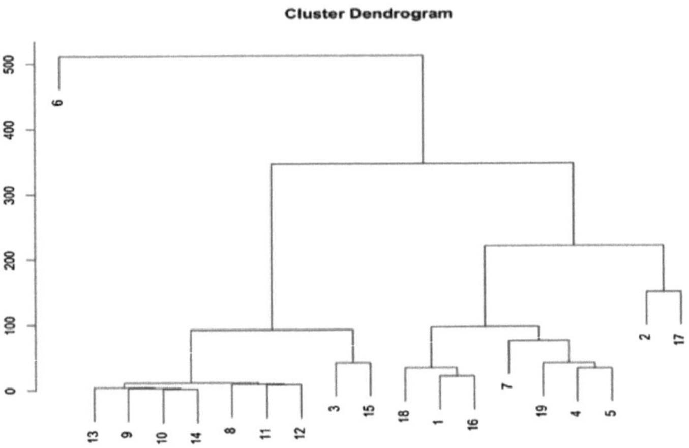

Fig. 5. Dendrogram of behavior clustering

Back to person behaviors, these 19 learners can be classified by their behaviors. Figure 5 are the cluster dendrogram of k-nearest neighbor data clustering algorithm.

Obviously from Fig. 5, four clusters are the most optimal, and each of them can have the following interpretation:

(Group-1) No Exercise group: including learners 3, 8, 9, 10, 11, 12, 13, 14, and 15, who do less exercise, and might not do exercise often.
(Group-2) Average Exercise group: including learners 1, 4, 5, 7, 16, 18, and 19, who have 2-to-3-hours regular exercise, i.e., do exercise stably.
(Group-3) Long-term Exercise group: including learners 2 and 17, who are capable of doing long term exercise.
(Group-4) Very Long-Term Exercise group: including only one learner (learner 6), who does less exercise, and might have capability to do very long-term exercise.

Such clustering gives many meaning interpretations. (A) Nearly half of the persons (Group-1) do not do exercises and need to be promoted; (B) About one-third persons will have regular exercises, which can be monitored continuously; (C) Only a few persons (3 persons in Group-3 and 4) have long-term exercise, whose exercise patterns can be further investigated.

6 Conclusion

This paper proposes a serial approach for analyzing the user behaviors of learners equipped with sports bracelets. When the step counts are recorded from mobile devices to cloud database, the behavior events and behavior states can be obtained. A daily behavior states are represented by a 0–5 digits string, which can be decomposed and clustered to find the behavior sub-states. The behavior length and behavior strength can be computed accordingly.

The behavior analysis flow chart is implemented and verified for a 19-learners pilot experiment in five months. The collected mobile data are processed to classify these 19 learners into four groups: no exercise (9 persons), average exercise (7 persons), long-term exercise (2 persons) and very long-term exercise (1 person) group. The resultant behavior models not only give learners' portraits, but can show their exercise guidelines.

Up to now, this study focuses on the development of behavior analysis methodology, and the present experiment is just a pilot study. To make this research more contributive, it is necessary to plan a bigger experiment for learners. And the special research issues about the learners need to be further investigated. Finally, the applications of mobile devices, not restricted to sports bracelets, will be the main trend of mobile learning in the near future.

References

1. Brown, E.: Who needs the Internet of Things? Linux.com (2016). Accessed 10 May 2018
2. Mohammadi, M., Al-Fuqaha, A., Sorour, S., Guizani, M.: Deep learning for IoT big data and streaming analytics: a survey. arXiv:1712.04301 (2017). Freely accessible
3. Wiki. Internet of Thing. Accessed 10 May 2018
4. Marwaha, J.: IoT and behavioral analytics: a perfect marriage of big data. Syntasa.com (2018). Accessed 10 May 2018
5. Kylasov, A, Gavrov, S.: Diversity of sport: non-destructive evaluation. In: Encyclopedia of Life Support Systems, pp. 462–491 (2011)
6. Bagheri, M. Movahed, S. H.: The effect of the Internet of Things (IoT) on education business model. In: 12th International Conference on Signal-Image Technology & Internet-Based Systems (2016)
7. Charise, B.G.: How many sensors inside a sports smart bracelet? Banggood.com (2015). Accessed 10 May 2018
8. Narins, E.: 8 ways you're using your fitness tracker wrong. Cosmopolitan.com (2014). Accessed 10 May 2018
9. Achamess: Log scale/transformation for sensory testing. Forum.painresearcher.net (2016). Accessed 10 May 2018
10. Altmann, J.: Observational study of behavior: sampling methods. Behavior **49**(3), 227–267 (2014)
11. Hume, S.: Fast string searching. Softw. Pract. Exp. **21**(11), 1221–1248 (1991)

AI Applications on Music Technology for Edutainment

Von-Wun Soo[1], Chih-Fang Huang[2(✉)], Yu-Huei Su[3], and Mei-Ju Su[4]

[1] Department of Computer Science, Tsing Hua University, Hsinchu, Taiwan
soo@cs.nthu.edu.tw
[2] Department of Information Communications, Kainan University, Taoyuan City, Taiwan
jeffh.me83g@gmail.com
[3] Director of Research Center for Music, Technology and Health, National Tsing Hua University, Hsinchu, Taiwan
yhsu@mail.nd.nthu.edu.tw
[4] Department of Biomedical Engineering, Yuanpei University of Medical Technology, Hsinchu, Taiwan
merri@mail.ypu.edu.tw

Abstract. Music composition for songs is difficult for people, due to the necessity of the complicated music composition theory and the combined artistic conception and emotion-based ideas. The emotional representation can define the valence and arousal coordinate, and it is possible to perform the mapping technique between music and emotion, according to lyrics emotion. The proposed emotion-based algorithmic music composition uses song lyrics emotion to classify music segments, and use the mapping between music and emotion. It can make people who even don't know music theory easily compose a song. Some demos finally show the result of the research. Therefore the proposed method can be applied to such fields as the popular songs composition, background music, musical edutainment, education musicale, etc. Some traditional sources of entertainment have embraced AI to compose music and create stage performances. AI will increasingly enable entertainment that is more interactive, personalized, and engaging. In the future, more sophisticated tools and apps will become available to make it even easier to compose music. The creation and dissemination of entertainment will benefit from the progress of technologies such as ASR, dubbing, and Machine Translation, which will enable content to be customized to different audiences inexpensively. This democratization and proliferation of AI-created media makes it difficult to predict how humans' taste for entertainment, which are already fluid, will evolve.

Keywords: Emotional representation
Emotion-based algorithmic music composition · AI-created media

1 Introduction

Automatic lyrics composition for a song is a challenging task that requires satisfying various constraints from the themes, styles and melody structures in the song.

T.-T. Wu et al. (Eds.): ICITL 2018, LNCS 11003, pp. 594–599, 2018.
https://doi.org/10.1007/978-3-319-99737-7_63

Kento et al. [1] showed that there were techniques adopted in Japanese lyrics writing. A lyric writer may also consider the singer's habit and the easiness of utterance to pronounce the words. As structural units of lyrics are basically verse, bridge, and chorus, we must be able to identify the melody segments as templates in which lyrics segment units can be filled. Therefore, segmenting or parsing a song into segmental structures is important. Unfortunately, we found that the music segmentation theory such as GTTM [2] can explain hierarchy structure for many pieces of classic music but cannot provide coherent and satisfying prediction on the phrase or sentence boundary for segmenting a melody especially for popular songs that usually require accompanying lyrics. Given a large set of common sense knowledge base, we had developed an evolutionary computation system [3] that learned to compose a modern poem in Mandarin Chinese for any simple topic as title. It could satisfy rhyme, level of oblique tone, antithesis and common sense semantics and come out poems with a fixed sentence sizes. With modern deep learning technology, it is now feasible to use end-to-end training techniques to train computers to learn to generate lyrics accompanying to a song without much human intervention. But it requires to prepare a huge set of parallel corpus on pair-wise melodies and lyrics first in order to train with a deep learning model. We have now established such a large corpus by accessing and downloaded from a public Karaoke database. We could then adopt semantic word embedding that encodes meaning of the lexicons in the lyrics first that match the emotion sense implicit in the song. The implicit emotion elements of a song can be usually interpreted using existing computational models [4] into points in a two dimensional VA space of valence and arousal. The VA emotion space can be annotated to correspond to fear, sad, joy, pleasure, anger, etc. that can be used as concepts clusters to link to other concept lexicons. We also need to construct a syntactic model for lyrics to ensure that the rhyme, metaphor, double meaning, double negatives, interrogatives, onomatopoeia, inversion, repetition, and rewording patterns can be properly expressed as well. Research on artificial intelligence has also gradually turned to the establishment of human-recognized, trustworthy intelligence systems. The performance of information processing algorithms has been accompanied by significant advances in hardware technology, such as perception, perception, and target recognition, in addition to the perception processing of video tagging and behavioral recognition. AI and Music can be utilized by edutainment and entertainment domain. On music edutainment domain, some innovative music technology products are for adjusting emotion like EMO and Last.fm, EMO is a music app which can be identified by your facial expressions of your emotions, then recommend music to fit your current mood at the moment. Last.fm is an aid from social tags, you will get a station full of songs that other Last.fm-ers have tagged as being appropriate to that emotion. At present, the concept of music therapy education is generally accepted, and research related to music, edutainment, and education has received more and more attention. For example, the Media Lab at the Massachusetts Institute of Technology (MIT) conducted a technical research and development of Music, Mind & Edutainment to successfully make cerebral palsy patients move through the muscles. And brain awareness, performing real-time music creation performance. When we establish a set of data that can test the effectiveness of music on human body, AI can find out the relevance of the physiological characteristics of music participants from these complex musical characteristics and optimize the real reaction of human music behavior. In this way, breakthroughs in the application of music therapy can be achieved and quickly become an industry. Such success will affect the development of AI-related industries. By combining social and edutainment data, some edutainment Apps can perform data mining, learning, and prediction from captured data. The convergence of data and functionality across applications will likely spur new and even obvious products, such as an exercise Apps that not only proposes a schedule for exercise but also suggests the best time to do it, and provides coaching to stick to that schedule. In addition to the application of music edutainment, AI music technology can also be applied to the entertainment and education industry. Driven by artificial intelligence, the Internet has used "user-generated content" as a viable source of information and entertainment, such as the AI smart game agent system. In response to emotions, virtual characters such as virtual singers are generated, and even integrated into video games or film scenarios to produce interactive video music or soundtracks, so that the sound effects are more realistic. Beyond aggregate performance statistics, on-field signals can be monitored using sophisticated sensors and cameras.

2 Method

In the field of psychology, there have been many tests of musical mood perception and explores the feelings that music brings to humans. When we want to implement music emotions at the program level, we need some emotional features to correspond with musical features in order to produce music that meets emotional needs. Our proposed method uses 2-D emotion coordinate to express the emotion situation, including both "positive emotion" and "negative emotion" for X-Axis as "Valence". In addition, "emotion active" and "emotion passive" can be in the Y-Axis as "Arousal" into the 2-D emotion coordinate [5, 6]. Figure 1 shows Thayer's arousal-valence emotion plane. The proposed method is based on the emotion-music mapping using the 2-D Emotion Plane.

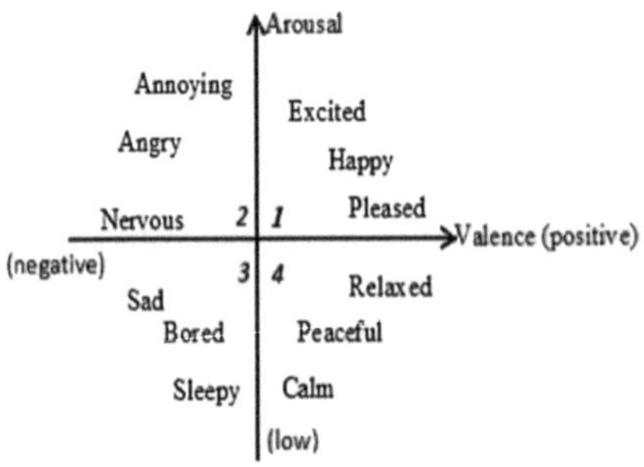

Fig. 1. Thayer's arousal-valence emotion plane [6]

In the past, there have been many studies that have summarized music into different emotions and expressed them in an emotional plane. Steven R. Livingstone and Andrew R. Brown [7] subdivided the four quadrants of the AV (Arousal and Valence) emotional plane into eight regions and classified the following six musical emotions: Happy, Excited, Angry, Sad, Depressed, Dreamy, as shown in Fig. 2. The more consistent musical characteristics in each area are proposed. Algorithmic Composition is a method of composing music using an algorithm. The basic concept is that the composer determines a set of rules, and then randomly generates music according to this set of rules. Due to the advancement of computing power in computers today, composers can use computer programs to deal with more complicated rules, making the possibility of composing the guidelines continue to advance with the advancement of science and technology. Therefore, the name Computer Automated Composition was later used to analyze the quantified music elements through the concept of musical parameterization, making it a variable in automatic composition. Our proposed method to perform the mapping techniques needs to perform the way to "map" or "transform" the song lyrics (or the users can define it by themselves) between "Music Emotion" (Happy, Excited, Angry, Sad, Depressed, Dreamy) and "Music Features" (Mode, Tempo, Pitch, etc.). Algorithmic Composition is a method of composing music using an algorithm. The basic concept is that the composer sets a set of rules and then randomly generates music according to this set of rules. Due to the advancement of computing power in computers today, composers can use computer programs to deal with more complicated rules, making the possibility of composing the guidelines continue to advance with the technology. Therefore, the name Computer Automated Composition was later used to analyze the quantified music elements through the concept of musical parameterization, making it a variable in automatic composition. When designing an automatic composition system, how to maintain these parameters within a limited range is a very important goal. Excessive restrictions will result in narrowing of results. Excessive freedom will result in no logic. Therefore, most of the composing systems will add "parameters" to the system control, among which the Markov Chain [8] is most often used by the

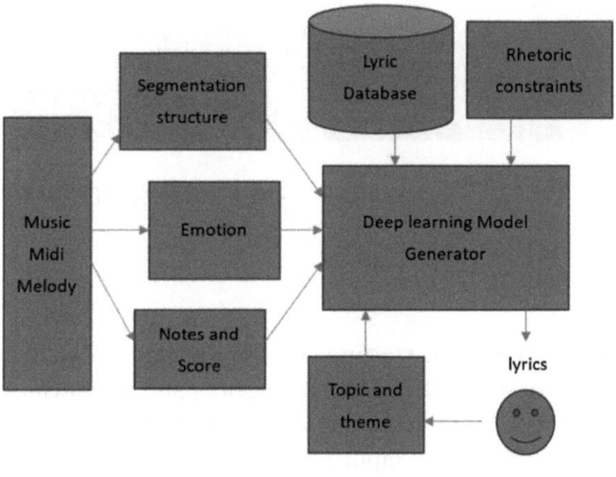

Fig. 2. The lyrics and music composition generated based on an emotion-based segment

automatic composer system. If the chord progression can be processed by Markov Chain, then other music features including Pitch and Tempo and be also used for this method. However music Mode such as Major or minor is not necessary to use Markov Chain, because it can be simply selected by the Music-Emotion definition. The Lyrics with the music segmentation structure emotion can be generated with the consistent Algorithmic Composition song generation. Please refer to Fig. 2.

3 Implementation

There are three main steps for our proposed method, including:

1. From the lyrics input by the user, determine the song pattern and match it with the number of words and paragraphs.
2. Analyze the user's lyrics, recommend the user to choose emotions, produce melody, chords, and speed that match the mood.
3. The resulting Midi file is output so that the user can go back to the more professional DAW (Digital Audio Workstation) to complete the work.

4 Result

Through the Chord Track function in Cubase music software, we can directly convert the generated data of our chord tracks into chord marks. Use Cubase's stave function to add lyrics to our MIDI file and output it. The complete melody and harmonics progress score is shown in Fig. 3. The listeners can easily feel the emotion of the music with a good correlation.

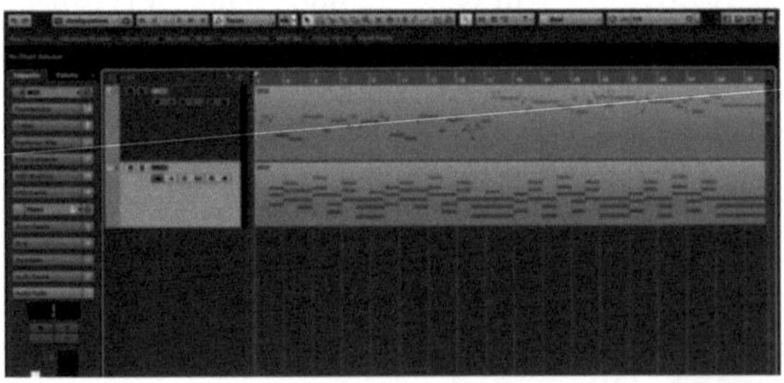

Fig. 3. The MIDI piano roll output by using the proposed method

5 Conclusion

In this study, the lyric mood is the starting point of the algorithmic composition system. First collect lyrics data or user's self-defined emotion, and ask music experts to identify, and then lyric data for word segmentation, sentiment analysis, emotional word comparisons, and classification, the user input lyrics are divided into positive and negative emotions. Through this emotional result, the user is recommended to choose six emotions: happy, depressed, sad, dreamy, angry, and excited. Through the analysis of the characteristics of the Chinese language music, the three characteristics of the song's tempo, range, and size are combined with the six emotions. Through the analysis of the Chinese music data, the melody rhythm, chord progression, and tempo are modeled. According to the lyrics input by the user, the rhythm matching device is used to select a suitable rhythm group, and a chord pairer is used to select a chord. Finally, a melody generator that combines Markov chains, imitations, and vocal tracts produces rhythms and chords in a given rhythm and chord. This system is implemented to reduce the threshold of song composition and provide a more convenient tool for songwriters, or even most of the music lovers. We think more other applications including music education, music edutainment, TV and movie soundtrack, game music, and even music therapy will be used in the future. In the future, we will emphasize AI for the music edutainment with our proposed method.

Acknowledgements. The authors would like to appreciate the support from Ministry of Science and Technology project of Taiwan: 106-2410-H-424-016.

References

1. Watanabe, K., Matsubayashi, Y., Inui, K., Goto, M.: Modeling structural topic transitions for automatic lyrics generation. In: 28th Pacific Asia Conference on Language, Information and Computation, pp. 422–431, Phuket, Tailand (2014)
2. Lerdahl, F., Jackendoff, R.: A Generative Theory of Tonal Music. MIT Press, Cambridge Mass. (1983)
3. Soo, V-W, Lai, T-Y, Wu, K-J, Hsu, Y-P: Generate modern style chinese poems based on common sense and evolutionary computation. In: Proceeding in TAAI (2015)
4. Coutinho, E., Trigeorgis, G., Zafeiriou, S., Schuller, B.: Automatically estimating emotion in music with deep long-short term memory recurrent neural networks. In: Working Notes Proceedings of the MediaEval 2015 Workshop (2015)
5. Russell, J.A.: A circumplex model of affect. J. Pers. Soc. Psychol. **39**(6), 1161–1178 (1980)
6. Thayer, R.E.: The Biopsychology of Mood and Arousal. Oxford University Press, Oxford (1989)
7. Livingstone, S.R., Brown, A.R.: Dynamic response: real-time adaptation for music emotion. In: Proceedings of the Second Australasian Conference on Interactive Entertainment, vol. 9, no. 2, pp. 105–111 (2005)
8. Hastings, W.K.: Monte Carlo sampling methods using Markov chains and their applications. Biometrika **57**(1), 97–109 (1970)

Building a Reconfigurable Subject-Free Learning Game System

Jun-Ming Su(✉) and Chia-Hao Wang

Department of Information and Learning Technology, National University of Tainan, Tainan, Taiwan
junming.su@gmail.com, sampoway6880@gmail.com

Abstract. The specially-designed educational game are effective for the improvement of the motivation and outcome of learning. However, the development of the learning game is the labor-intensive and time-consuming work (High Cost) and the application of the learning scope is limited to a specific learning subject (Learning Scope Limitation). The concept of the subject-free learning game is able to address the Learning Scope Limitation well, but the High Cost is still the pressing issue for all kinds of games. Therefore, in this work, a Reconfigurable Subject-free Learning Game System based on a Collaborative Subject-free Learning Game Scheme, called ReSfLGS, is developed, a reconfigurable scheme of which is able to reconfigure and integrate the various game content according to the proposed I/O protocol, the definition of which enables that various games can be controlled and communicated with ReSfLGS. Moreover, the game content is able to be efficiently created using the Web-based visualized authoring tool in ReSfLGS for addressing the High Cost issue.

Keywords: Game-based learning · Subject-free learning game · Reconfiguration Collaboration

1 Introduction

Learning motivation of students is an important factor for the effective learning. Currently, the Game-based Learning or Educational Game has shown the effectiveness for improving the learning motivation [1]. The popular scheme of applying Game-based Learning is to design the specific game context to perfectly meet the learning subject for efficiently leveraging the fun and meaningful learning, called specially-designed educational game [2–4]. However, the game development is the (1) labor-intensive and time-consuming works (High Cost) and (2) the learning scope is limited to a specific learning subject (Learning Scope Limitation). Moreover, to apply the off-the-shelf general purpose commercial games to the learning context and subjects [11] become a possible method, but to find a suitable game might not be easy [12].

Accordingly, to integrate learning subjects with subject-free games, the context and scenario of which are general purpose and not designed for the desired, specific learning subject, has also been investigated and show the potential effects, such as the [5, 6]. Similarly, A collaborative game, League of Learners (LoL), based on a Collaborative

T.-T. Wu et al. (Eds.): ICITL 2018, LNCS 11003, pp. 600–605, 2018.
https://doi.org/10.1007/978-3-319-99737-7_64

Subject-free Learning Game (CSfLG) Scheme in our previous study [7], had been proposed. CSfLG scheme integrates the learning with gaming by means of answering the test items for gaining game resources and to motivate students to collaboratively play and learn by means of the complementary design of the game roles. Its experimental results also showed the efficient and beneficial for students. However, the concept of the subject-free games seems to be able to address the Learning Scope Limitation well, but the High Cost is still a pressing issue for all kinds of Game-based Learning.

Therefore, in this work, in order to address the issues of the Learning Scope Limitation and High Cost, a Reconfigurable Subject-free Learning Game System based on CSfLG Scheme [7], called ReSfLGS, has been proposed and developed. ReSfLGS consists of the (1) Teacher-side system and (2) Learner-side system. In the former, a reconfigurable scheme is proposed to be able to reconfigure the various game content and integrate them with the ReSfLGS system according to the I/O protocol, the definition of which is able to enable that various games can be controlled and communicated with ReSfLGS. Moreover, in order to facilitate the construction of the subject-free game, the context and content of games are able to be efficiently created by means of our previous work, Collaborative Diagnostic Virtual Experiment System (CoDiVE) [8], for addressing the High Cost issue of the game developments. Consequently, the concept of the learning subjects with subject-free games can be realized and applied to learn the various subjects for the improvement of the learning motivation. Afterwards, a Game Task, including a subject-free game with the test items of a learning subject, can be defined and announced by teachers for the game-based learning application. Therefore, students can learn and play the announced Game Task through the Learner-side system in ReSfLGS. Currently, the ReSfLGS system has also been developed to show the workability. Thereby, students will be expected to be motivated in learning with the playing of subject-free game through the ReSfLGS system and teachers can understand the learning status through the gaming portfolio for improving the teaching and learning performance.

2 Related Works

The effectiveness of using games to motivate the motivation in learning has been proven. Therefore, a larger number of game-based learning applications have been proposed. In order to leverage the joyful playing and meaningful learning, most of them are designed based on the concept of the specially-designed educational game. For example, the games are specifically designed for learning the history [2] and ecology [9, 10]. Moreover, the problem of the specially-designed educational game is that its learning scope is limited to the specific learning subject. Accordingly, the concept of subject-free learning game, the game context of which is not relevant and limited to a specific learning subject, have also been proposed. Accordingly, the usage of the general-purpose commercial games in educational purpose seems to be the alternative method [11]. It may be able to address the problems of the high cost of the game development but it is not easy to find a suitable commercial game to adequately meet the context of the targeted learning course [12].

Lin et al. [5] applied the Monopoly Game to learn the concept of "Area of Circle" in Mathematics, where students were asked to answer the questions for gaining the opportunity of "rolling the dice". Similarly, the PaGamO [6] was developed to motivate students in doing the homework, the scheme of which was to ask students to answer the question for occupying the territory in the game world. A collaborative game, called League of Learners (LoL) [7], was our previous study and also developed based on a Collaborative Subject-free Learning Game (CSfLG) Scheme. The LoL game applied the concepts of the collaboration in a learning group and the complementary players' factors in a game to motivate the learners in learning the subject and playing the subject-free game. The experimental results of aforementioned studies showed the effectiveness of the improvement of motivation and learning. Accordingly, the concept of the subject-free game becomes the potential method for learning improvement. However, for those studies of the subject-free learning games, the high cost of the game development is still the pressing issue.

3 Reconfigurable Subject-Free Learning Game System

This paper proposes and develops a Reconfigurable Subject-free Learning Game System, called ReSfLGS. Figure 1 illustrates the architecture of ReSfLGS, which consists of the Teacher-side system and Learner-side system. Teacher-side system includes (1) the Management system to manage the (a) Game Content, (b) Item Bank, and (c) Game Task, and (2) the Server system to handle the run-time operation of the learning games according to the announced game task by the game task module. Learner-side system is designed based on the CSfLG scheme, which is our previous work, Collaborative Subject-free Learning Game Scheme [7].

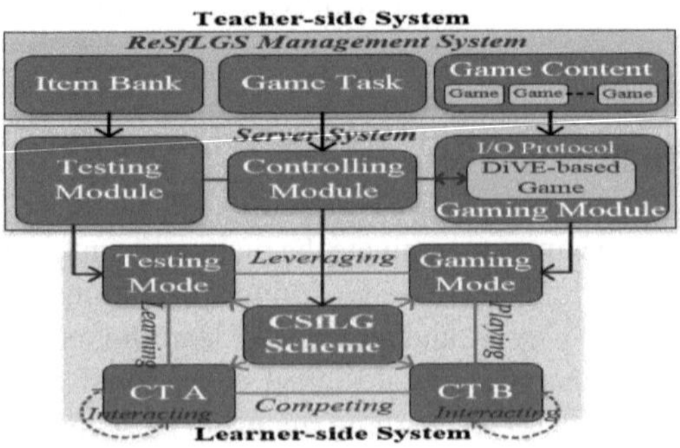

Fig. 1. Architecture of the Reconfigurable Subject-free Learning Game System (ReSfLGS).

3.1 Learner-Side System in ReSfLGS

For efficiently integrating the learning subject with subject-free game, the scenario of the learner-side system in ReSfLGS is designed based on Collaborative Subject-free Learning Game (CSfEG) Scheme [7] to leverage the meaningful learning and joyful gamming. As shown in Fig. 1, the CSfLG Scheme consists of (1) Learning, (2) Gaming, and (3) Interaction aspects, each of which is respectively designed and regarded as the (1) Testing Mode (Learning), (2) Gaming Mode (Gaming), and (3) Collaborative Team (CT) (Interaction) in ReSfLGS. In CSfLG Scheme, the method of asking students to correctly answer the test items in [Testing Mode] for gaining the resource in [Gaming Mode] is designed to leverage the meaningful learning in the test context and joyful playing in gaming context. Moreover, the method of asking students to play the complementary game roles, each of which has different game factors and skills, e.g., attacker or defender, is designed to enhance the interaction among students for maintaining the motivation and stickiness. In the CSfLG Scheme, each round of a Game Task requires two Collaborative Teams (CT), i.e., CT A and CT B in Fig. 1, to compete with each other, where each CT has two students at most, each of whom plays as either attacker or defender, to collaboratively compete with another CT for the wining of the gaming and learning.

3.2 Teacher-Side System in ReSfLGS

In ReSfLGS, the Teacher-side System designs the (1) Management system and the (2) Server system to realize the aforementioned CSfLG Scheme. The former consists of three functionalities, i.e., (a) Game Content, (b) Item Bank, and (c) Game Task, to create and manage the required resource and tasks for the learning and gaming, each of which is able to be handled by the corresponding functionality, i.e., (a) Gaming Module, (b) Testing Module, and (c) Controlling Module, in the latter.

Reconfigurable Scheme of Game Content. In the management system of ReSfLGS, the Game Content Management functionality is designed to reconfigure the various game content and integrate them into ReSfLGS for realizing the purpose of learning and playing with Subject-free Learning Game. In order to facilitate the construction of the game content, the context and content of games are able to be created by means of our previous work, Collaborative Diagnostic Virtual Experiment System (CoDiVE) [8]. It offers a Visualized Reusable Object-based Construction Scheme (VROCS) based on Object-Oriented Design Approach (OODA) and Rule-Based Control Approach (RBCA) to enhance the Reusability and Extensibility. In CoDiVE system, a Web-based visualized authoring tool, as a WYSIWYG style, has been developed to facilitate the construction of the Diagnostic Virtual Experiment (DiVE) by defining the associated attributes, actions, and control rules using the drop-down menu and be presented by 2D graphics and HTML5. Therefore, non-technical (game) designers can easily create the desired DiVE-based Game without the programming for addressing the high cost issue of game development [8]. As shown in Fig. 1, the DiVE-based Games can be regarded as the third-party software component and thus be integrated to third-party system based on the proposed I/O protocol in ReSfLGS, a control and communication method between the system and DiVE-based game content. Therefore, the DiVE-based Games can be efficiently created by the CoDiVE system and easily reconfigured and integrated by the Game Content Management functionality in the management system.

Management of Game Task and Item Bank. The test items associated with concept definition can be managed through the Item Bank functionality, where the word files of test items can be transformed into Web-based format and stored in the Item Bank for the usage of a Game Task. Afterwards, teachers can manage the game tasks through the Game Task functionality. For the announcement of a game task, teachers select the related test items as the game resource and a desired subject-free game to create a game task for the learning of students.

Process of Server System. In ReSfLGS, the Server System is designed to take over the execution of an announced game task, where the Controlling Module controls the main process and leverages the learning and gaming modules, i.e., Test Module and Gaming Module being in charge of the process of the test items and the communication of a DiVE-based game, respectively.

4 Implementation

The prototypical system of ReSfLGS has been developed and the screenshots of the Learner-side System is as shown in Fig. 2. In the Gaming Mode (Fig. 2.a), a DiVE-based game content is able to be integrated and controlled with ReSfLGS based on the I/O protocol, whereby students in the Collaborative Teams (CT A or CT B) can play the game, communicate with each other through the Message Panel, and change the types of mode through the button of Change Mode. In the Learning Mode (Fig. 2.b), the Test Items list will be shown and students can select and answer the test item for gaining the game resource. Currently, two DiVE-based game content have been created using the CoDiVE system and integrated into ReSfLGS using the Game Content management for showing the workability of ReSfLGS system.

Fig. 2. The screenshots of the gaming mode and the learning mode of the learner-side system in ReSfLGS.

5 Conclusion

In this work, a Reconfigurable Subject-free Learning Game System based on a Collaborative Subject-free Learning Game Scheme (CSfLG), called ReSfLGS system, is designed and developed to address the issues in terms of the high cost of game development and the limitation of learning scope. The reconfigurable scheme in ReSfLGS system is able to reconfigure and integrate the various game content according to the proposed I/O protocol for addressing the limitation of learning scope, and the Web-based visualized authoring tool is able to facilitate the construction of the game content for addressing the high cost of game development. In the near future, the ReSfLGS system is going to be applied to the actual class teaching and learning for the evaluation.

Acknowledgement. This research was supported by Ministry of Science and Technology of Republic of China under the number of MOST 106-2511-S-024-002-MY3 and MOST 105-2511-S-024-009.

References

1. Garris, R., Ahlers, R., Driskell, J.: Games, motivation and learning: a research and practice model. Simul. Gaming **33**, 441–467 (2002)
2. Egenfeldt-nielsen, S.: Beyond edutainment: exploring the educational potential of computer games. Ph.D. dissertion, IT- University Copenhagen, Denmark (2005)
3. Lo, J.-J., Ji, N.-W., Syu, Y.-H., You, W.-J., Chen, Y.-T.: Developing a digital game-based situated learning system for ocean ecology. In: Pan, Z., Cheok, A.D., Müller, W., El Rhalibi, A. (eds.) Transactions on Edutainment I. LNCS, vol. 5080, pp. 51–61. Springer, Heidelberg (2008). https://doi.org/10.1007/978-3-540-69744-2_5
4. Hwang, G.J., Wu, P.H.: Advancements and trends in digital game-based learning research: a review of publications in selected journals from 2001 to 2010. Br. J. Educ. Technol. **43**(1), 6–10 (2012)
5. Lin, C.H., Liu, E.Z.F., Chen, Y.L., Liou, P.Y., Chang, M., Wu, C.H., Yuan, S.M.: Game-based remedial instruction in mastery learning for upper-primary school students. Educ. Technol. Soc. **16**(2), 271–281 (2013)
6. PaGamO. https://pagamo.com.tw/. Accessed 01 June 2018
7. Su, J.M., Wu, K.M.: League of Learners (LoL)-a collaborative subject-free learning game scheme to leverage fun and meaningful learning: a study on potential and effect. In: The Proceeding of the Third International Conference on Educational Innovation Through Technology (EITT 2014), Brisbane, Australia, 27–29 October 2014, pp. 68–74 (2014)
8. Su, J.M., Huang, J.R.: Building a web-based visualized authoring system to collaboratively create reconfigurable and diagnostic virtual experiments in natural science. In: The 4th International Conference on Learning Technologies and Learning Environments, pp. 12–16, Okayama Convention Center, Okayama, Japan, pp. 358–362 (2015)
9. Marlow, M.: Games & learning in landscape architecture. In: 10th International Conference on Information Technologies in Landscape Architecture (2009)
10. Susaeta, H., Jimenez, F., Nussbaum, M., Gajardo, I., Andreu, J.J., Villalta, M.: From MMORPG to a classroom multiplayer presential role playing game. Educ. Technol. Soc. **13**(3), 257–269 (2010)
11. Panoutsopoulos, H., Sampson, D.G.: A study on exploiting commercial digital games into school context. Educ. Technol. Soc. **15**(1), 15–27 (2012)
12. Rieber, L.P.: Seriously considering play: designing interactive learning environments based on the blending of microworlds, simulations, and games. Educ. Technol. Res. Dev. **44**(1), 43–58 (1996)

Innovative Thinking Education and Future Trend Development

Discussion on the Teaching and Learning Innovation of Higher-Order Thinking

Chun-cheng Chen[1,2(✉)], Ming-chang Wu[1], and Ting-ting Wu[1]

[1] Graduate School of Technological and Vocational Education, National Yunlin University of Science and Technology, Yunlin, Taiwan
{wumc,ttwu}@yuntech.edu.tw

[2] Bachelor's Program in Software Engineering and Digital Innovation Applications, Fu Jen Catholic University, New Taipei, Taiwan
chen0001@ms3.hinet.net

Abstract. This study aims to explore the teaching and learning innovation by using higher-order thinking. Many studies have found that although there are significant and considerable effects in the teaching and learning of higher-order thinking, there still lacks elaboration and analysis of higher-order thinking in teaching thinking method, learning thinking method and curriculum thinking design. This study first elaborates the implications and characteristics of higher-order thinking, the thinking process of higher-order thinking and the level analysis of higher-order thinking. It then proposes the teaching strategies of higher-order thinking in teaching and learning, and combines the 3P Thinking approaches (Problem found, Definition problem and Problem solving), as well as the analytical teaching curriculum planning and goal practice. Finally, it discusses the nature of higher-order thinking and proposes specific strategies for applying higher-order thinking in university teaching.

Keywords: Higher-order thinking · Creative thinking · Critical thinking
Problem-solving capability · Curriculum innovation

1 Introduction

The mere acquisition of knowledge is not longer the purpose of the education provided by the school, and it is not the due goal or plan in school education [1]. Especially in today's education, how to think and what to think, and how to use thinking to solve problems and conduct curriculum planning design of higher-order teaching and learning is one of the key issues that both instructors and learners must take seriously.

In the innovation of teaching and learning in higher-order thinking, this study emphasizes how to import the subjective cognition and use skills of higher-order thinking into teaching and learning thinking, so that both instructors and learners can effectively promote their capabilities through complex creative thinking, critical thinking as well as the application of the problem-solving thinking. The so-called higher-order thinking is a kind of thinking that requires combining creative thinking, critical thinking and problem-solving capabilities so as to solve problems effectively after

T.-T. Wu et al. (Eds.): ICITL 2018, LNCS 11003, pp. 609–615, 2018.
https://doi.org/10.1007/978-3-319-99737-7_65

application of teaching and learning, analysis, judgment, and creation. This is also an innovation and research in teaching and learning that this study wants to emphasize and import. What are the significance and characteristics of higher-order thinking? In past related studies, it has been found that using higher-order thinking has considerable effectiveness and significance in teaching [2–8]. In addition, higher-order thinking was incorporated into the planning of the curriculum and the setting of teaching goals [3, 9]. More importantly, many studies mentioned that higher-order thinking is a kind of teaching method and strategy that can be trained [1, 9].

Yeung and Lam: argued that the instructors' innovation and understanding of the curriculum was often the key factor for success [10]. Therefore, this study expects that the use of higher-order thinking in teaching and learning can show different looks and innovations, so that instructors and learners can improve the quality and purpose of teaching through the importation of higher-order thinking.

2 Discussion on Higher-Order Thinking

2.1 The Implications and Characteristics of Higher-Order Thinking

Before talking about higher-order thinking, we should first define what is "Thinking". Thinking is a subjective cognition of human beings, and this cognition is to solve problems. However, the problem needs to be solved through learning, experience, and transformation into a meaningful process [11]. The reason why human beings are powerful is because they have the ability to think, but not necessarily we all know how to think, what to think and think correctly. The reason why people think is usually they want to correctly, effectively, and rationally solve the previous, present and future problems, so that thinking comes into being. However, thinking is indeed not an easy task, because the lack of information or incorrect information often affects the correctness and validity of thinking, leading to possible ineffective thinking. In other words, in the process of thinking, you must first acquire a considerable amount of knowledge and experience, and then convert it into the process that can solve the problem through the thinking process, which can be called thinking.

Higher-order thinking ability can be improved through systematic training, and it can significantly improve the ability to learn and solve problems [12]. Therefore, this study first took the six teaching objective indicators of Bloom, namely (1) knowledge, (2) comprehension, (3) application, (4) analysis, (5) synthesis, (6) evaluation as the principal, and then took the higher-order thinking characteristics of creative thinking, critical thinking and problem solving capabilities proposed by [13]. as the auxiliary to propose and revise it as "Teaching Objectives of 3P Thinking (3P: Problem found, Definition problem, Problem solving)".

The "Teaching Objectives of 3P Thinking" proposed in this study is mainly to re-simplify and classify the new three types of teaching indicators, namely (1) Problem found ((knowledge), (comprehension)); (2) Definition problem ((application), (analysis)); (3) Problem solving ((synthesis), (evaluation)) (Table 1).

Table 1. Teaching objectives of 3P thinking (Compiled and designed by this study)

Teaching objectives of 3P Thinking	Teaching objectives of Bloom	Teaching objectives of Chang, Li, Chen,& Chiu
Problem found	knowledge comprehension	creative thinking critical thinking Problem-solving bility
Definition problem	application analysis	
Problem solving	synthesis evaluation	

The comprehensive analysis of applying the "Teaching Objectives of 3P Thinking" proposed in this study in the teaching and learning of higher-order thinking is as follows:

2.2 Problem Found (Knowledge, Understanding/Creative Thinking)

As for how to achieve "Problem found", when instructors use the creative thinking of "Problem found", they should take the multiple intelligence as the main structure. As for designing the creative teaching with concrete feasibility, we should first change the habitual recognition that we are accustomed, because "habits affect the creative thinking". As long as you think it "as a matter of course", it produces habits, which seriously hinders the ability of "Problem found". When cognition changes habits, it naturally produces new thinking. When new thinking is created, it produces the angles, perspectives, and cognitions of treating things and extends different thinkings or ideas, which is a teaching method and strategy of "Problem found". If instructors can use this creative teaching method or strategy, they can effectively create new product inventions and explore humans' problem solving with originality and value to achieve the best problem-solving thinking.

2.3 Teaching of "Definition Problem" (Application, Analysis/Analytical Thinking)

Usually, most time is spent in "Problem found" and "Problem solving", and the importance of "Definition problem" is ignored. suggested that if unintended results occurred when problems were found or resolved, there was no clear and explicit definition on the problem [14]. As long as the problem is clearly defined, subsequent resolution of the problem will reduce a lot of unnecessary time and costs. As for "Definition problem", it requires to use the thinking ability. First of all, it is necessary to clearly and specifically define whether it solve the problem of "who", "what", "when", "where", or "which". This is a teaching method and strategy for defining problems.

2.4 Teaching of "Problem Solving" (Synthesis, Evaluation, Creation/Practical Thinking)

When "expectation - reality = gap", that is, there is a gap when expecting a possible phenomenon minus the various conditions and factors of reality. This "gap" is also a method or source waiting for us to solve the problem. How to conduct "Problem solving"? In the process of "Problem solving", what happens most often is that the idea produces various contradictions with actual practice. It may be technical problems and contradictions, production problems and contradictions, marketing problems and contradictions, business model problems and contradictions, cost problems and contradictions. indicated that education in this era should not only be content to train learners as the armchair critic, but should be the activists [15].

Only actual practice can find out what the real problem is. This is a teaching method and strategy for solving problems.

3 Conclusion and Suggestions

3.1 The Process and Influencing Factors of Higher-Order Thinking

In this study, it is found that the influencing factor in the process of higher-order thinking is that instructors and learners do not first define the thinking of the problem clearly. First: "Confirmation". That is, clearly "confirm" the problem first. This is the conflict on the "problem" between the instructor and the learner. Therefore, in order to solve this problem conflict for confirmation, instructors and learners should learn how to "ask questions"! It is even more necessary to "ask the right questions"! Asking questions: This study regards it as a basic capability that is currently lacking in education. As for asking questions, what is lacking for both instructors and learners is that they can not, does not want or dare to ask questions, so that instructors and learners may have a wrong cognition of the problem. Asking the right questions: This is "Problem found" in the "Teaching Methods of 3P Thinking" proposed by this study. When one cannot, does not want or dare to ask questions in response to problems, then it is relatively difficult to find out what the real problem is. Second: "Communication". This is "Definition problem" in the "Teaching Methods of 3P Thinking" proposed by this study. What instructors and learners still lack is how to clearly and definitely define problems. This requires effective communication. Conduct communication on the problems found and make clear definition before it can conduct the final "Problem solving". Third: "Implementation". This is "Problem solving" in the "Teaching Methods of 3P Thinking" proposed by this study. This study indicates that if the previous problem is not confirmed effectively and clearly, it may produce conflicts during conducting communication and definition of the problem. Finally, during the process of implementing "Problem solving", it may produce ineffective or worthless capabilities for "Problem solving". In sum, these are also influencing factors of the characteristic, process and improvement that the teaching and learning of higher-order thinking should have for this study.

3.2 When the Standard Answer Is Obtained, Higher-Order Thinking Is Stopped

According to Sternberg [16], IQ scores do not represent the level of intelligence. This study also suggests that "Having higher-order thinking does not necessarily require high intelligence", "having higher-order thinking does not necessarily require high academic qualifications" and "having higher-order thinking does not necessarily require much experience". Then extend "knowledge is power". Literally, knowledge is a kind of power, and there is no problem. However, if it is simply to acquire knowledge without using knowledge, it can not produce power. Therefore, according to the "Teaching Methods of 3P Thinking" proposed in this study, "Problem found", "Definition problem" and "Problem solving" should be the three steps that are required to cultivate higher-order thinking.

There are still many very traditional education and learning environments, in which the educator-oriented education is adopted, and this is a very serious and urgent problem requiring improvement [17]. Therefore, this study suggests that "School! It's a place to learn 'imitation'". Exams always test what teachers teach. However, think carefully, is this really the education we need? Especially after leaving school, the real problems encountered in daily life and work field, are usually not the content taught by teachers and textbooks. I often give the following example: "You can buy recipes for reference, but don't cook by indiscriminately imitating them." The vast majority of recipe content is to explain how much food material and how many kinds of seasonings need to be prepared. Recipes always explain what to do in the first step, what to do in the second step, and how long it takes for each step to cook, and finally delicious dishes as tasty as that in the recipe can be cooked. This study indicates that the focus of recipes is to explain the key of adding seasonings or the timing when cooking this dish to those who want to learn cooking, instead of just introducing the cooking steps. People who buy recipes to learn cooking are simply not familiar with the cooking approach and focus of this dish. If it only explains the process of cooking, this study argues that the value of such recipes is low. We can recall that famous chefs on TV added various kinds of seasonings during cooking in a timely manner according to their past experience and the actual amount of the dishes. Therefore, this study suggests that when the standard answer is obtained, the ability of higher-order thinking is stopped.

3.3 Self-examination of Higher-Order Thinking

Many people point out that the use of higher-order thinking in teaching and learning has a particularly significant and undeniable role in the learning motivation, learning effectiveness, learning ability, learning speed and achievement for learners [5]. In particular, teaching strategies of higher-order thinking always play an indispensable role in the significant learning effectiveness for learners [4]. Above all, the key is that instructors must develop more creative teaching methods and conduct continuous innovation in curriculum planning and design [18, 19]. Of course, in the process of implementing the teaching and learning of higher-order thinking, the most important thing is whether the instructors themselves have appropriate teaching concepts and whether they fully understand and agree with the curriculum reform [10]. In addition, instructors certainly play one of the most important roles in teaching and learning. In the main environment of education, the instructor is a promoter and even a master [6]. Teaching and learning can be effectively implemented only when instructors agree and understand the teaching philosophy and curriculum content. In contrast, in the learning process of higher-order thinking, learners need to use the guidance, demonstration, and presentation of the instructors, and then use the advanced thinking ability in innovation and criticism required for the higher level, and finally use the thinking of problem-solving ability to achieve the ultimate goal.

Finally, in the learning process of school education, results can only represent the achievement in the process of school learning. Only the results obtained outside the school are the real achievement.

References

1. Jónsdóttir, S.R.: Narratives of creativity: how eight teachers on four school levels integrate creativity into teaching and learning. Thinking Skills Creativity **24**, 127–139 (2017)
2. Brookhart, S.M.: How to Assess Higher-Order Thinking Skills in Your Classroom. ASCD, Alexandria (2010)
3. Saido, G.M., Siraj, S., Bin Nordin, A.B., Al_Amedy, O.S.: Higher order thinking skills among secondary school students in science learning. Malays. Online J. Educ. Sci. **3**(3), 13–20 (2015)
4. Heong, Y.M., Yunos, J.B., Hassan, R.B., Othman, W.B., Kiong, T.T.: The perception of the level of higher order thinking skills among technical educational students. In: 2011 International Conference on Social Science and Humanity IPEDR, vol. 5, pp. 281–285. IACSIT Press, Singapore (2011)
5. Lateef, A., Dahar, M.A., Latif, K.: Impact of higher order thinking skills of students on their academic performance. Pakistan association of anthropology, Islamabad. Pak. Sci. Int. (Lahore) **28**(Special Issue 2), 2013–2016 (2016)
6. Akshir Ab Kadir, M.: What teacher knowledge matters in effectively developing critical thinkers in the 21st Century curriculum? Thinking Skills Creativity **23**, 79–90 (2017)
7. Ramos, J.L., Dolipas, B.B., Villamor, B.: Higher order thinking skills and academic performance in physics of college students: a regression analysis. Int. J. Innovative Interdisc. Res. **4**, 48–60 (2013)
8. Nguyễn, T.M.T., Nguyễn, T.T.L.: Influence of explicit higher-order thinking skills instruction on students' learning of linguistics. Thinking Skills Creativity **26**, 113–127 (2017)
9. Yen, T.S., Halili, S.H.: Effective teaching of Higher-Order Thinking (HOT) in education. Online J. Distance Educ. e-Learn. **3**(2) (2015)
10. Yeung, S.Y.S., Lam, C.C.: Teachers' conception of curriculum integration: a problem hindering its implementation in Hong Kong. Educ. J. **35**(2), 1–36 (2007)
11. De Bono, E.: Lateral Thinking: Creativity Step by Step. Harper and Row, New York (1983)
12. De Bono, E.: Teach Your Child How to Think. Viking, London (1992)
13. Chang, Y.L., Li, B.D., Chen, H.C., Chiu, F.C.: Investigating the synergy of critical thinking and creative thinking in the course of integrated activity in Taiwan. Educ. Psychol. **35**(3), 341–360 (2015). https://doi.org/10.1080/01443410.2014.920079
14. Heong, Y.M., Yunos, J.B., Hassan, R.B., Othman, W.B., Kiong, T.T.: The perception of the level of higher order thinking skills among technical educational students. In: 2011 International Conference on Social Science and Humanity IPEDR, vols. 2, 5, pp. 281–285. IACSIT Press, Singapore (2011)
15. Hodson, D.: Time for action: science education for an alternative future. Int. J. Sci. Educ. **25**(6), 645–670 (2003)
16. Sternberg, R.J.: Beyond IQ: A Triarchic Theory of Intelligence. Cambridge University Press, Cambridge (1985)
17. Hoang, V.V.: Factors affecting the quality of English education at Vietnam National University, Hanoi. VNU J. Sci. **24**, 22–37 (2008)

18. Simplicio, S.C.: Teaching classroom educators how to be more effective and creative teachers. Education **120**(4), 675–680 (2000)
19. Lamas, E., Maria, A., Gomes, M.: Didactics–promoting collaborative work and personal learning environment: critical, creative and autonomous roles in a competitive society. Congrés International de Didàctiques **398**(2), 1–8 (2010)

An Adjustable Safety Device with Quick Return Structure for the Weightlifting Training

Keter Sheu[1] and Chun-chen Chen[2,3](✉)

[1] Department of Mechanical Engineering, National Cheng Kung University, No. 1, University Road, Tainan City 701, Taiwan
ketersheu@gmail.com

[2] Graduate School of Technological and Vocational Education, National Yunlin University of Science and Technology, Yunlin, Taiwan
chen0001@ms3.hinet.net

[3] Bachelor's Program in Software Engineering and Digital Innovation Applications, Fu Jen Catholic University, New Taipei, Taiwan

Abstract. According to statistics, most weightlifting training injuries occur in the training process, and the upper part of the body has most injuries, followed by the waist. For the injuries caused by weightlifting, light injuries harm muscles and joints, and severe injuries may result in permanent disability. The purpose of this study is to provide a protection measure for weightlifting exercise that allows the barbell to be lifted in the same way as the normal weightlifting process, when the force is provided by the user; but when the barbell is lowering, the support is provided from the mechanism of the product, so that the weightlifting unit hangs instead of falling to cause damage. The safety device of this study includes a one-way transmission unit, a winding transmission unit and a very light counterweight unit. When the barbell is lifted, the one-way transmission unit moves in the direction of the barbell without any resistance as the general freewheel. Now the main weight of the barbell is supported by the user, so the purpose of weightlifting training can be achieved. If the user stops the barbell lifting force, the one-way transmission unit generates a reversed supporting force, so that the barbell will not fall due to the user's stopping the force. This can ensure the user's safety during weightlifting training. This study adopts a mechanical structure with low cost, easy installation and a quick-return mechanism to complete the safety measures, which takes into account both the convenience and safety of the user.

Keywords: Weightlifting · Sports injuries · Safety structure · Training process

1 Introduction

Modern people are paying more and more attention to health and healthcare, and the sports atmosphere is also on the rise. Therefore, the establishment of gymnasiums is increasing too. Gymnasiums often have equipment for gravity training. Weight training is to train muscles and bones against gravity. The snatch action of weightlifting includes the process of pulling, lowering, shearing, and supporting shown in Fig. 1. Pulling: Pull the barbell up and keep it up until it is close to the body upright range [1].

T.-T. Wu et al. (Eds.): ICITL 2018, LNCS 11003, pp. 616–624, 2018.
https://doi.org/10.1007/978-3-319-99737-7_66

Lowering: Lower the center of body weight rapidly; Shearing: Put the center of body weight under the barbell in the process of lowering the center of body weight; Supporting: The center of body weight is lowering before the barbell has fallen.

Fig. 1. Weightlifting training

However, overloaded training methods of the weightlifters or their technical movements tend to cause sports injuries. According to statistics, most weightlifting injuries occur in the training process, and the upper part of the body has most injuries, followed by the waist. For the injuries caused by weightlifting, light injuries harm muscles and joints, and severe injuries may result in permanent disability [2] shown in Fig. 2.

Fig. 2. Weightlifting injury

The determination of weightlifting success and failure depends on whether the barbell is lifted and the arm is straightened (barbell rising phase). However, the weightlifting injury mainly occurs when the weight cannot be loaded (when the barbell falls unexpectedly). However, when performing weight training (e.g. weightlifting), the user often exerts excessive force, or cannot continue to exert force due to various factors after lifting. Then, the lifted barbell will quickly fall, resulting in the injuries in the user's muscles or bones. This is even worse for beginners for gravity training. There are many cases where users suffer severe injuries in the hands or the waist, and there are even cases where the injury cannot be recovered. Thus, weightlifting has concerns in its operational safety.

There is a study of "Programmable Controlled Group Force Device and Method Applied to Fitness Equipment" [3]. which uses a configuration of controlling the resistance unit to generate resistance to reduce the counterweight, and detects the strength of the cable to prevent barbell stall or other abnormal situation to ensure the safety of use. However, the structure of the device is only applicable to such equipment as the weight bench or the weightlifting chair, and the mechanism is driven by electricity and controlled by a program. Although it provides safety during gravity training, the cost of the device is high. If the power is turned off due to unpredictable factors, if the program operation is erroneous or the unit is shaken and the program is shut down, the safety device will be invalidated. And there are no other safety measures to prevent the power supply and the program from shutting down. This will cause the barbell to fall down quickly. Furthermore, the force measuring unit of the load cell that detects if the rope of the hanging barbell is stalled or abnormal needs the reaction distance and reaction time, otherwise it may cause misjudgment and cause the motor to pull the rope, which will greatly change the weight of the barbell, so that the benefit of weightlifting is not achieved. And if the reaction distance and reaction time are too long, the safety of the user cannot be ensured. If the user cannot immediately support the barbell at this time, the harm caused to the user will be unthinkable.

Another study is "A Sports Method and Module Unit for Elastoquake Motion with An Oscillating Amplitude" [4]. which is the combination of a transmission rope set on the motion unit connected to a shock-absorbing elastic-vibration motion module to allow the user to receive the vibration load from the elasto-kinetic movement module to provide the exercise for the trainer, and to adjust the elasto-shock motion and vibration amplitude for the trainer according to the physical condition during the exercise and the training arrangement. Although it adjusts the elasto-shock motion and vibration amplitude based on the state of the user, it is mainly a mechanism used to enhance the user's training, and there is not any relevant safety device or safety measure.

The "Light Weight Lifter" study [5]. includes a rubber base disc, a first counterweight disc, a second counterweight disc, and a wear-resistant collar. The rubber base disc is provided with a perforation for the first, the second counterweight discs to be respectively arranged on both sides of the rubber base disc. The first and the second counterweight discs are both provided with corresponding through holes and reinforced ribs. The anti-wear rub ring sets are arranged in the through holes, wherein the rubber base disc provides a sufficient diameter size, and the ribs of the first and second counterweight discs can increase the strength of the weightlifting disc. Because the diameter of the weightlifting disc is large enough to lift the height of the crossbar of the barbell off the ground, the chance of lumbar sports injury is reduced during the clean and jerk. However, this structure can reduce the lumbar sports injury, but this will change the structure of the original barbell. After the user lifts the barbell, if he or she cannot support or continue to exert force due to various factors, the barbell will still fall quickly. The safety issue cannot be addressed by this structure.

Another study provides a safety device for weightlifting [6], as shown in Fig. 3, which includes a frame body with a one-way transmission limiting unit and a free wheel set, and the free wheel set passes through a transmission shaft, and the transmission shaft is power-coupled to the one-way transmission limiting unit, so that the transmission

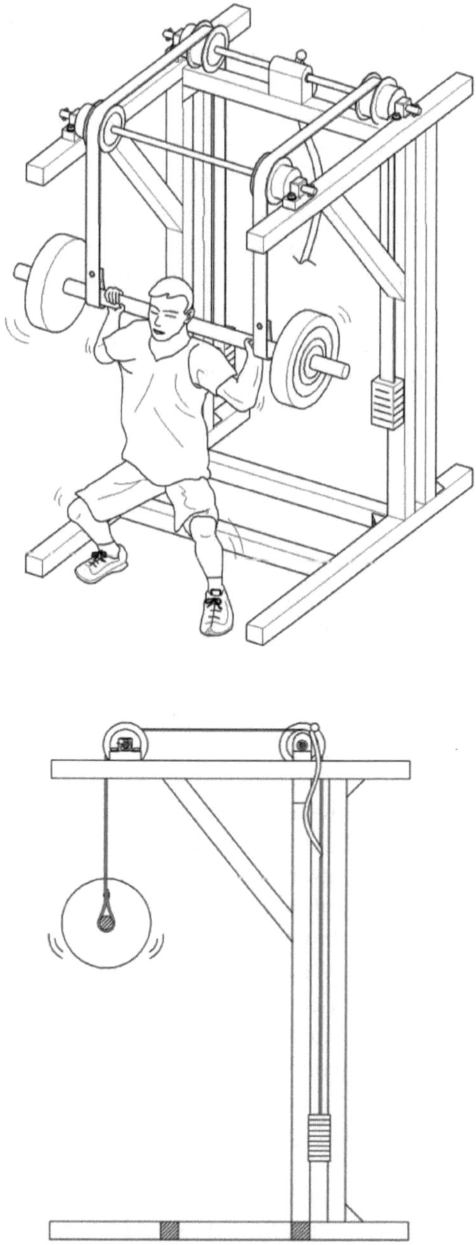

Fig. 3. Weight training protection mechanism

shaft is affected by a one-way transmission limiting unit to act. The one-way transmission limiting unit is provided with a clutch switching unit, so that the user can pull to switch the one-way transmission limiting unit to a one-way transmission mode or damping mode. In the one-way transmission mode, when the weightlifting unit is lifted by force, it is subject to a one-way transmission mechanism and is suspended without falling; in the damping mode, the weightlifting unit is slowed down due to the damping effect. However, a clutch switching unit needs to be added to switch the one-way transmission limiting unit from the one-way transmission mode to the damping mode, and this makes the operation inconvenient.

In addition, there are commercially available products such as the Smith Machine [8], which is a large-scale equipment necessary for the gym. It has a high and low security liner lock design (as shown in Fig. 3(a)) that allows users to do exercise within a safe range. This is because that the barbell can only slide up and down along both sides of the track without shaking back and forth. Once one's own tolerant weight is exceeded, the machine will generate a protection unit by rotating the barbell to catch the liner lock (as shown in Fig. 3(b). The precondition of using this machine is that you must set a proper height in advance by yourself, so that it will not hurt you. It is suitable for beginners. However, such a mechanism is a passive adjustment device and cannot produce active protection.

The purpose of this study is to solve the problem that conventional weightlifting devices are prone to causing serious sports injuries, and that their installation costs are high and they need to consume electricity. In addition, they rely solely on programs and power control without additional safety measures. If the program goes wrong or stops, or the power supply stops due to unforeseen factors, and the user fails to immediately support the barbell, the damage caused to the user will be unthinkable.

2 System Architecture

The purpose of this study is to provide a protection measure for weightlifting training that allows the barbell to be lifted in the same way as the normal weightlifting process, when the force is provided by the user, but the lowering of the barbell is supported by the mechanism of the product, so that the weightlifting unit hangs without falling to cause damage. Its architecture is shown in Fig. 4.

The safety device of this study includes a one-way transmission unit, a winding transmission unit, and a very light counterweight unit. When the barbell is lifted, the one-way transmission unit moves in the direction of the barbell without resistance as the general freewheel. Now, the main weight of the barbell is supported by the user, so the purpose of weightlifting training can be achieved. If the user stops the barbell lifting force, the one-way transmission unit generates a reversed supporting force, so that the barbell will not fall due to the user's stopping the force. This can ensure the user's safety during weightlifting training. This product uses a mechanical structure of low cost and easy installation to complete the safety measures, and has a fast-back type mechanism that can take into account both convenience and safety when it is operated by the user.

Fig. 4. Smith machine

Fig. 5. Adjustable safety device for weightlifting training

3 System Design

In order to achieve the above objectives, this study provides an adjustable safety structure for weightlifting training, as shown in Fig. 6. Where A is the body of the mechanism, B is the ratchet wheel positioning unit, C is the ratchet wheel, D is the one-way bearing, E is the C-line buckle ring, and F is the axis center. It contains a frame body, equipped with a ratchet unit that can adjust its resistance, and a winding transmission unit, which is in power connection with the ratchet wheel unit. One end of the winding transmission unit is connected to a weightlifting training unit for the user to perform weightlifting training, and the other end is connected to at least one counterweight. The weight of such counterweight is greater than the tension required to straighten the winding transmission unit, and the total weight of the weightlifting training unit is less than the resistance of the ratchet wheel set. Therefore, the weightlifting training unit is not affected by the resistance of the ratchet wheel set when it is lifted by force. When the upward force is no longer applied, the weightlifting training unit will not fall due to gravity. If the downward force is applied to the weightlifting training unit, so that the total weight of the gravity of the weightlifting training unit and the applied force is greater than the resistance of the ratchet wheel set, the weightlifting training unit will be forced to land.

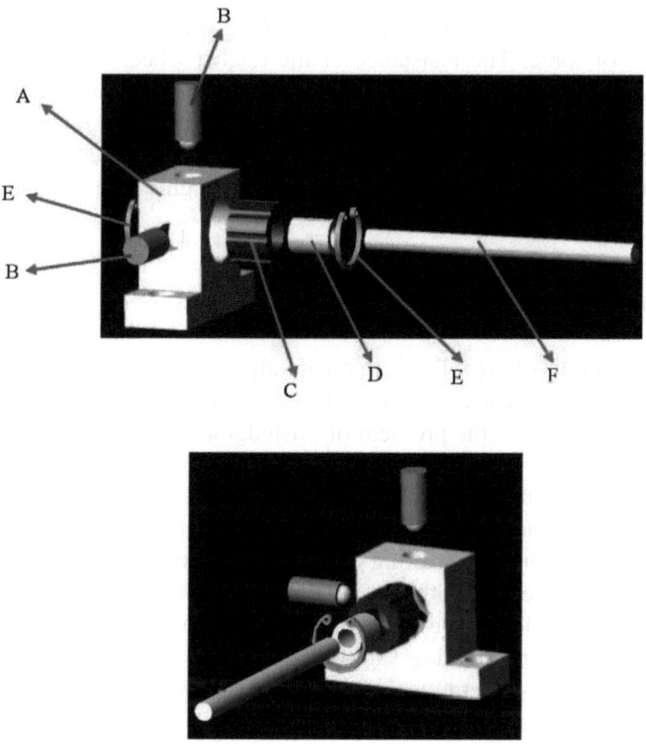

Fig. 6. Adjustable safety device for weightlifting training

According to the adjustable safety structure for weightlifting training described above, the ratchet wheel unit has a one-way transmission unit and a ratchet wheel set connected to the one-way transmission unit, and there is power connection between the winding transmission unit and the one-way transmission unit.

4 Experiments

The experimental photograph of this study is shown in Fig. 5. In this study, the one-way transmission unit and the ratchet wheel set are arranged coaxially, and the weight lifting training unit includes the one-way transmission unit connected to the direction of the winding transmission unit, and the other end of the winding transmission unit is equipped with counterweight. Therefore, when the user lifts the weightlifting training unit, the winding transmission unit is pulled by the counterweight that overcomes only the required tension of the winding transmission unit, and the action of lifting the weight-lifting training unit is mainly provided by the user. When the user cannot continue to apply upward force, the weightlifting training unit is suspended without falling. When the weightlifting training unit is to be reset, the weightlifting training unit only needs to be forced downwards for the resistance of the ratchet wheel set to reduce the gravity of the weight lifting training unit, so that the weightlifting training unit can be allowed to land at a slow speed, and the position of its landing can be adjusted according to the user's exertion of force. The resistance of the ratchet wheel set can be changed by adjusting the degree of tightening of the locking element, and the counterweight only needs to overcome the tension required for the winding transmission unit to straighten. For users, the weight change due to the change in the counterweight is very small for this weightlifting training unit, so it is suitable for the weightlifting training for beginners or players.

5 Conclusion

This study uses a ratchet wheel unit that can adjust its resistance to complete safety measures. It can automatically generate safety protection characteristics when the user operates. This study solves the problem of misjudgment or damage caused by the use of power and program control. The invention has a simple structure, it neither needs to consume any power or install electric equipment, nor has power control and other problems, which greatly reduces the cost, and can also more effectively achieve convenience and safety for the user in weightlifting training. The ratchet wheel unit has a one-way bearing and a ratchet wheel set with a pressure spring. Compared with the Smith machine that must rotate the cartridge to produce a protective action, it is more cost-effective than the previous weightlifting training safety device. It is easy to install and have such advantages of facilitating operational convenience and safety at the same time.

References

1. Wang, S.C.: Weight Lifting and Body Building. Sports Physiology Weekly (58) (2000)
2. Horrible Injuries on Weight Lifting Fields: Famous Italian Weight Lifter with Spine Severely Broken in Competition (Photos). http://blog.sina.com.cn/s/blog_4db6d74d0100fu6y.html
3. Chen, Y.J., Huang, C.H., Shih, C.W.: Programmable control force device and method used for fitness equipment. ROC Patent No. I268789 (2006)
4. Wang, S.C., Shih, C.H.: A Sports method and module unit for elastoquake motion with an oscillating amplitude. ROC Patent No. I330093 (2007)
5. Lin, C.Y., Uesaka, T.: Light weightlifting sheet. ROC Patent No. M345615 (2008)
6. Hsu, H.Y., Hsu, H.H., Lin, Y.D., Lin, S.H., Liu, C.C.: Safety device for gravity training. ROC Patent No. I330093 (2014)
7. Hsu, H.Y.: Adjustable weight lifting training safety structure. ROC Patent No. I439305 (2014)
8. Smith Machine. https://tw.matrixfitness.com/strength/plate-loaded/mg-pl62-smith-machine

An Innovative Trend of Sport Event in Environmental Perspective

Chun-Chu Yeh[1(✉)] and Chin-Huang Huang[2]

[1] Department of Tourism and Hospitality, TransWorld University, Yunlin, Taiwan
joyceyehh@gmail.com

[2] Graduate School of Technological and Vocational Education, National Yunlin University of Science and Technology, Yunlin, Taiwan
hch55@ntupes.edu.tw

Abstract. Hosting mega sport events will build of the events venues and infrastructure, and the operation of the events involve huge environmental resources, activities, and construction projects that might negatively affect cities' natural environment. Since Olympic Games would damage to the natural environment of host city. In order to protect the natural environment and mitigate the disturbance at host city, International Olympic Committee (IOC) introduced environment into the Olympic Games as the third pillar associated with sport and culture since 1996. The environment has become an important factor for hosting Olympic Games. Both host and non-host residents felt that environmental legacies were the most important aspect, as it was highly relevant to their quality of life. Mega sports events also potentially impact on local ecosystems. But the environmental impacts of sport events are difficult to assess quantitatively. This study introduces environmental concept into sports event to resolve the problem of estimation and help to offer benefit/cost analysis information sufficiently. The aim of this research is to discuss the evolution of sports event and environment. This research is also to construct a feasibility analysis method on the evaluation of sports event based on environment estimation methods.

Keywords: Sports event · Evolution · Environment · Sustainable development

1 Introduction

Olympic Games are the largest sports games in the world, with substantial economic, environmental, social, cultural, and political impacts for the host country, region, and city [1, 2]. The sports equipments also have a significant negative impact on the environment [3]. However, the environmental harm might caused by the exercise of outdoor sport activities [4]. Hosting mega sport events might negatively affect cities' natural environment because the built of the events venues and infrastructure and the operation of the events involve huge environmental resources, activities, and construction projects, even impact upon local ecosystem [5]. In order to reduce potential conflicts between the Games and the natural environment, International Olympic Committee (IOC) had added

T.-T. Wu et al. (Eds.): ICITL 2018, LNCS 11003, pp. 625–630, 2018.
https://doi.org/10.1007/978-3-319-99737-7_67

the environment component into the Olympic movement as the third pillar associated with sport and culture since 1996 [6].

Mitigating negative environmental impacts has become a major theme to mega events. The Torino Winter Games in 2006 included measures to reduce greenhouse gas emission, minimize water use in snow making, promote eco-friendly hotels, and with plans to offset carbon emissions. In 2006, FIFA's Green Goal program also aimed to make the World Cup the most environmentally friendly ever, working to reduce resource use and with plans to offset the 100,000 tonnes of carbon emissions [7]. The 2008 Beijing Summer Games had implemented a Green Olympics, and to promote environmental awareness for a zero net emissions games. For 2012 London Summer Games focused on a Sustainable Development Strategy to mitigate carbon emissions, waste and water use, and to use transport and material with environmental friendly [8]. In 2016 Rio Summer Games paid attention to environmental sustainability in planet save. The evolution of mega sports events promote from competition to environment preservation and sustainability development. However, the environment impacts of sports events are difficult to evaluate quantitatively [9]. This study tries to introduce the concept of environment economics research method to assess the contribution effects of sports events.

2 Sports Event and Environment

The IOC had stressed the importance of environmental considerations for planning and staging of Summer and Winter Games increasingly. Hosting mega sports event increased both the social and the environmental domains of quality of life. At low levels of perceived atmosphere, such as negative effects on environment damaged, decreased the hosting in psychological domain of quality of life [10]. Even the non-hosting residents identified that Olympic Games impacted the community included positive and negative on social and environment strongly [11]. During the 2008 Beijing Olympic Games, several meetings were hosted with environmental NGOs to discuss the implementation of a Green Olympics. The Beijing Municipality used the Olympics a vehicle to promote environmental awareness among citizens. Jin, Zhang, Ma, and Connaughton (2011) examined residents' perceived environmental impact of the Beijing Olympic Games, and found that the Games could positively enhance the environmental protection, which confirmed and supported the idea of the IOC [12]. Karadakis and Kaplanidou (2012) discovered that both host and non-host residents felt that environment legacies were the most important aspect, as it was highly relevant to their quality of life at pre, during and post stage [13]. The result was consistent with the findings of Andereck, Valentine, Vogt, and Knopf (2007), that the environmental category was the highest mean score in the importance for quality of life [14].

Quantifying the environmental impacts of mega sport events is important to sustainable development difficult to evaluate quantitatively for host city [9]. Next section will introduce the environmental economics methods to value the effect of environment in mega sports events.

3 Environmental Economics Method

The concept of environment preservation caused by the Exxon Valdez oil spill to injury the natural resources. Since the tanker Exxon Valdez ran aground and ruptured on Bligh Reef in Alaska's Prince William Sound. Nature resources injury would give rise to lose passive use values and the environment economists began to evaluate the non-use value [15]. Randall and Stoll (1983) established total economic value (TEV) framework for estimating environmental resources value [16]. TEV includes use value and nonuse value, and is the most popular model for estimating environmental resources. Olympic Games generate tangible and intangible impacted effects [17–19]. Walton, Longo, and Dawson (2008) estimated the residents' willingness to pay of intangible values for hosting 2102 Olympic Games [20]. Owen (2006), Barget and Gouguet (2007), and Yeh, Lin and Huang (2018) used the framework of TEV to estimate the economics value of sports event [21–23].

The TEV aggregates the main function-based economic values by a given ecosystem, which taking into account not only goods and services with market price but also those non price and market goods. The use value allows the best possible observation to be identified on the basis of consumer behavior with market price, which usually adopts travel cost method (TCM). While the non-use value cannot be estimated by market price directly, contingent valuation method (CVM) is always used to give nature an economic value by asking individuals to place explicit monetary values upon environmental goods [24].

However, the evolution of evaluating for nature resources is now established the economics of ecosystem and biodiversity (TEEB), that ideas developed in the Millennium Ecosystem Assessment (2005) and the first phase has demonstrated the significance of ecosystems and biodiversity and the threats to human welfare if no action is taken to reverse current damage and losses. The ecosystem services can be classified into provisioning services, regulating services, cultural services, and supporting services. Final ecosystem services are components of nature, directly enjoyed, consumed, or used to yield human well-being [25].

From the changes of hosting mega sports events, the ecosystem functions are impacted through the ecosystem services both positive and negative effects, and the final will bring the human well-being to people (see Fig. 1). That depends on our people need pay much attention to protect the environmental resources for sustainable development.

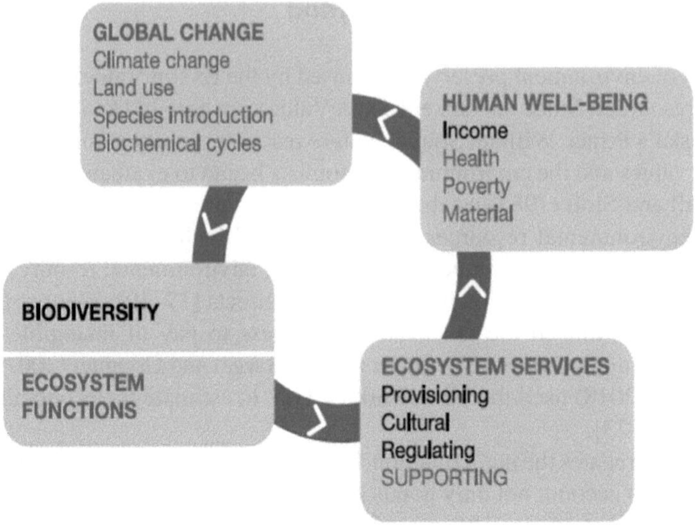

Fig. 1. Conceptual framework for biodiversity and global change effects on welfare under the ecosystem services approach. *Source*: adapted from MA 2005 (by *Simboloxico*)

4 Conclusion

Mega sports events influenced the host city, including tangible and intangible impacts on social, economic, political and cultural development, and environment, which contains both positive and negative impacted for community. The significant negative impacts on environment were found by IOC. In order to emphasis on sustainability development, IOC added the environment component as the third pillar in Olympic movement. The sports events the characteristics of public goods and include use and nonuse value, which cannot evaluate in market price. This study introduces the environmental economics methods to resolve the estimation problem, include all nonmarket impacts. The use value can be valued by TCM, while the non-use value cannot be performed by CVM. For the full information of costs and benefits for host cities, TEV model would results the precision decision making for sports organization. Furthermore, TEEB model will demonstrate the ecosystem functions of sports events clearly. Future research may try to adopt the concept of TEEB and non-market methods to analyze the cost and benefit of mega sports events.

References

1. Toohey, K., Veal, A.J.: The Olympic Games: A Social Science Perspective. Wallingford, Oxfordshire (2000)
2. Geeracrt, A.: It's not that easy BeingGreen: the environmental dimension of the European Union's sports policy. J. Sport Soc. Issues **40**(1), 62–81 (2016)

3. Subic, A., Mouritz, A., Troynikov, O.: Sustainable design and environmental impact of materials in sports products. Sports Technol. **2**, 67–79 (2009)
4. Wheeler, K., Nauright, J.: A global perspective on the environmental impact of golf. Sport Soc. **9**, 427–443 (2006)
5. Cantelon, H., Letters, M.: The making of the IOC environmental policy as the third dimension of the olympic movement. Int. Rev. Sociol. Sport **35**, 294–308 (2000)
6. Beyer, S.: The green olympic movement: Beijing 2008. Chin. J. Int. Law **5**(2), 423–440 (2006)
7. Stahl, H., Hochfield, C., Schmied, M.: FIFA Green Goal Legacy Report. Organizing Committee of the 2006 FIFA World Cup, Frankfurt (2006)
8. Weaver, M.: London 2012 Organizers Plan Greenest Games Ever. Guardian (2007)
9. Collins, A., Jones, C., Munday, M.: Assessing the environmental impacts of mega sporting events: two options? Tour. Manag. **30**, 828–837 (2009)
10. Pfitzner, R., Koenigstorfer, J.: Quality of life of residents living in a city hosting mega-sport events: a longitudinal study. BMC Public Health **16**, 1102 (2016). PubMed https://doi.org/10.1186/s12889-016-3777-3
11. Ritchie, B.W., Shipway, R., Cleeve, B.: Resident perceptions of mega-sporting events: a non-host city perspective of the 2012 London Olympic Games. J. Sport Tourism **14**(2/3), 143–167 (2009)
12. Jin, L., Zhang, J.J., Ma, X., Connaughton, D.P.: Residents' perceptions of environmental impacts of the 2008 Beijing Green Olympic Games. Eur. Sport Manag. Q. **11**(3), 275–300 (2011)
13. Karadakis, K., Kaplanidou, K.: Legacy perceptions among host and non-host Olympic Games residents: a longitudinal study of the 2010 Vancouver Olympic Games. Eur. Sport Manag. Q. **12**(3), 243–264 (2012)
14. Andereck, K.L., Valentine, K., Vogt, C., Knopf, R.: A cross-cultural analysis of tourism and quality of life perceptions. J. Sustain. Tourism **15**(5), 483–500 (2007)
15. Larson, D.M.: Can nonuse value be measured from observable behavior? Am. J. Agr. Econ. **74**(5), 1114–1120 (1992)
16. Rahdall, A., Stoll, J.: Existence value in a total valuation framework. In: Rowe, R., Chestnut, L. (eds.) Managing Air quality and Science Resources at National Parks and Wilderness Areas. Westview Press, Boulder (1983)
17. Preuss, H.: The conceptualization and measurement of mega sport event legacies. J. Sport Tourism **12**(3–4), 207–227 (2007)
18. Wicker, P., Hallmann, K., Breuer, C., Feiler, S.: The value of olympic success and the intangible effects of sport events-A contingent valuation approach in Germany. Eur. Sport Manag. Q. **12**(4), 337–355 (2012)
19. Wicker, P., Whitehead, J.C., Mason, D.S., Johnson, B.K.: Public support for hosting the olympic summer games in Germany: the CVM approach. Urban Stud. **54**(15), 3597–3614 (2017)
20. Walton, H., Longo, A., Dawson, P.: A contingent valuation of the 2012 London Olympic Games-A regional perspective. J. Sports Econ. **9**(3), 304–317 (2008)
21. Owen, J.G.: The intangible benefits of sports teams. Public Finan. Manag. **3**(6), 321–345 (2006)
22. Barget, E., Gouguet, J.J.: The total economic value of sporting events: theory and practice. J. Sport Econ. **8**(2), 165–182 (2007)
23. Yeh, C.C., Lin, C.S., Huang, C.H.: The total economic value of sport tourism in Belt and road development—an environmental perspective. Sustainability **10**(4), 1191 (2018). https://doi.org/10.3390/su10041191

24. Jones-Walters, L., Mulder, I.: Valuing nature: the economics of biodiversity. J. Nat. Conserv. **17**, 245–247 (2009)
25. MA-Millennium Ecosystem Assessment Ecosystems and Human Well-Being: Biodiversity Synthesis. World Resources Institute, Washington, DC (2005)

Concept Development of Personified Digital Prosthesis Teaching Model–Fused Application of Acupoint-Located Method by Anatomical Landmark and 3D Composition Method

Tzu-ching Weng[1,2(✉)] and Nyan-myau Lyau[2]

[1] Department of Beauty and Health Care, Min-Hwei College of Health Care Management, Tainan, Taiwan
A310@o365.mhchcm.edu.tw
[2] Graduate School of Technological and Vocational Education, National Yunlin University of Science and Technology, Yunlin, Taiwan
lyaunm@gemail.yuntech.edu.tw

Abstract. This paper aims to improve the plane meridian and acupoint figure omissions and gaps, and combines the acupoint-located method by anatomical landmark of traditional Chinese medicine with innovative 3D composition method to complete a highly personified digital prosthesis teaching model. This system is fabricated by using four techniques of computer drawing software Maya, such as modeling, material and texturing, lighting and render, it will contribute to the accuracy of acupoint location, and it can convey important academic and theoretical basis of acupoint, so as to clarify the interlaced and complicated human channel trends and acupoint locations, reducing the learning-use fall, and enhancing the efficiency and quality of teaching and learning.

Keywords: Maya · Acupoint location · Skull
Acupoint-located method by anatomical landmark

1 Introduction

Chinese medicine is the criteria of Chinese health preservation and care. Chinese medicine started from the earliest medical classic HuangdiNeijing of the Chinese nation. HuangdiNeijing is the first book recording the concept of meridian. Each acupoint in meridian has its own duty and location. The main physiological function of acupoints is to associate body surface and in vivo viscera, it is a preventive medicine of "prevention before disease", so it is learned and studied extensively [9, 12, 13]. The acupoint finger pressing is a noninvasive self-health care method. The common people can massage themselves for health care with hands and tools anywhere and anytime. Domestic medical health care related divisions have opened related courses. The key points of the courses include looking for the acupoint location, understanding the main function of acupoint and implementation method.

The present meridian and acupoint teaching materials are mainly textbooks, while print illustration and 3D meridian bronze figures are used as auxiliary teaching aids. The

T.-T. Wu et al. (Eds.): ICITL 2018, LNCS 11003, pp. 631–639, 2018.
https://doi.org/10.1007/978-3-319-99737-7_68

2D figures of human meridians and acupoints in the textbooks are generally hand drawn illustrations, which are usually inconsistent with the exact locations of human acupoints, so that the meridian and acupoint figures are for reference only, difficult for the students to learn intuitively. Therefore, the students can find out the correct acupoint locations by implementation with the teacher's explanation, the learning process takes some time, and then the students can find the essentials of point finding.

For the best curative effect of acupoint acupuncture and massage, the accuracy of acupoint location is crucial. It is known that the acupoint location shall be accurate. First of all, the reference object shall be calibrated. The Acupoint Names and Location published in Chinese Mainland in 2006 contain male and female acupuncture point wall charts. The wall charts indicate the locations of various acupoints. However, most of acupoints are located in bone gaps or pits, and generally in both ends and the center of bone gaps. The location of acupoint shall be confirmed according to the acupoint-located method by anatomical landmark. Therefore, the wall charts of Acupoint Names and Location are only illustrative, still lacking the trueness of human 3D space.

This paper aims to start the development research from the beginning, taking the head as subject, the 3D digital software Maya is combined with the acupoint-located method by anatomical landmark of Chinese medicine to overlay the head and skeletal system to complete a 3D highly personified acupoint-located body surface digital scale model, to remedy the deficiencies in current 2D meridian and acupoint figures, so that the students are easy to master the 3D space and skeletal system of human body, as well as to know the acupoint locations, reducing the fall of visual presence, enhancing the learning effect, and making the learning more lively and interesting.

2 Literature Review

2.1 Skeletal System

The anatomy involves the skeletal system. A normal adult has 206 pieces of bones. The human body is divided into 26 regions which are removable. The smallest bone of human body is located in the ear, and the biggest bone is the femur composing the thigh bone. The skull is divided into two kinds, which are the 8 pieces of cranial bone wrapping the head, and the 14 pieces of facial bone composing the face. The 8 cranial bones are the paired parietal bones and temporal bones and unpaired frontal bone, ethmoid bone, sphenoidal lane and occipital bone. In addition, the skull comprises other accessory bones, including the three small phonophores in middle ear and the hyoid of neck. The total number of human head bones and accessory bones is 29 [8], as shown in Fig. 1.

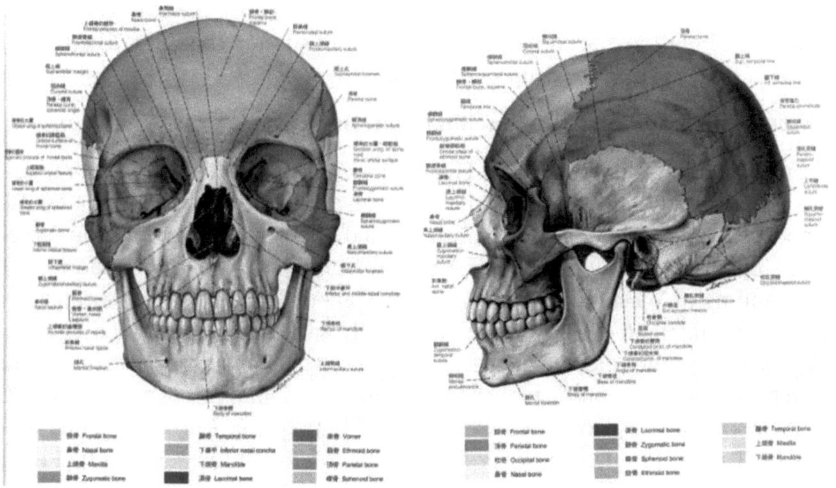

Fig. 1. Front and side views of skull

2.2 Meridians and Acupoints

(1) Head channels and acupoints

The head is the most important part of human body. The meridians throughout human body have 12 regular channels, 6 regular channels and the Ren and Du Channels flow into the head. The six regular channels are the Large Intestine Channel of Hand-Yangming, the Stomach Channel of Foot-Yangming, the Small Intestine Channel of Hand-Taiyang, the Bladder Channel of Foot-Taiyang, the Sanjiao Channel of Hand-Shaoyang and the Gall Bladder Channel of Foot-Shaoyang. There are 49 head acupoints on one side, and 98 on two sides. There are 15 the Ren and Du Channels acupoints. In addition, there are 3 extra-ordinary points on one side of head, and 6 acupoints on two sides, the head has 119 acupoints [5–7].

(2) Acupoint localization method

The locations of meridians and acupoints are mostly correlated with the texture of muscles and joint gaps, it is difficult to let the students understand the acupoint locations without the guidance of anatomy. The human body has 14 regular channels, 361 acupoints and more than 400 extrachannel points, about 4/5 of points can be located according to anatomical landmark directly [8].

On the human body surface, some portions of bones or muscles often form prominences or pits, which can be seen or felt, called landmark of body surface. The internal intramuscular bones can be seen through the landmark of body surface, providing the anatomy with visual and tactual comprehensions of spatial relation. The landmark of body surface contains fixed landmark and moving landmark, using the hand of the body to measure and conjecture the phenomena under the points. The clinical point seeking methods include bone proportional Cun, rough measurement by fingers and proportional unit of the body [7]. Among the human anatomical landmarks, the osseous landmark of body surface is the most accurate, the most significant and the most likely mastered landmark of body surface for acupoint location [9].

(3) **Discussion about acupoint teaching materials**

The meridians and acupoints from HuangdiNeijing have been existing for thousands of years. With the evolution of times, the meridian and acupoint teaching materials have been modified, but the content is still abstract, and the words are ancient and difficult to read, the students generally think the learning difficulty is high [10]. The Meridian Point Painted Dummy of Western Han unearthed in Tianhui Town, Jinniu District, Chengdu City, Chinese Mainland in 2012 is the historically earliest acupoint teaching model so far [11]. At the teaching site, the most frequently used teaching materials are the national standard Meridian Locations established by Chinese Mainland [12] and the New Color Graph Acupuncturology compiled by Professor Jaung-geng Lin from China Medical University, Taiwan [5]. The major problem in the Meridian Locations is that the illustrations don't correspond to the words, the anatomical landmarks involved in standard textural acupoint location are not displayed in the pictures, and there is no stereo display of superposed location among different layers, it is difficult for the students to correspond such illustrations to relative locations of 3D human acupoints. Huang (2007) indicated that the drawer himself may not know if the acupoint locations indicated in the meridian and acupoint figures are correct or not, because there is no landmark of body surface for reference [9]. On the other hand, there was no support from surface anatomy at that time, and there was no powerful drawing function of computer software, as shown in Fig. 2. The New Color Graph Acupuncturology has fluent text and luxurious 2D acupoint illustrations, and uses skeletal system as the reference indicator of acupoint location, so that the students are easy to understand the acupoint location from the text and icons, but the defect is no spatial presentation, as shown in Fig. 3.

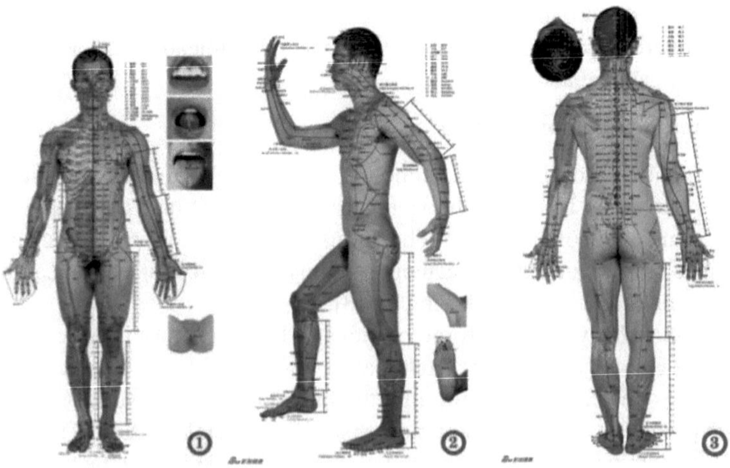

Fig. 2. CNS meridian locations on male meridian and acupoint figures

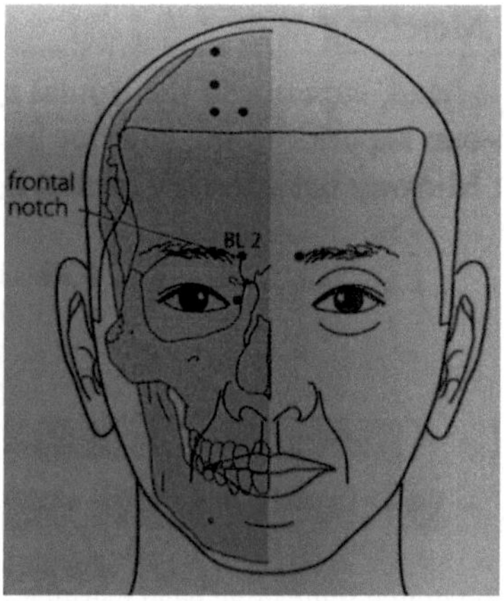

Fig. 3. Schematic diagram of New Color Graph Acupuncturology tsanchu point

2.3 Application of 3D Software

The 3D teaching has been used universally. Chou (2017) studied teaching and found that the remedial teaching strategy of 3D video and interactive response system can upgrade the students' achievements [13], because the 3D videos can attract the students' attention, contributing to learning. Oropeza, Sanchez and Villagomez (2015) found that the 3D videos in college orthodontics course have better effectiveness of instruction than the traditional method using slide projection [14]. Ferdig, Blan, Kratcoski and Clements used 3D teaching material in the senior high school biology to teach DNA structure. The results showed that the achievements of the students using 3D video learning were apparently better than that of the students who did not use 3D videos. The authors tried to use Maya software to develop the first generation 3D digital interactive head meridian learning system [7]. (Figures 4 and 5), which was imported into teaching and well accepted by the students.

Fig. 4. Front side of 3D digital interactive head meridian learning system

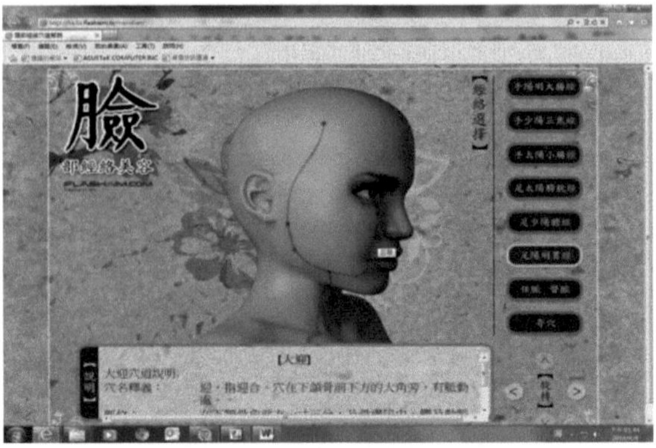

Fig. 5. Side of 3D digital interactive head meridian learning system

There are many kinds of 3D software, the Maya software is written by Alias Maya, it is an advanced and complex 3D calculator 3D animation software, used in digital effect creation of commercial design, industrial design, architectural design, artistic creation, on-line game, visual effects, 3D virtualization, TV production and movie effects. The special effects of the famous Star Wars series were produced by using Maya, and Spider-Man, Ice Age, Ice Age 2, The Lord of the Rings, Jurassic Park, Finding Nemo, Harry Potter, Monsters vs. Aliens, Avatar, and a lot of cinematographic works including Initial D [15].

Therefore, the meridian teaching must start from the structure of human meridians and acupoints, muscle texture and joint gaps. General graphs are two-dimensional plane, for illustration only, lacking three-dimensional curved surface and guidance of organizational interface for instructional practicability. This study will combine the quantifiable digital drawing technique with acupoint-located method by anatomical landmark of Chinese medicine to solve the problems in current acupoint teaching.

2.4 Summary

The acupoints are special positions where the qi and blood go in and out of human viscera meridians, as well as the disease response points and treatment stimulation points [16]. The accuracy of acupoint location influences the curative effect of subsequent acupuncture and massage. The researchers always try to integrate the experimental knowledge and theory of anatomy into the treatment manipulation of traditional Chinese medicine gradually, and use complementary form to promote the coevolution of the two sciences, and to perform the maximum effect of their combination.

In the view of the point 3D construction theory of traditional Chinese medicine, the anatomical structure of points is formed of multiple known normal tissues, such as skin, muscles, tendons, fasciae, nerves, blood vessels and lymphs, distributed in 3D space structure regularly to some extent. In traditional Chinese medicine and modern medicine, the acupoint location and morphological structure are described by using lots of words and hand drawn illustrations, structural diagrams of shot and scanned points. These methods only display the 2D anatomical structure of acupoints.

With the development of digital information technology, if the 3D view of human head can be represented by using 3D technology, and superposing the skeletal system of head, the osseous landmark of body surface is used as reference frame for acupoint location, the skin and bones are displayed in the same 3D space, the picture becomes layered and perspective, the students can perceive presence directly. This idea will help reduce the visual fall of current 2D meridian and acupoint figures. This digital teaching material learning will contribute to the students' learning.

3 Research Method

3.1 Research Process

The 3D head model is drawn by using Maya software according to the literature review results, and the head form is superposed with skull. Finally, the meridian and acupoint locations are marked according to osseous landmark of body surface. The development process is approximately divided into three stages. The flowchart is shown in Fig. 6.

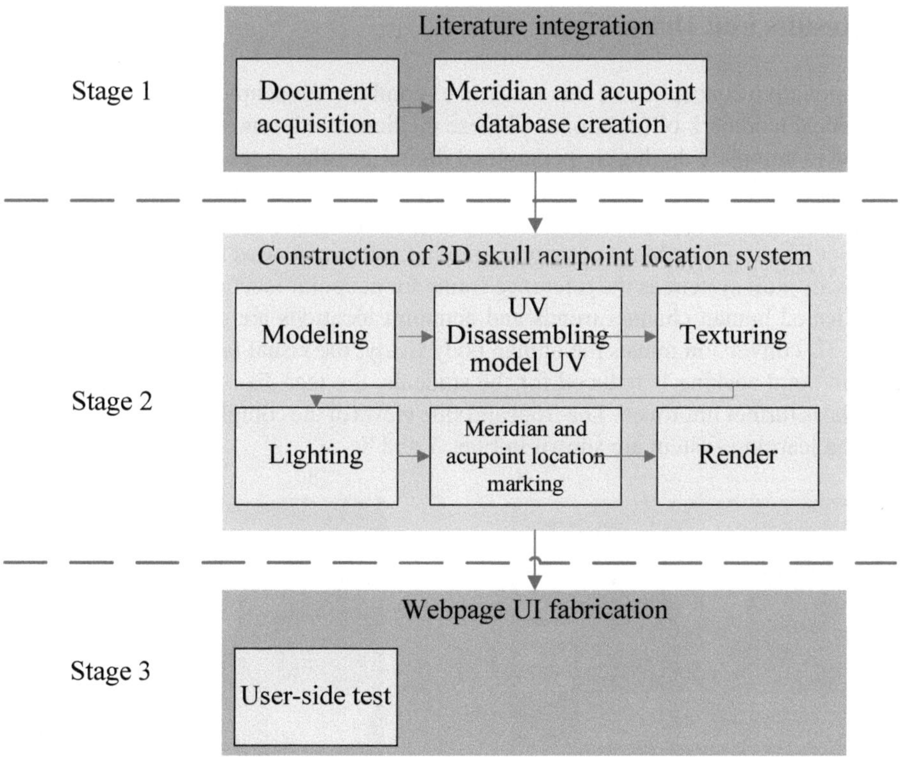

Fig. 6. 3D skull acupoint location system development construction process and method

The documents are compiled in Stage 1, the head acupoint locations to be developed are classified according to meridians to create an acupoint database for future use. The 3D skull acupoint location system is built in Stage 2, the techniques used include modeling, material and texturing, lighting, camera, channels and meridian point location marking, and render. The webpage UI is made in Stage 3.

3.2 Fabrication Method

In terms of the fabrication of the body surface location model, a round sphere is used as the basic head model, the lines are put on the sphere surface to form the curves of facial features. The face model is completed through the procedure, and a skull model is built in the same way. The 2D texturing coordinates are registered to previous 3D digital, the digital model and human body location coordinates are combined for accurate location. The head channels and acupoints are marked on the skull model by osseous body surface, and the 360° channels of entire model are reviewed. The face soft tissues, hard tissues in cranial bones, trends of channels and acupoints and point distribution, the points, lines and curved surfaces are combined with osseous body surface location, are designed systematically at a time, this personified digital prosthesis tissue teaching model is completed.

4 Results and Discussion

The innovative conception of this study is to combine the acupoint-located method by anatomical landmark of traditional Chinese medicine with innovative 3D composition method to complete the highly personified digital prosthesis teaching model. The new combination of old elements of traditional medicine is interpreted by 3D drawing technique, the acupoint-located method by anatomical landmark is used as the basis of acupoint location. The Maya computer drawing software is used to overlay the 3D head form with skull system as the reference frame for acupoint location. The interlaced and complicated human channel trends and acupoint locations are displayed clearly. The 2D-to-3D conversion makes the human body lively, the visual fall is reduced, the difficulty in point seeking is reduced for the students, the meridian and acupoint teaching material is further improved. The front and side views of the completed 3D skull acupoint location learning system are shown in Figs. 7 and 8.

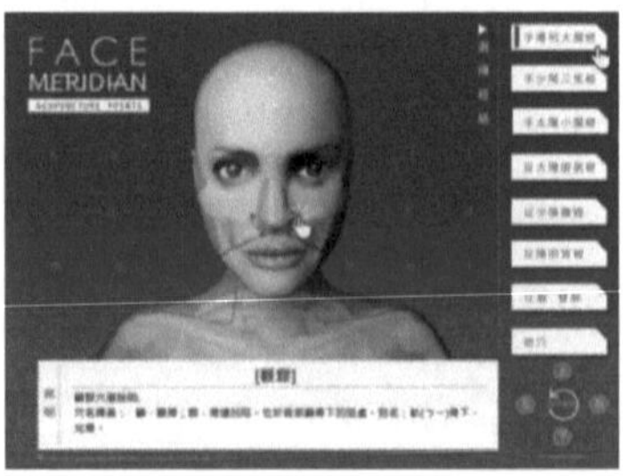

Fig. 7. Front view

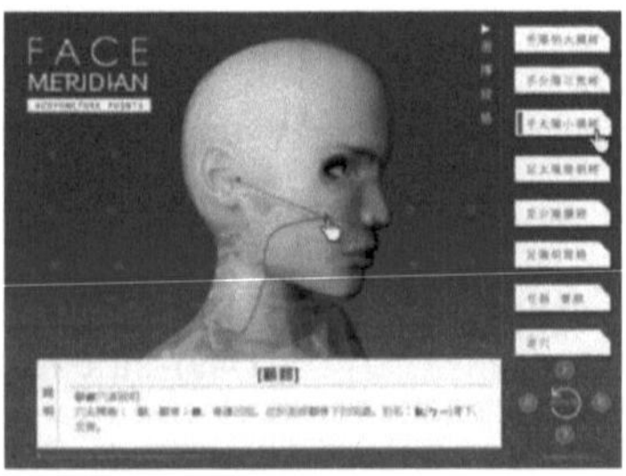

Fig. 8. Side view

As the body constitution system and channel system are complicated, this study only develops the head. The researchers can use this technique in the future to develop 3D acupoint and bone location system for other body parts, and can further discuss whether the characteristics of this system can enhance the students' learning attitude, willingness to use and learning satisfaction.

References

1. Yeh, M.L., Chang, Y.C., Huang, Y.Y., Lee, T.Y.: A randomized controlled trial of auricular acupressure in heart rate variability and quality of life for hypertension. Complement. Ther. Med. **23**(2), 200–209 (2015). https://doi.org/10.1016/j.ctim.2015.01.005
2. McFadden, K.L., Healy, K.M., Dettmann, M.L., Kaye, J.T., Ito, T.A., Hernandez, T.D.: Acupressure as a non-pharmacological intervention for Traumatic Brain Injury (TBI). J. Neurotrauma **28**(1), 21–34 (2011). https://doi.org/10.1089/neu.2010.1515
3. Wong, W.K., Chien, W.T., Lee, W.M.: Self-administered acupressure for treating adult psychiatric patients with constipation: a randomized controlled trial. Chin. Med. **10**, 10 (2015). https://doi.org/10.1186/s13020-015-0064-7
4. Putz, R., Pabst, R.: Sobotta: Atlas of Human Anatomy. Ho-Chi Publishing, Taipei City (2003)
5. Lin, J.G.: New Color Graph Acupuncturology. JyinPublishing, Taipei (2010)
6. Chiu, M.L.: Acupuncturology. JyinPublishing, Taipei (2004)
7. Weng, T.C., Chen, C.H.: Development of 3D digital interactive learning system of head meridians. J. Int. Esthetic Sci. **10**(3), 85–102 (2013)
8. Liang, D.Y., Li, X.C., Ma, T.M., Ren, L., Ren, P.: Model study between meridian acupoints and anatomical of relations. Chin. Arch. Tradit. Chin. Med. **27**(3), 596–597 (2009)
9. Huang, L.X.: Combined application of surface anatomy, imageology and authropometry to the study on standardization of acupoint location. Acupunct. Res. **4**, 91–93 (2007)
10. Feng, M., Peng, C., Tang, Y.F., Chao, H.C., Liang, S., Chang, Y.C.: Primary exploration of application of mobile learning to meridians and acupoints teaching. Health Vocat. Educ. **5**, 56–57 (2017)
11. Liang, F.R., et al.: Preliminary study on lacquer figure with meridian-points marked of the western Han dynasty unearthed in Laoguanshan, Chengdu. Chin. Acupunct. Moxibustion **1**, 91–93 (2015)
12. Sui, M.H., Liu, W.L.: Detailed Description of Use of the Latest National Standard Acupuncture Points. China Press of Traditional Chinese Medicine (2013)
13. Chou, C.: An analysis of the 3D video and interactive response approach effects on the science remedial teaching for fourth grade underachieving students. Eurasia J. Math. Sci. Technol. Educ. **13**(4), 1059–1073 (2017)
14. Oropeza, L.M., Sanchez, R.O., Villagomez, R.O.: Teaching-learning: stereoscopic 3D versus traditional methods in Mexico City. Ann. Rev. Cybertherapy Telemed. **13**, 37–43 (2015)
15. Maya, October 2017. Wikipedia. http://zh.wikipedia.org/wiki/Maya
16. Chiang, C., et al.: Primary exploration of development of integrating points with 3D digitized virtual human and assistance to acupoint anatomy teaching. Educ. Chin. Med. **5**, 32–33 (2011)

Exploration on Innovative Teaching and Information Technology Integration in College Physical Education

Long-Yu Lin[1,2](✉)

[1] Department of Leisure Business Management, Nan Kai University of Technology, Nantou, Taiwan
ttn@nkut.edu.tw

[2] Graduate School of Technological and Vocational Education, Yunlin University of Science and Technology, Yunlin, Taiwan

Abstract. Due to the changes of the environment and policy of higher education, the college-level Physical Education (PE) in Taiwan is now facing the bottleneck of drastic transformation. In order to address the dilemma and achieve educational excellence, the education community has been developing innovative teaching as an important solution. The integration of information technology in teaching has not only become a common sight at educational premises but also offered an important tool for innovative teaching. The integration of information technology in the development of Physical Education courses, however, has often been hampered by the nature of the sports discipline and competence of PE instructors. This study explored innovative teaching and integration of information technology based on the nature of PE courses in hope of offering a fresh perspective in the development of college PE courses.

Keywords: Physical education teacher · Creative teaching
Information literacy

1 Introduction

Since the amendment to the University Act was announced in 1994, there have been major changes to the existing system of compulsory college PE courses. In the past, PE courses were required for the undergraduate programs of all colleges and universities; at present, the colleges and universities determine whether they are required or selective courses. After the changes over the years, many colleges have mandated their PE courses to be required courses for the first two years of the undergraduate program, while some colleges only offer one year or none of required PE courses. Due to the autonomy granted to colleges by the University Act regarding PE courses, variation in years of PE coverage and more freedom allowed for students in choices of PE courses, the existing courses and their teaching content have become less popular among students, resulting in a continuous decline in the number of students enrolled in PE courses [1].

Due to the shift of College PE courses in their status from required ones to electives, coupled with a general decline in the number of students choosing PE electives, college

T.-T. Wu et al. (Eds.): ICITL 2018, LNCS 11003, pp. 640–647, 2018.
https://doi.org/10.1007/978-3-319-99737-7_69

students don't have enough sports activities, leading to a general decline in their fitness level and a deterioration of their life quality [2]. In response to the declining college PE, college PE instructors need think over how to secure positive changes to make PE classes popular again among college students. First of all, they need give full play to the competitive edge of PE by being student-oriented, meeting the demands of students and attracting them to choose PE electives. All course designs are student-oriented [3]. Therefore, domestic college PE classes, required or elective, have to adapt themselves in light of the social changes and student demands; PE instructors have to do what they can to provide diverse PE course content to meet student demands and stimulate their interest in PE electives [4]. Meanwhile, Ministry of Education gathered through invitation a group of experts and scholars in 2016 to discuss how to address various issues regarding the development of course innovations and lack of sports participation among students. This discussion was intended to promote regular exercises among college students, featuring diverse studies, self practice and interest-based planning. It was hoped that college students could integrate PE in their daily lives, and apply information technology; PE instructors should develop modularized courses of a high caliber to tackle the dilemma and challenge of the marginalization of college PE.

In face of policy changes and their impact on PE courses, College PE instructors could secure their jobs in education in the new era only by adjusting their out-of-date education methodology, making proper changes to their teaching content and methods, innovating PE courses and creating a new outlook in PE using modern technology.

2 Traditional PE Teaching vs. Innovative PE Teaching

Rigid traditional teaching methods usually do not stimulate interest in students and turn them into passive learners. Traditional PE teaching is delivered based on instructors' teaching experience over years in a fixed teaching model in accordance with a certain educational ideology. Such a fixed teaching model puts restraint on teaching innovations. Its long-term use also affects students' motivation, hampering the development of their creative thinking capability. Its freshness fades over time, causing a lack of interest in PE classes among students.

Traditional school PE courses are designed to help students learn sports skills. Although most of students obtain the skills in the end, their studies are usually limited to imitation or skill transfer while neglecting the learning at cognitive level, resulting in a lack of comprehension impeding further studies. In response to the problems in their PE teaching, colleges have adopted an important strategy to study how to make traditional teaching more effective and turn students from passive knowledge recipients to active learners seeking to improve their own knowledge, understanding and skills [5]. The traditional PE teaching, which tends to gives priority to sports skill learning and practice of basic movements, mainly follows the procedure of verbal instruction followed in turn by instructor demonstrations, student practices, error corrections and evaluations. Traditional PE teaching methodology, unable to deal with the drastic transformation in education, is going to be replaced by a more innovative one.

In PE teaching, instructors need adopt diverse teaching approaches in lively forms. While imparting knowledge, techniques and skills to students, PE instructors need focus on cultivating students' interest which lays a solid foundation for their future creativity. The initiative of students who are the dominant player in the learning process should be given full play in PE teaching. While imparting knowledge and techniques, PE instructors need to challenge their students to think actively. Only by thinking creatively to identify the association between knowledge and techniques can students develop their creative thinking capability. To foster creativities of students, instructors have to abandon their authoritative style of teaching in favor of another one in which students are allowed more freedom to learn to decide for themselves. A shift in teaching style is suggested from one in which instructors have a final say in choices of textbooks, teaching and evaluations to another one in which students learn by themselves. The rationale behind the suggestion is to help students lay a solid foundation in fundamentals before allowing them to practice, judge and decide by themselves, and finally create and design their self-study [6].

Innovative teaching refers to a teaching approach which is different from traditional teaching model for introducing innovative ideas. Or it could mean a new teaching model which makes a break from existing teaching model in its design and enables student to improve their studies and explore knowledge. Innovative teaching is originally designed to reform traditional teaching approaches to make them diverse and stimulate students' interest in studies. Innovation, always a teaching objective, is therefore of great significance and value to the improvement of teaching effectiveness as it not only provides diverse teaching materials and methods to instructors but also stimulate students' interest in studies with its creativities [6]. Therefore, instructors need recognize the contribution of innovation to both teachers and students in the first place, which shows their positive attitude toward innovation as a purpose of teaching. Constant learning offers them the best tool to improve their capabilities so as to master the principles and practice of innovation [7].

Instead of continuing traditional or existing teaching approaches, instructors need constantly update or change their teaching styles as required by innovative teaching. Instructors need adapt their teaching style to stimulate students' interest in studies and inspire creative thinking in students and accommodate their individual differences. To achieve innovative teaching, instructors must be creative by thinking out of the box and challenging traditions [8]. As college students tend to be increasingly self-aware and more self-motivated in studies now, college PE instructors need try to offer more tailored and thought-provoking content in their teaching design while providing opportunities for students to demonstrate their capabilities. In addition, instructors need embrace the emerging information-based society by integrating information technology in their teaching so as to provide unique and innovative teaching content to better meet students' demands. Through college innovative PE courses, students would be able to have a better understanding and fresh perspectives about PE studies, thus fostering their interest in them.

3 Innovative Teaching and Information Technology Integration

Learning refers to a process used to produce sustained changes in terms of learner's perception, attitude, knowledge or movement skills. Any meaningful learning entails the following factors such as learners' preparedness, prior knowledge and experience and motivation and the matching levels of information assimilation process and learners' learning capacity as well as the compatibility between new knowledge and experience with their existing counterparts [9]. Digital learning, however, focuses on learners by cultivating their self-discipline to help them become lifelong learners and finally knowledge creators [10]. Much more need to be done to promote digital learning as it is not easy to be carried out in large classes. Now it has become a hot topic in education to conceive a way to take the advantages of information technology to combine key teaching elements such as experience, participation, cooperation and sharing so as to develop an innovative teaching model and create an effective learning environment full of fun [11]. As required by modern education, instructors have to integrate digital learning approaches and technology in their teaching.

As constant innovations in information technology offer new application opportunities in all sectors and the digitalization continues to shape educational traditions, the latest educational methodology resulting from the educational reform over recent years holds that instructors need make full use of advanced information technology and engage in diversified reforms to meet the demands of the times [12, 13]. According to many evidence-based studies, advanced information technology indeed helps to improve teaching efficiency and learning results [14, 15]. Naturally advanced information technology has become a major tool for teaching innovations [16].

Chen and Kao pointed out in 2004 that the major difference between information technology integration in teaching and application of traditional educational technology in teaching lies in the fact that the latter is designed to simply change the teaching results to improve educational quality and efficiency while the former focuses on the process of both learning and teaching. In contrast with traditional teaching approaches, materials and media, information technology offers an important tool for instructors to use information equipment in their innovative teaching to achieve teaching objectives [17].

Hsieh suggested that knowledge and information serve as a tool and raw materials for educational innovations while innovations the soul of creativity. As an organized, systematic and ideal reform, innovation relies on rigorous analysis and continued research and improvement to create new educational content and approaches thus fostering students' interest in studies and improving their learning efficiency [18]. In order to take advantages of information technology applications by integrating them in educational designs, many studies have begun to attempt to use specific computer audio-video media in sports education and PE teaching to improve the motivation of learners [19].

The progress and development of information technology enrich and diversify information transmission, thus facilitating innovation and reform in various educational approaches. PE teaching is also expected to catch up with the times through constant innovations. Since the practicability of information technology is highlighted in information era, information technology has been converted into educational technology widely used in education. PE instructors, however, need ponder over how to properly use such technology in PE teaching.

4 Information Technology Integration in PE Teaching

According to Wang information technology integration in teaching is to integrate information technology in courses, teaching materials and teaching, making information technology an indispensable tool for both teaching and learning [20]. As defined by Ho information technology integration in teaching means that instructors use information technology in due course to aid their teaching, thus improving students' learning efficiency and their skills in using information technology as a tool to expand their scope of learning and communication [21]. It reveals that the purpose of information technology integration in teaching is to help student reach expected objectives in studies and obtain related information-based skills through combination of information technology and course studies [22]. To be specific, the information technology here refers to computer multi-media and internet technology. These media technology, digital in nature, offers multiple stimulations in forms of audio, video, sound and light, allowing for easy access, rapid processing and easy communication. If used to support delivery of teaching content and teaching tactics, information technology such as computer multi-media and internet could be viewed as a teaching tool. In this vein, information technology integration in teaching requires that instructors need learn not only how to use computer but also how to use computer to achieve teaching objectives more efficiently [23]. To integrate information technology in teaching, instructors need use information technology equipment as a tool to fully present teaching process and help students achieve learning objectives successfully.

In response to the changes in teaching environment, PE instructors have to employ information technology in their classes to prepare for course presentation, teaching aid, and diversifying teaching formats and tactics, thus effectively improving teaching quality [24]. Ho and Liao suggest that computers and boundless virtual cyberspace could be used to promote sports activities and also facilitate PE teaching and administration operations, leading to quality PE teaching, diverse development, tailored sports learning, high efficiency of sports administration, universal sports participation and public access to sports information [25].

Chang points out that it is very important to improve students' sports skills and movement by making repeated observation available to them. Carefully planned applications of multi-media in teaching clearly help build a professional image of PE teaching [26]. According to Tang computer multi-media help present in a lively manner such teaching contents as analysis of basic movement, appreciation and explanation of outstanding performance, field rules and analysis of in-class movement practice, so as to motivate students, provide more fun to classes and achieve teaching objectives [27]. In addition, information technology helps improve learning efficiency, as evidenced by the fact that multi-media-aided teaching allows for repeated presentation of correct demonstration movement in slow or fast motion or in still image [26].

Information technology integration in PE teaching helps student conduct focused observations from multiple perspectives and imitate movements while traditional teaching could only offer a presentation of movement from a single perspective, making it difficult to break down movement. With information technology integrated in PE teaching, learners could strengthen their weakness after class and observe and imitate movements on their own, allowing for learning based on their own needs [28]. In PE teaching process involving instructions, technique demonstration and movement and skill practice, instructors, with the assistance of information technology, could help students have a better understanding of movement skills and then master them. It is not difficult to imagine that such a unique teaching model could significantly improve students' learning efficiency [29].

As the contribution of information technology to teaching can't be denied, many scholars both at home and abroad have found through their studies that application of information technology in PE teaching has gone beyond the limitations which traditional teaching is subject to [30], thus improving students' learning efficiency. To reshape college PE, instructors, however, face such challenges as improvement of their competence in effective use of information technology, development of course content in light of students' needs, and development of proper course objectives.

5 Conclusion

It has been an unavoidable trend that college PE courses are changing from required courses to electives with a year-on-year decline of their duration as required courses. Sports administration departments across all universities and colleges are making changes in their PE curricula to offer recreational PE courses to meet the expectation of their students. Most universities and colleges, however, could not make significant changes due to lack of proper equipment. As a result, the PE courses they offer are mainly traditional sports programs. Therefore, innovation in PE course content, teaching materials and approaches is essential if traditional sports programs are to be made attractive and their stereotype is to be overturned. College PE instructors have to consider how to attract college students' interest in PE courses by introducing information technology in PE teaching content in light of current information application trend while pursuing course innovation.

The development of information technology and college students' interest in information technology are exerting an increasing impact on college students' skill learning. According to many research findings, information technology could motivate students and facilitate effective learning. PE courses are different from those in other disciplines in that PE courses mainly involve learning of dynamic skills. Information technology, if used properly to aid course delivery, does not go against the main purpose of PE teaching which is to learn sports skills. On the contrary, it could give play to its advantages as teaching innovation and broaden the scope of PE teaching.

In the wake of a series of educational reforms, innovative teaching and information technology integration tend to become an irreversible trend in the future PE teaching. As a result, college PE instructors are compelled by the educational reforms to adapt their teaching models in light of such a new trend. PE instructors are expected to make a clean break with out-of-date thinking, improve their competence in the use of information and properly employ information technology and media in their course design and evaluations, thus making their contribution to the development of college PE in Taiwan by reshaping PE teaching.

References

1. Wei, L., Chiu, J.C.: Country's athletics curriculum development in the institute of higher physical education eighth respond of preliminary study. J. Sports Health Leisure **6**, 133–139 (2014)
2. Lin, J.T.: The impact and influence of the explanation No. 450 from the meeting of justices of constitutional court on the PE structure. Sports Exer. Res. (40), 87–93 (1999)
3. Chang, Y.M.: Marketing. Hwa Tai Publishing Co. Ltd., Taipei City (1995)
4. Lin, M.L.: Application of somatics in College PE teaching. Sports Res. Rev. **80**, 20–25 (2005)
5. Tsai, T.H.: A tentative research on development strategy of sports teaching objectives. Nat. Pingtung Univ. Educ. PE **12**, 359–379 (2009)
6. Chang, C.H.: From creative PE teaching to creative thinking teaching. School Sports **15**(1), 14–19 (2005)
7. Huang, Y.C.: Creation of an environment for innovative PE teaching. School Sports **15**(1), 2–3 (2005)
8. Chang, S.C.: Teaching Principles: Combination and Application. Wu-Nan Book Inc., Taipei (2002)
9. Chang, C.C., Liang, C.Y., Shu, K.M., Chiu, Y.C.: Alteration of influencing factors of e-Learning continued intention for different degrees of online participation. Int. Rev. Res. Open Distrib. Learn. **16**(4), 33–61 (2015)
10. Rosenberg, M.J.: e-Learning: Strategies for Delivering Knowledge in the Digital Age. McGraw-Hill Press, New York (2001)
11. Lin, L.C., Chen, K.T., Li, Y.J., Tsao, H.H.: The trend of the use of innovative technology in digital learning. Pers. Mon. **327**, 45–55 (2012)
12. Singh, H.: Building effective blended learning programs. Educ. Technol. **43**(6), 51–54 (2003)
13. Cottrell, D.M., Robinson, R.A.: CASE4 blended learning in an accounting course. Q. Rev. Dist. Educ. **19**(2), 261–269 (2003)
14. Alavi, M.: Computer mediated collaborative learning: an empirical evaluation. MIS Q. **18**(2), 159–174 (1994)
15. Maki, R.H., Maki, W.S., Patterson, M., Whittaker, P.D.: Evaluation of a web-based introductory psychology course: I. Learning and satisfaction in on-line versus lecture courses. Behav. Res. Methods Instrum. Comput. **32**(2), 230–239 (2000)
16. Sun, P.C., Chou, C.H.: A research on teachers trying to innovate teaching with advance information technology. Sun Yat-Sen Manag. Rev. **19**(2), 423–465 (2011)
17. Chen, W.H., Kao, H.F.: A tentative research on the evaluation criteria for information application education. J. Leisure Exer. **122**, 133–147 (2004)
18. Hsieh, W.C.: New thinking in PE teaching. Taiwan Educ. Rev. Mon. **4**(11), 170–174 (2015)
19. Keller, J.M.: Motivation by Design. Unpublished Manuscript, Florida State University (1999)
20. Wang, C.S.: The significance and connotation of information technology integration in teaching. Inf. Educ. **80**, 23–31 (2000)
21. Ho, R.G.: The future development of IT-based education in light of the nine-year-plan for new courses. Inf. Educ. **85**, 5–14 (2001)

22. Chiu, C.H.: Practice of integration of information technology in teaching in primary and secondary schools. Inf. Educ. **88**, 3–9 (2002)
23. Shyu, H.Y., Wu, P.C.: Integration and implementation of information technology into classroom: current definitions, rationales and methods. Instr. Technol. Media **59**, 63–73 (2002)
24. Wang, C.C., Lin, C.D., Yang, T.C., Wang, Y.S.: Research on IT-aided teaching and innovative teaching by high school pe instructors in Taoyuan & Hsinchu. NCYU Phys. Educ. Health Recreation J. **14**(1), 46–54 (2015)
25. Ho, J.L., Liao, Y.G.: Virtual sports elementary school planning and construction. Teach. Technol. Media (50), 26–36 (2000)
26. Chang, Y.K.: The application of computer multimedia CAI in physical education teaching. Nat. Pingtung Teach. Coll. Educ. PE **5**, 119–135 (2001)
27. Tang, J.M.: Using computer multimedia computer systems to create fun sports lessons. Nat. Sports Q. **27**(4), 28–36 (1998)
28. Xiao, Y.Q., Chen, W.Z.: Computer aided instruction in physical education teaching. Teach. Technol. Media **46**, 36–42 (1998)
29. Chang, C.M., Shih, W.Y., Weng, H.S., Lay, Y.L.: The study on the differences between information technologies involved and traditional physical education pedagogies-example of table tennis backhand blocking technique. Chung Yuan Phys. Educ. J. **1**, 123–131 (2012)
30. Hao, K.C., Lin, P.Y.: Development of multi-media-aided basketball teaching system. Sports Exer. Res. **101**, 146–155 (2009)

Author Index

MIX
Papier aus verantwortungsvollen Quellen
Paper from responsible sources
FSC® C105338

If you have any concerns about our products,
you can contact us on
ProductSafety@springernature.com

In case Publisher is established outside the EU,
the EU authorized representative is:
Springer Nature Customer Service Center GmbH
Europaplatz 3, 69115 Heidelberg, Germany

Printed by Libri Plureos GmbH
in Hamburg, Germany